World War II and the Postwar Years in America

# World War II and the Postwar Years in America

## A Historical and Cultural Encyclopedia

VOLUME 2: J–Y

*William H. Young and Nancy K. Young*

ABC-CLIO

Santa Barbara, California • Denver, Colorado • Oxford, England

Copyright 2010 by ABC-CLIO, LLC

All rights reserved. No part of this publication may be reproduced, stored in a
retrieval system, or transmitted, in any form or by any means, electronic, mechanical,
photocopying, recording, or otherwise, except for the inclusion of brief quotations in
a review, without prior permission in writing from the publisher.

**Library of Congress Cataloging-in-Publication Data**

Young, William H., 1939–
  World War II and the postwar years in America : a historical and cultural encyclopedia
/ William H. Young and Nancy K. Young.
      p. cm.
  Includes bibliographical references and index.
  ISBN 978-0-313-35652-0 (alk. paper)—ISBN 978-0-313-35653-7 (ebook)
 1. United States—History—1933–1945—Encyclopedias.   2. United States—
History—1945–1953—Encyclopedias.   3. World War, 1939–1945—
United States—Encyclopedias.   I. Young, Nancy K., 1940–   II. Title.
  E806.Y73   2010
  973.91—dc22          2010021470

ISBN: 978–0-313–35652–0
EISBN: 978-0-313–35653–7

14  13  12  11  10    1  2  3  4  5

This book is also available on the World Wide Web as an eBook.
Visit www.abc-clio.com for details.

ABC-CLIO, LLC
130 Cremona Drive, P.O. Box 1911
Santa Barbara, California 93116–1911

This book is printed on acid-free paper ∞

Manufactured in the United States of America

# Contents

**VOLUME 1**

*Alphabetical List of Entries   vii*
*Guide to Related Topics   xi*
*Preface   xvii*
*Acknowledgments   xxi*
*Introduction   xxiii*

**The Encyclopedia, Entries A–I   1**

*Index   I-1*

**VOLUME 2**

*Alphabetical List of Entries   vii*
*Guide to Related Topics   xi*

**The Encyclopedia, Entries J–Y   417**

*Timeline for the 1940s   787*
*Selected Resources   801*
*Index   I-1*

# Alphabetical List of Entries

ABC (American Broadcasting Company)
Abstract Expressionism
Acuff, Roy
Advertising
All-Girl Orchestras
Andrews Sisters, The
Architecture
Art (Painting)
*ASCAP vs. BMI* Radio Boycott and the AFM Recording Ban
Atomic Bomb, The
Automobiles and the American Automotive Industry
Autry, Gene, and Roy Rogers
Aviation
Axis Sally and Tokyo Rose

Baby Boom
Baseball
Basie, Count
Basketball
Bebop (Bop)
Berlin Airlift, The
Best Sellers (Books)
*Best Years of Our Lives, The* (William Wyler)
Beverages
Black Market

Blackouts, Brownouts, and Dim-Outs
Bogart, Humphrey
Boogie-Woogie
Book Clubs
Bowling
Boxing
Boyd, William (Hopalong Cassidy)
Broadway Shows (Comedy and Drama)
Broadway Shows (Musicals)

Canteens
Cartoons (Film)
*Casablanca* (Michael Curtiz)
Children's Films
*Citizen Kane* (Orson Welles)
Civil Defense
Classical Music
Cold War, The
Cole, Nat King
Comedies (Film)
Comic Books
Comic Strips
Copland, Aaron
Costume and Spectacle Films
Country Music
Crime and Mystery Films
Crosby, Bing
Crosley Automobiles

Dance
D-Day
Design
Desserts, Candy, and Ice Cream
Disney, Walt
Drama (Film)
Drive-Ins: Movie Theaters, Restaurants, and Banks
DuMont Network

*Edgar Bergen/Charlie McCarthy Show, The*
Education
Eisenhower, General Dwight David
Ellington, Duke

Fads
Fashion
Fast Food
Film Noir
FM Radio
Folk Music
Food
Football
Frozen Foods

Games
GI Bill (Servicemen's Readjustment Act of 1944)
Godfrey, Arthur
Golf
Grocery Stores and Supermarkets

Health and Medicine
Hobbies
Hockey
Hope, Bob
Horror and Thriller Films
Horse Racing
Hot Rods and Drag Racing
House Un-American Activities Committee (HUAC)
*Howdy Doody Show, The*

Illustrators
Internment Camps (Relocation Centers)
*It's a Wonderful Life* (Frank Capra)

*Jack Benny Program, The*
Jazz
Jones, Spike
Jukeboxes
Juvenile Delinquency

Kinsey, Alfred C.
*Kraft Television Theatre*

Labor Unrest
Lawns, Lawnmowers, and Fertilizers
Leisure and Recreation
Levittown and Suburbanization
*Lone Ranger, The*
Louis, Joe

MacArthur, General Douglas
Magazines
Marshall, General George Catlett
MBS (Mutual Broadcasting System)
Miller, Glenn
Miranda, Carmen
Motorsports
Movies
Murphy, Audie
Musicals (Film)

Newspapers

Photography
Political and Propaganda Films
Posters
Pyle, Ernie, and Bill Mauldin

Race Relations and Stereotyping
Radio
Radio Programming: Action, Crime, Police, and Detective Shows
Radio Programming: Children's Shows, Serials, and Adventure Series
Radio Programming: Comedy Shows
Radio Programming: Drama and Anthology Shows
Radio Programming: Educational Shows
Radio Programming: Music and Variety Shows
Radio Programming: News, Sports, Public Affairs, and Talk

Radio Programming: Quiz Shows
Radio Programming: Soap Operas
Rationing
Religion
Restaurants
Rhythm 'n' Blues
Roller Derby
Roosevelt, Eleanor
Roosevelt, President Franklin Delano
Rosie the Riveter

Scrap Drives
Sculpture
Selective Training and Service Act of 1940 (Selective Service, or Draft)
Serial Films
Service Flags (Gold Stars and Blue Stars)
*Seventeen*
Shore, Dinah
Sinatra, Frank
Skating (Figure)
Skating (Roller)
Skiing
Smith, Kate
Softball
Songwriters and Lyricists
Spam
Spock, Dr. Benjamin O.
Steel Pennies (1943)
*Superman*

Swimming and Water Skiing
Swing

Technology
Television
Tennis
*Terry and the Pirates* (Milton Caniff)
*Texaco Star Theater* (Milton Berle)
*Toast of the Town* (Ed Sullivan)
Toys
Trains
Transportation
Travel
Truman, President Harry S.

UFOs (Unidentified Flying Objects)
United Nations, The
USO (United Service Organizations)

V-E and V-J Day
Victory Gardens
Voice of America

War Bonds
War Films
Westerns (Film)
"White Christmas" (Irving Berlin)
Women in the Military: WACs, WASPs, WAVES, SPARS, and Others

Youth

# Guide to Related Topics

**Art**

Abstract Expressionism
Advertising
Art (Painting)
Comic Books
Comic Strips
Design
Disney, Walt
Fashion
Illustrators
Magazines
Photography
Posters
Pyle, Ernie, and Bill Mauldin
Sculpture

**Architecture**

Architecture
Design
Drive-Ins: Movie Theaters, Restaurants, and Banks
Levittown and Suburbanization
Technology

**Aviation**

Aviation
Berlin Airlift, The
Technology
Transportation
Travel

**Comic Books and Strips**

Cartoons (Film)
Comic Books
Comic Strips
Illustrators
Newspapers
Serial Films
*Superman*
*Terry and the Pirates*

**Fads and Games**

Book Clubs
Dance
Fads
Games
Hobbies
Hot Rods and Drag Racing
Leisure and Recreation
Radio Programming: Quiz Shows
Skating (Roller)
Swing
Toys

**Food and Drink**

Advertising

Beverages
Canteens
Desserts, Candy, and Ice Cream
Drive-Ins: Movie Theaters, Restaurants, and Banks
Fast Food
Frozen Foods
Grocery Stores and Supermarkets
Health and Medicine
Rationing
Restaurants
Spam
USO (United Service Organizations)
Victory Gardens

**Government**

Atomic Bomb, The
Civil Defense
Cold War, The
Education
GI Bill (Servicemen's Readjustment Act of 1944)
Health and Medicine
House Un-American Activities Committee (HUAC)
Illustrators
Internment Camps (Relocation Centers)
Labor Unrest
Photography
Political and Propaganda Films
Posters
Race Relations and Stereotyping
Rationing
Roosevelt, Eleanor
Roosevelt, President Franklin Delano
Rosie the Riveter
Scrap Drives
Selective Training and Service Act of 1940 (Selective Service, or Draft)
Service Flags (Gold Stars and Blue Stars)
Steel Pennies (1943)
Trains
Transportation
Truman, President Harry S.
UFOs (Unidentified Flying Objects)
United Nations, The

USO (United Service Organizations)
Victory Gardens
Voice of America
War Bonds
Women in the Military: WACs, WASPs, WAVES, SPARS, and Others

**Individuals**

Acuff, Roy
Andrews Sisters, The
Autry, Gene, and Roy Rogers
Axis Sally and Tokyo Rose
Basie, Count
Boyd, William
Cole, Nat King
Copland, Aaron
Crosby, Bing
Disney, Walt
Eisenhower, General Dwight David
Ellington, Duke
Godfrey, Arthur
Hope, Bob
Jones, Spike
Kinsey, Alfred C.
Louis, Joe
MacArthur, General Douglas
Marshall, General George Catlett
Miller, Glenn
Miranda, Carmen
Murphy, Audie
Pyle, Ernie, and Bill Maudlin
Roosevelt, Eleanor
Roosevelt, President Franklin Delano
Shore, Dinah
Sinatra, Frank
Smith, Kate
Spock, Dr. Benjamin O.
Truman, President Harry S.

**Literature**

Best Sellers (Books)
Book Clubs
Comic Books
Illustrators
Magazines
Newspapers
*Seventeen*

Guide to Related Topics | xiii

**Magazines**

Advertising
Illustrators
Magazines
Photography
*Seventeen*

**Movies**

Autry, Gene, and Roy Rogers
*Best Years of Our Lives, The* (William Wyler)
Bogart, Humphrey
Boyd, William (Hopalong Cassidy)
*Casablanca* (Michael Curtiz)
Children's Films
*Citizen Kane* (Orson Welles)
Comedies (Film)
Costume and Spectacle Films
Crime and Mystery Films
Crosby, Bing
Dance
Disney, Walt
Drama (Film)
Drive-Ins: Movie Theaters, Restaurants, and Banks
*Edgar Bergen/Charlie McCarthy Show, The*
Hope, Bob
Horror and Thriller Films
House Un-American Activities Committee (HUAC)
*It's a Wonderful Life* (Frank Capra)
*Lone Ranger, The*
Miranda, Carmen
Movies
Murphy, Audie
Musicals (Film)
Political and Propaganda Films
Race Relations and Stereotyping
Serial Films
*Superman*
Television
War Films
Westerns (Film)

**Music**

Acuff, Roy
All-Girl Orchestras
Andrews Sisters, The
*ASCAP vs. BMI* Radio Boycott and the AFM Recording Ban
Autry, Gene, and Roy Rogers
Basie, Count
Bebop (Bop)
Boogie-Woogie
Broadway Shows (Musicals)
Classical Music
Cole, Nat King
Copland, Aaron
Country Music
Crosby, Bing
Dance
Disney, Walt
Ellington, Duke
FM Radio
Folk Music
Jazz
Jones, Spike
Jukeboxes
Miller, Glenn
Miranda, Carmen
Race Relations and Stereotyping
Radio
Radio Programming: Music and Variety Shows
Rhythm 'n' Blues
Shore, Dinah
Sinatra, Frank
Smith, Kate
Songwriters and Lyricists
Swing
Television
"White Christmas" (Irving Berlin)

**Musicians**

Acuff, Roy
Andrews Sisters, The
Autry, Gene, and Roy Rogers
Basie, Count
Cole, Nat King
Copland, Aaron
Crosby, Bing
Jones, Spike
Miller, Glenn
Miranda, Carmen

Shore, Dinah
Sinatra, Frank
Smith, Kate

**Newspapers**

Advertising
Atomic Bomb, The
Blackouts, Brownouts, and Dim-Outs
Berlin Airlift, The
Civil Defense
Cold War, The
Comic Strips
Newspapers
Pyle, Ernie, and Bill Maudlin
Rationing
Roosevelt, Eleanor
Roosevelt, President Franklin Delano
Scrap Drives
*Superman*
*Terry and the Pirates*
Truman, President Harry S.
UFOs (Unidentified Flying Objects)
USO (United Service Organizations)
V-E and V-J Day
Victory Gardens
War Bonds

**Organizations**

All-Girl Orchestras
House Un-American Activities Committee (HUAC)
USO (United Service Organizations)
Voice of America

**Radio**

Advertising
ABC (American Broadcasting Company)
*ASCAP vs. BMI* Radio Boycott and the AFM Recording Ban
*Edgar Bergen/Charlie McCarthy Show, The*
FM Radio
*Jack Benny Program, The*
Leisure and Recreation
*Lone Ranger, The*
Radio

Radio Programming: Action, Crime, Police, and Detective Shows
Radio Programming: Children's Shows, Serials, and Adventure Series
Radio Programming: Comedy Shows
Radio Programming: Drama and Anthology Shows
Radio Programming: Educational Shows
Radio Programming: Music and Variety Shows
Radio Programming: News, Sports, Public Affairs, and Talk
Radio Programming: Quiz Shows
Radio Programming: Soap Operas
Religion
Roosevelt, Eleanor
Roosevelt, President Franklin Delano
Shore, Dinah
Smith, Kate
*Superman*
Technology
Voice of America

**Social Issues**

Baby Boom
Berlin Airlift, The
Fads
Folk Music
GI Bill (Servicemen's Readjustment Act of 1944)
Health and Medicine
Juvenile Delinquency
Kinsey, Alfred C.
Labor Unrest
Race Relations and Stereotyping
Radio Programming: News, Sports, Public Affairs, and Talk
Religion
Roosevelt, Eleanor
Rosie the Riveter
Spock, Dr. Benjamin O.
United Nations, The

**Sports**

Baseball
Basketball

Bowling
Boxing
Golf
Hockey
Horse Racing
Hot Rods and Drag Racing
Motorsports
Roller Derby
Skating (Figure)
Skating (Roller)
Skiing
Softball
Swimming and Water Skiing
Technology
Tennis

### Suburbanization

Advertising
Architecture
Automobiles and the American Automotive Industry
Baby Boom
Best Sellers (Books)
Book Clubs
Design
Drive-Ins: Movie Theaters, Restaurants, and Banks
Education
Fast Food
Games
GI Bill (Servicemen's Readjustment Act of 1944)
Golf
Grocery Stores and Supermarkets
Lawns, Lawnmowers, and Fertilizers
Leisure and Recreation
Levittown and Suburbanization
Magazines
Newspapers
Radio
Radio Programming: Action, Crime, Police, and Detective Shows
Radio Programming: Children's Shows, Serials, and Adventure Series
Radio Programming: Comedy Shows
Radio Programming: Drama and Anthology Shows
Radio Programming: Educational Shows
Radio Programming: Music and Variety Shows
Radio Programming: News, Sports, Public Affairs, and Talk
Radio Programming: Quiz Shows
Radio Programming: Soap Operas
Skating (Figure)
Skating (Roller)
Technology
Television
Trains
Transportation

### Television

ABC (American Broadcasting Company)
DuMont Network
*Edgar Bergen/Charlie McCarthy Show, The*
Hope, Bob
*Howdy Doody Show, The*
*Jack Benny Program, The*
*Kraft Television Theatre*
Leisure and Recreation
MBS (Mutual Broadcasting System)
Technology
Television
*Texaco Star Theater* (Milton Berle)
*Toast of the Town* (Ed Sullivan)

### Theater

Broadway Shows (Comedy and Drama)
Broadway Shows (Musicals)
Copland, Aaron
Dance
Movies
Radio Programming: Drama and Anthology Shows
Songwriters and Lyricists
*Texaco Star Theater* (Milton Berle)

### Travel

Automobiles and the American Automotive Industry

Aviation
Crosley Automobiles
Trains
Transportation
Travel

## World War II

Advertising
All-Girl Orchestras
Atomic Bomb, The
Aviation
Axis Sally and Tokyo Rose
Berlin Airlift, The
*Best Years of Our Lives, The* (William Wyler)
Black Market
Blackouts, Brownouts, and Dim-Outs
Canteens
Civil Defense
Cold War, The
D-Day
Education
Eisenhower, General Dwight David
GI Bill (Servicemen's Readjustment Act of 1944)
Health and Medicine
Hope, Bob
Internment Camps (Relocation Centers)
Louis, Joe
MacArthur, General Douglas
Magazines
Marshall, General George Catlett
Miller, Glenn
Movies
Murphy, Audie
Newspapers
Photography
Political and Propaganda Films
Posters
Pyle, Ernie, and Bill Maudlin
Race Relations and Stereotyping
Radio
Radio Programming: News, Sports, Public Affairs, and Talk
Rationing
Roosevelt, President Franklin Delano
Rosie the Riveter
Scrap Drives
Selective Training and Service Act of 1940 (Selective Service, or Draft)
Service Flags (Gold Stars and Blue Stars)
Smith, Kate
Songwriters and Lyricists
Spam
Steel Pennies (1943)
Technology
Television
Toys
Trains
Transportation
Travel
Truman, President Harry S.
USO (United Service Organizations)
V-E and V-J Day
Victory Gardens
Voice of America
War Bonds
War Films
"White Christmas" (Irving Berlin)
Women in the Military: WACs, WASPs, WAVES, SPARS, and Others
Youth

# J

## JACK BENNY PROGRAM, THE

One of the most popular **radio** shows of the 1940s, its host and star first entered show business as a teenager in 1908, playing violin with some local Waukegan, Illinois, dance bands. At this time, he still used his real name, Benjamin Kubelsky (1894–1974). Three years later, Kubelsky had moved to performing in vaudeville theaters, although his parents forbade him to go on the road. A brief stint in the navy during World War I caused him to discover a talent for comedy and also brought about a change in names to the better-known Jack Benny.

Benny slowly established a good reputation as a comedian and worked his way up the vaudeville ladder, and he went to Broadway to perform in revues. He also appeared in a number of lackluster **movies** in the early 1930s. Good fortune came his way when he landed a spot on *The Ed Sullivan Show* in 1932, a network radio variety program with gossip columnist Ed Sullivan (1901–1974) as master of ceremonies; a large audience heard Benny on the air. Shortly thereafter, NBC (National Broadcasting Company) offered him a contract for a show of his own. The first broadcasts of *The Jack Benny Show* occurred in 1932; the program would remain a radio staple until 1955. Benny stayed with NBC until 1948 and then with CBS (Columbia Broadcasting System) until 1955. Reruns, called *The Best of Benny,* kept the show on the air until 1958. During all of those 23 years on radio, *The Jack Benny Program* usually ranked among the top shows in popularity. In 1950, Benny also moved to CBS **television,** another radio star making the transition to the new medium. For five years, he successfully straddled both radio and TV.

With his burgeoning popularity on the air, Hollywood rediscovered Jack Benny; he appeared in eight additional motion pictures during the mid- and later 1930s, and the 1940s saw him in another seven. He opened the decade with *Buck Bunny Rides Again,* a silly romp with much of the cast from the radio show. *Love Thy Neighbor* (1940) merely carries on the fun, and *Charley's Aunt* (1941) has him taking on the classic 1892 Victorian farce with considerable flair. With the war raging, *To Be or Not to Be* (filmed in 1941 but released in 1942) served as a strong anti-Axis comedy, with Benny and Carole Lombard (1908–1942) matching wits with both the Nazis and Shakespeare. *George Washington Slept Here* (1942) and *The Meanest Man in the World* (1943) stand as lesser efforts for Benny, but *The Horn Blows at Midnight* (1945), a film he delighted in panning on his radio show, redeemed his film career, although the comedian thereafter bowed out of moviemaking, except for occasional guest appearances.

Even with his active motion picture schedule, Benny devoted most of his creative efforts to his radio show. He and his writers created a handful of long-running characters, such as Rochester, Benny's put-upon black valet played by Eddie Anderson (1905–1977), and Mr. Kitzel, a recurring figure played by Artie Auerbach (1903–1957). Anderson's Rochester might raise an eyebrow in later years for racial stereotyping, but seldom did he kowtow to anyone, especially Benny. Auerbach's Kitzel spoke in a heavy Jewish accent but insulted no one's ethnicity. Since his role involved selling hot dogs, his classic "pe-e-ekle in the me-e-edle with the mustard on top" convulsed audiences, and the phrase quickly entered the language.

By the 1940s, such familiar names as tenor Dennis Day (ne Owen Patrick McNulty, 1916–1988), bandleader Phil Harris (1904–1995), vocal effects master Mel Blanc (1908–1989), and announcer Don Wilson (1900–1982) had all become regulars. Dennis Day played a featherbrained naïf, whose "Gee, Mr. Benny," always got a laugh. Phil Harris, on the other hand, took on the role of a hip, hard-drinking musician who mangled the language. He dubbed Benny "Jackson" and greeted him on the air with a "Hi'ya, Jackson." Even Don Wilson, ostensibly the announcer, became a comic personality during airtime. A large man, the cast made endless jokes about his girth, and he continually pleaded with Benny to allow the Sportsmen Quartet, another musical staple on the show, to sing the jingles for commercial products. Both made-up characters and real-life performers gave the program a strong sense of continuity.

As the cast of the show became established in radio, Benny worked to find a formula that would give the production a distinctive identity. Almost from the beginning, his real-life wife Sadye Marks (1906–1983) played Mary Livingstone throughout its run, first in a role as a fan and then as his wisecracking secretary; she became so well-known that she eventually changed her name legally. Contrary to popular belief, she did not play Benny's wife; his stage reputation as a notorious miser would not have allowed a spouse.

The writers connected with *The Jack Benny Program* also worked tirelessly to preserve the persona of its star. In time, they established several traits for Benny that endured into his days on television. He seemingly became the butt of his own jokes, and his mastery of timing enhanced the effect. His pauses, as he deliberated what had been said, were legendary. A miser in all things, his fictitious home contained a basement vault guarded by a ferocious polar bear ("He ate the gas man") named Carmichael, voiced by Mel Blanc. Given this cheap side to his evolving personality, he treasured his wheezy automobile, a vintage Maxwell, and Blanc, through his vocal antics, gave it life. Vain, he remained 39 forever, a running joke that never grew stale. Of course, the Jack Benny his writers created did not resemble the real man at all, and audiences knew this. But the fact that he would make fun of himself in a long, continuing series only added to the fun; it made the audience a part of the joke.

Given its radio popularity, *The Jack Benny Program* naturally attracted sponsors. From 1934 until 1942, Jell-O underwrote the program, followed by Grape Nuts cereals (1942–1944); Lucky Strike cigarettes served in this coveted capacity for the longest period, 1944 to 1955, and gave the production an alternate title, *The Lucky Strike Program.* But for millions of fans, it would always remain *The Jack Benny Program.*

*See also:* Advertising; Automobiles and the American Automotive Industry; Comedies (Film); Musicals (Film); Political and Propaganda Films; Race Relations and Stereotyping; Radio Programming: Comedy Shows; Radio Programming: Music and Variety Shows; *Toast of the Town* (Ed Sullivan)

**Selected Reading**
Benny, Jack, and Joan Benny. *Sunday Nights at Seven: The Jack Benny Story.* New York: Warner Books, 1990.
Dunning, John. *On the Air: The Encyclopedia of Old-Time Radio.* New York: Oxford University Press, 1998.

# JAZZ

In the days just prior to the entry of the United States into World War II, the big bands, the most popular musical force in the land, could do no wrong in the eyes of the mass audience. They exemplified **swing,** a melodic, danceable melding of jazz and popular music that had arisen during the early 1930s. Overwhelmed by the dominance of swing, much contemporary jazz went unheard by the listening audience, since the large record companies wanted top-selling artists like Tommy Dorsey (1905–1956), **Duke Ellington** (1899–1974), Benny Goodman (1909–1986), Harry James (1916–1983), and **Glenn Miller** (1904–1944). For example, clarinetist Artie Shaw's (1910–2004) hit swing version of "Begin the Beguine," a romantic tune written in 1935 by Cole Porter (1891–1964) and recorded by Shaw in 1938, remained a big seller well into the 1940s.

The same held true for night clubs, **dance** halls, and concerts. Owners, managers, and producers wanted customers, and those customers wanted, or so many assumed, the leading names in swing. These attitudes toward both recorded and live performances carried with them racial implications, because the successful (i.e., profitable) orchestras tended to be white, which meant, given the times, that their fans consisted of a preponderance of white patrons. In many ways, however, the foundations of swing, especially its propulsive beat and emphasis on instrumentalists, had come from jazz, which predated swing by several decades. Ironically, jazz existed in the background during swing's heyday, and many fine jazz artists and groups, mainly black, struggled for survival during the 1930s and early 1940s, muffled by the loud applause given their boisterous stepchild. During this time, swing and jazz often seemed synonymous terms, and the dividing line between the two formats often appeared fuzzy.

When **Count Basie** (1904–1984) and his band performed "One O'Clock Jump" (1937; reached its greatest popularity in the early 1940s) or Benny Goodman and vocalist Peggy Lee (1920–2002) collaborated on "Why Don't You Do Right?" (recorded 1942), the renditions delighted jazz and swing fans alike, and any discussions about jazz and swing differences carried the hallmarks of academic nitpicking more than anything else. Perhaps the greatest exemplar of popularly oriented swing was bandleader Glenn Miller. From the late 1920s, when he first appeared on the musical scene, he traced a career that steadily rose in public appeal. At the time of his death in 1944 while with the Army Air Force, the Glenn Miller Orchestra (both his civilian and later service bands) ranked No. 1 with most fans.

Diehard jazz aficionados might be dismissive—mere swing tunes—about Miller's "In the Mood" (1939) or "A String of Pearls" (1941), two of his biggest instrumental hits from the early 1940s, whereas those on the other side of the argument might be ecstatic, proclaiming them great dance numbers. Whatever one's leanings, however, most could agree that swing and jazz enjoyed a close kinship, at least into the 1940s.

But nothing lasts forever. When the public's adulation toward the highly structured and tightly arranged music featured by the leading swing orchestras slowly drew to a close in the waning days of World War II, jazz innovators started carving out new paths that distanced them from a style that had seemed, just a few short years earlier, destined to rule American music for the foreseeable future. The demise of many big bands simultaneously brought about the rise of countless small jazz groups in the 1940s, although the war and simple economics served to conceal much of this ferment from potential audiences until later in the decade and the return to peace.

The 1940s also served as a breeding ground for new musical expressions, ranging from a revival of traditional New Orleans styles to the most avant-garde experiments, especially in the area of modern (as opposed to traditional) jazz. For many musicians, the period represented a time of unparalleled opportunity, and these changes—some gradual, some almost overnight—occurred at the expense of the once-mighty big bands. They were reduced, if active at all, to playing a kind of diluted version of swing, mainly in the form of bland pop tunes and usually behind a name vocalist.

Another event, in this case a single 1939 recording, also deeply influenced the development of jazz. Tenor saxophonist Coleman Hawkins (1904–1969), a renowned veteran of the swing orchestra led by Fletcher Henderson (1897–1952) and countless small groups, in 1939 made a studio recording of "Body and Soul," a revival of a 1930 song composed by Johnny Green (1908–1989) that announced to the music world that momentous changes awaited contemporary music. After touching on the familiar melody, Hawkins launches into a long (two choruses, plus the coda) rhythmic improvisation that examines the harmonics of the song. Remarkably, given the abstract qualities and absence of a recognizable melody in his performance, "Body and Soul" became a hit. A master instrumentalist, Hawkins presaged the **bebop** revolution and its emphasis on chord structure and, in so doing, helped open the boundaries of jazz to a new generation of artists.

At the same time Coleman Hawkins was dissecting "Body and Soul," a young guitarist named Charlie Christian (1916–1942) joined the Benny Goodman orchestra. He quickly became a regular in the Goodman Sextet, an extension of the leader's former quintet. Backed by Goodman, clarinet; Lionel Hampton (1908–2002), vibraphone; Johnny Guarnieri (1917–1985), piano; Artie Bernstein (1909–1964), bass; and Nick

Fatool (1915–2000), drums, Christian's long, linear lines of improvisation, played over the more traditional 4/4 swing of the group, established new ways of listening to solo instruments, not unlike what Hawkins had achieved.

On another front, drummer Gene Krupa (1909–1973), formerly a star with Goodman in the 1930s, formed his own band in 1941 that spotlighted trumpeter Roy "Little Jazz" Eldridge (1911–1989) and vocalist Anita O'Day (1919–2006) and opened new vistas for contemporary popular music. They enjoyed a hit with a 1941 effort, "Let Me Off Uptown." Eldridge's piercing horn and O'Day's sassy singing would prove strong influences on a new generation of players and singers and indicated changes ahead. The close interplay between O'Day and Eldridge presented an additional facet to the evolving face of jazz in the 1940s, because she was white and he was black. More and more bands and groups became racially integrated, quietly and without fuss for the most part, and this long-overdue progress would continue throughout the decade.

While numerous others experimented with new approaches to jazz in small group settings, three adventuresome orchestras attempted to assimilate some of the innovations in modern music for big bands. Woody Herman (1913–1987) had been active in big band circles from the late 1920s onward, spending most of that time laboring as a reed-playing sideman. In 1936, he took over the leadership of the popular Isham Jones (1894–1956) orchestra and immediately faced the dilemma of whether to continue performing as a new Jones ensemble or to branch out into then-untried fields. Herman's ensemble chose the latter course and agreed to call the group The Band that Plays the Blues. With a carryover Decca recording contract giving them some financial security, the orchestra began to put on disks—appropriately enough, a number of blues-oriented compositions.

In 1939, The Band that Plays the Blues attracted considerable attention with the release of "Woodchopper's Ball." An up-tempo piece, it effectively captured the energy of the aggregation and established Woody Herman as a major new force in jazz and swing circles. In addition, he played clarinet on this tune, and the strength of his performance immediately put him into the charmed circle of clarinetists then dominated by Benny Goodman and Artie Shaw. Up to this time, the group's theme had been an older tune, "Blue Prelude" (1933). A new theme, "Blue Flame" (1941), thought to better represent the orchestra, replaced "Blue Prelude." A haunting number, its distinctive mood provided an impressive opener for the band.

Numerous club dates and more recordings followed, and by 1943 the renamed Woody Herman Orchestra boasted a loyal cadre of fans. The following year, a number of significant personnel changes took place, and Herman left Decca and signed a new contract with Columbia Records. For some time, the aggregation had been attempting increasingly modern compositions, and people took to calling this latest incarnation of the orchestra the First Herd. In time, the Second Herd would replace the First, the Third Herd the Second, and so on.

Herman's First Herd broke upon the scene with several dizzying numbers unlike anything previously heard. "Apple Honey" (1945), "Northwest Passage" (1945), "Bijou" (1945), and "Wild Root" (1945) serve as tantalizing samples of what the band could do. For the next several years, Woody Herman's orchestra would electrify listeners with its disciplined hysteria. Arrangers Ralph Burns (1922–2001) and Neal Hefti

(1922–2008) deserve much credit, as do soloists Bill Harris (1916–1973; trombone), Pete Candoli (1923–2008; trumpet), Flip Phillips (1915–2001; tenor saxophone), and the inimitable leader himself on clarinet. The experimentation, the sharp movement away from traditional swing arrangements as the band focused more on modern jazz, would continue into the postwar period, and Herman's Herds became ensconced as one of America's favorite orchestras. By eschewing traditional swing, Herman avoided the collapse then occurring among many bands that clung to the past.

Another newcomer, Stan Kenton (1911–1979) and His Artistry in Rhythm Orchestra, entered the turbulent jazz field in 1941. An early member of the growing roster of musicians signed with fledgling Capitol Records, pianist Kenton achieved modest success with cuts like "Artistry in Rhythm," "Artistry Jumps," and "Eager Beaver" (all 1943; all compositions by Kenton). In addition, from the beginning, he hired the best musicians and arrangers, including Pete Rugolo (b. 1915) at this time, and featured top vocalists such as Anita O'Day and June Christy (1925–1990) during the mid-1940s. Not satisfied with the status quo, Kenton sought out new avenues of expression and dubbed his efforts "progressive jazz," not swing or bebop. In the postwar years, Kenton continued to move forward and try new things and became known as an orchestral innovator of the first rank, one that commanded a devoted following.

On the heels of Stan Kenton came Boyd Raeburn (1913–1966). Another leader in the progressive jazz vein, Raeburn had led groups in the Midwest during the 1930s, and came to New York City in 1942 expecting to play some extended club engagements. Until this time, he had performed pretty much as the leader of a straight swing orchestra, but he made the risky choice of experimentation when a fire destroyed his existing book and he had little to lose. With modernist arrangers Johnny Richards (1911–1968) and George Handy (1920–1997) providing provocative charts, Raeburn took the plunge into new musical territory, a move that attracted others from the jazz community, including famed bebop trumpeter John Birks "Dizzy" Gillespie (1917–1993) in the 1944 edition of the band. Hardly a traditional dance orchestra any more, the Raeburn organization immediately gained critical kudos but little commercial success. Raeburn finally had to break up the group in 1948 for economic reasons; he had been too far ahead of his time. Raeburn went back to a traditional swing and dance ensemble in the 1950s.

While a number of artists moved into the fields of modern and progressive jazz, others looked fondly to the preswing past. Trumpeter Louis Armstrong (1901–1971), whose career paralleled the rise of jazz, successfully straddled both the old and the new, leading a series of small groups that could play anything from the music of the 1920s to the swing hits of the 1930s to the pop songs of the 1940s. No matter what he performed, his innate sense of rhythmic swing gave his numbers a jazz feel and introduced untold legions of people to the music.

In addition to Armstrong, a series of books by music historians that began appearing in the late 1930s; particularly, Ramsey and Smith's *Jazzmen* (1939) stirred interest in the performers and early days of jazz. These scholarly studies and anecdotal remembrances, coupled with a handful of record companies that reissued some classic sides by old-time musicians, led to a postwar revival of this form of jazz. A number of instrumentalists—mainly black, largely overlooked, and seemingly in the autumn of their careers, such as Sidney Bechet (1897–1959), George Brunies (1902–1974), Pops Foster (1892–1969), Bunk Johnson (1879–1949), George Lewis (1900–1968), and Kid Ory (1886–1973)—were rediscovered. At the same time, a group of mainly white, tradition-favoring musicians such as Wild Bill Davison (1906–1989), Bud Freeman (1906–1991), Art Hodes (1904–1993), Pee Wee Russell (1906–1969), and Muggsy Spanier (1906–1967) joined with these veteran players. Veteran guitarist Eddie Condon (1905–1973), owner of a popular New York club, served as an unofficial raconteur for the East Coast factions of the revival and led his own group of spirited jazzmen. As the 1940s progressed, the movement spawned a small but enthusiastic following, and interest in the roots of jazz grew throughout the 1940s.

While Condon and his followers held forth in New York, trumpeter Lu Watters (1911–1989) and His Yerba Buena Jazz Band, a California outfit that featured trombonist Turk Murphy (1915–1987) and pianist Wally Rose (1913–1997), led a similar revival on the West Coast during this period. Watters's group brought, they claimed, a kind of historical purity to their music. Other musicians joined in, including Bob Scobey (1916–1963) and his band, which featured the singing of Clancy Hayes (1908–1972). Regardless of location, these musicians tried to stay reasonably true to the authentic music of New Orleans in its early-20th-century heyday.

Many listeners, East and West Coast, lumped these efforts under the generic title Dixieland, and the music cultivated a core of dedicated fans during the later 1940s that has endured into the present. In 1949, a group of young musicians, after playing under several names in New Orleans, reorganized as The Dukes of Dixieland. What they perhaps lacked in the historical purity of their music, they made up for with enthusiasm. And for countless fans receptive to this kind of music, the band epitomized Dixieland and the New Orleans tradition as attested to by strong record sales. For many, the traditional revival signaled a desire to return to the beginnings of jazz, and the popularity espoused for New Orleans, Dixieland, or any of their variants amounted to a rejection both of big band swing and the many experiments taking place in the realm of more modern—and often less accessible—jazz styles.

Hollywood acknowledged this revival with a 1947 film, *New Orleans*. Musically, it stars Louis Armstrong, Billie Holiday (1915–1959), and Woody Herman, along with a number of fine sidemen, but, as several critics noted, the insipid story gets in the way of the music. Even Armstrong saw his career rise to new, successful heights when he played a concert at New York's Town Hall in 1947. From this event grew the Louis Armstrong All Stars, a well-named troupe of veteran musicians capable of playing in all mainstream styles. Armstrong's ensemble, which included trombonist Jack Teagarden (1905–1964) and drummer Sid Catlett (1910–1951), among others, delight club and concert audiences with their straight-ahead presentation and recorded extensively, continuing successfully on all counts into the 1950s.

Jazz is a music that constantly mutates and evolves. The newer postwar embodiments of jazz grew in clubs, jam sessions, in hotel rooms and buses on the road, drawing from all that went before it—the blues, stride piano, swing, from Louis Armstrong's amazing trumpet constructions to Benny Goodman's fluid clarinet stylings. It often took time to develop new expressions and find an appreciative audience, and so many modernists had to struggle, both creatively and economically.

***See also:*** *ASCAP vs. BMI* Radio Boycott and the AFM Recording Ban; Boogie-Woogie; Crosby, Bing; Classical Music; Country Music; Race Relations and Stereotyping; Radio Programming: Music and Variety Shows

**Selected Reading**

Gioia, Ted. *The History of Jazz.* New York: Oxford University Press, 1997.

McClellan, Lawrence, Jr. *The Later Swing Era, 1942 to 1955.* Westport, CT: Greenwood Press, 2004.

Ward, Geoffrey C., and Ken Burns. *Jazz: A History of America's Music.* New York: Alfred A. Knopf, 2000.

Young, William H., and Nancy K. Young. *American Music through History: The World War II Era.* Westport, CT: Greenwood Publishing Group, 2005.

# JONES, SPIKE

In the grim, early days of World War II, a bandleader came along who injected a welcome dose of humor into his performances. He went by the name Spike Jones (1911–1965), and he called his group the City Slickers, a play on the hillbilly music then receiving increased exposure that often employed gags and costumes for effect. In actuality, he was born in urban Southern California as Lindley Armstrong Jones. On stage, and usually attired in suits sporting outlandish patterns and colors, Jones and his City Slickers achieved fame—or notoriety—for comic renditions of both original materials and adapted old favorites.

As an adolescent, Jones played drums in bands he organized with his pals. In addition, he displayed dexterity in playing pots and pans or anything else handy that could be used to percussive effect. He graduated to more legitimate orchestras in the 1930s, experience that exposed him to **radio** shows and theater performances, all of which led to employment as a drummer in various name bands, including John Scott Trotter's (1908–1975) orchestra from 1937 to 1942. Trotter's aggregation, which long backed vocalist **Bing Crosby** (1903–1977) on his *Kraft Music Hall* radio program and on his Decca recordings, mainly played smooth, conventional pop music. Occasionally, however, Trotter's music veered off into raucousness.

The cause for this transition rested with comedian Bob Burns (1890–1956), a frequent guest on Crosby's show. Burns had crafted a unique musical instrument made from stove pipes and tubing that he referred to as a bazooka. When he blew into this ungainly contraption, it produced a hoarse, unharmonic ba-zoom. Trotter and his musicians would follow suit on their traditional instruments, and the audience loved it. U.S. soldiers in World War II also christened a handheld tubular antitank weapon a bazooka because of its resemblance to Burns's creation. This combination of sounds and popular response caught Jones's ear and triggered his imagination. He foresaw leading a band that featured comic music and offbeat instruments.

While still working for Trotter, Jones put together a pick-up band in order to do a little freelance work. The as-yet unnamed group showed promise, and RCA Victor signed Jones to a recording contract in 1941. The term "City Slickers" had perhaps been informally discussed, but it appeared on the label of their first Victor release, making it more or less official. Their first commercial success occurred with "Clink,

Clink, Another Drink," recorded early in 1942 and featuring the voice of Mel Blanc (1908–1989), "the man of a thousand voices" and most famous for creating the voices of most of the cartoon menagerie—Bugs Bunny, Tweety Bird, Sylvester the Cat, and others—seen in Warner Bros. animated features.

The band's road to fame continued in 1942 with a song to be featured in war-related animated cartoon. *Donald Duck in Nutzi Land,* which had been produced by the Walt Disney studios, employs a song called "Der Fuehrer's Face" (1942) throughout its roughly eight-minute running time. Shortly before the film's January 1943 release, the number had already been heard on radio and recordings cut just prior to the recording ban that went into effect in August 1942, a situation that lasted until November 1944. The song became especially popular in a version arranged for Spike Jones and the City Slickers.

This satire about "Der Fuehrer" (the Leader), as German dictator Adolf Hitler (1889–1945) was known, elicited an immediate and favorable response from the American public and promptly became the first charted hit for the band. The Disney organization, aware of the song's runaway success, renamed the cartoon utilizing the song's title. The soundtrack, however, plays another arrangement. Jones's recorded version, and the one most people knew at the time, uses some rather rude sound effects each time the word "*heil*" ("hail," as in hail to the chief) occurs, and it occurs numerous times. An improvised instrument called a birdophone announces, loud and clear, the band's opinion of Hitler immediately after each *heil.* The cartoon's version substitutes a more modest low note from a trombone, although anyone familiar with the City Slickers would know what had been omitted.

The success of "Der Fuehrer's Face" cast Jones and his musicians as hot properties in the music business. Their unique instrumentation, such as the birdophone, along with the anvilaphone (a dressed-up anvil) and the latrinophone (a toilet seat with strings), plus the sounds of gunshots (Jones frequently came on stage brandishing a six-gun), klaxons, car horns, foghorns, cowbells, pots and pans, washboards, and squeeze bulbs delighted listeners, as did the band's unique skills in creating Bronx cheers, raspberries, burps, belches, gurgles, and other impolite sounds. Carl Grayson (active 1940s) did the vocal honors on "Der Fuehrer's Face," although the talented Red Engle (1906–1965) usually performed the vocals during the early 1940s because he possessed many humorous voices. Winstead "Doodles" Weaver (1911–1983) kept the audience in stitches with his horse race routines, especially "Feetlebaum" (1947). Del Porter (1902–1977) wrote many of the band's early arrangements; Joe "Country" Washburne (1904–1974) followed him and expanded the City Slickers' wacky repertoire.

Many of the City Slickers' biggest hits were performed on radio during the recording ban. Fortunately for fans of Spike Jones's music, engineers preserved them on transcription disks, something those enforcing the ban permitted, provided they were not sold commercially. After 1944, these radio recordings could be transferred to regular records and purchased by the general public. Songs like "Little Bo-Peep Has Lost Her Jeep" (1942), "Siam" (1942), and "Hotcha Cornia" (1943; parody adaptation of a traditional 1800 Russian folk melody called "Otshi Tshornye" or "Dark Eyes") soon became available in stores. Shortly thereafter, the group claimed three successful hits with "Cocktails for Two" (1944; a parody of a 1934 tune of the same name), "You

Always Hurt the One You Love" (1944; a parody of a pop hit from that year), and "Chloe" (1945; a parody of a 1927 tune bearing the same name). Even the irrepressible Jones and his zanies had a song for the anticipated return of the troops in 1945: "Leave the Dishes in the Sink, Ma," a tune for which renowned comedian Milton Berle (1908–2002) received partial credit for the lyrics.

In the mid-1940s, Spike Jones strove to gain some musical legitimacy among his critics. All of his sidemen were accomplished musicians; if they had not been so, they could not have so skillfully distorted songs in the myriad ways that became their trademark. In 1945, he formed Spike Jones and His Other Orchestra. It played reasonably straight dance music, with few shenanigans. But the effort ended up costing him money out of his own pockets, because disappointed audiences continued to demand the City Slickers. In response, Jones gave up and returned to his old ways, forming *The Musical Depreciation Revue* in 1946, a touring show featuring the City Slickers once again. He hit his stride with 1948's hit, "All I Want for Christmas Is My Two Front Teeth," a novelty holiday tune featuring a nasal, childlike vocal by trumpeter George Rock (active 1940s and 1950s), in reality an extremely large man. But **rhythm 'n' blues,** rock 'n' roll, and a changed musical climate made Jones and his crew obsolete for new generations of listeners in the years ahead.

He ventured into **movies**—*Thank Your Lucky Stars* (1943), *Breakfast in Hollywood* (1946), *Ladies' Man* (1947), *Variety Girl* (1947), and several years later, his only starring role and his final film, *Fireman Save My Child* (1954)—but he usually had minor walk-on parts or maybe a featured number with the City Slickers. Radio, which had served Jones well in the early 1940s by carrying his music, landed the bandleader his own program, *The Spike Jones Show* in 1945 as a summer replacement on NBC (National Broadcasting Company). He then moved to **MBS (Mutual Broadcasting System)** in 1946 for several months, and then to CBS (Columbia Broadcasting System) in 1947 to 1948 for the *Spotlight Revue,* where he shared the microphone with Dorothy Shay (1921–1978), the "Park Avenue hillbillie," a popular comedy vocalist of the day. Shay departed in 1949, and the series' title became *The Spike Jones Show* for the remainder of the season. Neither his movie nor his radio career, however, equaled the success Jones found in recordings and personal appearances.

Spike Jones and His City Slickers, will be remembered as a wacky aggregation that delighted in parodying—some would say wrecking or destroying—music of any and all kinds. Just as his impudent "Der Fueher's Face" had amused millions in 1942, the band's many take-offs of more serious music kept listeners laughing and probably made it impossible for anyone to listen to a song in its original format without thinking of the shambles the City Slickers made of it.

*See also:* ASCAP *vs.* BMI Radio Boycott and the AFM Recording Ban; Cartoons (Film); Country Music; Radio Programming: Comedy Shows; Radio Programming: Music and Variety Shows.

**Selected Reading**

Mirtle, Jack. *Thank You, Music Lovers: A Bio-Discography of Spike Jones, 1941–1965.* Westport, CT: Greenwood Press, 1986.

Young, Jordan R. *Spike Jones Off the Record: The Man Who Murdered Music.* Albany, NY: Bearmanor Media, 2004.

# JUKEBOXES

Historians trace the origin of the term jukebox back to the days of slavery in the American South. In West Africa, "juke" meant disorder, wickedness, or a house of prostitution. With the transport of black Africans to the United States, the term took on new meaning: a cheap, rowdy **dance** hall, usually located on rural roads in the South. Even the dances became jukes. Sometimes the use of an alternative spelling "jook" allowed the place to be called a jook joint. In the late 1920s, coin-operated machines began to replace live music at many of these establishments; by the mid-1930s, the term "juke" had shifted from the dance halls and bars to the record machines found in them, and thereafter entered the language.

The development of the jukebox can be attributed to Thomas Edison (1846–1931) and his invention of the phonograph. His models played cylindrical recordings. The introduction of the more familiar flat disks offered Edison some competition and finally became the standard in the recording industry. A significant step forward occurred in 1916, when the John Gabel Manufacturing Company of Chicago, initially a manufacturer of player pianos, produced a coin-operated machine that handled 24 disks in sequence.

Even with the ability to hold more than one recording, problems existed. For example, only one side of a disk could be played, and the lack of a means to adequately amplify acoustic sound made the players impractical in the crowded public places where they were most likely to be found, such as bars and taverns. In addition, a coin chute that could detect false coins and, in turn, reject them had not yet been invented. Over the years, corrections to these faults finally enabled the Automatic Musical Instrument Company (AMI; founded in 1927) in Grand Rapids, Michigan, to introduce the first coin-operated, electrically amplified, 20-selection phonograph with a mechanical 10-record system that played disks on both sides. The modern jukebox had arrived

*By 1940, jukebox manufacturing had become a profitable business, and three major companies called upon their engineers and industrial designers to create the most up-to-date machines housed in creative and elaborate cabinets. This model is just one of many on the market at the time. (Photofest)*

By 1940, jukebox manufacturers were making a considerable profit from their machines. The **technology** had improved, and problems of amplification had been resolved. In addition to the Gabel Company and AMI, three other major manufacturers entered the industry within a few years of each other—the J. P. Seeburg Corporation (Seeburg, 1928), the Rudolph Wurlitzer Company (Wurlitzer, 1933), and the Rock-Ola Manufacturing Corporation (Rock-Ola, 1935). Rock-Ola went on to purchase the Gabel Company in 1949, and Rowe machines acquired AMI in 1959 to become known as Rowe/AMI. A number of much smaller firms also attempted to attract buyers but enjoyed little success.

In order to compete, all five major manufacturers worked closely with engineers and industrial designers in hopes of offering the most up-to-date machines housed in attractive cabinets. Clifford Brooks Stevens (1911–1995), perhaps best known for his **design** projects for Studebaker **automobiles** and Harley-Davidson motorcycles, worked with the Gabel Company in the late 1930s and early 1940s to create eye-catching cabinets. Paul M. Fuller (1897–1951), another well-known designer, worked for Wurlitzer and receives credit for giving the company an edge on the market prior to World War II in both large floor models and a special small version that could be placed in cramped quarters such as diners, **restaurants,** and taverns.

From 1942 until early 1946, the U.S. government halted jukebox production, along with many other luxuries, to free labor for defense jobs and materials for the war effort. Both the Seeburg Company and Wurlitzer converted their facilities to wartime efforts and each received three Army-Navy E (for excellence) Awards. Seeburg manufactured electrical equipment for the armed forces, while Wurlitzer provided interphone communication systems for aircraft. Its factories also supplied ramps, floors, doors, and miscellaneous wooden accessories. Rock-Ola became 1 of 10 civilian companies contracted to manufacture the M1 carbine, the most widely produced small arm of World War II.

But the war only served to bolster the popularity of jukeboxes. People wanted music for listening and for dancing, and in public places like bars and taverns these electronic marvels provided it for just a few cents a song. The orchestra led by Glenn Miller (1904–1944), a favorite of millions, even paid homage to AMI, Seeburg, and others with "Juke Box Saturday Night," a hit recording penned by Al Stillman (1906–1979) and Paul McGrane (active 1940s). The band plays imitations of then-current tunes being widely played on jukeboxes everywhere; the song also enjoyed featured billing in the Broadway musical *Stars on Ice,* a show that ran from 1942 to 1944. A rarely seen movie, *Juke-Box Jenny,* played movie theaters in 1942. A mediocre B picture, it nonetheless features some good swing musicians and the song, "Fifty Million Nickels Can't Be Wrong," along with a ludicrous glimpse of the jukebox business.

Once victory had been declared, the troops began returning home, jukebox components once again became available, and the country stood ready to celebrate. To take advantage of peacetime demand, all top five companies resumed manufacturing coin-operated machines. Almost half a million jukeboxes had played music in the United States in 1939; by the late 1940s, over 2 million of them took patrons' nickels (about 45 cents in 2008 money). New models sported names like *Night Club, Peacock, Singing Tower, Streamliner,* and *Throne of Music.* Insatiable, jukeboxes in the 1940s consumed over 13 million disks a year, or almost 15 percent of the total output of the nation's record companies.

In their quest for distinctive cabinets to house all the electronics inside a modern jukebox, Wurlitzer rejected the more traditional gothic and cathedral models, opting instead for a jazzy art deco look. The company's 1015 jukebox, referred to as the Bubbler and designed in 1946 by Paul Fuller, achieved a futuristic light and music show effect with colored bubble tubes that started at the bottom of the cabinet, rose vertically, and then arched over the top of the unit. Wurlitzer sold 56,000 of Bubblers in less than two years, a record that pushed the firm to a leadership position in the industry.

*Billboard* magazine, a widely read trade journal, began posting a weekly chart it called "Most Played in Juke Boxes," a listing of those individual songs available for coin-operated play. This coverage of the business underscored the importance given to jukeboxes; when people heard a song on a jukebox, they frequently bought the recording. Thanks to their heavy use, jukeboxes exerted a strong influence on the acceptance and sales of individual songs.

With the introduction of 45-rpm records in 1949 by RCA Victor, jukeboxes everywhere had to be significantly altered or new ones manufactured to make the switch from the traditional 10-inch 78-rpm disks to Victor's 7-inch 45s. In 1950, Seeburg introduced the M100B, the first jukebox to play 45-rpm records, creating tight competition between Seeburg and Wurlitzer. In 1954, Wurlitzer countered with a conversion kit that enabled the Bubbler and other company models to play the new records. The Bubbler continued to be in high demand throughout the decade; as a final statement about its iconic status, Wurlitzer celebrated the 40th anniversary of this remarkable machine by manufacturing it again in 1986 and dubbing it One More Time. On the outside it retained its classic design, but inside the new Bubbler held the latest technology.

Competing firms followed Wurlitzer's design example by opting for more colors, more bubbles, and more garish, eye-catching decorations; the gaudier the jukebox, the better people seemed to like it. Soon after the 1946 appearance of the Bubbler, Rock-Ola introduced its Magic Glow machine, which also employed an arch design and illuminated bright colors that did indeed have a magic glow. By 1948, the company had three models in this series.

American-made jukeboxes became synonymous with outlandish design, regardless of what company built them, and the illuminated arch established itself as a standard decoration. Seeburg's 3W-1 wallbox, or Wall-O-Matic, which made its debut in 1948, proved an exception; it nonetheless stands equal to the Bubbler as one of the most recognizable jukeboxes ever made. With its simple beige-colored cabinet, the 3W-1 could be hung on the wall of diner and restaurant booths or grace the establishments' counters. Small units and wall mounts were not new, but the 3W-1's 100 selections, 20 visible at a time, and a single coin chute for nickels, dimes, or quarters surpassed the usual 24- or 40-selection machines. It also featured Selectomatic, which added to the ease with which customers could pick and play their favorite songs. Businesses, of course, also enjoyed the increased number of times money dropped into the coin slots.

The makers of jukeboxes, like all manufacturers, regularly advertised their products in brochures and in trade journals such as the *Automatic Age Coin Machine Magazine.* Seeburg issued its own *Seeburg Illuminator* giving all of the latest news about its players. Wurlitzer distinguished itself in the industry by **advertising** in mass media publications. During World War II, company ads appeared in mainstream periodicals such as *Better Homes and Gardens* (founded 1922) and emphasized support for the war;

for example, from May to December of 1943, Wurlitzer published seven ads under the theme "For Victory, Invest in **War Bonds.**"

Starting in 1946, Wurlitzer expanded its advertising to include the widely distributed *Saturday Evening Post* (founded 1821), *American Weekly* (founded 1896), *Collier's* (1888), *True Confessions* (1922), *Liberty* (1924), *Life* (1936), and *Look* (1937). The advertisements all featured colored artwork by noted **illustrators.**

Along with its extensive ad campaigns mounted in the 1940s, Wurlitzer began using a new company logo. Officially known as "The Sign of the Musical Note," it features a trumpet-playing musical note wearing a top hat and standing in front of a spinning record. Widely seen on billboards and promotional giveaways as well as in magazine ads, the logo, referred to as "Johnny-One-Note," became immediately recognizable as representative of Wurlitzer. A 1937 Broadway musical, *Babes in Arms,* featured a song titled "Johnny One Note," with music by Richard Rodgers (1902–1979) and lyrics by Lorenz Hart (1895–1943), but any direct connection between the two remains uncertain.

Prior to the mid-1930s, Americans had fallen in love with technological advances; they expressed a growing demand for coin-operated music machines in public places and businesses that offered this form of musical entertainment. Five companies emerged in the early 1940s as the major players in what is referred to as the golden age of jukeboxes (1936–1950). Many hard-working industrial designers secured a number of design patents in a relatively short period of time, and postwar models appeared in large numbers, followed by effective marketing.

Jukeboxes peaked in the 1950s, and then a decline in demand for newer models set in during the 1970s. Eventually Seeburg stopped operations in the United States and Wurlitzer went out of business. AMI continued to function as Rowe International, and Rock-Ola sold its business in the 1990s to Glenn Streeter (active late 20th century) who, maintaining the Rock-Ola name, manufactures both commercial and home jukeboxes.

***See also:*** Art (Painting); *ASCAP vs. BMI* Radio Boycott and the AFM Recording Ban; Aviation; Broadway Shows (Musicals); Cole, Nat King; Country Music; Crosby, Bing; Leisure and Recreation; Magazines; Sinatra, Frank

**Selected Reading**

DeCillis, Tom. *Toms Zone: The inComplete Jukebox.* www.tomszone.com

Jukebox History. www.nationaljukebox.com/history.html; www.radiomuseum.org/forum/jukebox_history_of_coin-operated_phonographs.html

Lynch, Vincent, and Bill Henkin. *Jukebox: The Golden Age.* Berkeley, CA: Lancaster-Miller, 1981.

## JUVENILE DELINQUENCY

Adolescence can be a confusing age even in times of peace. The first years of World War II proved especially baffling for America's **youth,** since those under the legal draft age of 18 had no clear role to play in the national effort to win the war. They could participate when activities such as rationing, **scrap drives,** and **civil defense** programs got underway, but even this involvement did not lessen feelings of fear, anxiety, and being left out.

When the United States began drafting millions of young men into military service, industries actively recruited young people (as well as countless adults) to work in defense facilities that operated around the clock. Some teenagers saw this as an opportunity for freedom, money, and a sense of direction, and they quit school to obtain jobs. Suddenly members of the typical American family found themselves going in myriad directions: fathers off to war; mothers working; and teenagers either in school, working, or both.

Without supervision and with money in their pockets, these youthful workers, along with others still in school, began to spend more time away from home. The expectation among adolescent males of eventually having to fight, along with a general desire for an adventure, led some to acts of misconduct—primarily petty larceny, burglary, running away from home, car thefts, disorderly behavior, and malicious mischief—in numbers greater than prior to the war. Others, not involved in any wrongdoings and not counted in the data but caught up in current **fads** such as hot-rodding or wearing zoot suits, were mistakenly viewed by various adults as delinquents.

The rise in statistics about real juvenile delinquency also occurred among girls. For example, the Federal Bureau of Investigation (FBI) reported a 64 percent increase in the number of females under 21 arrested during the first six months of 1943 over the same time period of 1942. There had also been a significant jump in 1942 over 1941. Many adolescents of both sexes felt disoriented because of the war and likewise resorted to unlawful behavior involving petty larceny, incorrigibility, truancy, disorderly conduct, running away from home, and sex offenses. A particular concern for adults involved the practice of some young women to offer companionship, and often sex, to servicemen, all under the guise of patriotism.

The National Recreation Association published a pamphlet in 1943 called *Teen Trouble,* which describes this activity as an effective "get-your-man plan" used by girls around 14 and 15 years old. Known as V girls (victory girls), khaki-wackies, good-time Charlottes, and free girls, some even traveled to various military bases and port areas seeking intimate encounters. Venereal disease and pregnancy emerged as serious consequences for some.

Judges in large metropolitan areas across the country voiced concern about the increase in juvenile delinquency as measured by a sharp rise in the number of teenagers brought into court. Records of these cases indicated three wartime conditions as contributing factors: (1) parents absent from home because of fathers in the service and mothers with defense jobs; (2) rapid increases in teenage employment (much of it illegal in light of child labor laws); and (3) high wages paid to young people. The FBI reported that youthful offenders, however, stated lack of adequate recreational facilities as the primary cause of their misconduct.

In 1944, Dorothy Gordon (1889–1970), a **radio** journalist, interviewed a broad sample of adolescents between the ages of 15 and 17 enrolled in public, private, and parochial schools about their views on juvenile delinquency. These respondents, perhaps differing in experiences from youths with arrest records, seem unconcerned about inadequate numbers of recreation facilities. Instead, they suggested lack of sex **education** and gangster-oriented **movies** and literature as the major influences.

Many of these respondents probably had seen such films, because Hollywood had regularly produced gangster and crime motion pictures throughout the 1930s. These movies, like *Little Caesar* (1931), glamorize criminals and outline in great detail their encounters with law enforcement officials. Samuel Goldwyn's *Dead End* (1937) introduces six young actors called the Dead End Kids who portray unruly and incorrigible delinquents in a half-dozen productions made between 1937 and 1939. A seventh feature, *The Angels Wash Their Faces* (1939), brings a positive slant to a Dead End Kids picture when reform school successfully influences one of the kids to return home and help clean up corrupt businessmen.

By 1940, the motion picture industry became consumed by the war in Europe and greatly reduced the output of crime movies, although it did occasionally acknowledge the growing concerns about juvenile delinquency. For the most part, however, it concentrated on making films with patriotic themes. Pictures with juvenile characters and their stories seldom dealt with the real issues, but instead focused on how antisocial youth could be brought into mainstream society and help with the war effort. For example, *Sea Raiders* (1941), the last picture to feature the Dead End Kids (they became the East Side Kids in 1940 and the Bowery Boys in 1946), and Universal Pictures' *Junior G-Men of the Air* (1942) linked delinquency and the war by showing a group of boys in heroic acts helping to capture saboteurs and foreign agents. Three others, *The Penalty* (1941), *Johnny Holiday* (1949), and *Kid from Cleveland* (1949), focus on the results of sending delinquents to either reform schools or rehabilitative farms, steps guaranteed to produce model patriotic citizens.

Twentieth-Century Fox took a different slant in 1943 with a documentary titled *Youth in Crisis*. This production specifically links rising juvenile delinquency statistics to fathers in the military, mothers working, and employed teenagers earning money. The film also suggests answers: kids selling **war bonds** and joining 4-H clubs. RKO Radio Pictures followed with a similar movie in 1944, *Youth Runs Wild,* which seriously addresses the absence of parents in wartime and what appears to be an accompanying wave of juvenile delinquency.

On another front, Fredric Wertham (1895–1981), a respected New York psychiatrist, published *Dark Legend* in 1941. He based his book on the true story of a 17-year-old patient and murderer that Wertham described as a youngster with a sinister fantasy life based on popular culture outlets like movies, radio shows, and **comic books.** Writing in the later 1940s, Wertham published interviews and articles in such periodicals as *Collier's,* the *Saturday Review of Literature,* and the *American Journal of Psychotherapy.* In each, he pursued a common theme—that comic books posed a negative, possibly dangerous, influence on youth.

The comic book industry attempted to respond. A few publishers formed the Association of Comics Magazine Publishers and announced a Publishers Code with six standards as guides to self-regulate decency in their publications. Many of the larger comic book houses, however, declined membership and enforcement of the code failed. Wertham continued with his campaign and in 1954 wrote *Seduction of the Innocent,* a sensational book that led to a U.S. Senate hearing on the potential dangers caused by mass media. The publishers organized again and created the Comics Magazine Association of America and a new 12-point Comics Code Authority (CCA). Although the CCA succeeded in toning down the content of some comics, Wertham continued to rail against comic books for years thereafter.

Whatever the causes of juvenile delinquency during the 1940s, many commentators addressed the issue. At the end of 1943, *Life* magazine ran an article bearing the title, "Our Kids Are in Trouble." Alarmed communities across the country sought to find solutions. In the spring of 1944, *Look* magazine profiled a youth center in Moline, Illinois, and in October, Continental Pictures released *Youth Aflame,* which tells the story of the good Katie trying to help her wayward sister and other juveniles by opening the Jive Club. Soon Teen **Canteens** appeared across the country. Usually neighborhood based and located at facilities such as the YMCA, a church, community center, or empty building, these centers offered ping-pong tables, **jukeboxes, dance** floors, and Coke machines; they enforced age restrictions, usually 13 to 19, and opened Friday and Saturday evenings as well as several weeknights. Recognizing a marketing potential, the Coca-Cola Company had quickly distributed pamphlets on start-up procedures. As places for the teenage crowd to go, Teen Canteens carried a variety of distinctive names that reflected the youth culture of the day: the Jive Hive, the **Swing** Haven, Rhythm Rocker, or Boogie, to name a few.

Despite these valiant efforts, a steady increase in juvenile delinquency statistics continued throughout the war years, causing **President Harry S. Truman** (1884–1972) in December 1945 to acknowledge it as the most alarming problem for the country since the war. Early the next year, the Magazine Bureau of the Office of War Information (OWI) distributed "Magazine War Guide" to hundreds of magazine editors, urging them to educate the public about the situation by including articles about juvenile delinquency instead of continuing discussions about child care centers, a wartime issue.

By February 1946, Attorney General Tom Clark (1899–1977) had declared war on juvenile delinquency by appointing a 30-member national advisory panel to study the increase and make recommendations. Suggestions included a national conference to be attended by leading authorities on the subject; schools and agencies across the country organizing classes to help parents cope; prevention programs to be carried out by schools and social agencies; more traditional youth activities already provided by the scouts, YMCA, and YWCA, and churches increasing their activities with teenagers.

Juvenile delinquency—its statistics, possible causes—gained considerable media coverage, much of it sensational, during the later 1940s. According to the United States Children's Bureau, rates increased markedly during World War II and by 1947 had declined somewhat, especially in large cities such as Los Angeles, Philadelphia, and New York. During the 1950s, cases of juvenile delinquency again increased annually despite all the good efforts made during the 1940s.

*See also:* Best Sellers; Beverages; Comedies (Film); Crime and Mystery Films; Hot Rods and Drag Racing; Leisure and Recreation; Magazines; Political and Propaganda Films; Religion

**Selected Reading**

Devlin, Rachel. "Female Juvenile Delinquency and the Problem of Sexual Authority in America, 1945–1965." In *Delinquents and Debutantes, Twentieth-Century Girls' Cultures,* ed. Sherrie A. Inness, pp. 83–106. New York: New York University Press, 1998.

Juvenile Delinquency. *New York Times,* September 22, 1942; December 28, 1942; May 21, 1943; July 18, 1943, September 22, 1943; September 25, 1943; August 6, 1944; December 12, 1945, February 10, 1946; April 28, 1947; July 20, 1947; April 24, 1949. www.proquest.com

Savage, Jon. *Teenage: The Creation of Youth Culture.* New York: Viking, 2007.

# K

## KINSEY, ALFRED C.

Two controversial books, *Sexual Behavior in the Human Male* (1948) and *Sexual Behavior in the Human Female* (1953), made Alfred C. Kinsey (1894–1956), formerly an obscure researcher, famous outside his regular academic circles. Both books became **best sellers,** and profits from them went to finance the Institute of Sex Research at Indiana University in Bloomington, Indiana. Founded in 1947 by Kinsey, in affiliation with Indiana University, it evolved into The Kinsey Institute for Research in Sex, Gender, and Reproduction in 1982. It continues to actively promote interdisciplinary research on human sexuality in all its forms. The institute also houses an archive of more than 48,000 inventoried photographs. The bulk of this collection documents artistic and popular representations of the human body and various sexual behaviors.

In the 1948 and 1953 publications, Kinsey and his coworkers, Clyde Martin (b. 1918), Wardell Pomeroy (1913–2001), and Paul Gebhard (b. 1917), dared to challenge a prevailing silence that surrounded human sexuality in American society. Under the direction of Kinsey, the researchers set out to explore suspected contrasts between how people presented themselves to others as against the realities of their sexual behavior. The first book emerged from 5,300 personal interviews with white men, each encompassing over 300 questions, contained in 12,000 sets of data.

When Kinsey commenced this research in the early 1940s, he had already become established as a teacher, author, and researcher. After receiving a doctorate in sciences from Harvard University in 1920, he had joined Indiana University as an assistant professor of zoology. He quickly gained the rank of full professor; between 1922 and 1936, he published high school biology books and numerous papers on a small insect called the gall wasp. Within the scientific community, he had been named an outstanding scientist in *American Men of Science* in 1937.

One year later, Kinsey coordinated a course given by several instructors at Indiana University on marriage. Lecturing on the biological aspects of married life, Kinsey became frustrated when trying to answer students' questions about sex with no adequate facts for giving answers. In an attempt to fill this gap in knowledge about a basic human activity, Kinsey decided to conduct research into the sex patterns of men and women. He received enthusiastic support from the university president, Herman B. Wells (1902–2000), and funding from two sources—the National Research Council (founded in 1916) and the Rockefeller Foundation (founded in 1913).

After almost eight years of research and writing, the W. B. Saunders Company of Philadelphia published Alfred Kinsey's *Sexual Behavior in the Human Male,* 804 pages long and at the steep price of $6.50 ($58 in 2008 dollars). One day before the official release date, the *New York Times* carried a thorough and glowing review written by Howard A. Rusk (1901–1989), its medical book reviewer. *Time* magazine ran a long article about Kinsey and his findings on the day the publication appeared in book stores. The book sold over 200,000 copies during the first two months of its release and soon became available in six translations. In hopes of boosting sales, Saunders immediately increased its **advertising** budget and placed ads in both scientific journals and metropolitan **newspapers.**

As to the research, Kinsey and his associates had found that sex behavior for men differed across groups as defined by completed **education** and economic status. He reported that those who had attended college had kissed many women but had had intercourse with none, while males of lower educational levels engaged in more intercourse and less petting. For the sample, 85 percent had had premarital intercourse; nearly 70 percent had had relations with prostitutes; between 30 percent and 45 percent had experienced extramarital intercourse; and 37 percent had engaged in a homosexual experience between adolescence and old age.

From the initial success of the book, Kinsey concluded that people wanted information of this kind. Long-term reactions to such detailed data on human sexual behavior, however, also met with condemnation. Many of his fellow researchers found his methodology, his failure to use random sampling, and the fact that he interviewed only white men to be major flaws. Most were unwilling to support his work and even publicly denounced him and his research. Many in the general public expressed outrage that Kinsey refused to make moral judgments and only presented pure statistics.

Undaunted by criticism and disapproval, Kinsey and his colleagues continued their research with the intent of publishing a second volume on the sexual behavior of women. With over 18,000 personal interviews in their data bank, they utilized almost 6,000 that had been conducted with white women for their second publication. Scheduled to be available at book stores across the country on September 14, 1953, *Sexual Behavior in the Human Female* received advance publicity from *Time* magazine when it featured Kinsey as the subject of its August 24, 1953, cover story and picture.

Another lengthy and costly publication, 842 pages and $8 (almost $65 in 2008 dollars), the report on women, as with men, found a wide gap between the expected sexual conduct and actual behavior. The data showed that 62 percent of the women masturbated; 90 percent had petted; nearly 50 percent had experienced premarital intercourse; 26 percent had participated in extramarital intercourse; and 13 percent had engaged in at least one homosexual contact. Most often referred to as the Kinsey Reports, both books concluded that American men and women engage in sex before marriage and extramarital sex more often than anyone wanted to admit.

The book received an expected flood of mixed reviews. While some expressed horror and disgust that such intimate information would be asked of and reported on women, others thanked Kinsey for his openness and helpfulness of understanding sexual human behavior in the United States. By September 27, *Sexual Behavior in the Human Female* appeared in the No. 3 spot on the general list of best sellers. This, however, did not lessen the distress experienced by Kinsey because of letters of protest and belittling public statements made by noted figures such as Karl Menninger (1893–1990) of the famed Menninger Clinic and the up-and-coming evangelist Billy Graham (b. 1918). Problems for Kinsey escalated when the Rockefeller Foundation did not grant additional funding. Some people suggested that the United States Postal Service (USPS) ban the mailing of the newest book, and the U.S. Army refused to stock the book about women in military libraries in Europe.

Kinsey's personal sexual life had been in turmoil from childhood. The effects of being a married adult and also involved in homosexual relationships, along with the criticisms of his research, took their toll. In 1956, on the defensive more than ever, Kinsey, who had been in poor health for some time, began to experience a serious decline. Until his death, he nonetheless continued to actively attempt to raise money and conducted interviews and appeared in a taped interview on NBC (National Broadcasting Company) **television** on March 20, 1956, just a few months before his death in August.

Debate about the value of Kinsey's work continued long after his death. Some applauded him for his critique of Victorian morality and serving as the father of the sexual revolution of the 1960s, along with championing sex education and gay liberation. Others denounced him as a scientist and lamented the damage brought about by his reports on what they saw as the already deteriorating morals of the United States. In some circles, the debate continues into the 21st century. The books, however, remain available in libraries and from booksellers some 60 years later.

*See also:* Magazines; Photography; Religion

**Selected Reading**
Jones, James H. *Alfred C. Kinsey: A Public/Private Life.* New York: W. W. Norton, 1997.
Kinsey Book Reviews. *Time,* January 5, 1948; April 12, 1948; August 24, 1953. www.time.com/time/magazine/article; *New York Times,* January 4, 1948; August 30, 1953; September 24, 1953. www.proquest.com
*Kinsey Institute for Research in Sex, Gender, and Reproduction.* www.kinseyinstitute.org/

# KRAFT TELEVISION THEATRE

As American **television** attempted to define itself and find what appealed to viewers in the late 1940s, writers, producers, and directors experimented with a variety of dramatic formats, attempting to discover approaches that worked best in the new medium.

One such approach emerging out of these efforts gained the name "anthology dramas," a unique concept that received much critical praise but never achieved the popular success enjoyed by competing comedy and variety shows.

Instead of presenting a group of familiar characters—lawyers, doctors, police, and others—in continuing adventures, as has become the norm for much contemporary network programming, the anthology drama attempted to create an original, unrelated production for each weekly episode of a series. No characters would recur, no plot lines would carry over week to week, and no set formulas would dominate. These shows, such as *The Ford Television Theater* (CBS [Columbia Broadcasting System], others, 1948–1957), *Philco Playhouse* (NBC [National Broadcasting Company], 1948–1955), and *Studio One* (CBS, 1948–1958), presented both adapted and original scripts, usually an hour in length. They utilized the talents of the best writers and playwrights of the day and featured both unknown and star performers.

In the late 1940s, the three major networks launched virtually all their television productions from studios located in New York City. **ABC (American Broadcasting Company),** CBS, and NBC were headquartered there, which meant the people involved usually came from **radio** and Broadway backgrounds, not Hollywood. Given the limitations of cameras and equipment at the time, most shows of any kind had to adapt to these environs. Most writers therefore created plays that might easily have been written for the stage. Dialogue and intimacy preempted any emphases on action or elaborate sets, and seldom did a playwright attempt to present events occurring outside these confines.

*Kraft Television Theatre* (NBC, 1947–1958), a true pioneer among the anthology dramas, first appeared on home screens in the spring of 1947. The Kraft Foods Company, a major processor of cheeses and other dairy products, already possessed considerable experience in radio. The *Kraft Music Hall,* which premiered in 1933 on NBC radio with orchestra leader Paul Whiteman (1890–1967), soon became one of the biggest successes of the day, especially when **Bing Crosby** (1903–1977) hosted it from 1935 until 1946. Kraft had decided on this medium to promote its line of goods, and when sales took off following on-air advertisements, especially for Miracle Whip, a salad dressing and sandwich spread, the company soon sponsored a number of other shows.

J. Walter Thompson, Kraft's **advertising** agency, foresaw great potential with television and convinced the company to underwrite the largely (for the time) experimental *Kraft Television Theatre*. To give an idea of how new and untested television seemed to advertisers, Kraft in 1947 allocated about $3,000 a week to the TV show (about $29,000 in 2008 dollars) for time and talent, a piddling sum by modern entertainment standards. At that same period, Kraft paid up to $30,000 (approximately $290,000 in 2008 dollars) a week for time and talent on the radio version of *Kraft Music Hall*. Much higher fees soon replaced those early television costs as more and more people acquired TV sets and radio usage began to fall off.

In 1947, the beginning of the television boom and the debut of the *Kraft Television Theatre,* U.S. companies managed to manufacture only 180,000 sets for the year. Because broadcasters restricted most programming to the metropolitan New York City area, the small number of receivers caused no real hardship in the rest of the country. By 1948, however, true mass production commenced, and by mid-1949 over 2 million homes boasted sets. A year later, the numbers had more than doubled, to over 5 million sets. Kraft realized what this seismic change meant when sales of its products shown on the *Kraft Television Theatre* rose rapidly. The connections between advertising and television exposure were impossible to ignore.

Announcer Ed Herlihy (1909–1999), blessed with a mellifluous voice and a quiet, authoritative manner, did Kraft's commercials, both on radio and television, for 40 years. He introduced the *Kraft Television Theatre* each week, imploring listeners and viewers, in a dignified way, to try Kraft products and offering recipes that would show off the sponsor's line of goods. For television, the accompanying image showed hands preparing a dish while Herlihy, unseen, described the details involved. The "Kraft Hands" commercials have since become advertising classics.

Most sponsors saw the many anthology dramas as prestigious venues on which to sell their products. The association between the two, they hoped, would make a brand more appealing. These dramatic shows did not always earn the highest ratings, but consumers might nevertheless be impressed by who sponsored them and go out and buy the brand. It has been estimated that more people witnessed a live dramatic production of just one episode of the *Kraft Television Theatre* than the total attendance for the entire 1948 Broadway season.

Media historians, looking back over the early days of commercial TV, have dubbed the era of the anthology dramas, roughly 1949 to 1958, as a Golden Age of Television. The shows, new and fresh and featuring some of the best writing talents of the day, also enjoyed the freedom to be innovative, because producers were not as beholden during that brief period to the tyranny of ratings. Since no one had any previous television models on which to base these pioneering productions, actors, directors, and crews worked in the enviable environment of establishing their own standards. In many instances, they introduced a level of excellence that continues to impress anyone fortunate enough to view them today—often on a grainy kinescope recording, since few of these dramas from the late 1940s have survived—and realize what promise the young medium held.

*See also:* Broadway Shows (Comedy and Drama); Radio Programming: Music and Variety Shows

**Selected Reading**
Hawes, William. *American Television Drama: The Experimental Years.* Tuscaloosa: University of Alabama Press, 1986.
Sturcken, Frank. *Live Television: The Golden Age of 1946–1958 in New York.* Jefferson, NC: McFarland, 2001.

# L

## LABOR UNREST

American labor unions displayed unparalleled might during the 1940s. They achieved this through close ties with the Democratic Party, which had been in power since 1932, plus the labor shortages caused by World War II swelled union membership from roughly 10 million workers in 1940 to almost 15 million in 1945. Prior to the nation's entry into the conflict, labor disputes frequently dominated newspaper headlines. Thanks to the formation of the government's National War Labor Board (NWLB, 1942), union leaders agreed to a nonbinding no-strike pledge for the duration of the struggle. This did not, however, stop strikes or heavy media coverage during or after the hostilities. In 1947, Congress passed a controversial bill known as the Taft-Hartley Act; it placed restrictions on unions and their growing numbers in a response to public demands for action. Tempers ran high, with many believing that post-wartime strikes had damaged the U.S. economy and a prosperous postwar lifestyle that everyone desired; enough was enough.

In the world's preindustrial days, craftsmen in different trades formed guilds to maintain high-quality production standards. Early in the history of the United States, certain laborers continued the guild tradition while others organized as unions, which focused more on protecting common interests and improving working conditions. Shortly after the Civil War (1861–1865), the first national federation of unions formed the National Labor Union. Over the years, organizational changes occurred that resulted in the creation of the American Federation of Labor (AFL) in 1886; it functioned as the parent association for smaller unions, made up primarily of those engaged in skilled trades. William Green (1873–1952) held the position of president of the AFL from 1924 until his death. In 1938, the Congress of Industrial Organizations (CIO) was founded to give mass production workers, especially those in automobile and steel manufacturing, union representation. John L. Lewis (1880–1969) served as its president for the years

1935–1940; Philip Murray (1886–1952) followed Lewis, holding the position until his death in 1952; the same year as Green.

Labor unions addressed issues critical to their members and families, which frequently caused them to go without income during a strike, plus suffering the disdain of those who deplored unions. If strikes proved successful and income levels rose, many families benefited because that meant they moved economically from a laborer's status into the middle class. During strikes, consumers dependent upon products from laborers' work found that they had to do without, since labor stoppages halted production and drained inventories. In addition, meeting union pay demands could result in higher prices for consumers and possible reduction in their spending power.

When strikes took place in the 1930s and 1940s, folk singers, known for protest songs, frequently included labor numbers in their repertoires. The Almanac Singers, a folk trio composed of Pete Seeger (b. 1919), Lee Hays (1914–1981), and Millard Lampell (1919–1997), and frequently joined by Woody Guthrie (1912–1967), serve as an example. They held their first major New York City public appearance at Madison Square Garden in 1941 for the local striking Transport Workers' Union. From the success of this event, the group recorded four albums, including one of union songs. A year later, the Almanac Singers performed a new song they had written about the

TABLE 65. Major Labor Unions Active during the 1940s

| Union | Founded | President, Dates of Office | Comments |
| --- | --- | --- | --- |
| Brotherhood of Locomotive Engineers | 1863 | Alvanley Johnston (1875–1951); 1940s | First union formed among railroad workers |
| United Mine Workers of America | 1890 | John L. Lewis, 1920–1960 | Solicited Dubinsky and Hillman's assistance in forming a Committee of Industrial Organizations in 1935; it became the Congress of Industrial Organizations (CIO). |
| International Ladies Garment Workers Union | 1900 | David Dubinsky (1892–1982), 1932–1966 | Founding member of CIO |
| Amalgamated Clothing Workers of America | 1914 | Sidney Hillman (1887–1946), 1914–1946; Jacob Potofsky (1892–1979), 1946–1976 | Founding member of CIO |
| United Automobile Workers of America (UAW) | 1935 | Francis Dillon (active 1930s and 1940s), 1934–1946; Walter Reuther, (1907–1970), 1946–1970 | Completed goal of representing all automobile manufacturers in 1941, when Henry Ford (1863–1947) finally recognized UAW |
| Steel Workers Organizing Committee; became United Steel Workers | 1936 1942 | Philip Murray, 1942–1952 | Created after six years of divisive struggles to form a union |

*Despite a wartime no-strike commitment made by the leaders of America's major labor unions, laborers continued to protest their working conditions throughout World War II. In this photograph, policemen keep a watchful eye for possible trouble as American Federation of Labor (AFL) electricians defy the ban and picket the Consolidated Edison Company's building in New York City. (Library of Congress)*

United Automobile Workers of America (UAW) titled "UAW-CIO." A patriotic song, the lyrics tell of the UAW members' pride in being Americans and union members. It also came at a time when the Ford Motor Company, the last holdout among automobile manufacturers, allowed for unionization and membership in the UAW.

In 1942, Frontier Films released *Native Land*. Narrated by actor and singer Paul Robeson (1898–1976), the film celebrates patriotism and democracy. It also chronicles abuses suffered by farmers and laborers brought about by union-busting corporations and their spies. The 1930s trend of Hollywood **movies** and Broadway plays dealing with labor issues did not, however, continue into the 1940s because of the war and the need for solidarity.

Prior to the country's participation in World War II, government and industrial leaders had embarked on steps to ready the nation for a transition from consumer to war-defense production. Industries already committed to military contracts stepped up their work, while other manufacturers began to retool for wartime needs. In September 1940, Congress passed, and **President Franklin Delano Roosevelt** (1882–1945) signed, the **Selective Training and Service Act of 1940,** a bill that established mandatory military conscription for men identified as eligible. This resulted in labor shortages throughout the nation for all kinds of work and introduced large numbers of teenagers, blacks, women, Dust Bowl refugees, and other rural migrants to their first industrial jobs—a situation that changed the work environment and the experiences of these new workers.

During the 1940s, organized labor's strikes affected the lives of many citizens and threatened to weaken national security. For example, workers, including coal miners and employees of the New York City Transit company, staged strikes in 1941. Both proved particularly troublesome for the federal government. Coal drove 95 percent of the locomotives and furnished 62 percent of the nation's electric power. Without coal and **transportation** systems, the country could come to a virtual standstill. A walkout by employees of the Allis-Chalmers plant in Milwaukee occurred just as the firm had started to fulfill a contract to build turbines for the navy and created a major issue in defense readiness. A strike at the North American Aviation plant in California proved equally bothersome.

At this time, as the nation prepared for war, resources became scarce, hoarding of **food** and other products used on a daily basis took place, and Americans began to experience a rise in the cost of living—conditions that would continue until 1943. Responding to this multifaceted situation, the NWLB established the "Little Steel Formula," a 15 percent wage increase over January 1941 levels. Government acknowledged the need for more pay but at the same time placed controls on how much. The unusual name for this formula came about because authorities first applied it in a case involving four small companies—Republic Steel Company, Youngstown Sheet and Tube Company, Jones & Laughlin, and Inland Steel—collectively called Little Steel. Its implementation helped keep inflation in check in many areas of U.S. industry. "Big Steel," on the other hand, consisted of large companies such as U.S. Steel, Bethlehem Steel, National Steel, and Armco Steel. They, too, endured stormy labor relations during the 1940s.

In 1943, almost half a million coal miners, unhappy with how the formula restricted their pay, staged four strikes. John L. Lewis (1880–1969), president of the United Mine Workers of America (UMW), authorized the walkouts, which ranged from 48 hours to six days, despite the no-strike rule. At that time, a coal strike created the potential for a state of emergency, especially if it stopped **trains** from running, because they served as the main transport of soldiers across the country to ports of embarkation, as well as carrying civilian passengers and freight. The U.S. government immediately took over the mines. Operation reverted to the owners, and the miners returned to work with a settlement of a pay raise of roughly $1.50 (almost $19 in 2008 dollars) per day, along with increased opportunities for overtime work.

Tensions nevertheless rose in other sectors of the work world, and over 3,700 strikes involving almost 2 million workers occurred in 1943 and continued at a comparable level into 1945. New problems developed after World War II. During the years of the conflict, many workers had benefited from full employment, wages that kept up with inflation, and overtime pay. As soldiers returned home as fast as possible, they reentered civilian life under laws that provided, among many benefits, job reinstatement and seniority rights. Government officials and private-sector management faced the challenge of moving these veterans into the workforce while converting to consumer production.

Rapidly rising demand and limited supplies of both raw materials and finished products created inflationary pressures that once again required price controls. Labor wanted an immediate end to regulations in 1946, making it one of the most severe years of unrest in U.S. labor history. Hoarding and **black market** activity, similar to that which occurred in the early years of the war, reappeared. Strikes broke out in almost every industry as steel, automobile, electrical, lumber, shipping, and railroad workers walked off their jobs. They demanded higher wages, better working conditions, independence on the job, and increased fellowship with coworkers. Before it ended, over 4.5 million workers associated with nearly 5,000 labor disputes accounted for a loss of 116 million days of employment and production.

But three conflicts at this time also damaged labor solidarity and began to lessen union power. In 1946, two groups—coal miners in March and railroad workers in May—yet again threatened strikes that could have created drastic economic problems for the country; the importance of coal and trains had not diminished. Fortunately both the miners' and the railroad employees' grievances were accommodated and strikes averted but not without much agitation within the federal government, including a threat to take over the railroads.

A few months after settlements with both groups, John Lewis, who commanded total dedication from his UMW members, decided he wanted to change the settlement. To this end, in November he threatened to call out 400,000 miners. **President Harry S. Truman** (1884–1972) intervened by obtaining a court order to stop the proposed strike. Lewis ignored the order, and the miners walked out. Legal wheels turned immediately, with Lewis being cited for contempt of court and personally fined $10,000 (a little over $110,000 in 2008 dollars), along with a penalty for the union of $3.5 million (about $39 million in 2008 dollars). Even these steps did not immediately stop Lewis, and the strike continued for more than two weeks. Finally, on December 7, 1946, the anniversary of Pearl Harbor, Lewis summoned his men back to the mines, giving the federal government a victory over labor.

A strained relationship between labor and government ensued. Amid much publicity, both the general public and political leaders condemned organized labor's attempts to free itself from governmental restraints and ruin the economy. Congress responded in 1947 with the passage of the Taft-Hartley Act, which intended to discourage strikes by placing a number of restrictions on unions. Among the law's many regulations, it outlawed the hiring of union members only (closed shops), and required that new employees have sufficient time to decide whether to join a union. Heated debate surrounded the bill, sponsored by Ohio Republican Senator Robert Taft (1889–1953) and New Jersey Republican Representative Fred Hartley 1902–1969). Union leaders strongly opposed its passage, to no avail. President Truman sided with the unions and issued a veto, describing it as a "slave-labor bill." The strongly Republican Congress, however, used its authority to override the veto and did so, a setback for Truman.

The third struggle that damaged labor's solidarity developed around the appropriateness of allowing members of the Communist Party to serve as union leaders. Shortly after the end of World War II, a number of unions—mostly those within the

CIO—either had leaders that belonged to the Communist Party or adhered to that party's positions on political and economic issues. In 1947 and 1948, Philip Murray and Walter Reuther continually voiced concern that Communists who followed the party line did not reflect the political views of most of the workers they represented. In 1949, Murray and Reuther encouraged the executive board of the CIO to squelch the Communist influence, which resulted in the expulsion of 11 unions numbering 900,000 members, action that corresponded to the rising national concern over the developing **Cold War** between the United States and the Soviet Union.

The 1940s began with unprecedented power for organized labor in the United States. The creation of the Congress of Industrial Organizations broadened union membership to include mass production industries, and the labor movement grew rapidly. Membership rolls further increased because the federal government pressured employers to recognize unions. Workers gained paid vacation time that before had been available to only a few, as well as health and retirement benefits; wage gaps between highly- and less-skilled individuals therefore narrowed.

Turbulent relations between organized labor and President Truman during his administration brought about unrest at a level never before seen and resulted in legislation that placed new and tighter restrictions on unions. The decade ended with Reuther leading a CIO delegation to a London conference that established the International Confederation of Free Trade Unions in opposition to the Communist-dominated World Federation of Trade Unions. He became president of the CIO in 1952 and soon joined forces with George Meany (1894–1980) to bring about a merger of the AFL and CIO in 1955. Under Meany's leadership as the elected president of the new AFL-CIO, membership grew again, and organized labor celebrated a rebound from postwar political setbacks, gaining new security and increased influence in the political system.

*See also:* ASCAP *vs.* BMI Radio Boycott and the AFM Recording Ban; Automobiles and the American Automotive Industry; Aviation; Broadway Shows (Comedy and Drama); Folk Music; House Un-American Activities Committee (HUAC); Levittown and Suburbanization; Newspapers; Rationing; Rosie the Riveter

**Selected Reading**
Diggins, John Patrick. *The Proud Decades: America in War and Peace, 1941–1960.* New York: W. W. Norton, 1989.
Patterson, James T. *Grand Expectations: The United States, 1945–1974.* New York: Oxford University Press, 1996.
Zieger, Robert H. *John L. Lewis: Labor Leader.* Boston: G. K. Hall, 1988.
Zieger, Robert H., and Gilbert J. Gall. *American Workers, American Unions.* Baltimore: Johns Hopkins University Press, 2002.

# LAWNS, LAWNMOWERS, AND FERTILIZERS

Home lawns—for most, barely more than a plot of dirt with weeds and a little grass during the years up to and including World War II—went through a transformation with the return of peace. No longer just a small green patch, this outdoor space developed into carefully planned areas of lush grass and often included picturesque arrangements of trees, shrubs, and flower beds. Lawns flourished as a status symbol that represented the joys of postwar prosperity evidenced by home ownership. The yard, front and back, because of the regular use of the best seeds, fertilizers, pesticides, and herbicides available, now required meticulous upkeep. By the late 1940s, a new American pastime had been born.

Prior to the war, a number of homeowners aspired to have and maintain attractive lawns, but the onset of the conflict and the unavailability of items such as grass seed, mowers, gasoline, and rubber for hoses made both the maintenance of established lawns and the creation of new ones a challenge. In fact, by 1945, most lawns had fallen into disrepair, much to the chagrin of the lawn care industry.

One well-established company, O. M. Scott and Sons, which had been founded in 1868 as a local hardware and seed store, stands out among those firms that strove to keep this trade alive during the war. Scott and Sons entered the 1940s strictly as a seed business, although it did have a small mail-order component. Scott advertised its readiness to provide seeds, lawn mowers, fertilizers, and irrigation equipment for the home lawn. A company newsletter, *Lawn Care,* which dated back to 1928, attempted to educate the public on the value of a planted yard for the home. The firm found, to its surprise, that its customers included not only homeowners but also a number of military bases.

In fact, the federal government had been setting good landscaping examples for some time. New Deal projects of the Works Progress [after 1939, Projects] Administration (WPA; 1935–1943) and the Civilian Conservation Corps (CCC; 1933–1942) contributed to the attractiveness of public parks and playgrounds. With the war, the government continued as a good role model, carefully planting grass to keep down the dust around military bases, munitions factories, and federal housing projects.

The end of the war, however, changed everything. A rapid return to civilian-oriented production, along with U.S. assistance to both wartime allies and former enemies, helped create unprecedented postwar prosperity for the nation. As servicemen came home, the country witnessed an increase in marriages and births, a boom that shaped a common dream of home ownership, kids, pets, and a white picket fence surrounding a green lawn.

Suburban developers attempted to fulfill this dream with large planned communities across the country that offered added lawn space. For example, in Levittown, New York, one answer to the postwar demand for individual family homes, the builders utilized grass as a fast and cheap way to hide the scars of construction and then required the homeowners to keep their lawns healthy and trimmed. In turn, landscaped yards immediately became a part of the postwar suburbia, with peer pressure assuring that they stay well-kept, at least the yard fronting the street. Mowing soon became an activity or chore, depending on one's point of view, that sometimes supplanted the weekend **softball, tennis,** or **golf** game.

Before World War II, the care of a lawn befell mostly men; women tended the flower beds. During the war, those women, by necessity, moved from flower gardening to handling all lawn maintenance, and magazine articles and **advertising** reflected this change in roles. After the war, such information reverted to a focus on men but retained a balance in recognizing the involvement of both adult members of the household.

A key to achieving an impressive lawn rests on feeding it with the best nutrients possible; European inventions in the early part of the 20th century guaranteed high-quality fertilizer for American lawns. Fritz Haber (1868–1934), a German chemist and winner of the Nobel Prize in Chemistry in 1918, is perhaps best-known for his work with poison gas, but he also developed a method for synthesizing ammonia, a step necessary for the manufacture of fertilizers. Carl Bosch (1874–1940), a fellow German chemist and winner of the Nobel Prize in Chemistry in 1931, mastered the mysteries of large-scale production, giving the world the Haber-Bosch process that assured an abundant supply of nitrogen for making fertilizers.

With the sudden postwar interest in yards, the lawn care industry became a lucrative one, employing thousands of workers. It eagerly assisted in the development of better lawns by selling imported and hybrid grasses, power mowers, fertilizers, weed killers, herbicides, and an array of related necessities. The first gasoline-powered mower had appeared in 1919, but before World War II most neighborhoods relied on manually pushed models.

Following the war, however, as men returned home and resumed their maintenance chores (or acquired them for the first time), the lawn mower industry initiated a heavy advertising campaign celebrating the superiority of power mowers over push ones. In 1947, the Australian Victa Company introduced its first rotary models, and the ease of lawn maintenance moved up a notch. In a short time, the traditional reel-type mower became obsolete. From 1945 until mid-1948, yard equipment sold as fast as it could be produced. Sales jumped from $5 million in 1941 (about $71 million in 2008 dollars) to $100 million (about $860 million in 2008 dollars) in 1950.

The gardening industry also benefited from increasing rates of home ownership and the resulting rise in neatly kept lawns and gardens. Guidelines and tips appeared in magazine articles, gardening books, and advertisements. One such expert, Charles B. Mills (active 1940s.) of O. M. Scott and Sons, regularly contributed pieces to **magazines** such as *House Beautiful, Better Homes and Gardens,* and *House and Garden.* They all presented the lawn as nurturing, welcoming, beautiful, and safe; what more could a young couple just starting out want? In 1949, *House and Garden* estimated that 19 million people in the United States claimed to be active gardeners.

Neighbors saw their lawns as a means of imitating and outdoing each other, and standards for lawn appearance quickly evolved in the postwar years—grass of the right color, at the correct height, and with the absence of weeds. A flood of advertising and horticultural advice in popular magazines reinforced the importance of these standards. Thanks to the suburban home owners of the late 1940s, the care of the yard has become the weekend pursuit of millions of Americans.

*See also:* Baby Boom; Hobbies; Leisure and Recreation; Levittown and Suburbanization; Technology

**Selected Reading**
Jenkins, Virginia Scott. *The Lawn: A History of an American Obsession.* Washington, DC: Smithsonian Institution Press, 1994.
Nobel Prize Winners. www.nobelprize.org/

# LEISURE AND RECREATION

Leisure, a period of rest, pleasure, and freedom from work and other time-consuming responsibilities, played an essential role in the everyday life of Americans throughout the 1940s, both in war and peace. Armed with experiences gained from the Great Depression, people knew how to fill nonwork hours with amusements. Material shortages during World War II did not deter children or adults from searching for ways to engage in individual, participatory, and spectator activities. They responded to their inability to buy new **games** and recreation equipment by creating homemade ones. They also read voraciously, listened to the **radio,** went to the **movies,** played cards (especially bridge), worked crossword puzzles, and participated in activities and sports at schools, community centers, and neighborhood playgrounds. Old Monopoly sets and jigsaw puzzles, as worn as they may have been, continued to be favorite pastimes.

During the first half of the decade, everyone welcomed any diversion from the realities of the war; with the arrival of peace and prosperity, the nation's involvement with leisure and recreational opportunities exceeded prewar levels and laid the groundwork for even more playtime activities in the 1950s. Tables 66 and 67 illustrate the number of people participating in selected nonwork activities, the money spent on selected leisure pursuits, and the number of recreational areas in the United States during the 1940s. These statistics reveal both decreases and increases for 1943 to 1945, the most intense years of World War II. With millions of soldiers serving overseas, some numbers drop. The return of military personnel after the victory of the Axis powers created stresses and strains on all aspects of life but also contributed to steady postwar growth.

In Table 66, "Participation in Selected Recreational Activities," the game of **bowling** shows the kind of fluctuations that occurred during the war years. With countless

TABLE 66. Participation in Selected Recreational Activities, 1939–1949

| Year | Number of Bowlers (in thousands) | Hunting Licenses (in thousands) | Fishing Licenses (in thousands) | Motion Picture Average Weekly Attendance (in millions) |
| --- | --- | --- | --- | --- |
| 1939 | 535 | 7,511 | 7,858 | 85 |
| 1940 | 684 | 7,646 | 7,931 | 80 |
| 1941 | 874 | 7,913 | 8,004 | 85 |
| 1942 | 1,059 | 8,521 | 8,423 | 85 |
| 1943 | 895 | 8,081 | 8,029 | 85 |
| 1944 | 910 | 7,491 | 7,830 | 85 |
| 1945 | 1,048 | 8,191 | 8,280 | 85 |
| 1946 | 1,060 | 9,854 | 11,069 | 90 |
| 1947 | 1,415 | 12,067 | 12,620 | 90 |
| 1948 | 1,635 | 11,392 | 14,078 | 90 |
| 1949 | 1,821 | 12,759 | 15,479 | 70 |

*Source: Historical Statistics of the United States, Colonial Times to 1970.* Washington, DC: Census Bureau, U.S. Department of Commerce, 1975.

men serving in the armed forces, bowling experienced a decline in the number of participants for 1942 to 1943. By 1945, however, it had returned to its 1942 standing. Originally, a sport that primarily owed its popularity to America's males working class, women increasingly joined bowling's ranks in the 1920s and thereafter, so that by the later 1940s its image had changed. Women entered the industrial workforce in unprecedented numbers as men left their jobs for military service. These new employees frequently played on teams put together by factories, and bowling soon became a recreation for all, regardless of gender.

Hunting and fishing, two other popular recreational endeavors, had traditionally attracted mainly men. As more and more troops departed for the European and Pacific theaters, however, the number of issued licenses decreased from 1942 through 1944. And, unlike bowling, few women chose to take up these sports. Applications moved ahead slightly in 1945 and jumped dramatically in 1946, with peace and increasing numbers of servicemen returning home.

On the other hand, average weekly attendance at the movies, which now included both indoor and drive-in theaters, held steady from 1941 through 1945. Entertaining and cheap, this relaxing medium offered a chance for a brief respite from the tensions of war. Enough men remained stateside and regularly attended the movies—along with millions of women, adolescents, and children—that the absence of servicemen had little impact. In addition, first-run movies were also regularly shown at overseas bases. Many of the films produced during the war years reinforced the values and ideas that U.S. citizens proclaimed as important and validated the sacrifices they were willing to make. People felt good after attending a movie. In the immediate postwar years, audiences continued to increase, but attendance showed a significant drop in 1949; the impacts of **television** were just beginning to be felt.

TABLE 67. Municipal and County Park and Recreation Areas, 1939–1949

| Year | Baseball Diamonds | Softball Diamonds | Tennis Courts | Bathing Beaches | Swimming Pools | Golf Courses | Playgrounds under Leadership |
|---|---|---|---|---|---|---|---|
| 1939 | 3,846 | 8,995 | 11,617 | 548 | 1,181 | 358 | 9,749 |
| 1940 | 3,904 | 10,042 | 12,075 | 572 | 1,200 | 387 | 9,921 |
| 1941 | 3,951 | 10,061 | 12,262 | 583 | 1,278 | 366 | 9,646 |
| 1942 | 3,645 | 9,207 | 11,516 | 529 | 1,190 | 380 | 8,739 |
| 1943 | n.d. | n.d. | n.d. | n.d. | n.d. | n.d. | |
| 1944 | n.d. | n.d. | n.d. | 564 | 1,447 | 409 | 10,022 |
| 1945 | n.d. | n.d. | n.d. | n.d. | n.d. | n.d. | n.d. |
| 1946 | 4,323 | 10,034 | 11,847 | 618 | 1,449 | 340 | 11,559 |
| 1947 | n.d. | n.d. | n.d. | n.d. | n.d. | n.d. | n.d. |
| 1948 | 4,576 | 11,143 | 11,964 | 638 | 1,395 | 355 | 13,520 |
| 1949 | n.d. | n.d. | n.d. | n.d. | n.d. | n.d. | n.d. |

*Note:* n.d. = no data available.
*Source: Historical Statistics of the United States, Colonial Times to 1970.* Washington, DC: Census Bureau, U.S. Department of Commerce, 1975.

Recreational sports and physical activity at parks and playgrounds provide healthy outlets in both stressful and peaceful times. During the early years of the Depression, many recreational areas closed and few new ones were built. With the rise of the New Deal in the mid-1930s, this situation changed as various programs recognized the importance of such establishments. Lawmakers saw to it that new places were developed and provided the necessary personnel to supervise and coordinate activities. Table 67 shows how this movement continued through 1942 and the advent of World War II.

Concrete data for 1943 to 1945, 1947, and 1949, unfortunately, remain spotty, although existing evidence suggests many towns and cities established new recreational sites and initiated programs that offered a variety of activities for relieving anxieties during these years. Wartime gas **rationing** also necessitated limiting activities geographically. Teen centers, neighborhood adult programs, and industrial recreation opportunities flourished close to the participants' homes and neighborhoods.

After the war ended, returning soldiers added to local demand, and national and community leaders immediately acknowledged both the preventive and therapeutic value of recreational activities. Congress formed the Federal Interagency Committee in 1946 and charged it to oversee efforts to initiate and coordinate recreation at the federal level. Locally, communities across the country continued to increase the number of recreational parks and facilities, thus setting the stage for the 1950s, a decade when Americans experienced a significant increase in both disposable income and leisure time.

In addition to the numbers of people engaged in leisure activities and utilizing recreational sites, a review of money spent, as shown in Table 68, further demonstrates how Americans used their leisure time during the 1940s. The war, costly in all ways, nevertheless stimulated economic growth. On the down side, inflation rose 29 percent from 1939 to 1945, and the production of consumer goods was uneven. Americans

TABLE 68.  Personal Consumption Expenditures, 1939–1949 (in millions of dollars)

| Year | Radio and Television Receivers, Recordings, and Musical Instruments | Nondurable Toys, Sport Supplies | Wheel Goods, Durable Toys, Sports Equipment, Including Boats and Pleasure Aircraft | Books, Maps, Magazines, Newspapers, and Sheet Music |
|---|---|---|---|---|
| 1939 | $420 | $285 | $228 | $780 |
| 1940 | $494 | $306 | $254 | $823 |
| 1941 | $607 | $362 | $314 | $891 |
| 1942 | $634 | $404 | $306 | $994 |
| 1943 | $403 | $393 | $271 | $1,204 |
| 1944 | $311 | $459 | $323 | $1,330 |
| 1945 | $344 | $533 | $400 | $1,485 |
| 1946 | $1,116 | $840 | $793 | $1,688 |
| 1947 | $1,398 | $907 | $955 | $1,774 |
| 1948 | $1,450 | $1,076 | $965 | $1,958 |
| 1949 | $1,675 | $1,170 | $836 | $2,081 |

*Source: Historical Statistics of the United States, Colonial Times to 1970.* Washington, DC: Census Bureau, U.S. Department of Commerce, 1975.

nevertheless positively responded to governmental drives to buy savings bonds and stamps, and they still found money for fun times. The decline in dollars spent during the war years, as noted in columns two, three, and four, came more from the unavailability of many products than lack of interest or money.

Columns two and five show the dollars spent and suggest that highly popular leisure diversions involved reading and keeping up with the latest songs through sheet music and recordings. **Book clubs** proliferated during the decade; at their height, membership totaled 3 million. Estimates show that, by the end of the war, at least 49 million people (approximately one-third of the population) read at least one book a month. **USO (United Service Organizations)** clubs, always well stocked with books, fulfilled the purpose of serving the leisure needs of servicemen and industrial workers. Incorporated in 1941, USO branches flourished in many community settings. The soldiers who passed their free time at them contributed to the large number of readers and helped to promote book clubs as a successful 1940s fad.

Many other activities not mentioned in these tables helped Americans fill their idle time both during and after the war with pleasurable pursuits such as dancing, dating, picnicking, outdoor sports, and camping. Large numbers of people also followed both college and professional sports. The Sunday afternoon drive remained popular, but the rationing of gas caused many citizens to curb their use of **automobiles.** As always, children played hide-and-seek, jacks, hopscotch, jump rope, marbles, and a variety of other games.

**Golf** and **tennis,** both popular during the 1930s, waned during the 1940s. The suspension of all major professional golf and tennis tournaments between 1942 and 1945 affected these two sports and influenced this decrease, as did gas rationing. Material needed for the manufacture of golf balls was in short supply, and government campaigns encouraged golfers to recycle their metal clubs. The closing of over 25 percent of the nation's golf courses freed land for use as **victory gardens,** a wartime phenomenon that flourished throughout the war years.

Two new games, one outdoor and one indoor, appeared in the later 1940s to fill idle hours: Frisbee and Scrabble. In 1947, a pair of Californians constructed a flying disk from plastic and the Wham-O Manufacturing Company obtained the patent. Tossing a Frisbee got off to a slow start but gradually grew in popularity. Specialized Frisbee games developed after the 1940s have made the simple plastic disk an American institution.

A board game invented in 1933 by Alfred Butt and later to be called Scrabble, combined luck, skill, and a good vocabulary. Originally available only to the inventor's family, friends, and occasional purchasers, entrepreneur James Brunot in 1948 gave the game its famous name and manufactured and distributed it. Initially, his efforts lost money, but in 1952 sales finally soared. Scrabble, like Frisbee, went on to be a significant part of American popular culture.

Some nonwork ventures occupied people's free time, not necessarily for pleasure but to contribute directly to the war effort. Governmental officials encouraged everyone to collect anything that could be recycled into needed wartime materials. Youth-oriented agencies such as the Boy Scouts, Girl Scouts, Camp Fire Girls, and 4-H clubs, always on the lookout for new activities, spent many leisure hours gathering scrap metal, paper, and cooking grease; selling **war bonds** and stamps; and making supplies for USO centers.

While those back home during the war years entertained themselves as best they could, soldiers away from home also found their spirits lifted in a number of ways. In addition to attending traveling USO shows, listening to the Armed Forces Radio (AFR), watching movies, and reading, many soldiers collected and posted pinup girls on locker doors, walls of Quonset huts, and even inside their helmets. Quickly reaching the status of a fad, Hollywood stars like Betty Grable (1916–1973), Lana Turner (1921–1995), Ava Gardner (1922–1990), and Rita Hayworth (1918–1987) became favorite pinups, and soon their pictures, along with photos of many other attractive women, appeared on submarines, airplanes, and tanks. It has even been reported that someone painted a likeness of Rita Hayworth on the **atomic bomb** dropped on Hiroshima.

Although wartime rationing and restrictions had affected how both soldiers and civilians spent their leisure time during the first half of the 1940s, the lifting of wartime limitations and the reshaping of life in the immediate postwar years created new challenges. During this period, unlike during the Depression years and World War II, Americans had both time and money to pursue leisure and recreation as well as a surplus of pent-up demand and resources. The transition from a wartime economy to a peacetime one took several years, however, and leisure and recreational activities did not fully blossom until the 1950s.

*See also:* Architecture; Baseball; Drive-Ins: Movie Theaters, Restaurants, and Banks; Fads; Hot Rods and Drag Racing; Softball; Youth

**Selected Reading**

Giordano, Ralph G. *Fun and Games in Twentieth-Century America.* Westport, CT: Greenwood Press, 2003.
Kirdendall, Richard S. *The United States, 1929–1945: Years of Crisis and Change.* New York: McGraw-Hill, 1974.
Panati, Charles. *Panati's Parade of Fads, Follies, and Manias.* New York: Harper & Row, 1991.

# LEVITTOWN AND SUBURBANIZATION

The concept of a suburban development comprised of many houses laid out in a semblance of order, which many people associate with the years following World War II, had its beginnings long before the 1940s and 1950s. Since the early days of the republic, Americans have observed a love-hate relationship with their cities. As settlements along the East Coast grew into urban centers, the residents were already looking to the West, wanting to escape the crowded conditions they had created in their once-small towns. By the later 19th century, satellite towns ringed most larger communities, and people looked longingly at the open spaces beyond population centers.

Although the word "suburb" had long been a part of the language, referring to a residential area outside a city or town, the term "suburbanite" did not enter common usage until the 1890s. It identified those who chose to live in these gray areas—the marginal spaces just outside the city or, at the extremes, a borderland. At about the same time, the word "suburbia" also came into use, meaning not really within the confines of the traditional city, but not the rural countryside either. While language attempted to adapt, the cities and towns maintained their inexorable growth, pushing their boundaries ever outward, along with their peripheral areas, creating further pressures for expansion and broadening the linguistic interpretations of suburb.

Caught within this cycle, the imagery of the endless frontier lingered. Land developers promoted the concept of a cozy home situated on a plot of green away from the bustle of the crowded city, perhaps in a picturesque village. A man's job might be in town, but he and his family resided in an idyllic semirural setting. Endless illustrations in women's **magazines** advanced the idea of a picturesque "country" (suburban) house, and in the pre-automobile era, streetcar lines conveniently extended their tracks ever outward, giving birth to the commuter and the name "streetcar suburbs." With the rise of the motorcar, ribbons of concrete replaced rutted, dusty dirt roads, new homes in more spacious settings sprang up along the highways, necessitating additional road construction, and thus did the patterns of suburban growth become part of the American landscape.

By the late 1930s, suburbs surrounded every population center and had developed many of the amenities once associated with cities. Small clusters of commercial establishments provided at least minimal shopping, although a trip to the city or downtown offered greater selection and lower prices as a rule. Most suburbs, however, were predicated on access to an automobile to get anywhere, although commuter **trains,** streetcars, and extended bus lines continued to compete with the cars parked at virtually every suburban home. Despite the Great Depression and its economic turmoil, those who could continued to move to the beckoning suburbs. But then, as it did to so many aspects of American life, World War II stalled the construction of new highways, streets, and homes, while it momentarily altered modes of **transportation** with gasoline **rationing** and related **travel** restrictions.

The end of the war found most citizens with cash in their wallets and an urge to make up for lost time. As the soldiers and sailors flooded back to the States and resumed their civilian lives armed not with rifles but with the benefits of the **GI Bill,** a housing boom unlike any other had its beginnings in the immediate postwar years. Housing shortages abounded around the country as eager builders and real estate agents strove to meet the wants of all the ex-servicemen and their families.

While smiling developers unveiled plans for new housing tracts, Detroit announced its postwar lines of shiny new cars, and merchants across the land restocked their shelves with a vast array of goods they hoped consumers would find irresistible. The postwar years also announced the accelerated growth of suburbs fueled by government encouragement in the form of improved highways built with federal subsidies. In addition, the GI Bill offered returning veterans attractive terms for mortgages, and the Federal Housing Authority (FHA) favored offering loans to buyers wishing to buy in the suburbs. These two agencies allocated a disproportionate amount of money to suburban developments, about half of all their home financing, a practice that persisted from the 1940s until the late 1960s.

Throughout the war years, *Ladies' Home Journal* ran a monthly architect-designed "dream house" feature accompanied by drawings that usually showed it in a suburban setting with a spacious yard and space between the dwelling and its neighbors.

Immediately after the war, *Look* magazine carried a similar feature, helping to define buyer aspirations when they went home-shopping. And, although they were not rolling off the assembly lines yet, manufacturers ran ads touting fancy postwar appliances for those dream homes. These temptations, coupled with the **baby boom** and a housing shortage that dated back to the Great Depression, set the stage for unprecedented demands for new homes.

During the immediate postwar years and with money available, developers devoted about two-thirds of their new construction to residences located in suburban settings. And although big builders with numerous crews and all manner of equipment accounted for only 10 percent of all construction firms, these large operations erected fully 70 percent of new houses in the late 1940s, capitalizing on the economies of scale.

An enterprising father and his two sons—Abraham Levitt (1880–1962) and sons William (1907–1994) and Alfred (1912–1966)—envisioned in the still-rustic potato fields of west central Long Island, near Hempstead, an opportunity to create the definitive postwar subdivision. In the 21st century, disbelievers might find it hard to realize that much of the middle and eastern reaches of Long Island not that long ago housed little more than villages and productive farms. The famed American genre painter William Sidney Mount (1807–1868) often depicted these areas in his work—a land of tilled fields, sturdy barns, and livestock. Although the New York boroughs of Brooklyn and Queens might have occupied the western part of the island, their dense populations and the bucolic simplicity of Long Island's eastern sections were worlds apart. But proximity to the city, coupled with extended rail and streetcar lines, soon changed that. A number of towns grew rapidly in the central portions of the island during the latter half of the 19th century, including Garden City, an early planned community. In 1906, construction began on the pioneering Long Island Motor Parkway (now defunct), its use restricted to **automobiles,** a prescient nod to the future. But much open agricultural land also existed until the dawn of World War II.

In 1939, construction of the Long Island Expressway (or the L.I.E., as locals called it; the word "expressway" itself did not become a part of everyday speech until the late 1940s), which did not reach completion until the early 1950s, hastened commuters and travelers along much of the length of the island. The addition of other bridges and connectors changed the once rural land for all time, and increasingly easy access to New York City and environs would make the Levitts' vision the most famous of all postwar suburbs—and it lay only 29 miles from Manhattan.

Abraham Levitt, a real estate lawyer by profession, founded Levitt and Sons in 1929. The young company specialized in building substantial, upper-middle-class custom homes on Long Island in the years prior to World War II. From the start, Abraham took on few responsibilities aside from land acquisition, and turned over the day-to-day operation of the firm to son William. The father did engage in landscape **design,** insisting on allocating to each front yard in Levittown exactly two saplings, positioning them precisely like the ones on the neighbors' adjoining lawns.

Alfred Levitt, the younger son, quickly took a dominant hand in planning and designing the company's houses. He became knowledgeable in more efficient means of home building and eventually worked on the overall layout of Levittown, including the curving lanes (they were never called streets) that characterized the community. Alfred left the family firm in 1954 to pursue other construction projects.

William Levitt proved to be the most innovative of the three. When he assumed the presidency of Levitt and Sons in 1929 at age 22, he soon had landed a number of attractive contracts for the business. In 1941, with the industry booming in the United States as factories geared up for military production, William agreed to provide over 2,000 units to house defense workers in Norfolk, Virginia. Several similar commissions followed, and by war's end the company ranked among the nation's largest building firms. William also served with the navy's Seabees (the construction arm of the service) during the war, where he learned still more about mass-production techniques that he shared with Alfred.

With the end of the war, Levitt and Sons in July 1947 began breaking ground on some 4,000 acres of farmland Abe had acquired near Hempstead, Long Island. Using all the tricks of the trade, such as individual workers specializing in just a few tasks for optimum efficiency, the firm could build up to 30 houses a day by mid-1948, using a total of 27 prescribed steps in their construction. One crew might install bathtubs, another caulk windows, another paint trim, and so on. Working with a formula that approximated Speed + Efficiency = Cost Effectiveness, the Levitts built on concrete slabs; they saw no need to dig a basement. William and Alfred stressed the need for interchangeable parts that can be utilized in various configurations.

At first, the basic house in Levittown resembled a small Cape Cod cottage: 750 square feet on a 60-by-100-foot lot. It contained a kitchen, bath, living room–dining area, and two bedrooms; it did not include a garage or carport. An unfinished attic, however, could be expanded into one or two bedrooms with minimal remodeling. The Cape Cod, in 1948, cost $7,990 (about $71,350 in 2008 dollars). In 1949, they expanded their line of homes, offering a simple ranch-style house that measured 800 square feet and carried a price of $9,500 (about $85,900 in 2008 dollars). The company threw in for free a Bendix automatic washing machine and a small, 8-inch Admiral **television** set with the home. A carport also became available in 1950, an admission of the importance assigned automobiles by those who dwelled in the suburbs. For comparison, in 2008, the size of a new home in the United States averaged 2,500 square feet, or over three times larger than the original Levitt houses, and prices averaged $293,000, also a considerable jump, even when adjusting for inflation.

At first the Levitts built their homes for lease, but once they had the Veterans Administration for GI loans and the FHA for conventional financing on board in 1949, they changed to marketing houses for purchase at bargain prices. The company signed agreements with buyers that stipulated strict landscaping restrictions (no fences, no drying clothes outdoors except on racks supplied by Levitt, regular lawn mowing, etc.) along with the usual covenants about the care and upkeep of the house. These agreements also included a whites-only clause. Not until 1954 did the company allow racial integration of any kind, and Levittown for much of its early history remained primarily white. Also, through a gentleman's agreement then prevalent, the company did not sell to Jews, despite the religious heritage of the Levitts themselves. In time, they quietly dropped that unspoken restriction, but it nevertheless reflected some of the prejudices found in housing and real estate in the United States during the 1940s and 1950s.

*No postwar suburban development better exemplified the movement of people out of cities than did Levittown, New York. The first of over 17,000 cheaply-priced houses went up in the summer of 1947. This early aerial view suggests the enormity of Levittown, as well as the barrenness of the site and the close proximity of one dwelling to another. (Photofest)*

By the time painters sprayed the last panel and carpenters hammered home the last nail, Levittown, Long Island, comprised 17,410 houses, the largest suburban tract ever attempted in the United States. In 1951, a similar Levittown went up in Bucks County, Pennsylvania, near Philadelphia, with 17,311 homes. A Levittown in Willingboro, New Jersey, followed in 1958 with another 11,000 houses, and yet another in Puerto Rico, close to San Juan, in 1963, with 11,200. In all, the company erected almost 57,000 homes in those four Levittowns, and that does not include a number of other projects the firm undertook during the 1950s and 1960s.

While Levitt and Sons were busy on Long Island during the 1940s, other developers in places like greater Boston and Chicago, as well as Cleveland, Denver, Houston, Los Angeles, Phoenix, and Portland (Oregon) initiated subdivisions of their own, and they employed many of the cost-cutting methods the Levitts had pioneered. The rush to the suburbs had but begun in the later 1940s; the wave would crest in the years following Long Island's Levittown, but the lure of living beyond the immediate city continues to attract American families. As a result, a higher proportion of Americans currently reside in suburbs than live in rural areas and large cities combined.

Most planned communities, even those with contracts about lifestyles, did not plan for neighborhood stores. Developers simply overlooked this basic need, so focused were they on building houses. For Levittown, nearby Roosevelt Field, an airfield near Garden City, provided the perfect location for shopping. Open and flat, crews transformed the land into a vast collection of stores, the Roosevelt Field shopping mall. The airfield closed in 1951 and the new mall welcomed its first shoppers in 1956. Prior to its opening, Levittown residents had to decide which village or town—Hempstead, Garden City, or Hicksville—to visit for groceries, clothing, and almost everything else they might require.

Many suburban builders initially displayed in their planning—or lack thereof—an apparent antipathy toward pedestrian needs. They seemed more concerned with a need for unimpeded vehicular traffic flow, and the large shopping centers and malls with their acres of free parking catered to the automobile, not to anyone on foot. These retail outlets, however, lagged behind home construction and did not become commonplace until the 1950s and thereafter. Once they were up and running, such complexes nonetheless delivered the knockout blow to traditional downtown department-store shopping, and only those merchants that built suburban branches in the growing malls managed to survive.

In addition to the absence of retail facilities, early suburban subdivisions also brought about architectural monotony and bland neighborhoods, devoid of personality. "Cookie-cutter" designs and "ticky-tacky houses" became terms of disdain in the late 1950s and early 1960s for these tracts, but the critics came late; by that time, sprawling suburbs were a fact of American life, havens for young middle-class families striving to rise in the world. Although these new neighborhoods might possess economic and ethnic/racial homogeneity, most of them also became enclaves, excluding by restrictions and zoning those of lesser means and relegating them to decaying urban centers.

The decline of America's central cities only exacerbated urban flight by those who could afford to do so. Thus the suburbs prospered and the cities suffered economic neglect, with a resultant polarization between urban and suburban residents. Financial institutions gave no real thought to those below certain economic rankings; banks and savings institutions saw those in the lower social echelons as undesirable, probably unable to afford the money needed to purchase a starter house. And so they were ignored, left to the central city. Thanks to generous tax advantages and easy credit, the countless rising middle-class families were perceived as good risks, and developers welcomed them to the burgeoning suburban developments.

*See also:* Architecture; Grocery Stores and Supermarkets; Juvenile Delinquency; Lawns, Lawnmowers, and Fertilizers; Race Relations and Stereotyping

**Selected Reading**
Baxandall, Rosalyn, and Elizabeth Ewen. *Picture Windows: How the Suburbs Happened.* New York: Basic Books, 2000.
Duany, Andres, Elizabeth Plater Zyberk, and Jeff Speck. *Suburban Nation: The Rise of Sprawl and the Decline of the American Dream.* New York: North Point Press, 2000.
Hayden, Delores. *Building Suburbia: Green Fields and Urban Growth, 1820–2000.* New York: Vintage Books, 2004.
Jackson, Kenneth T. *Crabgrass Frontier: The Suburbanization of the United States.* New York: Oxford University Press, 1987.

# *LONE RANGER, THE*

In the early 1930s, George W. Trendle (1884–1972), the co-owner and manager of Detroit's station WXYZ ("the last word in **radio**"), had an idea for an adventure series he wanted to develop. He envisioned a mysterious cowboy who wandered the old West, punishing outlaws and securing quick justice for those in need. Working with veteran writer Fran Striker (1903–1962), the concept grew into *The Lone Ranger*, one of the most successful programs in the history of radio; the series would ultimately run for almost 3,000 episodes from 1933 until 1954.

When the show first came on the air in January 1933, it broadcast locally over WXYZ and regionally to a small group of Michigan stations. Audiences responded enthusiastically, and, when **MBS (Mutual Broadcasting System)** came into being in 1934 with WXYZ as a charter member, *The Lone Ranger* served as one of the most popular offerings of the new network. In time, MBS lost possession of the series when NBC (National Broadcasting Company) bought the rights to the show in 1942. The new ownership proved short-lived, however; a court-ordered breakup of a portion of NBC resulted in the creation of **ABC (American Broadcasting Company)** the following year, and in 1944 ABC commenced airing *The Lone Ranger*. The network carried the radio program until 1954 and the series' demise.

The Lone Ranger *could be heard first on radio in 1933; the series would continue over the air until 1954. This publicity shot depicts Brace Beemer astride Silver. Beemer would continue to portray the Lone Ranger until the show's end.* (Photofest)

Actor Brace Beemer (1903–1965) played the masked Ranger on radio throughout the 1940s, and he had as trusty companions his fabulous white stallion Silver ("Hi-Yo, Silver, away!") and a faithful Indian named Tonto, whose horse went by Scout ("Get 'em up, Scout!"). During this period, John Todd (1877–1957) took the role of Tonto. A recurring image in each episode involves the mysterious Ranger giving a silver bullet to those he has assisted. As he and Tonto ride away, Silver's and Scout's galloping hoofs in the background, the puzzled recipients study the silver bullet and ask, "Who was that masked man?" But, throughout the series, his real identity remains hidden.

Excitement, not mystery, however, dominated the broadcasts. Utilizing the exciting finale from Rossini's 1829 *William Tell Overture* as the opening theme for each show, listeners knew from the first bars that another episode was about to begin. Anyone who has ever listened to *The Lone Ranger* on radio cannot hear Rossini's composition without remembering the series, a perfect illustration of how popular culture freely borrows from the other arts. The use of **classical music** on many radio shows also illustrates how stations saved money; most music from the 19th century and earlier lacked copyright protection—that is, it could be played on the air for free. Trendle, well aware of such legal loopholes and notorious for his tight-fisted management at WXYZ, utilized the older classics whenever he could. He later introduced another successful adventure series, *The Green Hornet* (1938–1953), on Mutual and freely used Rimsky-Korsakov's *The Flight of the Bumble Bee* (composed 1899–1900) as the show's memorable theme. He also persuaded Fran Striker to do much of the scripting for this new addition to the network's catalog.

Striker, who came from the world of pulp publishing, had previously created a number of radio shows, so he should not be thought a novice when Trendle initially offered him *The Lone Ranger*. Always with an eye to making money, however, Trendle pressured Striker into signing a contract that gave the station owner all rights to the character, and the hardworking scriptwriter merely received a salary. Thereafter, Trendle always claimed he created and owned *The Lone Ranger* (as he did also with *The Green Hornet* and under similar contractual terms). Such shady business arrangements aside, Striker turned out to be a fast and prolific writer, and the challenge of coming up with three new stories a week seemed not to daunt him. If each plot were analyzed critically, a discerning listener would soon realize that each episode more or less replicates the others; by changing a name or a place, a clever author could sustain a character indefinitely.

Nevertheless, *The Lone Ranger* achieved such a high level of popularity that Trendle and Striker spun the series off into the **comic strips** in 1938; hundreds of **newspapers** carried the masked man's adventures throughout the 1940s, and cartoonist Charles Flanders (1907–1973) illustrated the stories during that time. The strip ran both daily and in Sunday editions until 1971. Despite this hectic schedule, Striker somehow found time to write 18 Lone Ranger novels, with seven of them appearing in book stores between 1940 and 1949.

Other media also took advantage of the series' success. Despite erratic publishing schedules, several **comic books** appeared on newsstands in the 1940s. Republic Pictures released two Lone Ranger serials: *The Lone Ranger* (1938; 15 episodes) and *The Lone Ranger Rides Again* (1939; 15 episodes). In 1940, the studio took the older serial and patched together a feature film called *Hi Yo Silver*. In deference to the times and changing tastes, a **television** version of the long-running radio program premiered in 1949 on home screens; a success in its own right, it remained on the air until the fall of 1957.

A pioneer in the early days of television, *The Lone Ranger* remained in the hands of ABC throughout its eight-year run. Once again, Trendle dictated many of the details concerning the show. He contracted actors Clayton Moore (1914–1999) and Jay Silverheels (1912–1980) to play the Lone Ranger and Tonto, insisting that Moore make his voice sound as close to Brace Beemer's distinctive voice as possible. He wanted viewers to consider the television series as a continuation of the radio version. The show made Moore and Silverheels early television celebrities, and *The Lone Ranger* became ABC's first big hit. Over the years, it went into syndication and can still occasionally be found in local broadcasting schedules.

*A televised version of* The Lone Ranger *came to home screens in 1949; it lasted until 1957. Clayton Moore, seen in this 1949 photograph—along with Jay Silverheels as Tonto, plus Silver—played the masked man in most of the episodes, and his voice matched radio's Brace Beemer reasonably well. (ABC/Photofest)*

To maintain audience interest in the radio show, advertisers on *The Lone Ranger* followed a common practice of the day by offering on-air premiums to listeners. In return for proofs of purchase (box tops, wrappers, etc.) of sponsors' products, a fan might receive "silver" bullets—usually cheap plastic or metal stampings—six-shooter rings, badges, and, in a reflection of the postwar era, a Lone Ranger **Atomic Bomb** Ring. All have become collectors' items.

One of the most successful and popular Westerns in the history of both radio and television, *The Lone Ranger* presented a mythic American West. The masked man's creed, jointly developed by Trendle and Striker and often invoked in the series—that all men are equal, one must sometimes fight for what is right, truth is the measure of all things, and similar homilies—gave the show something of an unusual tone. It supported their view that *The Lone Ranger* should do more than merely entertain; they wanted it to instruct and inspire children while appealing to an adult audience. For generations of listeners and viewers, at the first strains of the *William Tell Overture,* they knew they were in for another thrilling episode with one of their favorite American heroes.

*See also:* Advertising; Cold War, The; Leisure and Recreation; Radio Programming: Children's Show, Serials, and Adventure Series; Serial Films; Westerns (Film)

## LOUIS, JOE

Frequently at the center of both **boxing** and racial issues, Joe Louis (1914–1981), known as the "Brown Bomber," held the world heavyweight championship (175 pounds or more) for 12 years (1937–1949) and defended it more times than any other boxer in history. Probably as well-known as **President Franklin Delano Roosevelt** (1882–1945) during the 1930s and 1940s, people regarded Louis as an exemplary man. He adhered to strong moral principles, living and fighting clean, with no fixed fights and no gloating over a fallen opponent. In the ring, he demonstrated an ability to be powerful and quick with both hands and delivered deadly punches with a crushing left jab and hook.

Louis turned professional on July 4, 1934, when he knocked out Norwegian boxer Jack Kracken (active 1930s) in the first round; he did not lose another match until June 19, 1936. In a contest at Yankee Stadium with German boxer Max Schmeling (1905–2005), Louis suffered a sound beating that culminated in a knockout in the 12th round. He nevertheless continued to fight, and his next eight contests led to capturing the heavyweight title from James J. Braddock (1905–1974) on June 22, 1937, with a knockout in the 8th round.

Exactly one year later, Louis and Schmeling met for a second time amid heavy publicity that dubbed the event "the fight of the century." Increased awareness by the American public of German activities in Europe, along with the growing concern that the United States could be drawn into the conflict, added an element of patriotic intensity to the Louis-Schmeling bout. The press easily characterized the boxers as the "good" Louis versus the "bad" Schmeling, and more than half the **radio** owners in the United States listened to a fight that took on the symbolism of

*Heavyweight boxer Joe Louis immediately supported the entry of the United States into World War II and enlisted in the army in June 1942. Shown here in his military uniform, Louis worked in Special Services with the title of physical education instructor, a more prestigious position than those held by most blacks in the armed forces. (Photofest)*

democracy versus fascism. Louis delivered a sensational knockout just two minutes into the fight. He had quickly and soundly dispensed with a highly touted representative of Nazi Germany, and his victory comforted the nation and created a new hero who stood for America's best.

Following this event, Louis fought 17 additional matches, all of them wins. The United States entered World War II on December 7, 1941, and Louis immediately supported the effort. He donated his entire purse from a January 1942 fight with Buddy Baer (1915–1986) to the Navy Relief Fund and gave his earnings from a bout against Abe Simon (1913–1969) to the Army Emergency Relief Organization. When Louis enlisted in the army on June 5, 1942, he had been publicly recognized by Under Secretary of War Robert Patterson (1891–1952) and others for his acts of unselfishness and patriotism, adding to his status as a hero.

After completing basic training in the same segregated unit as Jackie Robinson (1919–1972), the first black to later play major league **baseball,** and fellow fighter Sugar Ray Robinson (1921–1989), the army assigned him to special services with the position of physical education instructor. He remained in the service until October 1, 1945. Instead of engaging in combat, he participated in 96 boxing exhibitions staged before more than two million troops.

Seeing the possibility of using this American icon to rally black citizens in support of the war, the government secured his assistance in a number of ways. In 1942, the War Department issued a poster that shows Louis in an army uniform carrying a rifle with a bayonet along with the slogan "We're going to do our part...and we'll win because we're on God's side." He could frequently be seen as a soldier in wartime newsreels, and, in 1943, he appeared in a cameo as himself, Sgt. Joe Louis, in a Warner Bros. Pictures production of Irving Berlin's (1888–1989) musical *This Is the Army*. These efforts achieved some black support for the war but not to the degree desired.

In 1944, Louis served as a consultant for the making of a propaganda documentary produced by the War Department titled *The Negro Soldier*. A clip from the second Louis-Schmeling fight appears early in the feature as a black preacher makes World War II an extension of that contest and suggests to the congregation that, if they love and support Joe Louis, then they must love and support America. *The Negro Soldier* experienced wide distribution to some 3,500 commercial theaters across the country, and the army chief of staff required all soldiers to see it. Reviews were mixed. Many raved about it, while others correctly felt that the film exaggerated and glorified the role of blacks in the war and described a compatibility between black and white soldiers that did not exist. Louis and others had hoped that the film would have a positive effect with regard to race relations, an end it did not fully achieve.

When Louis came out of the army, he signed a contract to defend his title against Billy Conn (1917–1993), the "Pittsburgh Kid." Interest in this match ran high, because the two had met in 1942 in what many call the greatest fight of all time. In that first bout, the spectators had watched in amazement as Conn outboxed Louis through 12 rounds, only to lose from a knockout in the 13th round. Louis repeated his feat, winning the 1945 contest with a knockout in the 8th round.

Before retiring on March 1, 1949, the champion defended his title three more times following the Conn fight. He defeated Tami Mauriello (1923–1999) in 1946 and Jersey Joe Walcott (1914–1994) twice, in 1947 and 1948. Then in late 1950, because of pressing financial problems including large debts and an assessment from the Internal Revenue Service (IRS) for $1 million (almost $9 million in 2008 money) in back taxes and penalties, Louis opted for a comeback. He lost the world heavyweight championship title to Ezzard Charles (1921–1975), who outpointed him in 15 rounds. Nevertheless, Louis continued to fight throughout 1951. In a match on October 26, Rocky Marciano (1923–1969) knocked him out in the 8th round, bringing Louis's career to a second and final end. Still needing money to settle with the IRS and to live on, he worked in Las Vegas as a casino host, wrestled professionally, and appeared on quiz shows. He died of a heart attack in 1981, at the age of 67.

Joe Louis ended his remarkable 17-year career with 68 wins and three losses, with 27 of those matches being championship bouts, a record. He won 54 of his fights by knockouts, including five in the first round. In 1941, he received the Edward J. Neil Trophy, awarded annually by the Boxing Writers Association of America to the boxer voted by membership to have been the best in that year. *The Ring* magazine, established in 1922, annually names a boxer as fighter of the year. It awarded that honor to Joe Louis four times—in 1936, 1938, 1939, and 1941. He narrowly lost to civil rights leader A. Phillip Randolph (1889–1979) in 1942, for the Spingarn Medal, bestowed for outstanding contributions to civil rights. The army, in 1945, awarded him the Legion of Merit for exceptional meritorious service and sacrifice, and in 1953 Hollywood released *The Joe Louis Story* starring boxer Coley Wallace (1927–2005) as the Brown Bomber.

The accolades have been many, but perhaps the most meaningful tribute to Joe Louis occurred when President Ronald Reagan (1911–2004) waived technical requirements for burial at Arlington Cemetery to allow Louis, one of the greatest fighters of all time, to be interred there. During a service with full military honors, hundreds of people came to pay their respects; in 1993, he became the first boxer honored on a United States postage stamp.

*See also:* Broadway Shows (Musicals); Musicals (Film); Race Relations and Stereotyping

**Selected Reading**
Bak, Richard. *Joe Louis: The Great Black Hope.* New York: De Capo Press, 1998.
Joe Louis fights. *Joe Louis vs. Billy Conn; Ringside Remembers; Joe Louis vs. Abe Simon II; Joe Louis vs. Jersey Joe Walcott Fight 2KO (Round 11); The Negro Soldier (1944); Joe Louis vs. Sky High Lee.* www.youtube.com
Sammons, Jeffrey T. Sammons. *Beyond the Ring: The Role of Boxing in American Society.* Chicago: University of Illinois Press, 1988.

# M

## MACARTHUR, GENERAL DOUGLAS

Born in Little Rock, Arkansas, into a distinguished military family, Douglas MacArthur (1880–1964) spent his entire professional life in the U.S. Army. In 1903, he graduated first in his class at the United States Military Academy at West Point and served in the army from 1903 to 1952. His first assignment out of West Point involved working with the Corps of Engineers in the Philippines, creating a lasting connection for him with the islands and with the corps. MacArthur went from the Philippines to Washington, DC, in 1916, to be the army's first public relations officer. When the United States entered World War I, he transferred to France as chief of staff for the 42nd Division, often called the "Rainbow Division" because of its wide geographical spread; historians attribute the nickname to MacArthur. His heroic service during World War I earned him the distinction of being among the most decorated U.S. officers of that war.

MacArthur returned home with an appointment to West Point as superintendent for the years 1919 to 1922. He married twice; first, in 1922 to Louise Cromwell Brooks (ca. 1890–1965) and then in 1937 to Jean Marie Faircloth (1898–2000). The couple had one child, Arthur, born in Manila in 1938.

After numerous promotions and various positions, including command posts in the Philippines, Major General MacArthur served as army chief of staff under President Herbert Hoover (1874–1964) and then military adviser to the government of the Philippines in 1935. The first of seven appearances on the cover of *Time* magazine occurred at this time. During his career, he associated with many talented officers, including **General George Catlett Marshall** (1880–1959) and **General Dwight David Eisenhower** (1890–1969). He retired from active service in December 1937 and accepted the appointment of field marshal of the Philippine Army, given by President Manuel Quezon (1878–1944). MacArthur became the only U.S. officer to hold this rank in any country.

*In this 1945 photo, General Douglas MacArthur, his famous corncob pipe ("barnyard meerschaum") firmly in place, can be seen in the recently liberated Philippines against the backdrop of Manila. (Bettmann/CORBIS)*

With the onset of World War II, **President Franklin Delano Roosevelt** (1882–1945) recalled MacArthur to active duty in July 1941. The president assigned him to serve as commander of the U.S. Army Forces Command in the Far East with the rank of lieutenant general, soon promoted to general. His initial efforts in the Philippines against an invasion by a superior Japanese force proved indecisive and ultimately disastrous. The Japanese easily destroyed most of the army's airplanes on the ground and tightened their grip on the islands. By January 1942, battered U.S. forces had retreated to the Bataan peninsula. Roosevelt, wanting to prevent America's most famous officer from falling prisoner to the enemy, ordered MacArthur to relocate to Australia as commander-in-chief of the Southeast Pacific area, specifically in charge of all land operations in Australia, the Philippines, New Guinea, and Papua. MacArthur left the Philippines at night aboard a B-17 bomber, devastated that deserting his men ran counter to an officer's duty; upon arrival in Adelaide, he said, "I shall return," a statement that captured the public's imagination and became the most famous words spoken during the war in the Pacific.

Between 1942 and 1944, MacArthur led Allied forces in the southwestern Pacific, pushing back the Japanese toward the Philippines. Finally, on October 20, 1944, MacArthur fulfilled his word. To the delight of photographers, he waded ashore at Leyte, complete with his recognizable crushed hat, open-collared shirt, aviator sunglasses, and corncob pipe, saying, "I have returned." The troops under his command quickly liberated the rest of the islands from enemy control. His next assignment involved overseeing a proposed land invasion of the Japanese home islands, tentatively scheduled for November 1945. When that became unnecessary because of two atomic bombs dropped in August—first on Hiroshima and, days later, on Nagasaki—MacArthur instead presided over the official surrender of the Japanese aboard the battleship USS *Missouri* on September 2, 1945. The ceremony marked the end of World War II.

By then one of the most decorated men in the army, MacArthur emerged as a famous military personality, admired and well-known to the American public. In 1944, he received the rank of General of the Army and a fifth star, along with three other generals—Marshall, Eisenhower, and Henry H. Arnold (1886–1950). Omar N. Bradley (1893–1981) became a five-star general in 1950.

MacArthur remained in Japan from 1945 to 1950, serving as the de facto ruler of that nation, since U.S. troops occupied it. In this capacity, he initiated a broad range of policies that dealt with disarmament, education reform, political stability, and economic recovery. To preserve national unity, MacArthur refrained from deposing Emperor Hirohito (1901–1989), but he reduced his authority to that of a figurehead. He also ordered that a new constitution be written, one that called for the election of a prime minister and the institution of a civilian government.

In June 1950, with the invasion of South Korea by North Korean troops, MacArthur was designated the commander of United Nations forces in the Far East. In the early months of the war, he brilliantly reversed a dire military situation with an assault behind enemy lines at Inchon and proceeded to drive the North Koreans back to the Yalu River along the China-Korea border. He wanted to continue into China, but orders prevented him from doing so. A retaliatory move by Chinese Communist soldiers in November 1950 swept over defending South Korean divisions, and a flanking move against UN forces led to the defeat of the U.S. Eighth Army and the longest retreat of any U.S. military unit in history. Still wishing to strike a retaliatory blow against China, one that possibly included the use of nuclear weapons, MacArthur found himself in sharp disagreement with **President Harry S. Truman** (1884–1972), his commander-in-chief, over military policy in Asia. In April 1951, and amid great controversy, Truman relieved MacArthur of his command because of insubordination.

Upon his return to the United States as one of the great generals of World War II and as the ousted commander in the Korean War, MacArthur delivered a farewell speech on April 19, 1951, before a joint meeting of the U.S. Senate and House of Representatives. Millions who listened and watched over **radio** and **television** heard an emotional closing when MacArthur quoted from a 19th-century barracks ballad that said, "old soldiers never die; they just fade away." He went on to say, "I now close my military career and just fade away" to tumultuous applause accompanied by tears in many eyes and a standing ovation.

MacArthur left the chambers to march in a parade in his honor on Pennsylvania Avenue. He appeared on the cover of *Time* magazine on April 30, and on May 1, the Veterans of Foreign Wars recognized him as he, along with Francis Joseph Cardinal Spellman (1889–1967), the Catholic archbishop of New York, stood in a place of honor viewing New York City's Fourth Annual Loyalty Day Parade, an event initiated in 1948 to demonstrate patriotism in opposition to other May 1 parades held by Communists and their followers. He continued to make speeches, leading many to anticipate his candidacy for president in the 1952 election, but General Eisenhower, his one-time aide, received the nod instead. The excitement did not last, and, as he had predicted, he faded from the public eye. General and Mrs. MacArthur lived quietly in New York until his death in 1964.

**See also:** Atomic Bomb, The; Cold War, The

**Selected Reading**

Manchester, William. *American Caesar, Douglas MacArthur, 1880–1964*. Boston: Little, Brown, 1978.

Perret, Geoffrey. *Old Soldiers Never Die: The Life of Douglas MacArthur*. Holbrook, MA: Adams Media, 1996.

"Truman." *American Experience: The Presidents*. PBS. www.pbs.org/wgbh/amex/presidents/video/truman_27_qt.html#v184

# MAGAZINES

From the early 19th century onward, magazines have occupied an important place in the cultural life of America. By the beginning of the 1940s, over 5,000 different periodicals circulated throughout the nation; at the end of the decade, despite a world war and the adjustments that came with peace, that figure had grown to over 7,000 titles circulating billions of annual copies. The general public knows little about the vast majority of these publications, because countless small-circulation periodicals (also known as "little magazines"), such as *The Bulletin of the Atomic Scientists of Chicago, The Butcher Workman, Tropical Fish Hobbyist, The Wooden Barrel,* and so on, cater to individual professions, businesses, and activities. Only a handful—perhaps 50 to 100 at the most—can be called general interest magazines, the high-circulation, quickly recognizable titles seen on drugstore, supermarket, and newsstand racks.

The **technology** that permitted the fast production and widespread circulation of general interest magazines had become well established by 1940. Linotype machines and web presses could print thousands of copies in almost no time, folding machines could put the final product together for distribution, and an efficient postal system could deliver mail virtually anywhere. With the onset of the 1940s, the total circulation of magazines with large, diverse readerships had grown close to 100 million. Just as important, **advertising** revenues, the lifeblood of any mass magazine, had begun rebounding from the doldrums of the Great Depression, despite suffering sharp declines in the early 1930s, the worst years of the crisis. Although still not as high as the precrash figures from 1929, revenues nevertheless had recouped sufficiently that the future looked bright. Of the titles that went under during the 1930s, enough new publications had come on the marketplace to offset those losses. Those that failed lacked both adequate circulation and advertising revenue, and sentiment alone could not sustain them.

The small percentage of popular, general interest magazines published tens of millions of copies with each issue—more than the output of all the little magazines combined—sending them to subscribers and selling them in high-traffic public venues. The more specialized periodicals, on the other hand, claimed select niche audiences instead of broad, general ones and therefore commanded far fewer readers per title. Any discussion of American mass magazines must therefore focus on limited samples of large-circulation publications, not the wider world of specialty periodicals.

Just a few titles—about 25 in all—led the way into the 1940s. Older, well-known journals, such as the *American* (founded 1911; ceased publication in 1956), *Better Homes and Gardens* (founded 1922), *Collier's* (1888; ceased publication in 1957), *Cosmopolitan* (founded 1886), *Good Housekeeping* (founded 1885), *House Beautiful* (founded 1896), *Ladies' Home Journal* (founded 1883), *Liberty* (1924; ceased publication in 1951), *McCall's* (founded 1897), *Reader's Digest* (1922), *Redbook* (1903), *Saturday Evening Post* (1821; ceased publication in 1969), and *Vogue* (1892) remained firmly ensconced in the magazine marketplace throughout the decade. Of all the weekly general interest magazines, only four could boast a steady circulation of over 1 million or more copies per issue: *Collier's, Liberty, Life* (founded 1936), and the *Saturday Evening Post.*

First appearing on newsstands in 1924, the now-forgotten *Liberty* initially appeared as the shared child of two metropolitan **newspapers,** the Chicago *Tribune* and the New York *Daily News.* It featured some of the tabloid sensationalism of its parent *Daily News* but never could develop a solid advertising base. It consistently lost money—even as it built a large circulation—and Bernarr Macfadden (1868–1955), a colorful multimillionaire made rich from other publishing ventures that had a combined monthly circulation of 7 million copies, finally bought the struggling weekly in 1931.

Under Macfadden's hand, *Liberty* gained readers, but it bore the reputation of being directed at the working class, not the more affluent middle class. Advertisers, rightly or wrongly, stayed away, placing their precious ad dollars in other publications they saw as potentially more profitable to them. Despite circulating a million or more copies each week, *Liberty* remained starved for advertising revenues. After a lingering decline throughout the 1940s, it finally expired in 1951. With its demise, the nation lost one of its most popular and unusual magazines, one that made no pretensions about being elitist or intellectual.

Periodicals such as the news magazine *Time* (founded 1923), the business-focused *Fortune* (founded 1930), and the general interest pictorial *Life* (founded 1936) magazine, all from the highly successful publisher Henry Luce (1898–1967), maintained their readership and advertising base throughout the 1940s. So did *Look* magazine (markedly similar to *Life*), which appeared on the scene in 1937 under the guidance of Cowles Publications in Des Moines, Iowa. It achieved success by following a relatively new approach for soliciting advertising: target marketing.

*Esquire,* a sophisticated men's magazine that premiered in 1932—the darkest year of the Great Depression—found the road to survival and ultimate success lay in knowing who read the periodical and then finding advertisers anxious to make appeals to that profile. Its editors designed the journal for a defined audience, men of some means and **education.** The sales staff then marketed *Esquire* to specific advertisers that carried products presumably attractive to this demographic. Whereas the big-circulation magazines appealed to a diverse market and carried a wide mix of ads, those periodicals that claimed (or targeted) a narrower socioeconomic readership could assure their advertisers a more receptive audience for specific products. The approach worked well; *Esquire* flourished, and target marketing has long since become commonplace in the publishing industry.

*Fortune* followed *Esquire*'s lead and shortly became one of the most advertising-heavy monthly magazines in the country. *Fortune*'s sister publication, *Time,* followed suit, especially in light of the challenges laid down by two new 1933 news-oriented entries, *Newsweek* and *U.S. News & World Report.* In 1936, *Life,* a pictorial journal of the week's events, entered the marketplace and provides the best example of target marketing. Its immediate acceptance by middle-class readers and resultant huge circulation convinced advertisers that *Life* held a key to reaching large, but specific, audiences. By 1939, and just three years old, *Life* could charge more for ad space than any of its competitors and had no lack of takers.

In addition to marketing their magazines to target groups, publishers also worked long and hard on the physical appearance of their publications. Throughout most of the first half of the 20th century, most magazine covers consisted of full-color reproductions of original works—oils, watercolors, pastels, drawings, cartoons, woodcuts, and so on. Although photographs and striking typography occasionally made up a cover, their use did not dominate the industry until well after World War II, when the economies of time and reproduction costs gave them a significant edge over the more expensive, hand-done alternatives.

Covers serve as a reader's introduction to a magazine, and so publishers lavished considerable expense on that aspect of their periodicals; an unattractive cover might deter a possible sale. But the subjects and their depiction also perform an additional task: they offer a quick, visual essay on styles, manners, and mores—any survey of magazine covers from the 1940s would reveal a wealth of information on countless aspects of ongoing American culture. Many such covers did not relate directly to the inside content of the magazine; they instead reflected the season (Christmas, Easter, etc.) or evoked moods—happy, humorous, nostalgic, sad, youthful—and often presented self-explanatory vignettes that stood on their own merits.

On the inside, mass-circulation magazines filled their pages with a blend of fiction and factual articles, accompanying the mix with an array of entertaining features such as puzzles, jokes and cartoons, interviews, photo essays, reviews, and the like. Their huge readership suggests they offered a form of journalistic escapism and that they succeeded in this role, but mainly they functioned as carriers of advertising.

All those journals published for the first time during the 1940s held true to the trend of more specialized than general interest magazines. Of the 28 publications listed in the table below, all from the period 1940 onward fashion themselves toward certain interests or groups of people and cover a wide range of interests, from sports to good eating, from history to hot rods, from organic farming to the world of teenagers. As would be expected because of the scarcity of paper during the years of World War II, only nine new titles appeared on newsstands between 1941 and 1945, with eight additional titles debuting between 1946 and 1949. They all had to face the specter of rising production costs in the postwar era: between 1944 and 1947, labor and materials, when taken together, rose on average 72 percent, a situation that would eventually put many already-borderline publications out of business.

The general lack of new magazines during the 1940s can be further explained by the continuing success of their predecessors. *Collier's, Life, Look, Reader's Digest,* and the *Saturday Evening Post* dominated the general market. In the face of strong showings by *Time, Newsweek,* and *U.S. News & World Report,* another newsmagazine would be a risky gamble. The women's market—with *Better Homes and Gardens, Cosmopolitan, Good Housekeeping, House Beautiful, Ladies' Home Journal, McCall's, Redbook,* and *Vogue*—offered little room for newcomers. As a result, most publishers looked to the more promising area of niche magazines, an ongoing attempt, not always successful, to find titles that would appeal to a specialized group of readers.

World War II signaled total involvement by the press, especially magazines. Until that time, no conflict had ever received such thorough coverage. In issue after issue, publishers filled the pages of their magazines with news, articles, and pictures, thus documenting the nation's part in the war. Discussion pieces, longer and more detailed than anything attempted by newspapers or **radio,** characterized much of this coverage. The postwar years, colored by anxiety about the future, saw a continuation of these analyses, and magazines in particular discussed in some depth the likelihood of World War III, especially atomic warfare.

TABLE 69. Representative American Magazines Founded in or around the 1940s

| Date Founded | Magazine | Comments |
|---|---|---|
| 1936 | *Life* (ceased regular publication in 1972) | Although *Life* predated the 1940s, it came to be an important magazine during the decade. In particular, it provided unparalleled photographic coverage of World War II. |
| 1937 | *Look* (ceased publication in 1971) | *Look*, which followed *Life* by just a year, also provided readers excellent **photography**, although it never equaled *Life's* popularity or circulation numbers. |
| | *Modern Photography* | Similar to *Popular Photography* [immediately below], but with only about half the circulation, *Modern Photography's* introduction suggests rising public interest in photography, especially with *Life* and *Look* available on newsstands. |
| | *Popular Photography* | Since its introduction in 1937, *Popular Photography* has dominated the field, with many how-to articles. |
| | *Woman's Day* | Introduced as a giveaway in A&P Food Stores to spur sales, this leading women's magazine went to 2 cents (about 30 cents in 2008 money) in 1937. During the war, because of its many practical recipes, circulation jumped to 4 million and has remained strong ever since. |
| 1938 | *U. S. Camera* | A competitor to *Modern Photography* and *Popular Photography*, its introduction so soon after the others further reflected rising interest among readers about this hobby. |
| 1939 | *Glamour* | Aimed at young, fashionable working women, *Glamour's* pages held more advertising than content, but its growing readership did not object, and heavy advertising became a hallmark of most women's **fashion** periodicals. |
| 1940 | *View* | An art and literature periodical, best remembered for advancing avant-garde topics to U.S. audiences, particularly surrealism. It ceased publication in 1947. |
| 1941 | *Ellery Queen's Mystery Magazine* | This monthly magazine contains short mysteries. Frederic Dannay (b. Daniel Nathan, 1905–1982) served as its first editor from 1941 until 1982. He, along with Manfred Lee (b. Manford Lepofsky, 1905–1971), created the fictional Ellery Queen as a pseudonym for writing detective stories of their own. |
| | *Gourmet, the Magazine of Good Living* | A monthly periodical with articles on good food and good wine, along with recipes. Earle R. MacAusland (1891–1980), one of its founders, served as editor-in-chief, 1941–1980. *Gourmet* ceased publication in 2009. |
| 1942 | *Negro Digest* | Similar to *Reader's Digest* in format, this black-oriented monthly offered condensed articles, books, and so on. A product of Johnson Publishing [see *Ebony*, below], it ceased publication in 1951, was revived in 1961, and was renamed *Black World* in the late 1960s. |

*(continued)*

TABLE 69. *(continued)*

| Date Founded | Magazine | Comments |
|---|---|---|
| | *Organic Farming and Gardening* | Published by Rodale Press, it promoted organic horticulture; the magazine early on called attention to the harmful effects of DDT and other pesticides. Its name changed to *Organic Gardening* in 1990. |
| 1944 | *Popular Crosswords* | This magazine capitalized on the American fondness for **games** and exemplifies many similar periodicals. |
| | **Seventeen** | Directed toward high school and college women, this popular monthly contains fashion news, beauty tips, and helpful information about growing up and getting along with others. |
| 1945 | *Commentary* | Published monthly, *Commentary* originally contained a preponderance of articles on Jewish affairs while strongly opposing Communism. |
| | *Congressional Quarterly* | Provides nonpartisan, in-depth coverage and analysis of U.S. congressional legislation, including floor votes. Widely read by politicians, government and business leaders, and educators. |
| | *Ebony* | A monthly pictorial news magazine for blacks modeled after *Life* magazine, the premiere issue sold 25,000 copies and served as a new vehicle for national advertisers to reach black consumers. Created by John H. Johnson (1918–2005), owner of Johnson Publishing, a leader in minority publications. |
| 1946 | *Highlights for Children* (popularly known as *Highlights*) | A magazine designed specifically for children by psychologist Garry Cleveland Myers (1884–1971), who also served as editor-in-chief. |
| | *Holiday* | One the first important postwar publications designed for a large audience, the glossy *Holiday* described itself as "the magazine of creative leisure" and would capitalize on the growing prosperity of the later 1940s. It published numerous works by noted authors about their travels. Later renamed *Travel-Holiday* in the early 1980s. |
| | *Sport* (ceased publication in 2000) | A new mainstream American sports magazine, this monthly periodical covered all sports and pioneered the use of color photography, offering full-page portraits of the stars of the day. It predated *Sports Illustrated* by eight years. |
| 1947 | *The Kiplinger Magazine* | The first national magazine to deal with personal finances; during the 1950s, the official name changed to *Changing Times*. The journal received its name from Austin H. Kiplinger (b. 1918), its founder. |
| | *Golf World* | A major **golf** publication that quickly became the leader in its field, its appearance in 1947 reflected the increased leisure time available to postwar golfers and the growing interest shown in this sport. |
| | *Road & Track* (often abbreviated *R&T*) | Initially published only six times between 1947 and 1949, and struggling, this now-monthly magazine for automobile enthusiasts focused on both production and race cars; |

| Date Founded | Magazine | Comments |
|---|---|---|
| | | professional drivers frequently contributed material. Its eventual success augured the postwar obsession with all aspects of motoring. |
| 1948 | *Hot Rod* | Created by Robert Peterson (1927–2007) on $400 and a belief in the postwar expansion of all automotive interests; the oldest magazine devoted to hot rods; this monthly publication supports the hobby as a legitimate endeavor and provides enthusiasts both a forum and a source of information. |
| 1949 | *American Heritage* | A quarterly periodical dedicated to covering the history of the United States; it evolved from *American Heritage: A Journal of Community History,* which ran from 1947 to 1949. By providing articles on many areas of American life, it had, by 1958, acquired a loyal readership of 300,000. Later (1954) expanded to six issues a year. |
| | *The Magazine of Fantasy and Science Fiction,* usually referred to as *F&SF* (first titled *The Magazine of Fantasy,* but only for one issue) | A monthly story anthology, edited by Anthony Bouher (1911–1968) and Francis McComas (1910–1978). It attracted fans of both fantasy and science fiction. |
| | *Modern Bride* (ceased publication in 2009) | A specialty magazine that served as a monthly source of information for brides-to-be and a place for advertisers to tout many different products. |
| | *Motor Trend* | Another automotive publication from *Hot Rod*'s Robert Peterson, who made a fortune by responding to the unparalleled growth of the automobile industry. *Motor Trend* appealed to the general car owner or buyer, extolling the virtues of all the latest models. |

As an example, novelist John Hersey (1914–1993) in 1946 wrote a 31,000-word article about the dropping of an **atomic bomb** on the Japanese city of Hiroshima in 1945 and its effects on six survivors. The *New Yorker,* a lively magazine about urban life and styles, chose to run *Hiroshima,* devoting the entire August 31, 1946, issue to Hersey's work. An immediate sensation, it sold out, newspapers excerpted it, radio stations carried readings from it, and a slim book soon followed. It took a leading magazine, however, to elicit this response.

In many ways, with their wide distribution and readership, magazines serve as national newspapers. Most papers, on the other hand, function on a more local or regional level and seldom, if ever, provide the space necessary for such extended pieces. Thus, the magazine falls into a unique middle ground between books and newspapers and fulfills a need for a mass medium that can be both timely and thorough.

*See also:* Advertising; Automobiles and the American Automotive Industry; Food; Hobbies; Hot Rods and Drag Racing; Leisure and Recreation; Motorsports; Movies; Youth

**Selected Reading**

Heller, Steven, and Louise Fili. *Cover Story: The Art of American Magazine Covers, 1900–1950.* San Francisco: Chronicle Books, 1996.

Janello, Amy, and Brennon Jones, *The American Magazine.* New York: Harry N. Abrams, 1991.

Peterson, Theodore. *Magazines in the Twentieth Century.* Urbana: University of Illinois Press, 1964.

Wood, James Playsted. *Magazines in the United States.* New York: Ronald Press, 1956.

# MARSHALL, GENERAL GEORGE CATLETT

Born into a Pennsylvania family that owned a prosperous coal business, George C. Marshall (1880–1959) graduated from Virginia Military Institute (VMI) in 1901 and went on to achieve a distinguished career in the military and diplomatic corps. Although he never led troops into combat during his 1901–1945 military service, Marshall, as an excellent organizer and motivator, held a variety of posts. **President Franklin Delano Roosevelt** (1882–1945) appointed him army chief of staff with the rank of four-star general in 1939.

In this position, Marshall held the final responsibility for building, supplying, and deploying over 8 million soldiers fighting in World War II and played a leading role in planning military operations on a global scale. He also served on a top policy committee appointed by Roosevelt in 1942 that supervised studies of atomic energy undertaken by U.S. and British scientists. This research would result in the **atomic bomb,** the most fearsome weapon of World War II. In December 1944, with the war grinding down and the Allies looking toward victory, Congress created a five-star rank called General of the Army. Marshall became the first recipient, followed within days by three other officers—**Douglas MacArthur** (1880–1964), **Dwight David Eisenhower** (1890–1969), and Henry H. Arnold (1886–1950). Omar N. Bradley (1893–1981) became a five-star general in 1950.

Once retired from the army, Marshall turned to a diplomatic career. While army chief of staff, he had participated in a number of conferences dealing with diplomatic issues, such as top-level discussions at Casablanca (1943), Cairo-Teheran (1943), Yalta (1945), and Potsdam (1945). In late 1945 and early 1946, shortly after the death of Roosevelt, he represented **President Harry S. Truman** (1884–1972) on a special mission to China, then torn by civil war. Marshall went to this position with prior experience, having served in Asia from 1924 to 1927.

Marshall became secretary of state in 1947 and, in a speech given at Harvard University on June 5 of that year, outlined a plan of economic and military aid to Western European nations. He carefully emphasized the humanitarian aspects of the plan—policies that would address hunger, poverty, desperation, and chaos.

But there was more to the intent; political motives lay behind the rhetoric. First, strengthening the European economies would, in turn, allow the citizens of those nations to buy American products. Second, money provided by the United States could be directed in ways acceptable to U.S. political interests, specifically, lessen the threat of Europeans turning to Communism. France had Communists in its cabinet, as did Italy, and the countries seemed susceptible to a Communist takeover, a condition that created great concern among government officials in Washington, DC.

Following Marshall's Harvard speech, the proposed plan underwent lengthy debate. Opponents questioned the necessity of such massive assistance, while those exhausted by two years of the **Cold War** voiced increasing alarm about Joseph Stalin (1878–1953) and his recent infiltration into Hungary and Czechoslovakia. Finally, in April 1948, Congress approved a 15-month appropriation of $6.8 billion ($60.7 billion in 2008 money). This unprecedented program became known as the Marshall Plan because of George Marshall's strong advocacy. Between 1948 and 1951, European countries received more than $13 billion ($117.5 billion in 2008 money) of economic, agricultural, and technical assistance from the United States.

In addition to enabling battered European countries to regain stability, the Marshall Plan also served as an impetus to the formation of the North Atlantic Treaty Organization (NATO) in 1949. After serving as secretary of state for two years, Marshall resigned and became the president of the American National Red Cross in 1949. In the early months of the Korean War (1950–1953), President Truman fired Defense Secretary Louis A. Johnson (1891–1966) and named Marshall as his replacement. Marshall served in that role for less than one year, retiring from public service in 1951. He represented the United States at the 1953 coronation of Britain's Queen Elizabeth II (b. 1926). For his world leadership, George C. Marshall received the Nobel Peace Prize that same year. He died in 1959.

**See also:** Berlin Airlift, The; D-Day; Political and Propaganda Films; Roosevelt, Eleanor; United Nation, The

**Selected Reading**

Kennedy, David M. *Freedom from Fear: The American People in Depression and War, 1929–1945.* New York: Oxford University Press, 1999.

Patterson, James T. *Grand Expectations: The United States, 1945–1974.* New York: Oxford University Press, 1996.

# MBS (MUTUAL BROADCASTING SYSTEM)

Organized in 1934 as a **radio** network, MBS (Mutual Broadcasting System) initially consisted of four stations: WOR in Newark, New Jersey (in 1941, WOR officially became a New York City–based station), WGN in Chicago, WXYZ in Detroit, and WLW in Cincinnati. Its founders hoped to compete with NBC (National Broadcasting Company) and CBS (Columbia Broadcasting System) networks. Although it never achieved the prominence or success of its considerably larger and better financed counterparts, MBS (often referred to as simply Mutual) nonetheless made its mark in American radio history during the 1930s and 1940s.

For a number of reasons, WXYZ left the fledgling network in the fall of 1935; a year later, WLW also departed. Although they were missed, Mutual rebounded and displayed rapid growth. By 1938, it counted 104 affiliates; shortly before that, the network added a regional group of stations in New England and had also reached the West Coast by adding several linked California stations. The end of World War II saw Mutual with 384 affiliates, and by 1950 it had achieved a remarkable 543 participants in its

A mustachioed Bud Collyer behind the MBS microphone. Mutual carried The Adventures of Superman *during the 1940s, and Collyer played both Clark Kent and the Man of Steel throughout the decade. (Photofest)*

collaborative system, a number of which also associated with NBC and CBS. Despite Mutual's impressive totals, it should be noted that NBC and CBS, although they had fewer linked stations, could always claim much larger audiences throughout the 1940s. They carried most of the prominent radio stars of the day, plus MBS counted many low-power affiliates in small markets.

Because of its somewhat informal structure and practice of sharing resources among its affiliates, Mutual, unlike NBC and CBS, had no central network studios and operated with a minimal staff. Each station remained an independent entity and could take advantage of opportunities unobtainable to those stations connected with NBC and CBS. For example, a Mutual affiliate might also offer selected NBC or CBS programming if it became available in certain regions. Occasionally, a show might be rejected by a local NBC or CBS station, in which case a Mutual affiliate could then broadcast it. As a result, Mutual and its partners practiced considerable flexibility in creating their broadcast schedules.

The MBS network itself, however, also offered a number of attractive programs to its associates. Among the most popular were *The Lone Ranger, The Adventures of Superman, The Shadow,* several colorful news commentators, audience participation quiz shows, and broadcasts of major sports events.

Before the creation of MBS, Detroit's WXYZ (which used the slogan, "the last word in radio") had in 1933 premiered a continuing Western series called *The Lone Ranger*. The tale of a mysterious masked man, a former Texas Ranger, the hero rides the plains doing good deeds, battling evil, and ensuring justice in the Old West. Almost from the inception of MBS in 1934, the various affiliates ran *The Lone Ranger,* and audiences estimated in the millions responded enthusiastically, making it a profitable network staple. Additional information about the series can be found elsewhere in this encyclopedia.

*The Lone Ranger* may have been Mutual's most successful offering, but *The Adventures of Superman,* which premiered on MBS in 1940, also boasted legions of devoted followers. Mutual carried the superhero's exploits throughout the 1940s; in 1950, **ABC (American Broadcasting Company)** obtained the broadcasting rights and ran the show until 1952. *The Adventures of Superman* consisted of 15-minute episodes broadcast around 5:00 in the afternoon, the preferred time for serials aimed at a youthful audience. Based on the comic book character created by Jerry Siegel (1914–1996) and Joe Shuster (1914–1992) in 1938, *Superman* in all its formats receives a more thorough discussion elsewhere in this encyclopedia; suffice it to say that the show proved a popular and enduring entry in the MBS lineup.

*The Shadow,* another audience favorite, had first been broadcast on radio in 1930, and it seemingly alternated between CBS and NBC in its early days. Initially, the "Shadow" title referred to a mysterious host for the show, but public curiosity caused producers to invent an actual character of that name. Walter B. Gibson (1897–1985, usually writing as Maxwell Grant), a prolific writer of pulp magazine fiction, in 1931 created the mysterious Lamont Cranston, also known as the Shadow, a man with the unique ability to "cloud men's minds" and thus render himself invisible. Gibson/Grant would continue to write the adventures at a remarkable rate, eventually churning out almost 300 novels for *The Shadow* magazine. For the radio productions, scriptwriters reduced Gibson's plots to workable 30-minute formats.

In September 1937, *The Shadow* moved to MBS and began a successful 17-year stay with the network. Orson Welles (1915–1985), still relatively unknown in 1937, played Cranston, and Agnes Moorehead (1900–1974) briefly portrayed Margo Lane, Cranston's lovely companion. By 1938, other actors had taken on the roles, but Welles and Moorehead had created the definitive characterizations, and subsequent players had to model themselves after the pair. Although Welles cannot take credit for the lines, "Who knows what evil lurks in the hearts of men? Ha, ha, ha, ha, ha…the Shadow knows!" his inimitable delivery made them unforgettable, and before long every listener knew them by heart and they became part of radio lore.

Although *The Shadow* magazine ceased publication in 1949, the Mutual series carried on a bit longer, but the impacts of **television** eventually doomed most radio drama, and *The Shadow* left the air in 1954. It did not enjoy a television sequel. Columbia Pictures, however, released a 15-episode serial of that name in 1940, but it more closely resembles the pulp magazine character than Mutual's radio version. Later in the decade and cashing in on the ongoing success of the MBS show, Monogram Pictures in 1946 produced three **movies** involving the Shadow: *The Shadow Returns, Behind the Mask,* and *The Missing Lady.* Each feature stars Kane Richmond (1906–1973) as Lamont Cranston, and they stand as typical B films of the era. Finally, in 1994, Hollywood made a big-budget, effects-filled picture bearing *The Shadow* name, but it bears little resemblance to either the pulp or radio versions.

Pure escapism, *The Lone Ranger, The Adventures of Superman,* and *The Shadow* demonstrated radio's unique ability to take outlandish plots and characters and make them believable in the imaginations of audiences. Times, however, change. *The Lone Ranger* left Mutual in 1942, when ABC offered better contractual terms for the Western. It eventually made its way to ABC television in 1949. *The Adventures of Superman* lasted until 1951 with MBS, but then likewise shifted to television and a long-running (1951–1957) series on ABC.

In addition to its popular dramatic series, MBS also boasted the talents of several colorful news commentators. Gabriel Heatter (1890–1972) became one of the most popular voices on the network, despite an unusually somber voice and delivery. He commenced a 30-year broadcasting career in 1932 on New York's WOR, one that spanned the Great Depression, World War II, and the Korean conflict. In an attempt to give his shows human interest, he developed a trademark opening line, "Ah, there's good news tonight!" What followed tended to be optimistic and uplifting, and audiences loved it.

He hosted programs such as *A Brighter Tomorrow* (1946–1947) and *Behind the Front Page* (1947–1948), shows built on stories taken from the news that had happy endings. His upbeat approach and curious style kept him ensconced at MBS until 1965.

If Gabriel Heatter gave the bright side of the news, Fulton Lewis Jr. (1903–1966) functioned as his opposite. A former newspaper reporter and an outspoken conservative, he opposed the New Deal, the Democratic Party, and anything else he thought of as liberal. In 1935, Lewis signed on with Washington, DC's WOL, by then a Mutual affiliate. As a strong isolationist on the eve of World War II, he opposed the country's participation in the conflict. Following the war, he aligned himself with anti-Communist groups and railed against what he perceived as left-wing subversion in the nation's affairs. Audiences either loved or loathed him, but they kept tuning in. His strident attacks finally caused MBS to drop him from its roster in 1961.

Mutual had yet another commentator of some note in Raymond Gram Swing (1887–1968), one of the most respected radio journalists in the nation. He had covered World War I for several Midwestern **newspapers** and broke into radio reporting sometime in the 1930s. He worked at WOR until 1939, at which time Mutual added him to its slate of news analysts. His extensive experience in foreign affairs served him well, and Swing quickly developed a devoted following. Unfortunately for the network, ABC contracted him and his expertise in 1942, and he would remain there for most of the decade.

A latecomer to Mutual's news offerings, *Meet the Press* may have been new to radio programming, but evolved as the archetype of all subsequent panel news shows. It premiered in 1945 and ran for five years. In 1952 NBC acquired broadcast rights and carried it until 1986, although by then *Meet the Press* had become far better known as a vehicle for television. In its original MBS format, Martha Rountree (1911–1999) served as moderator, and Lawrence Spivak (1900–1994) appeared as a permanent panelist. Rountree and Spivak coproduced it, and they can take credit for designing a format that has been imitated ever since.

The world of sports also received the Mutual network's attention. Starting in 1935, MBS provided the play-by-play for the World Series and **baseball**'s All-Star game. Each year until 1957, the network had exclusive rights to these major-league events. MBS also carried college **football** from Notre Dame, another association that would endure for many years.

With the decline of radio networks in the 1950s, the fortunes at the Mutual Broadcasting System fell on hard times. During the ensuing years, MBS went through a dizzying series of acquisitions, financial downturns, and format changes. By April 1999, the glory days of American radio had long since disappeared, and the newest set of owners formally retired the brand name Mutual.

*See also:* Comic Books; Magazines; Radio Programming: Action, Crime, Police, and Detective Shows; Radio Programming: Children's Shows, Serials, and Adventure Series; Radio Programming: Drama and Anthology Shows; Radio Programming: News, Sports, Public Affairs, and Talk; Serial Films; Westerns (Film)

**Selected Reading**

Barnouw, Erik. *A History of Broadcasting in the United States.* Vol. 1, *A Tower in Babel.* New York: Oxford University Press, 1966.

———. *A History of Broadcasting in the United States*. Vol. 2, *The Golden Web*. New York: Oxford University Press, 1968.

Dunning, John. *On the Air: The Encyclopedia of Old-Time Radio*. New York: Oxford University Press, 1998.

Lackman, Ron. *The Encyclopedia of American Radio*. New York: Checkmark Books, 2000.

## MILLER, GLENN

Born in the small Iowa town of Clarinda, future orchestra leader (Alton) Glenn Miller (1904–1944) started off his musical career as a modestly talented trombonist. He played in a number of regional Midwestern bands that toured for dancing in the mid- to late 1920s. Realizing his instrumental limitations early on, Miller began arranging for such leaders as Ben Pollack (1903–1971), Red Nichols (1905–1965), the Dorsey Brothers (Tommy, 1905–1956; Jimmy, 1904–1957), and Benny Goodman (1909–1986) in the first years of the **Swing** Era.

These experiences led to a position with the Ray Noble (1903–1978) orchestra in 1935, and this steady employment allowed Miller to polish his skills as an arranger. Two years later, he left Noble and organized a band of his own. In a decade crowded with different aggregations, Miller quickly realized that success demanded a distinctive sound that people would recognize and like. He experimented with various instrumental voicings, including riffs and fadeouts, techniques that would later serve as signatures of his band. He also discovered that a clarinet playing the melody an octave over the other reeds created a light, danceable sound. Commercial success, however, did not immediately fall on the heels of his discovery.

Miller's 1937 attempt at leading a band, although it hinted at things to come, went nowhere and he had to break it up. He continued to write arrangements and formed a second orchestra in 1938. This time around, Miller hired top sidemen and had the good fortune to land Ray Eberle (1919–1979), Marion Hutton (1919–1987), and the Modernaires (vocal group active 1930s and 1940s) as his vocalists.

This new Glenn Miller orchestra attracted some favorable attention and cut a number of recordings for several labels. These early efforts did not sell particularly well, nor did they produce quite the sound Miller had been looking

*One of the most popular bandleaders in the United States during the early 1940s, Glenn Miller tragically lost his life while serving in the Army Air Force. This 1940 picture depicts him in civilian dress, holding a cigarette, probably a Chesterfield, his radio sponsor at the time. (Photofest)*

for, but they nonetheless demonstrated that the new aggregation possessed the ability to play outstanding **dance** music. At the same time, Miller had developed a personable, easygoing stage manner that listeners and dancers enjoyed.

RCA Victor, a leader in the recording field, offered Miller a contract with its popular Bluebird label in the fall of 1938. For the first time, phonograph records captured the inimitable Miller sound, and, in the early months of 1939, the group enjoyed several hits. The band's engaging theme, "Moonlight Serenade" (composed and arranged that year by Miller), listeners found especially captivating, and people soon associated it with the band. A companion piece, "Sunrise Serenade," likewise had its admirers. Soon, other popular favorites like "Little Brown Jug," "Pennsylvania 6-5000," and "Tuxedo Junction" (all 1939) came out in quick succession on Bluebird disks and could be heard everywhere through **jukeboxes** and on the air; people crowded record shops trying to obtain copies. Network **radio,** which could not seem to get enough swing orchestras on the air to satisfy fans, discovered Miller at this time; CBS (Columbia Broadcasting System) radio in 1939 inaugurated *Moonlight Serenade* (also called *Music That Satisfies,* a nod to the sponsor, Chesterfield cigarettes), a 15-minute music show that broadcast three nights a week. It would run until 1942.

With the beginning of the 1940s, Glenn Miller had skyrocketed to success in the hotly competitive field of big band music and had displaced Benny Goodman, the former King of Swing, by topping every popularity poll. No letup appeared in sight; he played casinos, hotels, and ballrooms, packing in the audiences wherever he appeared. In a long stint at the Glen Island Casino, a lovely combination **restaurant** and ballroom overlooking New York's Long Island Sound, Miller continued to do radio programs by using a remote setup that allowed him to broadcast directly from his location. In early 1940, the band recorded one of its biggest hits, the up-tempo "In the Mood." Over the years, this recording would establish itself as one of the top-selling songs of the Swing Era and has remained a favorite of dancers.

Given his unprecedented popularity, Miller and his band performed in two film musicals released by Twentieth Century-Fox: *Sun Valley Serenade* (1941) and *Orchestra Wives* (1942). Lightweight, frothy entertainment characterizes both **movies,** but the band gets to perform some of its big hits of the day, such as "Chattanooga Choo Choo," "In the Mood," and "Moonlight Serenade" in *Sun Valley Serenade* and "At Last," "Kalamazoo," and "Serenade in Blue" in *Orchestra Wives.*

The outbreak of World War II in December of 1941 marked a turning point in both Miller's career and the music business in general. Some of the most prominent bandleaders of the day soon enlisted; for example, Tiny Bradshaw (1905–1958), Bob Crosby (1913–1993), Eddie Duchin (1909–1951), Wayne King (1901–1985), Clyde McCoy (1903–1990), and Artie Shaw (1910–2004), among others, switched their tuxedos for uniforms. Despite being at the height of his popularity in the states, Miller in 1942 tried to join the navy. Officials, however, would not allow him to enlist because of his age, 38 at the time. The army, however, yielded, and Glenn Miller donned an Army Air Corps uniform along with the rank of captain. These maneuvers thus gave birth to the most successful service ensemble of them all, a huge organization consisting of a 42-piece marching unit, a **jazz** combo, string accompaniment, and most famously, his 19-piece Army Air Force dance orchestra.

First stationed in the United States, Miller received an assignment to Great Britain shortly after the **D-Day** invasion of Normandy, France. Here he assembled an overseas band and gave hundreds of performances for U.S. forces. By now a major, Miller continued to record while in England, and his popularity showed no signs of slowing. But success would prove fleeting; a military plane carrying Miller from England to France disappeared in a storm over the English Channel in December 1944; authorities found no remains. Theories about the nature of his death have since abounded—accidental crash, weather, enemy action, a conspiracy of some sort, and so on—but no evidence supporting them has ever surfaced.

His various Air Force groups carried on under the leadership of sideman Ray McKinley (1910–1995) until they finally disbanded with the return of peace. Miller's civilian sidekick, vocalist and saxophonist Tex Beneke (1914–2000), had led a navy band in landlocked Oklahoma during the war. In 1946, after his discharge, and with the consent of the Miller estate, Beneke took over the leadership of the remains of the old Glenn Miller orchestra and so the dynasty nevertheless continued. In time, Beneke formed his own band and parted ways with the Miller estate. Other leaders, notably McKinley again, tried to carry on the tradition in the 1950s. Without their popular leader, however, the subsequent Glenn Miller bands have always seemed but shadows of the original.

During its brief heyday, the Miller aggregation epitomized versatility. Essentially a sweet band, it could play the slow, syrupy ballads, often accompanied by singers or vocal groups that made no attempt to "swing" the lyrics. But the orchestra could also perform jazz-tinged arrangements of up-tempo tunes that any swing band could envy. Miller successfully straddled both camps, a rare accomplishment.

*See also:* ASCAP *vs.* BMI Radio Boycott and the AFM Recording Ban; Musicals (Film); Radio Programming: Music and Variety Shows; Songwriters and Lyricists

**Selected Reading**
Grudens, Richard. *Chattanooga Choo Choo: The Life and Times of the World Famous Glenn Miller Orchestra.* Stony Brook, NY: Celebrity Profiles, 2004.
Simon, George T. *Glenn Miller and His Orchestra.* New York: Thomas Y. Crowell, 1974.
Yanow, Scott. *Swing: Great Musicians, Influential Groups.* San Francisco: Miller Freeman, 2000.

# MIRANDA, CARMEN

Born in a rural town in Portugal but raised in urban Rio de Janeiro, Brazil, Carmen Miranda (1909–1955) opened a small hat shop while still a teenager. She frequently sang on the job, and that exposure brought her some club dates, which in turn caused a local **radio** station to invite the budding vocalist to perform on the air. Miranda soon enjoyed considerable fame as a samba singer, and RCA Victor Records, hearing about her success, signed her to a recording contract. Her success with music then led to roles in six Brazilian **movies,** and producers in the United States took notice of her considerable talents. They invited the 30-year-old rising star north and, in 1939, Miranda, along with her musical group, Bando da Lua, appeared in *Streets of Paris,* a Broadway revue. On stage, she sang "South American Way," a Latin-tinged number composed by

*This studio still (probably Twentieth Century-Fox) shows the "Brazilian bombshell," Carmen Miranda, in one of her trademark tutti-frutti hats. Concoctions of tropical fruits and greenery, such millinery defied gravity and delighted her many fans. (AP Photo)*

the popular American songwriting team of Jimmy McHugh (1894–1969) and Al Dubin (1891–1945), and her performance would lead her to Hollywood.

She inked a contract with Twentieth Century-Fox the following year and appeared in *Down Argentine Way* (1940), her North American movie debut. A small role, but it allows her to perform several Brazilian numbers with her band, including "South American Way" again. Audiences immediately liked Miranda's infectious energy and asked for more, a request that the studio hurried to honor.

In 1941, she again appeared on American screens with *That Night in Rio*, a sequel of sorts to *Down Argentine Way*. Both films star Don Ameche (1908–1993), a popular leading man of the day, along with two stylish actresses, Betty Grable (1916–1973) in *Down Argentine Way* and Alice Faye (1915–1998) in *That Night in Rio*. Big-name celebrities daunted Miranda little, and her exuberance while on camera immediately put her in league with her costars. As proof, Twentieth Century-Fox quickly released a third 1941 picture, *Week-End in Havana*, teaming her once more with Alice Faye, with whom she now shared top billing.

These three films, pleasant trifles all, made Miranda a guaranteed box office draw, provided—in the eyes of her studio—she continue to play the fiery Latin stereotype. Now billed as the "Brazilian Bombshell," she next appeared in *Springtime in the Rockies* (1942), along with Betty Grable again, but as costar this time around. Another Technicolor Fox musical, it perhaps remains most notable for the music of Harry James (1916–1983) and his orchestra, one of the most well-received big bands of the later **Swing** Era. The film also has Miranda singing "Chattanooga Choo-Choo," a No. 1 hit from **Glenn Miller** (1904–1944) produced in the early 1940s, not in English but in her native Portuguese.

Fox teamed Alice Faye and Carmen Miranda for a third time in *The Gang's All Here* (1943), a frothy wartime picture. Busby Berkeley (1895–1976), the esteemed choreographer from many movies made during the 1930s, gives Miranda a standout **dance** number in "The Lady in the Tutti Frutti Hat." The tune, penned by Harry Warren (1893–1981) and Leo Robin (1900–1984), acknowledges the outrageous headwear worn by Miranda, usually huge arrangements of exotic fruit—especially bananas—piled high atop her head that had quickly become her trademark.

*Greenwich Village* came along in 1944. An exercise in nostalgia, it supposedly takes place in New York's famed artist and writers' neighborhood during the 1920s, which allows for such old chestnuts as "I'm Just Wild about Harry" (1921), "Swingin' Down the Lane" (1923), and "Whispering" (1920). But the producers also introduced "Give Me a Band and a Bandana," a decidedly upbeat 1944 tune scored for Miranda and her equally upbeat Latin dancing featuring typical Berkeley choreography. With each successive film, however, she also became more and more a caricature of herself. The hats grew bigger, the costumes more flamboyant, and her characterizations more shallow. But audiences continued to flock to her motion pictures and they made money.

*Something for the Boys* (1944), adapts Cole Porter's (1891–1964) Broadway musical of 1943 for the screen, and Miranda takes the role originally played by Paula Laurence (1916–2005). Bowing to Miranda's unique abilities, tunes like *Batuca Nega* and *Samba Boogie* replace some of the more traditional numbers from Porter's original score, and she gives them her expected zest and energy. The next year, 1945, saw no new releases featuring Miranda, and yet she had the distinction of reputedly being the highest paid woman in the United States, quite an accomplishment for someone who had come to the country just six years earlier.

Two so-so movies, *Doll Face* and *If I'm Lucky,* graced marquees in 1946. The first, about the days of burlesque, stars Vivian Blaine (1921–1995), and Miranda's name gets buried in the credits, although she performs another of her hits, "Chico Chico." *If I'm Lucky,* a vehicle for Blaine, also stars up-and-coming vocalist Perry Como (1912–2001), and Miranda again receives second billing, singing only a couple of forgettable numbers.

Despite its tantalizing title, 1947's *Copacabana* unfortunately comes across as a limp musical comedy. Unfortunate, because it headlines two talented entertainers, Carmen Miranda and the renowned Groucho Marx (1880–1977). They try their best, but an uninspired script coupled with inept direction does not allow them to rise above mediocrity. The picture also suggests that Miranda's once-bright star might be waning—*Copacabana* marks her first feature not produced by her long-time studio, Twentieth Century-Fox. Beacon Productions, a small operation that used United Artists for distribution, released the picture. Additionally, the movie was one of the last for Marx; except for an occasional feature and some cameos, he would shortly move on to new heights in radio and later **television.**

The slow downhill slide of Miranda's once-blazing career continued with *A Date with Judy* (1948). Based on the long-running (1941–1950) radio show of that name, the picture mainly revolves around teenage shenanigans instead of music or dancing. Miranda and Latin bandleader Xavier Cugat (1900–1990) show up more as window dressing than essential players, although "Cuenta la Gusta" adds some zest to events. The picture came with Miranda's move to Metro-Goldwyn-Mayer (MGM), one of Hollywood's largest studios, but executives and producers there showed little imagination with their new acquisition.

Her last two films, *Nancy Goes to Rio* (1950) and *Scared Stiff* (1953), put Miranda in the unaccustomed role of bit player. She mugs a bit and sings but hardly in the manner of her big production numbers from the past. She even has to play against the comedy team of Dean Martin (1917–1995) and Jerry Lewis (b. 1926) in *Scared Stiff.* The picture allows Lewis to do a spoof of her Latin character, a reflection of her faded career.

Miranda continued performing, making the rounds of night clubs and occasional television appearances. An unhappy personal life, poor health, and disappointments influenced her final years, and she died in 1955, just 46 years old, after suffering a heart attack during a television taping. A figure of the 1940s, Carmen Miranda helped introduce Latin music and dance to the United States and enjoyed a meteoric Hollywood career. She also influenced **fashion;** her elaborate turbans and thick platform shoes were soon adapted—in toned-down versions, of course—as essentials for the well-dressed woman of that era.

*See also:* *ASCAP vs. BMI* Radio Boycott and the AFM Recording Ban; Broadway Shows (Musicals); Songwriters and Lyricists; Musicals (Film)

**Selected Reading**
Gil-Montero, Martha. *Brazilian Bombshell: The Biography of Carmen Miranda.* New York: Dutton, 1989.
Tompkins, Cynthia M., and David W. Foster. *Notable Twentieth-Century Latin American Women.* Westport, CT: Greenwood Press, 2001.

# MOTORSPORTS

The sport of automobile racing, an attempt to get from point A to point B faster than anyone else, experienced significant growth and untold possibilities with the development of safe, practical internal combustion engines in the late 19th century. By the early 1900s, races had begun to occur that involved **automobiles,** along with occasional contests with motorcycles. Speedboats also got into the picture at times, as did primitive airplanes, all vying to be faster than their competition. Air races, however, seldom get grouped under the motorsport rubric; most enthusiasts reserve the term for motorized land vehicles.

Auto races had become a popular American spectator sport by the 1940s, and a number of annual events were eagerly awaited each season. In 1940, for example, two notable accomplishments occurred in the field of motorsports. First, at the Indianapolis 500-Mile Race held during the May Memorial Day weekend, Wilbur Shaw (1902–1954), already a well-established driver, raced an Italian Maserati and became the first man in the race's history to win the Indy 500 twice in succession, an achievement that cemented his status as a celebrity and brought considerable attention to the sport. A couple of months later, David Abbott "Ab" Jenkins (1883–1956), another professional driver and also the mayor of Salt Lake City, along with his relief driver, Cliff Bergere (1896–1980), completed 3,858 miles in 24 hours in Jenkins' Mormon Meteor III on Utah's Bonneville Salt Flats. Their performance, an average speed in excess of 160 miles per hour, broke a previous record set by Jenkins in 1937, and the new accomplishment endured until 1990.

The December 1941 entry of the United States into World War II brought a temporary halt to many sporting events. Gasoline **rationing** curtailed all motorsports and put countless drivers and mechanics out of work. But not for long, because many proved invaluable for defense work in aviation factories and allied industries. Racing resumed in 1946 with both old and new venues, along with increased safety precautions in an attempt to decrease the inherent dangers of the sport—a car spinning, flipping, or rolling could quickly cause an accident that might kill the driver or others, even spectators unlucky enough to be in its path.

The following list presents a brief overview of the major automobile, motorcycle, and power boat competitions enjoyed by participants and spectators alike during the decade.

*AAA Championship Trail Races.* Introduced in 1905 by the American Automobile Association (AAA), these races involved cars on dirt or unimproved tracks of a mile or more. The trails probably derived from the early days of auto touring, when many roads, such as they were, followed trails that had been first marked out years before the advent of the horseless carriage. As they grew in popularity, the AAA approved other locations and the tracks became much improved, but the name remained unchanged.

Both before and after World War II—virtually no racing of any kind occurred between 1942 and 1945—many of the Championship Trail drivers also participated in midget car races and events scheduled for larger cars, entering one kind of race during the week and another on weekends. Consistent winners included Wilbur Shaw, who captured the Championship Trail wins in 1937 and 1939 and finished first at the Indy 500 in 1937, 1939, and 1940, and Mauri Rose (1906–1981), who took the Championship Trail title in 1936 and won the Indy 500 in 1941, 1947, and 1948. Henry Banks (1913–1994), another outstanding driver, emerged victorious in the American Racing Drivers Club's midget car competitions in 1941 and took the AAA Championship Trails in 1950.

*Indianapolis 500-Mile Road Race.* Shortened to the Indianapolis 500, Indy 500, or The 500, this race has for many decades attracted both American and foreign drivers and cars. It reigns as one of the oldest motorsports events and a world-class auto race. It also holds the record for the highest number of deaths. The speedway, initially built in 1906 as a testing ground for road cars, consists of a–two-and-a-half-mile oval track. In 1909, 3 million paving bricks replaced the earlier, more dangerous surface of compacted stone, giving the track its nickname "The Brickyard," a term that still sticks despite its subsequent asphalt covering. Races have been held annually since 1911, with the exception of World War I, 1917–1918, and World War II, 1942–1945.

The 500 features a monetary prize divided between the owner of the car and the driver. In 1940, the purse equaled $30,000 (a little over $460,000 in 2008 dollars); by the end of the decade, it had risen to $65,855 (almost $596,000 in 2008 dollars). Usually, the driver receives additional prizes. For example, in 1940, Wilbur Shaw took home an electric refrigerator, a town car, a statue, a year's meal ticket at an Indianapolis restaurant, and the checkered flag that signaled his victory. Following an Indianapolis 500 tradition in place since 1936, his name and likeness was added to the Borg-Warner trophy, named for the U.S. automotive parts supplier. The speedway's Hall of Fame Museum permanently houses the trophy.

Cars that entered The 500 during the 1930s and 1940s usually had U.S.-built Offenhauser racing engines as their source of power. A strong, reliable motor that could stand the abuse of running at top speed for long periods of time, the "Offy" dominated race events throughout the decade. In 1949, WFBM-TV, an Indianapolis station (later WRTV), televised The 500 live, thereby exposing a wider range of people to the event.

Twelve cars finished the grueling test of man and machine, with Bill Holland (1907–1984) winning in a car powered by an Offenhauser engine. His victory set a record at the time of 121 miles per hour, and breaking speed records has continued to be a drawing feature for the race. Offenhauser motors, however, lost their dominance to other manufacturers in the 1960s but remained strong competitors until the 1970s.

As is frequently the case with successful sporting events, the Indy 500 provided more than the main attraction; even midget car races could be enjoyed. The 142,000 fans at the 1940 race and the 160,000 who attended in 1942 could also amuse themselves at a number of tent shows, ride Ferris wheels, or test their skills at roller skating rinks and shooting galleries. After the war, the Indy 500 continued to offer a variety of forms of entertainment in addition to the main event.

Among the drivers of the 1940s racing at Indianapolis were Rex Mays (1913–1949) and Ted Horn (1910–1948). Mays had taken the AAA championship in 1940 and 1941. He also competed in the Indy those two years, but a trophy and a speed record eluded him. Like Mays, Ted Horn never crossed The 500 finish line first but, after his rookie year, always placed second, third, or fourth. He went on to claim the AAA crown for three consecutive years, 1946 to 1948.

*Watkins Glen Grand Prix.* In 1948, road racing arrived in Watkins Glen, a small community in upstate New York. Cameron Argetsinger (1921–2008), a law student at Cornell University in nearby Ithaca, a sports car enthusiast and one of the first members of the Sports Car Club of America (SCCA, a 1944 renaming of the Automobile Racing Club), obtained permission from the Watkins Glen Chamber of Commerce and sanction from the SCCA to organize a road race in the area. He established a six-and-a-half-mile course using mostly paved roads that wound through the town and its environs, including a short dirt and gravel stretch at the site. After an unfortunate 1952 accident in downtown Watkins Glen, officials moved the race to a less congested area.

Fifteen cars started the 15-lap contest on October 2, 1948. In front of an estimated 10,000 viewers and with 11 cars completing the competition, Frank Griswold Jr. averaged 63 miles per hour in his Alfa Romeo and placed first. Briggs Cunningham (1907–2003), entering a race for the first time, came in second. Cunningham, another early member of SCCA, soon formed B. S. Cunningham, Inc., and between 1951 and 1955 built The Cunningham, an American sports car. For his cumulative motorsport accomplishments, Cunningham appeared on the cover of *Time* magazine in April 1954, and, during 1948 and 1949, membership in SCCA nearly doubled each year.

*Stock car racing.* Today, stock car racing ranks as one of the nation's most popular spectator sports. During Prohibition days, stock automobiles rolled off the production lines of Chrysler, Ford, and General Motors. A few of these cars that arrived in the mountainous parts of the Southeast underwent significant modifications. Carefully adjusted suspensions and shock absorbers enabled haulers of illegal moonshine to safely speed along windy mountain roads. Such alterations became something of a craft, and informal backroad racing offered a way of comparing equipment and driving skills.

From the 1900s to the 1930s, Daytona Beach, Florida, became known as a place to try to break land speed records, with numerous world records being established there. In 1935, however, these speed tests were moved to Utah's Bonneville Salt Flats, an area with a more consistent surface and less congestion. Daytona Beach officials, concerned about the loss of tourist trade, asked Sig Haugdahl (1891–1970), a local racer, to organize and promote a race for street-legal sedans on the hard-packed sand course. On March 8, 1936, drivers took the wheels of cars similar to those that carried moonshine, and the event receives credit as the first stock car race. William "Bill" France (1909–1992), a mechanic and racing driver, placed fifth at Daytona and in 1938 assumed management of the beach races. Fourteen more such races were held before the United States entered World War II.

After the war, France decided to concentrate on promoting racing instead of driving and, on February 21, 1948, formed a family-owned and operated business to be called the National Association for Stock Car Automobile Racing (NASCAR). The organization, still active and successful today, set out to schedule, sanction, and govern qualifying and championship auto racing events, a focus that has remained with NASCAR ever since.

NASCAR's first official season ran from February through November 1948 and consisted of 52 modified races. Fords, enhanced for racing, held first place positions in all of these events, and three drivers emerged as the top contenders, winning more than half of the events—Truman Fontell "Fonty" Flock (1921–1972) captured 15 of the races, Robert "Red" Byron (1915–1960) won 11, and Curtis Turner (1924–1970) collected 7 victories.

For NASCAR's second season, France arranged eight races using cars that the general public actually drove every day. Called the Strictly Stock Race—today known as the Sprint Cup Series—the inaugural event took place on June 19, 1949, in Charlotte, North Carolina, before a crowd of 13,000, and included one female driver, Sara Christian (1918–1980), among the first women to compete professionally in racing. At one point in the race, Christian let Bob Flock (1918–1964) finish in her car when his engine quit. In a July 1949 race, Louise Smith (1916–2000) and Ethel Mobley (1920–1984), joined Christian. She placed 18th, Mobley came in 11th, and Smith rolled her car.

In addition to having winners for each race, France devised a point system for determining a season's champion. In 1949, and until 1967, prize money and finishes determined the points won. A graduated system awarded 10 points for first place, 9 for second, and so on; he then multiplied scores by a percentage of the race purse. On this basis, for the 1949 season, Red Byron became the champion with 842 points. His earnings for the season hit a total of $5,800 (almost $52,500 in 2008 dollars).

*Midget auto racing.* Midget cars first appeared as racers in 1932. Smaller than the big racing models seen at major fairgrounds and the Indy 500, they were often home-built machines. Because of their size, they could be raced at small facilities such as the Bronx Coliseum in New York City, **baseball** diamonds, **football** fields, or playgrounds across the country. These neighborhood events introduced automobile racing to a larger public.

Early in the history of midget auto racing in the United States, four groups organized—the Badger Midget Auto Racing Association (1936), the American Racing Drivers Club (1939), the Rocky Mountain Midget Racing Association (1940), and the Bay Cities Racing Association (1942). These associations represented drivers and car owners when dealing with tracks and promoters.

Midget auto contests, considered a good starting point for those wanting to participate in stock car racing, offered a place to test and strengthen driving skills. Some drivers eventually abandoned midget racing for big-car events, while others participated in more than one motorsport. For example, Bill Schindler (1909–1952), known as Bronco Bill, began racing in 1931 in a sprint car, a high-powered vehicle designed primarily for running on a short oval or circular dirt or paved track. He moved from a sprint car to midgets, frequently racing daily at tracks up and down the East Coast. Over the course of his career, he won more midget races than any competitor and held the ARDC Midget-Car Season Championship for four years: 1940, 1945, 1946, and 1948.

*Motorcycle races.* The Hendee Manufacturing Company in Kings Mountain, North Carolina, today known as the Indian Motorcycle Company, produced its first bike in 1902, followed by Harley-Davidson in Milwaukee, Wisconsin, in 1903. The Harley-Davidson bike, built to be a racer, won its first race in Chicago in 1905. By 1949, riders on Harley-Davidsons won 19 of 24 national championship events, clearly differentiating the brand from its competitors.

The Federation of American Motorcyclists, formed in 1903, sanctioned early races and kept event records. The group folded in 1919 to be replaced by the American Motorcycle Association in 1923. A few of the events and their winners quickly gained prominence in the sporting world. Motorcycle sales had increased during the Great Depression, a time when many could not afford a car, and this provided decent-sized audiences for motorcycle racers and racing spectators during the 1940s.

The Daytona 200, launched in 1937 as the country's first major motorcycle road race, shared a 3.2-mile stretch of beach with stock car races and attracted drivers from both the United States and Canada. Americans won each year, except for Billy Mathews (1912–1980), a Canadian riding a British Norton motorcycle in 1941, the last year for the race because of World War II.

When the Daytona 200 returned in 1947, Bill France, in addition to his stock car racing responsibilities, managed and promoted this race. The event drew 184 racers. John Spiegelhoff (active 1930s and 1940s) won that first year, and Floyd Emde (1919–1994) took the honors in 1948, both on Indian bikes. Dick Klamfoth (b. 1928), riding a Norton, took the honors in 1949. By then, the track had been expanded to stretch for 4.1 miles.

In addition to the Daytona races, other categories of motorcycle competitions were created in the 1940s. The Langhorne (Pennsylvania) 100 Mile National offers a speedway event that takes place on a flat oval dirt track. The Pacific Coast TT race uses a time trial format on an oval track with a single jump followed by a right hand turn. Motocross events, the equivalent of road racing, run on a closed-circuit surface such as sand, mud, or grass. All of these variations have proved popular over the years, and both local and national events have grown in numbers.

*Speedboat racing* (also motorboat, powerboat, or hydroplane racing). Competition among the pilots (few use the term "driver" for boats) of motor-powered vessels dates back to the early 1900s. The events can consist of contests among two or more pilots and their boats or solo runs to challenge established speed records. Participants in motorboat racing tend to favor operating their powerful machines at high speeds. Many also take pleasure in building, maintaining, and improving engines and other equipment.

The sport can also be enjoyed by onlookers, and, during the 1940s, yachts frequently formed a substantial spectator fleet.

Representatives of yacht clubs in the Northeast region of the United States formed the American Power Boat Association (APBA) in 1903 to serve as a racing organization for enthusiasts. It held its first challenge cup race, known as the Gold Cup, in 1904 on the Hudson River in New York. In the following years, this annual event was held in other localities, and each year's winners could defend their victories on home waters.

By 1940, APBA also sponsored a number of races leading to the Gold Cup. Various yacht clubs offered regattas and heats featuring speedboat and hydroplane racing, giving potential Gold Cup entrants practice events. Even though the United States was not officially at war in the summer of 1941, only one boat entered, *My Sin,* piloted by owner Zalmon "Guy" Simmons Jr. (active 1920s to 1940s). Officials awarded Simmons the trophy after he ran one solitary heat. No events were held for the years 1942 through 1945.

In the postwar period, a record number of regattas and races drew entries and spectators that exceeded prewar statistics. Detroit hosted the 1946 Gold Cup, the first major motorboat event following the war, with a record 22 boats entering. The 1941 winner, *My Sin,* reappeared. But by then, popular bandleader Guy Lombardo (1902–1977) owned and piloted it, and he renamed it *Tempo VI.* Lombardo came in first, winning the race with a speed of 70.890 miles per hour, which bettered a 26-year-old record of 70.412 miles per hour held by motorboat builder and racer Garfield "Gar" Wood (1880–1971).

Lombardo, a speedboat aficionado and well-known in racing circles, won a number of official and unofficial events until 1953 and his retirement. He featured prominently in another popular competition, the President's Cup, held annually on the Potomac River in Washington, DC. In 1946, with **President Harry S. Truman** (1884–1972) watching from the deck of a navy day cruiser, 28-year-old Dan Foster (b. 1916), who perfected his racing skills as the pilot of a Lockheed P-38 fighter plane during World War II, took the event in *Miss Great Lakes* with Lombardo coming in second. Foster also won the Gold Cup piloting the same boat in 1948.

Speedboat racing in its early days could only be afforded by the wealthy, with many of the names of boat owners found in the Social Register; some served as the pilot in races, others hired experienced hands to operate the boat. In June 1948, a motorboat race running from Albany, New York, to a point near where 72nd Street in New York City comes close to the Hudson River, boasted a record fleet of around 200, with participants from as far away as California. A number of enthusiastic male owners entered, but the event also included a grandmother and a 15-year-old, both from Ohio. Six months later at the National Motor Boat Show held in New York, 238 exhibits attracted record crowds and rang up more than $5 million in sales (over $45 million in contemporary dollars), with some powerboats selling for as low as $3,000 (approximately $27,000 in 2008 dollars). A speedboat devotee no longer needed to be wealthy to own a powerful boat and participate in racing.

Motorsports as a recreational and competitive activity gained prominence during the 1940s, especially after World War II. NASCAR races and the Watkins Glen Grand Prix attracted drivers from all over the United States as well as other countries. Many drivers entered automobile racing of one form or another as midget car drivers before moving on to stock car racing and the bigger races, such as the Indianapolis 500. Records were broken only to be broken again, although a few held for several years. After World War II, more and more tracks appeared coast to coast, paving the way for expanded automobile racing opportunities such as drag racing, cross-country, hill climbs, and vintage sport cars. Powerboat events likewise grew in numbers and popularity. Advancements in **technology** and **design** constantly increased speed possibilities and influenced all motorsports—cars, motorcycles, and boats—well after the 1940s.

*See also:* Design; Hot Rods and Drag Racing; Leisure and Recreation; Skating (Roller); Television

**Selected Reading**
Golenbock, Peter. *American Zoom: Stock Car Racing—from the Dirt Tracks to Daytona.* New York: Macmillan, 1993.
Libby, Bill. *Great American Race Drivers.* New York: Cowles Book Company, 1970.
Motorsports. *New York Times,* January 12, 1941; August 16, 1941; December 21, 1941; May 9, 1942; July 4, 1942; August 18, 1946; June 29, 1947; June 13, 1948; October 3, 1948; January 9, 1949; September 18, 1949. www.proquest.com

# MOVIES

Fighting in Europe and Asia may have embroiled other nations in war, but the United States basked in a false peace in 1940. The Great Depression had come and mostly gone, industry boomed (although defense-related manufactures accounted for much of that prosperity), and the spectacular New York World's Fair promised "The World of Tomorrow." Hollywood, the nation's grand purveyor of dreams, turned out hundreds of films that entertained, relaxed, thrilled, created a chuckle or two, widened the eyes, or brought a tear and generally gave 1940 a feel, a look, of normalcy—or what the studios that created the films deemed normalcy.

Hollywood moved into the 1940s a company town—a locale where large production studios dictated what movie would be made, what crews would work, what directors would direct, what performers would star, what wages would be paid, and a myriad of other "whats" that ultimately determined what the public would see. The "Big Five" studios dominated the business, consisting of Metro-Goldwyn-Mayer (usually known as MGM), Paramount, RKO (never known as Radio-Keith-Orpheum, its original organizers), Twentieth Century-Fox, and Warner Bros. The "Little Three" followed—Columbia, Universal, and United Artists—and stood just below the Big Five in power, wealth, and importance.

Finally, a host of smaller studios—such as Colony, Lippert Pictures, Metropolitan Pictures, Monogram (and its subsidiary Allied Artists), Producers Distributing Corporation (succeeded by the similarly named Producers Releasing Corporation, or PRC), Republic Pictures, Screen Guild, Victory, and many others—also released commercial films, but they lacked the size and clout exercised by their larger counterparts. These studios carried the nickname "Poverty Row"; they seldom produced the highly publicized first-run hits, or A pictures, but instead filled out a double bill with cheaper, less important B movies. They nonetheless exercised control over their employees and productions, although not as rigidly as the larger operations.

The large studios additionally practiced what economists call vertical integration, whereby they not only owned their films, they also owned the distributors of the movies, and, in many cases, the theaters where they were shown. This explains the many glittering Paramounts, Warners, Foxes, and so on that could be found in major cities across the nation, the property of those studios whose names they bore in neon. Eventually, vertical integration would be challenged in the courts, with lawyers arguing that controlling all aspects of production, right down to owning the theaters, violated antitrust statutes. The arguments carried to the Supreme Court, which in 1948 ruled that vertical integration constituted a monopoly and must be ended, a decision that changed Hollywood profoundly and led to many upheavals in the movie business during the 1950s and beyond.

For the 1940s, however, the old practices more or less remained in place until the end of the decade. Statistics show that the movie capital's major studios released over 350 commercial, feature-length films in 1940; that number had dropped to some 230 in 1945, but the decrease came about because of the war and general belt tightening throughout the entertainment industry. By 1950, output had risen again, but just slightly, to approximately 265 pictures annually.

Attendance, one indicator of the medium's health, remained strong throughout the period. The Great Depression had wreaked havoc on ticket buyers, so that in the mid-1930s only about 40 percent of the population, or 49 million people, went to the movies with any regularity. By 1940 and improved economic times, the numbers had risen sharply, with some 61 million people going to theaters weekly, or almost half the population of 132 million. It has also been estimated that, on any given night during the conflict, over half a million servicemen were watching a movie somewhere.

At the end of hostilities in 1945, in excess of 85 million moviegoers—or 62 percent of all Americans—were purchasing tickets each and every week. When the veterans began to return home in the months following the war, the total reached an all-time high in 1946; estimates suggest that 87 million people a week saw the latest Hollywood offerings. But that year also marked a turning point; thereafter, attendance began a slow but steady decline. By the end of the decade, about 59 million people, or approximately 39 percent of a population of some 151 million, attended the movies weekly, certainly a substantial total but a deceptive one. Movie attendance dropped not just in numbers but, more importantly, as a percentage of the population. After 1950, the postwar **baby boom** caused the population to rise sharply, but the figures showing how many people went to the movies continued to drop, especially with the competition brought about by **television.** For the reminder of the 20th century, the decline would continue, never again approaching the figures achieved in the period 1940 to 1949.

The postwar years were not kind to the industry. Labor troubles struck the studios in 1946, and antitrust action by the courts, inflationary pay raises, and heavy overseas taxation took their economic toll. To cut expenses, most of the studios pared their bloated payrolls, an action that put thousands out of work. Several of the smaller studios still could not make ends meet and folded, and others merged with their former competitors.

Toward the end of the decade, amid mounting anti-Communist hysteria, the **House Un-American Activities Committee (HUAC),** a committee within the U.S. House of Representatives, held investigative hearings on the movie industry. In the charged political atmosphere of the time, members sought to find evidence of Communist infiltration of the film industry, both among employees working for studios and in the content of commercial films. Out of these hearings came the practice of blacklisting suspected Communists and the creation of a list of scapegoats, the so-called Hollywood Ten. In later years, most of the blacklisted individuals cleared their names but at great personal and professional expense. For some who died, the reprieves came too late, and many others never resumed their careers in filmmaking.

But with hundreds of productions and millions of people attending them throughout the 1940s, most leaders in the film industry tended to disregard any warning signs that things might change. Instead, Hollywood saw to it that its audience could choose from a wide variety of features. Naturally, from 1942 until 1945, the war preoccupied everyone, and the studios created many pictures devoted to the conflict. But movies also provide escapism, and so when people scanned the "what's showing" section of their **newspapers** or surveyed the marquees of neighborhood theaters, they could likely find something that offered a respite from the headlines of the day.

Other factors also enter into any discussion of motion pictures and the 1940s. An influx of talented European directors influenced both the content and techniques of the era's movies, frequently giving them a darker, more mature tone, especially in the realm of those dealing with criminals. Following World War I, a number began immigrating to the United States, driven from their home countries by repression and turmoil. The 1930s saw men like Fritz Lang (Vienna, 1890–1976), Otto Preminger (Vienna, 1906–1986), and Billy Wilder (Sucha, Austria, 1906–2002) establish themselves in Hollywood and begin to leave their mark on a succession of distinguished films. Lang directed pictures like *Western Union* (1941), *Ministry of Fear* (1944), *The Woman in the Window* (1944), and *Scarlet Street* (1945), whereas Preminger claimed *Laura* (1944), *Fallen Angel* (1945), *Forever Amber* (1947), and *The Fan* (1949). Wilder took credit for the classic *Double Indemnity* (1944) along with *The Lost Weekend* (1945), *A Foreign Affair* (1948), and many others.

The decade also welcomed a bevy of fresh stars making their debuts, both during and after the war. New names and faces like Alan Ladd (1913–1964), Veronica Lake (1919–1973), Robert Mitchum (1917–1997), Jane Russell (b. 1921), Robert Walker (1918–1951), Esther Williams (b. 1921), and countless others brightened screens around the country. They may not have entirely displaced the established stars from the 1930s—leading ladies and men like Bette Davis (1908–1989), Clark Gable (1901–1960), Cary Grant (1904–1986), and Myrna Loy (1905–1993)—who still enjoyed countless good roles throughout the 1940s and possessed undeniable box office appeal, but they announced the arrival of a new generation of movie actors ready to challenge any and all for the audience's favor.

After 1945 and the return of peace, no one wanted cinematic reminders of the recent conflict, so movies about the war and combat virtually disappeared. In their place came a spate of pictures dealing with the supposed evils of Communism and the growing tensions associated with a new threat to democracy, the **Cold War.** But these motion pictures filled a narrow niche, and more traditional categories, such as love and romance or cowboys and Indians, overshadowed them. Audiences wanted entertainment, and the industry complied.

Few science fiction films, traditional standbys on the Hollywood menu, received production during the 1940s. A handful—*One Million B.C.* (1940), *Doctor Cyclops* (1940), *The Invisible Woman* (1940), *The Invisible Man Returns* (1940), *Beginning or the End* (1947, dealing with the development of the **atomic bomb**)—constitute the best-known titles, a far cry from either the 1930s or the 1950s; perhaps the many movies that depicted the horrors of World War II, along with all the advanced **technology** that emerged from the conflict, served as adequate substitutes for the category.

For ease in reading, the broad topic area of movies has been broken into the period's principal film genres, and each receives separate treatment. The following 13 categories can be found alphabetically within the pages of this encyclopedia:

1. Cartoons (Film)
2. Children's Films
3. Comedies (Film)
4. Costume and Spectacle Films
5. Crime and Mystery Films
6. Drama (Film)
7. Film Noir
8. Horror and Thriller Films
9. Musicals (Film)
10. Political and Propaganda Films
11. Serial Films
12. War Films
13. Westerns (Film)

*See also:* *Best Years of Our Lives, The* (William Wyler); *Casablanca* (Michael Curtiz); *Citizen Kane* (Orson Welles); *It's a Wonderful Life* (Frank Capra)

**Selected Reading**
Doherty, Thomas. *Projections of War: Hollywood, American Culture, and World War II.* New York: Columbia University Press, 1993.
McLaughlin, Robert L., and Sally E. Perry. *We'll Always Have the Movies: American Cinema during World War II.* Lexington: University Press of Kentucky, 2006.
Muller, Jurgen. *Movies of the 40s.* Cologne, Germany: Taschen, 2005.
Thomas, Tony. *The Films of the Forties.* Secaucus, NJ: Citadel Press, 1975.

# MURPHY, AUDIE

The most decorated U.S. soldier of World War II, Audie Murphy (1924–1971), hardly seemed the type to become a bona fide combat hero. Born into a poor Texas farming family, he became a rifle sharpshooter, killing small game for his impoverished family. Following the December 7, 1941, attack on Pearl Harbor, he soon tried to enlist, but the military had to reject him on the basis of age. In June 1942, after altering his birth certificate so as to appear 18, he tried again, first with the U.S. Marines, and then with U.S. Army parachute forces. They both turned him down for physical reasons. Shy, small (five feet, five inches), slight of build (approximately 110 pounds), and babyfaced, no one foresaw his eventual ferocity on the battlefield.

The infantry branch of the army, not quite as selective as some others at the time, accepted his enlistment. He went through basic and advanced infantry training and in early 1943 received assignment to North Africa with the Third Infantry Division. His unit participated in the liberation of Sicily in the summer of 1943, where he received his initiation into combat. He demonstrated his marksmanship by killing two escaping Italian officers mounted on horseback.

Following the Sicilian campaign, Murphy's division went on to mainland Italy, starting at Salerno. Various encounters with German forces earned him promotion to sergeant as well as commendations. From Italy, Murphy and his troops participated in the invasion of southern France, where he again encountered the foe numerous times. In one engagement, Murphy single-handedly took out a machine gun nest and even turned the weapon on the Germans. For this, he received the Distinguished Service Cross, the second-highest medal awarded by the U.S. military.

More fighting won him more medals, plus a battlefield commission to second lieutenant. A sniper's bullet put Murphy in a field hospital for several weeks in the winter of 1944, but he returned to active duty in January 1945. His company, reduced to just a fraction of its original strength, encountered German resistance at Holtzwihr, a small village in eastern France near the Swiss border. Murphy ordered his soldiers to pull back in the face of superior forces, and he then proceeded to hold off the Germans, first with rifle fire, and then by operating the machine gun atop an abandoned tank. During this time, he was wounded in the leg but kept up his murderous fire. Out of ammunition, he rejoined his troops and rallied them in a counter attack that resulted in driving off the larger German force. For this heroic action, the army awarded Murphy the Congressional Medal of Honor, the nation's highest military honor. He also received a promotion to first lieutenant and removal from the front lines.

In all, Audie Murphy participated in campaigns in Sicily, Italy, France, and Germany. Records credit him with killing more than 225 Germans. He received over 30 medals from the United States plus several from France and Belgium. He earned every decoration the nation could offer—in addition to the aforementioned medals, he wore the Silver Star, the Bronze Star, the Oak Leaf Cluster, and three Purple Hearts for his combat wounds. He achieved all this before he had turned 21.

Murphy returned to the States in the summer of 1945 and received his service discharge in August. All of his honors got him on the cover of *Life* magazine in July 1945, an event that would influence his subsequent career path. Famed movie actor James Cagney (1899–1986) noted the *Life* cover with the youthful-looking Murphy on it and invited him to Hollywood for a screen test. Although the results did not look promising, Murphy stayed on and eventually gained a small role in *Beyond Glory,* a 1948 court-martial drama starring Alan Ladd (1913–1963). An inauspicious start, but it earned him a contract with Universal Pictures and another role in *Texas, Brooklyn and Heaven,* a 1948 comedy in which he plays a copy boy.

The following year proved a breakthrough for the young actor. The studio cast him in the lead for *Bad Boy* (1949; also known as *The Story of Danny Lester*). A film about a young man who gets into trouble, Murphy depicts a juvenile delinquent well, presaging a rash of such **movies** in the years following. Along with a string of B Westerns, 33 in all, his professional career peaked in the early 1950s with an adaptation of Stephen Crane's (1871–1900) novel *The Red Badge of Courage* (written in 1895; adapted for film in 1951) and a movie version of his 1949 autobiography, *To Hell and Back,* which had done well, spending 14 weeks on best seller lists. The latter picture, a rousing story, drew large audiences following its 1955 release and grossed several million dollars for the studio. Together, book and movie acquainted many people who did not know about Murphy's superlative war record. He eventually appeared in a total of 44 feature films.

The iconic American fighting man of World War II, Audie Murphy honored all soldiers with his bravery under fire. His distinguished service, however, came at considerable personal cost. A victim of what officials then called battle fatigue—a term more recently replaced by post-traumatic stress disorder (PTSD)—Murphy campaigned vigorously for adequate medical and psychological coverage for veterans throughout the postwar era.

*See also:* Best Sellers (Books); Juvenile Delinquency; War Films; Westerns (Film)

**Selected Reading**
Gossett, Sue. *The Films and Career of Audie Murphy.* Madison, NC: Empire, 1996.
Murphy, Audie. *To Hell and Back.* New York: Viking, 1949.

# MUSICALS (FILM)

The development of sound **movies** in the late 1920s added a new dimension to film production. Instead of relying on only the visual aspect of cinema, directors could integrate aural elements previously unavailable to them. The age of the movie musical had arrived.

By the 1940s, most of the mechanical problems presented by this new technology—proper placement of microphones, capturing individual voices in crowd scenes, accurate reproduction of sounds, and so on—had been overcome, and good storytelling and competent acting had again become primary concerns. In addition, the Hollywood studios had, during the 1930s, created a pantheon of movie stars associated almost exclusively with musicals. Singing and dancing greats like Fred Astaire (1899–1987), **Bing Crosby** (1903–1977), Marlene Dietrich (1901–1992), Alice Faye (1915–1998), Judy Garland (1922–1969), Al Jolson (1886–1950), Dick Powell (1904–1963), Eleanor Powell (1912–1982), and Ginger Rogers (1911–1995) had become household names, crooning and cavorting in one memorable musical after another.

A new galaxy of stars waited in the wings, ready for the 1940s. Along with those individuals mentioned above, people like Cyd Charisse (b. 1921), Betty Grable

(1916–1973), Rita Hayworth (1918–1987), Gene Kelly (1912–1996), Ann Miller (1923–2004), **Carmen Miranda** (1909–1955), Donald O'Connor (1925–2003), **Frank Sinatra** (1915–1998), Vera-Ellen (1921–1981), and Esther Williams (b. 1921), plus two particularly famous singing cowboys, **Gene Autry** (1907–1998) and **Roy Rogers** (1911–1998), graced countless motion pictures both during World War II and the postwar period. With such an array of talent, small wonder that the Hollywood musical remained a popular favorite, attracting audiences of all ages.

Even with the threat of war hanging heavy over the nation, the escapist pleasures of screen music and **dance** kept such gloomy thoughts at bay when the decade opened. Fred Astaire, Eleanor Powell, and George Murphy (1902–1992), another fine hoofer from the era, tap their way across some elaborate MGM sets in *Broadway Melody of 1940,* while a mostly Cole Porter (1891–1964) score provides a lovely backdrop. Made in late 1939 but not released until February 1940, the movie dishes up glamour and romance, a perfect recipe for that tense period. Even the still-youthful movie veterans Judy Garland (only 18 in 1940) and Mickey Rooney (b. 1920) brighten the screen with *Strike Up the Band,* a loose but light-hearted adaptation of George and Ira Gershwin's (1898–1937 and 1896–1983, respectively) 1927 Broadway hit of the same name.

Garland and Rooney came right back in 1941 with *Babes on Broadway,* another breathless romp through show business from the popular pair. *That Night in Rio* (April 1941) and *Week-End in Havana* (October 1941) brought together Alice Faye and Carmen Miranda, the latter famous for her tutti-frutti hats, conglomerations of tropical fruits that defy gravity. Both pictures qualify as mindless fluff, but their close release dates suggest the popularity the two actresses enjoyed then—and how studios wasted no time in getting out movies that might have box office potential.

In the spring of 1942, and with the nation struggling in the war, Paramount released *Holiday Inn,* a cheerful film that features Bing Crosby and Fred Astaire. A pleasant diversion from the grim headlines, its two debonair stars glide effortlessly through the story. Since the plot involves an inn that opens only for major holidays, the memorable Irving Berlin (1888–1999) score introduces tunes that use that theme, such as "Easter Parade" (written in 1933), "Let's Say It with Fire Crackers," "Happy Holidays," and "**White Christmas.**" Although the composer had written the song earlier for a never-released movie, no one knew it, and so *Holiday Inn* had the unique honor of launching what would become the most popular single recording of the 20th century. It so impressed the public that Paramount produced a second version in 1954, teaming Crosby with Danny Kaye (1913–1987) instead of Fred Astaire, and wisely titling the remake *White Christmas.*

As the country recovered from the initial shock of Pearl Harbor, a slight change in movie content rippled through Hollywood, one that can be seen in musical titles, if nothing else. The storylines may still involve romance and fluff, but the pictures suggest more topical concerns: *The Fleet's In, Star Spangled Rhythm, True to the Army, Yankee Doodle Dandy* (all 1942), down through *Anchors Aweigh* in 1945 and the return to peace. Uniforms and patriotism might have marked many of the wartime musicals, but the music and dancing remained true to the cause of entertainment.

Thus, *Stage Door Canteen* (1943; United Artists) and *Hollywood Canteen* (1944; Warner Bros.) ostensibly honor the good works done by show people at the New York

TABLE 70. Representative Film Musicals, 1940–1949

| Year | Film Titles | Stars |
|---|---|---|
| 1940 | Broadway Melody of 1940 | Fred Astaire, Eleanor Powell |
| | Dance, Girl, Dance | Maureen O'Hara, Lucille Ball |
| | Down Argentine Way | Betty Grable, Carmen Miranda |
| | If I Had My Way | Bing Crosby, Gloria Jean |
| | Lillian Russell | Alice Faye, Henry Fonda |
| | Little Nellie Kelly | Judy Garland, George Murphy |
| | Rhythm on the River | Bing Crosby, Mary Martin |
| | Second Chorus | Fred Astaire, Paulette Goddard |
| | Strike Up the Band | Judy Garland, Mickey Rooney |
| | Tin Pan Alley | Alice Faye, Betty Grable |
| 1941 | Babes on Broadway | Judy Garland, Mickey Rooney |
| | Birth of the Blues | Bing Crosby, Mary Martin |
| | Lady Be Good | Eleanor Powell, Robert Young |
| | Louisiana Purchase | Bob Hope, Victor Moore |
| | Moon Over Miami | Betty Grable, Don Ameche |
| | Sun Valley Serenade | Sonja Henie, Glenn Miller |
| | That Night in Rio | Alice Faye, Carmen Miranda |
| | Week-End in Havana | Alice Faye, Carmen Miranda |
| | You'll Never Get Rich | Fred Astaire Rita Hayworth |
| | Ziegfeld Girl | James Stewart, Judy Garland |
| 1942 | Broadway | George Raft, Pat O'Brien |
| | The Fleet's In | Dorothy Lamour, Betty Hutton |
| | For Me and My Gal | Judy Garland, Gene Kelly |
| | Holiday Inn | Bing Crosby, Fred Astaire |
| | My Sister Eileen | Rosalind Russell, Janet Blair |
| | Orchestra Wives | George Montgomery, Glenn Miller |
| | Star Spangled Rhythm | Victor Moore, Betty Hutton |
| | True to the Army | Ann Miller, Judy Canova |
| | Yankee Doodle Dandy | James Cagney, Walter Huston |
| | You Were Never Lovelier | Fred Astaire, Rita Hayworth |
| 1943 | Cabin in the Sky | Ethel Waters, Lena Horne |
| | Dixie | Bing Crosby, Dorothy Lamour |
| | Du Barry Was a Lady | Red Skelton, Lucille Ball |
| | The Gang's All Here | Alice Faye, Carmen Miranda |
| | Girl Crazy | Mickey Rooney, Judy Garland |
| | Stage Door Canteen | Cheryl Walker, William Terry |
| | Stormy Weather | Lena Horne, Cab Calloway |
| | Thank Your Lucky Stars | Eddie Cantor, Dinah Shore |
| | This Is the Army | George Murphy, Joan Leslie |
| | Thousands Cheer | Gene Kelly, Kathryn Grayson |
| 1944 | And the Angels Sing | Dorothy Lamour, Betty Hutton |
| | Follow the Boys | George Raft, Jeanette MacDonald |
| | Four Jills in a Jeep | Kay Francis, Martha Raye |
| | Going My Way | Bing Crosby, Barry Fitzgerald |

*(continued)*

TABLE 70. *(continued)*

| Year | Film Titles | Stars |
|---|---|---|
| | *Hollywood Canteen* | Bette Davis, John Garfield |
| | *Irish Eyes Are Smiling* | Dick Haymes, Monty Woolley |
| 1944 | *Lady in the Dark* | Ginger Rogers, Ray Milland |
| | *Meet Me in St. Louis* | Judy Garland, Margaret O'Brien |
| | *Pin Up Girl* | Betty Grable, Martha Raye |
| 1945 | *Anchors Aweigh* | Gene Kelly, Frank Sinatra |
| | *The Bells of St. Mary's* | Bing Crosby, Ingrid Bergman |
| | *Diamond Horseshoe* | Betty Grable, Dick Haymes |
| | *The Dolly Sisters* | Betty Grable, June Haver |
| | *Rhapsody in Blue* | Robert Alda, Joan Leslie |
| | *A Song to Remember* | Cornel Wilde, Merle Oberon |
| | *State Fair* | Jeanne Crain, Dick Haymes |
| | *Tonight and Every Night* | Rita Hayworth, Janet Blair |
| | *Weekend at the Waldorf* | Ginger Rogers, Lana Turner |
| | *Wonder Man* | Danny Kaye, Virginia Mayo |
| 1946 | *Blue Skies* | Bing Crosby, Fred Astaire |
| | *Centennial Summer* | Jeanne Crain, Cornel Wilde |
| | *Easy to Wed* | Esther Williams, Van Johnson |
| | *The Harvey Girls* | Judy Garland, Ray Bolger |
| | *The Jolson Story* | Larry Parks, Evelyn Keyes |
| | *Night and Day* | Cary Grant, Monty Woolley |
| | *People Are Funny* | Jack Haley, Rudy Vallee |
| | *Swing Parade of 1946* | Gale Storm, Phil Regan |
| | *Three Little Girls in Blue* | Vera-Ellen, June Haver, Vivian Blaine |
| | *Ziegfeld Follies* | William Powell, Fred Astaire |
| 1947 | *Copacabana* | Groucho Marx, Carmen Miranda |
| | *Down to Earth* | Rita Hayworth, Larry Parks |
| | *The Fabulous Dorseys* | Tommy and Jimmy Dorsey |
| | *Good News* | June Allyson, Peter Lawford |
| | *Hit Parade of 1947* | Eddie Albert, Constance Moore |
| | *I'll Be Yours* | Deanna Durbin, Tom Drake |
| | *I Wonder Who's Kissing Her Now* | June Haver, Mark Stevens |
| | *Mother Wore Tights* | Betty Grable, Dan Dailey |
| | *Variety Girl* | Bing Crosby, Bob Hope, many others |
| | *Welcome Stranger* | Bing Crosby, Barry Fitzgerald |
| 1948 | *A Date with Judy* | Jane Powell, Elizabeth Taylor |
| | *Easter Parade* | Fred Astaire, Judy Garland |
| | *The Emperor Waltz* | Bing Crosby, Joan Fontaine |
| | *On an Island with You* | Esther Williams, Peter Lawford |
| | *The Pirate* | Gene Kelly, Judy Garland |
| | *The Red Shoes* | Moira Shearer, Anton Walbrook |
| | *Romance on the High Seas* | Doris Day, Jack Carson |
| | *A Song Is Born* | Danny Kaye, Virginia Mayo |
| | *When My Baby Smiles at Me* | Betty Grable, Dan Dailey |
| | *Words and Music* | Mickey Rooney, Tom Drake |

| Year | Film Titles | Stars |
|---|---|---|
| 1949 | *The Barkleys of Broadway* | Fred Astaire, Ginger Rogers |
|  | *In the Good Old Summertime* | Judy Garland, Van Johnson |
|  | *It's a Great Feeling* | Doris Day, Dennis Morgan |
|  | *Jolson Sings Again* | Larry Parks, Barbara Hale |
|  | *Look for the Silver Lining* | June Haver, Ray Bolger |
| 1949 | *My Dream Is Yours* | Doris Day, Jack Carson |
|  | *Neptune's Daughter* | Esther Williams, Red Skelton |
|  | *Oh, You Beautiful Doll* | June Haver, Mark Stevens |
|  | *On the Town* | Gene Kelly, Frank Sinatra |
|  | *Red, Hot and Blue* | Betty Hutton, Victor Mature |

and Los Angeles clubs run by the **USO (United Service Organizations)** to serve the troops as they passed through these cities, but they also celebrate the stars themselves, those performers who took time out to mingle with anxious soldiers and sailors about to embark for foreign shores. Dozens of big names appear in the films and delivered free publicity for the two studios that had the players under contract and put them into these extravaganzas.

With the surrender of the Axis powers in 1945, the movie industry quickly shed its patriotic trappings and went back to nontopical entertainment. In the area of musicals, however, a touch of nostalgia, a return to the good old days before world wars, became a popular theme. *Centennial Summer* (1946) goes back to 1876 and the country's 100th birthday, whereas *Mother Wore Tights* (1947) resurrects vaudeville from the turn of the century. In fact, the popularity of *Mother Wore Tights* caused Twentieth Century-Fox to reunite the two leads, Betty Grable and Dan Dailey (1913–1978), for another exercise in nostalgia, *When My Baby Smiles at Me* (1948). Instead of vaudeville, the plot utilizes a close relative, burlesque. Both films incorporate much early popular music into their scores.

The decade ended by continuing a musical exploration of the past, those innocent years before the United States became a world power and had to contend with a new kind of conflict, namely the **Cold War.** Trifles like *In the Good Old Summertime, Look for the Silver Lining,* and *Oh, You Beautiful Doll* (all 1949) boasted sentimental scores containing chestnuts from yesteryear, and audiences much preferred them to anything raucous or modern. One of the best of this kind, *The Barkleys of Broadway* (1949), brought back to the screen a dance partnership that millions had loved during the 1930s: Fred Astaire and Ginger Rogers.

In a series of nine musicals the two made between 1933 (*Flying Down to Rio*) and 1939 (*The Story of Vernon and Irene Castle*), the duo set a virtually unmatched standard of dancing for film. They had worked for RKO in the 1930s, but MGM managed to land them *The Barkleys of Broadway.* Another exercise in nostalgia, this time on two levels—the biographical story of a dance team from before World War I and the reunion of Astaire and Rogers after an absence of 10 years, the motion picture clearly fits the mood and setting of so many musicals produced during the postwar era. Things would change but not until the 1950s.

The 1940s proved a fruitful decade for Hollywood musicals. The list above, hardly inclusive, leaves out dozens of pictures made on the cheap by small studios and cast largely with unknowns. They usually had short runs, made little money, and then disappeared. The quality musicals released by the major studios during the decade, however, have endured remarkably well and continue to be well received by critics and the moviegoing public alike.

*See also:* Broadway Shows (Musicals); Canteens; Comedies (Film); Costume and Spectacle Films; Shore, Dinah; Smith, Kate; Songwriters and Lyricists; Westerns (Film)

**Selected Reading**

Jones, John Bush. *The Songs that Fought the War: Popular Music and the Home Front, 1939–1945.* Waltham, MA: Brandeis University Press, 2006.

Smith, Kathleen E. R. *God Bless America: Tin Pan Alley Goes to War.* Lexington: University Press of Kentucky, 2003.

Springer, John. *All Talking! All Singing! All Dancing!* Secaucus, NJ: Citadel Press, 1966.

Young, William H., and Nancy K. Young. *American Music through History: The World War II Era.* Westport, CT: Greenwood Publishing Group, 2005.

# N

## NEWSPAPERS

Americans have traditionally relished theirs newspapers, from big-city dailies to country weeklies. Possessed of a colorful history that dates back to the Revolutionary days of the late 18th century and runs to the Roaring Twenties, newspapers ruled supreme and functioned as the nation's primary mass medium. With the onset of the 1930s, however, two challengers—**radio,** and to a lesser degree, **movies**—appeared, giving the press its first real competition.

Radio probably did more damage to the newspaper business than did either the Great Depression or World War II. Newspapers had traditionally been the average citizen's first choice for news, but radios were becoming omnipresent, a ready source for late-breaking stories. Plus radio, with its mix of news, sports, entertainment, and music, took up an increasing portion of **advertising** revenue—and unlike a daily paper, it came into homes for free. Radio's popularity skyrocketed during the 1930s, with about two-thirds of American homes possessing at least one receiver in 1935 to over 89 percent by 1945 and 95 percent by 1950. Unfortunately for the newspaper industry, no commensurate gains can be found. Many newspaper publishers therefore acquired radio stations as a way to stay profitable. They may have viewed their electronic rival with some disdain, but they also saw it as a surefire moneymaker and invested in stations accordingly. During the 1940s, newspaper interests owned, or were affiliated with, several hundred broadcast stations.

Readership and circulation, however, remained strong during the Depression decade and even displayed increases during that difficult economic time, although some papers fell by the wayside. The public stayed hungry for news throughout World War II, and newspapers did their best to satisfy it; not until the late 1940s did a new challenger—**television**—make its debut, but it took time to establish this electronic medium in homes, and so the decade closed with newspapers maintaining a seemingly unbeatable lead over any competition.

In reality, U.S. newspapers had commenced a long, slow 20th-century decline that first became noticeable during the 1920s. At the beginning of the 1930s, the nation boasted 1,942 daily newspapers, down from some 2,500 in the 1920s. With the onset of the 1940s, the figure had fallen to 1,878 dailies, a loss of 64 more papers. And when the decade drew to a close, 1,772 papers continued daily publication schedules, revealing that 106 additional newspapers had ceased publication. So, despite annual population increases, the number of daily newspapers had been steadily decreasing. Some of this loss can be accounted for by mergers or consolidation, and a number of papers went out of business because of the Depression-era economy, a situation that caused advertising revenues, the lifeblood of newspapers, to tumble, bringing about financial failure. In the war years, shortages, **rationing,** and price controls continued to restrain the economy, which in turn cut newspaper advertising and again put pressures on publishers. But the postwar period (1945–1949) witnessed a return to a robust consumer economy and subsequent advertising increases, but at least some newspapers seemingly ran counter to these events, because a significant number nevertheless closed their offices.

Ironically, daily circulation continued an upward climb that had been ongoing throughout the 20th century. By the late 1930s, circulation could be measured at about 41 million papers sold each day. Assuming, in a typical household, that two or three people read a newspaper on a regular basis, that 41 million number jumps to over 100 million, or well over half of the nation's population of 131.5 million in 1940. By the end of the decade, U.S. newspapers circulated almost 54 million daily copies, 13 million more than 10 years earlier. The country's population had also climbed, rising to 149 million at decade's end, so that the proportion of multiple readers remained stable. It can therefore be seen that people found the medium an essential source of news and entertainment.

Before drawing conclusions, however, some additional numbers need to be considered. The nation's 1940 population represented an increase of about 8 million over 1930, or about 7 percent. Between 1940 and 1950, the total jumped another 13 percent, to 149 million. Daily circulation, however, climbed from the aforementioned 41 million copies to 54 million, or a 33 percent increase. Those numbers, good news to publishers at the time, suggested that readership grew faster than the nation's population, meaning a higher percentage of Americans regularly read newspapers. But the figures proved an aberration, a momentary fluke. Despite their modest gains in circulation during the 1940s, newspapers would, in the long run, reflect a decline.

For a point of reference, in 2000, daily circulation stood at approximately 48 million daily copies, or 6 million fewer than a half-century earlier. But the U.S. population had climbed to 292 million, or almost double the 1950 figures. Even if three people read those 48 million papers, they constituted a distinct minority, and the declines have accelerated in the 21st century. In addition, the number of dailies published in 2000 had shrunk to 1,520, or 252 fewer daily newspapers than in 1950, and with no end to this numerical erosion in sight.

Despite the momentary bright spot about circulation in the 1940s, other factors struck the U.S. newspaper industry. The country, still suffering the aftereffects of the Great Depression, became mired in World War II and had to endure numerous hardships. Printing equipment, such as the huge presses required for big-city papers, were difficult to repair given shortages of replacement parts. Newsprint was in limited supply, and the draft took many employees away from their journalism jobs.

The Espionage Act and the Trading with the Enemy Act, both statutes dating from 1917 and World War I, remained on the books in 1941, when the nation again went to war. Both acts gave government the right to censor or block publications felt to be dangerous or supportive of enemies during a national crisis. In late 1941, shortly after Pearl Harbor, the War Powers Act gave the White House a sweeping mandate to censor all communication between the United States and other nations, friend or foe, and resulted in the creation of the federal Office of Censorship. In order to control any news deemed detrimental to the war effort, the government in 1942 printed *A Code of Wartime Practices for the American Press;* although it claimed to be voluntary, most editors and reporters adhered to its restrictions on covering troop movements, casualties, defense production, new **technology,** and the like. Broadcast journalists also respected its provisions. In a spirit of cooperation, reporters did not write stories on the successful development of radar and ongoing experiments that would lead to the first **atomic bomb.** Editors similarly hushed information about a host of other defense efforts. Some individuals in the news business might know about a new weapon or the deployment of troops overseas, but they were expected to maintain a discreet silence, and virtually everyone complied.

At its height of influence, the Office of Censorship employed over 14,000 people. Most of these workers examined mail and cable communications between the United States and the rest of the world. They also monitored telephone calls. Another federal agency, the Office of War Information (OWI), much larger and focused more on disseminating specific information about the war, complemented the work done by the Office of Censorship. The OWI, through its news bureau, provided press releases to selected reporters, news organizations, news **magazines,** and related groups. Much of the content contained in its materials could be classified as propaganda, providing a favorable, pro-U.S. interpretation of events, but the OWI frequently served as the only source of information available to reporters.

Despite the blanket of censorship that covered the nation during World War II, reporters nonetheless managed to give readers and listeners remarkably full coverage of the conflict throughout its duration. U.S. newspapers and magazines fielded over 500 correspondents abroad, and some, like Ernie Pyle (1900–1945), painted personalized vignettes of life on the front lines, while cartoonist Bill Mauldin (1921–2003) sketched mostly humorous comments from a foot soldier's point of view.

When the war drew to a close in 1945, the government lifted most domestic censorship. But the onset of the **Cold War** almost immediately thereafter presented new problems for U.S. journalists. Many government officials wanted news reports from Europe to be strongly, even stridently, anti-Communist in tone. The rise of the investigative powers of the **House Un-American Activities Committee (HUAC)** in the later 1940s chilled many reporters because they suspected—correctly, time would show—a wave of witch hunts would grip the committee as it sought to find evidence of Communist subversion within the country. These events would not transpire until the early

1950s for the most part, but a climate of fear nonetheless descended on many newspapers; censorship in wartime was understandable, but the Cold War, a war of rumors and innuendo, demanded new responses from a vigilant press.

In the world of newspaper publishing, relations between management and labor have been historically frosty, at best. The New Deal policies of **President Franklin Delano Roosevelt** (1882–1945) broadened the rules for collective bargaining, making it easier for employees to enter into contract negotiations, but they also heightened the chances for angry confrontation. The American Newspaper Guild, which was founded in 1933 to improve the bargaining power of employees, started as a small union. But it affiliated with the American Federation of Labor (AFL) in 1936 and then with the Congress of Industrial Organizations (CIO) in 1937, moves that considerably increased both its influence and membership, and making it the primary labor union responsive to the needs of those working in the newspaper field. For the remainder of the 1930s, guild chapters struck a number of papers for better wages and more equitable hours and **labor unrest** became the norm.

World War II brought about a nationwide no-strike agreement pledge, but in a peaceful 1946, workers forgot the pledge and labor problems became common in many segments of U.S. industry. For its part, the guild made a general minimum wage for newspaper employees a primary goal for the postwar period, one that it achieved in 1954 with about 90 percent of its contracts. The guild asked for a $100-per-week minimum for members; that figure translates to approximately $800 per week in 2008 dollars. Strikes against recalcitrant papers and management soon followed in 1946, a pattern that would continue into the 1950s. Members of sympathetic trade unions (such as pressmen, typesetters, typographers, and teamsters) joined their comrades in picketing selected papers, usually making production and deliveries impossible. The strikes generally ended as victories for the guild, and a series of crippling walkouts throughout the 1950s financially damaged several newspapers. In most cases, however, arbitration won the day.

Other forces also conspired to affect newspaper profitability. During the 1920s and 1930s, most cities with populations exceeding 100,000 residents claimed at least 2 rival papers; by 1940, 25 cities had lost that kind of lively competition and had become 1-newspaper towns. Even New York City, the most competitive of newspaper sites and home to many famous newspapers, felt the change. Earlier in the century, it had boasted some 20 competing dailies, but by 1940 the number had fallen to 7. Those places lucky enough to continue having 2 or more papers usually claimed both morning and evening editions, with the majority coming out in the late afternoon or evening. As Table 71 shows, that disparity continued throughout the decade; not until the 1980s did morning editions surpass their evening counterparts both in number and in popularity. In large metropolitan areas, the absence of heavy traffic simplified the distribution of a morning edition, plus advertisers liked the idea of readers perusing bright, fresh ad copy while they planned their shopping day.

Unlike most other developed nations, the United States never published a true national newspaper until the rise of *USA Today* and the *Wall Street Journal* in the latter years of the 20th century. Most books and many magazines enjoy nationwide distribution, but the vast majority of newspapers can claim at best a limited regional audience.

TABLE 71.  Number and Circulation of U.S. Newspapers

| | Daily Newspapers | | | | Sunday Newspapers | |
|---|---|---|---|---|---|---|
| | Morning | | Evening | | | |
| Year | Number | Circulation | Number | Circulation | Number | Circulation |
| 1939 | 383 | n.d. | 1,505 | n.d. | 524 | 31,519 |
| 1940 | 380 | 16,114 | 1,498 | 25,018 | 525 | 32,371 |
| 1941 | 377 | 16.519 | 1,480 | 25,561 | 510 | 33,436 |
| 1942 | 345 | 17,111 | 1.442 | 26,264 | 474 | 35,294 |
| 1943 | 333 | 17,078 | 1,421 | 27,315 | 467 | 37,292 |
| 1944 | 338 | 18,059 | 1,406 | 27,896 | 481 | 37,946 |
| 1945 | 330 | 19,240 | 1,419 | 29,144 | 485 | 39,680 |
| 1946 | 334 | 20,546 | 1,429 | 30,382 | 497 | 43,665 |
| 1947 | 328 | 20,762 | 1,441 | 30,911 | 511 | 43,151 |
| 1948 | 328 | 21,082 | 1,453 | 31,203 | 530 | 46,308 |
| 1949 | 329 | 21,005 | 1,451 | 31,841 | 546 | 46,399 |
| 1950 | 322 | 21,266 | 1,450 | 32,563 | 549 | 46,582 |

*Note:* Circulation figures are in thousands; figures as of October 1 of each year.
*Source: Historical Statistics of the United States, Colonial Times to 1970.* Washington, DC: Census Bureau, U.S. Department of Commerce, 1975.

In most cases, that means that, while countless people read newspapers, what someone reads in Chicago might differ from the choices an editor makes in San Francisco or New Orleans. National and international stories might be more or less identical, but state and local news would differ, as would local advertisements and features.

Given the apprehensions generated by the rise of Nazi Germany and the accompanying threat of a new world war, smaller papers that lacked overseas bureaus immediately felt themselves at a disadvantage. They could ill afford to send correspondents to cities far from their home bases. Thus, news syndicates like the Associated Press (AP) and United Press (UP) enjoyed significant growth. For a subscription fee paid by the papers, they would supply the reporters and detailed stories an individual newspaper could not hope to provide. Although both the AP and the UP trace their beginnings to the late 19th century, not until the World War II era did they come into their own. With more and more national and international news to cover, only these far-flung organizations could consistently file stories for their growing lists of subscribers.

Widespread syndication brought about a certain amount of standardization in U.S. newspapers. The syndicated features found in one paper could easily be found in another. This lessened the insularity of small-town dailies, bringing them more into the mainstream of American life. Standardization occurred not just with news stories; **comic strips,** horoscopes, crossword puzzles, bridge columns, the latest Hollywood gossip, advice columnists, box scores, and financial pages graced the paper because of syndication.

Even with the war, some syndicated columnists relied on gossip and celebrity watching for their appeal. Walter Winchell (1897–1972) probably ranks as the most colorful of this group. Over 1,000 papers in cities a considerable distance from the Great White Way carried his "On Broadway," a long-running column published from 1924 until 1963. Louella Parsons (1884–1972) and Hedda Hopper (1890–1966) followed close on Winchell's heels, at least in popularity during the 1940s. Both women contributed widely syndicated columns that focused almost exclusively on Hollywood and its stars. Their success helped maintain high circulation figures for movie magazines as well, ranging from the purely gossipy *Screen Romances* to the slightly more serious *Silver Screen*. In addition to their newspaper work, the two columnists reported over radio. Parsons hosted *Hollywood Hotel,* a mix of talent and gossip that premiered in 1934 and remained on the air until 1941. Never one to be outdone, Hopper parlayed her fame and influence into the popular *Hedda Hopper Show.* A 15-minute blend of chatter and celebrities, it began in 1939 and ultimately ran until 1951.

Other types of columnists also enjoyed significant syndication. For example, First Lady **Eleanor Roosevelt** (1884–1962) penned a long-running column series called "My Day." It began in 1935 and chronicled her thoughts and activities for many appreciative readers until 1962. Three other women writers monitored the nation's manners and mores. Emily Post (1872–1960) provided the last word on etiquette; her book *Etiquette,* published in 1922, joined the ranks of **best sellers** and made her famous. She also wrote about good manners for several magazines and, starting in the 1930s, published a popular newspaper column that could be found in over 150 papers until well into the 1940s. Dorothy Dix (b. Elizabeth M. Gilmer, 1870–1951) and Beatrice Fairfax (b. Marie Manning, 1873–1945) wrote advice-to-the-lovelorn features that also enjoyed wide followings. Dix had the distinction of being the highest-paid woman columnist of the 1930s and 1940s; she began writing in the 1890s, but her popular advice pieces did not begin until 1923; after they caught on, over 200 papers carried them. Fairfax likewise started young, and some consider her "Dear Beatrice Fairfax" column of the 1890s as the first newspaper advice series ever to run. An unsuccessful novelist, she wrote for newspapers to assure a steadier income. Fairfax left journalism in the 1920s but returned following the onset of the Depression and remained with her newspaper features until her death in 1945. All three women grew into unofficial arbiters of taste and behavior, their words anxiously studied by millions of readers who wanted to know about proper dining and dating.

The smart-alecky, quick-thinking newspaper reporter, along with his or her harried editor, has long been a stock character in much American popular culture. Movies, and later radio, have utilized this figure in comedies, mysteries, and even some Westerns. Throughout the 1940s, Hollywood released dozens of motion pictures, a few good, but mostly mediocre and forgettable, about journalists getting the big story. One of the best, *His Girl Friday* (1940), stars Cary Grant (1904–1986) and Rosalind Russell (1907–1976), a comedic remake of *The Front Page* from 1931. Fast paced with machine-gun dialog, it set the pattern for other newspaper films during the decade. *Public Enemies* (1941), *It Happened Tomorrow* (1944), *The Walls Came Tumbling Down* (1946), *Trespasser* (1947), *Call Northside 777* (1948), and *On Our Merry Way* (1948) serve as representative samples of the genre, although **Superman** (1948) should not be forgotten. Clark Kent, to hide his identity as the Man of Steel, works as a reporter on *The Daily Planet.*

*Newspaper reporters have long intrigued the public; American popular culture has often depicted them as wisecracking know-it-alls, and this still from the 1940 film comedy* His Girl Friday *serves as a case in point. Frequently fast and hilarious, it stars Cary Grant and Rosalind Russell as two newspaper people always on the alert for a fresh story and a way to beat out competing papers in acquiring it. (Claridge Pictures/Photofest)*

*City Desk* entertained radio listeners in 1941, and *The Front Page* reappeared as a broadcast series during 1948. A newspaper-oriented soap opera that could be heard on late afternoons was *Front Page Farrell,* on the air from 1941 to 1954. *Big Town,* more about crime than journalism, ran from 1937 to 1952, although a character named Steve Wilson, as a crusading editor, has the lead. *Casey, Crime Photographer* involves a newspaper photographer; his pictures usually give him clues about crimes, at which point he becomes more of a detective than a representative of the press. It premiered in 1943 and lasted until 1950 on CBS radio. Both movies and radio series tended to evolve into detective or crime stories; the ordinary, day-to-day experiences of a regular reporter probably would not present sufficient drama and excitement for most audiences.

The flush times the newspaper business enjoyed during the 1940s no doubt gave publishers a sense of never-ending prosperity, a feeling that readership and advertising volume would continue to rise with each passing year. From Pearl Harbor to the radioactive ashes of Hiroshima and Nagasaki, World War II filled the pages of U.S. newspapers with constant, important news stories. Even the first few postwar years were good to the industry. Advertisers, again able to promote consumer products, and with virtually no television to claim a percentage of every advertising dollar, poured money into the nation's newspapers, the dominant marketing medium of the day. Things would change down the road, but during the 1940s, the future looked rosy, indeed.

*See also:* Atomic Bomb, The; Comedies (Film); Crime and Mystery Films; Drama (Film); Photography; Pyle, Ernie, and Bill Mauldin; Radio Programming: Action, Crime, Police, and Detective Shows; Radio Programming: Drama and Anthology Shows; Radio Programming: News, Sports, Public Affairs, and Talk; Radio Programming: Soap Operas; Selective Training and Service Act of 1940 (Selective Service, or Draft); Westerns (Film)

**Selected Reading**

Emery, Edwin. *The Press and America: An Interpretive History of Journalism.* Englewood Cliffs, NJ: Prentice Hall, 1962.

Mott, Frank Luther. *American Journalism, A History: 1690–1960.* New York: Macmillan, 1962.

Schudson, Michael. *Discovering the News: A Social History of American Newspapers.* New York: Basic Books, 1978.

Wallace, Aurora. *Newspapers and the Making of Modern America: A History.* Westport, CT: Greenwood Press, 2005.

# P

## PHOTOGRAPHY

During the first half of the 20th century, technological advancements in the manufacture of cameras and film, coupled with improved developing processes and a growing interest in photography, created four distinct groups of camera users: (1) snapshot amateurs, (2) photojournalists and news photographers, (3) **fashion** and **advertising** photographers, and (4) artistic photographers. The craft offers aesthetic as well as utilitarian possibilities, dimensions that numerous individuals earnestly explored during the 1940s.

War photographers stand as a unique group for a set period of time. To cover World War II, the U.S. armed forces used both military and civilian photographers. The U.S. Signal Corps served as the home base for those in the military, except for the navy, which had its own Naval Aviation Photographic Unit, supervised from 1942 to 1945 by retired photographer Edward Steichen (1879–1973). During this time, he organized two wartime exhibits for the Museum of Modern Art: *Road to Victory* (1942), a pictorial portrait of the United States at war with a text written by his brother-in-law, poet Carl Sandburg (1878–1967), and *Power in the Pacific: Battle Photographs of Our Navy in Action* (1945), images taken by photographers in the naval unit. While supervising navy photographers, Steichen also shot pictures himself, which he compiled into *The Blue Ghost: A Photographic Log and Personal Narrative of the Aircraft Carrier U.S.S. Lexington in Combat Operation* (1947). Back in New York after completing his wartime duties, Steichen became director of the photography department at the Museum of Modern Art (MoMA).

Most of the civilian photographers came from *Life* magazine (founded 1936) or news services, such as the Associated Press (AP), INS (International News Service), Acme Newspictures, and *Life* magazine. During the course of World War II, 37 U.S. photographers lost their lives and 112 received wounds. Joe Rosenthal (1911–2006), working for the AP, captured one of the best-known pictures from the war, that of the U.S. flag being raised on the Pacific island of Iwo Jima on February 23, 1945, and first published in *Life*.

*Snapshot amateurs.* George Eastman (1854–1932) introduced his first Kodak camera in 1888 and sold his first Brownie, a simple box camera, in 1900. With an attractive price, the Brownie in its many variations experienced great popularity over its 70-year history. Many photographers started at a young age with a Brownie, and a few eventually turned the hobby into a profession, working for **magazines** and **newspapers.** Others branched out on their own, establishing studios and contracting for various assignments.

To kick off the 1940s, Eastman Kodak offered visitors to the 1939–1940 New York World's Fair a special Brownie for the low price of $1.25 (approximately $19 in 2008 dollars). The plastic case, designed by the famous Raymond Loewy (1893–1986), had the words "New York World's Fair" in raised letters on the front. It quickly became a collector's item.

The entry of the United States into World War II brought an abrupt change to the business of Kodak and other manufacturers of cameras. They moved from consumer goods to wartime products and government projects. An immediate contribution for the Allies from Kodak involved the development of Airgraph or V-Mail (for victory mail), a system for microfilming letters that conserved both weight and shipping space on cargo ships for the millions of letters sent both from home and abroad. One sack of V-Mail letters equaled over 37 sacks of conventional first-class letters written on regular paper.

In 1945, Kodak's consumer production resumed, and by 1946 three new Brownies were on the market: the Flash Six-20 for $6, the Target Six-16 Camera at $4, and the Target Six-20 Camera, which sold for $3.50 ($66, $42.50, and $37, respectively, in 2008 dollars). The company had also been marketing Kodachrome color film since the late 1930s, and a new photographer on the scene, Eliot Porter (1901–1990), experimented with this product for nature pictures. Until this time, most noted nature photographers, such as Ansel Adams (1902–1984) and Edward Weston (1886–1958), took only black-and-white shots. Porter went on to a distinguished career in color photography and achieved widespread recognition.

Eastman Kodak introduced Ektachrome in 1946, the first color film that amateur photographers could process themselves using special chemical kits, an invention that added to the number of people pursuing photography as a hobby. In May 1948, a widely distributed Kodak advertisement consisted of a group of Ektachrome pictures taken by the famous Edward Weston.

Two years later, the Polaroid Corporation, founded in 1937 by inventor Edwin H. Land (1909–1991), placed its first instant photography product, the Polaroid camera, on the market. The original model, initially available at Jordan Marsh, Boston's oldest department store, weighed in at five pounds when loaded with film and sold for $89.75; the film itself cost $1.75 for eight exposures (approximately $800 and $16, respectively, in 2008 dollars). Despite these high costs, on the first day, all 56 available units sold, and first-year sales exceeded $5 million ($44.6 million in 2008 dollars). This was good news for the struggling company; the return to peace had brought to an end its business of producing infrared filters, night-vision goggles, and other equipment for the armed forces.

*Photojournalists.* During World War II, photographs published in newspapers and magazines, and sometimes assembled in books, offered information, news, and propaganda, primarily about the home front and, secondarily, about the Pacific and European theaters. The mainstream magazines, such as *Life* and *Look* (founded 1937), primarily reported on the war from the angle of how it altered American lifestyles. For example, in 1939, before the United States entered World War II, only 10 of the 52 *Life* covers featured a military subject, usually a portrait of a general or an admiral. In 1942, with the United States officially involved, fewer than 50 percent of the *Life* covers depicted something related to the military aspect of the war, and, as in 1939, most of these were portraits of high-ranking officers. Articles and photographs about life at home—**victory gardens, scrap drives, blackouts, rationing,** and the latest fashion trends for the working woman—appeared regularly.

By 1943, however, covers relating to the war on the battlefields appeared and acknowledged ordinary fighting men and women, such as pilots, foot soldiers, PT-boat skippers, bomber crews, and the WACs (Women's Army Corps) and the WAVES (Women Accepted for Voluntary Emergency Service). Attention to events and people at home also continued, showing the latest fashions, along with high school graduations, dancing the lindy hop, and the latest gossip about celebrities such as Rita Hayworth (1918–1987) or **Frank Sinatra** (1915–1998).

The United States Office of War Information (OWI, 1942–1945), headed by Elmer Davis (1890–1958), a popular **radio** news reporter, took up the task of coordinating government information services, primarily for the home front. OWI personnel developed **posters,** radio programs, and newsreels intended to promote patriotism, recruit women into defense jobs, and warn citizens about foreign spies. Like the picture magazines, OWI photographers documented America's mobilization during the first years of the war, concentrating on subjects such as aircraft factories and women in the workforce.

Margaret Bourke-White (1904–1971), Robert Capa (1913–1954), Walker Evans (1903–1975), Dorothea Lange (1895–1965), Helen Levitt (1913–2009), W. Eugene Smith (1918–1978), and Weegee (b. Arthur Fellig, 1899–1968) can be called photojournalists because they used their cameras to offer illustrated stories about people, events, and the conditions of life. All of these individuals were featured in exhibits at museums or art galleries, and publishers collected their images in book format.

Most of the photojournalists in Table 72 worked for magazines. During World War II, Robert Capa went to Europe to cover the war and could thus be classified as a war photographer. His *Battle of Waterloo Road* chronicles wartime life in Britain with numerous images of London. Capa readily traveled with U.S. soldiers, which resulted in some daring pieces. His advice to other wartime photojournalists was, "If your pictures aren't good, you're not close enough."

Two distinguished photographers, Margaret Bourke-White and W. Eugene Smith, also exposed themselves to dangerous situations. Bourke-White spent time in wartorn Europe and Russia, resulting in the three publications noted in Table 72. Smith twice sustained injuries in the war, with the first occurring in 1942 as he simulated battle conditions for a picture for *Parade* magazine. He also received a serious wound when he

TABLE 72. Representative Photojournalists, 1940–1949

| Photographer | Exhibits and/or Magazine Work | Publications | Other Significant Accomplishments |
|---|---|---|---|
| Margaret Bourke-White | Best-known picture: Any one of many taken of U.S. industries (1920s to 1950s) | 1939: *North of the Danube* 1941: *Say, Is This the U.S.A.?* (on industrialization of the nation) 1942: *Shooting the Russian War* | Principal photographer for *Fortune* magazine 1941: First foreign photographer to chronicle Soviet industrialization and the only foreign photographer present during the German bombing of Moscow 1942: First official woman photographer for U.S. Army Air Corps |
| Robert Capa | Photographs appeared in *Collier's Weekly* and *Life* magazines Best-known picture: "Death of a Loyalist Soldier" (1936) | 1941: *The Battle of Waterloo Road* 1942: *Slightly Out of Focus* 1948: Pictures in John Steinbeck's (1902–1968) *A Russian Journal* | 1944: Set a standard for close-up photography during World War II, landing with U.S. soldiers on Omaha Beach on D-Day, June 6 1947: Along with others, formed the Magnum picture agency, a photographic cooperative |
| Walker Evans | Photographs appeared in *Fortune* magazine 1948: *Walker Evans Retrospective* at the Art Institute of Chicago Best-known picture: Any one of many taken of migrant workers in the South (1936) | 1941: *Let Us Now Praise Famous Men*, with text by James Agee (1909–1955). 1943: Art reviews for *Time* magazine | 1940: Received Guggenheim Fellowship to return to the South and photograph tenant farmers. 1959: Received a second Guggenheim Fellowship to produce a book of pictures of life in the United States |
| Dorothea Lange | 1942: *Sixty Prints by Six Women Photographers* at the Museum of Modern Art (MoMA) Best-known picture: "Migrant Mother" (1936) | 2006: Gordon, Linda and Gary Y. Okihiro publish *Impounded: Dorothea Lange and the Censored Images of Japanese American Internment*, which contains some of the 800 pictures taken of Japanese Americans in internment camps in 1943. | 1941: Guggenheim Fellowship, the first awarded to a woman 1945: Became a faculty member in the first Fine Arts Photography Department at the California School of Fine Arts (CSFA) 1952: A founder of the magazine *Aperture* with Ansel Adams, Minor White (1908–1976), and several others |

| | | |
|---|---|---|
| Helen Levitt | 1940: Picture titled "Halloween" included in inaugural exhibit of the Photography Department at MoMA<br>1943: *Helen Levitt* at MoMA<br>Best-known picture: "Halloween" (1939) | 1945–1946: *In the Street*, a film<br>1946–1947: *The Quiet One*, a film | 1940s: Worked as a film editor and extended her photographic practice into this medium<br>Numbered among the first to use color in fine art photography<br>1944–1945: Worked in the Film Division of the Office of War Information |
| W. Eugene Smith | *Life* magazine cover of Marines blowing up a Japanese cave on Iwo Jima, April 9, 1945<br>Best-known picture: "Walk to the Paradise Garden" (1946) | 1948: *Life* magazine photo essays "Country Doctor: His Endless Work Has Its Own Rewards" | |
| Arthur Fellig, or "Weegee" | 1941: "Murder Is My Business" at the Photo League, New York<br>1943: "Action Photography" at MoMA includes five Weegee photos.<br>1948: *50 Photographs by 50 Photographers* at MoMA<br>Best-known picture: "The Critic" (1943) | 1945: *Naked City*<br>1946: *Weegee's People* | 1948: Completed *Weegee's New York*, the first of several short features |

accompanied troops on the invasion of Okinawa in May 1945. He did not fully recover until 1947, returning to the staff of *Life.*

Among the representative photographers in the preceding table, Walker Evans is considered to be one of the premier documentary photographers of the 20th century. Much of his work, as with Lange, clearly came from his understanding of and concern about social justice issues. He recorded the conditions of white sharecroppers in the rural South during the Great Depression for an article in *Fortune* magazine, but the staff voiced some discomfort with the content and the project changed to a book, *Let Us Now Praise Famous Men* (1941), published by Houghton Mifflin. It went virtually unnoticed at the time, selling only 300 copies. The publication eventually gained popularity with a reprinting in 1960. Evans joined the staff of *Fortune* magazine in 1945 and became its special photographic editor in 1948.

Also dedicated to addressing social justice through photography, Dorothea Lange produced her strongest images during the years she worked for the Farm Security Administration (FSA, 1937–1943). In 1943, she completed another forceful collection of pictures on the internment of Japanese Americans despite having to work under numerous governmental restrictions. At the end of the year, as she completed her work, the U.S. Army confiscated her almost 800 shots and negatives and held them until shortly after the war, when they went to the National Archives.

As a brash press photographer, Arthur Fellig, better known as Weegee, cruised the streets of New York in the early morning hours taking sensational and graphic pictures of people involved in or watching crime scenes, accidents, fires, and other disasters. In 1947, he moved to Hollywood offering technical assistance to that industry and sometimes playing minor roles in the **movies.**

Helen Levitt also roamed the streets of her native New York to photograph children and street life. Except for a brief time in Mexico City in 1941, nearly all of her work depicts Manhattan. She worked often in poor neighborhoods, and an unusual series of photos taken from 1938 through 1948 focuses on children's chalk drawings and messages on city sidewalks and streets. In the early 1940s, she began working as a film editor and soon became a filmmaker.

Mention should be made of two other American documentary photographers active during the 1940s: Minor White (1908–1976) and Russell Lee (1903–1986). White assisted with FSA projects before being drafted into the U.S. Army in 1942. After an honorable discharge in 1945, he moved to California and, in addition to his photographic work, helped found *Aperture,* a quarterly photography magazine, serving as its editor for many years. Russell Lee started his career with FSA, a member of that government organization from 1936 until 1942. He, too, joined the army for the remainder of World War II and afterwards spent much of his time teaching, starting with the Missouri Photo Workshop in 1948.

*Fashion photographers.* By the 1940s, a number of women's and fashion periodicals, such as *Harper's Bazaar* (founded 1867), *Vogue* (founded 1892), *Mademoiselle* (founded 1935), and *Glamour* (founded 1939) had prospered and offered work opportunities for photographers so inclined. Two, Irving Penn (1917–2009) and Richard Avedon (1923–2004), made names for themselves. Penn, in 1943, became an assistant to Alexander Liberman (1912–1999), art director at *Vogue.* Initially he suggested photographic designs for covers but soon took the pictures himself. An innovator, Penn posed subjects against a simple gray or white backdrop, and his cover picture for the October 1, 1943, issue of *Vogue* consisted of a still life of a big brown leather bag, beige scarf and gloves, lemons, oranges, and a huge topaz. It cemented Penn's photographic career. In addition to fashion photography, he did portraits of personalities such as Martha Graham (1894–1991), Marlene Dietrich (1901–1992), and Georgia O'Keeffe (1887–1986).

After serving in the Merchant Marine from 1941 to 1942, Richard Avedon enrolled in a design course at New York's New School for Social Research and at the same time began working at *Harper's Bazaar*. He soon joined Penn as the most prominent of the younger generation of fashion photographers that frequently shot outdoors. Avedon eventually shifted to the studio setting and developed an effective white-backdrop style. He remained at *Harper's Bazaar* until 1965, when he went to *Vogue*.

*Photographic artists.* Ansel Adams and Edward Weston, two younger photographers inspired by the pioneering work of Alfred Stieglitz (1864–1946), probably the most influential American photographer of the early 20th century, wanted to put photography on an artistic plane equal with painting. Both Adams and Weston, in 1931 joined with five others—Imogen Cunningham (1883–1976), William Van Dyke (1906–1986), John Paul Edwards (1884–1968), Henry Swift (1891–1962), and Sonya Noskowiak (1900–1975)—to form Group f/64. Intending to adhere to what they called "pure photography," the organization explored the artistic potential of their craft, experimenting with light and form. Their work, while popular with many, also raised photography to the level of elite art.

Group f/64 dissolved in 1935, but Adams and Weston continued to focus on the group's principles: to use only the most basic equipment and natural light for their sharply focused and carefully framed images of objects, such as peppers, an artichoke half, flowers, sand dunes, mountains, and rock formations. The two also shot landscapes, particularly of the American West, where they did most of their photography. In addition, Weston gained fame for his imaginative and artistic studies of nudes. Both men also taught and wrote about photography. They directed the first *U.S. Camera* Yosemite Photographic Forum in 1940 and regularly had articles in specialized publications such as *Camera Craft, Popular Photography,* and *Aperture*.

Ansel Adams' career spanned over 50 years, and his photographs appeared in numerous books and portfolios. He remained faithful to clarity and precision in his work. Edward Weston started experiencing symptoms of Parkinson's disease in 1946 and two years later made his last photographs at Point Lobos, California; in 1952; his *Fiftieth Anniversary Portfolio* was published. He died at his home on January 1, 1958.

Photography in the 1940s changed in many ways. Amateur photographers found a number of new cameras and new films available for purchase. Documentary photography came into its own and World War II produced many memorable images, including the raising of the American flag over Iwo Jima, the mushroom cloud over Hiroshima, and the haunting pictures of Nazi death camps. Professional photographers offered images that glorified the country's mountains and meadows, while also paying attention to cityscapes and neighborhoods. Museums established photography departments for the first time and displayed solo exhibits for the more notable artists. Pictures

TABLE 73. Representative Artistic Photographers, 1940–1949

| Photographer | Exhibits | Publications | Other Significant Accomplishments |
|---|---|---|---|
| Ansel Adams | 1940: *A Pageant of Photography*, Golden Gate Exposition in San Francisco<br><br>1943: Manzanar Relocation Center pictures at MoMA, New York City. | 1940: *A Pageant of Photography*, introduction by Adams<br><br>1944: *Born Free and Equal: The Story of Loyal Japanese-Americans* (pictures taken at Manzanar Relocation Center, California | 1940: Helped the Museum of Modern Art (MoMA) form a Photography Department<br>1941: Photographed some of the National Parks and Indian reservations for the Department of the Interior to be used as murals for decoration in their building in Washington, DC<br>1942–1945: Consultant for the armed forces carrying out photographic assignments including making prints of secret Japanese installations in the Aleutian Islands<br>1945: Founded and became the first director of the California School of Fine Arts. Dorothea Lange, Imogen Cunningham, and Minor White accepted an invitation to become faculty members.<br>1946: Along with Lange, White, and others, founded *Aperture* magazine<br>1946 and 1948: Guggenheim Fellowships to photograph all of the U.S. National Parks and Monuments<br>1949: Consultant for the Polaroid Corporation. |
| Edward Weston | 1940: *A Pageant of Photography*.<br><br>1946: Western Retrospective, MoMA, New York City | 1940: *California and the West*.<br>1941: Illustrated a new edition of Walt Whitman's *Leaves of Grass* with photographs taken in the South and East<br>1946: *Edward Weston*, edited by Nancy Newhall<br>1947: *Fifty Photographs* | **1940:** Guggenheim Fellowship |

were even taken from space. In 1946, the Johns Hopkins University Applied Physics Laboratory strapped a 35-millimeter motion picture camera to a V-2 missile and shot it into the air at White Sands Missile Range. Ascending to a height of 65 miles, the camera, in a steel case, snapped a picture every one and a half seconds and soon fell straight back to Earth, unharmed. When technicians put the frames together, the view covered a million square miles or more at a single glance, a glimpse of things to come in future years.

*See also:* Hobbies; Internment Camps (Relocation Centers); Technology

**Selected Reading**
Green, Jonathan. *American Photography: A Critical History 1945 to the Present.* New York: Harry N. Abrams, 1984.
Hulick, Diana Emery, with Joseph Marshall. *Photography—1900 to the Present.* Upper Saddle River, NJ: Prentice Hall, 1998.
Newhall, Beaumont. *The History of Photography, from 1839 to the Present.* Boston: Little, Brown, 1982.
Turner, Peter. *History of Photography.* New York: Exeter Books, 1987.

# POLITICAL AND PROPAGANDA FILMS

Always fearful of alienating potential audiences or running afoul of the strictures enforced by the Hollywood Production Code, the various movie studios throughout the 1930s presented a united front and avoided any stories that might offend the political sensibilities—real or imagined—of other nations. Despite the news from Asia involving Japanese imperialism and the loss of freedoms in Germany and Italy under Hitler and Mussolini, American **movies** followed a path of strict impartiality. But shortly before the German invasion of Poland in the fall of 1939 and the continuing Japanese incursions in the Far East, a crack appeared in the industry's armor when a few producers and screenwriters declared war on the Axis powers.

In 1938, producer Walter Wanger (1894–1968), working through United Artists, released *Blockade* (1938), a film about the Spanish Civil War. It stars Henry Fonda (1905–1982) as a Spanish soldier, although the movie never explicitly states which side—the Nationalists or the Republicans—he supports. The Code forbade political endorsements, but the script eventually makes clear that Fonda's on the "good" side, the Republicans. This created problems, because Germany and Italy openly supported the Nationalists, whereas Russia backed the Republican cause. This situation brought about an outwardly noncommittal film, but alert audiences could quickly ascertain that Fonda's character fought for the Republicans.

The following year, *Idiot's Delight* spoke out against war in any form, which might seem a safe position, but even pacifism makes a political statement, especially in the tense days before open hostilities, and so the picture upset some in the movie industry. *Idiot's Delight* appeared tame when compared to *Confessions of a Nazi Spy, Espionage Agent,* or *Hitler—Beast of Berlin* (all 1939). Both *Confessions of a Nazi Spy* and *Espionage Agent* came from feisty Warner Bros.; the first stars Edward G. Robinson (1893–1973), the second features Joel McCrea (1905–1990), two leading actors of the day. *Hitler—Beast of Berlin,* a little-known film, originated with Producers Distributing Company (PDC), a tiny, independent studio. Each of these movies, from their titles on, makes no secret about loyalties, and although they raised a number of hackles, especially among isolationists, they indicated the increasingly ideological stance that motion pictures would take as the world descended into chaos.

In 1940—a new year, a new decade, and World War II a reality in Europe—Hollywood shed what remained of its former reticence and more or less caved in to those supporting the Western democracies. Topicality became fashionable (and profitable). United Artists adapted *Personal History,* a best-selling 1935 memoir by journalist Vincent Sheean (1899–1975). Outspoken in its antipathy toward Hitler's Germany, the studio turned it into a breathless chase thriller called *Foreign Correspondent* (1940). The Nazi villainy remains intact, it boasts Alfred Hitchcock (1899–1980) as the director, uses pre-occupation Holland as its setting, and Joel McCrea returns as a character relentlessly pursued by Nazis.

*The Mortal Storm* presents the theme of flight from the Nazis, one found in several movies made in the early 1940s; it features James Stewart (1908–1997), while *Escape* (1940) stars Robert Taylor (1911–1969) as a son attempting to free his mother from a German concentration camp. *Pastor Hall* (English, 1939; released in the United States in 1940 by United Artists) also exposes the reality of concentration camps. Initially rejected by British censors as too anti-German, *Pastor Hall* promptly gained permission to be shown after September 1939 and the beginning of the European war. American review boards also fretted about its political leanings but granted it full release as the conflict progressed.

Torn loyalties propel *Four Sons* (1940), the chronicle of a German Czech family. Naturally, the worst of the four sons reveals his Nazi sympathies, thereby setting off a tragedy that leaves no one untouched. In *The Man I Married* (1940; also called *I Married a Nazi*), Joan Bennett (1910–1990) learns her husband, played by Francis Lederer (1899–2000), embraces the goals of Hitler's Third Reich. She must then determine to leave him and take their son to the United States. On a lighter note, comedian Charlie Chaplin (1889–1977) skewered Adolf Hitler (1889–1945) in a brilliant satire titled *The Great Dictator* (1940).

With the onset of 1941, England stood alone and increasingly beleaguered, but not until the end of the year would the United States actually become a combatant. In the meantime, Hollywood continued to release movies that showed support for the English; their plots often served as virtual recruiting tools for the armed forces. *A Yank in the R.A.F., International Squadron* (both 1941) and *Captains of the Clouds* (1942) tell tales of eager Americans, anxious to see action, enlisting in either the British or Canadian air forces. On the home front, one adventure-filled picture after another played at neighborhood theaters, urging anyone of age to sign up for a branch of military service. The movies covered a broad range—*I Wanted Wings* (1941), *Dive Bomber* (1941), *Flying Tigers* (1942), *Air Force* (1943), *The Memphis Belle: A Story of a Flying Fortress* (1944; documentary)—and carried the message of service to one's country.

Thus, when the United States entered World War II as a combatant, the movie industry could already claim a colorful menu of pro-war motion pictures; all that remained was to shed the last remnants of neutrality and charge ahead with action-packed features that left no question where loyalties stood. The production of more subtle, politically oriented films came to a virtual halt, only to be revived after 1945 with a bevy of pictures that tried to capture the anxieties of the postwar years, especially the beginnings of the **Cold War.**

For the duration of the conflict, Hollywood dutifully produced dozens upon dozens of war stories, almost all of which show Americans and their allies to be good and the Axis to be uniformly bad. There exists, however, a double standard regarding perceptions of the enemy forces. Occasionally, a German soldier or two might be given sympathetic qualities. In *The Moon Is Down* (1943), an adaptation of John Steinbeck's (1902–1968) popular 1943 novel of the same name, the story involves the Nazi occupation of Norway. Several of the German invaders question the war and attempt to get along with the Norwegian civilians. Although their efforts prove futile—the townspeople thwart them at every turn—the soldiers are at least humanized. The movies grant no such qualities to members of the dreaded Gestapo or SS (the initials refer to *Schutzstaffel,* or special police forces); they are shown as inherently evil and beyond redemption.

An additional double standard, one with racial overtones, applies to Germans forces and their Japanese counterparts. In movies of the era, some of the Germans at least possess a modicum of culture and often emerge as interesting characters even as villains; the Japanese, on the other hand, usually come across as primitive beasts, and screenwriters spent little time humanizing them. Duplicitous and capable of unspeakable acts of savagery, neither officers nor enlisted men receive three-dimensional personalities; characterization of any kind becomes obvious only by its absence. Propaganda traditionally works best by painting the enemy in the most negative and simplistic terms; to be seen as evil and cruel is, however, one thing; to be depicted as evil and cruel and subhuman is quite another.

Because the war so occupied the nation's consciousness, the movie industry felt no hesitation in referring to it in every conceivable kind of film. Frothy musicals, like *The Fleet's In* (1942), *This Is the Army* (1943), and *Four Jills in a Jeep* (1944), certainly entertained audiences, but they also reminded people about the ongoing conflict. Similarly, low-budget B mystery series and **Westerns** often reference the war, as in *Counter-Espionage* (1939; it features The Lone Wolf, the hero of a long-running detective series), *Enemy Agents Meet Ellery Queen* (1942; another popular crime series), *Sherlock Holmes and the Secret Weapon* (1943), *Charlie Chan in the Secret Service* (1944), and *Hands Across the Border* (1944), the last a Roy Rogers (1911–1998) Western. Hillbilly comedienne Judy Canova (1913–1983) outwits a Nazi spy ring in *Joan of Ozark* (1942); Tarzan of the Apes fights the Nazis in *Tarzan Triumphs* (1943), a particularly grisly episode in that long-running series; and Blondie, of comic-strip fame, does her part on the home front in *Blondie for Victory* (1942). In short, all genres of American film incorporated, at one time or another between the late 1930s and 1945, references to World War II. The messages they carried tended to be the same: support the nation's war effort in every way.

All wars eventually draw to a close, and after 1945 the movie industry had lost an urgent topic. Occasional films about World War II continued to be produced, but they now constituted a distinct minority. On the other hand, the adjustments that returning service personnel and civilians had to make in peacetime provided the impetus for four outstanding motion pictures of the mid-1940s: ***The Best Years of Our Lives*** and *Till the End of Time* (both 1946), *Crossfire* and *Gentleman's Agreement* (both 1947). The ironic title of the first refers to a group of people reuniting at the close of the war. For many, their best years—which would include youth, family, and careers—were spent in combat or waiting for loved ones. Produced just after the German and Japanese surrenders, the film accurately captures a moment in U.S. history when millions of people had to readjust their lives, best or otherwise, and begin anew. It deservedly won Academy Awards for best picture, best director (William Wyler, 1902–1981), best actor (Fredric March, 1897–1975), best screenplay (Robert E. Sherwood, 1896–1955), plus three other Oscars.

*Till the End of Time* has much in common with the more famous *Best Years of Our Lives*. It, too, tells about several veterans returning home and the problems they face in moving from military to civilian life in a once-familiar environment. Somewhat uneven and melodramatic—it ends with a confrontation with a group of racial bigots—it nonetheless portrays the period well.

The following year, two other pictures addressed social issues that had been suppressed during the war. Each deals with anti-Semitism, until then a taboo topic for Hollywood, and returning veterans. Both films seem dated a half-century after their release, but admirers at the time viewed them as cutting-edge films dealing with social problems. Dated or not, *Crossfire* and *Gentleman's Agreement* led the way for a number of motion pictures that would tackle previously whispered or unspoken topics.

The film industry may have taken pride in its daring, but some of that self-importance needs tempering. The producers of *Crossfire* adapted it from a novel titled *The Brick Foxhole* (1945), a book that frankly discusses homophobia. Written by Richard Brooks (1912–1945), no studio at that time would venture to challenge the Hollywood Production Code that forbade any overt references to or depictions of homosexual behavior. So Brooks, who also served as screenwriter, changed his theme to anti-Semitism and got the go-ahead for the project, but *Crossfire* had significantly changed from *The Brick Foxhole*.

The problem of racial intolerance, which has plagued the country since its founding, awaited inspection by the film industry, but little happened in the immediate postwar years. No doubt most studio executives at that time wished that all movies featuring black characters—in itself, something of a rarity—would present America's racial climate as benignly as did Walt Disney (1901–1966) in his 1946 release, *Song of the South*. Ostensibly a children's film, it contains a mix of live action and cartoons and appears to be set in a timeless South. A naive white boy played by Bobby Driscoll (1937–1968) befriends Uncle Remus, a wise elderly black man played by James Baskett (1904–1948), and learns that "everything is satisfactual" at the plantation. This racial pairing has been, and continues to be, presented in a number of motion pictures. The realities of that time to the contrary, segregation and intolerance have no place in this cinematic never-never land, provided people know their place in the scheme of things.

In the Hollywood of 1946, no one wanted to investigate the real racial climate, with the result that, until the end of the decade, virtually no cinematic attempts were made to peel back the veneer of harmony shown in most pictures. A muted attempt occurred in 1948 when an offbeat picture, *The Boy with Green Hair,* showed in movie houses around the country. Dean Stockwell (b. 1936) stars as an orphaned **youth** whose hair inexplicably turns green. Immediately ostracized by his peers for being different, the film creates a fable about individuality and tolerance. Easily translated into cultural terms, it challenged conventional beliefs and stirred some controversy because it espouses pacifism.

A year later, the release of *Lost Boundaries* and *Pinky* opened the gates wider. Both deal with the topic of "passing," a term that means a person of one race attempting to be accepted as a member of another racial group. In the past, at least in the United States, this situation usually translated as a light-skinned black individual taking on the outward identity of a white person. Too often, in fear of white resentment, the film studios denied choice roles to blacks. Two exceptions to this practice existed: For pictures targeted at primarily white audiences, if the part called for a stereotype such as a maid, butler, cook, or **jazz** musician, black actors could fill those roles. The second exception occurred with movies produced for black audiences. From the 1920s until the 1960s, a handful of small studios produced so-called race movies that featured all-black casts. Usually made on miniscule budgets and starring largely unknown actors, they normally played at theaters catering to black audiences, but at least they provided an outlet for talented performers otherwise denied full participation in American moviemaking.

For Hollywood in the 1940s, passing more often involved a white performer applying some makeup and taking the screen role of a black character. *Lost Boundaries* and *Pinky* illustrate this long cinematic tradition. The first picture stars Mel Ferrer (b. 1917), a white actor, playing a black doctor who chooses to pass himself as a white physician in a small New England town. In *Pinky,* Jeanne Crain (1925–2003), also white, learns of her black heritage while living in the South. The plots of both films proceed to detail how these individuals deal with the disclosure of their true identities and how those around them receive this news. The pictures portray a United States still caught up in questions and attitudes about race and suggest how difficult any resolution of the subject would prove.

When news of casting for *Pinky* made the show business rounds, entertainer Lena Horne (b. 1917), herself a fair-skinned black, campaigned for the title lead but lost the part to Jeanne Crain because the plot involves a love affair between Pinky and a white doctor played by William Lundigan (1914–1975). Twentieth Century-Fox, the studio producing the film, felt that true interracial love scenes (i.e., between Horne and Lundigan) on screen would upset audiences but that anything with Crain and Lundigan, since both are white, would be permissible. It took years after the 1940s before a love scene between two people of different races occurred on screen.

Another pair of 1949 pictures also employ racial themes; *Intruder in the Dust* and *Home of the Brave.* The first, a movie adaptation of William Faulkner's (1897–1962) novel of the same name published in 1948, concerns a black man unjustly accused of murder. More a portrait of prejudice in the old South, it explores little new territory but does allow several statements about the need for tolerance and gives a disquieting picture of what life could be for blacks in the days before the civil rights movement.

*Home of the Brave,* on the other hand, tells of a dangerous mission undertaken by a group of marines in the Pacific during World War II. Standard fare, until the troops learn one of their comrades, James Edwards (1918–1970), is black. Considerable tension grows out of this revelation, and prejudice almost ruins the mission. By the end, the men have learned that their previous black stereotypes are false, and for soldiers to survive, they must work together, regardless of race. Although both of these pictures might seem to some terribly dated for contemporary times, at their release in 1949 they took an enlightening step ahead for commercial movies.

While these foregoing movies that deal with social ills kept many in the industry busy, Hollywood momentarily lacked an issue that would offend no one. But postwar current events quickly provided the fodder for a host of new and controversial movies. After the treaties ending World War II had been signed, relations between Russia and the Western nations deteriorated—a situation that led to the Cold War. Allies became enemies, and Hollywood had found a new focus.

While the usual quota of comedies, Westerns, mysteries, musicals, and all the rest continued to flow from the studios, moviemakers also began to gear up for a different kind of film: the anti-Communist picture. It started slowly. In 1948, *Sofia, Walk a Crooked Mile,* and *The Iron Curtain* graced marquees. The first two involve foreign locales, vital atomic secrets, and covetous Communist spies. Except for the Communist angle, they rank as mediocre thrillers. The last, a more effective drama, features Dana Andrews (1909–1992) as a disenchanted Communist agent who wants to change allegiances and the misunderstandings that arise from his decision. The plot allows the screenwriters the opportunity to serve up lots of propaganda about Communism and Soviet subversives in the nation's midst. Not at all unlike the movies from the late 1930s, such as *Confessions of a Nazi Spy* (1939), which stirred up strong anti-German feelings, this new generation of motion pictures fit in well with the hysteria then building in some quarters about the threat from the Soviet Union.

The success of *The Iron Curtain* assured more of the same, and 1949 saw *Conspirator, I Married a Communist, The Red Danube,* and *The Red Menace,* each advertising "shocking but true" revelations about the growing Communist threat. With the advent of the 1950s, the floodgates opened wide, and numerous pictures detailing Communist subversion were produced, reinforcing what citizens read in books, **magazines,** and **newspapers.** Ongoing congressional investigations sought evidence of widespread Communist conspiracies at home and abroad, outspoken legislators demanded security checks and loyalty oaths from U.S. citizens, and it all gave rise to a collective paranoia that has come to be called the Red Scare.

In a fascinating bit of political hindsight, the **House Un-American Activities Committee (HUAC)** in 1947 initiated a series of hearings that predate the above anti-Communist movies. The HUAC investigation sought to find a link between selected American movies and the spreading of Communist propaganda. The films that stirred the queries and drew the most congressional ire consisted of the following five titles: *Mission to Moscow* (1943), *The North Star* (1943), *Days of Glory* (1944), *Song of Russia* (1944), and *Counter-Attack* (1945). All of these movies had been made when the Soviet Union stood shoulder to shoulder with the other Western allies in order to defeat Germany. They show ordinary Soviet citizens in a positive light, and little ideology can be discerned in any of them. The propaganda revolves around the mutual desire to defeat the common enemy.

TABLE 74. Selected Political and Propaganda Films, 1940–1949

| Year | Film Titles | Stars |
|---|---|---|
| 1940 | *Escape* | Robert Taylor, Norma Shearer |
| | *Escape to Glory* | Pat O'Brien, Constance Bennett |
| | *Foreign Correspondent* | Joel McCrea, Laraine Day |
| | *Four Sons* | Don Ameche, Alan Curtis |
| | *The Great Dictator* | Charlie Chaplin, Paulette Goddard |
| | *I Married a Nazi* (also known as *The Man I Married*) | Joan Bennett, Francis Lederer |
| | *The Mortal Storm* | James Stewart, Robert Young |
| | *Night Train to Munich* | Rex Harrison, Paul Henreid |
| | *Pastor Hall* | Wilfrid Lawson, Marius Goring |
| | *Waterloo Bridge* | Vivien Leigh, Robert Taylor |
| 1941 | *Dangerously We Live* | John Garfield, Raymond Massey |
| | *49th Parallel* | Richard George, Eric Portman |
| | *I Wanted Wings* | Ray Milland, Brian Donlevy |
| | *International Squadron* | Ronald Reagan, William Lundigan |
| | *Man Hunt* | Walter Pidgeon, Joan Bennett |
| | *Paris Calling* | Randolph Scott, Basil Rathbone |
| | *Sergeant York* | Gary Cooper, Walter Brennan |
| | *So Ends Our Night* | Fredric March, Magaret Sullavan |
| | *Underground* | Philip Dorn, Jeffrey Lynn |
| | *A Yank in the R.A.F* | Tyrone Power, Betty Grable |
| 1942 | *Berlin Correspondent* | Dana Andrews, Virginia Gilmore |
| | *Casablanca* | Humphrey Bogart, Ingrid Bergman |
| | *Desperate Journey* | Errol Flynn, Ronald Reagan |
| | *Joan of Ozark* | Judy Canova, Joe E. Brown |
| | *Joan of Paris* | Alan Ladd, Paul Henreid |
| | *Joe Smith American* | Robert Young, Marsha Hunt |
| | *Mrs. Miniver* | Greer Garson, Walter Pidgeon |
| | *Nazi Agent* | Conrad Veidt, Anne Ayars |
| | *Saboteur* | Robert Cummings, Priscilla Lane |
| | *The War Against Mrs. Hadley* | Edward Arnold, Fay Bainter |
| 1943 | *Edge of Darkness* | Errol Flynn, Ann Sheridan |
| | *For Whom the Bell Tolls* | Gary Cooper, Ingrid Bergman |
| | *Hitler's Children* | Tim Holt, Bonita Granville |
| | *Hitler—Dead or Alive* | Ward Bond, Paul Fix |
| | *Hitler's Madman* | John Carradine, Edgar Kennedy |
| | *Mission to Moscow* | Walter Huston, Ann Harding |
| | *The Moon Is Down* | Cedric Hardwicke, Lee J. Cobb |
| | *The North Star* | Anne Baxter, Dana Andrews |
| | *This Land Is Mine* | Charles Laughton, Maureen O'Hara |
| | *Watch on the Rhine* | Bette Davis, Paul Lukas |
| 1944 | *Days of Glory* | Gregory Peck, Tamara Toumanova |
| | *Dragon Seed* | Katharine Hepburn, Walter Huston |
| | *The Fighting Sullivans* | Anne Baxter, Thomas MItchell |
| | *The Hitler Gang* | Robert Watson, Sig Ruman |

*(continued)*

TABLE 74. *(continued)*

| Year | Film Titles | Stars |
|---|---|---|
| | The Purple Heart | Dana Andrews, Richard Conte |
| | The Seventh Cross | Spencer Tracy, Hume Cronyn |
| 1944 | Since You Went Away | Claudette Colbert, Jennifer Jones, Shirley Temple |
| | Song of Russia | Robert Taylor, John Hodiak |
| | Tomorrow the World | Fredric March, Skip Homeier |
| | The White Cliffs of Dover | Irene Dunne, Van Johnson |
| 1945 | Back to Bataan | John Wayne, Anthony Quinn |
| | A Bell for Adano | John Hodiak, Gene Tierney |
| | Betrayal from the East | Lee Tracy, Nancy Kelly |
| | Blood on the Sun | James Cagney, Sylvia Sidney |
| | Counter-Attack | Paul Muni, Larry Parks |
| | Hotel Berlin | Faye Emerson, Raymond Massey |
| | The House on 92nd Street | Lloyd Nolan, Leo G. Carroll |
| | The Story of G.I. Joe | Burgess Meredith, Robert Mitchum |
| | They Were Expendable | John Wayne, Robert Montgomery |
| 1946 | The Best Years of Our Lives | Fredric March, Myrna Loy |
| | Cloak and Dagger | Gary Cooper, Lilli Palmer |
| | Hitler Lives (short documentary) | |
| | I See a Dark Stranger | Trevor Howard, Deborah Kerr |
| | The Searching Wind | Robert Young, Sylvia Sidney |
| | The Stranger | Edward G. Robinson, Orson Welles |
| | Till the End of Time | Guy Madison, Dorothy McGuire |
| 1947 | Crossfire | Robert Young, Robert Mitchum, Robert Ryan |
| | Gentleman's Agreement | Gregory Peck, Dorothy McGuire |
| 1948 | The Boy with Green Hair | Bobby Driscoll, Pat O'Brien |
| | The Iron Curtain | Dana Andrews, Gene Tierney |
| | The Search | Montgomery Clift, Ivan Jandl |
| | Sofia | Gene Raymond, Mischa Auer |
| | Walk a Crooked Mile | Louis Hayward, Dennis O'Keefe |
| 1949 | Conspirator | Robert Taylor, Elizabeth Taylor |
| | The Fountainhead | Gary Cooper, Patricia Neal |
| | Home of the Brave | James Edwards, Lloyd Bridges |
| | I Married a Communist | Robert Ryan, Laraine Day |
| | Intruder in the Dust | Claude Jarman Jr., Juano Hernandez |
| | Lost Boundaries | Mel Ferrer, Beatrice Pearson |
| | Pinky | Jeanne Crain, Ethel Waters |
| | The Red Danube | Walter Pidgeon, Ethel Barrymore |
| | The Red Menace | Robert Rockwell, Barbara Fuller |
| | The Third Man | Orson Welles, Joseph Cotton |

But in 1947, the Union of Soviet Socialist Republics, a former friend, had taken on a new role—that of foe. Led by Representative J. Parnell Thomas (1895–1970; R-N.J.), and with a young Richard Nixon (1913–1994) serving as a member, the committee sought to prove how these pictures spouted the insidious Communist line. In this quest they failed, but the hearings did reveal that the congressional members knew precious little about the content of the movies in question.

This investigation would drag on until 1958 and then quietly disappear with no real evidence that any motion pictures ever knowingly served as a vehicle of political propaganda and attempted to seduce the population with lies and disinformation. It did, however, bring about the practice of blacklisting in the film industry, create a group of victims called the Hollywood Ten, and ruin a number of careers.

All motion pictures to a degree reflect their times. No one in Hollywood attempted to ignore World War II, the defining event of the 1940s, with the result that it affected the content of virtually every movie made during the period 1940 to 1945. Either as background or foreground, the conflict painted these years in stark blacks and whites, allowing easy distinctions, such as us versus them, good versus evil, and freedom versus totalitarianism. The postwar period, however, blurred the certainties of just a few years earlier. Social and political issues, swept under the rug during the fighting, began to appear on screens. Race relations, the menace of Communism, propaganda, loyalties, the role of movies in a changing world—no easy answers arose for these new problems, and American filmmakers reflected the uncertainty and unease in their productions.

*See also:* Autry, Gene and Roy Rogers; Cartoons (Film); Crime and Mystery Films; Drama (Film); Film Noir; Horror and Thriller Films; Musicals (Film); Race Relations and Stereotyping; War Films

**Selected Reading**
Cripps, Thomas. *Making Movies Black: The Hollywood Message Movie from World War II to the Civil Rights Movement.* New York: Oxford University Press, 1993.
Higham, Charles, and Joel Greenberg. *Hollywood in the Forties.* New York: A. S. Barnes, 1968.
Koppes, Clayton R., and Gregory D. Black. *Hollywood Goes to War: How Politics, Profits, and Propaganda Shaped World War II Movies.* New York: Free Press, 1987.
Manvell, Roger. *Films and the Second World War.* New York: Dell, 1974.

# POSTERS

Historians generally agree that 17th- and 18th-century broadsides, which conveyed information and could be posted in highly visible spots, serve as a prelude to today's poster. The development of lithography in the 19th century made for even easier and cheaper mass production. Most consider an advertisement made in 1867 by French artist Jules Cheret (1836–1932) that announced a theatrical performance by Sarah Bernhardt (1844–1923) to be the first modern commercial poster. By 1940, the poster relied heavily on graphic **design** and served as a commercial or public service announcement to be used in a variety of ways—promote an event, an entertainment, a product, an idea, or facts or stir emotions and create a sentiment, such as patriotism. Once it has been widely reproduced and displayed in a public place, a poster can have immediate and far-reaching impact.

During World War II, the United States Office of War Information created and issued volumes of posters dealing with a wide range of topics relevant to fighting the war successfully, both on the battlefield and on the home front. Proper eating habits for soldiers and civilians served as an important theme in the early years of the conflict. (Library of Congress)

This art form had been successfully used by U.S. government officials during World War I to rally support for the country's participation in the conflict. Likewise, during the Great Depression, the Federal Art Project (FAP), a division of the New Deal's Works Progress Administration (WPA, 1935–1943), turned out a compelling number of posters from an impressive list of designers. Their works effectively advertised a broad array of cultural, educational, and recreational activities and could be seen at many places, such as school and community centers, commercial complexes, in government buildings, and on buses and subways.

In light of its success, the FAP was moved in 1943, its final year of existence, from under the administration of the WPA to the Department of Defense. There, it brought valuable expertise to the United States Office of War Information (OWI). Organized in June 1942, the OWI designated a Graphics Division to produce posters to again link the home front with the battlefield and attempt to inspire a sense of patriotism and support for the war from all citizens. Prominent artists and **illustrators** such as James Montgomery Flagg (1877–1960), Norman Rockwell (1894–1978), Ben Shahn (1898–1969), Stevan Dohanos (1907–1994), and John C. Atherton (1900–1952) contributed to the war poster campaign, which called men to military service, urged women to work in defense-related jobs, recommended that those on the home front grow and can their **food,** warned that loose conversations could give information to spies, and strongly urged everyone to hate the nation's ruthless enemies.

Within the government agencies in Washington DC, the U.S. Department of the Treasury and the War Production Board (WPB) joined the OWI in poster projects. Posters also began to emerge from nongovernmental sources, such as businesses, industries, and **advertising** agencies, causing OWI officials to voice concern about the mechanics of monitoring and controlling so much poster production.

Debate also persisted between two groups of OWI personnel over design and guidelines that would be issued to those designing and printing posters. One group saw posters as war art with stylized or abstract images and symbolism, while others, especially advertising specialists, wanted posters to have a realistic, familiar, and homey look similar to the ads that regularly appeared in **newspapers** and **magazines.** Under the direction of Francis E. (Hank) Brennan (1910–1992), former art director of *Fortune* magazine and head of the OWI Graphics Division, the parties reached a compromise.

Posters would use war graphics that combined the styles of contemporary design with the aims of the government.

From these decisions, the OWI, to enforce its oversight responsibility, issued six war information themes that could be used in poster campaigns: (1) the nature of the enemy, offering negative descriptions of the Axis forces; (2) the nature of the Allies, showing the close ties of the United States to Great Britain, the Soviet Union, and China, and ennobling their forces; (3) the need to work, emphasizing different ways Americans must labor for the war to be won; (4) the need to fight, depicting a fearless waging of war, which would lead to victory; (5) the need to sacrifice, with citizens giving up all luxuries and contributing their spare time to the war effort; and (6) Americans telling the story of democracy and its freedoms. These guidelines were to be followed by both government and nongovernment groups.

Some of the government agencies proceeded to hire artists and illustrators to work for them while also commissioning others to assist in certain areas. Artist Jes Wilhelm Schlaikjer (1897–1982) became the War Department's official artist with a studio in the Pentagon. He created powerful recruitment posters that featured heroic, handsome figures in dramatic conflict situations. Arthur Szyk (1894–1951) produced patriotic posters for the U.S. Department of the Treasury's war bond drives and also designed wartime stamps for the postal service.

During 1942, the first full year of World War II, most posters retained the characteristic of war art using dark, somber colors and harsh messages, such as "When you ride ALONE you ride with Hitler! Join a Car-Sharing Club TODAY!" By 1943, advertising specialists had gained ground and shaped the appearance of most of the posters. The written content still adhered to the recommended messages of sacrifice and struggle, but symbolism and abstract images had been replaced by commercial illustration standards of literal representation and emotional pull. One states, "Do with less—so *they* will have enough! **RATIONING** GIVES YOU YOUR FAIR SHARE," and shows a smiling soldier lifting his cup in thanks to the viewer. Another, with the words "We'll have lots to eat this winter, won't we Mother?" "Grow your own/Can your own," depicts a brightly dressed mother and daughter obviously happy to be together producing many beautiful jars of canned food.

A famous poster from World War I, the presentation of Uncle Sam pointing to the viewer and saying "I WANT YOU for the U.S. ARMY, ENLIST NOW," drawn by James Montgomery Flagg in 1916, had been reissued before the United States entered World War II on December 7, 1941, since it did not seem dated or in need of improvement. The OWI engaged Flagg and others to produce additional recruitment posters for all the military services, works that utilized war graphics and symbolism.

While the OWI concentrated on messages that would enlist men to fight, the U.S. Department of the Treasury turned to the Outdoor Advertising Association of America for assistance in addressing the issue of paying for the war. John C. Atherton's image of two hands shaking (one representing the government and the other a citizen) above the words "BUY a share in America" appeared on a 48-foot billboard in New York City at the corner of Forty-Second Street and Fifth Avenue in July 1941. Carl Paulsen (active 1940s) also offered a billboard image. His had the American flag dominating the available space with a caption below that read "Buy U.S. WAR SAVINGS BONDS & STAMPS now." Reported to be one of the most popular World War II poster images, it appeared along highways at more than 30,000 locations across the country in the spring of 1942. It reappeared in the summers of 1942 and 1943. To meet an almost overwhelming demand from the public for copies, the Government Printing Office printed and distributed 4 million small color reproductions.

In addition to Flagg and Paulson, untold numbers of artists—some famous, others unknown—provided designs for both the OWI and the U.S. Department of the Treasury. Cyrus C. Hungerford (1888–1983), a well-established editorial cartoonist with the *Pittsburgh Post-Gazette,* in 1941 devised the line "Production Soldiers," alluding to Americans on the home front who also served Uncle Sam. Employing stylized images and symbolism, Hungerford created a series of posters portraying civilian defense workers as a part of America's defense team.

Henry Koerner (1915–1991) started painting in 1943 and designing posters provided him much-needed steady work, even after he became a GI in 1945. He entered National Defense Poster Competitions in 1941 to 1943, sponsored by the Museum of Modern Art (MoMA) in New York City. The museum hoped to inspire many artists to create posters that would encourage citizens to support the war effort. Each year the designs could be seen at MoMA and army recruiting stations, as well as on billboards throughout the country. Koerner was one of several winners with his piece "Someone talked!" Falling under the theme of the nature of the enemy, the poster tells of the importance of not having loose war-related conversations that might reach the ears of spies and thus endanger U.S. soldiers. After V-E Day, Koerner went to Germany to sketch the Nuremberg trials for the U.S. government. Once back in the United States, Koerner's career as a serious artist grew. He gained fame in the 1950s and in the decades following for his portraits of celebrities, many of them appearing on the covers of *Time* magazine.

Some poster art work first surfaced in other artistic forms. Norman Rockwell's series of famous paintings, known collectively as *The Four Freedoms* and commissioned by the *Saturday Evening Post,* graced the covers of four issues of the magazine. Completed within six months, *Freedom of Speech, Freedom of Worship, Freedom from Want,* and *Freedom from Fear* were launched on a nationwide tour in April 1943 in support of selling **war bonds.** Following that tour, the government printed 4 million copies of the paintings as posters.

U.S. industries also got into the act of sponsoring posters that carried one or more of the approved themes. The Westinghouse War Production Co-Ordinating Committee commissioned illustrator J. Howard Miller (ca. 1915–1990) to design a poster to be displayed in its defense plants in hopes of inspiring and boosting the morale of the company's many women employees. The resulting painting and poster, "We Can Do It," presents a determined female worker beneath those words looking straight at the viewer with a raised arm flexing her bicep. Miller did not present his work as **Rosie the Riveter,** the name that eventually represented the millions of working women during the war, but his depiction became one of the most enduring to emerge from World War II; people assumed that "We Can Do It" depicts Rosie. Norman Rockwell, however, did intentionally provide *Saturday Evening Post* with a Rosie the Riveter for the magazine's May 29, 1943 cover, an image that also graced posters.

The war may have had a strong hold on poster production, but Hollywood also relied heavily on the medium to advertise current and upcoming releases. During the

1940s, movie posters fell into three categories: lobby cards, teaser posters, and character posters. Lobby cards helped to lure customers into the theater to see the movie. Usually produced in sets of eight by the movie studio and displayed in the lobby, they showed the title of the film, the leading actors and actresses, credits, and glimpses of key scenes. Teaser posters did exactly that. As an early promotional instrument, the poster would contain a basic design or image without revealing too much, but at the same time causing the viewer to want to see the movie. A character poster, the third category, featured a role seen in the film and generally gave the name of the actor playing the part or showed the actor painted realistically so he or she could be recognized.

Before 1940, each Hollywood studio maintained an exchange office in major cities across the country. New releases, along with studio-produced advertising, would be sent to the exchange office for distribution to theaters. Once a theater had shown a movie for its three-or four-day run, the film reels, along with the promotional materials, went back to the exchange office to be forwarded to the next scheduled theater. Eventually, the **movies** themselves, along with any paper advertising still intact, went back to their respective studios.

The National Screen Service (NSS), founded in 1920, set out as a business to assist the studios with advertising. Initially NSS only produced movie trailers, or previews, on behalf of all the studios. Gradually the agency added other forms of advertising and, by 1940, had acquired exclusive contracts with movie companies to produce and distribute all three kinds of posters.

Artists and graphic designers, most of whom worked anonymously, created countless movie posters. Others, such as Norman Rockwell, William L. Rose (b. 1909) and Bill Gold (b. 1921), received credit for their work. During the 1940s, Norman Rockwell's signature appeared on posters for *The Magnificent Ambersons* (1941), *The Song of Bernadette* (1943), *Along Came Jones* (1945), and *The Razor's Edge* (1946). William L. Rose drew for magazines such as *Collier's* while also turning out posters for ***Citizen Kane*** (1941), *Cat People* (1942), *Nocturne* (1946), and *Out of the Past* (1947). Bill Gold started his career in 1941, working for Warner Bros. He became the head of poster design in 1947, and some of his better-known work at the time included *Yankee Doodle Dandy* and ***Casablanca*** (both 1942) and *Night and Day* and *The Big Sleep* (both 1946). In the late 1950s, he launched his own business and by 2000 had designed thousands of movie posters.

Whereas war poster production ceased when the war ended, poster design and production for the movies and other commercial enterprises continued. Throughout the war years, posters pertaining to the conflict had high visibility—on boards in front of city halls, on fences, on buildings, on billboards, at train and bus stations, in government buildings, at **USO (United Service Organizations)** centers, in factories, in hotel lobbies, in eating establishments, in the windows of vacant stores—anywhere and everywhere a poster could be placed. Theater managers generally restricted movie posters to inside and immediately outside the buildings where a film played.

The war posters expressed a sense of urgency and asked citizens to become involved. They served a vital communication function and promoted an important art form. Produced by government agencies and commercial firms, posters conveyed messages through a combination of emotional illustrations and memorable phrases of text.

Movie posters throughout the 1940s highlighted the outstanding performers of the day and the story told by the film in hopes of drawing patrons into theaters for an evening of escapism from the realities of the times.

*See also:* Art (Painting); Bogart, Humphrey; Boxing; Cold War, The; Education; Scrap Drives; Trains; V-E and V-J Day; Victory Gardens

**Selected Reading**
Gallo, Max. *The Poster in History.* New York: American Heritage, 1972.
Judd, Denis. *Posters of World War Two.* New York: St. Martin's Press. 1973.
Nourman, Tony, and Graham Marsh. *Film Posters of the 40s.* London: Aurum Press & Reed Poster, 2002.

# PYLE, ERNIE, AND BILL MAULDIN

These two individuals, the first a war correspondent, the other a cartoonist, recorded World War II in a shared manner: they focused their work from the day-to-day perspective of the foot-slogging infantryman, not from the lofty vantage point of generals and tacticians. In retrospect, they made the conflict personal, up close and intimate, instead of one consisting of massed battles, huge bombing raids, and mechanized chaos.

No other journalist enjoyed quite the following that Ernie Pyle (1900–1945) built with his columns about everyday GIs fighting a faraway war. Born in rural Indiana, Pyle missed World War I, except for three months in the Naval Reserve in 1918. During the 1920s, he held a desk job with a small Washington, DC, newspaper. Anxious to write, he left the capital and traveled around the country. Upon his return to Washington, he wrote columns about **aviation** and became expert in the field. The Scripps-Howard newspaper chain, impressed with Pyle's abilities and style, gave him a job writing nationally about the passing scene in the United States. Out of these experiences, spanning 1935 to 1941, came a posthumous book of his reflections, *Home Country* (1947).

With the outbreak of war in December 1941, Pyle quickly responded and landed an assignment as a war correspondent. Scripps-Howard agreed to run his columns, and, before long, over 300 **newspapers** carried his observations of the war. Pyle first started writing from England and soon shifted to North Africa, graphically describing the desert warfare between tanks and infantry. When U.S. troops invaded Sicily, he accompanied them, staying with the soldiers on up the boot of Italy, including during the bloody Anzio beachhead. After **D-Day** and the Normandy landings of 1944, he followed them across France and the bloody encounters among the rural hedgerows. With victory in Europe in sight and the final destruction of the Third Reich assured, Ernie Pyle took a short break stateside and then began island hopping with troops in the Pacific. In April 1945, while riding in a Jeep on the island of Okinawa, a Japanese machine gun found him; he died instantly, and his GI comrades had lost a friend. Pyle lies buried in the National Cemetery of the Pacific in Honolulu, Hawaii; a monument also remembers him on Okinawa. The government awarded him a Purple Heart for his injuries, one of few civilians so honored.

Out of the many columns Pyle wrote chronicling these events, four anthologies of his writings emerged: *Ernie Pyle in England* (1941), *Here Is Your War: Story of G.I. Joe* (1943), *Brave Men* (1944), and *Last Chapter* (1946). Once he got into describing the gritty lives of soldiers on the front lines, Pyle had found his niche. Not as instantaneous as the war reports heard on **radio,** but more detailed and often more moving, his writings from close to the front lines attracted a wide, devoted audience.

Given his popularity, Hollywood's United Artists studio, working closely with the War Department, which supplied both equipment and numerous soldiers for bit parts, created *The Story of G.I. Joe* (1945), a loose adaptation of Pyle's 1943 book of the same title. It stars Robert Mitchum (1917–1997) as a U.S. officer who leads a company of infantrymen from North Africa to Italy. In the course of his duties, he keeps encountering Ernie Pyle, played by Burgess Meredith (1907–1997). The correspondent profiles many of the men and establishes a good rapport with them, just as he did in real life. A superior war movie, it also pays homage to the memory of the popular journalist.

Pyle expressed great affection for the humble combat infantryman, and how this fellow—until recently a civilian with no military background—coped with the drudgery and horrors of modern warfare. Sometime humorous, other times tragic, but always employing vignettes filled with human interest, he described a war the headlines usually missed. Critics agreed, and Pyle received a Pulitzer Prize for correspondence in 1944.

If Ernie Pyle captured in words the lives of U.S. combat soldiers, Bill Mauldin (1921–2003) accomplished much the same, but in pictures. Born and raised in New Mexico and Phoenix, Arizona, Mauldin studied drawing at the Chicago Academy of Fine Arts under the legendary Ruth VanSickle Ford (1897–1989). In 1940, still in his teens, he joined the U.S. Army and received assignment to the 45th Infantry Division. When the unit shipped overseas, Mauldin found himself in the Mediterranean theater and participated in campaigns in Sicily and Italy. His commanders allowed him to draw cartoons for the divisional newspaper, and they proved a success. During his time in Italy, Mauldin's growing popularity among the troops was such that the army saw fit to give him space in *Stars and Stripes,* the official newspaper of the U.S. military.

Wider circulation only increased Mauldin's appeal among soldiers; he soon operated more or less on his own, touring the front lines in a Jeep and gathering ideas and stories for his cartoons. Not that he shirked his duties; he even gained a Purple Heart from shrapnel wounds in Italy. In time, Mauldin made sergeant, and the army, in appreciation for his many morale-boosting contributions, awarded him the Legion of Merit in 1945.

More important than medals and citations, Mauldin created two memorable characters, Willie and Joe. Two weary, usually unshaven, foot soldiers, or dogfaces, often mired over their ankles in mud or cringing in a foxhole while artillery bursts over their heads, they personified the U.S. infantry. Ready with a wry comment about their situation, they groused and griped, but they got the job done. No matter where or what it might be, the pair brought a quiet humor to an otherwise grim war, a humor much appreciated by their real-life counterparts.

Six new panel cartoons appeared each week in *Stars and Stripes,* eagerly awaited by GIs who may well have been in similar mud or foxholes hours before the new issue of the newspaper became available. The punch lines seldom favored imperious, by-the-book officers, but always stood up for the enlisted man. Mauldin apparently caught the ire of a few martinets, but those more knowledgeable in the high command got him off the hook, recognizing his positive effect on morale among the troops. Willie and Joe simply offered up observations shared by most soldiers slogging through yet another combat zone.

In time, United Feature Syndicate released his cartoons to stateside newspapers, and they were received by an equally enthusiastic civilian audience. In 1945, with peace in sight, publisher Henry Holt issued *Up Front,* a collection of Mauldin's best work, the same year that Ernie Pyle's *Brave Men* came out. Pyle even wrote an admiring sketch of Mauldin in *Brave Men,* pointing out how the cartoonist understood what foot soldiers endured on a daily basis. Mauldin contributed a running text to his book, much of which reads like the captions beneath his drawings, and the book climbed the best-seller charts, as did Pyle's volume. *Up Front* also won the 1945 Pulitzer Prize for editorial cartooning.

Although it took somewhat longer, Hollywood, this time with Universal Pictures, told about Willie (as played by Tom Ewell, 1909–1994) and Joe (David Wayne, 1914–1995) in a humorous, slapstick way with *Up Front* (1951). At its release, a new war, the Korean conflict, raged, and perhaps the producers thought a light-hearted view of war and soldiers would attract audiences. They apparently judged somewhat correctly, because Universal made a sequel, *Back at the Front,* the following year. Harvey Lembeck (1923—1982) took over the role of Joe. The two **movies,** so different in tone from the newspaper cartoons on which they were based, failed to capture Mauldin's quiet respect that he displayed for his two tired dogfaces, replacing it with shenanigans of one sort and another, and the artist disassociated himself from the pictures, refusing to see the final cuts. The fact that a major studio thought that Mauldin's cartoons still had a following nonetheless suggests how popular they had been throughout much of World War II.

Following the war, Mauldin continued cartooning, appearing on the editorial pages of many newspapers. He tried politics as an unsuccessful candidate for Congress and did some acting (*The Red Badge of Courage,* 1951) but finally settled in at the *St. Louis Post-Dispatch* and then the *Chicago Sun-Times.* He also won a second Pulitzer in 1959.

*See also:* Best Sellers (Books); Comic Strips; Illustrators; Radio Programming: News, Sports, Public Affairs, and Talk

**Selected Reading**
Mauldin, Bill. *Up Front.* New York: Henry Holt, 1945.
Mauldin, Bill. www.lambiek.net/artists/m/mauldin_bill.htm
Pyle, Ernie. *Brave Men.* New York: Henry Holt, 1944.
Pyle, Ernie. www.journalism.indiana.edu/resources/erniepyle/

# R

## RACE RELATIONS AND STEREOTYPING

As they had in the past, U.S. minorities during the 1940s suffered from oppressive attitudes and acts of discrimination and hostility. Segregated schools, **restaurants,** lodging, housing, public **transportation,** recreational and entertainment facilities, even drinking fountains, represented the norm. In 1941, **President Franklin Delano Roosevelt** (1882–1945) issued an executive order banning discrimination in plants with federal government defense contracts; in his January 6, 1942, State of the Union address, he warned the American public that "We must be particularly vigilant against racial discrimination in any of its ugly forms." He then desegregated federal buildings in Washington, DC, and appointed some black leaders to respectable offices, small steps toward guaranteeing equal rights for all citizens, but not enough to make a significant difference at the time.

The months preceding the Japanese attack on Pearl Harbor found the United States preparing for war with soaring industrial production and marked growth in the armed forces. Nevertheless, people of color, roughly 10 percent of the population, continued to be excluded from the rising prosperity of the nation and advancement within the army and navy. According to the United States Census Bureau, in 1940, blacks represented 9.8 percent of the total population; American Indian, Eskimo, and Aleut, 0.3 percent; and Asian and Pacific Islanders, 0.2 percent. The Census Bureau at that time included figures for individuals of Hispanic origin with the totals for white, or Caucasian, citizens. Because of the somewhat negligible number of other minorities, discrimination and stereotyping of blacks overshadowed attitudes toward other racial groups in American life during the 1940s.

As the country's involvement in the European war became inevitable, black Americans faced a two-front battle—at home and overseas in the armed forces. The National Association for the Advancement of Colored People (NAACP), a civil rights group

*Segregation reigned in the armed forces, and many black soldiers worked in lowly noncombat jobs during World War II. Submitting to pressure from the National Association for the Advancement of Colored People, President Roosevelt directed the Army Air Force to train black military personnel as pilots and technicians. This action resulted in the formation of four squadrons that came to be called the Tuskegee Airmen. (AP PHOTO/PAULA ILLINGWORTH)*

founded in 1909, regularly attempted to end segregation and acquire equality for all. The organization's strategies consisted of working through the courts and lobbying legislative bodies. By the early 1940s, with the minor exception of President Roosevelt's executive orders, matters had not much changed. Jim Crow, a term taken from a 19th-century plantation song and used to express racial discrimination, continued to reign, especially in the South. Even the military held to its World War I practices of segregation, declaring blacks unfit for the front lines and combat. Both enlistees and draftees found themselves in all-black service or supply units working as cargo handlers or cooks under the supervision of white officers and confined to their own mess halls and barracks.

Amid the unrest concerning military service, Roosevelt in 1941 relented to pressure from civil rights leaders to establish a means for testing the combat readiness of blacks; he directed the U.S. Army Air Corps (later that year it became known as the Army Air Force) to train black military personnel as pilots and technicians. The government constructed Tuskegee Army Air Field in Alabama at a site near the historically black Tuskegee University; there it activated four squadrons destined to be called the Tuskegee Airmen. The test proved a success; 997 cadets earned their pilot wings before the program closed in 1946. The men saw action in North Africa and Europe, and the 332nd Fighter Group received a Presidential Unit Citation in March 1945.

Despite these results, segregation in the armed forces continued with only a few exceptions. **General Dwight David Eisenhower** (1890–1969) temporarily desegregated the army in 1944 in order to have a sufficient number of troops for the Battle of the Bulge. More than 2,000 black soldiers volunteered to fight. Likewise, the navy, toward the end of the war, desperate for additional personnel, integrated briefly. Also, black nurses could now administer to white soldiers in England.

Some parties saw the training of the Tuskegee Airmen as a step forward, but black military personnel still encountered discrimination and intolerance both at home and in the services. Nevertheless, many blacks felt called upon to support their country at this critical time, and before the war's end more than half a million had served in Europe, including well-known sports stars like boxers Beau Jack (1921–2000), Bob Montgomery (1919–1998), welterweight and middleweight title holder Sugar Ray Robinson

(1921–1989), and heavyweight **boxing** champion **Joe Louis** (1914–1981). Louis, who had joined the army in June 1942, immediately set out to support the war effort in a number of ways and particularly wanted to secure the help and support of black citizens. Louis appeared on a recruiting poster, could frequently be seen as a soldier in newsreels, and in 1944 served as a consultant when the War Department made a filmed propaganda documentary titled *The Negro Soldier.* He and others had hoped that the picture would have a positive effect with regard to race relations both at home and in the military, an end that it did not fully achieve.

Aside from his service work, Louis, along with other black athletes such as track and field star Jesse Owens (1913–1980), holder of four gold Olympic medals, hoped to advance racial equality by earning respect and maintaining their celebrity status both during and after the war. Ironically, despite the negative effects of a segregated military, World War II had a positive impact on blacks participating in sports. The diversion of American manpower to the war created vacancies on professional and amateur teams, which blacks occasionally filled. In the sport of **baseball,** Satchel Paige (1906–1982) and his Negro Baseball All-Star Team gained the opportunity to compete against major league champions; the Negro Collegiate All-Stars of **Football** saw games against the titleholder of the National Football League (NFL).

This trend continued after the war; by the early 1950s, most major sports were integrated. In 1946, the color line fell in the National Football League when the Los Angeles Rams (formerly in Cleveland) signed Kenny Washington (1918–1971) and Woody Strode (1914–1994), while the Cleveland Browns signed Marion Motley (1920–1999) and Bill Willis (1921–2007). Jackie Robinson (1919–1972) made headline news in 1947 as the first black player accepted in major league baseball. Larry Doby (1903–2003) and Satchel Paige quickly followed, joining the Cleveland Indians in 1948. That same year, Alice Coachman (b. 1923) earned the honor of being the first American black woman to win an Olympic gold medal (for the high jump). Integration occurred in professional **basketball** in 1950 with the inclusion of Charles "Chuck" Cooper (1926–1984), Nathaniel "Sweetwater" Clifton (1922–1990), and Earl Lloyd (b. 1928) in the National Basketball Association (NBA). Althea Gibson (1927–2003) became the first black woman to compete in the National Championships of Tennis (later the United States Open) at Forest Hills in Queens, New York, in 1950.

Frustrated with the ineffectiveness of lobbying for rights by the NAACP, labor and civil rights leader A. Philip Randolph (1889–1979) organized a national, black-led march to the capitol in Washington, DC, for July 1, 1941. Estimates that the event would draw over 100,000 people concerned Roosevelt, fearing that the march would upset the perceived feeling of national unity during wartime. As a preventive measure, one week before the protest, he issued Executive Order 8802 establishing the first Fair Employment Practices Committee (FEPC), an agency with the responsibility of eliminating racial discrimination in government. Randolph then decided the march unnecessary and cancelled the event, but he immediately established the March on Washington Movement (MOWM) as a means of holding the FEPC accountable. Throughout the summer of 1942, MOWM held mass rallies of orderly protest in St. Louis, New York, and Chicago.

Randolph's strategies of involving ordinary people instead of political elites departed from the practices of other civil rights groups. Because of his success, his counterparts began to recognize the significance of grassroots black politics and the ability of a black-led mass movement to achieve change. The MOWM continued to interact with the FEPC until 1942, when Roosevelt changed the agency from an independent investigative body to a committee under congressional oversight, an action that reduced the committee's ability to assist the MOWM in its efforts, and the MOWM ceased operations in 1947.

Violent, spontaneous racial protests occurred in Detroit during the spring of 1943. Tensions had been building over the construction of a federal housing project for blacks next to a white Polish American neighborhood. Emotions climaxed on a June day, when more than 100,000 people, white and black, attempted to find relief from the heat at a municipal park on Belle Isle in the Detroit River. Fighting erupted between the two groups and continued intermittently for 12 hours, but without serious injuries. Unfounded rumors the next day caused more violence, and events quickly escalated, resulting in the deaths of 25 blacks and 9 whites; it took 6,000 federal troops to bring the riot to an end. That same year, tensions rose in other cities; Beaumont, Texas; Mobile, Alabama; and New York City were among those urban sites that endured race riots.

Various entertainment outlets reinforced long-held myths that blacks displayed low intelligence, criminal tendencies, and physical inferiority; these persisted throughout the 1940s. **Radio,** a major purveyor of popular culture at the time, aired programs that presented blacks in unattractive ways, but what should have been an issue of racial stereotyping seldom entered any discussions about the shows.

For example, *Amos 'n' Andy,* one of the most popular programs in the history of the medium, aired from 1929 to 1960, alternating between NBC (National Broadcasting Company) during 1929–1939 and 1943–1948, and CBS (Columbia Broadcasting System) in 1939–1943 and 1948–1960. An instant hit for its two white creators and actors, Freeman Gosden (1899–1982) and Charles Correll (1890–1972), the script called for a stereotypical "Negro dialect" and presented blacks as unreliable, lazy, and hapless individuals. Gosden and Correll soon supplemented Amos and Andy by adding others to the cast, including Kingfish, Lightnin', Calhoun, Sapphire, and Madame Queen. Its popularity reached such heights that movie houses would time the showing of newsreels and the main feature so as to pause in an unobtrusive way and air the radio program to its patrons through speakers mounted in the auditorium.

*The Beulah Show* told the story of Beulah, a meddling, simpleminded black maid who worked for Fibber McGee. The role of Beulah went to two white men: first, Marlin Hurt (1905–1946) from 1945 to 1946 and, second, Bob Corley (1924–1971), from February to August 1947. Their presence created a double insult—a transgendered blackface. In November 1947, CBS changed things by casting Hattie McDaniel (1895–1952), a successful, award-winning black performer, as Beulah. She took the role to **television** in the 1950s.

*The Jack Benny Program,* another popular show, ran on CBS (1932–1933; 1949–1958) and NBC (1932; 1933–1948) radio from 1932 to 1958. It introduced Rochester, Benny's gravel-voiced black valet, in 1937. Played by Eddie Anderson (1905–1977), script writers portrayed Rochester as a servant with little status, the butt of much humor at the hands of Benny, but he also came across as a clever man in his own right. As with *Amos 'n' Andy,* white America accepted these behaviors as normal.

Other minority performers, frequently played by white actors, had limited exposure on radio, and their shows regularly moved from one network to another. Two characters, however, sustained long careers and popularity over several years. The long-running **Lone Ranger** Western series (1933–1942, Mutual; 1942–1944, NBC; 1944–1956, ABC) introduced Tonto, supposedly a Potawatomi Indian. Tonto played the crucial role of faithful sidekick to the Lone Ranger.

Charlie Chan, a Chinese American detective, came from the pen of author Earl Derr Biggers (1884–1933) in a series of mysteries that ran from 1925 to 1932. Immensely popular, these tales soon made the transition to sound films in 1931, and many motion pictures followed. Between 1940 and 1949, 29 Charlie Chan movies thrilled audiences. White actors made to look Asian play Chan—Sidney Toler (1874–1947) in 23 productions followed by Roland Winter (1904–1989) in 6. The detective could also be heard on radio from 1932 until 1948. Again, a white actor—in this case, Ed Begley (1901–1970)—even on the invisible medium of radio, portrayed Chan.

When newspaper **comic strips** included minorities in their storylines, the figures also tended to be presented in a stereotypical manner and held subordinate roles. Kenneth Kling's (1895–1970) *Joe and Asbestos* (1925–1926, 1928–1966) features Joe Quince, a white character, picking real horses for actual races, with his picks always winning. Soon after the strip's first appearance, Kling gave Joe a companion, a black stable boy named Asbestos. An Al Jolson–style caricature, Asbestos might have been acceptable at the time but would today be considered politically incorrect.

Lee Falk (1911–1999), creator of *Mandrake the Magician* (1934 to present) did somewhat better in showing respect. Mandrake, another white hero, fights criminals and other villains with Lothar, a black character, serving as his crime-fighting companion. Mandrake met Lothar during travels in Africa, and the pair are reported to be among the first interracial team of crime fighters. Falk also created *The Phantom* at the same time as *Mandrake.* A muscular white man clad in purple tights and wearing a mask, the Phantom battles evil in the African jungle on "The Dark Continent." Guran, a member of the pygmy tribe, serves as his loyal helper, not unlike Lothar in the *Mandrake* series or Tonto in the Lone Ranger serials. In each of these strips, the minority characters perform as subservient figures. The comics also offered renderings of other American ethnic or racial groups. Fred Harman's (1902–1982) successful strip *Red Ryder,* which ran from 1938 to 1963, paired a Navaho Indian tyke, Little Beaver, with the tough cowpoke Ryder, creating a hackneyed image of Native Americans as inferior to whites, a role similar to those given blacks, but this time in drawings.

The movies likewise presented stereotypes and adopted past racial images. Lincoln Perry (1902–1985), through his portrayal of a character known as Stepin Fetchit, became America's first black movie star and millionaire. He acquired the distinction and riches at a heavy price. Perry made 54 films between 1925 and 1976, always as a befuddled, mumbling, worthless fool. Although he reached his peak popularity in the mid-1930s, Perry, frustrated with constant battles with Twentieth Century-Fox concerning equal pay, walked away from Hollywood in 1940. He returned to appear in five motion pictures between 1945 and 1949, declared bankruptcy in 1947, went back to Hollywood sporadically during the 1950s and 1970s, and then faded into obscurity.

During the 1940s, despite some protests from black leaders concerning stereotypical negative images, Hollywood gave all black actors exaggerated dialects and made them up with exaggerated lips and bulging eyeballs. Scripts called on them to be ignorant, lazy, conniving people, but ones with great rhythm for dancing. Further insult came when studios had white actors and actresses in blackface playing the roles of blacks. One example among many can be found in Paramount Picture's highly successful *Holiday Inn* (1942) starring Bing Crosby (1903–1977), Fred Astaire (1899–1987), Marjorie Reynolds (1917–1997), and Virginia Dale (1917–1994). Crosby and Reynolds, along with a chorus and orchestra, appear in blackface for a demeaning musical number titled "Abraham," a song in honor of President Abraham Lincoln (1809–1865) and the ending of slavery. Even children's cartoons such as Bugs Bunny in *All This and Rabbit Stew* (Warner Bros., 1941) or Universal Pictures' *Scrub Me Mama with a Boogie Beat* (1940) reinforce negative images of blacks.

In contrast to most mainstream Hollywood productions, a film genre called "race movies" or "race pictures" existed in the United States between 1915 and 1950. It consisted of movies aimed at all-black audiences featuring all-black casts, produced primarily in West Coast or Northern cities, and most often financed by white-owned companies and scripted by white writers. These motion pictures presented characters in roles usually reserved for whites, such as doctors, lawyers, soldiers, cowboys, and powerful gangsters, but in a curious turnaround gave them stereotypical black servants and chauffeurs.

Businessman and publisher John H. Johnson (1918–2005), himself black, created the first mass **magazines** that celebrated black culture and lives through positive images. On November 1, 1945, the debut issue of *Ebony,* a pictorial news magazine modeled after *Life* magazine, hit the newsstands of Chicago. The premiere issue sold 25,000 copies and served as a new vehicle for national advertisers to reach black consumers. Johnson had started his publishing career with *Negro Digest* in 1942. Similar to *Reader's Digest* but aimed at black readers, it took a serious look at racial issues. Both *Ebony* and *Negro Digest* originally sold for 25 cents per issue (approximately $3 in 2008 dollars), a relatively high price in an era of 5-cent and 10-cent periodicals.

Publication of the *Negro Digest* ceased in 1951, being replaced by *Jet,* a similar magazine. Early issues of *Ebony* featured stars such as Lena Horne (b. 1917) and Dorothy Dandridge (1922–1965) and over the years offered articles about notable black celebrities and sports figures. It occasionally presented works by well-established literary figures such as author Langston Hughes (1902–1967) and poet Gwendolyn Brooks (1917–2000). Johnson's magazines proved so successful that in 1972 the Magazine Publishers Association selected him as magazine publisher of the year, and 10 years later he became the first black to appear on the Forbes 400 list of the wealthiest Americans.

Minorities in general did not fare as well as whites in **advertising.** Food products especially at one time used blacks as a part of their labeling. The Quaker Oats Company provides an example. It developed a logo for pancake flour, syrup, and other breakfast foods known to consumers as Aunt Jemima. The company also employed a number of different women over the years to be Aunt Jemima at state and national fairs. Originally, this smiling Mammy image served as a female version of Uncle Tom, a servant presented in unflattering ways and always at the beck and call of whites. Since her first appearance in 1893, Aunt Jemima has undergone significant changes and, according to Quaker Oats, has become racially neutral; some observers, knowing the heritage of the logo, might disagree. Other products utilizing images of blacks on their packages during the 1940s include Uncle Rastus for Cream of Wheat (hot cereal), and Uncle Ben (rice products). All of these images appear on the products' packages, advertisements in magazines and on billboards, and even made it to children's **toys** as dolls.

Attitudes and acts of discrimination, hostility, and oppression toward blacks were not limited to just this group; other minorities living in the United States had similar experiences. By 1940, Native Americans had suffered a long history of grievances, including loss of their rightful lands and tribal authority, poverty, ill health, and inadequate **education.** The Indian Reorganization Act of 1934 brought some improvement. It recognized tribal ceremonies and practices, allowing tribes to write their own constitutions for self-governance. They could also assume ownership of reservation lands. By 1945, a total of 95 tribes had written constitutions and 70 had formed business corporations to develop reservation resources. Compared with earlier decades, matters had improved, but poverty, disease, and unemployment continued to run at higher levels than among other American minorities.

As a group, Native Americans offered strong support for war-related efforts, with 25,000, including 800 women, serving in the armed forces. The Wind Talkers unit from the Navajo tribe served as communication personnel and spoke in a code derived from their untranslatable language. They made another major contribution to winning World War II by taking part in every assault made by the marines from 1942 to 1945.

In the wake of the attack by Japan on Pearl Harbor on December 7, 1941, tensions mounted and many people blindly concluded that all Japanese Americans living on the West Coast somehow constituted a threat to national security. On February 19, 1942, President Roosevelt issued an executive order calling for the relocation of between 110,000 and 120,000 individuals of Japanese decent residing in California, Oregon, Washington, and southern Arizona. The War Relocation Authority (WRA) administered the program and, by October of that year, had constructed 10 **internment camps** in California, Arkansas, Idaho, Wyoming, Colorado, Utah, and Arizona to house the detainees for the remainder of the war. Tremendous financial losses occurred for these citizens, because homes, farms, and businesses were liquated on short notice and most personal property had to be left behind; it frequently mysteriously disappeared, probably by theft, despite government promises to protect it.

In addition to the relocation, the Federal Bureau of Investigation (FBI) arrested nearly 2,000 Japanese Americans. Only one man ever received a conviction, and that for the crime of forgetting to register as a business agent of a Japanese importing firm. During the war, the FBI also arrested thousands of white Germans and Italians, but they suffered no relocation as happened on the West Coast.

Conditions for the interned Japanese Americans finally changed on December 18, 1944, when a California state court, after two years of litigation, decided that a civilian agency such as the WRA had no constitutional authority to incarcerate law-abiding citizens. Two weeks later, authorities declared the camps closed, and by March 1946, all occupants had been released.

Mexican Americans and other Hispanics who lived primarily in the Southwest, like blacks and Native Americans, had been ill treated for most of their time in the United States. During the 1940s, they continued to experience segregation in schools, public accommodations, and neighborhoods, along with discrimination in the workplace in terms of working hours, pay, training, and advancement. The country's entry into

World War II sent millions of U.S. soldiers overseas and created severe labor shortages causing some employers to be more tolerant of hiring Mexican Americans.

Biases, however, persisted—especially on the West Coast, where a series of events culminated in what is known as the Zoot Suit Riots. It started with many Mexican adolescents, along with some black and white youths, sporting a new **fashion** fad—zoot suits.

Their attire consisted of long, fitted jackets with outsized lapels and padded shoulders and trousers with a high waist and legs full in the thigh and pegged to ankle-hugging tightness, a statement of teenage rebellion. At about the same time of the appearance of this new dress code, E. Duran Ayers (active 1940s), newly appointed head of the Los Angles Foreign Relations Bureau, reported to a grand jury on the "Mexican element," describing this group as "individuals with wild and violent tendencies, no matter how much education or training they might receive."

Shortly thereafter, zoot-suiter Henry Leyvas (1923–1971) and some of his friends were arrested and found guilty of murder. Led by local tabloids, the public cried for justice and vengeance against anyone so dressed. The Los Angeles police answered with a roundup of over 600 Mexican Americans, all charged with crimes such as suspicion of assault and robbery. In June 1943, against this backdrop of interracial hostility, 11 sailors on leave reported they had been attacked by a group of zoot-suited Mexican **youth.** In response, more than 200 sailors and marines on passes to Los Angeles wreaked havoc for three nights in Mexican neighborhoods, while military and civilian authorities looked the other way. The U.S. Navy and Marine Corps command staff finally intervened, confining sailors and marines to barracks and declaring Los Angeles off limits to all military personnel.

Despite continuing segregation and acts of discrimination during the 1940s, movement toward equality for all advanced, albeit at a glacial pace. From the outset of World War II, roughly 1 million black citizens, primarily from the rural South, moved to the industrialized North and to the West Coast. Although their new locations sometimes imposed housing restrictions, which created segregated and inadequate living conditions, they still provided greater possibilities for jobs and better schools for children to attend than did their previous places of residence.

Doors that opened during and after the war created opportunities toward economic mobility, but not enough to prevent noticeable gaps in income across racial groups. The number of blacks working in manufacturing jumped from half a million to 1.2 million. Another 2 million joined the federal civil service. At the same time, the number of working black women in domestic services declined from 72 percent of their number to 48 percent. Additionally, many of those men who fought in the war returned home with new job skills, relocated in new communities, and pursued new careers. Barriers still existed, just not as many. Housing continued to be a problem, and while developers and realtors initially prevented minorities from buying homes in the fast-growing postwar suburban developments like **Levittown,** the first black reporter gained entrance to a presidential press conference and his fellow citizens had access to the United States Senate press gallery for the first time.

Throughout the 1940s, A. Philip Randolph, the NAACP, and other civil rights organizations continued to fight for civil rights. In 1948, **President Harry S. Truman** (1884–1972) signed an executive order establishing the President's Committee on Equality of Treatment and Opportunity in the Armed Forces. The U.S. military, however, kept black soldiers in separate units until the early 1950s and the Korean War. Segregation officially ended in the military when authorities abolished the last all-black unit in 1954; that same year, the Supreme Court in *Brown v. the Board of Education,* struck down the separate-but-equal school systems in the United States. Even though MOWM closed its doors in 1948, it served as a model for the 1963 March on Washington, where the Reverend Martin Luther King Jr. (1929–1968) gave his famous "I Have a Dream" speech.

*See also:* Crime and Mystery Films; Fads; Leisure and Recreation; MBS (Mutual Broadcasting System); Newspapers; Radio Programming: Children's Shows, Serials, and Adventure Series; Radio Programming: Comedy Shows; Radio Programming: Music and Variety Shows; Westerns (Films)

**Selected Reading**
Bayor, Ronald H. *Race and Ethnicity in America: A Concise History.* New York: Columbia University Press, 2003.
Davis, Thomas J. *Race Relations in the United States, 1940–1960.* Westport, CT Greenwood Press, 2008.
Our, Alan M. *Blacks in the Army Air Forces During World War II.* Washington, DC: Office of Air Force History, 1977.
Patterson, James T. *Grand Expectations: The United States, 1945–1974.* New York: Oxford University Press, 1996.

# RADIO

For many media historians, the 1930s and 1940s reigned as radio's golden age. Untold millions of Americans listened to their receivers each and every day, making broadcasting far and away the most pervasive form of mass communication ever developed up to that time. Radio leveled regional and social differences and barriers by its very ubiquity. Varied shows, bold experiments, and high production values marked this period, yet the early 1950s found traditional commercial radio on the ropes, vanquished by **television** in just a few years, and soon reduced to a bland menu of music and news. The once-mighty medium increasingly became a conduit for recorded music and little else, and disc jockeys emerged as the primary voices on the air.

Despite this postwar setback, during the years 1930 to 1949, radio grew at a remarkable rate. The percentage of American homes with radio receivers went from about 46 percent in 1930 (over 13 million sets) to over 80 percent by 1940 (almost 29 million sets). Even with World War II and a shortage of new receivers, the numbers kept growing, reaching 88 percent of homes in 1945 (over 33 million sets). With postwar prosperity and the increased availability of consumer goods, at least one radio could be found in almost 95 percent of homes (almost 40 million sets) by 1949. Today, the figure approaches 100 percent, with most residences claiming multiple receivers.

During that same period, the number of commercial AM (amplitude modulation) stations on the air jumped from 618 broadcasters in 1930 to 765 in 1940, and then to 1,912 AM stations in 1949—and all this growth came about despite a crushing economic depression and war-imposed shortages. In addition, 727 FM (frequency modulation) stations had also come into existence by 1949, giving the nation 2,639 radio outlets at the end of the period, and these proliferating broadcasters fiercely competed for listeners. Remarkable statistics in themselves, it must be remembered that radio as a popular medium has been around only since the early 1920s.

Thanks to national networks—NBC (National Broadcasting Company), CBS (Columbia Broadcasting System), and **MBS (Mutual Broadcasting System)**—that grew up in the 1930s, electronically and culturally linking the nation and allowing millions to share in the same programming, radio brought a virtual nonstop menu of entertainment, music, news, and sports into the home. In addition, growing numbers of consumers viewed neither cars nor car radios as luxuries. Both had evolved into necessities, right along with **food** and shelter, and the car radio became as important as the one in the living room. As a result, more and more vehicles purchased during this period came so equipped. From the moment they arose in the morning until they turned off the lights at night, Americans everywhere—at home, on the job, on the road—could stay tuned.

As radio became part and parcel of the everyday lives of Americans, the medium assumed a unique importance. Unlike **movies** and print media, radio, with no admission price or fees per program, gave the illusion of being free. A twist of the dial brought in just about anything a listener might want, and detailed schedules in **newspapers** and **magazines** assured the public that no one might miss a favorite show.

As a point of comparison, approximately 80 million Americans attended the movies each week during the 1930s, despite a numerical drop during the worst days of the Great Depression; those numbers grew during World War II to 85 million, peaking at 90 million in 1946–1947. At the end of the decade, and also because of the impacts of television, the figures plummeted to 60 million weekly and continued their drop thereafter. But not even the film industry, churning out hundreds of features yearly, could approach radio's appetite for dozens of shows each day, hundreds each week, thousands by the end of a year. The quality may have been wildly uneven, but the breadth of selections was unparalleled.

*See also:* Automobiles and the American Automotive Industry; FM Radio; Radio Programming: Action, Crime, Police, and Detective Shows; Radio Programming: Children's Shows, Serials, and Adventure Series; Radio Programming: Comedy Shows; Radio Programming: Drama and Anthology Shows; Radio Programming: Educational Shows; Radio Programming: Music and Variety Shows; Radio Programming: News, Sports, Public Affairs, and Talk; Radio Programming: Quiz Shows; Radio Programming: Soap Operas; Technology

**Selected Reading**
Barfield, Ray. *Listening to Radio, 1920–1950.* Westport, CT: Praeger, 1996.
Barnouw, Erik. *A History of Broadcasting in the United States.* Vol. 1, *A Tower in Babel.* New York: Oxford University Press, 1966.
———. *A History of Broadcasting in the United States.* Vol. 2, *The Golden Web.* New York: Oxford University Press, 1968.
Maltin, Leonard. *The Great American Broadcast: A Celebration of Radio's Golden Age.* New York: New American Library, 2000.
Sterling, Christopher H., and John M. Kitross. *Stay Tuned: A Concise History of American Broadcasting.* Belmont, CA: Wadsworth, 1990.

# RADIO PROGRAMMING: ACTION, CRIME, POLICE, AND DETECTIVE SHOWS

During the late 19th century, American publishers began issuing countless dime novels, cheap little volumes—initially a dime, but later often available for as little as a nickel (or about $2.50 and $1.25 in 2008 dollars)—filled with violent tales of action and adventure. Aimed principally at an audience of boys and young men, but if sales serve as any indicator, popular with other readers as well. The dime novels, printed on low-quality pulp paper and poorly bound, featured a pen-and-ink cover illustration depicting an exciting event from the pages within, such as a leap from a cliff; a damsel in distress; guns and fisticuffs; or a mad chase with horses, stage coaches, locomotives, or anything else that might lure a prospective buyer. The crude tales evolved into pulp **magazines,** big sellers at newsstands and kiosks that continued the tradition of garish covers promising thrills and chills for only a dime or so.

Both Hollywood and, later, the **radio** networks, always alert to trends that might attract audiences, strove to duplicate these early pulp successes. One of the most popular radio shows of both the 1930s and the 1940s featured *The Shadow,* a wily crime fighter who possessed the power to "cloud men's minds," thereby rendering himself invisible. Street and Smith, publishers of numerous pulp magazines, in 1930 sold CBS (Columbia Broadcasting System) on the idea of creating a radio show based on one of its most successful titles, *The Shadow.* An invisible hero presented no problems for an aural medium, and the series quickly built a large audience; it stayed on the air until 1954, an unusually long run for any show.

Battling crime, invisibly or more traditionally, proved a profitable road to travel for series producers. *True Detective,* another popular pulp magazine, debuted in print in 1924; by 1929, its stories, purportedly based on real events, could be heard on the air. Except for occasional breaks, *True Detective Mysteries* did not sign off until 1958, another long-lived show.

With their theme of "crime does not pay," *The Shadow* and *True Detective Mysteries* spawned many another crime series. *Gang Busters* introduced audiences to wailing police sirens, screeching tires, and the rat-tat-tat of a tommy gun and served as the first of many police-oriented shows. Violence and realism characterized *Gang Busters,* and legions of listeners relished the mix, keeping it on the air until 1957.

By the end of the 1930s, crimes and criminals had established a substantial niche in American broadcasting. With the onset of the 1940s, the period might well be called the decade of the detective. Classic sleuths like Sherlock Holmes and Charlie Chan had already made their mark on radio schedules, but a new breed, the hardboiled detective, moved en masse into network time slots during this period. Inspired by the pulps and writers like Raymond Chandler (1888–1959; *Adventures of Philip Marlowe*), Earle Stanley Gardner (1889–1970; *Perry Mason*), Dashiell Hammett (1894–1961; *Adventures of Sam Spade, Adventures of the Thin Man*), Ellery Queen (shared pseudonym of Frederic Dannay, 1905–1982, and Manfred Lee, 1905–1971, and also the name of their fictional detective; *Adventures of Ellery Queen*), Rex Stout (1886–1975; *Adventures of Nero Wolfe*), and a host of nameless other authors, the radio detective had his day.

Throughout the war years, these new private eyes appeared with some regularity. Top radio actors (or voices) usually played them, such as Ray Collins (1889–1965; *Crime Doctor*), Hugh Marlowe (1911–1982; *Ellery Queen*), Santos Ortega (1899–1976; *Perry Mason*), Les Tremayne (1913–2003; *The Thin Man*), and many others. Often, one actor would initiate a role, another would then take it, and possibly another and another before the series had run its course, but such was the hectic nature of network radio during the 1930s and 1940s.

In the postwar period, still more sleuths came along. Dick Powell (1904–1963), a former song-and-dance man in Hollywood musicals of the 1930s, established a radio reputation as a wisecracking private eye. He first played in *Rogue's Gallery,* a short-lived series (1945–1947) that allowed him to polish the tough-guy persona that he brought to the later *Richard Diamond, Private Detective,* Powell's best-remembered show. These roles resembled similar ones he played in several well-received **movies** at the time: *Murder, My Sweet* (1944), *Cornered* (1945), and *Johnny O'Clock* (1947).

Frank Lovejoy (1912–1962), another motion picture actor, could be heard on radio often. His instantly recognizable gravelly voice first caught people's attention in *Gang Busters,* and he gave Mr. Malone, the titular hero of *Murder and Mr. Malone,* a gruff authority. He went to other radio productions in the 1950s, the same time that his film career blossomed. Alan Ladd (1913–1964)—like Frank Lovejoy, a veteran of both radio and the movies—created a syndicated series called *Box 13* in 1948. He wrote and starred in the show, a continuing tale about a for-hire adventurer named Dan Holiday. Clients wrote to "Box 13" when seeking Holiday's assistance, and the ensuing exploits allowed Ladd to burnish his reputation as an action entertainer.

Sam Spade, the most famous of Dashiell Hammett's many characters, finally came to radio in 1946. Actor Howard Duff (1913–1990), who parlayed network success into a movie career, took on the role of the hardboiled gumshoe in 1946 and retained it until 1950, becoming, in the process, one of the most memorable of radio detectives. Wildroot Cream Oil, a hair dressing for men, sponsored the show until its demise in 1950.

Finally, two relatively unknown actors rose to considerable fame amid all the private eyes populating the airwaves in the later 1940s: J. Scott Smart (1902–1960) and Jack Webb (1920–1982). Smart played Brad Runyon, a heavyset investigator in *The Fat Man.* Smart himself weighed in at well over 250 pounds and had a deep voice that seemingly emanated from his considerable depths. The program's opening, "There he goes, he's stepping on the scales. Weight, 227 pounds; fortune [pause], danger," served as one of those classic radio bits everyone came to know. Smart boasted an extensive radio background, mainly character roles, when he came to *The Fat Man* in 1946. But he quickly molded a distinctive personality for Runyon, and the show enjoyed good ratings for its five-year run. Hollywood released a so-so low-budget feature, *The Fat Man,* in 1951, which wisely stars the rotund Smart; the picture, however, later became notable primarily as the first film in which Rock Hudson (1925–1985) receives screen credits.

Still a youthful 26 when he broke into radio with *Pat Novak, for Hire* in 1946, Jack Webb worked to establish an identity for Novak, one that consisted mainly of

TABLE 75. Selected Action, Crime, Police, and Detective Programming on American Radio, 1940–1949 (Arranged Chronologically)

| Selected Artists/Performers and Shows | Dates |
|---|---|
| *True Detective Mysteries* | 1929–1930; 1936–1939; 1944–1958 |
| *The Shadow* | 1930–1954 |
| Basil Rathbone, others, in *Sherlock Holmes* | 1930–1950; 1955–1956 |
| Ed Begley in *The Adventures of Charlie Chan* | 1932–1948 |
| Frank Lovejoy, others, in *Gang Busters* | 1935–1957 |
| *Famous Jury Trials* | 1936–1949 |
| *Big Town* | 1937–1952 |
| *Mr. Keen, Tracer of Lost Persons* | 1937–1955 |
| *Adventures of Ellery Queen* | 1939–1948 |
| *I Love a Mystery* | 1939–1941; 1943–1944; 1949–1953 |
| *Mr. District Attorney* | 1939–1954 |
| *Crime Doctor* | 1940–1947 |
| *Adventures of the Thin Man* | 1941–1950 |
| *Adventures of Bulldog Drummond* | 1941–1954 |
| *Adventures of Mr. & Mrs. North* | 1942–1955 |
| *The Whistler* | 1942–1955 |
| *Counterspy* (also known as *David Harding, Counterspy*) | 1942–1957 |
| *Adventures of Nero Wolfe* | 1943–1951 |
| *Molle Mystery Theater* | 1943–1954 |
| *The Falcon* | 1943; 1945–1954 |
| John Larkin in *Perry Mason* | 1943–1955 |
| *Nick Carter, Master Detective* | 1943–1955 |
| Chester Morris in *Boston Blackie* | 1944–1950 |
| Herbert Marshall in *The Man Called X* | 1944–1952 |
| *Michael Shayne, Private Detective* | 1944–1953 |
| *The FBI in Peace and War* | 1944–1958 |
| Dick Powell in *Rogue's Gallery* | 1945–1947 |
| *Casey, Crime Photographer* | 1945–1950 |
| *The Saint* | 1945–1951 |
| *This Is Your FBI* | 1945–1953 |
| Jack Webb in *Pat Novak, for Hire* | 1946–1949 |
| Howard Duff in *Adventures of Sam Spade, Detective* | 1946–1951 |
| J. Scott Smart in *The Fat Man* | 1946–1951 |
| *Let George Do It* | 1946–1954 |
| Jack Webb in *Johnny Modero: Pier 23* | 1947 (partial season) |
| *Call the Police* | 1947–1949 |
| *Adventures of Philip Marlowe* | 1947–1951 |
| Frank Lovejoy in *Murder and Mr. Malone* | 1947–1951 |
| *The Big Story* | 1947–1954 |
| *Official Detective* | 1947–1957 |
| Alan Ladd in *Box 13* | 1948–1950 |
| Brian Donlevy in *Dangerous Assignment* | 1949–1953 |
| Dick Powell in *Richard Diamond, Private Detective* | 1949–1953 |
| *Broadway Is My Beat* | 1949–1954 |
| Jack Webb in *Dragnet* | 1949–1956 |

hard-bitten one-liners. That trait—terse dialogue and sarcasm—worked well, and Webb polished it, first in the brief (1947) *Johnny Modero: Pier 23* and then in his best work, *Dragnet*. In that series, Webb played Detective Sergeant Joe Friday, a Los Angeles police officer, and his characterization propelled him to fame. He went on to a later **television** series of the same name, and several movies, including, not surprisingly, *Dragnet* in 1954. Webb, something of a one-note actor, seldom strayed far from his tight-lipped, unsmiling Friday character. As with the opening of *The Fat Man*, *Dragnet* also featured a memorable introduction, in its case, four musical notes—dum-de-dum-dum—that signaled a new episode.

Mysteries and detective yarns took up much network programming during the 1940s. Aural extensions of two literary traditions, pulp magazines and crime novels, they found receptive audiences, and many titles carried over from the 1930s. Freely employing sound effects and fast-paced plots, often with tough-as-nails heroes, these many series provided escapism and thrills on a nightly basis. When television began to make inroads at the end of the decade, the new medium likewise looked to similar sources. By the early 1950s, this once-flourishing radio genre had all but disappeared, replaced by images of TV cops and private eyes.

*See also:* Best Sellers (Books); Bogart, Humphrey; Crime and Mystery Films; Film Noir; Illustrators; Musicals (Film)

**Selected Reading**

Dunning, John. *On the Air: The Encyclopedia of Old-Time Radio.* New York: Oxford University Press, 1998.

Hilmes, Michele, and Jason Loviglio, eds. *Radio Reader: Essays in the Cultural History of Radio.* Florence, KY: Routledge, 2002.

Lackman, Ron. *The Encyclopedia of American Radio.* New York: Checkmark Books, 2000.

Maltin, Leonard. *The Great American Broadcast: A Celebration of Radio's Golden Age.* New York: Dutton, 1997.

# RADIO PROGRAMMING: CHILDREN'S SHOWS, SERIALS, AND ADVENTURE SERIES

From the earliest days of commercial **radio,** producers created programming targeted at juveniles. One of the first, *Coast-to-Coast on a Bus* (it began in 1924 as *The Children's Hour*), laid the framework for many successive children's programs: mix music, patter, and brief stories in order to hold the attention of young listeners. Milton Cross (1897–1975), the famed host for the Saturday afternoon broadcasts of the Metropolitan Opera from 1931 to his death, served as the bus conductor and took great pride in the show.

Two other radio personalities, Ed McConnell (1893–1954) and "Uncle" Don Carney (ne Howard Rice, 1897–1954), modeled their productions, *Smilin' Ed and His Buster Brown Gang* and *Uncle Don,* after the pattern established by *Coast-to-Coast on a Bus.* All three continued into the 1940s, and only the advent of **television,** with its visual component, doomed that form of programming. (Many people believe that Uncle Don, thinking his microphone was turned off, muttered over the air some curse words about his attitudes toward his listeners. But this bit of media lore actually predated Uncle Don's show and has since been applied to virtually everyone who has hosted a children's program. According to www.snopes.com, the leading source for debunking such manufactured claims, no evidence substantiates the incident. Myths, however, possess lives of their own, as do Uncle Don's purported comments.)

Cowboy shows also enjoyed a following. Screen stars **Gene Autry** (1907–1998) and **Roy Rogers** (1911–1998), probably the best-known among youngsters, enjoyed high ratings with their programs. Autry, billed as America's Favorite Cowboy," led the way with *Melody Ranch,* which debuted on CBS in 1940. It blended humor, Western tales, and music. Although Autry had to absent himself from the show from 1944 and 1945 for military service, the network and Wrigley's Doublemint Gum, his continuing sponsor, welcomed him back after the war. *Melody Ranch* continued for another 11 years as a regular CBS offering, finally heading for its last roundup in 1956.

Roy Rogers (1911–1998), the "King of the Cowboys" and Autry's chief rival in the 1940s, also made the transition to radio. *The Roy Rogers Show* premiered in 1944 on **MBS (Mutual Broadcasting System**). Accompanied by the popular Dale Evans (1912–2001), dubbed the "Queen of the West" and also his wife in real life, the program likewise appealed to a youthful audience by mixing music, comedy, and drama but never achieved the success of *Melody Ranch.* Burdened by an erratic schedule and far fewer affiliates, *The Roy Rogers Show* struggled along until 1955.

For the 1940s, the leading form of children's programming concerned serials and adventure series. Serials involved continuing, episodic stories that ran for months at a time. Adventure series, on the other hand, usually presented complete, self-contained stories with each broadcast. The cast of characters continued, reappearing from week to week, ready for fresh new thrills.

Two of the first serials, taken from the popular **comic strips** of the day, *Little Orphan Annie* (1930–1942) and *Buck Rogers in the 25th Century* (1932–1940; 1946–1947), made their debuts in the early 1930s. Both weekday offerings, *Little Orphan Annie* grew out of the strip penned by Harold Gray (1894–1968), and *Buck Rogers* came from a newspaper series of the same name by author Philip Nowlan (1888–1940) and artist Dick Calkins (1895–1962). The success of these pioneering serials caused competitors to appear on station schedules shortly thereafter.

Usually broadcast during the late afternoon, after school but before dinner, serials guaranteed sponsors a returning audience by crafting their stories to end on a suspenseful, cliff-hanging note with each 15-minute episode. The heroes tended to be earnest young American boys; Annie proved an exception, and did not bring about an influx of similar heroines. More characteristically, Jack Armstrong received billing as the "All-American Boy," a lad that led a group of admiring pals from adventure to adventure.

TABLE 76. Representative Children's Programming, 1940–1949 (Arranged Chronologically)

| Artists/Performers and Shows | Dates |
| --- | --- |
| *Coast to Coast on a Bus* (also known as *The Children's Hour*) | 1924–1948 |
| Ed McConnell, *Smilin' Ed and His Buster Brown Gang* (also known as *The Buster Brown Show*) | 1929–1941; 1944–1953 |
| Don Carney (ne Howard Rice; 1897–1954), *Uncle Don* | 1929–1949 |
| Nila Mack (1891–1953), creator/director, *Let's Pretend* (originally *The Adventures of Helen and Mary*) | 1929–1954 |
| Ireene Wicker (1906–1987), *The Singing Story Lady* (stories accompanied by music for young children) | 1931–1941; 1945 |
| Mary Small (1922–1976), *The Mary Small Show* (music) | 1933–1937; 1941–1946 |
| *The Cinnamon Bear* (children's fantasy) | 1937–1955 |
| Gene Autry (1907–1998), *Gene Autry's Melody Ranch* | 1940–1943; 1945–1956 |
| Isabel Manning Hewson (active 1940s and 1950s), *Land of the Lost* (children's fantasy) | 1943–1948 |
| Roy Rogers (1911–1998), *The Roy Rogers Show* | 1945–1956 |
| *Adventures of Archie Andrews* (juvenile comedy; adapted from a popular comic strip) | 1945–1953 |
| *Juvenile Jury* (children's panel show) | 1946–1953 |
| *Lassie* (animal adventures) | 1947–1950 |

Cowboy legend Tom Mix (1880–1940) did not appear in the serial bearing his name; instead, professional radio actors impersonated him, but youngsters, gathered about a radio and hanging on every word, did not mind. The imaginary worlds created in the late-afternoon serials relied on a willing suspension of disbelief (often assisted by good sound effects) for their success.

The later serials of the war years, and also the self-contained adventure shows, became more realistic, more contemporary, and lost some of the innocence that had characterized those of the 1930s. Axis villains popped up with some regularity, and spies and secret weapons colored the plots. Don Winslow battled enemy ships and planes, Captain Midnight commanded the Secret Squadron, Terry left the pirates behind and focused on his Army Air Force duties, and Hop Harrigan ranged from Berlin to Okinawa. Schuyler (Sky) King came along too late for the war, but his Western flying adventures nevertheless provided thrills aplenty.

The radio serial died a lingering death in the late 1940s and early 1950s. A long-standing tradition for kids home from school, the excitement of waiting for the next episode of a favorite program began to pale amid the newfound wonders of a newly acquired **television** set.

Often relegated to inconvenient time slots and sometimes erratic in their scheduling, children's programming and their audience somehow found one another. The shows could be gentle and sweet (*Coast-to-Coast on a Bus*, *Let's Pretend*) or as violent as anything created in evening prime time for more mature audiences (*Terry and the*

TABLE 77.  Representative Radio Serials and Adventure Series, 1940–1949 (Arranged Chronologically)

| Title | Dates |
|---|---|
| *Little Orphan Annie* (serial) | 1930–1943 |
| *Buck Rogers in the 25th Century* (serial) | 1932–1940; 1946–1947 |
| *Jack Armstrong, the All-American Boy* (serial) | 1933–1951 |
| *The Lone Ranger* (series—self-contained stories) | 1933–1954 |
| *The Tom Mix Ralston Straight Shooters* (serial) | 1933–1951 |
| *Adventures of Frank Merriwell* (series—self-contained stories) | 1934–1949 |
| *Jungle Jim* (serial) | 1935–1952 |
| *Adventures of Dick Tracy* (serial) | 1934–1939; 1943–1947 |
| *The Green Hornet* (series—self-contained stories) | 1936–1952 |
| **Terry and the Pirates** (serial) | 1937–1939; 1941–1948 |
| *Don Winslow of the Navy* (serial) | 1937–1940; 1942–1943 |
| *Challenge of the Yukon* (series—self-contained stories) (also known as *Sergeant Preston of the Canadian Mounted Police,* 1951–1955) | 1938–1955 |
| *Captain Midnight* (serial) | 1939–1949 |
| *Mandrake the Magician* (serial) | 1940–1942 |
| *Adventures of Superman* (serial) | 1940–1951 |
| *The Sea Hound* (serial) | 1942–1944; 1946–1948; 1951 |
| *Hop Harrigan* (serial) | 1942–1950 |
| *Red Ryder* (series—self-contained stories) | 1942–1951 |
| *The Cisco Kid* (series—self-contained stories) | 1942–1956 |
| *Chick Carter, Boy Detective* (serial) | 1943–1945 |
| *Tennessee Jed* (serial) | 1945–1947 |
| *Sky King* (serial) | 1946–1954 |

*Pirates, Red Ryder*). But they had legions of fans, and sponsors were quick to be associated with the popular programs. By the 1950s, however, most of the children's shows had been cancelled, victims of the mass transition to television.

*See also:* Classical Music; Country Music; Radio Programming: Educational Shows; Westerns (Film); Youth

**Selected Reading**
Dunning, John. *On the Air: The Encyclopedia of Old-Time Radio.* New York: Oxford University Press, 1998.
Nachman, Gerald. *Raised on Radio.* Berkeley: University of California Press, 1998.
Stedman, Raymond William. *The Serials: Suspense and Drama by Installment.* Norman: University of Oklahoma Press, 1971.

# RADIO PROGRAMMING: COMEDY SHOWS

Throughout World War II, commercial **radio** provided a nonstop diet of entertainment. Along with music and variety shows, comedy programs dominated the evening hours, that time when listenership was at its greatest. Many of the most popular and enduring shows had their beginnings in the 1930s and simply carried over into the 1940s, but new comedians also found radio to their liking, especially in continuing series that came to be called situation comedies.

Amid the laughter, both shows and sponsors acknowledged the country's increasing involvement with the war. Patriotism—support your country, support the troops at home and abroad, buy bonds, save scrap, obey rationing restrictions, give blood—became a repeated theme, just as cheerfulness and good spirits provided some escape from the grim realities of combat. Most shows mixed these seemingly contradictory ideas skillfully, leaving the audience laughing in the best comic tradition.

Two pioneers of broadcasting, Freeman Gosden (1899–1982) and Charles Correll (1890–1972), created one of radio's first comedies, the trailblazing *Amos 'n' Andy*, in 1928. Although Gosen and Correll were white, their fictional cast—including Amos and Andy themselves, plus countless others—consisted of black characters. One of the first depictions of black life in then-segregated America, *Amos 'n' Andy* soon became one of the era's biggest hits, sustaining itself for over 30 years. A precursor of many of the situation comedies that dominated much programming in the immediate postwar period, its reliance on running gags and memorable characterizations made it a national favorite with all audiences.

From 1932 to 1958, comedian Jack Benny entertained radio listeners with his top-rated weekly show. A veteran of vaudeville, he knew how to fill the time with a mix of patter, music, sketches, and jokes. With a cast of regulars and loyal sponsors, The Jack Benny Program enjoyed consistently large audiences. (Photofest)

Veteran comedians like Fred Allen (1894–1956), Jack Benny (1894–1974), and **Bob Hope** (1903–2003) reached their greatest fame on radio, telling jokes and laughing along with their guests while being topical yet generally avoiding anything of much substance. Usually accompanied by some buoyant music, their humor served as a good pick-me-up during the war years. In a similar vein, three husband-wife teams—Goodman and Jane Ace (1899–1982; 1897–1974) on *Easy Aces,* George Burns and Gracie Allen (1896–1996; 1905–1964) on *The Burns and Allen Show,* and Jim and Marian Jordan (1896–1988; 1898–1961) on *Fibber McGee and Molly* brought domestic humor to the airwaves.

TABLE 78.  Selected Comedy Programming on American Radio, 1940–1949 (Arranged Chronologically)

| Selected Artists/Performers and Shows | Dates |
|---|---|
| Freeman Gosden and Charles Correll, *Amos 'n' Andy* | 1928–1960 |
| Goodman Ace and Jane Ace, *Easy Aces* | 1930–1948 |
| Chester Lauck and Norris Goff, *Lum and Abner* | 1931–1954 |
| Jack Pearl, *The Jack Pearl Show* | 1932–1936; 1948–1951 |
| Art Van Harvey and Bernardine Flynn, *Vic and Sade* | 1932–1946 |
| Ed Wynn, *The Texaco Fire Chief; The Perfect Fool* | 1932–1947 |
| Fred Allen, *The Fred Allen Show* | 1932–1949 |
| George Burns and Gracie Allen, *Burns and Allen* | 1932–1950 |
| Jack Benny, **The Jack Benny Program** | 1932–1958 |
| Bob Hope, *The Pepsodent Show* (other titles) | 1935–1959 |
| Jim Jordan & Marian Jordan, *Fibber McGee and Molly* | 1935–1959 |
| Milton Berle, *The Milton Berle Show* (other titles) | 1936–1949 |
| Fanny Brice, *Baby Snooks* | 1936–1951 |
| Edgar Bergen, *Edgar Bergen/Charlie McCarthy Show* | 1936–1956 |
| *The Tommy Riggs and Betty Lou Show* | 1938–1940; 1942–1943 |
| *Stop Me if You've Heard This One* | 1939–1948 |
| Penny Singleton and Arthur Lake, *Blondie* | 1939–1950 |
| *The Aldrich Family* | 1939–1953 |
| Red Skelton, *The Red Skelton Show* | 1939–1953 |
| *That Brewster Boy* | 1940–1945 |
| Bud Abbott and Lou Costello, *The Abbott & Costello Show* | 1940; 1942–1949 |
| *Meet the Meeks* | 1940–1949 |
| Henry Morgan, *Here's Morgan* | 1940–1950 |
| *A Date with Judy* | 1941–1950 |
| *Duffy's Tavern* | 1941–1951 |
| *The Great Gildersleeve* | 1941–1956 |
| *It Pays to Be Ignorant* | 1942–1951 |
| *Junior Miss* | 1942–1954 |
| Art Linkletter, *People Are Funny* | 1942–1959 |
| Joan Davis, *Leave It to Joan* | 1943–1950 |
| *Meet Corliss Archer* | 1943–1954 |
| Jack Carson, *The Campbell's Soup Program* | 1943–1956 |
| Alan Young, *The Alan Young Show* | 1944–1949 |
| William Bendix, *The Life of Riley* | 1944–1951 |
| Ozzie and Harriet Nelson, *Adventures of Ozzie & Harriet* | 1944–1953 |
| Eddie Bracken, *The Eddie Bracken Show* | 1945–1947 |
| *Adventures of Archie Andrews* | 1945–1953 |
| *Beulah* | 1945–1954 |
| Don Ameche and Frances Langford, *The Bickersons* | 1946–1951 |
| Marie Wilson, *My Friend Irma* | 1947–1954 |
| *Life with Luigi* | 1948–1953 |

Ventriloquist Edgar Bergen (1903–1978), always accompanied by his dummy Charlie McCarthy, made *The Edgar Bergen/Charlie McCarthy Show* a top hit for 20 years. It mattered little that audiences could not see the two, the illusion somehow worked. Another program akin to the Bergen/McCarthy series was *The Tommy Riggs and Betty Lou Show*. It featured the bivocal talents of Tommy Riggs (1908–1967), an entertainer who created Betty Lou, an imagined youngster who accompanied Riggs in his adventures. Riggs employed no dummy but relied on his voice alone for Betty Lou. Hardly the hit that Bergen achieved, it nonetheless illustrated the imaginative power of radio.

Using plots built around characters or events, situation comedies usually ran for 30 minutes on a weekly basis. Each new episode introduced a fresh story, although the cast and characters continued from week to week. The aforementioned *Amos 'n' Andy* established many of the conventions governing the genre, and it reached its height of popularity from roughly 1940 to 1950, although a number of series survived into the next decade. *Blondie, Duffy's Tavern, The Great Gildersleeve, Leave It to Joan, The Life of Riley,* and *The Adventures of Ozzie and Harriet* (which also starred another real-life couple, Ozzie and Harriet Nelson, 1906–1975; 1909–1994) reflect the variety to be found in situation comedies. In addition, a disproportionate number of programs focused on adolescents: *The Aldrich Family, A Date with Judy, Meet Corliss Archer, Junior Miss,* and *The Adventures of Archie Andrews*. Since many writers, educators, members of the medical community, and social critics took a heightened interest in the teenage years during the 1940s, the increasing representation of young adults in the entertainment field merely reflected this concern.

Always popular, radio comedies provided a respite from the cares of the day. From simple to sophisticated, they introduced new talents to the American public, as well as sustaining the careers of numerous entertainers whose lives went back to vaudeville and silent films.

*See also:* Comedies (Film); Comic Books; Comic Strips; Education; Health and Medicine; Race Relations and Stereotyping; Radio Programming: Music and Variety Shows; *Texaco Star Theater* (Milton Berle); War Bonds

**Selected Reading**

Barnouw, Erik. *A History of Broadcasting in the United States.* Vol. 1, *A Tower in Babel.* New York: Oxford University Press, 1966.

———. *A History of Broadcasting in the United States.* Vol. 2, *The Golden Web.* New York: Oxford University Press, 1968.

Dunning, John. *On the Air: The Encyclopedia of Old-Time Radio.* New York: Oxford University Press, 1998.

Lackman, Ron. *The Encyclopedia of American Radio.* New York: Checkmark Books, 2000.

# RADIO PROGRAMMING: DRAMA AND ANTHOLOGY SHOWS

Many **radio** shows, regardless of genre, that made their debuts during the 1930s proceeded to carry over into the 1940s. Good production values, along with effective scripting and top-rated stars, attracted substantial audiences and pleased sponsors. Music, comedy, and variety shows might be reliable standbys, but dramatic offerings grew in number during both decades, proof the medium could sustain a broad range of programming.

Anthology shows relied on constantly changing stories and characters instead of a continuing cast and connected stories. One week an ongoing series might present a classic tale by an established dramatist. The following week could offer a contemporary script by a new, unknown writer. Both serious and comedic productions often occurred within weeks of one another, and the overall appeal of particular pieces depended on audience preferences. With such a mixture on the season's program, quality varied; no show guaranteed a masterpiece each and every broadcast.

*The First Nighter Program,* which gave the illusion of an opening night at a fictional theater "off Times Square," featured a pleasant host (played by several actors over its long run) who informed the audience about the show. Although most of the *First Nighter* productions tended toward light, romantic comedies, they had a professional sheen, and the program continued on the air until 1953, one of the most successful anthologies.

Many other serious dramatic shows entered station schedules. In 1934, *The Lux Radio Theater* (Lux, a product of Lever Brothers, was a popular beauty soap of the day) premiered on NBC (National Broadcasting Company); shortly thereafter, it switched to CBS (Columbia Broadcasting System), where it remained for 20 years, a staple of network radio. This top-ranked anthology had as its host famed Hollywood director Cecil B. De Mille (1881–1959) until 1945. Each week, the series presented one-hour adaptations of leading motion pictures, utilizing, as often as possible, the same stars as had appeared in the movie version. The show served as an ideal way of publicizing films while at the same time illustrating the close connections between the two media, radio and **movies**.

Similar anthology-type shows likewise made their first appearances during the 1930s and carried over into the 1940s. With the war years, still more debuted—*Armstrong Circle Theater, The Radio Reader's Digest,* among others—with the last-named taking stories from the popular magazine and dramatizing them. Hallmark Cards began sponsoring this program in 1946, and it evolved into *The Hallmark Playhouse* in 1948, running until 1953, when it changed titles to *The Hallmark Hall of Fame;* it lasted until 1955. During the immediate postwar years, and before **television** took anthology drama to new heights, *The Ford Theater, Hollywood Star Preview, Family Theater,* and *Radio City Playhouse* also continued the tradition of presenting new and different dramatic productions on a weekly basis.

Four other shows presented dramatic tales of an entirely different kind. *Lights Out* pioneered the thriller/horror genre in 1934, something that radio, relying on the power of a listener's imagination, did extremely well. Originally on NBC, it shifted networks from 1942 onward, closing out its radio career on **ABC (American Broadcasting Company)** in 1947. Sound effects of a macabre nature—stabbings, breaking bones, violent deaths, and whatever else technicians needed to devise for aural thrills—characterized this popular, long-running series. Often more fright-inducing than anything the movies could openly show on the screen, *Lights Out* provided the sounds and listeners filled in the rest.

TABLE 79. Selected Drama and Anthology Programming on American Radio, 1940–1949 (Arranged Chronologically)

| Selected Artists/Performers and Shows | Dates |
| --- | --- |
| *Death Valley Days* (Western dramas) | 1930–1951 |
| *The First Nighter Program* | 1930–1953 |
| *Grand Hotel* | 1933–1940; 1944–1945 |
| *Irene Rich Dramas* (also known as *Woman from Nowhere*) | 1933–1944 |
| *Lights Out* (thriller, horror) | 1934–1947 |
| *Lux Radio Theater* | 1934–1955 |
| *Helen Hayes Theater* (also known as *The Electric Theater*) | 1935–1949 |
| *The Columbia Workshop* | 1936–1947 |
| *Silver Theater* | 1937–1944 |
| *Grand Central Station* | 1937–1953 |
| *Dr. Christian* | 1937–1954 |
| *The Campbell Playhouse* (originally *Mercury Theater on the Air,* 1938) | 1938–1941 |
| *Curtain Time* | 1938–1949 |
| *Screen Guild Players* | 1939–1951 |
| *Philip Morris Playhouse* | 1939–1953 |
| *Suspense* (thriller, horror) | 1940; 1942–1962 |
| *Inner Sanctum Mysteries* (thriller, horror) | 1941–1952 |
| *Stars Over Hollywood* | 1941–1954 |
| *Armstrong Circle Theater of Today* | 1941–1954 |
| *Radio Reader's Digest* (later *The Hallmark Playhouse* and then *The Hallmark Hall of Fame*) | 1942–1955 |
| Lionel Barrymore, *Mayor of the Town* | 1942–1949 |
| *Command Performance* (produced by Armed Forces Radio Service for military personnel overseas) | 1942–1949 |
| *Hollywood Star Time* | 1944; 1946–1947 |
| *Ford Theater* | 1947–1949 |
| *Hollywood Star Preview* (also known as *Hollywood Playhouse*) | 1947–1950 |
| *Escape* (thriller, horror) | 1947–1954 |
| *Family Theater* | 1947–1956 |
| *Radio City Playhouse* | 1948–1950 |

In 1941, NBC introduced *Inner Sanctum Mysteries* (most fans remember it simply as *Inner Sanctum*), a series in many ways similar to *Lights Out*. Opening with the sound of a creaking door, it welcomed the listener into a world of chills and even some ghoulish humor. Performers loved the show because it allowed for exaggerated dramatics, and it enjoyed a long radio life. CBS, which became the primary network for this kind of production, gained the broadcasting rights to *Inner Sanctum* in 1943, keeping it until 1950. It survived on ABC for an additional year, but the creaking door finally closed permanently in 1952. Old-time radio buffs will immediately recognize the trademark door, squeaks and all, possibly one of the most memorable of sound effects.

*Suspense* came on the air over CBS affiliates in 1942. Supposedly a crime series, it usually paid lip service to a mystery of some kind but concerned itself more with keeping audiences in a state of nervous apprehension—thus its title. Each week a new story would unfold, building listener anxiety, and resolution came only in the final minutes of the broadcast. Although it guaranteed no happy endings, top actors took roles on the show, just as on *Inner Sanctum.* Audiences, obviously fond of the scary nature of the scripting, kept *Suspense* in the CBS lineup until 1962, making it one of the last dramatic shows still being broadcast in the waning days of commercial radio.

Well aware of the devoted followings these shows created, CBS in 1947 introduced *Escape.* Usually not as bloodcurdling as its predecessors, the producers relied more on skillful plotting than sound effects. The stories, however, could be equally hair-raising and keep an audience on the edge of its seat. Despite its title, the tales frequently dwelt on the seeming impossibility of escape from situations or events. Unfortunately, CBS apparently could never find an ideal time for the show and moved it about without much rhyme or reason. Fans therefore faced the challenge of finding *Escape* at a given time or day, and yet the network kept it on the air, albeit erratically, until 1954.

On virtually any given evening, listeners could find dramatic anthologies or stand-alone dramas on their radio dials. These shows often displayed a high level of artistic creativity and allowed scriptwriters considerable latitude. The lack of a visual element in broadcasting gave production crews an opportunity to devise all manner of sound effects to compensate for its absence, resulting in an auditory experience that made audiences exercise their imaginations. Good writing and good sound, coupled with good actors, often resulted in exceptional radio programming.

*See also:* Broadway Shows (Musicals); Horror and Thriller Films; Magazines; Radio Programming: Comedy Shows; Radio Programming: Music and Variety Shows; Television

**Selected Reading**
Dunning, John. *On the Air: The Encyclopedia of Old-Time Radio.* New York: Oxford University Press, 1998.
Hilmes, Michele, and Jason Loviglio, eds. *Radio Reader: Essays in the Cultural History of Radio.* Florence, KY: Routledge, 2002.
MacDonald, J. Fred. *Don't Touch That Dial! Radio Programming in American Life, 1920–1960.* Chicago: Nelson-Hall, 1979.
Nachman, Gerald. *Raised on Radio.* Berkeley: University of California Press, 1998.

# RADIO PROGRAMMING: EDUCATIONAL SHOWS

In the early days of American **radio,** visionaries held great expectations about the educational potential of the new medium. Over 200 stations, many affiliated with colleges and universities, received broadcasting licenses to produce educational shows during the early 1920s. More than half were gone within a few years, their disappearance caused by financial constraints within their sponsoring institutions. Commercial stations took up some of the slack, but educational broadcasting continued to suffer throughout the Great Depression.

By the onset of the 1940s, only 35 educational stations remained on the air. Many of these utilized but a fraction of their available time to present anything fitting the educational description, focusing instead on entertainment. Several national committees, formed to study the relative absence of such stations, argued for creating separate, not-for-profit bandwidths on the AM (amplitude modulation) dial that would be reserved for educational purposes, but commercial interests, more concerned with profits than public service, disdained the idea and it floundered. Finally, with the introduction of new FM (frequency modulation) bandwidths, the Federal Communications Commission (FCC) allocated space at the low end of the FM broadcast band for noncommercial stations, which would include educational broadcasters. On a traditional analog FM dial, reading from left to right, the range extends from 87.5 megahertz (MHz) to 108 MHz. The low end of the range typically includes nonprofit stations from 87.5 to 92 MHz. Bandwidths above that become the domain of commercial interests. Today, most National Public Radio (NPR) stations, along with religious broadcasters, can be found at the numerically lower segment of the dial.

World War II put a halt to any expansion of FM broadcasting and the potential growth of educational stations. With the postwar years and growing prosperity, the future looked bright. Various organizations representing schools and allied academic pursuits, and led by the National Association of Educational Broadcasters, pushed for new FM station licenses, with the result that, from 1949 to 1950, almost 90 educational FM stations had come on the air. Most of them again had connections with colleges and universities. But these new start-up stations encountered unforeseen difficulties, including access to a large audience.

With the postwar buying spree to acquire consumer goods, radio manufacturers had directed their energies into mass producing ever-cheaper AM receivers, selling tens of millions of small, plastic table models between 1945 and 1949. Virtually all of these receivers, however, carried AM signals only, ignoring the FM market. Electronics companies allocated less than 6 percent of radio production to FM receivers. In addition, the readjustments made to FM bandwidths just prior to World War II rendered most existing FM receivers obsolete. To cap it off, postwar FM sets cost three to four times more than the cheap AM models rolling off assembly lines in the later 1940s. Not until late in the decade did combination AM-FM radios begin to appear in stores, in limited numbers and at much higher prices than AM-only units. Thus the dream of numerous FM stations broadcasting educational content to large, receptive audiences had to be put on hold until the 1950s and the creation of a larger consumer pool.

As Table 80 indicates, despite the promise and allure of educational programming, it seldom had much impact on actual station schedules. Among those programs that did come on the air, much of their content revolved around cooking and household advice, as found in *Women's Exchange, Neighbor Nell,* and *The Jack Berch Show*. They could be heard primarily in the morning or afternoon hours and targeted women in the audience. Others, like *The American School of the Air* and *The Music Appreciation Hour,* fulfilled the early goals of providing educational materials through radio and were heard in schools as well as homes. Historical dramatizations that combined top actors and good sound effects made the past come alive in NBC's *Cavalcade of America* and two memorable CBS productions, *You Are There* and *Hear It Now*.

**TABLE 80.** Selected Educational Programming on American Radio, 1940–1949 (Arranged Chronologically)

| Selected Hosts/Performers and Shows | Dates |
|---|---|
| *Betty Crocker* (cooking) | 1924–1953 |
| Walter Damrosch (1862–1950), *The Music Appreciation Hour* (music education) | 1928–1942 |
| Alma Kitchell (1893–1997), *Women's Exchange* (other titles) (household advice) | 1928–1942 |
| Everett Mitchell (1898–1990), *The National Farm and Home Hour* (agricultural reports, advice) | 1928–1958 |
| Allen Prescott (active 1930s–1940s), *The Wife Saver* (household hints) | 1929–1943 |
| Robert Ripley (1890–1949), *Believe It or Not* (unusual facts and information) | 1930–1948 |
| John MacPherson (1977–1962), *The Mystery Chef* (recipes, cooking advice) | 1930–1948 |
| Robert Trout (1909–2000), *The American School of the Air* (history, geography, and others; supplement to school courses) | 1930–1948 |
| Mary Lee Taylor (active 1930s–1950s), *The Mary Lee Taylor Program* (cooking, household advice) | 1933–1954 |
| Nellie Revell (1872–1958), *Neighbor Nell* (other titles) (household advice) | 1934–1943 |
| *Cavalcade of America* (dramatized history) | 1935–1953 |
| John J. Anthony (1902–1970), *Mr. Anthony—The Goodwill Hour* (marital, social, and financial advice) | 1936–1961 |
| Dave Elman (active 1930s–1940s), *Hobby Lobby* (information about various hobbies) | 1937–1946; 1949 |
| Jack Berch (active 1930s–1950s), *The Jack Berch Show* (household hints) | 1937–1954 |
| Albert Mitchell (active 1930s–1950s), *The Answer Man* | 1937–1956 |
| Katharine Lenroot (1891–1982), *The Child in Wartime* (child rearing advice) | 1942 |
| *The Man Behind the Gun* (war drama, military documentary) | 1942–1944 |
| John Daly (1914–1991), others, *You Are There* (historical recreations) | 1947–1950 |
| Edward Arnold (1890–1956), *Mr. President* (historical drama) | 1947–1953 |
| Edward R. Murrow (1908–1965), *Hear It Now* (historical recreations) | 1950–1951 |

As it did with so much radio programming, **television** delivered the knockout blow to educational broadcasting over the airwaves. The ability to add a visual component to aural content made most TV shows infinitely more appealing, especially to children. Watching an expert chef prepare a complex recipe surpassed, for most people, hearing that same chef describe each step in its preparation; scenes from history proved superior to reading from a text; and, from an important economic standpoint, sponsors for educational television could more easily be found than sponsors for educational radio. By the end of the 1940s, only a handful of shows survived, and most of them disappeared within a few years.

*See also:* Education; FM Radio; Food; Radio Programming: Children's Shows, Serials, and Adventure Series; Radio Programming: News, Sports, Public Affairs, and Talk; Radio Programming: Quiz Shows

**Selected Reading**
Dunning, John. *On the Air: The Encyclopedia of Old-Time Radio.* New York: Oxford University Press, 1998.
Sterling, Christopher H., and John M. Kitross. *Stay Tuned: A Concise History of American Broadcasting.* Belmont, CA: Wadsworth, 1990.

# RADIO PROGRAMMING: MUSIC AND VARIETY SHOWS

As American commercial **radio** went through the stages of defining itself in the late 1920s and early 1930s, producers frequently looked to the still-thriving vaudeville stage for inspiration. Music, comedy—variety—became the hallmark of many pioneering shows broadcast on the new medium. *The A & P Gypsies, The Happiness Boys,* and *The Ipana Troubadors* mixed music and patter, but in front of a microphone instead of from a theater stage. Fred Allen (1894–1956), Eddie Cantor (1892–1964), Jimmy Durante (1893–1980), and Al Jolson (1886–1950), veteran vaudevillians all, easily made the move into the radio studio, and their network shows enjoyed long runs. Audiences and sponsors liked their material, making music and variety one of the primary categories of radio programming during the 1930s and into the 1940s.

A look at Table 81 reveals the diversity of programming that occurred within this category and also illustrates how many of the listed shows had their beginnings in the 1930s or earlier and continued into the following decade. Even **country music** and cornpone humor had their niche, with *The National Barn Dance* and *Grand Ole Opry* setting records for longevity.

At the beginning of the 1940s, a number of new music and variety programs made their debuts, some reflecting the popularity of big bands and their vocalists. **Dinah Shore** (1917–1994), Ginny Simms (1915–1994), and **Frank Sinatra** (1915–1998) all came from this background, whereas Judy Canova (1913–1983) claimed a varied musical past, including **movies** and vaudeville, and ably carried on the traditions of country humor.

Knowing that maintaining troop morale constituted an important part of military strategy, the Armed Forces Radio Service (AFRS) began to take shape in 1942. Envisioned as a service for U.S. troops overseas, it at first used the broadcasting facilities of nations friendly to the United States. In time, however, AFRS began installing its own transmitters, creating a network that, by the end of 1943, consisted of over 300 outlets operating in 47 countries. That number swelled to over 800 outlets by 1945. Many of these AFRS stations operated in a mobile capacity, following troops through their campaigns, often close to the front lines. Portable transmitters, usually mounted on trucks, allowed these makeshift stations to inform and entertain soldiers, sailors, and pilots virtually anywhere.

Although AFRS broadcast prerecorded programming, the service also carried news and special events, such as sports, by shortwave relay. Its menu included a fair share of comedy and variety shows, but mainly it featured music, especially material found on V-Disc recordings. When and wherever troops turned their radio dials to an AFRS station, they could usually pick up the latest popular tunes.

On the home front, larger stations often retained studio bands. These groups did yeoman service and could feature lineups that included some of the best instrumentalists in the business. Their job consisted of playing for live commercials, providing background music for dramatic shows, backing singers and vocal groups, and generally being available whenever someone called for live music. More often than not, what they played

*Swing remained king in the early 1940s, and many radio shows featured big-name musicians. This picture shows (from the left) trombonist and bandleader Tommy Dorsey, the popular disc jockey Martin Block, and guest baseball star Joe DiMaggio. Although DiMaggio had no particular music credentials, he lent celebrity status to the proceedings. (Photofest)*

could be categorized as mundane. Few listeners considered the studio band the star of a show; who they accompanied received the attention. Studio orchestras nonetheless provided stable employment for countless musicians during the war years.

By the late 1930s, band remotes—direct wires from a radio station to a hotel or dance pavilion—were old hat for many orchestra leaders. Remotes allowed the music to be transmitted directly to a participating station, which in turn would broadcast it to unseen listeners, often recording the proceedings in the process. If a band got lucky, the station would have a network affiliation, and so the program went out to countless affiliates and helped mightily in making the aggregation known to a wide audience. In fact, just such a remote setup assured the success of bandleader **Glenn Miller** (1904–1944). He and his orchestra had played innumerable dances and had even cut some forgettable recordings for the Brunswick label. Despite the activity, the group seemed unable to inspire any great enthusiasm among listeners. In the summer of 1939, Miller landed a contract to play the Glen Island Casino, an elegant restaurant and ballroom on Long Island Sound. A series of remote broadcasts from that venue captured the attention of millions, which in turn sparked a flurry of best-selling Bluebird records, and soon Glenn Miller rocketed to the top in terms of popularity.

TABLE 81. Selected Music and Variety Programming on American Radio, 1940–1949 (Arranged Chronologically)

| Selected Artists/Performers and Shows | Dates |
|---|---|
| Various hosts, *The National Barn Dance* | 1924–1970 |
| Various hosts, *Grand Ole Opry* | 1925 to present |
| *Cities Service Concerts* | 1927–1944 |
| Lanny Ross, *The Lanny Ross Show* (other titles) | 1928–1942; 1946–1952 |
| Guy Lombardo, *The Guy Lombardo Show* | 1928–1946; 1949–1956 |
| *The Voice of Firestone* | 1928–1956 |
| Rudy Vallee, *Rudy Vallee Show, The Fleischmann Hour, The Sealtest Hour* (other titles) | 1929–1947 |
| Paul Whiteman, *Paul Whiteman Presents, Forever Tops* (other titles) | 1929–1952 (erratic) |
| Ben Bernie, *Ben Bernie, The Old Maestro* (other titles, including *The War Workers' Program,* 1941–1943) | 1930–1943 |
| Harry Frankel, *Singin' Sam, the Barbasol Man* | 1930–1947 |
| Morton Downey, *Songs by Morton Downey* (other titles) | 1930–1951 |
| **Bing Crosby,** various titles, including *The Music That Satisfies, Kraft Music Hall, The Chesterfield Show, Philco Radio Time* | 1930–1956 |
| Arthur Tracy, *The Street Singer* | 1931–1942 |
| Andre Kostelanetz, *Tune Up Time* (other titles) | 1931–1949 |
| Fred Waring, *Fred Waring and His Pennsylvanians* | 1931–1950 |
| *American Album of Familiar Music* | 1931–1951 |
| **Kate Smith,** *The Kate Smith Hour* | 1931–1952 |
| Eddie Cantor, *The Chase and Sanborn Hour* (other titles) | 1931–1954 |
| Al Jolson, *Kraft Music Hall, The Lifebuoy Program* (other titles) | 1932–1949 |
| *Manhattan Merry-Go-Round* | 1932–1949 |
| Various hosts and formats, *The Camel Caravan* | 1932–1949 |
| Mildred Bailey, *The Mildred Bailey Show* (other titles) | 1933–1945 |
| Eddie Duchin, *The Eddie Duchin Show* | 1933–1948 |
| Jimmy Durante, *The Jimmy Durante Show* | 1933–1950 |
| Don McNeill, *The Breakfast Club* | 1933–1954 |
| Pat Barrett, *Uncle Ezra's Radio Station* | 1934–1941 |
| Phil Spitalny, *The Hour of Charm* | 1934–1948 |
| Edward Bowes, *Major Bowes' Original Amateur Hour* | 1934–1952 |
| Bob Crosby, *The Camel Caravan* (also known as *The Bob Crosby Show*) | 1935–1950 |
| Horace Heidt, *The Horace Heidt Show* | 1935–1953 |
| Martin Block, other disc jockeys, *Make-Believe Ballroom* | 1935–1954 |
| Various hosts, *Your Hit Parade* | 1935–1957 |
| Jessica Dragonette, *Saturday Night Serenade* | 1936–1948 |
| Sammy Kaye, *Sammy Kaye Show* (other titles) | 1937–1946; 1950–1956 |
| Kay Kyser, *Kay Kyser's Kollege of Musical Knowledge* | 1937–1949 |
| *The NBC Symphony* | 1937–1953 |
| Various hosts, including Fred Allen, *The Texaco Star Theater* | 1938–1946 |
| Various hosts and formats, *The Fitch Bandwagon* | 1938–1948 |
| Glenn Miller, *Glenn Miller Show* (various titles including *Chesterfield Time, Sunset Serenade,* and *I Sustain the Wings*) | 1939–1944 |

| Selected Artists/Performers and Shows | Dates |
|---|---|
| Alec Templeton, *The Alec Templeton Show* | 1939–1948 |
| Dinah Shore, *The Dinah Shore Show* (other titles) | 1939–1955 |
| Various hosts, *Maxwell House Coffee Time* | 1940–1944 |
| *Gay Nineties Revue* (aka *Gaslight Revue*) | 1940–1945 |
| *Chamber Music Society of Lower Basin Street* | 1940–1952 |
| Donald Voorhees, *The Telephone Hour* | 1940–1958 |
| *Spotlight Bands* (produced by Armed Forces Radio Service for military personnel at home and abroad; also carried by network radio for civilians, it played under the title *Victory Parade of Spotlight Bands*) | 1941–1946 |
| Bob Burns, *The Arkansas Traveler* | 1941–1947 |
| Various hosts, *American Melody Hour* | 1941–1948 |
| Tom Breneman, *Breakfast in Hollywood* | 1941–1949 |
| *The Prudential Family Hour* | 1941–1949 |
| Ginny Simms, *Ginny Simms Show* (other titles) | 1941–1952 |
| *Stage Door Canteen* | 1942–1945 |
| *GI Journal* (produced by Armed Forces Radio Service for military personnel at home and abroad) | 1942–1946 |
| Judy Canova, *The Judy Canova Show* | 1943–1953 |
| Frank Sinatra, *The Frank Sinatra Show* (other titles) | 1943–1954 |
| Various artists, *The Chesterfield Supper Club* | 1944–1950 |
| **Spike Jones,** *Spike Jones and His City Slickers Show* | 1945–1949 |
| *Harvest of Stars* | 1945–1950 |
| Arthur Godfrey, *Arthur Godfrey Time* [in addition, *Arthur Godfrey's Talent Scouts]* | 1941–1945; 1945–1972; 1946–1956 |
| *The Railroad Hour* | 1948–1954 |

If, however, big band **swing** failed to meet a person's expectations, a further twist of the dial would reveal endless additional musical choices. Radio may have been perceived by many as appealing to the lowest common denominator, but in reality both the networks and local stations once saw **classical music** as a staple of radio programming. Not until the 1950s did serious composition commence its long, slow decline as a part of the broadcasting day. Many stations, including the networks, felt that programming featuring serious music increased the prestige behind the call letters, with the result that even tiny, low-power outlets usually carried some classical offerings, although everyone involved knew such shows drew a limited audience.

NBC (National Broadcasting Company) had its own NBC Symphony Orchestra, under the baton of the famed Arturo Toscanini (1867–1957); the program ran from 1937 until 1954. The equally renowned Leopold Stokowski (1882–1977) often conducted in Toscanini's absence. Not to be outdone, CBS arranged with the New York Philharmonic Orchestra, led by John Barbirolli (1936–1941) and Artur Rodzinski (1942–1947), for broadcasting rights. The show aired on Sunday afternoons.

Other classically oriented performances found on the networks during the 1940s included such groups as the distinguished Boston Symphony Orchestra, the Cleveland Symphony Orchestra, the Indianapolis Symphony Orchestra, along with *The Voice of*

*Firestone, General Motors Concerts, The Ford Sunday Evening Hour,* and *The Treasure Hour of Song.* Of course, no mention of classical music on radio would be complete without acknowledging Saturday afternoons and performances by the Metropolitan Opera. Premiering in 1931 on NBC, this show became a ritual for opera lovers everywhere and continued broadcasting throughout the war years and thereafter. Hosted by the urbane Milton Cross (1897–1975) from its beginnings until 1975, and sponsored by Texaco from 1940 onward, *The Metropolitan Opera* became one of the longest-running shows in radio history, a tribute to its unstinting quality of production.

By the end of the decade, the programming of popular music to the exclusion of other formats displayed a marked increase, rising to over 75 percent of the average broadcast day on most stations. The variety show, so important in radio's early days, also faded away. High production costs and the competition raised by similar programming on **television** sealed its doom. With the rise of FM (frequency modulation) around that same time, alternative forms of music, especially classical, could again be heard with some regularity. The popular song, the hit, had in the meantime come to dominate the AM airwaves.

*See also:* Advertising; Andrews Sisters, The; *ASCAP vs. BMI* Radio Boycott and the AFM Recording Ban; Broadway Shows (Musicals); FM Radio; Restaurants

**Selected Reading**

Dunning, John. *On the Air: The Encyclopedia of Old-Time Radio.* New York: Oxford University Press, 1998.

Jones, John Bush. *The Songs that Fought the War: Popular Music and the Home Front, 1939–1945.* Waltham, MA: Brandeis University Press, 2006.

Lackman, Ron. *The Encyclopedia of American Radio.* New York: Checkmark Books, 2000.

Young, William H., and Nancy K. Young. *American Music through History: The World War II Era.* Westport, CT: Greenwood Publishing Group, 2005.

# RADIO PROGRAMMING: NEWS, SPORTS, PUBLIC AFFAIRS, AND TALK

Entertainment—music and variety, comedy and drama—may have occupied a major part of the typical broadcasting day during the 1940s, but **radio** also served as an important carrier of news and information. The networks and their affiliates considered the coverage of current events a responsibility, an attitude reinforced by the FCC (Federal Communications Commission), the overseer of radio content. Most Americans still looked to their daily **newspapers** for a broader selection and more in-depth coverage of stories, but for breaking news and continuous updates, people increasingly listened to their radios. World War II, with its constantly shifting mosaic of campaigns, victories, and defeats, provided the medium a unique opportunity to demonstrate its importance in the timely reporting of daily happenings.

As the international situation deteriorated and the conflict grew in intensity, radio supplied late-breaking bulletins. Entertainment might remain radio's primary function, but listeners sought information along with escapism. Edward R. Murrow (1908–1965), for example, a member of the CBS (Columbia Broadcasting System) radio news team, brought unequalled sincerity and gravity to his reports. In mournful tones, he described the darkest days of late 1939 after war had broken out across Europe. His depictions of the London Blitz—sirens wailing in the background, the drone of enemy aircraft, the sound of exploding bombs—remain classic. Murrow's nightly introduction, "This...is London," foretold worse to come.

On the air, many newscasters, the word itself a relatively new coinage that often replaced "reporter" or "journalist" beginning around 1939, redefined the traditional image of a newspaper reporter. Along with Murrow, a significant number of newscasters rose to prominence during the course of World War II. This new breed, weaned on electronic newsgathering instead of newspaper beats, had begun to realize radio's potential during the 1930s and brought a measure of distinction to the networks. They introduced a personal aural style to their scripts and often added interpretive commentary to ongoing stories. News on the radio, no less colorful than that found in many newspapers, also offered the personality of the speaker.

**Some Notable Newscasters of the 1940s (Arranged Alphabetically)**

*Martin Agronsky* (1915–1999). While covering the war in Europe for NBC (National Broadcasting Company), Agronsky joined the new **ABC (American Broadcasting Company)** network in 1943; he remained there into the 1950s and pioneered **television** coverage of political events.

*Mel Allen* (1913–1996). Allen covered the New York Yankees' games throughout the 1940s, but he also did a number of radio shows for the Armed Forces Radio Service (AFRS) while in the army from 1943 to 1945. In addition, he announced most of the World Series and All-Star contests played in the 1940s and 1950s.

*Walter "Red" Barber* (1908–1992). A popular sportscaster, Barber served as the voice of the Brooklyn Dodgers throughout the 1940s. Later in the decade, he also made his first forays into television but remained at heart a radio announcer, continuing with baseball patter until 1966.

*Morgan Beatty* (1902–1975). A commentator as well as a reporter, Beatty anchored NBC's *News of the World* from 1944 to 1967.

*Boake Carter* (1899–1944). A veteran news correspondent, Carter freely editorialized during the 1930s, bringing himself some notoriety but costing the support of sponsors and eventually the backing of CBS. He later made noncontroversial war broadcasts over the **MBS (Mutual Broadcasting System)** until his death in 1944.

*Charles Collingwood* (1917–1985). One of "Murrow's Boys," a group of newscasters recruited by Edward R. Murrow and associated with CBS during the war years, Collingwood covered many events during the conflict. He later moved to CBS television.

*John Daly* (1914–1991). A distinguished newsman, busy on many fronts during World War II, Daly nonetheless reached his largest audience as the urbane host of *What's My Line?* a popular television quiz show that ran on CBS from 1950 to 1967.

*Elmer Davis* (1890–1958). A prominent announcer on CBS beginning in 1939, he left the network in 1942 to assume the post of director of the Office of War

Information (OWI). He returned to radio, but with ABC, in 1945, and remained a top reporter until 1955.

*Alex Dreier* (1916–2000). A wartime reporter for NBC, Dreier remained with the network until 1956, when he moved to ABC and its television news operation.

*Don Dunphy* (1908–1998). A sportscaster, Dunphy covered the busy New York **boxing** scene from 1939 until 1981, providing ringside commentary on over 2,000 bouts, including a long tenure with Gillette's popular *Fight of the Week*.

*Douglas Edwards* (1917–1990). A fixture at CBS, Edwards joined the network in 1942; he rose through the ranks, anchoring several news programs. The network tapped him to be the primary announcer on its nightly television news broadcast when it premiered in 1948. He would remain at the helm of the show until 1962.

*Richard Harkness* (1907–1977). Harkness worked with NBC from 1943 until 1970, covering myriad news events.

*Joseph C. Harsch* (1905–1998). A print reporter for the *Christian Science Monitor* from 1929 to 1988, Harsch concurrently worked with CBS radio during the 1940s and later for NBC and ABC. His wide-ranging reports about the war and the rise of Communism made him an influential radio commentator.

*Gabriel Heatter* (1890–1972). A popular Mutual newsman remembered for his colorful opening line, "Ah, there's good news tonight!" Even in the bleakest days of the war, Heatter could find some optimistic bits in the reports he read. He remained with the network from 1935 to 1961.

*Richard C. Hottelet* (b. 1917). The last survivor of the famed Murrow's Boys, he could boast of being briefly imprisoned by the Gestapo, covering **D-Day,** getting shot down and bailing out over Germany, as well as later meeting many of the principals of the **Cold War.** He has remained active into the 21st century.

*Chet Huntley* (1911–1974). Huntley first worked with CBS, beginning in 1939 as a news reporter. He moved to ABC in 1951 but achieved his greatest fame as the partner of David Brinkley (1920–2003) on NBC's highly rated television news show, the nightly *Huntley-Brinkley Report,* which premiered in 1956.

*Ted Husing* (1901–1962). Another pioneering sportscaster, Husing's ability to speak rapidly but understandably allowed him to cover the action in a game and not fall behind. He worked primarily at CBS, but in 1946 left the network and became a successful radio disc jockey. He also continued with limited sports broadcasting into the 1950s.

*H. V. Kaltenborn* (1878–1965). A radio veteran, Kaltenborn began his career as an announcer with CBS in 1928 and joined NBC in 1940, remaining there until 1955. Highly esteemed in his profession and a learned, multilingual man, he offered analyses of events along with straight reportage and could talk with most world leaders without the aid of a translator.

*Larry LeSueur* (1909–2003). Yet another of Murrow's Boys, LeSueur in World War II made the first broadcast from liberated Paris. In the postwar era, he won awards for the quality of his reporting from the **United Nations.** He later worked with the **Voice of America.**

*Clem McCarthy* (1882–1962). A famous sportscaster specializing in calling **horse racing** and boxing matches, usually for NBC. Millions of radio listeners could immediately recognize his distinctive, gravelly voice.

*Edward R. Murrow* (1908–1965). The dean of radio journalists during the 1940s, Murrow joined CBS in 1935; his job involved recruiting promising young reporters, who came to be called Murrow's Boys, in order to build an effective news team for the network. Active throughout Europe in the dark days preceding World War II, he eventually took the microphone himself and gave memorable descriptions of the German takeover of the continent; his live broadcasts from London during the 1940 Blitz electrified his growing audience. He later flew aboard U.S. bombing missions over enemy territory, giving listeners at home an intimate presentation of the air war. He also described, in chilling detail, the liberation of some of the Nazi concentration camps. In the postwar era, Murrow worked with the CBS evening news and in 1950 created and narrated *Hear It Now,* a weekly radio newsmagazine that recreated top stories through tapes and skillful editing. But the show came too late for radio, and Murrow therefore made the aural visual by designing *See It Now* in 1951, a change that marked his move to television and the beginnings of a second distinguished career.

*Eric Sevareid* (1912–1992). A newspaper reporter recruited by Edward R. Murrow for CBS, Sevareid covered the war from unusual places. His plane went down in Burma and he had to trek through uncharted jungles to make his escape; he later reported from the rugged mountains of Yugoslavia while camped with partisans fighting the Nazis. After the war, Sevareid could be heard regularly with the evening news, but he also created special reports for CBS, again traveling widely. After 1950, he moved to television as a correspondent.

*William L. Shirer* (1904–1993). A long-time European correspondent and one of the first newsmen hired by Edward R. Murrow, Shirer, like many other reporters at this time, came from a print background. A close associate of Murrow's from the beginning, the two made many broadcasts from Europe, their main focus. Shirer spent considerable time in Berlin in the early days of the war before the United States became involved, and he compiled his reports in *Berlin Diary,* a 1941 best seller. He continued with CBS until 1947, when he and Murrow had a falling-out; he then briefly went with MBS but finally left broadcasting altogether to focus on writing.

*Frank Singiser* (1909–1982). A former radio pitchman for various products and an announcer on *Your Hit Parade* in 1935, Singiser became a successful newscaster for Mutual in 1938 and continued there throughout the war and on into the 1950s.

*Howard K. Smith* (1914–2002). After a brief stint with newspapers, Smith became one of Murrow's Boys in 1940. He served as a CBS correspondent based in Berlin before the entry of the United States into the war. His 1942 book, *Last Train from Berlin,* sold well and details events immediately following those presented in William L. Shirer's *Berlin Diary,* published the preceding year. Smith enjoyed a distinguished later career from 1962 to 1979 as a newscaster and anchor for ABC television.

*Bill Stern* (1907–1971). Along with Red Barber, Bill Stern reigned as one of the leading sportscasters of the 1940s. As host of *The Colgate Sports Newsreel,* Stern got to tell stories, interview athletes, and entertain celebrity guests. The show ran on NBC from 1937 until 1953. In addition, he also regularly covered boxing matches and **baseball** games. In the 1950s, he went with ABC and its televised sports offerings.

*John Cameron Swayze* (1906–1995). Listeners first heard Swayze's voice in 1944 on the West Coast through NBC's Los Angeles news division; in 1947, the network moved him to its New York offices. Two years later, he had been tapped to anchor its new television news offering, *The Camel News Caravan.* For a short while, Swayze possessed one of the best-known faces on TV. He lost that distinction when NBC replaced him in 1956 with the team of Chet Huntley and David Brinkley and inaugurated *The Huntley-Brinkley Report.* He continued to be seen, however, thanks to numerous commercials and occasional appearances on entertainment shows.

*Raymond Gram Swing* (1887–1968). A print journalist, Swing broke into radio in 1932 covering the national elections. After refusing a job at CBS (the one Edward R. Murrow eventually took), he signed on with Mutual as a commentator, speaking to his radio audience learnedly about the oncoming war. He left Mutual in 1942, taking his considerable expertise to NBC, and later ABC, for much of the remainder of the decade.

*Lowell Thomas* (1892–1981). Thomas's radio career encompassed 46 years, running from 1930 until 1976. After a colorful career as a world traveler and author, he had established his fame and signed with CBS as a news announcer. Two years later, he went with NBC, remaining there until 1947, and then returned to CBS until his retirement. One of the highest-paid newsmen anywhere, Thomas also lectured widely and wrote books about his adventures. His voice can be heard narrating the Fox Movietone newsreels, seen nightly in countless theaters. He always closed his broadcasts with his trademark phrase, "So long until tomorrow."

*Robert Trout* (1909–2002). Among his many accomplishments over a long career, Trout coached Edward R. Murrow on how to talk into a microphone effectively. Already at CBS when Murrow came on board, Trout remained with the network until 1948, anchoring many news specials, particularly the 1944 D-Day invasion of Europe. He broadcast for NBC until 1952 and then returned to CBS. For many years, he also hosted *The American School of the Air,* a long-running (1930–1948) educational program on CBS. In the meantime, Trout also moved into television news for both NBC and CBS.

Another kind of journalist also gained an audience during the 1930s and 1940s: the electronic gossip columnist. Coming from backgrounds with the newspaper tabloids and movie fan **magazines** that had become established reading during the Roaring Twenties, writers like Jimmy Fidler (1900–1988), Hedda Hopper (1885–1966), Louella Parsons (1881–1972), Drew Pearson (1897–1969), Adela Rogers St. Johns (1894–1988), Ed Sullivan (1901–1974), and Walter Winchell (1897–1972) created gossip-oriented shows that audiences loved. Relying on tidbits and innuendo about the most popular (or notorious) celebrities of the day, these rumormongers became celebrities in their own right, occasionally engaging in real and fabricated on-air feuds with one another.

On the other hand, serious discussion shows, their topics often taken from current headlines, also found a place on station schedules. Usually categorized as public affairs programming, they attracted experts in various fields, and lively conversations ensued.

TABLE 82. Selected Public Affairs and Talk Programming on American Radio, 1940–1949 (Arranged Chronologically)

| Selected Columnists, Hosts, and Shows | Dates |
|---|---|
| Eleanor Roosevelt (1884–1962) (talk) | Various years, irregular, 1930–1951 |
| Walter Winchell, *Walter Winchell's Jergens Journal* (news and gossip) | 1930–1957 |
| Various hosts, especially Westbrook Van Voorhis (1903–1968), *The March of Time* (dramatized interpretations of world events) | 1931–1945 |
| John Howe (active 1930s and 1940s), moderator. *The University of Chicago Round Table* (public affairs) | 1931–1955 |
| Ed Sullivan, *The Ed Sullivan Show* (celebrity gossip) | 1932–1946 |
| Jimmy Fidler, *The Jimmy Fidler Show* (gossip) | 1934–1950 |
| Mary Margaret McBride (1899–1976), *Mary Margaret McBride* (talk and interviews) | 1934–1954 |
| George V. Denny Jr. (1899–1959), *America's Town Meeting of the Air* (public affairs) | 1935–1956 |
| Theodore Granik (1906–1970), *Mutual Forum Hour* (also known as *American Forum of the Air*) (public affairs) | 1935–1956 |
| *We, the People* (human interest) | 1936–1951 |
| Fulton Lewis Jr. (1903–1966), *Top of the News from Washington* (political commentary) | 1937–1957 |
| Hedda Hopper, *The Hedda Hopper Show* (gossip) | 1939–1951 |
| Drew Pearson, *Drew Pearson Comments* (news and commentary) | 1941–1953 |
| *Leave It to the Girls* (talk) | 1945–1949 |
| Galen Drake (1906–1989), *This Is Galen Drake* (news and commentary) | 1945–1958 |
| Tex McCrary (1910) and Jinx Falkenburg (1919–2003), *Hi Jinx, Tex and Jinx* (talk) | 1946–1959 |
| Various hosts, *Meet the Press* (public affairs) | 1947–1956 |

With the rise of television, most of this form of radio broadcasting either disappeared by the mid-1950s or made the transition to the new medium.

The postwar era seldom offered the day-to-day drama that World War II had provided, but with the sizable corps of newscasters the networks had assembled during the war years, they were reluctant to part with their services. Five-, 10-, and 15-minute newsbreaks became commonplace on stations around the nation, with occasionally longer morning and evening presentations. And then television entered the scene in the later 1940s and quickly introduced news shows of its own. As noted above, many of the best-known reporters moved to the new medium, although some performed double duties, broadcasting on both radio and television slots, at least for a time.

By the end of the decade, with television clearly in the ascendancy and radio in decline, stations cut back news-oriented programming. Brief, on-the-hour summations of the biggest stories, seldom without any analysis, along with box scores and short stock market reports, became the rule. Wire feeds replaced staff reporters, usually read by disc jockeys or other non-news station announcers. The heyday of radio news, 1939 to 1947—less than a decade in length—had drawn to a close.

*See also:* Best Sellers; Football; Louis, Joe

**Selected Reading**

Cloud, Stanley, and Lynne Olson. *The Murrow Boys: Pioneers on the Front Lines of Broadcast Journalism.* New York: Mariner Books, 1997.

Dunning, John. *On the Air: The Encyclopedia of Old-Time Radio.* New York: Oxford University Press, 1998.

Edwards, Bob. *Edward R. Murrow and the Birth of Broadcast Journalism.* Hoboken, NJ: John Wiley, 2004.

# RADIO PROGRAMMING: QUIZ SHOWS

The first **radio** quiz shows, which premiered in the 1930s, promised no great wealth; most awarded inconsequential prizes to winners, and some offered no prizes at all. The era of huge cash awards did not come until the 1950s and the rise of **television.** Radio quizzes served as prelude to the likes of TV's scandal-ridden, big-money shows such as *$64,000 Question* (1955–1958; 1955's $64,000 would be equivalent to approximately $514,000 in 2008 dollars.) and *Twenty-One* (1956–1958).

An early, informal radio quiz originated with *Vox Pop,* which made its debut in 1935 and ran until 1948. Interviewers would question passersby on city streets, and the respondents' spontaneous answers constituted most of the show. Correct answers to silly questions might earn $5 or so (about $75 in 2008 dollars) and perhaps an inexpensive token from a local store. But the formula (question + correct answer = reward) proved popular on the air, and many other shows soon followed suit.

*Professor Quiz* and *Dr. I.Q.,* two other pioneers that also carried into the 1940s, come much closer to the modern concept of a quiz program. Oriented toward awarding correct answers instead of giving interviews, contestants had to respond to serious questions within a specified time limit. Winners were awarded silver dollars on the spot, although the amounts were initially in the $25 range (or about $375 in 2008 dollars). As the audiences for *Professor Quiz* and *Dr. I.Q.* grew, so did the prizes, and the 1940s saw occasional winnings in excess of $3,000 (more than $43,000 in 2008 dollars). Different actors, largely unknown outside radio circles, played the resident hosts, but the rapid-fire format remained the same.

Writer and critic Clifton Fadiman (1904–1999) hosted *Information, Please!* and newspaper and magazine columnists Franklin Pierce Adams (1881–1960; he used the pen name FPA in much of his writing) and John Kieran (1892–1981) served as two of the erudite panelists on this long-running show. Fadiman asked questions submitted by listeners, and the panel—other intellectuals joined Adams and Kieran on a revolving basis—would proceed to give witty and extended answers. No prizes went to the panelists, but small awards—including a set of the *Encyclopaedia Britannica* and, in a wartime patriotic gesture, **war bonds**—were given to those people whose questions stumped the experts. For the panelists, clever banter sufficed (along with a healthy salary for the regulars), and moderator Fadiman cheerfully joined in the ongoing conversations.

Music played a role in several shows. Bandleaders Kay Kyser (1905–1985) and Sammy Kaye (1910–1987) fronted programs that focused more on **dance** tunes than braininess; Kyser's *Kay Kyser's Kollege of Musical Knowledge* asked silly questions of participants, whereas Kaye's *So You Want to Lead a Band?* allowed members of the audience a chance to conduct, with the winners receiving batons. In *Beat the Band,* listeners submitted questions to be asked of the musicians in the house orchestra; if a question "beat the band," the lucky listener received the grand sum of $20 (about $265 in 2008 dollars).

Two virtually identical shows, *The Singing Bee* and *Singo,* had contestants guessing song titles and putting them together to create stories. Winners could win $4 to $8 (or $50 to $100 in 2008 dollars), typical of the prizes awarded in those days. Finally, *Stop the Music,* a latecomer to the radio quiz rolls, enticed listeners with larger monetary prizes. The house band would begin playing a familiar pop song, and then suddenly host Bert Parks (1914–1992) would shout "stop the music!" over the air. A random telephone call would then be placed, and if the answering party had been listening to the show and could identify the song, he or she became eligible to guess the name of another song, usually something obscure. A second correct identification led to huge jackpots of $20,000 or more (or over $180,000 in 2008 dollars). Missing the question meant that the jackpot grew until the next call.

Many other quiz shows dotted station calendars during the later 1940s. Youngsters got into the act with the popular *Quiz Kids,* a durable show that went on for 13 seasons. Borrowing from the format established by *Information, Please!* a panel of five exceedingly bright young people, all under 16 years of age, weekly amazed audiences with their breadth of knowledge and math skills. The panelists changed, the three winningest ones advancing to the next week's production, the remaining two replaced with fresh faces. The moderator, Joe Kelly (1902–1959), previously a host with *The National Barn Dance,* kept matters down to earth and reasonably understandable for listeners. Each panelist received a $100 war bond for his or her efforts.

One of the last quiz shows to be heard on radio mixed snappy repartee with its questions. Comedian Groucho Marx (1890–1977), a former vaudevillian and movie star, finished out his career as the amusing host and interviewer of *You Bet Your Life.* Unlike most radio shows of the 1950s, *You Bet Your Life* survived until 1959, well into the television era. In fact, it also went to television in 1950, and viewers could watch, on prerecorded film, the radio show. This process of broadcasting the audio portion of a television production has come to be called simulcasting. Although the radio version ended in 1959, the TV series played until 1961. People listened to (and watched) *You Bet Your Life* for the exchanges between Groucho and his guests, not for the questions, which were usually inconsequential, or for the prizes, which consisted of small amounts of money. If, however, a contestant could not seem to answer anything correctly, Groucho would wind up the proceedings with "Who was buried in Grant's tomb?"

With only a few exceptions, quiz shows on radio during the 1940s attracted listeners least of all for the prizes. Instead, these programs found steady audiences because of their hosts, panelists, or format. The sophisticated wit displayed on *Information, Please!* the remarkable intellects of *The Quiz Kids,* and the shenanigans found on a number of musically oriented programs kept people coming back for more. Easy and inexpensive (with the exception of the big-money entries, of which there were

**TABLE 83.** Selected Quiz Show Programming on American Radio, 1940–1949 (Arranged Chronologically)

| Selected Artists/Performers and Shows | Dates |
|---|---|
| *Vox Pop* (also known as *Sidewalk Interviews*) | 1935–1948 |
| *Professor Quiz* | 1936–1948 |
| *True or False?* | 1936–1956 |
| *Battle of the Sexes* | 1938–1941; 1941–1943 |
| *Information, Please!* | 1938–1952 |
| *Kay Kyser's Kollege of Musical Knowledge* | 1938–1949 |
| *Dr. I.Q.* | 1939–1950 |
| *Pot O' Gold* | 1939–1940; 1946–1947 |
| *The Singing Bee* | 1940–1941 |
| *Beat the Band* | 1940–1944 |
| *Can You Top This?* | 1940–1951 |
| *Double or Nothing* | 1940–1953 |
| *The Quiz Kids* | 1940–1954 |
| *$64 Question* (also known as *Take It or Leave It*) | 1940–1956 |
| *Truth or Consequences* | 1940–1956 |
| *Singo* | 1942–1944 |
| *It Pays to Be Ignorant* | 1942–1951 |
| *Bob Hawk Show* (also known as *Thanks to the Yanks*) | 1942–1953 |
| *Ladies Be Seated* | 1944–1950 |
| *The Missus Goes A Shoppin'* | 1944–1950 |
| *Quick As a Flash* | 1944–1951 |
| *Give and Take* | 1945–1954 |
| *Break the Bank* | 1945–1955 |
| *House Party* | 1945–1956 |
| *Queen for a Day* | 1945–1958 |
| *Winner Take All* | 1946–1949 |
| *So You Want to Lead a Band?* | 1946–1950 |
| *Twenty Questions* | 1946–1954 |
| *Grand Slam* | 1947–1953 |
| *Strike It Rich* (also known as *Strike It Lucky*) | 1947–1955 |
| *Hit the Jackpot* | 1948–1950 |
| *Sing It Again* | 1948–1951 |
| *Stop the Music* | 1948–1955 |
| Groucho Marx, *You Bet Your Life* | 1948–1956 |

few) to produce, with simple sets and little scripting, quiz shows also pleased sponsors and networks. As a result, they sustained themselves well throughout the decade and primed listeners for the onslaught of quiz shows that would appear on television screens in the 1950s.

***See also:*** Book Clubs; Country Music; Magazines; Newspapers; Radio Programming: Comedy Shows; Radio Programming: Educational Shows; Radio Programming: Music and Variety Shows; Swing

**Selected Reading**

Douglas, Susan J. *Listening In: Radio and the American Imagination.* Minneapolis: University of Minnesota Press, 2004.

Dunning, John. *On the Air: The Encyclopedia of Old-Time Radio.* New York: Oxford University Press, 1998.

Hilmes, Michele. *Radio Voices: American Broadcasting, 1922–1952.* Minneapolis: University of Minnesota Press, 1997.

Nachman, Gerald. *Raised on Radio.* Berkeley: University of California Press, 1998.

# RADIO PROGRAMMING: SOAP OPERAS

Music, along with comedy and variety, may have dominated American **radio** programming during the 1940s, but soap operas held their own as well. Continuing stories that introduce vividly emotional characters and plotting—unfaithful husbands, conniving wives, romantic triangles, ungrateful children—all presented in melodramatic fashion, along with a helping of pathos and even an occasional dash of bathos, they usually focus on the tormented love lives of their many characters. These programs emerged as a major component of the broadcasting day early in the 1930s and lessened in popularity not at all with a new decade, a world war, and returning prosperity.

Christened soap operas because leading soap companies, such as Procter and Gamble, Lever Brothers, Colgate-Palmolive, and others, sponsored most of them, plus their emotion-laden plots brought to mind some characteristics of opera. Canny broadcasters and sponsors, working on the supposition that women would form most of the radio audience for these programs, positioned them in the late morning and early afternoon hours, before the kids came home from school or husbands from work. In creating these shows, producers surmised that men would not only be unavailable, but also that they would be uninterested, allowing the soaps to develop as a small but significant niche area of radio created for women.

For housewives and anyone else with idle time on their hands, although clearly the huge soap opera audiences went beyond stereotypes, the daily stories dished up a large helping of escapism. Writers deliberately featured molasses-like pacing in their plotting; if a listener missed an episode or two, it required little or no catching up, and their simple structure and black-and-white characters required minimal attentiveness. True to their perceived audience, these shows emphasized women—their love lives, their families, and the trials and tribulations of contemporary domestic life. Most of these serials displayed blatant gender biases, but listeners ignored that aspect or did not see themselves reflected. Whatever the answer, audiences maintained a high level of enthusiasm and remained remarkably faithful to their favorites, tuning in week after week and, in many cases, year after year.

Like most **movies** of the period, soap operas of the 1940s broke no cultural boundaries and instead affirmed traditions: marriage, family, and friends. Moralistic, conservative, and frequently set in rural locales, the stories took a varied set of characters and cast them into dramatic situations, and it followed that good, solid American values eventually won the day, although the convoluted plots might require a seeming eternity to reach resolution. When a story finally wound down, the primary players squared their shoulders and resolutely marched on to the next problem, reassured by the verities expressed along the way in the story. There existed no problem too great, no situation too complex, for their simplistic solutions. And, although the crises may be never-ending, listeners enjoyed the certitude that when a story eventually reached its inevitable conclusion, a new calamity awaited in the succeeding episode.

Several individuals, especially writer Irna Phillips (1901–1973) and the production team of Anne and Frank Hummert (1905–1996; 1882–1966), rose to become leading names in the genre. Phillips, often called the mother of the soap opera, developed *Painted Dreams* for Chicago's WGN in 1930. It ran until the early 1940s and generally receives credit as the first true radio soap opera. Serendipitously, it also had a detergent, Chipso Soapflakes, as one of its sponsors. Utilizing the techniques of melodramatic love stories then appearing in women's **magazines** as well as some romantic film antecedents, Phillips touched a nerve in her listening audience and penned a succession of similar serials, such as *Today's Children* (1933–1937, 1943–1950), *The Guiding Light* (1937–1956), *The Right to Happiness* (1939–1960), and several others, most of which enjoyed long runs during the 1940s (see table below).

Whereas Phillips wrote millions of words a year when creating scripts for her multiple shows, Anne and Frank Hummert did not write their many series, but instead created an agency devoted to their production. The couple reportedly demanded much of their writers and performers but, by maintaining high standards, assured quality technical values. Sponsors agreed, and the Hummerts accounted for over half the **advertising** revenue generated by soap operas. At times, their agency simultaneously supervised as many as 15 different serials (see table below). Popular titles like *Just Plain Bill* (1932–1955), *Ma Perkins* (1933–1960), *The Romance of Helen Trent* (1933–1960), and *Our Gal Sunday* (1937–1959) came from the efficient Hummert operation. For Irna Phillips and Anne and Frank Hummert, along with any other individuals with a successful background in the genre, the rise of **television** simply presented fresh opportunities for expansion. As radio declined, more than half a dozen series made the transition to the new medium and went on entertaining audiences just as they had in years past.

Few series involved big-name actors; cheaply produced and with small budgets, the soap opera world worked on the proverbial shoestring. Players would breathlessly rush from studio to studio, soundstage to soundstage, in order to act out their assigned roles in multiple dramas.

Table 84 lists, alphabetically, with dates and networks, 46 of the more popular and enduring soap operas that could be heard during the 1940s. A number of others also existed during this time, but many had brief runs or were syndicated, available only to those stations that subscribed to them for a fee. By the early 1950s, only about 29 radio soap operas remained on the air (NBC [National Broadcasting Company] with 14, CBS [Columbia Broadcasting System] with 14, **ABC [American Broadcasting Company]** with 1), and by 1959 the number had shrunk to 14, with 5 on NBC and 9 on CBS. The ABC network had by that time dropped all soap opera programming. NBC canceled the last of its productions in late 1959, leaving CBS the lone carrier of the soaps, and, in November 1960, an era came to a quiet close when it simultaneously axed its handful of remaining shows.

TABLE 84. Selected Soap Operas on American Radio during the 1940s (Arranged Alphabetically)

| Title | Network(s), Dates, Comments |
| --- | --- |
| *Against the Storm* | NBC, 1939–1942; Mutual, 1949; ABC, 1951–1952 |
| *Arnold Grimm's Daughter* | CBS, 1937–1938; NBC, 1938–1942; produced by Anne and Frank Hummert |
| *Aunt Jenny's True Life Stories* | CBS, 1937–1956 |
| *Aunt Mary* | NBC, 1942–1951 |
| *Bachelor's Children* | CBS, 1936–1941; NBC, 1941–1942; CBS, 1942–1946 |
| *Backstage Wife* | Mutual, 1935–1936; NBC, 1936–1955; CBS, 1955–1959; produced by the Hummerts |
| *Big Sister* | CBS, 1936–1952 |
| *Brave Tomorrow* | NBC, 1943–1944 |
| *Bright Horizon* | CBS, 1941–1945 |
| *The Brighter Day* | NBC, 1948–1949; CBS, 1949–1956; scripted by Irna Phillips; went to TV, 1954 |
| *David Harum* | NBC, 1936–1947; CBS, 1947–1950; NBC, 1950–1951; produced by the Hummerts |
| *Front-Page Farrell* | NBC, 1942–1954; produced by the Hummerts |
| *The Guiding Light* | NBC, 1937–1946; CBS, 1947–1956; scripted by Phillips; went to TV, 1952 |
| *Hilltop House* | CBS, 1937–1941, 1948–1955; NBC, 1956–1957 |
| *John's Other Wife* | NBC, 1936–1942; produced by the Hummerts |
| *Joyce Jordan, M.D.* | CBS, 1938–1945; NBC, 1945–1948; ABC, 1951–1952; NBC, 1955 |
| *Just Plain Bill* | CBS, 1932–1936; NBC, 1936–1955; produced by the Hummerts |
| *Life Can Be Beautiful* | NBC, 1938; CBS, 1938–1946; NBC, 1946–1954 |
| *The Light of the World* | NBC, 1940–1950 |
| *Lone Journey* | NBC, 1940–1943, 1946–1947; ABC, 1951–1952 |
| *Lora Lawton* | NBC, 1943–1950; produced by the Hummerts |
| *Lorenzo Jones* | NBC, 1937–1955; produced by the Hummerts |
| *Ma Perkins* | NBC, 1933–1942; NBC and CBS, 1942–1949; CBS, 1949–1960; produced by the Hummerts |
| *Myrt and Marge* | CBS, 1931–1942 |
| *One Man's Family* | NBC, 1932–1959; an evening show instead of daytime |
| *The O'Neills* | Mutual, 1934–1935; CBS, 1935–1941; NBC, 1942–1943; went to TV, 1949 |
| *Our Gal Sunday* | CBS, 1937–1959; produced by the Hummerts |
| *Pepper Young's Family* | NBC, 1936–1959 |
| *Portia Faces Life* | CBS, 1940–1941; NBC, 1941–1951; went to TV, 1954 |
| *The Right to Happiness* | NBC, 1939–1940; CBS, 1940–1941; NBC, 1941–1956; CBS, 1956–1960); scripted by Phillips |
| *The Road of Life* | NBC, 1937–1954; concurrent with CBS, 1938–1942, 1945–1947, 1952–1954; CBS, 1954–1958); scripted by Phillips; went to TV, 1954 |
| *The Romance of Helen Trent* | CBS, 1933–1960; produced by the Hummerts |
| *Rosemary* | NBC, 1944–1945; CBS, 1945–1955 |
| *Second Husband* | NBC, 1937; CBS, 1937–1946; produced by the Hummerts |
| *The Second Mrs. Burton* | CBS, 1941–1960 |

*(continued)*

TABLE 84. *(continued)*

| Title | Network(s), Dates, Comments |
|---|---|
| *Stella Dallas* | NBC, 1938–1955; produced by the Hummerts |
| *The Story of Mary Marlin* | NBC, but often CBS, 1935–1945; ABC, 1951–1952 |
| *This Is Nora Drake* | NBC, 1947–1959 |
| *Today's Children* | NBC, 1933–1937, 1943–1950; scripted by Phillips |
| *Valiant Lady* | CBS, 1938; NBC, 1938–1942; CBS, 1942–1946; ABC, 1951–1952; produced by the Hummerts; went to TV, 1953 |
| *Wendy Warren* | CBS, 1947–1958 |
| *When a Girl Marries* | CBS, 1939–1941; NBC, 1941–1951; ABC, 1951–1957 |
| *Woman in White* | NBC, 1938–1940; CBS, 1940–1942; NBC, 1944–1948; scripted by Phillips |
| *Woman of Courage* | NBC, 1939–1942 |
| *Young Dr. Malone* | NBC, 1939–1940; CBS, 1940–1960; went to TV, 1958 |
| *Young Widder Brown* | NBC, 1938–1956; produced by the Hummerts |

Soap operas flourished on radio until the early 1950s and only foundered with the surging popularity of television. As late as 1949, the networks still devoted dozens of hours a week to such afternoon programming, with most episodes running 15 minutes in length and competing series often occupying the same time slots so listeners would have to make choices. By the following year, however, the bottom began to fall out, and the decline of the genre gained momentum. It proved a lingering death, however; radio executives convinced themselves that soap operas remained unique to the medium, and they stubbornly continued to produce the shows throughout the 1950s, even occasionally introducing new ones as old favorites died out.

*See also:* Leisure and Recreation; Radio Programming: Drama and Anthology Shows

**Selected Reading**
Cantor, Muriel G., and Suzanne Pingree. *The Soap Opera.* Beverly Hills, CA: Sage, 1983.
Dunning, John. *On the Air: The Encyclopedia of Old-Time Radio.* New York: Oxford University Press, 1998.
Higby, Mary Jane. *Tune in Tomorrow.* New York: Cowles Education, 1968.
Hilmes, Michele. *Radio Voices: American Broadcasting, 1922–1952.* Minneapolis: University of Minnesota Press, 1997.

# RATIONING

With the 1941 entry of the United States as a combatant in World War II, everyday life for Americans changed significantly. The war affected how they spent their time, where they worked and traveled, and what they ate; plus they suffered the stress associated with having loved ones fighting overseas. The conflict called for patriotic sacrifices, and virtually everyone readily accepted the challenges.

Some of these changes came about because of Japanese conquests in Asia and unsafe shipping conditions across the Pacific Ocean. Important goods such as silk, rubber, and shellac from that part of the world could no longer reach the United States.

In addition, German submarines in the Atlantic and Caribbean, along with a shortage of ships, hindered the transport of sugar, tropical fruits, and other imports from Cuba, Puerto Rico, and Central America.

Because of dire shortages in England and Russia, Congress passed the Lend-Lease Act on March 11, 1941, a move that allowed the president to ship weapons, **food,** or equipment to any country whose struggle against the Axis assisted U.S. defense. This involved taking supplies away from the American home front in order to aid struggling allies abroad. As the war progressed, the U.S. military also needed vast quantities of food and other goods. These pressures caused scarcities among many consumer items and a corresponding increase in prices for what remained.

Along with these problems, however, some of the war-related changes could be viewed as positive. For example, being at war meant more jobs and, in many cases, higher wages. Together, however, these conditions—competition brought about by a shortfall of products, rising costs, and growing employment with money to spend—laid a foundation for inflation. To address these issues, rationing, a method of guaranteeing equitable distribution of limited supplies at any given time, while also controlling prices, became a reality of everyday life.

Prior to Pearl Harbor, **President Franklin Delano Roosevelt** (1882–1945) coped with ways of leading the nation through these difficult times. He displayed particular concern about consumer and economic woes, especially runaway inflation. In April 1941, the president issued an executive order that established the Office of Price Administration (OPA). He charged the agency to find ways to prevent rapid increases in prices and accompanying spirals in the cost of living. Struggling with how best to carry out its responsibilities, the OPA capitalized on the power of **advertising** to focus initially on encouraging Americans to spend their money on **war bonds,** an act that would divert income away from purchasing products and at the same time provide funds for some of the cost of the war.

Although the resultant bond drives met with immediate success, it nevertheless became clear that bonds alone would not solve all the challenges associated with shortages of goods; something else had to be done. Shortly after the declaration of war, the passage of the Emergency Price Control Act on January 30, 1942, gave the OPA authority to freeze retail prices. Three months later, the agency issued the General Maximum Price Regulation, which set the cost of 60 percent of all civilian food items at March 1942 levels. The OPA now had legislation and guidelines for a War Ration Program.

To implement rationing across the country, officials instructed all the counties in the 48 states to form ration boards. Staffed by some 300,000 volunteers, these workers soon began tracking the prices on 90 percent of the goods sold in more than 600,000 retail stores. Local schools became sites for the distribution of numbered war ration books; for example, book 1 became available in 1942, followed by books 2 and 3 in 1943, and so on. Given to every man, woman, and child, including infants, each contained an individual serial number along with red and blue stamps. As the war progressed and more consumer items fell onto the ration lists, the government added brown, green, and black stamps. Together with cash, they allowed citizens to purchase designated goods.

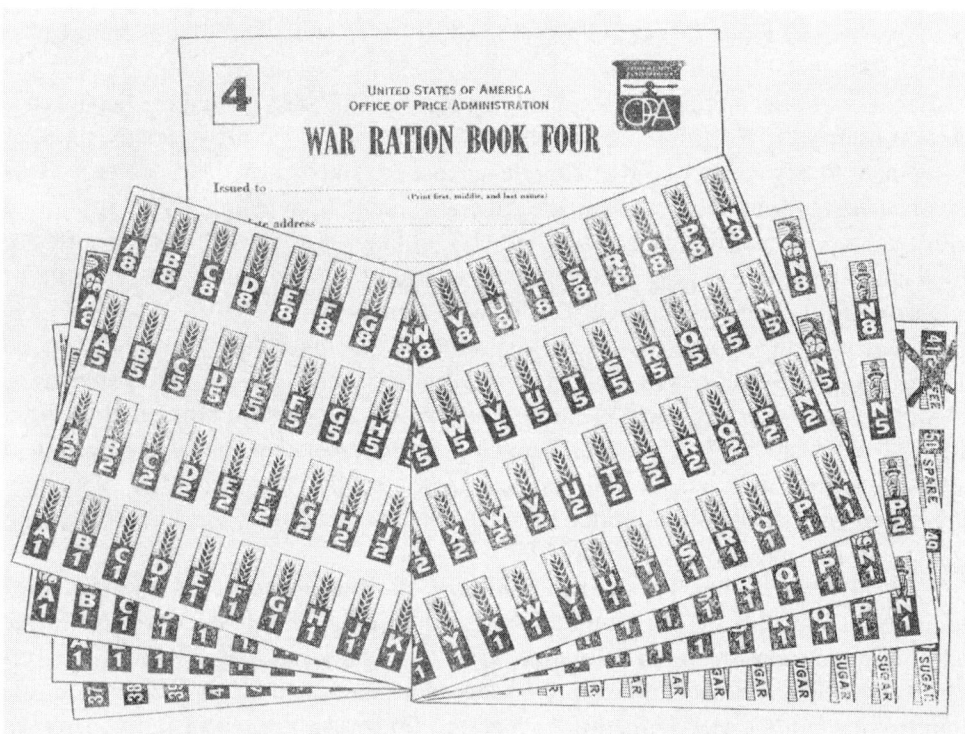

*A war ration program went into effect in March 1942, and shortly thereafter every man, woman, and child received books of ration stamps to be used for purchasing designated goods. (AP Photo)*

Consumers traded red stamps for meats, while the blue and green stamps covered canned, bottled, and frozen fruits and vegetables, juices, soups, baby food, catsup, and dry beans. Brown stamps could be used for butter, cheese, lard, and fats, and black ones served as spares for any cost adjustments. In addition to their colors, ration stamps displayed military or patriotic symbols, including drawings of an airplane, an artillery piece, a tank, an aircraft carrier, an ear of wheat, and the Statue of Liberty torch. The use of stamps might require change from the merchant to the consumer; to accommodate this, red and blue tokens made of a thin compressed wood material and about the size of a dime fulfilled that function. Like small change, they could be applied toward future purchases.

Details on how the program worked evolved over time as more and more products joined the list of rationed goods. Initially, the system involved a fixed point system for each item. Later a revision introduced a more flexible arrangement that allowed for a reduction or increase in points depending on scarcity. Eventually, the program contained four types of rationing, based on the commodity and its level of availability: (1) stamps used for point rationing for food, (2) uniform (the same for everyone) coupon rationing for shoes and sugar, (3) differential (allotments varied according to need) coupon rationing for fuel oil and gasoline, and (4) certificate rationing for **automobiles,** tires, and rubber boots.

Basic instructions, along with the motto "If you don't need it, DON'T BUY IT," appeared on the back of many stamp books. Eventually, the ration books also requested that everyone salvage their tin cans and waste fats. More detailed directions, information that the consumer found necessary for wise shopping, as well as knowing what to do in case of hospitalization or the death of a ration book holder, were issued separately by the OPA.

The homework required for maximizing the use of the ration program could be exhausting. For example, the stamps and coupons had expiration dates, a device intended to prevent hoarding but one that added another piece of information to remember. Because the stamps became unusable at the end of four weeks, everyone had to make monthly trips to the ration book distribution site. With the introduction of the flexible points system, it became necessary for shoppers to master an ever-changing point value for specific products; one week ground beef might be seven points and then become nine points the following week.

To aid the frustrated shopper, Consumers Union, publishers of the widely known and respected *Consumer Reports*, issued the weekly *Bread and Butter Magazine* from 1941 to 1947. It kept people informed about rationing changes, supplies, prices, and potential shortages. The gathering of information did not stop there. Sometimes ration boards offered special deals, such as being able to use a certain coupon on a specific date for a designated product. These particulars could appear at any time in **newspapers** or on lists posted at stores and thus required that someone in the household seek out these details on an almost daily basis. The following table illustrates samples of such announcements.

The first rationing occurred in January 1942 and covered tires. Lack of supplies from the Far East and low U.S. stockpiles along with increased military needs for rubber necessitated a number of measures. The government quickly placed a freeze on the sale of tires as well as a ban on recapping. Automobile owners with more than five tires per car were asked to turn in their extras to a service station; many communities held **scrap drives** for rubber, while industry geared up to try to find a substitute

TABLE 85.   Representative Newspaper Rationing Announcements

| Date | Announcement |
| --- | --- |
| Tomorrow | Coffee coupon No. 25 expires. Last day to use No. 4 "A" coupons for four gallons of gasoline. |
| March 22 | Coupon No. 26 in Ration Book No. 1 becomes valid for one pound of coffee until April 25. |
| March 25 | Processed food stamps for April, D, E, and F in Ration Book No. 2 become valid. The monthly quota of 48 points remains unchanged. Budget these through April 30. |
| March 31 | Last day to use A, B, and C point coupons for processed foods in Ration Book No. 2. Deadline for first tire inspection for "A" cards. |
| April 12 | Last day for No. 4 fuel oil coupons. |
| June 15 | Last day for coupon No. 17 good for one pair of shoes. |

Source: Lingeman, Richard. Don't You Know There's a War On? *The American Home Front 1941–1945.* New York: Thunder's Mouth Press, 1970, pp. 256–257.

or a synthetic. Despite Americans' love for their automobiles and the accompanying freedom of the open road, most people willingly complied with the tire restrictions. Some even put their cars away for the duration. Rubber nevertheless remained in short supply, causing the OPA to consider additional measures.

In May 1942, the agency announced gas rationing for the East Coast, mainly because of a fuel shortage caused by the sinking of a large number of tankers by German submarines in the Atlantic. Meanwhile, a commission appointed by Roosevelt to evaluate the rubber situation reported that the only way to save tires was to limit mileage for the entire country. By December 1, almost one year after the attack on Pearl Harbor, the president ordered nationwide gas rationing as well as a ban on pleasure driving and a 35-mile-per-hour speed limit on all of the nation's highways.

Depending on needs, civilians could obtain stickers for display on their cars or trucks that identified one of a number of classifications of gas ration coupons. These classifications entitled the holder to different quantities each week: an A sticker owner received the lowest gas share of four gallons a week—enough, the government estimated, to permit 60 miles of driving. By 1944, because of enormous military demands for gas, authorities lowered the basic allotment back home to two gallons a week. B stickers were issued to workers essential to the war effort, such as those in the military industry, and allowed them to purchase eight gallons a week, while C sticker drivers—ministers, doctors, and others important to the quality of life for civilians—received whatever they required. Commercial truck drivers earned a T sticker, which signified as much gasoline as needed for their work. Last, X stickers provided unlimited amounts of gas for police, firefighters, and civil defense workers. Somehow, federal legislators also qualified for X stickers, a situation that produced an uproar and a cry of scandal from the American public, but Congress did not relinquish the privilege.

Tire and gas rationing did bring about a noticeable decline in cars on city streets as well as some adjustments in daily life. In addition, **blackouts, brownouts, and dim-outs** greatly reduced night driving. In the East, milk delivery changed from every day to every other day, newspapers made only one delivery of editions to newsstands, and department stores curtailed their deliveries. On the good side, the auto death rate fell dramatically, but localities conversely struggled with a decline in money because of a drop in gasoline tax revenues.

A ban on any extended pleasure driving meant just that. The auto tourist trade vanished, because a car owner with an A sticker had only enough gasoline for what the OPA called essential business. This included necessary shopping, attending church or synagogue services or funerals, receiving medical attention, taking trips for family or occupational necessities, and handling emergencies involving a threat to life, health, or property.

Recognizing gas rationing as an opportunity for making money, professional criminals produced counterfeit ration coupons that they sold in a variety of ways to individual consumers and service station operators. By buying on the **black market,** individuals could get more gasoline than their legitimate quota. Service station owners used extra coupons to cover selling fuel above the ceiling price. Some truck drivers who had more than enough gasoline for their work sold any excess coupons to filling station owners, who could then fill the tanks of preferred customers without collecting coupons.

Even though difficult to enforce, OPA sleuths attempted to identify gas rationing and pleasure driving violators, and in some communities took coupons from drivers who stopped for a soft drink when making a trip that qualified as essential, parked in front of nightclubs and **restaurants,** or drove to a symphony concert. Recognizing the enforcement problems, the government cancelled the ban on pleasure driving in September 1943. Throughout the years of limited gasoline, most Americans looked for ways to conserve and coped by forming car pools and share-the-ride clubs or using public transit. Many found that their worn-out prewar cars and tires could last another year, especially if they limited their use to just the most necessary trips.

Food rationing was another story and probably had a greater impact on American life than did gas rationing. Sugar, the first table item to become scarce, made it to the ration list in April 1942, with an average allowance of 8, later 12, ounces per person per week. Some complained and incorrectly accused the government of not knowing what it was doing, asserting that a scarcity of sugar did not exist. But most realized the seriousness of the matter and found ways to tolerate the situation. Many people reduced the amount of sugar they put in drinks and food or used substitutes such as saccharin and corn syrup. Homemakers baked less and canned fewer preserves, and some bought from bakeries in order to save their own ration stamps. Restaurants filled their sugar bowls only half full and asked patrons to show their patriotic spirit by limiting how much they used.

Coffee rationing of one pound per person every five weeks followed in November 1942. Hotels and restaurants stopped offering refills, and railroad dining cars served coffee only at breakfast. Some coffee drinkers used chicory to stretch their supply, while others brewed their grounds a second time. As a product with limited availability, coffee acquired an aura of luxury, and frequently people used their stamps to buy coffee as a wedding or other special gift. Even some non–coffee drinkers turned to having one cup a day, seeing it as a special treat. Coffee rationing ceased in July 1943, when supplies increased.

The need for food by the military, especially canned goods, greatly decreased the amount available for civilians on the home front. In 1943, one-half of the entire production of canned food went to U.S. troops overseas, and a freeze on the selling of canned meats and fish began on February 2 of that year. By March 1, other kinds of canned goods—milk, fruit, vegetables, jams, and jellies—along with dried fruits, beans, and frozen foods, joined the list of rationed foods. **Victory gardens** became a popular way for those at home to add much-needed fruits and vegetables to their tables.

The government limited butter sales on March 22, 1943, and meat rationing followed a week later with a multitude of regulations and associated problems. Even before this rationing began, meat had been scarce because farmers held back their stock, waiting for higher prices. The demand from the armed forces—soldiers reportedly ate four and a half pounds of meat each week, those in the navy reportedly ate seven pounds each week—required civilians to reduce their consumption. The initial rationed portion per person of 28 ounces per week plus 4 ounces of cheese seemed meager to most, with the exception of vegetarians.

Meat rationing especially vexed butchers. The OPA provided them with 24 pages of directions for precise cutting of meat with the intention of ensuring uniformity. If a

T-bone steak had a certain regulated price and red stamp points cost, then T-bone steaks everywhere should be alike. Butchers complained that cutting meat by a ruler became time consuming and resulted in waste, while shoppers felt overwhelmed when trying to understand the various cuts with bone in or bone out and the associated costs.

Even with rationing, meat remained scarce, and many felt lucky to get frankfurters containing fillers made from soybeans, potatoes, or cracker meal. Horse meat, muskrat, and rabbit, unusual items in the American diet, sold in some areas of the country. *Life* magazine attempted to help by publishing articles such as "Raising Rabbits for Meat Is a Helpful Patriotic Hobby" (January 4, 1943) and "How to Prepare Variety Meats" (January 11, 1943). The scarcity and rationing of meat created a chain effect shortage for poultry. Pork, on the other hand, remained plentiful until late in the war, when it too made the ration list.

Laborers voiced concern about not getting enough meat and other food for the energy they expended in their work. Miners, led by John L. Lewis (1880–1969), struck on four different occasions, voicing their dissatisfaction with both low wages and inadequate food. In June 1945, the government belatedly increased the miners' ration to twice the standard amount. Lumberjacks in the state of Washington also struck for higher meat rations. Sheep herders, whose jobs took them far from stores for extended periods, found their rations inadequate and received an increase from 48 points for canned goods to 288 points. Unfortunately, some individuals who simply could not understand the rationing system often went without their allotments.

In addition to tires, gasoline, and food, the War Ration Program encompassed other items Americans believed important to their well-being. New typewriters, bicycles, automobiles, shoes, and household appliances became unavailable early in the war, and those already in the supply pool for purchase required a certificate showing need. Clocks, because of the requisitioning of brass and copper, made it to the shortage list, a condition that created some major theft problems and enabled telephone wake-up services to flourish.

Fuel oil rationing started just in time for the winter of 1942–1943 with an initial allotment based on a complicated formula involving a dwelling's square footage. Simplification came later so everyone received about two-thirds of what they used in 1941, or enough to keep the house or apartment at 65 degrees. In the Northwest, firewood and coal were added to the ration list in 1943.

As with the war bond campaigns, government-sponsored ads, **radio** shows, **posters,** and pamphlets asked Americans to comply with and contribute to the War Ration Program, and they did so without complaint. Nevertheless, announcements of a new item joining the ration lists frequently led to panic buying and hoarding. Within a day, depleted store shelves intensified scarcity and set the stage for the black market; these shady enterprises offered rationed items on the sly at higher prices. Consumers felt increased hardships when nonrationed goods such as whiskey, canned beer, cigarettes, milk, and paper became hard to find because of lowered production and related shortages. These conditions again offered opportunities for illegal entrepreneurs.

By the end of 1943, industrial activity for the military had decreased, and production of civilian items such as irons, stoves, and refrigerators slowly resumed. The summer of 1944 brought good news about the war, and the OPA lifted the rationing of canned goods and meat, except for beef steaks and roasts. But a temporary halt in the Allied advances during December 1944 crushed the hopes of ending the war soon. The government restored rationing, black market trading became more open, and Congress, fearing another major food crisis, extended the OPA's authority until June 1946, a date that turned out to be months beyond the **V-E and V-J day** celebrations in 1945.

With the declaration of war against Japan on December 8, 1941 (December 11, 1941, against Germany and Italy), the economy of the United States shifted overnight to war production; consumer needs and goods took a back seat to military production. Rationing, needed to control supply and demand and possibly decrease public anger over shortages, became a reality in the spring of 1942 and continued until 1946. It required a shared sacrifice from all citizens and deeply affected the American way of life.

*See also:* Hobbies; Labor Unrest; Leisure and Recreation; Magazines; Motorsports; Technology; Transportation; Travel

**Selected Reading**
"How to Use Your War Ration Book." *Genealogy Today.* U.S. Government Printing Office 16-26649-1. www.genealogytoday.com/guide/ww2/book_one_intro.html
Lingeman, Richard. *Don't You Know There's a War On? The American Home Front 1941–1945.* New York: Thunder's Mouth Press, 1970.
Winkler, Allan M. *Home Front U.S.A.: America during World War II.* Wheeling, IL: Harlan Davidson, 1986.
"World War II Rationing Collection, 1942–1946." New York State Library. www.nysl.nysed.gov/msscfa/sc22912.htm

# RELIGION

The 1940s can be seen as a decade of growth for mainline religions as well as evangelistic movements. Circumstances during the 1930s, a period of economic unrest and social turmoil, along with wartime and postwar events of the 1940s, laid the stage for increased religious affiliation within the general population. The Great Depression (1929–1933), with its accompanying economic hardships, had created a state of despair and sense of hopelessness for some citizens. New Deal programs developed by **President Franklin Delano Roosevelt**'s (1882–1945) administration, however, benefited many and allowed Americans to begin to regain national confidence, only to be confronted then by the rise of European fascism, a militaristic Japan, and other ideological challenges.

The United States' sudden entry into World War II in December 1941 ignited new concerns among its citizens about their national heritage, including its religious traditions. Almost four years later, the **atomic bomb,** the final surrenders, and the return of peace changed American life yet again. Industrial expansion, which had begun in the prelude to war, accelerated and pushed forward a strong economy, allowing a large number of families to move from urban centers to new and larger homes in the suburbs, thanks to improved roads and affordable **automobiles.** At the same time, the **television** industry opened countless new opportunities and provided a window to postwar affluence.

Data from the federal government, the Gallup Poll, and church reports document different aspects of Americans' involvement with faith communities. U.S. Census Bureau statistics for 1940 to 1949 tracked membership of four major Protestant bodies—Presbyterian, Episcopal, Methodist, and Southern Baptist—as well as Seventh-day Adventist and Roman Catholic. In addition to membership totals, which grew somewhat equally for all selected bodies, the bureau reported the value of construction contracts made with religious groups in general. Money spent dropped between 1940 and 1945 because of wartime shortages but strongly rebounded after the war. Statistics for other religious groups present in the United States, such as Buddhist, Old Catholic and Polish National Catholics, Eastern churches, and Judaism, did not become available until 1951.

The Gallup Poll conducted three surveys giving the percentage of the total population that belonged to a specified church. These reports show a small increase over the decade, rising from 72 percent of the population to 76 percent in 1947. For those citizens who did profess a religious preference, Gallup classified 69 percent as Protestant and 22 percent as Roman Catholic, a clear majority of total religious memberships.

The above statistics leave unanswered the decade's history of church attendance. Reports quoted in the *New York Times* indicate growing church attendance during the 1940s. At the time, most city dwellers could easily walk or use public **transportation** to get to houses of worship. For others, however, rubber and gasoline shortages along with **rationing** caused **travel** to be restricted to absolute necessities and probably prevented some from participating in church services. For those unable to attend church, both independent and network **radio** provided broadcasts of worship services and other religious programs that audiences could enjoy in the comfort of their living rooms. This kind of programming had steadily drawn increasing numbers of listeners during the 1930s, a trend that continued throughout the 1940s.

Independent stations across the country regularly carried Sunday church services close to or at 11:00 a.m. Radio networks aired long-time favorites as well as new programs in slots anywhere from 8:00 a.m. to 6:00 p.m. on Sundays, as well as on some weekdays. The choices varied, with something for almost everyone, whatever the preference. For example, the Columbia Broadcasting System aired *The CBS Church of the*

TABLE 86. Growth of Selected American Religious Bodies, 1940–1949

| Year | Roman Catholic Membership | Percentage Change | Selected Protestant Groups Membership | Percentage Change | Value of Construction Contracts for Religious Buildings |
|---|---|---|---|---|---|
| 1940 | 21,403,000 | | 16,782,000 | | $46 million |
| 1945 | n.d. | | n.d. | | $35 million |
| 1949 | 26,718,000 | +20% | 20,615,000 | +19% | $276 million |

*Note:* n.d. = no data available.
*Source: Historical Statistics of the United States, Colonial Times to 1970.* Washington, DC: Census Bureau, U.S. Department of Commerce, 1975, pp. 392, 624.

*Air,* dating back to 1931. Its format replicated actual church services and attempted to cater to all denominations and faiths. Two broadcasts each Sunday, made it possible to hear one denominational service in the morning and another in the afternoon. *Radio Bible Class* on **MBS (Mutual Broadcasting System)** was exactly that, an instructional class on Sunday mornings that the network carried. It came on the air early enough that audiences could tune in at home prior to departing for an 11:00 a.m. service. Musical programs such as *The Gospel Singer* and *Hymns for All Churches,* both of which aired several times a week over the years, also proved popular. The table below provides an overview of religious-oriented programming carried by the major networks; it does not include independent stations or syndicated programs.

The radio programs listed above allowed some ministers to become well-known, while elevating others to celebrity status. In May 1948, *The National Radio Pulpit,* which first broadcast in January 1923 on New York's independent WEAF, celebrated 25 years of broadcasting. NBC (National Broadcasting Company) carried it for 22 of those years, making it at the time the oldest such program on the air. Ralph W. Sockman

TABLE 87. Religious Network Radio Programs during the 1940s

| MBS | CBS | NBC | ABC |
|---|---|---|---|
| *The Old-Fashioned Revival Hour,* 1930s–1944 | *The CBS Church of the Air,* 1931–1960s | *National Radio Pulpit,* 1926–1962 | *The Old–Fashioned Revival Hour,* 1949–1960s |
| *The Lutheran Hour,* 1935–1956 | *The Mormon Tabernacle Choir,* 1932–1960s | *National Vespers,* 1929–1943 | *National Vespers,* 1943–1954 |
| *Radio Bible Class,* 1940–1957 | | *The Catholic Hour,* 1930–1960s | *Message of Israel,* 1943–1950 |
| *The Pilgrim Hour,* 1942, 1944–1947. This was a supplementary broadcast of *The Old-Fashioned Revival Hour* | *Hymns of All Churches,* 1936–1938; 1941–1942 | *The Gospel Singer,* 1933–1943 | *Hymns of All Churches,* 1945–1947 |
| | *Greenfield Chapel Choir,* 1937–1943 | *Religion in the News,* 1933–1950 | *Hour of Faith,* 1943–1950 |
| *The Voice of Prophecy,* 1942–1954 | *Wings over Jordan,* 1939–1954 | *Message of Israel,* 1935–1943 | *The Lutheran Hour,* 1949–1951 |
| *Reverend John E. Zoller,* *The Wesley League,* 1943–1946 | | *Hymns of All Churches,* 1938–1941, 1942–1946 | *The Baptist Hour,* 1949–1950 |
| *The Back to God Hour,* 1948–1956 | | *Hour of Faith,* 1942–1943 | |
| *Christian Science Talks,* 1949–1956 | | *Greenfield Chapel Choir,* 1943–1945 | |

*Source:* Dunning, John. *On the Air: The Encyclopedia of Old-Time Radio,* New York: Oxford University Press, 1998, pp. 571–574.

(1889–1970), a United Methodist minister, served as the officiating pastor and regularly stood before the microphone from 1936 until the end of its run in 1962. *Time* magazine, in its January 21, 1946, issue, identified Sockman as the No. 1 Protestant radio pastor in the United States, based on the volume of his fan mail, some 4,000 letters each week. Sockman, in addition to his radio show and Manhattan church responsibilities, regularly traveled the country on lecture tours and wrote best-selling books on Christian life, including *Live for Tomorrow* (1943), *Date with Destiny; A Preamble to Christian Culture* (1944), and *The Lord's Prayer* (1947).

Fulton J. Sheen (1895–1979), an American bishop representing the Roman Catholic Church, hosted *The Catholic Hour* (NBC) on Sundays at 6:00 p.m. for 20 years, 1930 to 1950, and received credit for converting many listeners to Catholicism, including some widely known people such as dramatist, war correspondent, and politician Clare Boothe Luce (1903–1987), industrialist Henry Ford II (1917–1987), and actress Virginia Mayo (1920–2005). *Time* magazine, again in its January 21, 1946, issue, referred to Sheen as "the golden-voiced Msgr. Fulton Sheen" and reported that he received 3,000 to 6,000 letters weekly. In 1950, he moved from radio to the new medium of television and appeared on *Time*'s cover on April 14, 1952; over the course of his career, Sheen wrote some 73 books.

Another prominent minister, radio personality, and author from the period, Norman Vincent Peale (1898–1993), received degrees from Ohio Wesleyan and the theological school at Boston University. Originally ordained a Methodist minister, Peale changed to the Dutch Reformed Church, known today as the Reformed Church in America, and served as pastor at the Marble Collegiate Church in Manhattan for 52 years (1932–1984). His fame evolved from a regular airing of his sermons on radio, which focused on a positive approach to modern living. He also published several best-selling books, including *The Art of Living* (1937), *Confident Living* (1948), and his most famous, *The Power of Positive Thinking* (1952). In 1945, Peale and his wife, Ruth Stafford Peale (1906–2008), founded the Foundation for Christian Living and distributed the first issue of *Guideposts* magazine, which today has one of the largest circulations of any religious periodical.

In addition to the representatives of mainstream denominations, radio also aired Protestant evangelistic services that went beyond providing a worship service. These programs contained zealous preaching of the Christian gospel with the intent of winning or reviving a person's commitment to Christ and offered choral music, singers of spirituals, and distinguished soloists, in addition to a crusading sermon. Evangelists, perhaps more than mainline pastors, recognized the potential of radio for reaching large numbers of people and converting them to the speaker's cause. Following the success of Aimee Semple McPherson (1890–1944), the first woman to preach sermons over radio, evangelists eagerly took to the medium soon after its widespread establishment in the early 1920s. By the 1940s, two men—Charles E. Fuller (1887–1968) and William Franklin "Billy" Graham (b. 1918)—successfully used radio to become well-known internationally and to significantly advance their ministries.

Charles Fuller, first a member of the Presbyterian Church and then a Baptist minister, gained fame as the host and speaker on *The Old-Fashioned Revival Hour*. Beginning in 1928, he broadcast from Calvary Church, in Long Beach, California, and could only be heard on the West Coast. Because of his growing audience, he resigned his pastoral position in 1933 and formed the Gospel Broadcasting Association to preach and strengthen his radio ministry. By virtue of being self-employed, he needed money and thus used his radio programs to ask his listeners for contributions; they responded generously.

By 1940, Fuller had contracted to pay the Mutual network for coast-to-coast airing of his hour-long show. The weekly services, held before a live audience in California, were transcribed and broadcast the following Sunday with the transcriptions circulated both in the United States and abroad. The content remained the same as it had been for years: a sermon, a choral group performing old-time gospel hymns, a male quartet, and occasional appearances by guest celebrities talking about their experiences in their faith. This format became the prototype for other evangelistic shows. The years during World War II were lucrative ones for Fuller and the *Old-Fashioned Revival Hour.* Contributions amply covered GBA expenses and payments to Mutual; Fuller even added stations overseas to carry the program to U.S. soldiers in Europe.

Mutual, unlike the other major networks that offered slots without commercial sponsorship or **advertising,** sold time for religious programming and in 1943 came under increasing pressure from the Federal Council of Churches (founded in 1908 as an ecumenical fellowship of major Protestant and Orthodox faith groups) to change its policies. Despite Fuller's distinction as Mutual's highest-paying customer, the network decided in 1942 to limit paid-time religious programs on Sundays to half an hour. Fuller accepted a 30-minute slot for *The Pilgrim Hour,* which had previously aired during the afternoon for an hour. When Mutual in 1944 decided to cancel any religious programming after 12:00 p.m., Fuller moved the more popular *Old-Fashioned Revival Hour* to independent stations. The program returned to network radio with **ABC (American Broadcasting System)** in 1949 and remained there for over a decade.

Whereas Fuller pioneered radio evangelism, Billy Graham, an ordained Baptist minister, became the star. Graham received his **education** from a fundamentalist network of schools, completing a bachelor's degree in 1943 from Florida Bible Institute. Following graduation, he served briefly as the minister at the Village Church in Western Springs, Illinois. The following year, with financial backing from this church, he added a failing local radio show, *Songs in the Night,* to his responsibilities and hired George Beverly Shea (b. 1909) as director of radio ministry. Over the decades, Shea became the musical mainstay for Graham's crusades. Also in 1944, Graham worked as the first full-time employee for the Youth for Christ movement, founded that same year by fellow minister and evangelist, Torrey Johnson (1909–2002). Graham traveled as a field representative in an effort to coordinate religious rallies being held for young people in the United States and Canada.

At age 30, Graham moved to St. Paul, Minnesota, to serve for one year as the president of Northwestern College, giving him the distinction of being the youngest person ever to serve in that position at the college. In 1949, while in Los Angeles, he launched what he thought would be a three-week revival. Held in large circus tents erected in a parking lot, his preaching received extensive coast-to-coast front-page coverage by the

Hearst **newspapers,** and the crusade grew from three to seven weeks. Overnight, Billy Graham had become a person of national prominence, with articles about him appearing in both *Time* and *Life* **magazines.**

George Carson Putman (1914–2008), a prominent radio commentator, conducted a poll for New York City's WOR in 1947. Designed to determine the city's most influential citizens, William Ward Ayer (1892–1985), minister at Calvary Baptist Church in Manhattan (1936–1950), ranked third, outpaced only by Cardinal Francis Spellman (1889–1967) and **Eleanor Roosevelt** (1884–1962). Ayer, educated at the Moody Bible Institute, Lincoln College, and the Northern Baptist Seminary of Chicago, could be heard for more than 41 years in New York over the airwaves. During his tenure at Calvary, the *New York Times* and the *Herald Tribune* ran Monday morning summaries of his Sunday sermons.

With denominations and ministers acquiring more and more radio air time, issues arose regarding the role of radio in promoting specific faiths and the use of commercial sponsorship or advertising as a part of religious programs. It addition to these matters, some religious leaders, especially those representing evangelistic groups, became concerned about the appearance on radio of people they deemed to be crackpots and fly-by-night operators. Radio station owners likewise found religious material at times to be controversial and difficult to handle.

As a consequence of these operational questions, prominent evangelistic ministers, both those with radio shows and those without, formed a number of councils: (1) the American Council of Churches of Christ (1941), (2) the National Association of Evangelicals (NAE, 1942), and (3) the National Religious Broadcasters (1944), an affiliate of NAE. All three of these evangelistic-oriented groups worked toward self-regulating the production side of religious programs and securing radio time for their programs to ensure a continuing presence.

Mainline denominations also became active and created four groups: (1) the Protestant Radio Conference (1945, an association of Protestant denomination leaders who oversaw a religious broadcast entity in Atlanta); (2) Joint Religious Radio Commission (1945, five Protestant denominations working to coordinate their radio work); (3) Religious Radio Association (1946, included representatives from Protestant, Jewish, and Roman Catholic faiths); and (4) the Protestant Radio Commission (1948), which took on the responsibility of overseeing *The National Radio Pulpit* and other programs of the Federal Council of Churches of Christ in America (1908, an ecumenical fellowship of major Protestant and Orthodox churches).

Since the days of the Pilgrims, many have debated religious rights, particularly in the context of public prayer. In 1933, a highly visible use of this basic element of most religions began with the first prayer service attended by a U.S. president-elect held before the swearing-in ceremony. In addition, all presidential inaugurations since 1937 have included one or more prayers delivered by members of the clergy.

In times of crisis, many people link prayer and patriotism, and some past presidents, including Thomas Jefferson (1743–1826), James Madison (1751–1836), and Abraham Lincoln (1809–1865), offered public prayers during difficult times. Franklin Roosevelt is particularly known for his **D-Day,** June 6, 1944, delivery of "A Prayer in

Dark Times." In the days following Roosevelt's example, large numbers of Americans visited churches to pray for the success of the Allied attempt to liberate Europe and also offered blood to the Red Cross.

While churches and their congregations threw support behind the national effort to end World War II victoriously, they also gave their official blessing to conscientious objectors (COs), people who refuse to participate as combatants in war because of their beliefs. Many World War II COs came from three Protestant churches: the Society of Friends (Quakers), Mennonites, and Brethren—sects that historically have advocated pacifism as a part of their basic doctrine. A majority of the conscientious objectors registered as noncombatants, individuals with military status and benefits but not assigned to fighting duties. Most COs held positions in units like the medical corps. Others accepted alternative service in Civilian Public Service from 1941 to 1947. These individuals worked in a variety of areas including land reclamation, firefighting, forest and park service, public health, and hospitals.

Perhaps one of the most important contributions made by religious bodies to support the war involved providing chaplains to the various branches of the armed forces. Governmental guidelines required Protestant, Catholic, and Jewish clergy at all military camps, with one for every 1,200 soldiers. Their duties included conducting worship services, participating in patriotic ceremonies, providing classes for religious instruction, acting as counselors to service personnel, visiting the sick and injured, and officiating at baptisms, marriages, and funerals. To accelerate the procurement of Protestant ministers to serve as chaplains, the federal government worked closely with the Federal Council of Churches and created a clearinghouse to handle applications and placement. The Roman Catholic Church and the Jewish Welfare Board provided similar assistance in finding priests and rabbis. Congress in 1941 appropriated almost $13 million (approximately $190 million in 2008 dollars) for the erection of chapels on service posts and camps throughout the nation.

Everyday life and popular culture reflected the growth experienced by religion in the United States during the 1940s. Church membership and attendance rose, and religious programming on radio expanded and acquired more listeners. Each year, with the exception of 1941, *Time* magazine annually dedicated at least two of its covers to a religious topic or leader, such as Cardinal Spellman, (February 25, 1946), and Mormon leader George A. Smith (1870–1951) on its July 21, 1947 issue. "God Bless America," composed by Irving Berlin (1888–1989) in 1918 and sung and recorded by Kate Smith (1907–1986) in 1938, emerged as one of the most inspiring songs of World War II; in some ways, it served as a second national anthem, while Frank Loesser's (1910–1969) "Praise the Lord and Pass the Ammunition" (1942) turned out to be a popular hit. Some of the choral groups appearing on religious programs, such as the choir on *Old-Fashioned Revival Hour,* released recordings and experienced successful sales. Enthusiasm about religion continued into the 1950s with nationally known religious figures such as Bishop Fulton Sheen, Billy Graham, Norman Vincent Peale, and Charles E. Fuller taking their religious programs to television, and entertainer and singer Tennessee Ernie Ford (1919–1991) closed his TV show and personal appearances with a religious number.

*See also:* Best Sellers (Books); Levittown and Suburbanization; Selective Training and Service Act of 1940 (Selective Service, or Draft)

**Selected Reading**
Ahlstrom, Sidney E. *A Religious History of the American People.* New Haven, CT: Yale University Press, 1972.
Church Attendance. *New York Times,* January 18, 1942; January 3, 1946; December 18, 1946. www.proquest.com
Hangen, Tona J. *Redeeming the Dial: Radio, Religion, and Popular Culture in America.* Chapel Hill: University of North Carolina Press, 2002.
Packard, William. *Evangelism in America, From Tents to TV.* New York: Paragon House, 1988.

# RESTAURANTS

Americans who wanted to eat out in 1940 had an array of possibilities in the kinds of **food** served and the dining facilities provided. They even had a guide, *Adventures in Good Eating* by Duncan Hines (1880–1959), which had made the best seller lists in 1939. Descriptive names of eateries varied—restaurants, cafeterias, tea rooms, hamburger stands, drive-ins, delicatessens, inns, lodges, taverns, soda fountains—with offerings that ranged from sit-down, home-cooked meals served family style to a quick bite on the run, from specialties of the region to ethnic restaurants. Whatever the kind of place, ownership could easily range from local mom-and-pop operations to national chains and franchises.

Prior to the 1920s and 1930s, the word restaurant referred to establishments that provided table service and fine cuisine prepared by chefs and skilled cooks; some also offered an orchestra or band that played music for both listening and dancing. These kinds of places still existed in the 1940s, but the more casual operations with simpler foods gained popularity both before and after World War II.

The growth of a variety of restaurants coincided with increased activity on the nation's roads and highways and a corresponding upward change in the number of people choosing to eat out. From 1930 to 1940, car ownership had grown, and the totals for automobile miles of **travel** rose from 206 billion to 302 billion. During the 1930s, astute businessmen such as Howard Johnson (1896–1972) and Maurice and Richard McDonald (1902–1971, 1909–1998) saw an opportunity to meet the emerging interest among people on the go with dining facilities different from those of the past.

Howard Johnson serves as a good example. He started out selling 28 flavors of ice cream at a soda fountain in a small corner drugstore in Quincy, Massachusetts, but soon opened a beachfront ice cream stand and added hotdogs to his fare. Next came a family restaurant, again in Quincy, with menu additions of fried clams, chicken pot pies, and baked beans served in a comfortable and recognizable setting. By 1935, he had a franchise agreement with an acquaintance to operate a Howard Johnson's Family Restaurant on Cape Cod. This kind of business contract allowed a retail business owner, such as Johnson, to expand operations without a large outlay of capital. At the same time, the operator of the new business was able to invest with little risk on an unknown venture and could guarantee the customers a recognized trademark, a uniform product, and quality service. Over the next four years, through franchises, the number of Howard Johnson's grew to 107 and continued upward during 1940 and 1941; such phenomenal growth provided evidence of Americans' growing interest in eating out.

While Johnson experienced success in the restaurant business with a somewhat varied menu and table service for New England and East Coast families, the McDonald Brothers took a different approach with their hamburger drive-in restaurants in California. They provided their customers, primarily young families and teenagers looking for a fast-served but good hamburger with French fries and a milkshake—food to be eaten in the car or taken to a park or home.

In the meantime, cosmopolitan areas, such as Hollywood, Chicago, and New York City, supplied a larger customer base with broader interests than many smaller communities. This gave rise to a wider variety of eateries, including ethnic restaurants. For example, the Pagoda Chinese Restaurant, still operating in the 21st century, opened in Hollywood in 1940 and, with its ornate glitter and red and gold vinyl, was considered to be one of the most modern and finest Chinese restaurants in the West.

Following the 1941 attack on Pearl Harbor by the Japanese and the subsequent entry of the United States into World War II, the food industry, like many other businesses on the edge of expansion, experienced challenges. The **rationing** of many foods and gasoline, along with a shortage of workers, initially proved worrisome at a time when demand for restaurant services increased. The removal of millions of men from the workforce from December 1, 1941, to December 31, 1946, for deployment in the armed forces resulted in a tripling of the number of women workers. Frequently putting in overtime with more pay, these women found restaurants an attractive alternative to preparing and eating a meal at home. Also, families trying to cope with the constraints of rationing and having difficulty providing certain meals, such as the expected Thanksgiving dinner, turned to eating establishments for what they could not prepare at home.

After concerted efforts by leaders in the restaurant industry, the Office of Price Administration (OPA) allowed food businesses some variation in the ration points needed for certain items, which in turn enabled them to meet the growing demand. Subsequently, from 1939 to 1946, restaurant sales across the country quadrupled. But even with overall success for the restaurant industry as a whole, some individual operations struggled. For example, during the first years of the war, and before OPA stepped in to help, Howard Johnson's closed the doors at 188 sites, leaving only 12 operating at the end of the conflict. The company survived by providing commissary food, including ice cream, to military installations, defense plants, and schools.

Mindful of potential problems, some entrepreneurs, such as Ike Sewell (1903–1990) of Chicago, nevertheless took risks and grabbed at what seemed to be wartime opportunities. Having dabbled in the restaurant business as a sideline to his job as a salesman with Standard Brands, Sewell embarked on what he saw as a successful venture. In 1943, he and Ric Riccardo (active 1940s), who had recently returned from Italy, opened Pizzeria Uno, a pizza restaurant that offered Chicago, and the country, the first deep-dish pizza and the beginning of an American fascination for this food. The chain remains in operation in the 21st century.

The war finally ended in 1945, and U.S. industries quickly reverted to commercial output as citizens rushed to pamper themselves and compensate for the hardships endured for the preceding four years. Mass production supported the cry for new and convenient commodities, and returning veterans and others invested in businesses, including restaurants, that could met the new consumer demands.

Restaurants with success under their belts, and those that had struggled during the war to stay afloat, anticipated growth, and some flourished. Howard Johnson's, by 1947, had reopened most of its closed sites, along with 200 additional new ones. The number grew to 400 by 1954. New chains appeared across the American landscape and included Dwarf House, now known as Chick-fil-A (1946), Shoney's (1947), Marie Callender's (1948), Coco's (1948), and Bob Evans (1948).

Restaurants benefited when automobile sales skyrocketed and provided **transportation** for getting to work, visiting friends and relatives, and taking family vacations—times when people frequently included dining away from home as a part of the excursion. To the detriment of the restaurant business, the resurgence of normal working hours, along with returning veterans and their spouses having babies, meant a growing interest in home and family. New houses with new appliances in new kitchens invited families to eat at home, not out. Also, as the decade drew to a close, sales of televisions soared, creating a powerful incentive for families to stay at home during mealtime and in the evening.

Returning veterans had another effect on the food industry. The New Haven Restaurant Institute, not a restaurant but a school, opened in New Haven, Connecticut, in 1946, with 50 students and a faculty consisting of a chef, a baker, and a dietitian. It marked the beginning of a long history of preparing chefs and bakers for the restaurant and bakery industry. Established to offer vocational training to World War II veterans who had served as cooks in the armed forces, the institute experienced immediate growth and, in 1947, moved to a larger building adjacent to Yale University and changed its name to the Restaurant Institute of Connecticut. It became the Culinary Institute of America in 1951, and, with a booming food services industry during the 1950s and 1960s, moved to a larger facility, its current home, at St. Andrew-on-Hudson in Hyde Park, New York in 1969.

The 1940s stand as a decade with both highs and lows for the restaurant industry. At the beginning of the decade, the automobile had clearly affected eating habits, and the restaurant business responded by catering to that situation. Howard Johnson's Family Restaurants owe their pre- and postwar success to being located along major highways. World War II offered some interruptions and challenges for the industry, but for many consumers it was easier to eat out, allowing many eateries to profit. The restaurant business declined nationwide during the postwar years, even with the introduction of new chains. At the same time, the industry laid the groundwork for rapid growth, especially in the area of **fast-food** operations, in the decades to come.

*See also:* Automobiles and the American Automotive Industry; Baby Boom; Beverages; Desserts, Candy, and Ice Cream; Frozen Foods; Leisure and Recreation; Technology; Television

### Selected Reading

"Howard Johnson International, Inc." Funding Universe. www.fundinguniverse.com/company-histories/Howard-Johnson-International-Inc-Company-History.html

Levenstein, Harvey. *Paradox of Plenty: A Social History of Eating in Modern America.* New York: Oxford University Press, 1993.

The Culinary Institute of America. www.ciachef.edu/admissions/about/history.asp

# RHYTHM 'N' BLUES

In the immediate postwar years, younger black audiences, initially so fond of modern **jazz** and **bebop** because they represented a revolt against what they considered the sterility of most white big bands, began to search out other innovative musical formats. Most bebop did not prove particularly danceable, and much modern jazz often seemed too cerebral for general audiences. Pop songs, clichéd, predictable, and more often than not performed by white vocalists for white listeners, also failed to stir most young blacks uprooted from the South and living in urban, industrialized communities to the north. The war, particularly defense jobs, had taken them and their families away from traditional Southern music.

A group of mainly black artists, some veteran performers of many years' standing and some as young as the listeners they wanted to reach, sought to appeal to this restless minority audience. Many of these musicians hailed from a blues tradition, and they sought to create a blend of styles that took from the blues, gospel church music, folk, country, barroom and honky-tonk tunes, **boogie-woogie,** and even from jazz and **swing.** What they developed came to be called rhythm and blues (often shortened to rhythm 'n' blues or abbreviated as R & B).

The major record companies, always alert to perceived social and musical movements, had begun a policy in the 1920s and 1930s of calling most music they viewed as aimed at black audiences as "race records." The smaller independent labels, many of them catering to small, niche audiences (including black listeners), likewise followed the race record approach, making their disks sometimes difficult to find in larger shops. Often, record stores in predominantly white neighborhoods or communities did not carry these recordings at all. A customer wanting a particular song by a black artist might have to order it. This kind of segregation even carried over to the airwaves; white **radio** stations tended not to play what they considered black music. Similarly, most **movies** with largely black casts seldom played mainstream theaters but were relegated to those located in minority neighborhoods. As far as concerned American popular culture, the forces of segregation strove mightily to keep racial groups apart.

In such a racially repressive climate, rhythm and blues began quietly, a musical form about which the majority population knew little. Even *Billboard* magazine, a periodical that supposedly tracked all the hits of the day, had no category for this new music until 1949—some years later than the style's inception and steadily growing popularity. Until then, *Billboard* had employed an awkward, catchall category it called Juke Box Race Records in which jazz, blues, novelty tunes, and anything else the editors thought appealed primarily to black audiences could be lumped.

In terms of popularity, rhythm 'n' blues can be thought of as a postwar phenomenon, but one that can trace its beginnings to the war years. It blossomed in the late 1940s, a time of ferment and change for much American music. Designed for uptempo dancing and stressing a strong, punctuated beat impossible to miss, R & B often featured singers, both solo and in groups, sometimes called shouters, screamers, or criers, depending on the style they utilized. The lyrics, however, carried little importance. Wailing, honking saxophones, played fast, loud, and long, accompanied by a steady, thumping rhythm section, provided the basic ingredients, and the words to a tune often got lost amid the excitement generated by the band.

Pianist Jay McShann (1916–2006), leader of a Kansas City-based orchestra noted for playing jump blues, began moving in the direction of what would eventually be called rhythm and blues in the late 1930s. His charts featured up-tempo numbers for dancing, and he enjoyed a minor hit with "Jumpin' Blues" in 1942. No one, however, exemplified this evolving genre better than Louis Jordan (1908–1975). Nicknamed the King of the Jukebox for his many hits on **jukeboxes** in black neighborhoods, Jordan successfully produced records that also crossed racial lines and attracted white listeners. His band, which he called the Tympany Five, counted titles like "Ain't Nobody Here but Us Chickens," "Caldonia (What Makes Your Big Head So Hard?)" "Choo

TABLE 88. Some Outstanding Performers in the Field of Rhythm 'n' Blues, 1940–1950

| Name and Dates | Specialty | 1940's Hits |
| --- | --- | --- |
| Gene "Jug" Ammons (1925–1974) | Tenor sax | "My Foolish Heart," 1949 |
| Earl Bostic (1913–1965) | Alto sax | "Temptation" and "Flamingo," late 1940s |
| Roy Brown (1925–1981) | Singer | "Rockin' at Midnight," 1948 |
| Ruth Brown (1928–2006) | Singer | "So Long," 1949 |
| Arnett Cobb (1918–1989) | Tenor sax | In the late 1940s, called the "wild man of the tenor sax" |
| Floyd Dixon (1929–2006) | Pianist, singer | "Wine, Wine, Wine," and "Too Much Jelly Roll," both late 1940s |
| Fats Domino (b. 1928) | Piano, organ | "The Fat Man," 1949 |
| Wynonie Harris (1915–1969) | Singer | "Drinking Wine, Spo-Dee-O-Dee," 1947; "Good Rockin' Tonight," 1948 |
| John Lee Hooker (1917 2001) | Guitar, vocals | "Boogie Chillen," 1948; "Moanin' Blues," 1949 |
| "Bullmoose" Jackson (1919–1989) | Tenor sax, vocals | "I Love You, Yes I Do," 1948 |
| Illinois Jacquet (1922–2004) | Tenor sax | Noted for his extended solos on Lionel Hampton's signature "Flying Home," 1940s |
| Big Jay McNeely (b. 1928) | Tenor sax | "Deacon's Hop" and "Wild Wig," both 1949 |
| Jack McVea (1914–2000) | Tenor sax | "Open the Door, Richard," 1947 |
| Amos Milburn (1927–1980) | Singer, pianist | "Chicken Shack Boogie," 1948 |
| Roy Milton (1907–1983) | Leader, singer | "RM Blues," 1945 |
| Wild Bill Moore (1918–1983) | Tenor sax | "We're Gonna Rock, We're Gonna Roll," 1948 |
| Hal Singer (b. 1919) | Tenor sax | "Cornbread," 1948 |
| Big Joe Turner (1911–1985) [Turner often performed with pianist Pete Johnson (1904–1967)] | Blues singer | "Roll 'em, Pete" and "Chains of Love," early 1940s |
| Eddie "Cleanhead" Vinson (1917–1988) | Alto sax, singer | "Kidney Stew Blues" and "Old Maid Boogie," both 1947 |
| Aaron "T-Bone" Walker (1910–1975) | Guitar, vocals | "Stormy Monday Blues," 1947 |
| Jimmy Witherspoon (1920–1997) | Blues singer | "Ain't Nobody's Business," 1949 |

Choo Ch' Boogie," and "Five Guys Named Moe" (all from the mid-1940s) among its crossover successes.

Real commercial acclaim, however, eluded most bands attempting to emulate the rhythm 'n' blues style during the early 1940s, but that did not stop musicians from forming groups and cutting records. Among the larger aggregations that made forays into the genre, those led by Tiny Bradshaw (1905–1958), Lionel Hampton (1908–2002), Buddy Johnson (1915–1977), Lucky Millinder (1910–1966), and Todd Rhodes (1900–1965) became the best-known during these formative years. Countless small combos, too numerous to mention, also raised public consciousness about the music, and the individual soloists from these groups occasionally rose to considerable celebrity.

The suggestive, often raunchy, lyrics found in many blues and rhythm 'n' blues tunes prevented disc jockeys from playing particular records on the air. And without airplay, a considerable part of the R & B audience might never hear the songs.

Despite the obstacles of limited radio exposure and a perceived white bias against race music, small, independent record companies sprang up to capture the sounds of rhythm 'n' blues. Over 400 new labels came into being (but only a handful survived) during the 1945 to 1950 period; for little money, an entrepreneur could record an artist, press 500 or so copies of the performance, and sell them in black-owned record shops. That limited pressing might well be the only evidence that a specific label ever existed. In the meantime, the major record companies (RCA Victor, Columbia, Capitol, and others) looked the other way, releasing less than 10 percent of R & B titles during this time. Success rode on singles, not albums, and all singles until the late 1940s were released on 10-inch, 78-rpm records. Not until the widespread introduction of the 7-inch, 45-rpm single around 1949 did the situation change.

The following list identifies a few of the leaders among the hundreds of independent labels that recorded rhythm 'n' blues performers during the 1940s. Many of these companies also owned subsidiaries with still other names. Some lasted for most of the decade, others enjoyed only a brief moment of success; some merged with their competitors, and some simply disappeared from the marketplace.

Collectively, the musicians and promoters of rhythm 'n' blues launched a revolution, just as did the players then taking up the new sounds of bebop and other forms of modern jazz. With few exceptions, however, the major accomplishments of the individuals listed above would take place later in the 1950s, and not the 1940s. The decade, especially the years immediately following World War II, served as a time when the genre defined itself and set standards. The biggest names in commercial rhythm 'n' blues, such as Chuck Berry (b. 1926), Lloyd Price (b. 1933), Little Richard (b. 1935),

TABLE 89. A Sampling of Independent Record Labels Featuring Rhythm 'n' Blues

| Acorn | Black & White | Imperial | Modern |
| --- | --- | --- | --- |
| Aladdin | Chess | Jubilee | Regent |
| Allegro | DeLuxe | Jukebox Records | Savoy |
| Atlantic | Excelsior | King | Swingtime |

B. B. King ("Blues Boy," b. 1925), and numerous others, did not come on the R & B scene until the early 1950s. But with its emphasis on a strong rhythmic format, or beat, and because of its appeal to young people, rhythm 'n' blues paved the way for rock 'n' roll, arguably the dominant musical form for the last half of the 20th century.

*See also:* ASCAP *vs.* BMI Radio Boycott and the AFM Recording Ban; Radio Programming: Music and Variety Shows; Race Relations and Stereotyping; Technology

**Selected Reading**
Ennis, Philip H. *The Seventh Stream: The Emergence of Rocknroll in American Popular Music.* Hanover, NH: Wesleyan University Press, 1992.
Ewen, David. *All the Years of American Popular Music: A Comprehensive History.* Englewood Cliffs, NJ: Prentice Hall, 1977.
Gillett, Charlie. *The Sound of the City: The Rise of Rock and Roll.* New York: Pantheon Books, 1983.

# ROLLER DERBY

A lively contact sport, Roller Derby first appeared in the United States in the 1920s. It consists of teams skating around a banked oval track (flat tracks can also be used) in a contest that combines elements of ice **hockey, football,** rugby, and a bicycle race. Its popularity grew after a 1935 event in Chicago conceived by Leo Seltzer (1903–1978) and billed as a Transcontinental Roller Derby. Seltzer, a successful entrepreneur and promoter of Depression-era **dance** marathons, saw a financial opportunity to replace this waning fad with something new. He recruited 25 skating teams to compete against one another as they attempted to be the first to complete a race on a track in the Chicago Coliseum. They skated around the course until they had covered a distance equal to that between New York and San Diego, approximately 3,000 miles.

In this new sport, audiences witnessed for the first time women competing under the same rules of play as men. The Transcontinental winning team of Clarice Martin (active 1930s and 1940s) and Bernie McKay (active 1930s and 1940s) finished the distance on September 22 after skating for 493 hours and 12 minutes, or slightly more than 20 days. From his success in Chicago, Seltzer took Roller Derby on the road to five other cities, steadily gaining fans along the way and ending in New York.

By 1939, **radio** stations aired Roller Derby contests. Team size increased from two to five members, with men and women playing on separate teams, alternating their play during a match. The sport continued to grow during the 1940s.

Then, as today, a Roller Derby starts with the teams tightly bunched in what is called a jam. The objective is for one or two of the skaters to break away from the pack, catch, and hopefully pass the skaters of the other team within a timed period, while members of each team try to block any advances by the opposition. In 1940, sportswriter Damon Runyon (1880–1946), who had been covering the games, realized that the occasional massive collisions and crashes that occurred created the most excitement among the mostly working-class spectators. He urged Seltzer to modify the rules to maximize physical contact and exaggerate the hits and falls.

*Physical contact, sometimes of a violent nature, drew large crowds to both women's and men's roller derby events. Here Gerry Murray (left), the captain of a Chicago team, and Midge Brashun, playing for Brooklyn, fight for the lead position in a 1947 match in Chicago. (Bettmann/CORBIS)*

Following Runyon's advice, matches became known as bouts, and the play depended more on dramatic embellishments than athletic skill, resulting in a form of entertainment instead of a true sport. Because the rules allow a certain amount of roughhousing, skaters readily engage in pushing, shoving, and pulling hair (helmets would come years later); broken wrists and concussions became an expected aspect of a good Roller Derby.

As predicted by Runyon, the followers of derbies went wild for the heightened violence of the sport, and 50 cities hosted contests for a combined total of more than 5 million spectators in 1940 alone. The growth of fan clubs accompanied this enthusiasm, some offering newsletters to their members. The *Roller Derby News,* renamed *Roller Rage* in the early 1940s, became popular for keeping fans informed about the exploits of their favorite teams. The entry of the United States into World War II, however, interrupted the sport's ascent when many skaters enlisted in the armed forces and crowds dwindled.

After the war's end in 1945, interest in becoming a member of a Roller Derby team, as well as attending an event, resumed, and growth continued through the remaining years of the decade. A number of communities on the East Coast organized local leagues and in 1949 the National Roller Derby League formed with six clubs: the New York Chiefs, Brooklyn Red Devils, New Jersey Jolters, Philadelphia Panthers, Washington-Baltimore Jets, and the Chicago Westerners. The league's first-season, week-long playoffs at Madison Square Garden in New York City sold out.

CBS (Columbia Broadcasting System), encouraged by the increasing number of fans, decided to feature Roller Derby on its fledging **television** network. Contests would be easy to capture on camera, given the confined space of the track. Beginning on November 29, 1948, matches, primarily between the New York Chiefs and Brooklyn Red Devils, aired weekly. Although few people owned television sets at the time, the broadcasts could be seen in bars and storefront windows. At the conclusion of CBS's 13-week run, the **ABC (American Broadcasting Company)** bought the rights and, in 1949, began a Roller Derby series that only ceased in 1951 because of scheduling disputes.

After the debut of Roller Derby on television, stars such as Midge "Tuffy" Brashun, Elmer "Elbows" Anderson, and Gerry Murphy (all active 1940s and 1950s) became household names. By 1952, interested parties had formed the Roller Derby Hall of Fame in New York City and inducted its first members, Johnny Rosasco and Josephine "Ma" Bogash (both active 1940s and 1950s).

Roller Derby, with all of its action, also received attention from Hollywood. Paramount Pictures produced a one-reel short subject, *Roller Derby Girl* in 1949. Nominated for an Academy Award, it lost to another Paramount production, *Aquatic House Party,* another short, about performing seals. Twentieth Century-Fox offered a full-length feature *The Fireball* (1950) starring Mickey Rooney (b. 1920). It tells the story of a kid who runs away from an orphanage and becomes a Roller Derby star. Marilyn Monroe (1926–1962), in one of her first credited performances, appears as a friend of Rooney's in a small role.

During the later 1940s, Roller Derby briefly threatened to replace wrestling as television's favorite sport, but as the action became more stylized, the novelty began to diminish. Early in the 1950s, attendance suffered a dramatic fall and television networks stopped broadcasting derbies. With declining interest and little likelihood of the sport continuing on the East Coast, Leo Seltzer moved from New York to Los Angeles. There he helped form two West Coast teams, the LA Braves and the San Francisco Bay Bombers. Bouts were held but with limited success, until the late 1950s, when Seltzer and his son, Jerry (b. 1932), syndicated Roller Derby to West Coast television stations. Interest waned again in the early 1960s with some revival occurring in the 1970s.

*See also:* Fads; Radio Programming: News, Sports, Public Affairs, and Talk; Skating (Roller)

**Selected Reading**
Coppage, Keith. *Roller Derby to Roller Jam.* Santa Rosa, CA: Squarebooks, 1999.
National Museum of Roller Skating. www.rollerskatingmuseum.com
National Roller Derby Hall of Fame. www.rollerderbyhalloffame.com
Roberts, Randy, and James Olson. *Winning Is the Only Thing: Sports in America since 1945.* Baltimore: Johns Hopkins University Press, 1991.
Roller Derby Events. *New York Times,* September 11, 1936; August 18, 1946; November 28, 1948. www.proquest.com

# ROOSEVELT, ELEANOR

At age 21, Anna Eleanor Roosevelt (1884–1962), best-known as Eleanor, married a distant cousin, **Franklin Delano Roosevelt** (1882–1945). At the time, she had recently returned to the United States from England, where she had completed her **education** at Allenswood, a school for girls. Once back home, she participated in charitable activities deemed appropriate for a young educated woman from a well-established and wealthy New York family. As a married woman, she moved from those community activities to family matters, raising five children; backing her husband's political career as he won elections to the New York State Senate in 1910, New York governorship in 1928, and president of the United States in 1932, 1936, 1940, and 1944; and assisting him as he struggled with infantile paralysis (polio).

By 1940, in addition to the care and support she offered to family and others while fulfilling the duties of first lady for seven years, Eleanor had become an accomplished person within her own right, earning respect for her myriad activities as a social activist for **youth,** women, blacks, and the downtrodden; humanitarian; newspaper and magazine columnist; prolific author; teacher; lecturer; and **radio** personality.

Always mindful of world affairs and the hostilities and oppression growing in Europe, Roosevelt used her pen to voice opposition to the injustices occurring in other countries. For example, *Christmas: A Story,* published by Alfred A. Knopf in 1940 and first written for *Liberty Magazine,* tells of a family living in Nazi-occupied Holland gaining strength from their faith and the meaning of Christmas. At this time, in addition to her writing, Roosevelt joined other Americans, such as authors John Dos Passos (1896–1970) and Upton Sinclair (1878–1968), in the newly formed Emergency Rescue Committee and attempted to assist European refugees with relocation. She also worked with the U.S. Committee for the Care of European Children founded by Quaker Clarence Pickett (1884–1965) in 1940. This group focused on removing British children from cities heavily bombed by the Germans and assisting German Jewish refugee children. Both groups were hampered in their work to bring children to the United States because of quota restrictions contained in the Immigration Act of 1924. Nevertheless, throughout World War II, Eleanor Roosevelt worked tirelessly on refugee issues.

First Lady Eleanor Roosevelt, a woman of principle, revealed in her writings convictions on issues that she deemed pertinent to a democracy and a way of life for its citizens. In *The Moral Basis of Democracy* (1940), released by Howell, Soskin Publishers,

*United Nations delegate and chair of the UN Human Rights Commission, former first lady Eleanor Roosevelt poses for a picture outside UN headquarters in New York City. (Photofest)*

she elaborates on her long-held belief that civil rights serve as the litmus test of a democracy. Just one year earlier, she had acted on this opinion when she withdrew her membership from the Daughters of the American Revolution (DAR) and arranged for Marian Anderson (1897–1993), an accomplished black contralto, to give an open-air concert at the Lincoln Memorial. This followed a refusal by the DAR to allow Anderson to perform at its Constitution Hall in Washington, DC.

During the World War II years, life on the home front occupied much of Roosevelt's time. She played an important role in the establishment of the Fair Employment Practices Committee established by Executive Order 8802 on June 25, 1941. It outlawed racial discrimination in industries that received defense contracts, urged equal treatment for blacks in the military, and serves as only one example of many presidential decisions strongly influenced by the first lady. She was particularly ardent about the continued implementation of New Deal polices and programs, a position that she maintained and argued for throughout the conflict.

Just a few hours after the early morning attack by Japanese aircraft on Pearl Harbor in December 1941, Eleanor Roosevelt went ahead with her scheduled weekly radio broadcast. She took the opportunity to acknowledge the fear and concern sweeping the nation, urged calmness and determination in carrying out the ordinary business of the day, and asked for support in the war effort.

On the West Coast, high anxiety prevailed, with hysterical fear directed toward Japanese Americans living in the region. The federal government responded by establishing 10 relocation centers to house people of Japanese ancestry. Always acknowledging what was happening and how it affected those at home, Eleanor wrote "A Challenge to American Sportsmanship," which appeared in *Collier's* magazine on October 16, 1943. The piece supports the federal government's decision to establish **internment camps,** but also urges everyone to view "our Japanese problem objectively" and to remember that "we cannot progress if we look down upon any group of people among us because of race or religion." She had first iterated this position in 1942, when she wrote an article titled "What Are We Fighting For?" for *American Magazine,* in which she stated that the war was about fighting for freedom, which had to include freedom from racial discrimination.

Whenever Roosevelt had the opportunity, she urged citizens to volunteer in the war effort in any way they could. She briefly served as deputy director of the Office of Civilian Defense (OCD). Upon accepting the job, she immediately became the scapegoat for those critical of her and her husband's administration. Both Republicans and Southern Democrats accused her of using the $100 million (approximately $1.3 billion in 2008 dollars) appropriated for the OCD to place "unfortunate idle rich people" in civilian defense jobs. She resigned, realizing that she could be more effective in an unofficial capacity. In her daily column "My Day," which ran in many newspapers, and in her speeches and radio broadcasts, she supported the war loan drives, **scrap drives, victory gardens,** and **USO (United Service Organizations)** activities and **canteens,** always mindful of voicing encouragement and boosting American morale. She offered encouragement to all those fighting in the war, answered letters received from soldiers, and traveled to military bases in England, the South Pacific, and New Zealand.

Eleanor Roosevelt stressed the necessity of women going to work to fill in the job gaps created by the large numbers of men enlisting or being drafted. Despite labor-pool needs and Roosevelt's support of women working, many Americans voiced opposition because they clung to the belief that mothers belonged at home. To address the issue of children being left at home unsupervised, or sleeping in cars parked in the defense plant parking lot, the first lady advocated the establishment of day care centers and takeout kitchens at war defense industries. Under Community Facilities Grants legislation passed by Congress in 1942, President Roosevelt, at his wife's urging, approved the construction of four government-sponsored child care centers.

Dedicated to this cause, Mrs. Roosevelt immediately embarked upon a campaign to get private industry to follow the federal government's example. She met with Edgar F. Kaiser (1908–1981), chairman of the Kaiser Company. In 1939, Kaiser had established a shipbuilding company with seven yards on the West Coast, four in Richmond, California, and three on the Columbia River in the vicinity of Vancouver, Washington, and Swan Island, near Portland, Oregon. High production from these plants was essential to the outcome of the war, and, thanks to Roosevelt's efforts and Edgar Kaiser's commitment, the Kaiser Company built state-of-the-art 24-hour day care centers—two in Portland and two in Richmond. As a bonus, Kaiser employees could also pick up a fully cooked meal from a takeout kitchen to have with their family that evening. Descriptions and reports of the Kaiser day care facilities and programs indicate they provided exemplary child care and early childhood education. Estimates indicate that, thanks to Eleanor Roosevelt, the Kaiser and government centers served up to 1.6 million children during the war. The two centers in Richmond, operated by he Richmond School District, continue to function as child care facilities in the 21st century.

Roosevelt's speeches, writing, and radio appearances did not stop with the end of the war. She continued with her syndicated column, "My Day." Running six days a week since 1935, it appeared in **newspapers** across the country until shortly before her death in 1962. *If You Ask Me,* a monthly question-and-answer column, appeared in the *Ladies Home Journal,* June 1941 to May 1949, and then moved to Mc*Call's,* where it remained until 1962. Appleton-Century published an anthology of her "My Day" columns in 1946 in a book under the same title. A regular on radio since shortly after her husband's 1933 inauguration, she continued to be heard until 1951. She teamed with her daughter Anna Roosevelt Boettiger (1906–1975) for a show called *Eleanor and Anna Roosevelt.* A popular program, it aired three times a week from November 1948 through September 1949 on **ABC (American Broadcasting Company)** radio.

Even with all of the preceding in place, following the death of Franklin in April 1945 Eleanor faced the question of "What now?" She quickly moved from the White House to her apartment in New York City, and over the remaining years of her life resided there and at Springwood, the family estate in Hyde Park, New York. She lent her name to Democratic Party fundraisers, hosted events commemorating Franklin Roosevelt's major accomplishments, and campaigned for local, state, and national political candidates. By 1949, she had completed the writing of *This I Remember,* the story of her 12 years in the White House published by Harper, and her second autobiography. The first, *The Autobiography of Eleanor Roosevelt* came out in 1937 and covered her life up to 1924.

**President Harry S. Truman** (1884–1972) appointed her as a delegate to the **United Nations,** providing her the means for finding a new, postwar public role. As such, she made major contributions to the human rights of individuals around the globe. She became head of the UN Human Rights Commission in 1946, a position she held for seven years. Roosevelt also oversaw the drafting and unanimous passage of the Universal Declaration of Human Rights, an accomplishment that further embellished her international reputation.

Eleanor Roosevelt's final presidential appointment came in 1961, when President John F. Kennedy (1917–1963) appointed her as chair of the President's Commission on the Status of Women. She accepted the job with strong credentials: her work on the Universal Declaration of Human Rights, her lifetime defense of a woman's right to both economic opportunity and fulfilling the traditional role in the family, and her continuous efforts to respect and work for the betterment of all people. Anna Eleanor Roosevelt—first lady of the United States, first lady of the world, diplomat, and humanitarian—held this position until her death in 1962 at the age of 78.

*See also:* Magazines; Radio Programming: News, Sport, Public affairs, and Talk; Race Relations and Stereotyping; Rosie the Riveter; War Bonds

**Selected Reading**
Eleanor Roosevelt Papers Project. www.gwu.edu/~erpapers/
Goodwin, Doris Kearns. *No Ordinary Time: Franklin and Eleanor Roosevelt: The Home Front in World War II.* New York: Simon & Schuster, 1994.
Lash, Joseph P. *Eleanor: The Years Alone.* New York: W. W. Norton, 1972.
———. *Eleanor and Franklin: The Story of Their Relationship, Based on Eleanor Roosevelt's Private Papers.* New York: W. W. Norton, 1971.

# ROOSEVELT, PRESIDENT FRANKLIN DELANO

The 1940 election of Franklin D. Roosevelt (1882–1945), frequently referred to as FDR, to his third consecutive term as president of the United States brought to an end an unwritten two-term presidential tradition. At the Democratic Party's 1939 convention, Roosevelt easily won the nomination against Henry A. Wallace (1888–1965) by 946 to 147 votes. He then chose Wallace as his running mate and went on to defeat Republican Wendell Willkie (1892–1944), winning 38 of the 48 states and gaining 54.8 percent of the popular vote. Roosevelt again won the party's nomination in 1944 and captured a fourth term as president, with 53.5 percent of the vote while carrying 36 states. The surprise in the 1944 election involved the selection of **Harry S. Truman** (1884–1972) as Roosevelt's choice for vice president; at the urging of the party, he dropped Wallace after one term because many politicians saw Wallace as too liberal.

Franklin Roosevelt came to his first presidential term in 1933 well prepared. After studying as a child under the guidance of his parents and private tutors, he enrolled at age 14 in Groton School, a prestigious boarding school in Groton, Massachusetts. From there he matriculated to Harvard University, receiving a BA degree in history in 1903. Two years later, he married a distant cousin, Anna **Eleanor Roosevelt** (1884–1962); the couple had six children, five of whom lived beyond infancy.

Roosevelt next pursued law at Columbia University but never graduated. He nonetheless passed the New York bar examination in 1907 and briefly practiced before entering politics in 1910, when he won a seat in the New York State Senate; he achieved reelection two years later. President Woodrow Wilson (1856–1924) appointed him to be assistant secretary of the navy, a position he held from 1913 to 1920.

Before assuming these positions Franklin had early on pursued various hobbies that he continued throughout his life. He exhibited a strong interest in stamp collecting, perhaps influenced initially by his mother's ongoing collection. After becoming president, Roosevelt asked cabinet members traveling abroad to save him interesting foreign stamps. He also had Postmaster General James A. Farley (1888–1976) send the first sheets of new issues to him, always paying for them. He even designed some stamps, encouraged various commemoratives, and frequently received gifts of stamps or exchanged them with fellow philatelists.

*Meeting at Yalta in the Soviet Crimea on February 9, 1945, (from the left) Winston Churchill, Franklin D. Roosevelt, and Joseph Stalin take a break from their talks that dealt with a defeated Germany and other postwar issues. (Photofest)*

From a very young age, he also developed a passion for boats and sailing and learned how to make working toy models. He became a skilled sailor and over his lifetime collected thousands of books, manuscripts, pamphlets, and articles on U.S. naval history. As president, whenever he could and despite his paralysis, Roosevelt enjoyed short excursions aboard the presidential yacht *Sequoia* or on his sailing yacht *Amberjack II*. His **hobbies** provided another way for him to connect with a significant number of his fellow citizens.

Stricken with infantile paralysis (polio) in the summer of 1921, Roosevelt became paralyzed from the waist down. For the rest of his life, in an attempt to overcome the disease, he spent as much time as he could in Warm Springs, Georgia, **swimming.** Although the waters did not provide a cure, the activity strengthened his upper body, enabling him to walk with some form of assistance, such as a cane or the arm of a companion. During this time, he maintained a political presence with the skillful help of both his wife and his political adviser, Louis Howe (1871–1936). He concealed his physical limitations as best he could and in 1928 moved into the New York governor's mansion in Albany. Reelected to that position in 1930, he also began to campaign for the presidency and the 1932 election.

Following his inauguration in 1933, FDR, determined to pull the country out of an unprecedented economic depression, during his first 100 days called a special session of Congress. He introduced and oversaw a flurry of New Deal legislation, including a massive program headed by the Works Projects Administration (WPA; 1933–1943), which provided jobs for laborers, artists, writers, musicians, and authors. The Civilian Conservation Corps (CCC; 1933–1942) employed thousands of young men, and the Social Security Act, passed in 1935, created federal unemployment compensation and old-age and survivors' benefits.

In carrying out his many duties, Roosevelt strongly believed in the importance of direct communication with the American public and capitalized on the use of **radio** and film. On March 12, 1933, he initiated his "Fireside Chats," a series of evening radio broadcasts made from either the White House or his home at Hyde Park, with each devoted to a single issue. Thousands of letters arrived at the White House following a chat; Roosevelt's staff saw to it that cameras recorded his radio broadcasts and excerpts then appeared at theaters in the newsreel segment seen between two Hollywood features. The announcement of the showing of one at a movie house guaranteed an increase in the number of patrons seeking admission. He presented a total of 30 such chats, 16 during the 1940s, with the first on National Defense (May 26, 1940) and the last focusing on the Fifth War Loan Drive (June 12, 1944).

By 1939, Roosevelt's presidential attention had increasingly moved away from issues at home to foreign affairs, and his one and only Fireside Chat that year dealt with the European War. Soon fierce debate over aid to England consumed the conversations of many across the country. Antiwar activists, convinced that assistance to Britain would draw the United States into the war, grew in numbers. In the Fireside Chats of the 1940s, Roosevelt dealt with various aspects of the war effort, mentioning freedom of the seas, war loan drives, wartime conferences, the home front, and plans for peace. These topics outnumbered discussions of other pressing issues at the time, such as economic policies and inflation.

On December 29, 1940, Roosevelt delivered a chat that has become known as his "arsenal for democracy" speech. In his comments, he stressed national security and the common cause, all in an attempt to undercut his opponents and set a tone for the introduction of legislation called the Lend-Lease Bill. In his closing lines, Roosevelt proclaims that "not the American government, but the American people have the power to turn the tide of the European war" and that "we must be the great arsenal of democracy."

One week later, on January 6, 1941, in his annual State of the Union message, Roosevelt continued with the theme of America's role in the world conflict and of the fundamental purposes of American democracy. This resulted in another famous speech, called the "Four Freedoms," in which Roosevelt articulated the basic principles of the U.S. political system: freedom of speech, freedom of worship, freedom from want, and freedom from fear. In the early months of 1943, four issues of the popular *Saturday Evening Post* magazine carried illustrator Norman Rockwell's (1894–1978) rendering of Roosevelt's four freedoms. In April, officials sent the paintings on a nationwide tour as a part of a war bond drive and Rockwell's works became the subject of a popular series of **posters.**

On March 11, 1941, soon after the Four Freedoms speech, Congress signed into law legislation that the Roosevelt administration called the Lend-Lease Act. In order to assist other countries militarily, the bill allowed Roosevelt to "sell, transfer title to, exchange, lease, lend or otherwise dispose of articles to any country he decided was vital to U.S. security." An early component of this bill, a "destroyers-for-bases" deal between Roosevelt and British Prime Minister Winston Churchill (1874–1965), drew mixed reaction from Congress and the American public. In the long run, Roosevelt received praised for his skill in obtaining permission from the British to build seven airfields and six bases on their soil in exchange for 50 aging U.S. destroyers. By the time the war ended, the Lend-Lease program had assisted some 38 countries, with Great Britain receiving the largest share. The total figure given for this aid ranges from $13.5 to $20 billion (approximately $178 billion to $264 billion in 2008 dollars).

As the war intensified in Europe, Roosevelt and Churchill decided to meet. Through arrangements made by Secretary of Commerce Harry Hopkins (1890–1946), a frequent and close presidential advisor, the two leaders met aboard British and U.S. naval vessels anchored in Placentia Bay, Newfoundland, Canada, on August 9–12, 1941. From their discussions, a statement of agreement called the Atlantic Charter outlined the two country's war aims. The document became the basis for a Declaration of the United Nations signed on January 1, 1942, by China, the United Kingdom, the United States, and the Union of Soviet Socialist Republics at a conference held in Washington, DC. Eventually 22 other nations would add their endorsement. The original signers of the declaration agreed to stand as united nations in fighting the Axis powers—Germany, Italy, and Japan—making the document the first to officially use the term "**United Nations.**"

Shortly after Roosevelt's meeting with Churchill, Japan launched a surprise attack on Pearl Harbor. Japanese aircraft sank eight battleships, three light cruisers, three destroyers, and four auxiliary craft; 2,403 service people died, with 1,178 left wounded. The next day, at 12:30 p.m., Roosevelt delivered his "Day of Infamy" speech, the title coming from his declaration that December 7 will be remembered as "a date which will live in infamy." Within an hour, Congress passed a formal declaration of war against Japan. Four days later, Germany and Italy declared war on the United States, giving President Roosevelt, as commander-in-chief of all U.S. armed forces, a war to fight on two fronts—the Pacific and European theaters. World War II would dominate the remaining years of FDR's presidency.

Three wartime conferences played a large part in the course that World War II followed and provided some firsts for a U.S. president. Roosevelt's attendance at a meeting held in Casablanca, Morocco, January 14–24, 1943, made him the first U.S. president to travel to Africa and the first to leave the country during a time of war. Churchill also attended; Soviet Premier Joseph Stalin (1878–1953) declined. By January 24, agreement had been reached that unconditional surrender would be demanded of Germany, Italy, and Japan and that a massive cross-channel invasion of Europe would be undertaken.

Stalin joined Roosevelt and Churchill for a second conference held at the Soviet embassy in Tehran, Iran, from November 28 to December 1, 1943. Here the Big Three decided to proceed with the invasion of Europe, tentatively set for May 1944. The leaders met for a final wartime conference at the Black Sea resort of Yalta in the Soviet Crimea on February 4–12, 1945. Their focus involved postwar issues: how to treat a defeated Germany, the future of Poland, Eastern Europe, Japanese-occupied East Asia, and the structure of a new United Nations organization.

In addition to building an alliance against the Axis powers and providing leadership in wartime conferences, FDR took an active role in choosing the principal field commanders for World War II. They included **General George Catlett Marshall** (1880–1959), **General Dwight David Eisenhower** (1890–1969), and **General Douglas MacArthur** (1880–1964), as well as several other outstanding officers. Successful campaigns in North Africa in November 1942 and in Sicily and Italy in 1943 eventually led to the **D-Day** landings on Normandy beaches in France on June 6, 1944. By April 1945, victory in Europe appeared certain.

While World War II raged, FDR continued to keep U.S. citizens informed about ongoing events. In addition to his effective use of radio and newsreels, he carefully worked with the Washington news media. He averaged two press conferences per week during his four-term presidency, for a total of 997 meetings. At these gatherings, he usually conveyed an attitude of informality, calling the reporters by their first names and frequently engaging in humorous exchanges. He almost always managed to offer some dramatic news that warranted front-page coverage. Because of FDR's pleasant routine, the press tended to present his policies in a favorable light, and photographers never showed him in an awkward position.

Despite, and because of, World War II, Franklin Roosevelt made some significant civil rights decisions, many suggested by Eleanor. Throughout his administration, he appointed a number of black men and women to administrative positions. Known as the Black Cabinet, these individuals primarily assisted as advisors from New Deal agencies. Perhaps the most famous, educator Mary McLeod Bethune (1875–1955), served as director of the National **Youth** Administration's Division of Negro Affairs (1935–1943).

Beginning in 1941, Roosevelt issued a series of executive orders designed to guarantee racial, religious, and ethnic groups equal opportunity when securing defense jobs and serving in the military. By the end of the war, the number of black workers in manufacturing and government jobs had increased significantly. For example, the number of black individuals serving as federal employees more than doubled from 8.4 percent in 1938 to 19 percent in 1944. Roosevelt advocated the admission of blacks into better positions in the military. Between 1940 and 1945, blacks in the armed forces increased from 5,000 to 920,000, and black officers grew from 5 to over 7,000. Previously, almost every black soldier received a lowly assignment to a service unit, such as **food** services. By 1945, they held more responsible jobs, receiving placement with artillery, tank, and infantry commands; a selected few served as pilots.

On the other hand, in Executive Order 9066, Roosevelt made the final decision on the military's authority to declare areas from which any or all persons, regardless of their citizenship, could be excluded. This resulted in the imprisonment of between 110,000 and 120,000 Japanese American citizens in 10 bleak **internment camps;** many remained there until after the war. Also the government confined some 5,000 Germans and Italians, both citizens and aliens, to camps at Fort Lincoln near Bismarck, North Dakota, and Fort Missoula, Montana.

A president that serves for 12 years has many opportunities to make significant appointments. Roosevelt, by naming Frances C. Perkins (1882–1962) as secretary of labor, 1933 to 1945, gave the country its first woman cabinet member. She, along with Secretary of the Interior Harold L. Ickes (1874–1952), have the honor of being the only two who retained their cabinet chairs for the entire time Roosevelt served as president. Cordell Hull (1871–1956) held the record as the longest-serving secretary of state, carrying out the responsibilities of the office for 11 years, 1933 to 1944. Henry Wallace, who had served as vice president during FDR's third term, held the positions of secretary of agriculture from 1933 to 1940 and secretary of commerce in 1945. President Roosevelt appointed eight Justices to the Supreme Court of the United States, five during the 1940s. Only George Washington (ca. 1732–1799), who named 10, exceeded him in the number of court appointments. In 1941, FDR promoted Harlan Fiske Stone (1872–1946) from Associate Justice to Chief Justice. He would remain in that position until 1946.

Throughout his life, FDR dealt with a variety of personal health issues, including routine childhood diseases, typhoid fever, pneumonia, influenza, surgery for appendicitis, and a tonsillectomy. Despite these ailments and the physical disability caused by polio, medical records indicate that he had great vitality and remained reasonably healthy and active up to 1943. Pictures and records indicate that following the Tehran Conference in November of that year, his condition rapidly declined. In early 1944, his doctor made a diagnosis of hypertension, heart disease, cardiac distress, and acute bronchitis. He did not shirk his duties. Despite the regimen of a low-fat diet, weight reduction, and medication, Franklin Delano Roosevelt died at Warm Springs from a massive cerebral hemorrhage on April 12, 1945, just one month before V-E Day. A funeral train brought his body back to Washington, DC. After the official ceremonies, another train carried him to Hyde Park for interment. Thousands of citizens lined the tracks as his cortege passed.

*See also:* Aviation; Axis Sally and Tokyo Rose; Blackouts, Brownouts, and Dim-Outs; Photography; Political and Propaganda Films; Race Relations and Stereotyping; Radio Programming: News, Sports, Public Affairs, and Talk; Religion; Rosie the Riveter; Scrap Drives; Toys; V-E and V-J Day; Victory Gardens; War Bonds; War Films

**Selected Reading**
Beschloss, Michael. *The Conquerors: Roosevelt, Truman and the Destruction of Hitler's Germany, 1941–1945.* New York: Simon & Schuster, 2002.
Gies, Joseph. *Franklin D. Roosevelt: Portrait of a President.* Garden City, NY: Doubleday, 1971.
Goodwin, Doris Kearns. *No Ordinary Time: Franklin and Eleanor Roosevelt: The Home Front in World War II.* New York: Simon & Schuster, 1994.
Graham, Otis L., and Meghan Robinson Wander, eds. *Franklin D. Roosevelt, His Life and Times: An Encyclopedic View.* New York: G. K. Hall, 1985.

# ROSIE THE RIVETER

This iconic name, representative of the millions of working women in wartime America, did not take hold until late in 1942. Prior to that, calls to women to join the growing workforce did not employ Rosie or any other name; many pleas were made—"Take His Place," "Get a War Job!" "Do the Job HE Left Behind," "It's a Woman's War, Too!"—but they did not yet have Rosie as a symbol.

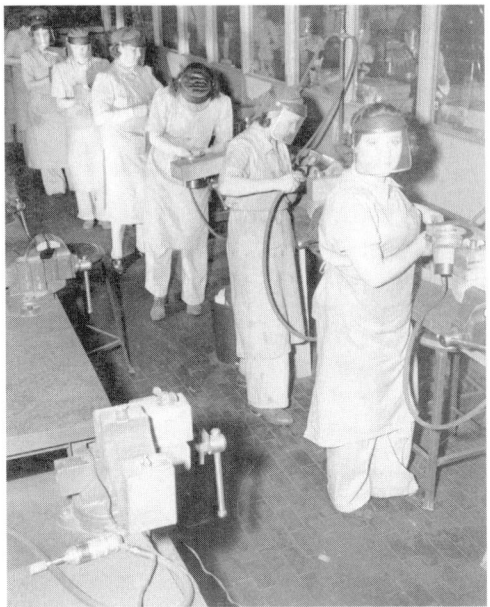

*When wartime manpower shortages depleted available factory workers, American women flocked to newly available jobs once reserved for men. Here women operate tools on an assembly line. With the end of the war in 1945, most such jobs reverted to men, and women again had to seek employment in more traditional settings. (Photofest)*

Illustrator J. Howard Miller (ca. 1915–1990) received a commission earlier in 1942 from the Westinghouse War Production Co-Ordinating Committee to create a morale-boosting poster for its various defense plants that employed growing numbers of women. His painting, "We Can Do It!" depicts a determined-looking, bandanna-topped worker beneath those words, raising her right arm and flexing her bicep, and it quickly attracted a wide circle of admirers. The artist used a woman named Geraldine Hoff Doyle (b. 1924) as his model, but he based his painting on a wire photo he saw of her working at a Michigan factory. Not until much later did Doyle discover that she had become one of the most enduring images to emerge from World War II. Famous as Miller's poster was, it did not purport to be Rosie, although over time many people have assumed his painting depicts her.

Rosie first received widespread mention in a popular song written toward the end of 1942. "Rosie the Riveter," with words and music by Redd Evans (1912–1972) and John Jacob Loeb (1910–1970), joined a rush of war-oriented music then filling the airwaves. Originally introduced by a vocal group called the Four Vagabonds, along with recordings by popular bands like the one led by Kay Kyser (1906–1985), it did not make the music charts as a big hit but clearly had an impact on public perceptions about women moving into the workforce. Apparently inspired by a woman named Rosalind Walter (active 1940s) who worked on airplanes at the Grumman Aircraft Corporation's Long Island plant, Evans's and Loeb's lyrics portray Rosie "rain or shine . . . a part of the assembly line," a faithful, hard-working employee, the equal of any man. Other sources, however, credit Rosina Bonavita (active 1940s), an employee at the Consolidated Vultee Aircraft (Convair) factory in San Diego, as the person responsible for the genesis of the song, although her work as a riveter came after the publication of the music's lyrics. East Coast or West Coast, the image of Rosie nonetheless took hold as an admirable home-front notable.

With the fictitious Rosie assuming a place in the nation's consciousness, Hollywood in 1943 released a short (three-minute) musical film that bore the title *Rosie the Riveter*. As would be the case of anything so brief—called in those days a "soundie"—it elicited little attention. That same year, however, Universal Pictures released *Follow the Band*, a feature-length film that utilizes the talents of numerous musicians but skimps on plot. Nonetheless, its soundtrack includes "Rosie the Riveter" as performed by guitarist Alvino Rey (1908–2004) and His Orchestra. This exposure helped further popularize both the song and the idea of women working in nontraditional jobs.

One year later, in 1944, another feature called *Rosie the Riveter* played theaters around the country. This Republic offering stars Jane Frazee (1918–1985) as a hardworking individual trying to hold down a defense job and deal with wartime housing shortages. Its musical score, despite the title, fails to include Evans's and Loeb's by-now famous tune, but instead has two innocuous pieces, "I Don't Want Anybody at All" and "Why Can't I Sing a Love Song?" But by this time, Rosie had become as famous as many real-life military heroes.

Norman Rockwell (1894–1978), at the time far and away the best-known and most popular illustrator in the country, added to Rosie's renown when he painted a humorous portrait of her in full working garb. His efforts graced the cover of the *Saturday Evening Post* on May 29, 1943. He took as his inspiration not anyone from a factory, but instead looked back to the Renaissance and Michelangelo's famous 16th-century Sistine Chapel ceiling. One of the artist's creations shows the prophet Isaiah, and Rockwell borrowed this pose to depict his version of Rosie.

He did, however, use a local Vermont woman, Mary Doyle Keefe (b. 1928) as his model. But the end result hardly resembled the petite neighbor he had hired for five dollars a day to pose (about $60 in 2008 dollars). Rockwell's Rosie—and he clearly identifies her as Rosie the Riveter, the name emblazoned on her lunch pail, riveting gun across her ample lap—has a classical monumentality, with massive arms and torso, yet she also projects a certain femininity with dainty curls in her red hair, painted nails and lipstick, and a lace hanky tucked in her coveralls as she delicately eats her ham sandwich. He also gives her a halo above her pushed-up visor and goggles, and her penny loafers disdainfully rest upon a ragged copy of *Mein Kampf.* Some time thereafter, Rockwell wrote Mary Doyle Keefe and apologized for making her several sizes larger, although she had never expressed any irritation about his artistic license.

Finally, a genuine Rosie emerged, thanks to the efforts of movie actor Walter Pidgeon (1897–1984). In 1943, he had been asked by the government to locate sites for promotional films encouraging the sale of **war bonds.** His task took him to Ypsilanti, Michigan, and the huge Ford aircraft plant located at Willow Run. In the course of his inquiries, he met Rose Will Monroe (1920–1997), busy at work riveting. Pidgeon quickly realized that Monroe put a real face on Rosie, and she subsequently appeared in several government-produced short films.

For the remainder of the war, many and varied images of Rosie the Riveter, both actual and imagined, could be found in factories, post offices, **magazines,** and anywhere else that people, especially women, might notice her. Her message—that even demanding defense work served as an entirely appropriate venue for women in times of national need—did not go unheeded. In 1940, about 12 million women held jobs of various kinds; by 1945 and the end of the war, over 18 million women worked, a number that represented over one-third of the total labor force. In defense-related sites, the places Rosies might likely be found, the increase grew by over 400 percent.

With peace, many industries urged their women employees to leave in order to create job slots for returning veterans. Many, but by no means all, followed this advice. In

1947, two years after the end of hostilities, almost 16 million women continued working, marking a significant and permanent change in the composition in the ranks of U.S. labor. Most of the stereotypes about helpless housewives, incompetent workers, lack of innate skills, inability to do heavy work, and all the rest came to an end during World War II and the influx of women into the ranks of factory workers. No small thanks for this change must go to the popular images of Rosie the Riveter.

*See also:* Art (Painting); Fashion; Illustrators; Musicals (Film); Radio; Radio Programming: Music and Variety Shows

**Selected Reading**
Colman, Penny. *Rosie the Riveter: Women Working on the Home Front in World War II.* New York: Crown Publishers, 1995.
Honey, Maureen. *Creating Rosie the Riveter: Class, Gender, and Propaganda during World War II.* Amherst: University of Massachusetts Press, 1984.
Rosie the Riveter (2 parts). www.youtube.com/watch?v=xo5KOCMDe68; www.youtube.com/watch?v=flWvxW4HgwQ

# S

## SCRAP DRIVES

The United States Office of Civilian Defense (OCD), created in May 1941, encouraged the American people to participate in a wide-ranging recycling program to benefit defense efforts. On the home front, citizens frequently participated in this program through scrap drives. With the country's active entry into World War II on December 7 of that year, the drives intensified. Among the most-needed items were rubber, all types of metal, kitchen grease, paper (books, **newspapers** and **magazines**), rags, and silk hosiery. Various industries then turned the collected commodities into weapons and other war-related products. In addition to providing essential materials, scrap drives gave ordinary people a way to feel involved, viewing their participation as a patriotic duty by contributing their time and their goods.

Most communities engaged in extensive publicity campaigns to identify items that could be donated and to stimulate involvement. Newspapers ran articles and cartoons; the government provided **radio** commercials, **posters,** and advertisements; movie theater owners cooperated by holding matinees with admission consisting of a certain amount of copper or other metal instead of money.

The War Production Board (WPB) identified school yards as collection sites, which easily allowed children to become part of the program. The WPB also provided curriculum suggestions such as writing essays or working out conversion figures to determine how many tin cans it would take to supply the tin needed for producing certain items. *Scholastic Magazine,* a periodical distributed to most schools then, offered articles that gave information on how to search attics and garages for salvage, described the mechanics of organizing scrap drives, and encouraged children to write letters to their parents and neighbors about the importance of this effort. The magazine also told of a government pamphlet containing a play script titled "War Against Waste Day" that could be performed by children.

Organized school and neighborhood clubs offered another way for children and young people to be involved in scrap drives and other patriotic efforts. In many cases, fictional heroes from the **comic strips** offered inspiration for these groups. For example, in the comic strip *Little Orphan Annie,* Annie became commander-in-chief of the Junior Commandos, a scrap-collecting organization for children that provided official cards, giveaways, posters, and songs. Advancement in rank from private to eventually captain came with how much tin and fat a member collected. Other media promoted children's participation, such as *Jack and Jill* magazine, which published a six-part story called "The Scrapper's Club" that told of a group of young people that found and alerted authorities about an abandoned trolley perfect for recycling and serving as an example of what others could do.

Of all the materials needed, rubber had appeared on the list before the war commenced. Supplies from the Dutch East Indies became scarce and could no longer be delivered to the United States

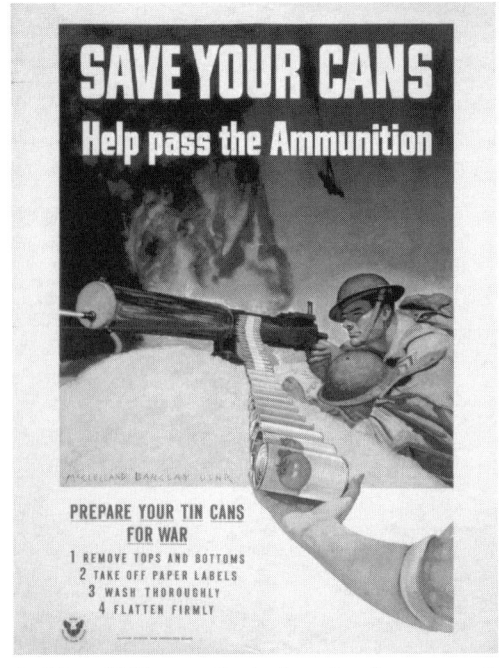

*In May 1941, months before the Japanese attack on Pearl Harbor, the federal government implemented scrap drives to collect materials that could be recycled into manufacturing military equipment for defense efforts. A variety of posters explained this effort; this one shows how tin cans can be turned into ammunition for a soldier's machine gun. (Library of Congress)*

when Japanese forces controlled that area. Catchy mottos such as "Save Rubber to Help Slap the Jap" were employed to increase collection participation. Discarded automobile tires, along with old rubber heels and soles from shoes, galoshes, and boots; rubber bands; car trunk and floor mats; and scrap rubber from manufacturing plants could easily push a community's rubber collection to millions of pounds. Steps that shifted rubber from the consumer market to the manufacturing world included a freeze on the sale of tires for the general public, a ban on recapping, and the requirement of a **rationing** certificate to purchase shoes and, in special cases, new tires. Recycled rubber, however, proved to be of inferior quality to the naturally occurring variety, and the eventual development and production of a synthetic did more than salvaging to help the United States win World War II.

In terms of metal, tin cans appeared high on the list of precious items because it could be used on aircraft instrument panels, bearings, and for solder in electrical equipment. Not harmed by salt water, tin became the ideal container lining for shipping food overseas to military personnel. This metal became so valuable that the WPB on October 19, 1942, issued a mandatory order for any city with a population of 25,000 or more to collect cans. Other scrap metal came from a variety of sources—slot machines, hammers, knives, keys, razors, daggers, revolvers, iron doors and fences, **toys,** ornamental metal on monuments, cannons, toothpaste tubes, and refrigerator cabinets. Many people, particularly children, peeled the tinfoil from gum and cigarette wrappers, creating a tinfoil ball large enough to be accepted at the collection site. Even the U.S. monetary system changed because of scrap drives. Copper went to war in 1943, when the Department of the Treasury began issuing **steel pennies** in lieu of the more familiar variety.

Prior to World War II, glycerin, like rubber, a critical material needed for the manufacture of gunpowder, came primarily from Pacific areas under Japanese control. Imported fats and oils also appeared on scarcity lists. Thus, the WPB urged homemakers to lead an effort to collect cooking grease to manufacture explosives. Three pounds of fat could provide enough glycerin to make a pound of gunpowder. In many communities, Boy and Girl Scouts and Camp Fire Girls helped the "fat campaign" by going house to house to collect their neighbors' saved grease.

By 1943, increased demand by the armed forces created a paper shortage. War activities requiring paper included packaging for shells, blueprint paper for drawing plans for new weapons, and paper milk bottles shipped to army camps. Magazines and books used an inferior quality paper, but collection centers nonetheless accepted them.

Even women's fashions became a part of the war story. Silk stockings had become a scarce item before the war started because of escalating prices set by Japan in the late 1930s. The DuPont Chemical Company answered this crisis in 1938 with the invention of nylon fiber, which provided an alternative for silk in hosiery and other products. Along with their leftover cooking grease, women were asked to turn in their silk stockings in order to make powder bags in naval and artillery guns and their nylon hosiery for the manufacture of parachutes and tow ropes for gliders. During the war, without stockings for proper dress, some women resorted to applying makeup to their legs and then taking a pen and drawing a seam line down the back of the calf so it appeared as if they were wearing them.

Scrap drives highlighted the value of recycling waste materials and reducing the consumption of war-related resources. The effort gained popularity, and numerous national drives occurred between 1941 and 1943. Many large companies such as Sears, Roebuck supported these efforts. With success, local drives proceeded on their own during 1944 and 1945. Towns and cities across the country developed a strong community spirit, sometimes with fierce competition among groups to collect the largest amount of products vital to the U.S. war effort. Historians debate just how much scrap drives contributed to winning the war; some believe that their importance has been exaggerated in the public memory. Either way, however, scrap drives did not slow the American embrace of product obsolescence, causing the continuous buying and consumption of new products as opposed to recycling and reusing.

*See also:* Advertising; Automobiles and the American Automotive Industry; Fashion; Technology; Youth

**Selected Reading**
Lingeman, Richard. *Don't You Know There's a War On? The American Home Front, 1941–1945.* New York: Thunder's Mouth Press, 1970.

Strasser, Susan. *Waste and Want: A Social History of Trash.* New York: Macmillan, 2000.
Winkler, Allan M. *Home Front U.S.A.: America during World War II.* Wheeling, IL: Harlan Davidson, 1986.

# SCULPTURE

In the United States, sculpture can be found in various forms and settings. Prior to 1940, it consisted primarily of decorative art objects made from marble or precious metals that resided in museums and the homes of the wealthy; folk art, such as weathervanes and wooden figureheads constructed for ships; busts and statutes formed from stone or clay that adorned public structures and large estates; decorative fountains; and sculpted copper and bronze on buildings. For the average American, sculpture meant traditional, realistic statues seen outside courthouses, in parks, and on the grounds of large homes.

The Work Projects Administration (WPA; 1935–1943), a New Deal program, provided jobs for a large number of artisans who produced countless numbers of paintings, murals, and sculptures. Displayed in public places across the United States, this undertaking exposed increasing numbers to fine art. In Washington, DC, alone, approximately 300 pieces of representational sculpture came to stand before many of the capital's buildings or on their grounds.

Two well-known sculptors during this time were James Earle Fraser (1876–1953) and Paul Manship (1885–1966). Fraser, remembered for his earlier works that included the Indian Head, or Buffalo, nickel (1913) and a seated horseman, *End of the Trail* (1915), had become a prolific creator of large-scale public monuments. For the 1939–1940 New York World's Fair, he made a 60-foot-tall plaster statue of George Washington (1732–1799), one of 160 pieces of sculpture displayed throughout the fair grounds. Washington anchored the central intersection of the main walkway, Constitution Mall, and faced the Trylon, a needlelike pyramid, and the Perisphere, a hollow sphere, designed by the New York architectural firm of Harrison and Fouilhoux (Wallace Harrison and Jacques-Andre Fouilhoux, 1895–1981 and 1879–1945, respectively). The Trylon and Perisphere, the symbols of the fair, accounted for two of a small number of purely abstract sculptures distributed throughout the fairgrounds.

In the same area, the *Time and Fates of Man* sundial and *Moods of Time* fountain by Paul Manship had been installed. At the time, the sundial ranked as the largest in the world. In 1934, Manship had sculpted the gilded *Prometheus,* which overlooks the skaters at New York City's Rockefeller Center.

Following the closing of the fair, Fraser completed seven large-scale works before his death. He executed four of them in the 1940s: an equestrian sculpture of Theodore Roosevelt (1858–1919), erected in Central Park in Manhattan (1940); one of Albert Gallatin (1761–1849), the longest-serving secretary of the Treasury (14 years), standing at the Department of Commerce Building in Washington, DC (1947); another of Benjamin Franklin (1706–1790) for the Franklin Insurance Company in Springfield, Illinois (1948); and finally a depiction of Thomas Edison (1847–1931) for Greenfield Village in Dearborn, Michigan (1949).

In addition, Jo Davidson (1883–1952), working primarily on portrait busts, sculpted the heads of the famous, including several of **President Franklin Delano Roosevelt** (1882–1945). He also did a likeness of singer **Frank Sinatra** (1915–1998) in 1946. The American Academy of Arts and Letters in Manhattan held a retrospective show of Davidson's work that same year.

Yet another American sculptor, Gutzon Borglum (1867–1941), became famous for a monumental work on Mount Rushmore in the Black Hills of South Dakota. Swinging from ropes or clinging to precarious positions on the sides of the mountain, he and his crew carved the heads of four presidents of the United States—George Washington, Abraham Lincoln (1809–1865), Thomas Jefferson (1743–1826), and Theodore Roosevelt. The project commenced in 1927 and did not reach completion until October 1941, a few months after Borglum's death. Numerous delays had kept the task, with its 60-feet-high busts and noses 20 feet long and mouths 18 feet wide, behind schedule for much of its duration.

Also in the Black Hills, sculptor Korczak Ziotkowski (1908–1982) in 1948 began carving his memorial to Chief Crazy Horse of the Sioux tribe. Ziotkowski had worked with Borglum on Mount Rushmore and took on this project to commemorate an Indian hero at the request of Sioux Chief Henry Standing Bear (ca. 1874–1953). Still far from completion in the early years of the 21st century, the final planned dimensions call for a piece 641 feet high and 563 feet wide. The head of Crazy Horse measures 87 feet high, outdistancing those of the nearby presidents by 27 feet.

Not all American sculptors subscribed to the traditional, despite its known popularity. Starting in the 1930s and continuing through the 1940s, sculpture, in the hands of some, moved away from strictly representational objects to abstract shapes that existed for their own sake with the intent to inspire, as well as surprise or shock, the viewers. Sculptors began to broaden both the materials and techniques they used as they joined in the avant-garde movements of surrealism, **abstract expressionism,** and constructivism. Four men—Alexander Calder (1898–1976), Joseph Cornell (1903–1972), Isamu Noguchi (1904–1988), and David Smith (1906–1965)—had productive careers during the 1940s and represent those artists who introduced new aesthetic approaches to sculpture.

*Alexander Calder.* Born in Philadelphia, Calder reigns as one of the most famous and popular American sculptors. He held miscellaneous jobs as a draftsman, engineer, and insurance company investigator before studying at the Art Students League in New York. He then embarked upon a multifaceted career as a sculptor, painter, illustrator, printmaker, and designer. In 1932, he exhibited his first suspended sculpture, which utilized motors to give it motion. The French artist Marcel Duchamp (1887–1968) called Calder's piece a "mobile," a term that stuck. Calder abandoned the mechanical aspects of this new art form when he realized that he could **design** a structure that undulated on its own from air currents. His first public commission for a mobile came in 1937 and consisted of a pair built for a new theater that opened in the Berkshire Museum in Pittsfield, Massachusetts. That same year he constructed his first large bolted "stabile," a nonmoving structure, to be placed outdoors.

Extremely productive during the 1940s, Calder created **toys,** jewelry, mobiles, and stabiles—the last two ranging from miniature to monumental. They easily found homes in museums and public places in many cities in the Western world. In 1943, he attempted to enlist in the Marine Corps to work with camouflage designs, but the examination board rejected him. Up to this time, Calder had primarily employed wire, sheet metal, and bronze as his materials, but the wartime scarcity of metal forced him to experiment with carved wood. This resulted in yet another original form of sculpture, wooden pieces anchored by wire and arranged in three dimensions, giving viewers a sense of the cosmos; thus the name "constellations."

Between 1939 and 1950, six Calder retrospective exhibits were held, three in the United States and three in Paris. In 1949, he constructed his largest mobile to date, *International Mobile,* for the Philadelphia Museum of Art's Third International Exhibition of Sculpture. The following year, Hollywood star Burgess Meredith (1907–1997) narrated *Works of Calder,* a film that Meredith also produced. The camera shows Calder at work in his shop, followed by shots of resultant pieces intercut with images from nature to illustrate the source of the sculptor's inspiration. Calder continued to be active until his death, which came shortly after the opening of a major retrospective show at the Whitney Museum in New York, in 1976.

*Joseph Cornell.* A self-taught sculptor, collage artist, and experimental filmmaker, Joseph Cornell lived the first 14 years of his life in Nyack, New York. He moved with his mother and sickly younger brother to Queens, New York, in 1917. Forced by the death of his father to take financial responsibility for his family, Cornell worked at a variety of jobs during the 1920s and 1930s, with textile design becoming the most permanent. He started assembling collages, almost by accident, as an after-work recreational pursuit at his kitchen table; constructing shadow boxes soon followed.

A natural collector, he accumulated a stash of advertisements, **fashion** shots, antique prints, art reproductions, photo spreads of singers and starlets, maps, and miscellaneous found objects long before he assembled his first collage or built his first shadow box. Widely read, Cornell regularly browsed used book shops, antique shops, and art galleries, where he became acquainted with Surrealist art dealer Julien Levy (1906–1981).

In the early 1930s, Cornell showed some of his collages to Levy, who, impressed by their romantic, sensual, and sophisticated qualities, included them in a survey of new surrealist artists at his gallery. Cornell's entries received a warm reception and cemented his future as a sculptor. In 1936, he made his first shadow box, and in 1938 his "Untitled (Soap Bubble Set)" appeared in an exhibit "Fantastic Art, Dada and Surrealism" at the Museum of Modern Art (MoMA). It ranked as one of the favorites in the show.

Two years later, Cornell resigned from his textile job and accepted some freelance illustration and layout jobs for **magazines** such as *House & Garden* (founded 1901) and *Vogue* (founded 1892), where he would continue intermittently until 1957. During World War II, he worked at a defense plant while continuing to work on his artistic assemblages in the evenings. Cornell often spent several years on his boxes, which came with two variants—resting on a table horizontally or hanging vertically on a wall. The tabletop boxes generally had lids that opened for viewing. Those intended for a wall show their contents to the viewer through transparent glass fronts.

Cornell admired screen and stage personalities and corresponded with his favorites. Despite his shyness, he sometimes met them backstage after attending a performance.

Using these opportunities to collect memorabilia, he then made elaborate, often romantic, boxes loaded with items, such as pictures of the star, hairpins, a scrap of clothing, or other keepsakes he had acquired. Examples include a vertical *Penny Arcade for Lauren Bacall* (early 1940s) and a horizontal *Homage to the Romantic Ballet* (1942).

Frequently, Cornell presented his boxes as a series: the Pharmacy group consists of drug store paraphernalia, while the Medici unit shows members of the Florentine family through ghostly reproductions of painted portraits. Other creative activities included writing and publishing articles in small-circulation magazines, most often *View* (founded 1940) and *Dance Index* (founded 1927). From 1950 until his death, Cornell continued to make collages. In the 1960s, he stopped building new boxes and instead reconstructed old ones.

*Isamu Noguchi.* California-born Japanese Irish Isamu Noguchi (1904–1988) completed his first sculpted piece in the mid-1920s. Over the course of his career he also worked as a designer, architect, and craftsman. Because he lived on the West Coast, he occasionally created busts of celebrities, such as George Gershwin (1898–1937) and Ginger Rogers (1911–1995), and fellow artists Martha Graham (1894–1991) and Berenice Abbott (1898–1991).

A turning point in his career came when he won an international competition to design a cast relief to stand above the entrance to the Associated Press building at Rockefeller Center in New York City. On April 29, 1940, he observed the installation of *News,* a stainless steel art deco plaque celebrating five journalists getting a scoop. He also had designed *Chassis Fountain* for the Ford Motor Company pavilion at the 1939–1940 New York World's Fair. Throughout his career, he continued to design fountains and always considered the water to be as important a material as the other elements.

Following his work in New York City, Noguchi resumed living in California shortly before Japan attacked Pearl Harbor in December 1941. He quickly returned East, which saved him from being rounded up with other Japanese Americans for relocation to **internment camps.** Wanting, however, to contribute to the war effort, he agreed to voluntarily enter the Poston, Arizona center with the intention of involving the refugees in arts and crafts; he hoped his instruction would provide them with skills that they could use once released. Noguchi entered Poston on May 12, 1942, just four days after it opened. The experience turned out to be a difficult one for him, and almost immediately Noguchi asked to leave, a process that took seven months.

Once again in New York, he did some stone carving with *Leda,* a stark geometric shape and his first piece after emerging from the camp. The next summer he carved *Noodle* out of stone, following it with *Time Lock.* In 1944, Noguchi began a series of works consisting of almost flat, interlocking shapes similar to constructions seen in surrealist paintings. Many critics consider *Kouros,* made from pink marble and standing nearly 10 feet tall, to be one of his masterpieces. During this time he also produced a series called *Lunars,* abstract, freestanding sculptures that incorporate hidden electric lights that produce glowing effects through openings. In 1946, MoMA included him in a show titled *Fourteen Americans.*

In addition to working as a sculptor, Noguchi occasionally designed stage sets. His first appeared in 1935 for Martha Graham and her early *Frontier.* In 1944, he accepted another request from Graham to design a set for *Appalachian Spring,* which she choreographed to music by **Aaron Copland** (1900–1990). Noguchi continued to design sets for the Martha Graham Dance Company, one in 1945 and again in 1946.

Active until his death at the age of 84, Noguchi worked with many materials, such as stone, stainless steel, driftwood, bones, paper, string, wire, wood, and plastic, and fashioned his sculptures in a variety of free forms. In addition to projects in the United States, he frequently traveled to Italy and Japan carrying out commissions in those countries.

*David Smith.* Born in Indiana, Smith (1906–1965) initially aspired to be a painter but switched to sculpture in 1931, making his first constructions from found objects. At the end of 1939, MoMA asked him for a loan of his *Blue Construction* for its sculpture garden. The piece had been displayed in the Contemporary Arts Building at the New York World's Fair. In November 1940, the Willard Gallery in Manhattan gave him his second solo show and the beginning of a decade of increased recognition. Subsequent shows of bronze and cast iron pieces almost became an annual event—1941, Minneapolis, St. Paul, and Kalamazoo; 1942, Minneapolis; 1943, Manhattan; and 1946, Manhattan—and art critics announced the inevitability of Smith becoming one of America's greatest artists. In 1947, the American Association of University Women sponsored a traveling retrospective exhibition of Smith's work.

The 1940 exhibit at the Willard consisted of 15 medallions cast in bronze. Called *Medals for Dishonor,* they offer a statement of protest in their depiction of the horrors of war. Two years later, as an alternative to military service, he took a welding job at the American Locomotive Company plant in Schenectady, New York, assembling M7 tanks and locomotives. He managed to continue with his sculpture, but on a limited basis. As a substitute to working with metal, which officials reserved for defense use, he learned to work with marble at a firm that made cemetery monuments.

Smith owned a farm in upstate New York at Bolton Landing on Lake George and in 1944 moved there to work full-time on his artwork. From then until the end of the decade, he experimented with the possibilities of forged and fabricated steel and bronze and welded metal in many variations. Frequently his sculpture contains miniature dramas or scenes such as *Widow's Lament* (1942–1943), in which a frame with four boxes convey four separate events in the widow's life. *Cockfight* (1945), in a vertical format, tells the story suggested by its title. *Jurassic Bird* (1945) is a linear, open-form composition, a drawing in air.

Much of Smith's work after 1949 came in series such as *Agricola*—22 sculptures produced over several years that incorporate farm tools and machinery and allude to agricultural life. The *Tanktotem* sculptures incorporate commercial boiler tops. He was at the height of his career when, in 1965, he died from injuries received in a vehicle accident on a road near Bennington, Vermont.

A number of sculptors during the 1940s, including those already mentioned, successfully utilized new approaches in both materials and techniques. Motion became a possibility, either by motorizing a sculpture or constructing it so that it moved with the wind or from the touch of a hand. Objects formed and gathered in a box told a story much as a painting might do. Welding and a paper-thin sheet of metal now allowed for freestanding and flat pieces to stand in sharp contrast with heavy monumental figures.

In the succeeding decades, sculptors such as Louise Nevelson (1899–1988) and Richard Lippold (1915–2002) took inspiration from these modern pioneers and combined the monumentality of the past and the abstraction of the 1940s. Another, Jose de Rivera (1904–1985), created elegant flowing linear forms in highly polished metal.

Many traditional sculptors, however, continued to execute realistic carvings, and most Americans who acknowledged an interest in sculpture professed a preference for recognizable figures and objects. For the 1949 Third Sculpture International show in Philadelphia, which displayed sculptures executed since 1940, judges selected 250 pieces out of 1,000 entries; 216 came from American sculptors. The exhibit reflected most of what had been happening during the decade, but pictures accompanying a May 15 review in the *New York Times* showed only monumental realistic figures. Despite the efforts by some to expand the form of expression to include constructivism, abstract sculpture, and surrealism, the decade ended in favor of traditional representative sculpture.

*See also:* Architecture; Art (Painting), Dance; Illustrators; Photography; Rationing

**Selected Reading**

Aspinwall, Margaret, ed. *200 Years of American Sculpture.* New York: Whitney Museum of American Art, 1976.

Calder, Alexander, and Jean Davidson. *Calder: An Autobiography with Pictures.* New York: Pantheon Books, 1966.

Duus, Masayo. *The Life of Isamu Noguchi: Journey without Borders.* Princeton, NJ: Princeton University Press, 2004.

Marcus, Stanley E. *David Smith: The Sculptor and His Work.* Ithaca, NY: Cornell University Press, 1983.

# SELECTIVE TRAINING AND SERVICE ACT OF 1940 (SELECTIVE SERVICE, OR DRAFT)

On June 10, 1940, **President Franklin Delano Roosevelt** (1882–1945), in a speech to the graduating class at the University of Virginia, raised the issue of the United States needing a system for drafting men into military service. He deplored the worldwide ramifications of an act carried out that same day by Italy's Benito Mussolini (1883–1945) when he declared war against France and Great Britain. In Roosevelt's remarks to both the assembled students and the nation by way of **radio,** he stated that the United States would "have equipment and training equal to the task of any emergency defense." His stand that the United States could not exist in a state of isolation, a justification for a peacetime draft, had strong critics, among them clergy, individual citizens, labor leaders, and assorted politicians.

Reactions from members of Congress ranged from enthusiastic endorsement to expressions of concern that this step would draw the United States into the European conflict. Shortly after Roosevelt's talk, matters in Europe swiftly deteriorated. Germany gained major victories in the summer of 1940 as France fell and Great Britain came under aerial and maritime siege. In September, Germany, Italy, and Japan signed the Tripartite Treaty; they would henceforth be known as the Axis powers.

Over the course of the summer, pictures of Nazi bombers and burning London appeared in **newspapers** and **magazines** across the United States, and public support for conscription changed from 50 percent in a June Gallup Poll to 71 percent by September. It had become clear that the United States had to prepare for the worst, and Congress acted quickly. On September 17, 1940, the headline on the front page of the *New York Times* read, "Proclamation Calling for Draft Registration on Oct. 16, The First Peacetime Draft in American History Becomes Law."

Not the first draft for the country but the first one enacted in peacetime, conscription had been employed by the United States during two previous conflicts. Both Union and Confederate officials had enforced a draft at the time of the Civil War, a decision that met with much criticism because many people considered it an infringement on individual freedom and personal liberty. The practice ended with the conclusion of the war. The 65th United States Congress created the Selective Service Act of 1917, giving President Woodrow Wilson (1856–1924) the power to draft men for military service as a part of the country's participation in World War I. Officials again discontinued conscription in 1920; with the onset of World War II, the government required new legislation to guarantee sufficient numbers for fighting yet another war.

The Selective Training and Service Act of 1940, passed by the 76th United States Congress, required all men ages 21 to 35 to register for a service period of 12 months. Certain occupations, including ministers, farmers, miners, commercial sailors, and railroad workers, received an exemption. The use of a lottery system for drafting individuals began in Washington, DC, when Secretary of War Henry L. Stimson (1867–1950), blindfolded, drew the card of the first inductee from a large glass bowl. Initially, students received a deferment, but this practice stopped in July 1941. Conscientious objectors (COs), about 25,000 for the duration of the war, could opt out by accepting alternate noncombatant service through the government's Civilian Public Service (CPS), performing in such areas as medical services, forestry projects, conservation, and the like. Numerous church-related organizations, including the Society of Friends (Quakers), Seventh-Day Adventists, Brethren, and Mennonites also participated in these efforts. For the most part, however, Americans viewed mandatory conscription as a necessary and patriotic duty, and many men enlisted before being called.

On December 7, 1941, the United States suffered the Japanese attack on Pearl Harbor. Congress issued a declaration of war the following day against Japan and then included Germany and Italy three days later, all of which led to an extension of the time for military service. Individuals would remain on active duty for the duration of the conflict, plus an added requirement of six months of service in the Organized Reserves. In November 1942, the age range for inductees, previously 21 to 35, changed to 18 to 45 years of age.

Various musicians soon expressed their take on the selective service system and the possibility of the United States becoming involved in a world conflict. For example, the Prairie Ramblers of *The National Barn Dance* recorded "I'll Be Back In A Year, Little Darlin'" (1941), words and music by Ben Shelhamer Jr., Claude Heritier, and Russ Hull (all active during the 1940s). A response titled "I'll Be Waiting For You, Darlin'" (1941), words and music by Russ Hull, was performed by artists such as Louise Massey (1902–1983) and the Westerners as well as Patsy Montana (1912–1996).

As conditions concerning a global war intensified, Bradley Kincaid (1895–1989) and Buck Nation (active 1940s) offered "I Won't Be Back In A Year Little Darling," a more realistic statement about current conditions. Other pop songs describing the transition from civilian life to that of a soldier reflected the times and briefly enjoyed radio play, along with releases of sheet music.

In July 1942, composer Irving Berlin's (1888–1989) patriotic musical, *This Is the Army,* opened on Broadway. Based on *Yip! Yip! Yaphank,* a 1917 skit Berlin had put together while a draftee himself, it tells the story service life in the army for both new recruits and officers through songs and skits. After a two-and-a-half-month run, *This Is the Army* closed on Broadway, and the cast set off on a tour across the United States. Once on the West Coast, Warner Bros. produced a filmed version released in 1943.

Other studios supported the troops in documentaries, features, and shorts. Metro-Goldwyn-Mayer issued two short films in 1941 and another in 1942 that related to those signing up for service. *You Can't Fool a Camera* (1941) consists of several very different pieces of footage. The film starts out showing photographic proof of unusual facts such as when horses gallop, all four hooves leave the ground, but by the time the short ends, it offers close-ups of the studio's major stars and a tribute to those who have joined the armed forces. In *Holiday Greetings* (1941), actor Lewis Stone (1879–1953) urges moviegoers to appreciate those in the U.S. armed forces who will be spending the Christmas holidays overseas away from their families. *Victory Quiz* (1942), a Pete Smith (1892–1979) Specialty, offers a series of multiple-choice questions such as "When was the parachute invented?" The movie intersperses news footage of the U.S. armed forces in action along with humor, Smith's real specialty.

Universal capitalized on the popularity of the comedy team of Bud Abbot (1895–1974) and Lou Costello (1906–1959) by releasing *Buck Privates, In the Navy,* and *Keep' em Flying* in 1941, all of which depict recruits adjusting to military life. Across the way, Paramount Pictures also released a war-related comedy in 1941 titled *Caught in the Draft.* It stars Bob Hope (1903–2003) and Dorothy Lamour (1914–1996). Hope plays a movie star trying to avoid the draft who falls in love with the colonel's daughter; in a typical slapstick manner, he accidentally enlists in the army, embarking on a service career that contains more laughs than serious intentions.

For those more prone to reading than going to the **movies,** Marion Hargrove (1919–2003) in 1942 published a collection of his humorous autobiographical newspaper columns about basic training under the title *See Here, Private Hargrove.* An immediate best seller, Metro-Goldwyn-Mayer released a film adaptation of the book in 1944 with Robert Walker (1918–1951) and Donna Reed (1921–1986) taking the lead roles.

The law requiring the induction of eligible men into military service changed conditions for those remaining on the home front. Active involvement by celebrities and the activities of ordinary citizens selling **war bonds** helped to finance the war; **rationing** and **scrap drives** provided ways to divert manufacturing resources from peacetime uses to defense production; and millions of women, personified as **Rosie the Riveter,** went to work in the jobs vacated by men fighting in the war.

As to overseeing the drafting and enlistments of personnel for military service, two individuals served as director of the Selective Service System. First, Clarence Dykstra (1883–1950), a civilian, carried out the responsibilities from October 1940 to April 1,

1941. U.S. Army Major General Lewis Hershey (1893–1977) became the second director, from July 31, 1941, to April 15, 1947. Each man faced challenges during his tenure; at the height of its operations, the Selective Service System had 27,371 paid employees and 184,325 volunteers, with 6,642 local boards handling the process while 469 boards listened to appeals.

One immediate problem occurred in the initial round of inductions; a large number failed the required physical examination. From the first 1 million men, 40 percent, or about 400,000, were rejected because of nutritional deficiencies. This crisis within the military created a national "healthy eating drive" directed by Paul V. McNutt (1891–1955), head of the Federal Security Agency. After study by various committees, Roosevelt announced the creation of the Office of Health Defense and Welfare, which would be headed by McNutt. This new agency embarked upon a massive campaign using newspaper and magazine articles, **posters,** curriculum materials for schools, conferences, short films, and professionals to educate the public about healthy menu planning, cooking, and eating.

A second issue had to do with a segregated army. The Selective Training and Service Act of 1940 stated that it should be the duty of every male citizen of the prescribed age range to present himself for registration; the act prohibited racial discrimination. Both the army and navy, however, continued to follow their established practice of segregation and did not allow blacks at the front lines or in combat. Both enlistees and draftees found themselves in all-black units working at subservient jobs under the supervision of white officers. Additionally, black units were restricted to their own mess halls and barracks.

The National Association for the Advancement of Colored People (NAACP), a civil rights group founded in 1909, actively attempted to end segregation in the armed forces. Its tactics included lobbying and personal appeals to various members of Congress, all to no avail. The NAACP also planned a March on Washington for July 1, 1941, expecting to draw over 100,000 people. A week before the protest, an alarmed President Roosevelt issued an executive order establishing the first Fair Employment Practices Committee (FEPC). In return, the organizers canceled the march and established the March on Washington Movement as a way to hold the FEPC to its promise of desegregating the armed forces.

World War II ended in 1945, the draft the following year. By that time, over 10 million men had been inducted into the armed services. The original act expired in 1947, making the joining of a branch of the armed forces voluntary instead of mandatory. Records still needed to be maintained, and Major General Hershey's title changed to director of the Office of Selective Service Records.

Soon after the Axis surrendered, tensions and political conflicts developed between the Union of the Soviet Socialists Republics and the Western powers, including the United States. Concern among the leaders of the armed forces in the early months of this **Cold War** brought about the passage of a new selective service act in 1948, the second one to be passed in peacetime. It required all men aged 18 to 26 to register, and those between 19 and 26 years became eligible for 21 months' service followed by five years of reserve duty. General Hershey's titled reverted to Director of the Selective Service System, a position that he continued to hold until 1970.

Also in 1948, **President Harry S. Truman** (1884–1972) issued Executive Order 9981 that established the President's Committee on Equality of Treatment and Opportunity in the Armed Forces. The order would address inequalities in all branches of service brought about by race, color, **religion,** or national origin. Blatant signs of segregation continued for several more years and black soldiers only gradually moved out of their units into integrated fighting groups. Finally, in October 1954, the secretary of defense announced that the last racially segregated unit in the armed forces had been abolished.

Heavy postwar budget cuts for defense purposes restricted 1948 conscriptions to 100,000 men. In June 1950, the **United Nations,** with the participation of the United States in what diplomats called a "police action," entered the Korean War. This brought the United States directly into another war and caused the number of armed forces inductees to greatly increase once again.

*See also:* Atomic Bomb, The; Aviation; Axis Sally and Tokyo Rose; Berlin Airlift, The; Best Sellers (Books); Broadway Shows (Musicals); Canteens; Civil Defense; Cole, Nat King; Education; Eisenhower, General Dwight David; Food; Louis, Joe; MacArthur, General Douglas; Marshall, General George Catlett; Race Relations and Stereotyping

**Selected Reading**
Selective Service Act of 1940. *New York Times,* June 11, 1940; September 17 through October 15, 1940; April 1, 1947. www.proquest.com
*Selective Service Act of 1948.* 80th Cong., 2d sess., HR Rep. 2438. www.loc.gov/rr/frd/Military_Law/pdf/act-1948.pdf
Young, William H., and Nancy K. Young. *American Music through History: The World War II Era.* Westport, CT: Greenwood Publishing Group, 2005.

# SERIAL FILMS

Across the country, in the late morning or early afternoon on any given Saturday, kids started milling about the box office at their local movie theater. Clutching a dime (or maybe 15 cents, but seldom more in the 1940s—a dime in the 1940s equals approximately $1.10 in 2008 dollars), they waited for the attendant to pull back the curtain behind the glass enclosure, the announcement that the theater was now open for the Saturday matinee. A weekly ritual fondly remembered by generations of Americans, these special shows were designed for a youthful audience and usually differed from a theater's main bill.

This tradition had its beginnings in the 1900s and the early days of silent films. By the 1930s, and with the addition of sound and occasional color, the Saturday shows had taken on a format that would be followed for the next 20 or so years. When children (and their parents) found in the early 1950s that **television** offered similar diversions on Saturday mornings, the weekly trek to a neighborhood theater drew to a close, and with it a chapter in American life.

In the matinees' heyday, roughly 1930 to 1950, that dime for admission bought two features, usually a B Western and maybe a low-budget comedy or detective picture, several **cartoons,** a short or a newsreel, previews, and the next installment of an ongoing weekly serial. Mom got the children out of the house for awhile, and the kids got more than three hours of thrills, chills, and a laugh or two.

The **Westerns** they saw, as well as other film genres, receive discussion elsewhere in this encyclopedia. The serials, however, deserve separate attention because of their unique qualities. Back in 1912, the idea of a continuing, or episodic, visual narrative grew out of the enormously popular serializations of popular short stories and novels that **magazines** of the day featured week-by-week or month-by-month. As the **movies** gained ever-larger audiences and studios and directors searched for new ways to keep their patrons entertained, the idea of creating similar continuing tales seemed a logical one.

In 1912, actress Mary Fuller (1888–1973) achieved unexpected stardom in *What Happened to Mary?* generally conceded to be the first American film serial. Consisting of 12 reels, each of which told more of the story, the cliffhanging ending to each part left the audience waiting for the next thrilling part. By the 1940s, the conventions of the form had been well established: individual episodes (also called chapters by some studios) should run about 15 to 20 minutes, and the full story should contain 12 to 15 installments, or last about one-fourth of an entire year when seen on a weekly basis. The stories should be constructed in such a way that if a person missed an episode, some brief background filler in the subsequent installment would make events clear, including how the main characters got out of whatever dilemma the story had previously placed them.

This suspenseful, episodic structure almost guaranteed a return audience each and every week. In the long stretch from Sunday to Saturday, serial fans could debate how they imagined their heroes would escape the newest fiendish plans laid by the villains. A clear offspring of the penny dreadfuls and dime novels of the 19th century, movie serials rose to extraordinary popularity alongside the garish pulp fiction so beloved by generations of readers.

Three Hollywood studios dominated in the production of serials: Columbia, Republic, and Universal. Of the three, Columbia Pictures ranked as a major studio, whereas Republic and Universal tended to be in the second tier, seldom boasting big-name stars or major box office hits. Despite its success with feature-length Hollywood fare, Columbia maintained a tradition of releasing a wide variety of shorter material, such as Three Stooges comedies, variety shorts, cartoons, and numerous serials. In 1956, faced with dwindling interest in the genre and competition from television, Columbia produced its last serial, *Blazing the Overland Trail.*

Once a major player in Hollywood circles, Universal Pictures had fallen on hard times during the 1930s and became known for cheap Westerns, comedy series, melodramas, and a house specialty, horror pictures. Changes in ownership and various financial arrangements kept the company going, and Universal eventually became a pioneer in the area of television production. Although the studio produced many serials in the 1930s and early 1940s, it got out of the field in 1946 with *The Mysterious Mr. M,* abandoning several serials in various stages of completion.

Republic Pictures came into being in 1935 when several small studios merged, including Consolidated Film Industries, Mascot Pictures, Invincible Pictures, Monogram Pictures, Majestic Pictures, Liberty Pictures, and Chesterfield Pictures. They fell into the category of "Poverty Row" studios, an industry term identifying those companies that eked out their incomes with generally mediocre, low-budget features of any and all kinds. Mascot Pictures brought to the marriage considerable experience in the production of serials, and the newly formed Republic Pictures conglomerate quickly put that expertise to use. From the mid-1930s until 1955 and *King of the Carnival,* the studio's last serial, Republic outproduced both Columbia and Universal.

During the 1940s, the Columbia-Republic-Universal triumvirate jointly created almost 100 serials, or more than 9 new productions a year. As a rule, Republic would turn out about 4 of these, followed by Columbia with 3, and Universal would contribute 2 titles. In any given year, these numbers might vary slightly, but the totals suggest how large the serial industry had become.

TABLE 90. Representative Movie Serials from the 1940s

| Year | Title | Number of Chapters | Stars | Studio |
|---|---|---|---|---|
| 1940 | *Adventures of Red Ryder* | 12 | Don "Red" Barry, Tommy Cook | Republic |
| | *Drums of Fu Manchu* | 15 | Henry Brandon, William Royle | Republic |
| | *Flash Gordon Conquers the Universe* | 12 | Buster Crabbe, Carol Hughes | Republic |
| | *The Green Archer* | 15 | Victor Jory, Iris Meredith | Columbia |
| | *The Green Hornet* | 13 | Gordon Jones, Keye Luke | Universal |
| | *King of the Royal Mounted* | 12 | Allan Lane, Robert Strange | Republic |
| | *Mysterious Doctor Satan* | 15 | Edward Ciannelli, Robert Wilcox | Republic |
| | *The Shadow* | 15 | Victor Jory, Veda Ann Borg | Columbia |
| | *Terry and the Pirates* | 15 | William Tracy, Jeff York | Columbia |
| | *Winners of the West* | 13 | Dick Foran, Anne Nagel | Universal |
| 1941 | *Adventures of Captain Marvel* | 12 | Tom Tyler, Frank Coghlan Jr. | Republic |
| | *Don Winslow of the Navy* | 12 | Don Terry, Walter Sande | Universal |
| | *The Green Hornet Strikes Again!* | 15 | Warren Hull, Keye Luke | Universal |
| | *Holt of the Secret Service* | 15 | Jack Holt, Evelyn Brent | Columbia |
| | *The Iron Claw* | 15 | Charles Quigley, Joyce Bryant | Columbia |
| | *King of the Texas Rangers* | 12 | "Slingin' Sammy" Baugh, Neil Hamilton | Republic |
| | *Sea Raiders* | 12 | Billy Halop, Huntz Hall | Universal |
| | *Sky Raiders* | 12 | Donald Woods, Billy Halop | Universal |
| | *The Spider Returns* | 15 | Warren Hull, Mary Ainslee | Columbia |
| | *White Eagle* | 15 | Buck Jones, Raymond Hatton | Columbia |
| 1942 | *Captain Midnight* | 15 | Dave O'Brien, Dorothy Short | Columbia |
| | *Gang Busters* | 13 | Kent Taylor, Irene Hervey | Universal |
| | *Junior G-Men of the Air* | 12 | Billy Halop, Huntz Hall | Universal |
| | *King of the Mounties* | 12 | Allan Lane, Gilbert Emery | Republic |
| | *Nyoka and the Tigermen* | 15 | Kay Aldridge, Clayton Moore | Republic |
| | *Overland Mail* | 15 | Lon Chaney Jr., Noah Beery Jr. | Universal |

*(Continued)*

TABLE 90. *(continued)*

| Year | Title | Number of Chapters | Stars | Studio |
|---|---|---|---|---|
| | *Perils of the Royal Mounted* | 15 | Robert Stevens, Nell O'Day | Columbia |
| | *The Secret Code* | 15 | Paul Kelly, Anne Nagel | Columbia |
| | *Spy Smasher* | 12 | Kane Richmond, Marguerite Chapman | Republic |
| | *The Valley of Vanishing Men* | 15 | Bill Elliott, Slim Summerville | Columbia |
| 1943 | *The Adventures of Smilin' Jack* | 13 | Tom Brown, Rose Hobart | Universal |
| | *Adventures of the Flying Cadets* | 13 | Johnny Downs, Bobby Jordon | Universal |
| | *The Batman* | 15 | Lewis Wilson, Douglas Croft | Columbia |
| | *Daredevils of the West* | 12 | Allan Lane, Kay Aldridge | Republic |
| | *G-Men vs. The Black Dragon* | 15 | Rod Cameron, Roland Got | Republic |
| | *The Masked Marvel* | 12 | William Forrest, Louise Currie | Republic |
| | *The Phantom* | 15 | Tom Tyler, Jeanne Bates | Columbia |
| | *Secret Service in Darkest Africa* | 15 | Rod Cameron, Joan Marsh | Republic |
| 1944 | *Black Arrow* | 15 | Robert Scott, Adele Jergens | Columbia |
| | *Captain America* | 15 | Dick Purcell, Lorna Gray | Republic |
| | *The Desert Hawk* | 15 | Gilbert Roland, Mona Maris | Columbia |
| | *The Great Alaskan Mystery* | 13 | Milburn Stone, Marjorie Weaver | Universal |
| | *Haunted Harbor* | 15 | Kane Richmond, Kay Aldridge | Republic |
| | *The Mystery of the Riverboat* | 13 | Robert Lowery, Eddie Quillan | Universal |
| | *Raiders of Ghost City* | 13 | Dennis Moore, Wanda McKay | Universal |
| | *The Tiger Woman* | 12 | Linda Stirling, Allan Lane | Republic |
| | *Zorro's Black Whip* | 12 | Linda Stirling, George J. Lewis | Republic |
| 1945 | *Brenda Starr, Reporter* | 13 | Joan Woodbury, Syd Saylor | Columbia |
| | *Federal Operator 99* | 12 | Marten Lamont, Helen Talbot | Republic |
| | *Jungle Queen* | 13 | Lois Collier, Ruth Roman | Universal |
| | *Jungle Raiders* | 15 | Kane Richmond, Eddie Quillan | Columbia |
| | *Manhunt of Mystery Island* | 15 | Richard Bailey, Linda Stirling | Republic |
| | *The Master Key* | 13 | Milburn Stone, Jan Wiley | Universal |
| | *The Monster and the Ape* | 15 | Robert Lowery, George MacReady | Columbia |
| | *The Purple Monster Strikes* | 15 | Linda Stirling, Roy Barcroft | Republic |
| | *The Royal Mounted Rides Again* | 13 | Bill Kennedy, George Dolenz | Universal |
| | *Secret Agent X-9* | 13 | Lloyd Bridges, Keye Luke | Universal |
| 1946 | *Chick Carter, Detective* | 15 | Lyle Talbot, Julie Gibson | Columbia |
| | *The Crimson Ghost* | 12 | Charles Quigley, Linda Stirling | Republic |
| | *Daughter of Don Q* | 12 | Adrian Booth, Kirk Alyn | Republic |
| | *Ghost Riders of the West* | 12 | Robert Kent, Peggy Stewart | Republic |

| Year | Title | Number of Chapters | Stars | Studio |
|---|---|---|---|---|
| | *Hop Harrigan* | 15 | William Bakewell, Jennifer Holt | Columbia |
| | *King of the Forest Rangers* | 12 | Larry Thompson, Helen Talbot | Republic |
| | *Lost City of the Jungle* | 13 | Russell Hayden, Jane Adams | Universal |
| | *The Mysterious Mr. M* | 13 | Dennis Moore, Byron Foulger | Universal |
| | *The Scarlet Horseman* | 13 | Paul Guilfoyle, Peter Cookson | Universal |
| | *Son of the Guardsman* | 15 | Robert Shaw, Ray Bennett | Columbia |
| 1947 | *The Black Widow* | 13 | Carol Forman, Bruce Edwards | Republic |
| | *Jack Armstrong* | 15 | John Hart, Rosemary La Planche | Columbia |
| | *Jesse James Rides Again* | 13 | Clayton Moore, Linda Stirling | Republic |
| | *The Sea Hound* | 15 | Buster Crabbe, Jimmy Lloyd | Columbia |
| | *Son of Zorro* | 13 | George Turner, Peggy Stewart | Republic |
| | *The Vigilante: Fighting Hero of the West* | 13 | Ralph Byrd, Lyle Talbot | Columbia |
| 1948 | *Adventures of Frank and Jesse James* | 13 | Clayton Moore, Steve Darrell | Republic |
| | *Brick Bradford* | 13 | Kane Richmond, Rick Vallin | Columbia |
| | *Congo Bill* | 15 | Don McGuire, Cleo Moore | Columbia |
| | *Dangers of the Canadian Mounted* | 12 | Jim Bannon, Virginia Belmont | Republic |
| | *G-Men Never Forget* | 12 | Clayton Moore, Roy Barcroft | Republic |
| | *Superman* | 15 | Kirk Alyn, Noel Neill | Columbia |
| | *Tex Granger, Midnight Rider of the Plains* | 15 | Robert Kellard, Peggy Stewart | Columbia |
| 1949 | *The Adventures of Sir Galahad* | 15 | George Reeves, Nelson Leigh | Columbia |
| | *Batman and Robin* | 15 | Robert Lowery, Johnny Duncan | Columbia |
| | *Bruce Gentry* | 15 | Tom Neal, Judy Clark | Columbia |
| | *Federal Agents vs. Underworld, Inc.* | 12 | Kirk Alyn, Rosemary La Planche | Republic |
| | *Ghost of Zorro* | 12 | Clayton Moore, Pamela Blake | Republic |
| | *The James Brothers of Missouri* | 12 | Keith Richards, Robert Bice | Republic |
| | *King of the Rocket Men* | 12 | Tristram Coffin, Mae Clarke | Republic |
| | *Radar Patrol vs. Spy King* | 12 | Kirk Alyn, Jean Dean | Republic |

A title alone cannot always convey the content of a movie, but some generalizations can be made from the foregoing list. Characters from **comic books, comic strips,** and **radio** shows, all of which enjoyed considerable popularity at the time, often made the move to the serial format. For example, from the pages of comic books came *Batman* (and later Robin), *Captain America, Captain Marvel,* and **Superman.** The daily strips in **newspapers** across the land provided, among others, *Brenda Starr, Brick Bradford, Don Winslow, Flash Gordon, The Phantom, Secret Agent X-9, Smilin' Jack,* and **Terry** *and the Pirates.* The crossovers with radio supplied *Captain Midnight, Gang Busters, Jack Armstrong,* and *The Shadow.*

Many serials, although not taken directly from other sources, owe much of their plotting and characters to common areas of popular culture. Movie Westerns made possible such titles as *Winners of the West, Daredevils of the West, Ghost Riders of the West, The Vigilante: Fighting Hero of the West,* and many others, equally self-explanatory. Science fiction supplied monsters and secret, advanced weaponry in adventures like *The Purple Monster Strikes, King of the Rocket Men,* and *Radar Patrol vs. Spy King,* while World War II provided a convenient, catchall category, as in *King of the Royal Mounted, Sky Raiders, The Secret Code,* and many others.

As long as the action continued at a nonstop, breakneck pace, the cliffhangers thrilled, and the directors spent little time with characterization or romance, serials filled the bill for youthful audiences. Most of them provided a woman to costar with the male lead, an obvious device designed to appeal to girls, although the script usually limited her to a role in which she lends moral support, gets conveniently captured, and screams at appropriate moments. But someone like Linda Stirling (1921–1997) nonetheless built a career in serials and even occasionally received top billing, as in 1944's *Tiger Woman.* All in all, serials enjoyed a devoted following, and they filled an inimitable movie niche in the 1940s.

*See also:* Children's Films; Costume and Spectacle Films; Crime and Mystery Films; Horror and Thriller Films; Political and Propaganda Films; Radio Programming: Children's Shows, Serials, and Adventure Series; War Films; Youth

**Selected Reading**
Cline, William C. *In the Nick of Time: Motion Picture Sound Serials.* Jefferson, NC: McFarland, 1984.
Fernett, Gene. *Hollywood's Poverty Row, 1930–1950.* Satellite Beach, FL: Coral Reef Publications, 1973.
Lahue, Kalton C. *Continued Next Week: A History of the Moving Picture Serial.* Norman: University of Oklahoma Press, 1964.
Stedman, Raymond William. *The Serials: Suspense and Drama by Installment.* Norman: University of Oklahoma Press, 1971.

# SERVICE FLAGS (GOLD STARS AND BLUE STARS)

During the war years of 1941 to 1945, a pedestrian walking any residential street in any American town, large or small, would notice small rectangular banners or flags displayed in the front windows of countless homes. Each flag, usually cotton or wool but sometimes silk or synthetics, consisted of a field of white bordered in red. One or a number of stars, blue or gold, were affixed vertically to the white area. A blue star represented a loved one on active duty; gold symbolized a family member lost while in the service of the country. Sometimes both blue and gold stars appeared on a single flag, with the gold star(s) always uppermost. These combinations showed a family with sons or daughters still actively serving (the blue) along with any losses (the gold).

Such symbols, called service flags, reminded people at home about the human cost of war and the need not to forget those who serve their country, sometimes with their lives. Hardly a new idea, the first service flags appeared in 1917, toward the end of World War I. Unofficial remembrances at first, the flags gained government approval in the 1920s. Standardized over time, they achieved their greatest popularity during World War II.

Several organizations formed in support of the banners. In 1928, the Gold Star Mothers Club officially formed after years of informally meeting. Open to the mothers of service personnel who died while on active duty, it also extended nonvoting membership to fathers. The Blue Star Mothers Club formed in 1942. Although open to mothers, fathers could obtain associate status. Its numbers swelled to 30,000 mothers during the war, making it the largest of its kind. Seeking recognition for their sacrifices and losses, the Gold Star Wives Club organized in 1945, welcoming the spouses of servicemen killed in the line of duty.

Although the display of gold or blue star banners has fallen off in recent years, the use of such service flags remains permissible for the parents or spouses of those serving in the United States military. And, at the time of World War II, the practice enjoyed wide support.

**See also:** Canteens

**Selected Reading**
"Service Flags." www.serviceflags.com

## *SEVENTEEN*

This monthly magazine, established to speak directly to high school and college women, first appeared on newsstands in September 1944, a time when many American teenagers had acquired sufficient money to assert significant consumer power. Editor-in-chief Helen Valentine (1893–1986), a mother and grandmother when she assumed her editorial duties, christened the new periodical in honor of Booth Tarkington's (1869–1946) seminal 1916 novel of the same name. Not the first magazine to acknowledge teenage girls as an audience, it quickly surpassed its competitors and reached an extraordinary number of youthful readers by devoting its entire contents to them.

The premier issue included, among other things, a celebrity feature on musician Harry James (1916–1983); a photomontage of crooner **Frank Sinatra** (1915–1998); a Hollywood gossip column; film, book, and record reviews; and columns titled "First Date Quiz" and "Why Don't Parents Grow Up?" *Seventeen* sold 400,000 copies in six days after starting with an initial print run of 530,000. Its monthly circulation exceeded 1 million copies by February 1947. Colorful covers promised the latest **fashion** news, beauty tips, and helpful information about growing up and getting along with others. Inside section headings organized these leads into categories such as "What You Wear," "Having Fun," and "How You Look and Feel."

But *Seventeen* went beyond clothes and cosmetics. It approached its readers in articles such as "Your Mind," "Getting Along in the World," and "What Are You Doing About the War?" as serious, intelligent, thinking young women interested in current affairs and aware of their future responsibilities. It educated them to the importance of responsible adulthood, of being informed, thinking, participating, and voting citizens.

To develop the magazine in a planned manner, the publisher, Walter Annenberg (1908–2002), invested substantial resources in three directions: (1) to create and describe a typical teenage reader, whom the staff called Teena, (2) to assure a high volume of **advertising,** and (3) to increase the size of the readership. To this end, in 1945, the publisher engaged a firm to conduct market research on the topic of what the magazine's audience and other **youth** expected to see and read. The results, provided in a pamphlet, *Life with Teena,* indicated that teenage girls had an interest in reading about relationships, both with boys and friends, and understanding parents. It confirmed that this audience consisted of affluent white girls who had money and were ready to spend it on clothes, jewelry, and cosmetics. Also, the study revealed that if they should run out of cash, parents could be counted on to supply it. The editorial staff used this information, coupled with the magazine's intent to reach "wholesome" girls between the ages of 13 and 18 who dressed neatly and conservatively for high school and dates as guidelines for articles, columns, and accepted advertisements.

For the manufacturers and advertisers, the *Seventeen* staff published a booklet titled "Who Is Tenna? Judy Jeckyll or Formalda Hyde?" in which they outlined the magazine's intent to run age-appropriate advertisements geared toward the image described as Teena. The publication also suggested that manufacturers could profit by regularly creating new teenage-specific products, sure items to sell not only to the readers but also their friends—get one teenage girl to buy and wear a product, and her friends will follow. As a final step in *Seventeen*'s sales plan, its promotional staff brought together an advertising advisory board charged to assist in establishing uniformity in the magazine's advertising and editorial presentations.

Shortly after *Seventeen*'s appearance on the market, World War II ended, soldiers returned home and soon thereafter married, many to *Seventeen* readers who had just graduated from high school. The magazine, in hopes of capitalizing on the postwar prosperity and continuing to attract as many readers as possible, broadened its articles to ones that would interest young wives and homemakers. Accepted advertisements now included engagement rings, appliances, china and silver, furniture, carpet, and linens. Careful planning and awareness of changing times paid off. By 1949, *Seventeen,* an advocate of youth consumerism, had reached a circulation of 2.5 million, thereby achieving a level of readership that exceeded the numbers for any other teen girl–focused publications for many years to come.

*See also:* Fads; Magazines

**Selected Reading**
Savage, Jon. *Teenage: The Creation of Youth Culture.* New York: Viking, 2007.
Schrum, Kelly. *Some Wore Bobby Sox: The Emergence of the Teenage Girls' Culture.* New York: Palgrave Macmillan, 2004.
———. "'Teena Means Business': Teenage Girls' Culture and *Seventeen* Magazine, 1944–1950." In *Delinquents and Debutantes, Twentieth-Century American Girls' Cultures,* ed. Sherrie A. Inness, pp. 134–163. New York: New York University Press, 1998.

# SHORE, DINAH

Remembered as a major star on network **television** from the early 1950s through the 1980s, Dinah Shore (1916–1994; née Frances Rose Shore) actually broke into the entertainment business at the end of the 1930s. That aspect of her career, largely forgotten today, save for some longtime fans, involved **radio** and recordings. For much of the decade, she reigned as one of the most popular female vocalists of the 1940s. Born in Tennessee, her parents encouraged her to pursue a singing career. She took time out for college at Nashville's Vanderbilt University and, after graduating in 1938, traveled to New York City in search of opportunities.

At auditions, she sometimes sang "Dinah," a 1924 standard from the Broadway show *Kid Boots*. People everywhere knew the song, which made the screenings go more easily and led Frances to take Dinah as her stage name. In 1939, she landed a singing job at WNEW, a leading New York radio station. She worked at times with another rising young vocalist, **Frank Sinatra** (1915–1998), as well as with Xavier Cugat (1900–1990), a popular bandleader who specialized in music with a Latin flavor. These varied experiences led to a recording contract with RCA Victor, a leading label.

*Dinah Shore rose to fame as a popular vocalist during the late 1930s. Able to sing in many styles, she enjoyed excellent stage presence, which led comedian Eddie Cantor to hire her for his NBC variety show. Here she stands behind the network's microphone while appearing on Cantor's program. (NBC/Photofest)*

After a brief stint with Ben Bernie (1891–1943) and his orchestra on CBS (Columbia Broadcasting System) radio in 1939, Shore gained her own 15-minute series, *The Dinah Shore Show*, which ran at various times (and with slight title changes) until 1943. More importantly, as far as her career went, she became a feature attraction on *The Chamber Music Society of Lower Basin Street* in 1940. The show, which premiered on NBC (National Broadcasting Company) network radio in early 1940, delighted listeners by taking a tongue-in-cheek approach to music in all genres, especially the classics, and thus its long-winded, satirical title. Occasionally abbreviated **CMSLBS**, it proved an instant hit with **jazz** and **swing** lovers and remained on the air until the fall of 1944, a long run for music shows.

Everyone seemed to have fun on the show, and the quality of musicianship would be hard to equal. Professionals all, they doubled on numerous instruments, which gave the in-house bands—usually the Dixieland Octet and the Woodwindy Ten, not counting guests—an opportunity to perform in many styles. Guest artists, often the cream of 1940s New York jazz, dropped in often, and "Mademoiselle Diva" Dinah Shore had a chance to sing with some of the best musicians of the day.

Shore's excellent stage presence brought her to the attention of comedian Eddie Cantor (1892–1964), who hosted his own top-rated variety program and had long been a fixture on network radio. He promptly signed her as vocalist for *The Eddie Cantor Show* in 1940, and she stayed with him for a year, as well as continuing with her series and the *Chamber Music Society of Lower Basin Street.* Cantor urged her to record an old Russian folk song he had come across, and the modernized result, now called "Yes, My Darling Daughter" (1941), enjoyed sensational sales. It soon became her theme song, and the ensuing national exposure on radio and recordings launched her into the front ranks of popular singers.

By 1943, she had graduated to a full half-hour evening offering on CBS called *The Birdseye Open House.* Various guest stars dropped by and chatted and performed. It stayed on the air until 1946, although it shifted to NBC. In the midst of her increasingly busy radio and recording schedule, Hollywood expressed an interest in Shore for possible motion picture roles. Since she could do her radio programs as easily on the West Coast as the East, she moved to California and began a new side to her multifaceted career.

Because the war dominated all aspects of American life, the movie industry had, by 1943, shifted into high gear as far as the production of films designed to raise public morale. Warner Bros., a leading studio, decided to create a filmed revue that would showcase its stable of stars and demonstrate its patriotism. *Thank Your Lucky Stars* (1943) did just that, giving more than two dozen Warner Bros. players some screen time. Although not under contract to the studio, Shore, by virtue of her growing celebrity, also appears in this, her movie debut. She sings three songs written by the team of Arthur Schwartz (1900–1984) and Frank Loesser (1910–1969): "How Sweet You Are," "Thank Your Lucky Stars," and "The Dreamer" (all 1943). Both she and the movie received good reviews, and other offers followed.

*Follow the Boys* (1944), a picture similar to *Thank Your Lucky Stars,* parades many of the actors associated with Universal Studios. Both of these pictures salute the efforts of the **USO (United Service Organizations)** to bring top entertainment to U.S. troops. Shore, in fact, would later receive a USO Medallion Award for her visits to soldiers on the front lines. In the movie, she performs the standard "I'll Get By" (1928) and a new tune, "I'll Walk Alone." Again, both she and the film received a warm reception.

That same year, she appeared in her first acting role by costarring in *Up in Arms* with comedian Danny Kaye (1913–1987). A farcical musical set in the wartime present, Shore plays an army nurse. In the course of the plot, she sings two songs penned by Harold Arlen (1905–1986) and Ted Koehler (1894–1973), "Tess's Torch Song" and "Now I Know." The latter garnered an Academy Award nomination for best song but lost out to "Swingin' on a Star," another fine composition from the 1940s.

With the success of *Up in Arms,* she soon appeared in another picture, this time a kind of hybrid Western-musical-comedy called *Belle of the Yukon,* which came out at the very beginning of 1945. With a miscast Randolph Scott (1898–1987) and burlesque queen Gypsy Rose Lee (1911–1970) in the leads, Shore plays second fiddle. But she gets to sing two good songs by Jimmy Van Huesen (1913–1990) and Johnny Burke (1908–1964), "Like Someone in Love" and "Sleighride in July." As was the case with "Now I Know," "Sleighride in July" received an Academy Award nomination for best song, losing to "It Might as Well Be Spring."

Following that flurry of moviemaking, Shore did no more feature films for the remainder of the decade, aside from occasionally appearing on screen (as herself) for a guest number or undertaking some voiceovers for a few animated shorts. Instead, she married Western actor George Montgomery (1916–2000) in 1943 and returned to her recording and radio interests.

She headlined a variety program on NBC called *The Ford Show* during the 1946–1947 season. From that, she went to *Call for Music* in 1948, where she shared microphones with composer-lyricist Johnny Mercer (1909–1976) and trumpeter-bandleader Harry James (1916–1983). Philip Morris cigarettes, with its distinctive advertising of "Call for Philip Morris!" sponsored the production. She also did a brief show for Pabst Blue Ribbon Beer that lasted into 1949. Like virtually everyone else in show business, Shore knew the days for variety programming on radio were numbered, and she began to look to television as a new medium on which to practice her talents.

In the fall of 1951, *The Dinah Shore Show* made its debut on NBC-TV. After that, she never looked back. Shore became permanently entrenched in television, seldom off the small screen for the next 30-odd years. But that success came from her wide range of experience, especially radio and recordings. One of the most popular vocalists of the decade, Dinah Shore excelled in all her endeavors, yet always exuded an air of casualness and small-town sincerity.

*See also:* ASCAP *vs.* BMI Radio Boycott and the AFM Recording Ban; Broadway Shows (Musicals); Canteens; Movies; Musicals (Film); Radio Programming: Music and Variety Shows); Songwriters and Lyricists

**Selected Reading**

Cassiday, Bruce. *Dinah! A Biography of Dinah Shore.* New York: Franklin Watts, 1979.

Dunning, John. *On the Air: The Encyclopedia of Old-Time Radio.* New York: Oxford University Press, 1998.

## SINATRA, FRANK

Born in Hoboken, New Jersey, in an Italian working-class neighborhood, Francis Albert Sinatra (1915–1998) eventually became the leading male vocalist in American popular music of the postwar era. His extraordinary career began in the last years of the 1930s, but much of his fame and fortune occurred after 1950. Sinatra rocketed to early prominence with the big bands, went through a flat period in the later 1940s, and then rebounded in the second half of the 20th century, emerging as a multitalented entertainer and one of the biggest names in show business.

An avid student of the vocalist's art, during his later teenage years he listened to the **radio** broadcasts and recordings made by many singers, especially **Bing Crosby** (1903–1977) and Billie Holiday (1915–1959). This exposure encouraged Sinatra to emulate breathing and stylistic techniques, but he avoided outright imitation. Possessed of a tenor voice as an adolescent, it would later mature into the baritone range. Thus equipped, he focused on pursuing a career in music and dropped out of high school at age 15.

His skinny good looks and obvious talent got him bookings in small New Jersey nightclubs during the later 1930s. Although his voice remained somewhat high, Sinatra demonstrated an ability to phrase his words with the music played by the band behind him, and on romantic ballads he seemingly caressed the lyrics, creating an intimacy between him and the listener. The crooners of the early 1930s—Rudy Vallee (1901–1986), Russ Columbo (1908–1934), and, of course, Crosby—had also exploited this gift of creating a romantic atmosphere within the confines of a three-minute popular song, the average playing time of most 78-rpm records then manufactured.

One of several breaks came for Sinatra in 1935, when he and three friends, calling themselves the Hoboken Four, entered a radio talent contest. *The Original Amateur Hour,* a popular program of the day, had premiered in New York City in 1934; it offered a showcase for untried, nonprofessional singers, musicians, actors, comedians, tap dancers, mimics, and so on to be heard by a large audience. The NBC (National Broadcasting Company) radio network had picked it up for national distribution in 1935, and it quickly became one of the most popular shows on the air.

*Rivaled only by Bing Crosby during the 1940s, Frank Sinatra became one of the great entertainers of the 20th century. In this picture, taken early in the decade, a young Sinatra holds sheet music of tunes he recorded and perhaps muses about his phenomenal success. (Photofest)*

*The Original Amateur Hour* featured Major Edward Bowes (1874–1946), a genial, easygoing man, as host for the proceedings on stage. Thousands of optimistic people, young and old, flocked to New York for auditions to appear on the enormously successful program. Hopes sprang eternal in those Depression-era years, and Sinatra and his buddies gave a rendition of Cole Porter's (1891–1964) "Night and Day" (1932), a song destined to be a regular part of his future repertoire. Only a tiny percentage of winners ever advanced much beyond their brief moments on the program, but the Hoboken Four proved to be one of the lucky acts. The victory put the quartet on the road under the auspices of Bowes and his producers, but Sinatra soon tired of the routine, quit, and returned to New Jersey.

Soon thereafter, he branched out on his own. While scrabbling for jobs from the mid-1930s on, Sinatra had landed a waiter's position at the Rustic Cabin, a well-known Englewood, New Jersey, roadhouse. Close to New York City, the establishment boasted radio remotes of its performers, allowing listeners beyond its confines to enjoy them. In 1938, the club promoted Sinatra to singing waiter, and thanks to this **technology,** numerous people heard Sinatra's interpretations of popular songs. He also sang on several 15-minute shows broadcast by local New York stations. In the spring of 1939, Harry James (1916–1983), a virtuoso trumpeter and leader of a newly formed **swing** orchestra, caught one of the young waiter's broadcasts and soon thereafter offered him a contract to perform with his band.

As was the custom with many bands in the late 1930s, James had a vocal group, the Music Makers, as part of his orchestra. Sinatra joined the aggregation in mid-1939 and took the role of lead singer. Within a short time, the James band cut its first recordings for the Columbia label, and Sinatra had the vocal honors on two sides, "From the Bottom of My Heart" and "Melancholy Mood." With the Swing Era in full flower at the time, the records enjoyed respectable sales but nothing sensational. He and the James band also recorded, along with a number of other titles, "All or Nothing at All" in 1939, but it too did little at the time. After Sinatra had emerged as a full-fledged star several years later, Columbia re-released the tune in 1943 and it became an enormous hit, a song that would be long associated with him.

Despite a close friendship with Harry James, Sinatra felt compelled to leave the orchestra when trombonist Tommy Dorsey (1905–1956), leader of another top-flight swing ensemble, offered him a substantial raise at the end of 1939. This new association would mean great things for the vocalist. Expert arrangements, fine musicians, and a chance to sing some of the best tunes of the day made everything jell, and in the first months of 1940, Frank Sinatra found himself one of the hottest properties in the country.

Just as Harry James had featured the Music Makers with his band, Dorsey had a vocal group called the Pied Pipers, a quartet that featured the fine voice of Jo Stafford (1917–2008). When Dorsey hired Sinatra, he promptly made him a member of the Pied Pipers. One of his first RCA Victor (Bluebird) recording sessions with Dorsey, conducted in May 1940, included "I'll Never Smile Again," a lush ballad that suited Sinatra's romantic style well. It rapidly climbed the charts to the No. 3 position, his first bona fide hit. In time, many more top-ranked tunes would come from Sinatra, but "I'll Never Smile Again" signaled the real beginning of his lengthy professional career.

The overnight popularity achieved by Sinatra presaged a groundswell of change that would alter the face of popular music as the 1940s progressed. Vocalists, men and women, and vocal groups as well had begun to upstage the bands. The instrumentals remained important, but audiences expected singers to take center stage. In time, they would begin to front many of the bands and often received top billing on marquees and record labels.

Sinatra's skill at intonation gave any ballad an intimate quality, a talent that would make him a rival to Bing Crosby, at the time the leading singer in popular music. During his tenure with Dorsey, Sinatra also demonstrated that he could go beyond just crooning romantic ballads. He performed a moderately up-tempo rendition of "Oh! Look at Me Now" in 1941 that did well on the charts, as well as a popular rendition of "Dolores." With "This Love of Mine" (1941), the vocalist both wrote the lyrics and sang them, suggesting his talents exceeded merely standing in front of a microphone. As the table below suggests, his many fans nevertheless preferred the slower love songs during the early, formative period of his career.

By December 1942, audiences, especially teenage girls, could not get enough of "that skinny kid from Hoboken," and managers booked him at New York's Paramount

TABLE 91. Top-Rated Songs Performed by Frank Sinatra, 1940–1949

| Year | Song | Notes |
|---|---|---|
| 1940 | "I'll Never Smile Again" | with Tommy Dorsey Orchestra |
|  | "We Three, My Echo, My Shadow, and Me" | with Tommy Dorsey Orchestra |
| 1941 | "Oh! Look At Me Now" | with Tommy Dorsey and Connie Haines |
|  | "This Love of Mine" | with Tommy Dorsey Orchestra |
|  | "Do I Worry?" | with Tommy Dorsey Orchestra |
| 1942 | "Just As though You Were Here" | with Tommy Dorsey Orchestra |
|  | "Take Me" | with Tommy Dorsey Orchestra |
| 1943 | "There Are Such Things" | with Tommy Dorsey Orchestra |
|  | "In the Blue of Evening" | with Tommy Dorsey Orchestra |
|  | "You'll Never Know" | with Bobby Tucker Singers |
|  | "All or Nothing at All" | with Harry James Orchestra (originally recorded in 1939) |
|  | "It Started All Over Again" | with Tommy Dorsey Orchestra |
|  | "People Will Say We're in Love" | a cappella choral arrangement |
|  | "It's Always You" | with Tommy Dorsey Orchestra |
| 1944 | "I Couldn't Sleep a Wink Last Night" | a cappella choral arrangement |
|  | "I'll Be Seeing You" | with Tommy Dorsey Orchestra (originally recorded in 1940) |
| 1945 | "Saturday Night (Is the Loneliest Night of the Week)" (originally recorded in 1940) | with Axel Stordahl Orchestra |
| 1946 | "Oh! What It Seemed to Be" | with Axel Stordahl Orchestra |
|  | "Five Minutes More" | with Axel Stordahl Orchestra |
|  | "They Say It's Wonderful" | with Axel Stordahl Orchestra |
| 1947 | "Mam'selle" | with Axel Stordahl Orchestra |
| 1948 | no songs charted |  |
| 1949 | no songs charted |  |

Theater. Bobby-soxers, as many called them, made Sinatra their new musical rage, and their screams and swoons when he came on stage foreshadowed the later reactions of adolescents toward celebrities like Elvis Presley (1935–1977) and the Beatles. Police had to be summoned to maintain order with the huge crowds anxious to get a glimpse of "the sultan of swoon." When he made a return engagement at the Paramount in the fall of 1944, some 25,000 screaming teens awaited him.

Riding the crest of his blossoming career, Sinatra left Tommy Dorsey in 1943 and moved to a solo contract with Columbia Records. Arranger-conductor Axel Stordahl (1913–1963), a long-time associate, became his musical director. Whereas the Dorsey band featured the usual assortment of reeds and horns, Stordahl favored arrangements that utilized string sections and choral groups. The AFM (American Federation of Musicians) recording ban ran from 1942 to 1944 and took place at the time Sinatra moved to Columbia, with the result he cut some of his first sides a cappella, usually with a chorus behind him. The AFM fortunately did not include vocalists in its restrictions. The arrangements Sinatra used effectively hide the absence of instrumentalists, surprising many listeners that he lacks traditional musical accompaniment.

By the end of 1943, the ban had lost much of its force, and nine months later terms had been reached with all the major record producers. Sinatra returned to the recording studio with a full orchestra in attendance and Stordahl arrangements in hand. But by that time, however, the Swing Era had peaked, and new trends in American popular music were replacing the Tin Pan Alley standards of the 1930s and early 1940s. The remainder of the decade would be difficult for Sinatra in terms of recording hit tunes. Despite this setback, and unknown to anyone at the time, the period of Sinatra's greatest musical acclaim still lay ahead in the 1950s and beyond.

During his early career, Sinatra could frequently be heard on network radio. *Songs by Sinatra,* which aired on CBS (Columbia Broadcasting System) stations from 1942 to 1947, usually in 15-minute or half-hour segments sponsored by Old Gold cigarettes, reminded listeners of his records. Rival NBC landed him for *Light-Up Time,* a similar show sponsored by Lucky Strike cigarettes, which ran from 1949 until 1950. In addition, Sinatra performed both as a soloist and a regular member of the vocal ensemble on *Your Hit Parade* during 1943–1945 (CBS) and 1947–1949 (NBC), a long-time radio favorite on Saturday nights. He could be heard singing anything from a serious love song to the latest novelty number.

But as he slipped in the music charts during the later 1940s, Sinatra cultivated new areas for his talents. Just as Bing Crosby had discovered the lure of Hollywood, Sinatra likewise found the **movies** appealing. In 1941 and 1942, he had appeared in two music shorts with Tommy Dorsey and his aggregation, but received no on-screen credits; he simply fills the role of anonymous band vocalist. The next year, 1943, he made his debut as an actor in *Higher and Higher,* a lightweight, nondescript musical. Aside from singing "I Couldn't Sleep a Wink Last Night," Sinatra basically shows himself to be a rather wooden newcomer to motion pictures. Similarly, the bland *Step Lively,* a musical remake of the Marx Brothers' 1938 *Room Service,* hardly improves on the original.

In 1945, however, Metro-Goldwyn-Mayer (MGM) gave Sinatra a better, more challenging role. The studio teamed him with dancer Gene Kelly (1912–1996) and singer-actress Kathryn Grayson (b. 1922) in *Anchors Aweigh,* a bouncy musical about two sailors on leave. Thanks to some technological wizardry, Kelly dances with Jerry Mouse, the costar of the many *Tom and Jerry* **cartoons.** Sinatra croons "I Fall in Love Too Easily," one of several songs that allowed the picture to win an Academy Award for best score. His acting also shows considerable improvement.

MGM pulled out all the stops in 1946 with *Till the Clouds Roll By,* a fictionalized biography of famed, recently deceased composer Jerome Kern (1885–1945). Practically all of the musical stars from the mammoth studio can be glimpsed at one time or another in this overblown film. Sinatra has virtually no screen time, appearing toward the very end performing in a finale spectacular. He sings Kern's "Ol' Man River," hardly the best choice for his more intimate singing style, but he gives it his best.

*It Happened in Brooklyn* (1947) continued Sinatra's streak of tepid **musicals.** Kathryn Grayson reappears, and veteran vaudevillian Jimmy Durante (1893–1980) has a good supporting role. In the picture, Sinatra sings "Time After Time," destined to be one of his signature songs, and he and Grayson even perform some operatic numbers—in Italian—but the sentimentality of the plot never allows the picture to rise above mediocrity.

A different studio, RKO Radio Pictures, saddled Sinatra with the part of a priest in *The Miracle of the Bells* (1948). Bing Crosby could do these roles well, but this kind of casting hardly fit Sinatra's image. Costarring Valli (Alida Valli, 1921–2006), a popular Italian actress who made only a few American movies, the contrived plot about a supposed miracle may have played successfully in the immediate postwar years but has not aged well, although everyone remains serious and spiritual throughout.

A better picture, but only marginally, follows *The Miracle of the Bells*. Titled *The Kissing Bandit* (1948), it has Sinatra playing the son of a bandit whose trademark involved kissing his victims. Not much of a vehicle for anyone in the film, but it kept him in front of movie cameras.

The following year, Sinatra found his stride again, thanks to better screenplays and direction. He appears first in *Take Me Out to the Ball Game,* another MGM musical production that teams him with Gene Kelly again. Esther Williams, best known for her aquatic skills, costars, and the studio even finds an opportunity to dress her in a bathing suit beside a hotel pool. A sprightly plot keeps things going, and the movie served as a prelude to Sinatra's best cinematic effort of the 1940s, *On the Town* (1949).

Based on *Fancy Free,* a famed 1944 ballet with music by Leonard Bernstein (1918–1990) and choreography by Jerome Robbins (1918–1998), the production moved first to Broadway in 1949 as *On the Town*. Its film adaptation came that same year, with Sinatra and Gene Kelly (their third pairing), along with Vera-Ellen (1921–1981), Ann Miller (1923–2004), Jules Munshin (1915–1970), and a fine supporting cast. Another tale of sailors on the town, the picture shows that Sinatra continued to polish his acting and had mastered some modest dancing skills to add to his resume.

Although he appeared in nine motion pictures in a span of seven years during the 1940s, only three of them—*Anchors Aweigh, Take Me Out to the Ball Game,* and *On the Town*—have endured reasonably well. But that wealth of experience prepared him for meatier roles in the 1950s, especially more dramatic, nonsinging parts. In 1953, he won an Academy Award for best supporting actor with his performance in *From Here to Eternity* as a young soldier in Hawaii at the dawn of World War II. In all, Frank

TABLE 92. Frank Sinatra Feature Films, 1940–1949

| Year | Title | Notes |
| --- | --- | --- |
| 1943 | *Higher and Higher* | Song: "I Couldn't Sleep a Wink Last Night" |
| 1944 | *Step Lively* | |
| 1945 | *Anchors Aweigh* | with Gene Kelly, Kathryn Grayson |
| 1946 | *Till the Clouds Roll By* | MGM studio spectacular |
| 1947 | *It Happened in Brooklyn* | with Kathryn Grayson; song: "Time After Time" |
| 1948 | *The Miracle of the Bells* | with Valli |
|  | *The Kissing Bandit* | |
| 1949 | *Take Me Out to the Ball Game* | with Gene Kelly, Esther Williams |
|  | *On the Town* | with Gene Kelly, Jules Munshin |

Sinatra appeared in over 60 films in just about every genre, an acting career that lasted into the 1980s.

While he made movies, Sinatra also continued to sing. In 1953, and in light of declining sales, Columbia Records did not renew his contract. Sinatra proceeded to sign with Capitol, and there he established a close working relationship with arranger Nelson Riddle (1921–1985). The two created a series of singles and albums in the 1950s and 1960s that dramatically turned his sagging musical career around and provided one hit after another. He also branched out into **television,** both as frequent guest and host of his own shows in 1950 to 1951 and 1957 to 1958.

From a boyish band singer in the 1930s, Frank Sinatra in the latter half of the 20th century became one of the most successful entertainers ever. He eclipsed Bing Crosby, becoming Ol' Blue Eyes, The Voice, the Chairman of the Board, leader of the Rat Pack—familiar nicknames for the vocalist who reinvented himself. The foundation for all this later acclaim, however, had been established in the 1940s, when he commenced a phenomenal show business career that other entertainers could only envy.

*See also:* ASCAP vs. BMI Radio Boycott and the AFM Recording Ban; Broadway Shows (Musicals); Dance; Fads; Fashion; Jazz; Radio Programming: Music and Variety Shows; Songwriters and Lyricists; Swimming and Water Skiing

**Selected Reading**

Freedland, Michael. *All the Way: A Biography of Frank Sinatra.* New York: St. Martin's Press, 1998.
Mustazza, Leonard. *Frank Sinatra and Popular Culture.* Westport, CT: Greenwood Press, 1999.
———. *Ol' Blue Eyes: A Frank Sinatra Encyclopedia.* Westport, CT: Greenwood Press, 1999.
O'Brien, Ed, and Scott Savers. *Sinatra: The Man and His Music: The Recording Artistry of Francis Albert Sinatra, 1939–1992.* Austin, TX: TSD Press, 1992.

# SKATING (FIGURE)

Ice skating, a pleasant cold-weather activity requiring the wearing of strap-on runners or boots with metal blades in order to glide on ice, has for centuries provided a welcomed outdoor diversion for children and adults. City parks in cold northern communities in the United States usually feature a frozen pond or lake for such purposes, and evenings find families skating or roasting marshmallows on nearby camp fires. For example, even before the 1870 completion of Central Park in New York City, a skating pond opened, quickly became a top attraction, and continues so today. In 1936, skating enthusiasts were provided a second spot for their sport, this time a man-made outdoor rink at Rockefeller Center. Advances in mechanical means of freezing and maintaining ice allowed for this installation at that time. Since its completion, the rink has drawn overflow crowds almost daily.

Skating arrived in North America from Europe in the mid-1700s; as it gained in popularity, many skaters became frustrated with just going in circles around the ice. Trial and error led to alterations to the blade that enabled skaters to break out of a circle and make elaborate figure eights and other geometric or grapevine designs. Some began to focus on cutting certain figures with an emphasis on doing it "properly."

Private skating clubs and associations were organized and many built rinks. These groups established standards and rules, provided teachers and coaches, and conducted competitions. By 1892, several European countries had organized the International Skating Union (ISU). The U.S. Figure Skating Association, formed in 1921 (and today known as U.S. Figure Skating), has been a member of ISU since 1923. Under its auspices, world figure skating championships have been held annually since 1896, except during the two world wars and in 1961 after a plane crash killed the entire U.S. team. The years 1944 and 1945 saw the U.S. Figure Skating Championships put on hold after enlistments and the draft sent many of the male skaters off to war. Female skaters and adolescents of both sexes continued to compete, and various ice-show companies held events in major cities. Some groups, in a spirit of patriotism, designated at least one performance per season in honor of service personnel. For example, on November 30, 1942, a show called the Ice Follies opened all the seats at Madison Square Garden to those in uniform at no charge.

European and U.S. ice skating competitions produced celebrities. One, Sonja Henie (1912–1969), a native of Norway, emerged as one of the most famous skaters in the world. She placed first in the world singles championship contests for 10 straight years starting in 1927 and received gold medals for singles skating in the 1928, 1932, and 1936 Olympic Games. She moved to Los Angeles in 1936, and by 1940 had easily advanced from success in competitive skating to a lucrative career as a movie star, organizer, and principal performer in her own traveling ice shows and revues. She skated in 12 **movies,** all light comedies advertised as "musical icetravaganzas," including *Sun Valley Serenade* (1941), *Iceland* (1942), *Wintertime* (1943), *It's a Pleasure* (1945), and *The Countess of Monte Cristo* (1949). On the road, the "Hollywood Ice Revue," which starred Henie, toured the United States and drew large crowds. Its January 16, 1940, show at Madison Square Garden in New York City attracted an audience of 16,500, the largest reception the city had ever accorded her.

When in New York, Henie did not limit her skating to Madison Square Garden. The Center Theater, located near Rockefeller Center, originally opened in 1932 as a movie theater. It was soon overshadowed by Radio City Music Hall and underwent renovations to accommodate musical ice shows. It reopened in October 1940 as an ice theater with the presentation of a Sonja Henie production, *It Happens on Ice* (1940–1942). In collaboration with arena owner and sports promoter Arthur Wirtz (1901–1983), Sonja Henie provided similar shows at the Center Theater throughout the 1940s. They included *Stars on Ice* (1942–1944), *Hats Off to Ice* (1944–1946), *Icetime* (1946–1947), and *Howdy, Mr. Ice* (1948–1949); each attracted millions of patrons during their runs.

Young girls credited Henie for kindling in them an interest in skating. One, Mabel Fairbanks (1916–2001), a black woman from New York City, reported that seeing Sonja Henie in a movie in 1938 convinced her that she wanted to be a skater. But Fairbanks encountered major obstacles because of her race; most importantly, she could not join a skating club, the source of both training and entry into competitive events. Maribel Vinson Owen (1911–1961), U.S. Figure Skating title holder in the 1920s and 1930s, learned of Fairbanks' desire to skate and secretly coached her. That gesture, however, did not solve the competition issue. In order to skate, Fairbanks then attempted to join ice companies, but she again encountered discrimination. She therefore decided to form her own show. She moved to Los Angeles and, during the 1940s, performed at nightclubs such as Ciros and other local venues. She eventually became a coach, giving free lessons to those too poor to pay. In the context of the civil rights movement of the 1960s, Mabel Fairbanks helped to open doors for blacks to become professional skaters.

Other women skaters made their way to the West Coast to be in movies in the early 1940s. Gladys Lyne Jepson-Turner (1923–2005), skater, dancer, and swimmer, came to the United States from England in the late 1930s. She toured with the Ice Capades in 1940 and became known as Belita, the Ice Maiden. She had a minor appearance in the movie *Ice-Capades* (1941), moved on to a more prominent spot in *Silver Skates* (1943), and achieved top billing in *Lady, Let's Dance* (1944). Hoping to maintain a postwar acting career, she accepted a role in a **film noir** production titled *Suspense* (1946), which combined skating with a serious plot. For the remainder of her movie career, which extended into the 1950s, she abandoned skating pieces for dramatic vehicles.

Republic pictures, in hopes of competing with Twentieth-Century Fox's successful Sonja Henie movies, brought the modestly successful Vera Helena Hruba (1921–2003) from Prague, Czechoslovakia, to Hollywood to star in *Ice-Capades* and *Ice-Capades Revue* (1942). Not satisfied with the outcome, the studio changed Hruba's surname to the easily pronounced, Ralston, taken from the name of a popular breakfast cereal, and cast her in more serious roles. These performances, however, proved difficult because of Vera Ralston's limited English and heavy accent.

Not all successful skaters journeyed to Hollywood. Some achieved fame just with their skating. Richard "Dick" Button (b. 1929), when only 14 years old, placed second in his first competition and quickly developed an enviable amateur record. From 1946 to 1952, he reigned as the U.S. men's champion. He became the first American to win the men's world figure skating championship in 1947 at age 18. In 1949, he received the James E. Sullivan Memorial Award given annually to the most outstanding amateur athlete, and in 1948 and 1952 he added back-to-back Olympic gold metals to his accomplishments. In addition to his status as champion, Button became famous as the first skater to perform two figure skating executions called a double axel and a flying camel. He briefly toured with Ice Capades and Holiday on Ice; since 1962, Button has worked as an expert commentator on figure skating for ABC's (American Broadcasting Company) *Wide World of Sports*.

Gretchen Merrill (1925–1965) won six U.S. National Championships in the period 1943 to 1949, and in 1947, at the first World and European Championships held after World War II, took home, respectively, silver and bronze medals. During the war, she frequently performed for military personnel. Eugene Turner (b. 1921) placed first in the 1940 and 1941 U.S. Figure Skating Championships. His 1943 enlistment in the U.S. Army Air Force interrupted his career; after the war, he became a coach and skated professionally as a partner with Sonja Henie. Robert Specht (1921–1999), with partner Joan Mitchell (1926–1992), placed third in the U.S. pairs figure skating competition in 1941 and captured first in the men's single competition the following year. After serving in the air force during World War II, he skated for many years with Ice Capades.

For those who retired from competition but wanted to continue to skate, ice shows offered several possibilities. One, known as the Ice Follies, founded by the Shipstad brothers, Eddie (1907–1998) and Roy (1911–1975), and Oscar Johnson (ca. 1900s–1960s), gave its first performance in 1936 in Tulsa, Oklahoma. The show combined figure skating and theater and featured the Ice Folliettes, chorus girls who executed a kick line and other skating productions with complete precision and elaborate props.

The Ice Follies offered a popular comic ice skating duo with the stage names Frick and Frack. Frick, Werner Groebli (1915–2008), and Frack, Hans Mauch (1919–1979), came to the United States from Switzerland in 1938, having established some of their antics in performances in London. Their slapstick routines with mock collisions and blade-close misses caused *Life* magazine to call them the "Clown Kings of the Ice." Their stage names became a slang expression meaning two people who are closely linked in some way. The entire Ice Follies troupe, along with Frick and Frack, appeared in a 1939 movie titled *The Ice Follies of 1939* starring Joan Crawford (1905–1977), James Stewart (1908–1997), and Lew Ayres (1908–1996). The movie turned out to be a flop, but Frick and Frack went on to more successful Hollywood films, including *Silver Skates* (1943) and *Lady, Let's Dance* (1944).

The immediate success of the Ice Follies, despite one failed Hollywood movie, inspired other entrepreneurs to follow suit. In 1940, John H. Harris (active 1940s), the owner of a skating rink in Pittsburgh, Pennsylvania, noticed that his **hockey** crowds swelled when he booked a figure skater to perform between game periods. Borrowing from vaudeville, he hired skaters, comedians, clowns, jugglers, barrel jumpers, and scantily clad showgirls as a part of the extravaganza. The performance usually began with an Olympic skater recently turned professional gliding out onto the ice for a dramatic interpretation of a classical piece of music. This would be followed by beautiful women Harris dubbed the Ice Ca-pets. An immediate success, the show became known as the Ice Capades and moved from a hockey game interlude to a touring show in direct competition with the Ice Follies and Sonja Henie productions. The Ice Capades added a new twist with the introduction of operettas and musicals to the ice show format.

Holiday on Ice joined the ranks in 1943 and over the years employed skaters who were not particularly well-known. Each year the program had a different theme, such as "Winter Carnival" or "Candyland," and always included a traditional element of a spinning wheel in which the skaters link arms with each other, one by one, and in the process lengthen the spokes, which spin around a center point. Although Holiday on Ice originated in the United States, since 1970 it has toured only in Europe and Latin America.

The January 1940 cover of *Child Life* magazine features a young boy and girl decked out in warm clothing, scarves, gloves, and new skates. With smiles on their faces, they gleefully glide along while being chased by a sliding dog. A line of other young skaters can be seen in the background. Throughout the decade, *Life* magazine offered elaborate layouts about the best-known ice figure skaters, all giving testimony to the popularity of activities on ice. Sonja Henie and Dick Button, perhaps two of the greatest figure skaters of all time, contributed to the growing interest in skating, as did the various show companies formed during the 1940s, and the four U.S. hockey teams.

*See also:* Classical Music; Dance; Fashion; Leisure and Recreation; Magazines; Race Relations and Stereotyping; Technology

**Selected Reading**
Copley-Graves, Lynn. *Figure Skating History: The Evolution of Dance on Ice.* Columbus, Ohio: Plataro Press, 1992.
Whedon, Julia. *The Fine Art of Ice Skating: An Illustrated History and Portfolio of Stars.* New York: Harry N. Abrams, 1988.

# SKATING (ROLLER)

Two varieties of roller skates—traditional four-wheel, or quad, and in-line—have constituted most of the history of this recreational and sporting footwear. Quad roller skates with wooden or composite wheels, a Dutch invention, have been around for many years. They usually consist of a metal frame clamped and locked to the soles of a pair of shoes with a special key. This variety can also be purchased as a pair of boots permanently attached to skate frames. Both kinds of quad skates have four wheels, arranged in a manner similar to the tires of a car. In 1863, James Leonard Plimpton (1828–1911), a New England businessman, improved on earlier inventions by creating a safer model that allowed the wearer to steer by simply leaning to the left or right. Toe stops made their debut in 1876. By the late 19th century, ball bearings allowed the wheels to rotate smoothly, greatly improving the ride.

In-line skates, often called Rollerblades after the current popular trade name, also date back to the 1800s. They, too, have a toe stop and can have anywhere from two to five wheels arranged in a single line. This skate lost favor shortly after its invention but experienced a rediscovery in 1980 because of an interest by **hockey** players and skiers for a way to continue training out of season. Traveling on smooth terrain on either kind of roller skate can be a form of recreation, a means of **transportation,** or a competitive sport.

Following Plimpton's invention, roller skating initially served as a popular pastime for men and women. Children and teenagers immediately joined the ranks of skaters, and in 1937 a group of skating rink owners formed the Roller Skating Rink Operators Association (RSROA), later known as the Roller Skating Association. Many skating rinks provided weather-protected space with live organ music and soda fountains. RSROA's promotional efforts included sponsoring amateur competitions; Cincinnati, Ohio, hosted the first one in 1938. The following year, Detroit served as the location for national figure roller skating championships, while Mineola, New York, sponsored **dance** roller skating contests. Together, these two forms of roller skating are often referred to as artistic skating. In 1940, RSROA brought figure and dance skating championships, along with speed as a third element, into one event held in Cleveland, Ohio. Almost 500 enthusiasts attended.

Various popular culture outlets began advancing roller skating during the 1930s, efforts that broadened the ranks of skaters during that time. For example, Hollywood released two shorts—*Around the Equator on Roller Skates* (1932, Universal Pictures) and *Eddie Duchin and Orchestra* (1933, Warner Bros.). In the latter, which takes place in a nightclub, the staff and orchestra wear roller skates. Paramount countered in 1938 with a cartoon, *A Date To Skate,* which has Popeye taking his girlfriend Olive Oyl roller skating. Children's novelist Ruth Sawyer (1880–1970) contributed a book, *Roller Blades,* in 1936, which tells of the life of Lucinda Wyman in the 1890s, a girl who enjoys skating around New York City.

RSROA, wanting to capitalize on the interest shown in their competitions, repeated the 1940 program the following year and attracted twice as many participants. That same year, a roller skating short from Universal Pictures, *In the Groove,* included a roller skating vaudeville team known as the Lightning Trio. From this success, roller skating hit it big in 1942, when Paramount Pictures produced *My Favorite Blonde.* The movie stars **Bob Hope** (1903–2003); the popular comedian skates with Percy, his remarkable roller skating penguin partner.

The Chicago Roller Skate Company, founded in 1905, and the largest roller skate manufacturer throughout most of the 20th century, featured a variety of skates, including its Betty Lytle Shoe Skates. Betty Lytle (active 1940s) had attained celebrity status in the world of roller skating, and many rinks offered membership in the Betty Lytle Dance and Figure Club.

**Newspapers** decided that roller skating had attained enough popularity to serve as a way to increase readership. In 1940, the *New York Journal-American* initiated a twice-a-week column devoted to roller skating. **Magazines** also covered the activity. Throughout the decade, *Life* magazine regularly ran features with pictures of children skating on neighborhood sidewalks, as well as dads and their daughters, mothers and their sons, individuals, and couples at indoor rinks. The photographs tell the story of roller skating, showing people of all ages arriving at the rink and changing into skates, tentatively moving out onto the floor, falling and being assisted by attendants, smiling as they later successfully circle the rink, and finally relaxing at the refreshment stand.

World War II affected everyday life in the United States in a number of ways, most noticeably with the advent of **rationing.** In mid-1942, production of most **toys** requiring quantities of steel and rubber in their manufacture ceased—a restriction that created a time of no more new metal items, including roller and ice skates. For kids who had usable skates and time to play after school and before dinner, gas rationing proved advantageous, because less traffic permitted safer skating on city streets. Rationing also necessitated that adults park their **automobiles** and use other means of transportation to get places. For short distances, roller skates became an option.

Officials gave recreation a high priority for military personnel throughout the war, and, when possible, bases included roller skating areas. During and after World War II, recreation facilities competed for patrons looking for ways to enjoy life. Skating rink owners developed promotional gimmicks such as special days for various groups, contests, and free days for servicemen and -women. Some rinks provided instructors to assist anyone who had lost a leg or had been otherwise injured in combat. The personnel at city parks advertised skating as something good for children to do; others held roller skating pageants to raise money for charities such as the March of Dimes. Interest grew and necessitated the building of additional rinks. Roller skating, in all its forms, had established itself as a healthy family activity, an identity that continued throughout the 1950s and 1960s.

*See also:* Advertising; Beverages; Leisure and Recreation; Photography; Skating (Figure); Skiing

**Selected Reading**
Brooks, Lou. *Skate Crazy.* Philadelphia: Running Press, 2003.
Phillips, Ann-Victoria. *The Complete Book of Roller Skating.* New York: Workman Publishing, 1979.

# SKIING

This popular outdoor activity, once primarily a sport for the wealthy had, by the 1940s, attracted growing numbers of people from varied walks of life. Prior to the 1930s, climate and geography also limited skiing to those who lived in mountainous regions with snowy winters. Evidence of increasing interest can be gleaned from various aspects of everyday life at this time—a 1940's die-cut paper toy of the comics' Captain Marvel Jr. outfitted on skis; the December 1940 cover of *Child Life* magazine presenting a skiing Santa Claus; a 1941 Charles Addams (1912–1988) cartoon in *The New Yorker* magazine showing single ski tracks going around both sides of a tree; *The Art of Skiing,* a 1941 Walt Disney Goofy cartoon; the 1940/1941 Sears catalog selling women's skiing outfits; and a February 1945 *Life* magazine cover and photo essay featuring ski clothes.

Three events during the 1930s caught the attention of potential skiers and contributed to the sport's mounting popularity: (1) the 1932 Winter Olympic Games, (2) the invention of chair and T-bar lifts, and (3) enterprising railroad ventures. The Olympics at Lake Placid, a small village deep in the Adirondacks of New York state, offered its snowy slopes, a ski jump, and speed skating facilities, a perfect setting for the games. A daily broadcast over the nationwide NBC (National Broadcasting Company) and CBS (Columbia Broadcasting System) **radio** networks, as well as newsreel features on Movietone News, took these winter sports events, including skiing, to households across the country.

Skiing requires determination and stamina, and, before the availability of mechanical assistance, many chose cross-country skiing over downhill; it was simply too difficult to get to the top of a slope for a decent run. Those who preferred alpine skiing had to contend with holding on to a rope tow; not an impossible task but not the most comfortable experience, either. Also, a coast down a mountainside on heavy and clumsy wooden skis could defeat the smoothness of the ride. The installation of the world's first chair lift at Sun Valley, Idaho, in 1936, offered a welcome convenience for being carried to the top. As the 1930s drew to a close, New Hampshire, Massachusetts, Vermont, California, Oregon, Washington, Utah, Wyoming, and Montana also featured ski areas with chair lifts ready to accommodate an estimated 1 million skiers. Those enthusiasts, however, would have to wait until after World War II for lighter, better skis.

Getting to a ski area could be as much of a problem as making it to the top of a slope. In Colorado and Utah, enterprising entrepreneurs occasionally used mining camp **trains** to carry skiers to high elevations; not necessarily fancy conveyances but a helpful means of **transportation.** In 1931, the East Coast Boston and Maine Railroad instituted 12 weekend ski train excursions to Franconia, New Hampshire, a step above the trains used in the West. Upon arrival at the ski area, the added touch of instruction at the modest Peckett's Inn encouraged novice skiers to give the sport a try.

The third and most ambitious undertaking of promoting skiing came from Union Pacific Railroad chairman, businessman, politician, and diplomat W. Averell Harriman (1891–1986). Recognizing Americans' growing interest in winter sports, especially skiing, and also wanting to bring travelers back to hopping on a train instead of stepping into their cars, Harriman in 1936 led Union Pacific in building an elaborate ski resort with a 220-room lodge and private cottages, **swimming** pools, and ski runs with superb snow conditions at Sun Valley, Idaho. The plan also included a ski train to transport customers from distant metropolitan areas. Once at the resort, visitors were offered all the amenities of skiing along with outstanding dining and the best of entertainment. The resort closed to paying customers during World War II to serve as a convalescent facility for the U.S. Navy. It reopened to the public in December 1946, but one floor of one wing of the lodge remained a medical clinic until 1961.

Once Sun Valley opened, Hollywood soon arrived. Stars came as guests and to entertain, and Twentieth Century-Fox validated this new winter wonderland and all of its activities with a musical comedy shot on location called *Sun Valley Serenade* (1941). The storyline involves the entertainment offered at the resort, including the staging of an ice show. The cast includes Norwegian-born figure skating champion Sonja Henie (1912–1969), popular **swing** bandleader **Glenn Miller** (1904–1944), and comedian Milton Berle (1908–2002). On a lighter side, but indicative of the growing interest in skiing among Americans during the 1940s, Paramount Pictures issued the animated *I'll Be Skiing Ya* (1947), starring Popeye and his girlfriend Olive Oyl.

Stories of skiing and ski areas at the local level, along with the latest information and newest tips, came from bulletins and newsletters published by ski clubs and associations under titles such as *The Ski Bulletin, The National Ski Weekly,* and *Western Skier.* In 1938, editor, publisher, and skier William T. Eldred (1913–1965) of Schenectady, New York, wrote numerous articles on skiing in his *Empire State Ski News* and by 1948 had acquired two West Coast periodicals, *Western Skiing* and *Ski Illustrated.* A merger of the three gave the country its first national ski magazine titled *Ski.*

Unfortunately, along with the fun of skiing, accidents occur and, by 1938, Charles Minot "Minnie" Dole (1899–1976), with strong support from the National Ski Association president Roger Langley (1901–1976), organized a group in the Northeast to patrol runs and assist injured skiers. Called the National Ski Patrol, the volunteers functioned as a committee of the National Ski Association (founded 1905; today the United States Ski Association), and the idea quickly spread to other parts of the country.

In November 1939, while most American skiers were on the slopes for pure enjoyment, Finnish ski-mounted soldiers carried out warfare in severe winter conditions. They glided through their native forests and fought the invading Soviet Union, a feat that caught the attention of Charles Dole. He, as did many other Americans, realized that the United States was preparing for the possibility of a global conflict. Dole sent letters to **President Franklin Delano Roosevelt** (1882–1945) and **General George Catlett Marshall** (1880–1959) offering to recruit experienced skiers to help train U.S. troops in similar tactics on skis.

General Marshall bought Dole's idea and secured a formal agreement with the National Ski Patrol to serve as an advisor to the War Department. *Life* magazine chronicled some of the activity in its January 20, 1941, issue with a cover picture and photo essay about an experimental army ski patrol. The activation of a complete unit dedicated to mountain warfare training first occurred in November 1941, at Fort Lewis, Washington. Men already in the army with skiing and mountaineering experience constituted its first members. Dole and fellow patrol members went to work seeking volunteers to serve in other units and brought some of the country's most accomplished skiers and competent instructors into the 10th Mountain Division, activated on July 15, 1943. Prepared to fight and survive under the most hostile winter conditions, the unit saw action in Italy and the Alps.

In 1945, ski periodicals predicted that the postwar years would bring the greatest influx of skiers that the United States had ever known, and indeed they did, creating a building boom of ski resorts led primarily by members of the 10th Division who had returned to civilian life to work as ski instructors, ski school directors, and Olympic and college coaches. Three, Friedl Pfeifer (1911–1995), Johnny Litchfield (b. 1917), and Percy Rideout (active 1930s–1950s), settled in Aspen, Colorado, and helped to usher in what would become a big-time ski industry for the state. In 1945, they launched the Friedl Pfeifer Ski School, reorganized as the Aspen Skiing Corporation in 1946, and installed two chair lifts. Aspen soon became a top-ranked American high-mountain resort.

Next on the list for development and another 10th Mountain alumni project, Arapaho Basin, opened in 1946, under the leadership of Larry Jump (1913–1989) and Sandy Schauffler (active 1930s–1950s). At first, the basin catered to day skiers from the Denver area and initially used only a rope tow; Jump and Schauffler added two chair lifts for the 1948–1949 season. Finally, in the late 1950s, Peter Seibert (1924–2002), also from the 10th Mountain Division, started construction of Vail Ski Resort in Colorado, another prominent and successful undertaking.

In 1948, the Olympic Games held at St. Moritz, Switzerland, offered downhill (or alpine) and slalom skiing (racing between poles placed close together) for the first time as separate events. Gretchen Fraser (1919–1994), the first American skier to receive Olympic medals in the sport, earned a gold in the slalom and a silver in downhill.

Howard Head (1914–1991), an aircraft engineer, went skiing for the first time in 1947, and experienced much difficulty because of the heavy wooden skis. Because of his immediate love of the sport and frustration about the skis, he left his job and devoted all of his time to making a lighter ski. Concentrating on the use of aluminum and plywood, Head made several attempts to perfect his product. By the end of the winter of 1947, and after several trial runs made by pro skier Neil Robinson (active 1930s–1960s), Head fashioned a ski as strong as a wooden one but half as heavy. In 1949, he started selling his Head standard ski, the first commercially successful aluminum ski on the market. Within a couple of years, the Head Ski Company, with its strong and easy-to-control skis, became a major supplier to enthusiasts far and wide.

One final technological innovation from the General Electric Company pushed the number of skiers higher yet—an estimated three million in the United States by 1948. In the late 1940s, its research labs produced white artificial snow in a cold chamber, and, by 1952, machines for replicating this procedure appeared on the market. Grossinger's resort in the Catskill Mountains of New York state, covered its slopes with manmade snow and led the industry by initiating early season skiing.

Although skiing as a sport had flourished during the 1930s, it diminished some during World War II. Most skiing news centered on the U.S. ski troops, especially the 10th Mountain Division and its success in crippling several German divisions. During the postwar years, skiing, like all else in the United States, returned to normalcy, and those involved in the ski industry offered a number of improvements: lighter, more durable, and faster skis; synthetic materials to replace cotton and wool in ski clothing; and destination ski resorts such as Sun Valley, Idaho, and Aspen, Colorado. Skiing had definitely taken on a new glamour, and many Americans with extra dollars to spend responded favorably.

*See also:* Automobiles and the American Automotive Industry; Comic Books; Comic Strips; Fashion; Leisure and Recreation; Magazines; Movies; Newspapers; Skating (Figure); Technology

**Selected Reading**
Berry, I. William. *The Great North American Ski Book.* New York: Charles Scribner's Sons, 1982.
Needham, Richard. *Ski: Fifty Years in North America.* New York: Harry N. Abrams, 1987.

# SMITH, KATE

A native of Greenville, Virginia, a small town near Staunton, Smith (born Kathryn Smith, 1907–1986) spent her early years in Washington, DC. While still a child, she sang for U.S. troops based in the capital area during World War I. In the mid-1920s, Smith broke into professional show business, appearing as a character named Tiny Little in a 1926 Broadway musical, *Honeymoon Lane*. Her strong contralto voice impressed producers, and she gained billing as a stage comedienne, subsequently appearing in *Hit the Deck* (1927–1928) and *Flying High* (1930). She also cut some recordings during this period, but they gained no notice.

Through the efforts of a canny talent agent named Ted Collins (1900–1964), Smith in 1930 signed with Columbia Records, an important breakthrough for the young vocalist. Collins soon thereafter became her manager, a position he would hold until his death. In 1931, Smith released her first recorded hit, a contemporary tune called "River, Stay Away from My Door." The success of this recording, along with Collins's continuing astute direction, brought her to the studios of CBS (Columbia Broadcasting System) and network **radio,** where she quickly achieved the rank of queen of the airwaves. Promoters billed her as "the songbird of the South," a tag that stayed with her for the remainder of her long career.

Her work with CBS commenced with *Kate Smith Sings,* a 15-minute show destined to survive under other titles and with shifting timeslots for many years. Although she already had one show under way, Smith added *The Kate Smith Hour* (also known as *The Kate Smith A & P Bandwagon* and *The Kate Smith Show*), a guest-filled variety offering in 1936; with time and schedule changes, it ran until 1947. That year, she switched to **MBS (Mutual Broadcasting System)** for a resumption of *Kate Smith Sings;* it ran through 1949 and had a brief revival in 1951.

*A popular recording artist and radio personality, Kate Smith stayed active throughout the 1940s. She is shown here singing Irving Berlin's "Alexander's Ragtime Band" as part of her CBS radio show,* The Kate Smith Hour *(Photofest)*

As if her musical shows did not suffice, in 1938 Smith introduced *Speaking Her Mind* and *Kate Smith's Column* on CBS. Daytime talk shows filled with folksy wisdom and practical advice, they coalesced into *Kate Smith Speaks* the following year, continuing until 1947. Her talk format proved popular, and after her move to MBS, she continued the program; it stayed on the air until 1951. A deeply conservative woman, Smith espoused homespun American values, wholesomeness, and patriotism—themes that gave her a solid following over the years.

A tireless stumper in drives for **war bonds,** Smith collected some $600 million (roughly $7.4 billion in 2008 dollars) for the Allied cause, making her one of the most successful fundraisers of all time. At one point, in September 1943, she gathered $39 million (roughly $485 million in 2008 dollars) in pledges during a marathon CBS radio broadcast that spanned 18 hours; no other individual had ever raised as much in a single attempt.

Smith, like so many entertainers, eventually made the move to **television.** *The Kate Smith Hour* premiered on NBC in the fall of 1950. A late afternoon show, it did well enough that, one year later, the network gave her a prime-time show with *The Kate Smith Evening Hour.* Because she also kept her afternoon program, she had the distinction of having two series on television, plus her *Kate Smith Sings* and her talk programs on radio. After her TV shows ran their course, she remained a frequent guest on many variety shows, a testament to her continuing popularity.

As a performer on radio, on television, and in live appearances, Smith opened her performances with a hearty "Hello, everybody!" and closed with a farewell "Thanks for listenin'." In her early series, *Kate Smith Sings,* she introduced "When the Moon Comes Over the Mountain" in 1931. The song quickly became her signature piece and remained so until her death in 1986. Her extensive radio exposure led Smith to Hollywood; she broke into the **movies** with *The Big Broadcast* (1932), a picture that features the stars of radio. She appears in a cameo singing, of course, her radio theme, "When the Moon Comes Over the Mountain." Smith then starred in a first-run feature called *Hello, Everybody!* Despite her presence, the film did poorly at the box office, and it finished Smith's short-lived venture into motion pictures, at least for the 1930s. In 1943, she made a brief appearance in *This Is the Army,* another variety musical with a mix of film stars and celebrities. Based on composer Irving Berlin's (1888–1989) stage production of the same name, it served as a patriotic flag-waver for the war years.

In retrospect, Kate Smith's early recording career, as far as hit singles go, fared little better than her film efforts. Not until 1940 and "The Woodpecker Song" (taken from the popular Woody Woodpecker cartoon series) did she next have a hit. A few charted songs followed in the 1940s—"I Don't Want to Walk without You" (1942), "Seems Like Old Times" (1946), "Now Is the Hour" (1947), and others—and her numerous additional records and albums sold steadily and in sufficient quantities that producers displayed little reluctance to employ her, given her immense popularity on radio. In time, she recorded over 3,000 songs, many of them during World War II. She favored sincere ballads that touch on loneliness, separation, and a hope for better times ahead.

One particular Kate Smith recording from the late 1930s merits attention for the 1940s. Some 20 years earlier, at the close of World I in 1918, Irving Berlin wrote a song he called "God Bless America" for an army camp show, *Yip, Yip, Yaphank.* Dropped from the final score, the tune languished in a trunk until Berlin exhumed it in 1938. He saw the ominous signs foretelling World War II and wanted to give the nation an unabashedly patriotic song for those dark days. His resurrected composition emerged as one of the most inspiring songs of the era. In addition, Berlin knew exactly who should perform it. Recognizing her considerable fame and talent, he granted Kate Smith exclusive rights to the words and music to "God Bless America," and she introduced it to the nation on Armistice Day, November 11, 1938, by singing it on *The Kate Smith Hour.*

Smith's performance spurred an overwhelming audience response that soon made Berlin's forgotten number into a virtual second, unofficial national anthem for the war years. Her powerful, optimistic rendition of his lyrics lifted people's spirits whenever they heard it. She recorded "God Bless America," along with "The Star-Spangled Banner," in 1939 for RCA Victor, and the disk became an instant standard, played over and over again on stations everywhere. Both Smith and Berlin generously turned over any royalties they might receive to the Boy and Girl Scouts of America, a substantial gift, given the song's reception ("The Star-Spangled Banner," already in the public domain, accrued no royalties). Smith went on to perform Berlin's composition countless times thereafter for bond drives and any other occasion that called for stirring people's patriotic feelings, plus she made it a weekly staple on *The Kate Smith Hour*. Throughout the conflict, her rendition brought her the admiration of millions, and it not surprisingly turns out to be the song she performs in *This Is the Army*.

By the end of the 1940s, Kate Smith found herself ranked among the most influential women of the era. Over the years, "the first lady of radio" had received numerous honors, her music and talk shows had audiences in the millions, and she had attained the status of a national treasure. World War II only served to burnish her reputation, and "God Bless America," like "When the Moon Comes Over the Mountain" before it, would always be associated with her. When she died in 1986, her grave bore the inscription, "This Is Kate Smith—This Is America."

*See also:* ASCAP vs. BMI Radio Boycott and the AFM Recording Ban; Broadway Shows (Musicals); Cartoons (Film); Musicals (Film); Radio Programming: Music and Variety Shows; Songwriters and Lyricists

**Selected Reading**

Dunning, John. *On the Air: The Encyclopedia of Old-Time Radio.* New York: Oxford University Press, 1998.

Hayes, Richard K. *Kate Smith: A Biography, with a Discography, Filmography, and List of Stage Appearances.* Jefferson, NC: McFarland, 1995.

Jones, John Bush. *The Songs that Fought the War: Popular Music and the Home Front, 1939–1945.* Waltham, MA: Brandeis University Press, 2006.

Smith, Kathleen E. R. *God Bless America: Tin Pan Alley Goes to War.* Lexington: University Press of Kentucky, 2003.

# SOFTBALL

Two versions about the origin of softball in the United States exist, each giving different dates and places for the first game. Both report it being played some time in the 1880s, utilizing a gymnasium in the Midwest during inclement weather as an alternative to **baseball.** Players used a ball larger and softer than a regular baseball. Legend also has it that a Chicago fire department officer reinvented the game for outside play in 1895. Exactly wherever and whenever the sport began, it soon became an outdoor game and spread rapidly in the early years of the 20th century. It even served as a popular form of recreation for U.S. soldiers—or doughboys as many called them then—fighting in World War I.

Something of a softball craze swept the United States following a single-elimination tournament held in conjunction with the 1933 Chicago World's Fair. Organized by sportswriter Leo Fischer (1897–1970) of the *Chicago American* and Chicago sporting goods salesman M. J. Pauley (active 1930s), the two advertised the event with stories written and submitted by Fischer to the wire services. Sixteen teams of men and eight for the women's division came from around the country. By the end of the third and final day, more than 350,000 people had taken advantage of free admission, and softball had established a firm foundation as a sport for both players and spectators.

Following Chicago's lead, the 1939–1940 New York World's Fair offered all-women and all-men teams in competition. Officials alternated the play of games in the area of special events, and good-sized crowds showed up every Saturday and Sunday. Shortly after the closing of the fair, Columbia Pictures Corporation released a short feature titled *Loveable Trouble* (1941). The story revolves around a scheme to secure funds to finance a women's softball team made up of chorus girls, an idea that did not succeed in the film, and the movie likewise did not do much to advance the sport. Its release, however, reflected growing interest in softball.

Initially, teams in various regions of the country referred to the game with different names—kitten ball, mush ball, diamond ball, and indoor baseball. In those formative years, bats varied in length and balls came in many sizes. With the organization of the Amateur Softball Association (ASA) in 1933, uniformity arrived, along with the recognized name of softball. Standardized rules became official. Given its popularity, softball replaced baseball on the list of the 10 most popular sports for women's college intramurals.

*Jo Kennedy, the no-hit, no-run softball queen from Fort Worth, Texas, winds up for a fireball in this 1944 shot. (AP Photo)*

The ASA reported in 1940 that more than 5 million people regularly engaged in a game of softball, and sporting goods manufacturers estimated that they annually spent some $20 million (almost $307.5 million in 2008 money) on the sport. Both men and women played on a variety of teams—church, neighborhood, and community—with factory and office teams contributing heavily to the growing number of players.

Children also enjoyed the sport, and some, after playing in their backyards with friends, would frequently join a recreation center team. Little League teams for baseball and softball had been organized in Williamsport, Pennsylvania, in 1938, with competition commencing in 1939. They became another source of play for children; by 1948, the program had expanded to 94 teams, and the next year to a total of 307.

All of this growing interest and active participation in softball necessitated more playing fields. In 1940, the total number of softball diamonds in municipal and county parks stood at 10,042 compared to 3,904 for baseball. Construction of new facilities occurred throughout the decade, resulting in 12,266 facilities for softball and 5,502 for baseball in 1950. Differences in field size require separate playing areas and the smaller softball diamond pares the distance between bases by 30 feet.

The nation's involvement in World War II affected softball in both negative and positive ways. Kapok, a fine, silky fiber that comes from a tropical tree and used in the manufacture of softballs, became scarce because of a reduction in its importation and the wartime **rationing** program. The military needed available kapok to produce, among other things, life preservers. For the duration of the conflict, softballs therefore had to be made from reclaimed kapok or any soft fabric that would hold together as a core stuffing, such as cocoa fiber or cotton.

But service officials also recognized the importance of recreational outlets at all training facilities, camps, and military hospitals, and toward this end softball became an integral part of the sports programs carried on by the armed forces. With the rationing of kapok enforced, any military requests for supplies received priority. The ASA nonetheless offered assistance in organizing U.S. service camp programs and, when it could, provided softball equipment.

On the home front, with the war in progress, a wide range of individuals and groups came together to raise money for the cause, and sporting events served as a popular venue. One such occasion in New York City in 1945 consisted of stars from Broadway shows, both men and women, playing a comedy softball game against a team of writers, with the proceeds going to the Red Cross War Fund. Softball games continued as a means of raising money after the war. In May 1947, teams from the Senate and the House of Representatives played an exhibition game before a crowd of 25,000. **President Harry S. Truman** (1884–1972) threw out the first ball, and the money raised went to the District of Columbia Police Boys Club.

In the postwar years, many high schools and colleges added women's softball to their sports programs. In August 1946, the *New York Times* reported on that year's season: men's and women's involvement in the game accounted for an estimated 9 million players on 600,000 teams played before 150 million spectators. A children's book, *The Dooleys Play Ball* by juvenile author and sports enthusiast Marion Renick (1904–1983) and released in the spring of 1949, tells the story of a family in which everyone plays softball. The book also includes charts and drawings that illustrate the fundamentals of the game to help its readers learn to play.

The fast-pitch softball game, whereby the pitcher throws the ball underhand as fast as he or she wishes and can, dominated the sport until the 1950s. At this time, officials also adopted standardized rules for a second kind of softball game to be called slow pitch. The rulemakers specified that the ball would be thrown in an arc rather than directly over the plate and that the arc had to be between 6 and 12 feet above the ground.

As the decade ended, softball continued to be widely enjoyed by both players and spectators. The 1950s saw growing interest in the slow-pitch variation, and the 1960s brought fans their first televised games, an all-star tournament played in Clearwater, Florida, on July 1, 1961, and broadcast by the **ABC (American Broadcasting Company) television** network.

*See also:* Broadway Shows (Comedy and Drama); Broadway Shows (Musicals); Leisure and Recreation; Youth

**Selected Reading**
Dickson, Paul. *The Worth Book of Softball: A Celebration of America's True National Pastime.* New York: Facts on File, 1994.
Plummer, Bill. *The Game America Plays.* Seattle: Amica, 2009.

Softball Games. *New York Times,* May 13, 1940; April 27, 1943; August 4, 1946; July 1, 1961. www.proquest.com

# SONGWRITERS AND LYRICISTS

The 1940s may have suffered World War II, the beginnings of the **Cold War, labor unrest,** and rising inflation, but the decade could also claim the creation of some of the best and most enduring popular music of the 20th century. Among the many reasons contributing to this situation, credit must be given to a remarkably talented group of songwriters and lyricists that continued a tradition of excellence dating back to the 1920s and 1930s. From the **Jazz** Age to the **Swing** Era, and then mixing maturity with youthful experimentation in the 1940s, the best of American music displayed consistent imagination, respect for the past, and a keen understanding of popular taste.

"The great American songbook," a term that has gained considerable usage in more recent years (as in "_____ sings the great American songbook" or "_____ plays selections from the great American songbook"), refers to the lyrics and tunes that have become established over time and known to many. Upon hearing these compositions, people with any knowledge of the music of the 1930s and 1940s can immediately recognize a few bars, maybe even sing a few lines. These songs, usually called standards, hold a special place among fans of this period and occupy a disproportionate amount of space in American musical history.

As a rule, novelty songs (such as 1941's "The Hut-Sut Song," 1946's One-zy, Two-zy," 1948's "All I Want for Christmas Is My Two Front Teeth," along with numerous others) may enjoy a brief period of great popularity and become momentary hits, but they usually fade in memory and become a footnote to a particular era. A standard, on the other hand, transcends time and accrues a growing following as years pass. For example, many of the compositions of composer Richard Rodgers (1902–1979) and his one-time partner, lyricist Lorenz Hart (1895–1943), have long since become songbook standards, as have the words penned by Rodgers's later colleague, Oscar Hammerstein II (1895–1960). Perhaps other names have not enjoyed the renown of Rodgers and Hart or Rodgers and Hammerstein, but such pairings as songwriter Jule Styne (1905–1994) with lyricist Sammy Cahn

*One of the more prolific—and possibly the most successful—of the large crop of notable American songwriters and lyricists from the 1940s was Johnny Mercer. In this photograph, taken late in the decade, Mercer holds the music to "On the Nodaway Road," a trifle he had penned some years earlier. (Photofest)*

(1913–1993), Harry Warren (1893–1981) with Al Dubin (891–1945), Jay Livingston (1915–2001) with Ray Evans (1915–2007), and others have resulted in still more standards.

Many composers, of course, choose to work independently, as do a sizable percentage of lyricists, and one collaborates with the other as opportunities and commissions demand. Thus, Johnny Mercer (1909–1976), one of the premier musical wordsmiths of the 1940s, sometimes wrote his own music, but more often than not he would partner with the best composers of the day, such as Harold Arlen (1905–1986), Jerome Kern (1885–1945), or Hoagy Carmichael (1899–1981). A significant number of individuals did both, writing both music and lyrics, perhaps feeling more comfortable putting words to melodies they themselves have composed, thereby not having to second guess or try to interpret what someone else intended. Irving Berlin (1888–1989), Cole Porter (1891–1964), and Frank Loesser (1910–1969) worked in this manner, and certainly the results of their efforts have borne the test of time.

Table 93 lists, alphabetically by year, a limited selection of the tremendous outpouring of popular music during the 1940s. Most of the songs have achieved the status of standards and should at least invoke some passing familiarity with most readers.

The music in the foregoing list became charted hits shortly after their initial release. "Chattanooga Choo Choo" (1941), thanks in part to the movie *Sun Valley Serenade* (also 1941) and the remarkable popularity of the **Glenn Miller** Orchestra, soon sold over 1 million records—the first tune on RCA Victor's Bluebird label to do so. "I've Heard That Song Before" became the No. 1 song for 1943, outranking some formidable competition. The next year, "Swinging on a Star" (1944) repeated the feat, as did "The Gypsy" in 1946 and "Near You" in 1947. "Buttons and Bows," a cheery tune from 1948 and featured in the movie comedy *The Paleface,* likewise reached the vaunted No. 1 position. A typical **Gene Autry** (1907–1998) Western, *Riders in the Sky* (1949), boosted "Ghost Riders in the Sky" to first place, further evidence of the close tie-ins between **movies** and music during the decade. Although it did not reach No. 1 on the charts, Anton Karas's (1906–1985) haunting instrumental theme music from the suspense thriller *The Third Man* (1949) achieved a comfortable place in the top 10 for 1950. In a time notable for hits by vocalists and vocal groups, "*The Third Man* Theme" ran counter to prevailing tastes and claims no contributing lyricist.

A cursory reading of Table 93 should also reveal that certain names—among composers, the likes of Hoagy Carmichael (1899–1981), **Duke Ellington** (1899–1974), and Jimmy Van Heusen (1913–1990) and among lyricists, such luminaries as Johnny Burke (1908–1964), Mack Gordon (1904–1959), and Paul Francis Webster (1907–1984)—reappear with some frequency. When added to the other composers and lyricists mentioned previously, it becomes clear that much of the enduring music of the 1940s emerged from the talents of a distinguished few.

The war years, 1941 to 1945, had a curious impact on American music. Composers and lyricists wrote uncounted numbers of songs about the conflict, the majority of them forgettable tunes like "Allegiance to the Red White and Blue" (1942), "Be a Hero, My Boy" (1943), "Dear God, Watch Over Joe" (1944), "If the Boys Come Home for Christmas, We'll Have a Happy New Year" (1943), "Since He Traded His Zoot Suit for a Uniform" (1942), and "We'll Go Back to Faithful Dobbin (Just to Help the

TABLE 93. Representative Popular Songs of the 1940s by Year, Composer, and Lyricist

| Year | Title | Composer and Lyricist |
|---|---|---|
| 1940 | "How High the Moon" | Morgan Lewis (music), Nancy Hamilton (words) |
| | "I Concentrate on You" | Cole Porter (words and music) |
| | "I'll Never Smile Again" | Ruth Lowe (words and music) |
| | "In a Mellotone" | Duke Ellington (music), Milt Gabler (words) |
| | "The Last Time I Saw Paris" | Jerome Kern (music), Oscar Hammerstein II (words) |
| | "The Nearness of You" | Hoagy Carmichael (music), Ned Washington (words) |
| | "Pennsylvania 6-5000" | Jerry Gray (music), Carl Sigman (words) |
| | "Polka Dots and Moonbeams" | Jimmy Van Heusen (music), Johnny Burke (words) |
| | "Taking a Chance on Love" | Vernon Duke (music), John Latouche (words) |
| | "When the Swallows Come Back to Capistrano" | Leon Rene (words and music) |
| 1941 | "Bewitched (Bothered, and Bewildered)" | Richard Rogers (music), Lorenz Hart (words) |
| | "Blues in the Night" | Harold Arlen (music), Johnny Mercer (words) |
| | "Boogie Woogie Bugle Boy (of Company B)" | Hughie Prince (music), Don Raye (words) |
| | "Chattanooga Choo Choo" | Harry Warren (music), Mack Gordon (words) |
| | "Georgia on My Mind" | Hoagy Carmichael (music), Stuart Gorrell (words) |
| | "How about You?" | Burton Lane (music), Ralph Freed (words) |
| | "I Got It Bad (and That Ain't Good)" | Duke Ellington (music), Paul Francis Webster (words) |
| | "Oh Look at Me Now" | John de Vries and Joe Bushkin (words and music) |
| | "Take the 'A' Train" | Billy Strayhorn (words and music) |
| | "Violets for Your Furs" | Matt Dennis (music), Tom Adair (words) |
| 1942 | "Comin' in on a Wing and a Prayer" | Jimmy McHugh (music), Harold Adamson (words) |
| | "Der Fuehrer's Face" | Oliver Wallace (words and music) |
| | "I Left My Heart at the Stage Door Canteen" | Irving Berlin (words and music) |
| | "I'm Old Fashioned" | Jerome Kern (music), Johnny Mercer (words) |
| | "Lamplighter's Serenade" | Hoagy Carmichael (music), Paul Francis Webster (words) |
| | "Moonlight Becomes You" | Jimmy Van Heusen (music), Johnny Burke (words) |
| | "Praise the Lord and Pass the Ammunition" | Frank Loesser (words and music) |
| | "Serenade in Blue" | Harry Warren (music), Mack Gordon (words) |
| | "Skylark" | Hoagy Carmichael (music), Johnny Mercer (words) |
| | "Tangerine" | Victor Shertzinger (music), Johnny Mercer (words) |
| 1943 | "Do Nothin' 'Till You Hear from Me" | Duke Ellington (music), Bob Russell (words) |
| | "I Had the Craziest Dream" | Harry Warren (music), Mack Gordon (words) |
| | "I'll Be Around" | Alec Wilder (words and music) |
| | "I've Heard That Song Before" | Jule Styne (music), Sammy Cahn (words) |
| | "My Shining Hour" | Harold Arlen (music), Johnny Mercer (words) |
| | "Oh, What a Beautiful Mornin'" | Richard Rodgers (music), Oscar Hammerstein II (words) |
| | "Oklahoma!" | Richard Rodgers (music), Oscar Hammerstein II (words) |

| Year | Title | Composer and Lyricist |
|---|---|---|
| 1943 | "One for My Baby (and One More for the Road)" | Harold Arlen (music), Johnny Mercer (words) |
| | "Poinciana" | Nat Simon (music), Buddy Bernier (words) |
| | "Speak Low" | Kurt Weill (music), Ogden Nash (words) |
| 1944 | "Ac-Cen-Tchuate the Positive" | Harold Arlen (music), Johnny Mercer (words) |
| | "The G.I. Jive" | Johnny Mercer (words and music) |
| | "Moonlight in Vermont" | Karl Suessedorf (music), John Blackburn (words) |
| | "Rosie the Riveter" | Redd Evans and John Jacob Loeb (words and music) |
| | "Saturday Night Is the Loneliest Night of the Week" | Jule Styne (music), Sammy Cahn (words) |
| | "Sentimental Journey" | Ben Homer, Les Brown, and Bud Green (words and music) |
| | "Spring Will Be a Little Late This Year" | Frank Loesser (words and music) |
| | "Swinging on a Star" | Jimmy Van Heusen (music), Johnny Burke (words) |
| | "The Trolley Song" | Hugh Martin (music), Ralph Blane (words) |
| | "What Are You Doing the Rest of Your Life?" | Burton Lane (music), Ted Koehler (words) |
| 1945 | "It Might As Well Be Spring" | Richard Rodgers (music), Oscar Hammerstein II (words) |
| | "It's Been a Long, Long Time" | Jule Styne (music), Sammy Cahn (words) |
| | "June Is Bustin' Out All Over" | Richard Rodgers (music), Oscar Hammerstein II (words) |
| | "Laura" | David Raskin (music), Johnny Mercer (words) |
| | "Memphis in June" | Hoagy Carmichael (music), Paul Francis Webster (words) |
| | "Nancy (with the Laughing Face)" | Jimmy Van Heusen (music), Phil Silvers (words) |
| | "On the Atchison, Topeka, and Santa Fe" | Harry Warren (music), Johnny Mercer (words) |
| | "These Foolish Things (Remind Me of You)" | Harry Link, Holt Marvell, and Jack Strachey (words and music) |
| | "We'll Be Together Again" | Carl Fischer (music), Frankie Laine (words) |
| | "You'll Never Walk Alone" | Richard Rodgers (music), Oscar Hammerstein II (words) |
| 1946 | "Come Rain or Come Shine" | Harold Arlen (music), Johnny Mercer (words) |
| | "Five Minutes More" | Jule Styne (music), Sammy Cahn (words) |
| | "The Gypsy" | Billy Reid (words and music) |
| | "(I Love You) For Sentimental Reasons" | William Best (music), Deke Watson (words) |
| | "Let It Snow! Let It Snow! Let It Snow!" | Jule Styne (music), Sammy Cahn (words) |
| | "Oh! What It Seemed to Be" | Bennie Benjamin, George Weiss, and Frankie Carle (words and music) |
| | "The Old Lamp-Lighter" | Nat Simon (music), Charles Tobias (words) |
| | "Ole Buttermilk Sky" | Hoagy Carmichael and Jack Brooks (words and music) |
| | "They Say It's Wonderful" | Irving Berlin (words and music) |
| | "To Each His Own" | Jay Livingston and Ray Evans (words and music) |
| 1947 | "The Anniversary Song" | Al Jolson and Saul Chaplin (words and music) |
| | "Ballerina" | Carl Sigman (music), Bob Russell (words) |
| | "Chi Baba-Baba, Chi-Baba (My Bambino Go to Sleep)" | Mack David, Al Hoffman, and Jerry Livingston (words and music) |

**TABLE 93.** *(continued)* *(continued)*

| Year | Title | Composer and Lyricist |
|---|---|---|
| 1947 | "Huggin' and Chalkin'" | Kermit Goell and Clarence Leonard Hayes (words and music) |
| | "I Wish I Didn't Love You So" | Frank Loesser (words and music) |
| | "Linda" | Jack Lawrence and Ann Ronell (words and music) |
| | "Mam'selle" | Edmund Goulding (music), Mack Gordon (words) |
| | "Near You" | Francis Craig (music), Kermit Goell (words) |
| | "Smoke! Smoke! Smoke! (That Cigarette)" | Merle Travis and Tex Williams (words and music) |
| | "You Do" | Mack Gordon and Josef Myrow (words and music) |
| 1948 | "Buttons and Bows" | Jay Livingston (music), Ray Evans (words) |
| | "I'll Dance at Your Wedding" | Ben Oakland (music), Herb Magidson (words) |
| | "It's Magic" | Jule Styne (music), Sammy Cahn (words) |
| | "Love Somebody" | Alex Kramer and Joan Whitney (words and music) |
| | "Manana (Is Soon Enough for Me)" | Peggy Lee and Dave Barbour (words and music) |
| | "Nature Boy" | Eden Ahbez (words and music) |
| | "Now Is the Hour" | Dorothy Stewart, Macwa Kaihau, and Clement Scott (words and music) |
| | "On a Slow Boat to China" | Frank Loesser (words and music) |
| | "A Tree in the Meadow" | Billy Reid (words and music) |
| | "Woody Woodpecker" | George Tibbles and Ramey Idriss (words and music) |
| 1949 | "'A'—You're Adorable" | Buddy Kaye, Fred Wise, and Sidney Lippman (words and music) |
| | "Again" | Lionel Newman (music), Dorcas Cochran (words) |
| | "Far Away Places" | Joan Whitney and Alex Kramer (words and music) |
| | "Ghost Riders in the Sky" | Stan Jones (words and music) |
| | "Mule Train" | Jimmy Lange, Hy Heath, and Fred Glickman (words and music) |
| | "My Darling, My Darling" | Frank Loesser (words and music) |
| | "Rudolph, the Red-Nosed Reindeer" | Johnny Marks (words and music) |
| | "Slippin' Around" | Floyd Tillman (words and music) |
| | "Some Enchanted Evening" | Richard Rodgers (music), Oscar Hammerstein (words) |
| | "That Lucky Old Sun" | Beasley Smith (music), Haven Gillespie (words) |
| 1950 | "A Bushel and a Peck" | Frank Loesser (words and music) |
| | "Chattanoogie Shoe Shine Boy" | Harry Stone and Jack Stapp (words and music) |
| | "Dear Hearts and Gentle People" | Sammy Fain (music), Bob Hilliard (words) |
| | "If I Knew You Were Comin' (I'd've Baked a Cake)" | Al Hoffman, Robert Merrill, and Clem Watts (words and music) |
| | "Mona Lisa" | Jay Livingston (music), Ray Evans (words) |
| | "Music! Music! Music!" | Stephen Weiss and Bernie Baum (words and music) |
| | "Rag Mop" | Johnnie Lee Wills and Deacon Anderson (words and music) |
| | | Charles Randolph Green (words and music) |
| | "The Thing" | Anton Karas (music) |
| | *The Third Man* Theme" | Spencer Ross (music), Gordon Jenkins and Mitchell Parrish (words) |
| | "Tzena, Tzena, Tzena" | |

U.S.A.)" (1942). Only a handful of war-oriented melodies captured much public attention, although several government agencies implored songwriters to create martial music that would instill a fighting spirit in those who heard them.

Clearly, the public, both uniformed and civilian, displayed little interest in that direction, preferring a more sentimental approach to those old standbys of love, romance, and loneliness. In addition to the few obviously topical tunes listed in the foregoing table, a few others had a slight impact on overall record and sheet music sales during World War II; they include "(There'll Be a) Hot Time in the Town of Berlin (When the Yanks Go Marching In)" (1943; words and music by Joe Bushkin and John De Vries), "Remember Pearl Harbor" (1942; music by Sammy Kaye and Don Reid, lyrics by Don Reid), and "There's a Star Spangled Banner Waving Somewhere" (1942; words and music by Paul Roberts and Shelby Darnell [pseudonym of Bob Miller]). By and large, however, people did not want musical reminders of the conflict.

On another note, Irving Berlin's classic "**White Christmas**" remains associated with the war years, but it does not appear in the listing because he created it in the late 1930s for a failed movie project. Berlin resurrected it—he seldom discarded unused compositions—for 1942's *Holiday Inn,* a film musical starring **Bing Crosby** (1903–1977) and Fred Astaire (1899–1977). "White Christmas" shortly thereafter became the top song for 1942 and then enjoyed renewed popularity in 1945 and 1946, finally taking its place as a holiday staple for many years to come.

Musical preferences change over time, and today's hit becomes tomorrow's forgotten melody. A transitional decade, 1940s swing lost its following, as did the major vocalists and groups. The postwar years witnessed the rapid rise of many alternative formats, including **bebop (bop), country music,** and **rhythm 'n' blues.** But nothing in music ever truly dies; these new styles, once unaccustomed ears adjusted to them, gained acceptance and established their own traditions, often borrowing from that which went before. In so doing, they joined the ongoing and always interesting parade of American popular music.

*See also:* ASCAP *vs. BMI* Radio Boycott and the AFM Recording Ban; Broadway Shows (Musicals); Comedies (Film); Crime and Mystery Films; Dance; Fads; Fashion; Horror and Thriller Films; Jukeboxes; Radio Programming: Music and Variety Shows; Shore, Dinah; Sinatra, Frank; Smith, Kate; Westerns (Film); Youth

**Selected Reading**
Furia, Philip. *The Poets of Tin Pan Alley: A History of America's Great Lyricists.* New York: Oxford University Press, 1990.
Jasen, David A. *Tin Pan Alley: The Composers, the Songs, the Performers and Their Times.* New York: Donald I. Fine, 1988.
White, Mark. *'You Must Remember This...': Popular Songwriters 1900–1980.* New York: Charles Scribner's Sons, 1985.
Zinsser, William. *Easy to Remember: The Great American Songwriters and Their Songs.* Jaffrey, NH: David R. Godine, 2000.

# SPAM

The name given Hormel Foods Corporation's 1937 addition to its canned meat line of sausages, ham, chili, and beef stew. The word comes from letters in "spicy" and "ham," which describe the basic taste of the product. Originally called Hormel Spiced Ham, the company held a contest to create a more distinctive name. The winner, Broadway performer Kenneth Daigneau (active 1920s and 1930s), received the grand prize of $100 (approximately $1,440 in 2008 dollars).

Hormel, founded in 1891 by George A. Hormel (1860–1946) in Austin, Minnesota, experienced steady growth throughout the early years of the 20th century, with sales offices opening in nearby cities and as far away as Georgia and Texas. A second meat-packing facility began operating in Los Angeles in 1928, and by the end of the Great Depression, 14 distribution centers guaranteed availability of all Hormel products, including Spam, across the nation.

The Hormel Corporation gave the U. S. government strong support in both world conflicts, producing sausages and other meats specifically for World War I, a precedent that it adhered to during World War II. Even before the December 7, 1941, attack by the Japanese on Pearl Harbor, Hormel had contracted to provide 15 million cans of Spam per week for the newly enacted Lend-Lease program. This plan allowed **President Franklin Delano Roosevelt** (1882–1945) to ship **food,** weapons, or other equipment to any country whose opposition to the Axis nations (Germany, Italy, and Japan) assisted U.S. defense. Spam, an easily transportable meat product high in fat and salt and boasting an indefinite shelf life, served as a perfect food item for this purpose.

Before the war ended, Hormel had issued approximately 100 million pounds of Spam, more than half of its total production, to provide rations to U.S., Soviet, and European troops, as well as European citizens needing food. Soviet premier Nikita Khrushchev (1894–1971), in his book, *Khrushchev Remembers* (1970), credits Spam with the survival of the Soviet army during the conflict.

For the U.S. armed forces' basic K rations, Spam, a staple, constituted a significant portion of both breakfast and supper units. GIs called it "ham that failed the physical." The 486th Bomb Group of the Army Air Force, in addition to eating the meat on a regular basis, created "Slammin' Spammy," a bomb-throwing pig, as nose art on one of their B-24 aircraft.

Spam and Hormel benefited from unsolicited coverage in a wide variety of publications. Throughout the war, *Time* magazine carried articles informing the public about Spam and its versatility. For example, in the October, 5, 1942, and April 15, 1946, issues, the editors mention Spam as a primary meat for the troops' suppers. Details of a party held in Rome, published on September 11, 1944, reports "dabs of Spam, corned beef, and Vienna sausage" as the featured food. On March 20, 1944, a reporter let it be known that in England some members of the House of Commons, off the record, referred to the United States as "Uncle Spam."

When it first appeared on the market, Hormel called Spam "the Miracle Meat," and at the height of meat **rationing,** *Woman's Day,* along with other well-known **magazines** published primarily for women, reminded readers that Spam provided an easy answer to the high cost and scarcity of meat. A few creative ideas about preparing Spam dishes linked it with many other foods, such as Spam 'n' Spaghetti, 'n' Limas, 'n' Eggs, or 'n' Waffles. Other possibilities frequently reported by the company and food columnists included Grilled Spam and Vegetables, Spam Barbecue, and Sam Western Salad—all of this, of course, in addition to its original intent, Spam sandwiches.

Hormel effectively promoted this product through extensive **advertising.** The company placed ads in "Jessie's Notebook," a regular display ad feature in the *New York Times,* which informed readers of Spam's many uses: a handy dish to serve to the family, hot or cold; an interesting party food by just adding tomato slices, prepared mustard, and French dressing to the platter; or an unusual presentation when cut into thin strips with onion and celery and served over rice as Spam Suey.

A pioneer in this kind of advertising, Hormel developed a singing **radio** commercial, as did the Pepsi-Cola Company. The Spam number, sung to the tune of a traditional Scottish folk song, "My Bonnie Lies Over the Ocean," reminds listeners of its being "a miracle canned meat, which tastes fine and saves time." Not only did Hormel use radio for airing commercials, in 1940 and 1941, it sponsored NBC's (National Broadcasting Company) *Burns and Allen,* a comedy show starring the husband and wife team of George Burns and Gracie Allen (1896–1996; 1895–1964). Spammy the pig, the company mascot, frequently made guest appearances on the show, and the couple also appeared in print advertisements.

Hormel's best-selling meat even got coverage in ads for other businesses. For example, *Puck, The Comic Weekly,* in order to suggest its value as a promotional medium, bought space in the *New York Times* to solicit advertising for its Sunday comic strip supplement. The editors of *Puck* pointed out that the Hormel Company had not only advertised in the weekly since 1939 but had increased its frequency, recognizing the value of exposure in the Sunday comics.

Spam sales soared during World War II, and the product continued to gain in popularity during the postwar years. With peace, many U.S. businesses emphasized the need to hire male war veterans, but Hormel developed a plan to hire women. A competitive drum and bugle corps composed of female veterans from all branches of the armed forces, evolved into a traveling caravan. Its talented members carried out door-to-door sales during the day and performed an assortment of musical productions in the evening, as well as entertaining on radio. The troupe started out in 1946, with 12 women, and when it disbanded in 1953, numbered 60 individuals. Known as the "Hormel Girls' Band and Chorus," the group rapidly gained popularity, and the company credited the aggregation with doubling the sales of its packaged foods, especially Spam.

The introduction of Spam to the public in 1937 proved to be a significant event for the American diet for decades to come. It served as a staple for both the troops fighting the war and the folks back home, and it continues to reign as a convenience food firmly rooted in the nation's food culture along with hamburgers, hot dogs, apple pie, and ice cream.

*See also:* Beverages; Comic Strips; Desserts, Candy, and Ice Cream; Radio Programming: Music and Variety Shows; Rosie the Riveter; Women in the Military: WACs, WASPs, WAVES, SPARS, and Others

**Selected Reading**
Armstrong, Dan, and Dustin Black. *The Book of SPAM.* New York: Atria Books, 2007.
Spam. *New York Times,* January 16, 1944; August 26, 1948; May 19, 1949. www.proquest.com
Spam. *Time Magazine,* October 5, 1942; March 20, 1944; September 11, 1944; April 15, 1946; October 4, 1948; May 19, 1949.

Wyman, Carolyn. *Spam: A Biography: The Amazing True Story of America's "Miracle Meat."* Fort Washington, PA: Harvest Books, 1999.

## SPOCK, DR. BENJAMIN O.

The eldest of six children born into a well-to-do Connecticut family, Benjamin O. Spock (1903–1998) learned a great deal about baby and child care through personal experience with his siblings. He attended Yale University, where he rowed with an eight-man crew; at the 1924 Paris Olympics, the team won a gold medal. He went on to Columbia University's College of Physicians and Surgeons, earning an MD in pediatrics. He also studied psychiatry and, during World War II, served as a psychiatrist in the medical corps of the U.S. Naval Reserve. Following the war, he held chairs at several universities.

With his combined expertise in pediatrics and psychiatry, and convinced that many popular child-rearing theories were flawed, Spock in 1946 published *The Common Sense Book of Baby and Child Care* (hardcover edition). It also came out in a 25-cent (about $2.75 in 2008 dollars) paperbound version that year titled *The Pocket Book of Baby and Child Care.* He could not have chosen a better time to publish: riding the crest of the postwar **baby boom** and an immediate best seller in both formats, *Baby and Child Care* enjoyed phenomenal sales almost from the first days of publication. By 2000, Spock's book—revised several times, including a 1957 editing to make the text more gender neutral—had sold over 50 million copies around the world in many languages and has continued to do well and remain in print into the 21st century.

Prior to the publication of Spock's classic, most guides to the care of infants and small children stressed parental control and discipline. Prevailing theory held that a child's behavior had to be carefully guided by its parents, and understanding motivations or needs was unnecessary. Spock, on the other hand, wanted parents to realize that a child's behavior (or misbehavior) grew out of natural impulses; as a child sought to explore its own autonomy, it would be natural to disobey certain limitations the parent had imposed. Rather than being upset and punishing the child, parents had to enforce appropriate limits but also allow the child freedom to expand its limited horizons. Children that get away with anything turn out spoiled and unhappy, but those raised in restrictive environments will have their natural curiosity stifled and will likewise be unhappy. Finding the middle way between extremes becomes the challenge to parents. As he says in his now-famous opening to the book, parents need to relax; they already know more than they think they know.

Laid out like a reference book—"The Father's Part," "Schedules," 'Crying in the Early Weeks" (Spock famously counsels that allowing a baby an occasional healthy cry will not hurt it, and constantly attending to a crying baby only encourages it to cry more), "Aggressiveness and Timidity," "Fat Children," and so on for some 160 entries—Spock dispenses gentle, reasonable advice regarding all aspects of growth from infancy to adolescence. Mothers and fathers responded enthusiastically, making *Baby and Child Care* the most successful guide to parenting ever written, and certainly one of the biggest **best sellers** in the history of American publishing.

Not all readers, however, responded so favorably. A few conservative clergy accused Spock of encouraging "permissiveness" (a term he uses early in the book but not in the positive way some believed), of straying from biblical injunctions about sparing the rod and spoiling the child. But their tirades usually evolved from a hasty or careless reading of the text. Others picked up on the theme of permissiveness, including a handful of Congressmen, a few of whom linked Spock to the Communist menace during the dark days of the **Cold War.** Much of the criticism, however, came later during the 1950s and 1960s, a time when youthful rebellion became a topic of considerable debate. Opponents of his book and its influence accused Spock of contributing to the social ills of the day. The feeling among critics seemed to be one of regret; had Spock's ideas not taken hold so successfully, then contemporary **youth** would not be out protesting, dressing inappropriately, listening to rock 'n' roll, disrespecting their elders, and doing all those other things that upset adults.

Despite these complaints about *Baby and Child Care*—a minority opinion, by the way—parents by the millions wore out their paperback copies of the guide. As the hardcover title states, Spock had set out to write a guide based on common sense, and he achieved remarkable success with that goal. Over the years, the marketing of the book has undergone some changes. Whereas the covers of early editions from the 1940s to 1960s stressed the title *Baby and Child Care,* more recent printings have greatly enlarged Spock's name as author, and the title appears in much smaller type. "Dr. Spock" ("Benjamin" also disappeared) or just "Spock's" strike the eye, working on the assumption that potential buyers will know the correct title once they see the author's surname.

In his later years and approaching retirement, his fame assured by the fabulous success of his book, Benjamin Spock pursued a somewhat different course of activities. He became involved with a number of peace movements during the Vietnam conflict of the 1960s and 1970s and could be found at numerous rallies advocating an end to the war. He advised young men on their draft responsibilities and how to avoid military service, a posture that drew the ire of many, including federal officials. Sentenced to prison in 1968 for aiding and abetting draft resisters, his sentence was shortly reversed upon appeal. Spock kept on protesting, including nuclear weapons and cuts in social services—a far cry from the pediatrician who dispensed folksy advice on raising children. Feisty until the end, Benjamin Spock died in 1998.

*See also:* Atomic Bomb, The; Book Clubs; Education; Juvenile Delinquency

**Selected Reading**
Maier, Thomas. *Dr. Spock: An American Life.* New York: Basic Books, 2003.
Spock, Benjamin. *The Pocket Book of Baby and Child Care.* New York: Pocket Books, 1946.

# STEEL PENNIES (1943)

Toward the end of 1942, a difficult war year for the United States, the government realized essential defense industries faced a shortage of copper—a strategic material in many products, especially shell casings. To reduce federal copper consumption and thus make more of the metal available for manufacturing purposes, officials at the Department of the Treasury decided that the composition of the traditional Lincoln penny would be drastically altered, going from a mix of 95 percent copper and 5 percent tin and zinc to one that contained no copper at all. Throughout 1943, the U.S. Mint produced pennies stamped from 100 percent steel, which came to be called "steelies." In order to keep them shiny longer, they received a thin coating of rust-resistant zinc.

The government minted these new pennies only that one year, making them something of a collectors' item as time passed and they fell out of general circulation. The temporary discontinuance of traditional copper pennies helped alleviate the shortage, and 1944 saw the reintroduction of the more familiar copper coin. In the meantime, officials estimated that the savings in copper during 1943 totaled the amount needed to make over 1.25 million shell casings for heavy artillery. Even with these economies, scarcities persisted, and from 1944 through 1946, the government allowed the U.S. Mint to utilize discarded cartridge casings instead of new, pure copper in the manufacture of pennies. These used casings contained significant amounts of brass (a mix of copper and zinc) from which the copper could be extracted, so salvaging them meant they could be recycled into coinage.

Despite the savings in copper that occurred in 1943, the public generally disliked the steel pennies. The zinc tended to discolor and look drab, not unlike slugs, and many people actually thought they were made of lead. This disfavor caused the government to launch an attempt to remove them from circulation, a program that began in 1945. For something as common as a penny, steel or copper, total success in any recall could never be achieved; from 1945 until 1965, when the effort ended, the mint reclaimed only about 15 percent of them. Because the Philadelphia Mint churned out 684.6 million of the steelies, the Denver Mint 217.7 million, and the San Francisco Mint 191.6 million, over 1 billion steel pennies circulated by the end of 1943. Reclaiming 15 percent of them, or about 164 million pennies, still constituted quite a feat.

In the years following World War II, the price of copper rose significantly, causing the manufacturing of pennies to cost more than their individual worth. Although the government never again reverted to steel coins, it did make changes in the composition of the familiar Lincoln-head cent. Today the so-called copper penny actually contains 97.5 percent zinc, with a 2.5 percent copper plating, a change that occurred in 1982.

The 1943 steel penny remains legal, and now and then shows up, albeit in ever-decreasing numbers. Dealers and suppliers have stashed away untold millions of them, and one in reasonably good condition is worth perhaps a nickel or a dime to a collector and considerably more if uncirculated (anyone can purchase uncirculated coins, dependent on availability, directly from the U.S. Mint, reputable dealers, and other numismatists). In contrast, a regular copper penny from the 1940s has a worth of just a few cents to a collector, or little more than its face value.

One exception needs to be noted: The U.S. Mint erroneously manufactured a handful of 1943 pennies that contain the traditional copper-zinc ratio. Officials quickly caught the error, and only a few continue to exist, but they can be worth thousands of dollars in good condition. Over the years, unscrupulous individuals have labored to alter 1943 steelies in order to make them appear to be their infinitely more valuable copper counterparts. They have utilized copper plating, dipped them in chemicals to discolor the zinc and impart a reddish or amber hue, and even resorted to disfiguring the dates on genuine copper pennies from the 1940s to make them appear to read 1943. An easy test for authenticity exists: a magnet will attract a real steel penny but has no effect on a copper one.

Although calls for abolishing the penny arise every so often (worthless, it's a nuisance, and so on), the U.S. one-cent piece has so far resisted them. Even the now-relatively rare 1943 steelie has its supporters, making the lowly penny a hardy survivor in the history of U.S. coins.

*See also:* Hobbies

**Selected Reading**
"Pennies/Cents." Collecting-US-Coins.com. www.collecting-us-coins.com/pennies-cents/penny-cent.html
"Steel Wartime Pennies." USMintQuarters.com. www.usmintquarters.com/steelcents.htm

## *SUPERMAN*

The concept of a superhero, an outwardly normal person able to overcome any and all obstacles by remarkable means, has been around since time immemorial, but not until the late 1930s and on into the 1940s did a comic book figure called Superman embody the idea in visual form.

Variations on the superhero had been a staple of popular pulp **magazines** for many years. These larger-than-life heroes opposed the worst evildoers one could imagine. Lester Dent (1904–1959; writing under the pen name Kenneth Robeson) created Doc Savage, The Man of Bronze, a figure that thrilled readers in the 1930s in one breathless tale after another. Savage relied on his physical prowess and an array of futuristic weapons to get out of endless predicaments that would have stymied lesser heroes. More sinister, perhaps, but just as exciting, *The Shadow* stories of Walter B. Gibson (1897–1985; writing as Maxwell Grant) involved the adventures of a mysterious playboy named Lamont Cranston. Instead of amazing athletic abilities, Cranston could "cloud men's

*A typical 1940s cover from DC Comics featuring Superman. The shadowy background of tanks and artillery links him to the war effort, and the American eagle perched on his left arm adds a patriotic note. (DC Comics/Photofest)*

minds" and thus seemingly make himself invisible to society's enemies, easily penetrating their lairs in order to bring them to justice.

Two high school chums from Cleveland, writer Jerry Siegel (1914–1996) and artist Joe Shuster (1914–1992), had been trying to interest comic book publishers in just such a figure, sustaining themselves with forgotten **comic strips** like *Doctor Occult, Federal Men, Slam Bradley,* and *Spy.* After knocking unsuccessfully on many doors, Siegel and Shuster in the spring of 1938 convinced the firm of Detective Comics, better known as DC, to allot space for an illustrated adventure narrative they called *Superman* in the premier issue of *Action Comics.* Often called the Man of Steel, Superman represented the first of a new breed of imaginary, fictional characters that would come to be called superheroes in the world of **comic books.**

The publishers must have been pleased with the pair's work; not only did the company run the story, a frame from the tale graces the cover; it depicts Superman lifting up an automobile while its dislodged and terrified passengers scatter in all directions. This muscular man, decked out in blue tights and a flowing red cape, receives no identification, and curious readers would have to look inside the comic book to find out his name.

Within a few pages, the comic introduces Superman. The tale, longer than usual for a comic book, briefly alludes to Superman's origins on the doomed planet Krypton, his escape to Earth, and how the Kents of Smallville became his adoptive parents. Readers learn he can leap (flying would come later) "an eighth of a mile in a single bound" and outrun speeding cars and **trains.** It tells of his assuming the role of Clark Kent, an apparently meek reporter with *The Daily Planet* (initially called *The Daily Star*), the leading paper in Metropolis. The plot has him stop a lynching, save an innocent man from the electric chair, capture the guilty parties, stop bullets and knives with his tough skin, and have a date with colleague Lois Lane. And that just summarizes the first *Superman* tale.

Siegel and Shuster's *Superman* captivated readers and helped to reinvigorate a struggling comic book industry. Too many cute anthropomorphic animals, too many reprints from previous newspaper strips, and too little inventiveness had flattened interest in the format. Customers wanted something new, and *Superman* sparked their interest. A succession of stories by Siegel and Shuster followed, fleshing out details about Superman's past. His abilities, such as leaping and running, were replaced by the authors with the gift of flight, along with such additional powers as X-ray vision and extraordinary hearing. Sales of *Action Comics* skyrocketed, and in 1939 Superman gained his own comic book, his name finally splashed brightly across the cover. By 1940, its circulation had surpassed 1 million copies per issue and continued climbing. An American icon had been born, one that flourished throughout the 1940s and beyond.

Overnight, other publishers took notice of this newcomer. Competitors of DC in the comic book field began looking for writers and artists for superheroes of their own and soon readied their own versions of *Superman. The Arrow, The Batman* (the article would shortly be dropped), *Captain America, Captain Marvel, The Crimson Avenger,* and a host of other caped and costumed superheroes hit newsstands soon thereafter, setting the stage for a comic book revolution.

As excitement grew over this unique character, newspaper comic syndicates wasted no time in approaching DC Comics and the authors about the possibility of a daily strip featuring Superman. The McClure Syndicate won the rights to distribute the character, and in January 1939, just months after *Superman*'s initial success as a comic book, it began running in daily **newspapers.** At first, Siegel and Shuster tried to do it all, but cartoonist Shuster quickly realized that he could not maintain the pace of drawing for both comic strips and comic books. Plus, in the fall of 1939, McClure added a Sunday version, given the enthusiastic reader response to the dailies. By 1941, two years after its inception as a comic strip, *Superman* appeared in well over 200 newspapers.

As a result, Shuster turned over more and more of the inking, coloring, and lettering chores to assistants, which accounts for some of the differences between the comic book Superman and his comic strip twin. Despite the hectic times, Siegel continued to do most of the writing for both formats. In 1943, however, he received his draft notice, and other writers had to step in. Slowly, Siegel and Shuster did less original work on *Superman* as staff writers and artists assumed more of the load. By 1947, Shuster ceased to work with *Superman;* Siegel followed suit in 1948 amid financial disputes with DC. Despite the loss of the two originators, the strip continued in hundreds of newspapers until 1966. Siegel and Shuster moved on to other projects, but they never again achieved the success they had enjoyed with *Superman.*

In the meantime, **radio** producers, already filling the airwaves with late afternoon serials aimed at youthful listeners, correctly foresaw that this character could be adapted to an aural format. In February 1940, *The Adventures of Superman* could be heard on New York's WOR; two years later, buoyed by strong listenership, it became an offering on the **MBS (Mutual Broadcasting System)** network. The show remained with MBS until 1949, at which time **ABC (American Broadcasting Company)** took the reins. It stayed with ABC until 1951, when it left radio for good. Bud Collyer (1908–1969) served as the voice of the Man of Steel until 1950.

Jerry Siegel had no part in the scripting for *The Adventures of Superman;* that job fell into the hands of other writers, although the show retained the flavor of its comic strip backgrounds. Broadcast at first three times a week, it soon became a daily 15-minute serial, usually heard somewhere between 5:00 p.m. and 6:00 p.m. Producers and advertisers cherished this time slot because children would be listening to the radio while awaiting dinner. Many similar offerings could be found at this hour, guaranteeing a large audience. Kellogg's Pep, a popular breakfast cereal of the day that reputedly provided energy (or pep) to anyone consuming it, sponsored the boundlessly energetic *Superman* throughout most of the 1940s.

The radio version, heard by millions of fans, introduced an opening sequence of memorable lines, used on virtually every broadcast, that have become a part of American speech:

"It's a bird!" "It's a plane!" "It's...Superman!"

Random House, a prominent book publishing firm, decided to capitalize on the excitement surrounding Superman and contracted with George F. Lowther (1913–1975), a little-known scriptwriter and dramatist, to pen *The Adventures of Superman* in 1942. Lowther, who had written episodes of the *Superman* radio series, knew many of the biographical details surrounding the superhero and thus felt comfortable expanding upon them in a novel. The title, taken from the radio show instead of the comic book or newspaper strip, reflects the huge listening audience the serial enjoyed at the time. It can be assumed that too many writing commitments tied down Jerry Siegel, and thus the choice of Lowther to retell the story; the equally busy Joe Shuster, however, contributed a number of drawings to the novel. An unusual and overlooked item in the *Superman* canon, Applewood Books in 1995 published a facsimile edition of Lowther's original work.

Hollywood should have immediately recognized the potential in such a visually showy character, but belatedly took advantage of the *Superman* phenomenon. The Fleischer Studio produced and released 17 cartoons collectively titled *The Adventures of Superman* between 1941 and 1943. Each runs for 10 minutes, and Bud Collyer reprises his Mutual network radio role by doing the voiceovers for the animations. Following these cartoons, several years passed before another *Superman* picture appeared.

In 1948, Columbia Pictures released a 15-episode serial titled, simply, *Superman*. It stars Kirk Alyn (1910–1999) as the Man of Steel. Apparently the serial fared well enough at Saturday matinees—the venue where most serials played in those days—that Columbia followed it with *Atom Man vs. Superman* in 1950, another 15-part saga with Alyn again in the lead. The Atom Man turns out to be none other than the notorious Lex Luthor, Superman's archenemy, in disguise. Lots of science fiction devices, including some early flying saucers, add to the excitement of this film.

The next year, Lippert Pictures, a small studio, released *Superman and the Mole-Men,* a low-budget feature. It most notably introduces movie audiences to George Reeves (1914–1959), an actor who would find his niche playing Superman on **television** two years later.

Still in its infancy, television nonetheless seized upon the superhero for his potential in a visual medium. Production for a weekly series commenced in 1951, but the first shows were not broadcast until early in 1953. Carried through a syndicate instead of a network, *Superman* eventually comprised 104 half-hour episodes and ran until 1957. George Reeves, clad in a padded but slightly baggy set of tights, became so closely associated with the character that he reportedly received no offers for any other roles.

By and large, the reign of the comic book superheroes began in the early 1940s amid concerns about the impending war. Like most of his cohorts, regardless of medium, Superman stormed into the fray when World War II broke out. He fought arrogant Nazis and badly caricatured Japanese villains, always emerging victorious, whether it be in comic books and newspaper strips or on the air. The war may have ended in 1945, but it carried on for another year or so in the comics as publishers and syndicates used up stories written before the cessation of hostilities, so Superman continued to bash the enemy for a several months thereafter.

With peace, most superheroes lacked any common foes. Many comic books featuring such characters ceased publication, but Superman continued, too popular to be dropped, albeit with different adventures and villains. Characters like the Prankster, the Toyman, and Mr. Mxyztplk taunted the Man of Steel (Mr. Mxyztplk, more mischievous than evil, debuted in the newspapers in 1944, seven months before his first comic book appearance), and the radio version introduced kryptonite in 1943, the one thing that can weaken Superman's powers. During the mid-1940s, a youthful Superboy also briefly appeared but never achieved the success of his older counterpart.

By and large, the later 1940s marked a continuation of remarkable inventiveness, despite the loss of Shuster and Siegel on the creative end of things. Competent new staffers carried on the traditions, and most readers, listeners, and viewers probably noticed little, if any change. Doubtless his disguise as the mild-mannered Clark Kent fit the adolescent fantasies of countless admirers in the way he could move from an ineffectual Kent character to someone capable of the most incredible deeds. It might have been a daydream, one that eventually touched millions in all its formats, and thus Superman moved into the 1950s as a widely recognized and successful product of American popular culture.

*See also:* Radio Programming: Children's Show, Serials, and Adventure Series; Serial Films; Youth

**Selected Reading**
Bridwell, E. Nelson. *Superman: From the Thirties to the Seventies.* New York: Bonanza Books, 1971.
Dooley, Dennis, and Gary Engle, eds. *Superman at Fifty! The Persistence of a Legend!* Cleveland, OH: Octavia, 1987.
Goulart, Ron. *Over Fifty Years of American Comic Books.* Lincolnwood, IL: Mallard Press, 1991.
Grossman, Gary. *Superman: From Serial to Cereal.* New York: Popular Library, 1977.

# SWIMMING AND WATER SKIING

Whether a dip in a pool, a summer vacation at the beach, or a Sunday afternoon swim in a lake or river, for those with access to water, swimming offers both a pleasant pastime and good exercise. U.S. census reports show that for communities with a population of 20,000 and more, the number of pools in municipal and county parks and recreation areas grew 26 percent from 1940 to 1950, with the same change for public beaches. This increase in providing places to swim, however, served primarily the white population of the country.

During the 1940s, segregation ruled when it came to the use of public swimming pools, and communities addressed the issue either by building separate facilities for whites and minorities, setting aside separate days for different racial groups, or excluding all but whites entirely. As soon as World War II ended, representatives from the National Association for the Advancement of Colored People (NAACP) and other groups interested in promoting racial equality began to protest pool segregation. Two early and significant pool desegregation contests occurred in Warren, Ohio (1945), and Montgomery, West Virginia (1946), but in many communities it would not be until well after the 1954 *Brown v. Board of Education* that towns and cities across the country opened their swimming pools to black citizens.

Water sports garnered their share of publicity during the 1940s from swimmers in synchronized performances featured in **movies,** entertainment offered by water shows, and the success of American swimmers at the 1948 Olympic Games. Johnny Weissmuller (1904–1984) and Esther Williams (b. 1921), first swimmers and later movie stars, contributed to a growing fascination with the sport. Weissmuller gained

*Whether in a community park or on a luxury cruise ship, pools were popular spots for swimming and socializing during the 1940s. (Photofest)*

national attention in the 1924 Olympics when he won three gold medals and one bronze, followed in the 1928 games with two gold medals. Also, in 1928, he reigned as the first person ever to swim the 100-meter event in less than a minute. In addition to these honors, he had achieved 36 national championships before retiring from active swimming in 1932 to star in his first Tarzan film. He completed 12 such features by 1948, and boys and young men, jumping into a river or swimming pool in good cannonball form, could be heard imitating the famous Tarzan yell given by Weissmuller before plunging into a jungle pool.

In 1941, at the San Francisco World's Fair, Weissmuller starred in Billy Rose's (1899–1966) Aquacade in choreographed duet swims with Esther Williams, a relatively unknown American Athletic Union (AAU) champion in the 100-meter freestyle. She had been picked to be a member of the United States 1940 Olympic swim team in games scheduled for Tokyo. Officials canceled this venue because of the looming global conflict, but Williams then won out over some 75 entries for the Aquacade. Scouts from Hollywood's Metro-Goldwyn-Mayer (MGM) studio noticed her in the show because of her flashy smile and shapely legs, which resulted in her appearance in two motion pictures, *Andy Hardy's Double Life* (1942) and *A Guy Named Joe* (1943).

Williams' third film and first swimming movie, *Bathing Beauty* (1944), placed her second to the lead, Red Skelton (1913–1997), and launched a successful career in film

**musicals** that feature elaborate swimming and diving performances. Her grace and skill inspired many young girls to take up the activities. Appearing in eight motion pictures during the 1940s, she initially continued in the No. 2 spot against stars Van Johnson (1916–2008) in *Thrill of a Romance* (1945) and *Easy to Wed* (1946) and William Powell (1892–1984) in *The Hoodlum Saint* (1946). With *Fiesta* (1947), however, she achieved top billing, a position she held for the rest of the decade, with the exception of a nonswimming film, *Take Me out to the Ball Game* (1949), in which **Frank Sinatra** (1915–1998) receives top billing.

The first presentation of Billy Rose's Aquacade occurred in 1937 at the Great Lakes Exposition in Cleveland. He moved his music, **dance,** and swimming show to the New York World's Fair in 1939, where it ranked for two years as one of the outstanding entertainment attractions for fairgoers. The Aquacade did equally well at the San Francisco Golden Gate International Exposition later in 1940. At both exhibitions, Johnny Weissmuller starred, and Gertrude Ederle (1905–2003) enjoyed cameo appearances. A celebrity in her own right, Ederle in 1926 had laid claim to the honor of being the first woman to swim across the English Channel. Esther Williams also joined the Aquacade troupe on the West Coast.

In addition to synchronized swimming, water skiing serves as a basic aspect of water shows. The inspiration for skiing on water goes to Ralph Samuelson (1904–1977), credited as the inventor of the activity. At a 1922 showcase event on Lake Pepin, a wide portion of the upper Mississippi River between Minnesota and Wisconsin, he showed off his creation. Advancement from a one-man performance to an organized water skiing show occurred at Atlantic City's Steel Pier in 1928. That same year, Richard "Dick" Pope Sr. (1900–1988) awed spectators in Miami by jumping from a long, low, slanted ramp while wearing water skis.

As interest grew, several individuals in addition to Samuelson attempted to manufacture the perfect water ski. In 1925, Fred Waller (1886–1954), working in Astoria, New York, for Paramount Pictures, invented and patented skis to support a movie camera on water. He quickly adapted the skis to accommodate feet and secured actress Clara Bow (1905–1965) for pictorial **advertising.** Waller went on to develop Vitarama, a widescreen film format shown at the New York World's Fair. Vitarama proved to be the forerunner of Cinerama, popular in the 1950s.

A third individual, Don Ibsen (active 1930s–1950s), offered yet another version of water skis in 1928. Operating on the West Coast, he created a show called the Ski-Quatic Follies, which he took throughout the country to both entertain audiences and promote his product. Elaborate costuming served as an integral part of the show and made the Ski-Quatic Follies unique, setting a standard for future endeavors undertaken by others. All three inventors offered workable skis, but, because Waller got a patent for his and the others did not, he frequently receives credit for the invention.

Pope and his wife Julie (d. 1988) founded Cypress Gardens near Winter Haven, Florida, in 1936 and initially concentrated on developing it as a botanical garden. With the entry of the United States into World War II, Dick joined the navy, leaving Julie and their children to operate the site. In 1942, a group of soldiers visited the gardens, and Julie organized a water ski show featuring her youngsters and others. That exhibition gave birth to what would become Cypress Gardens' key attraction: an elaborate mixture of complex water skiing demonstrations and maneuvers. In 1947, Cypress Gardens featured A. G. Hancock (active 1940s–1950s) and Dick Pope Jr. (1930–2007), respectively, as the first barefoot water skiers. The Popes also hosted the Dixie Water Ski Tournament, and Charles R. "Chuck" Sligh (active 1940s–1970s) proceeded to set a water ski jump record of 49 feet in 1947. The next year the first water ski pyramid joined the show, and soon a 12-person pyramid became the closing act at Cypress Gardens, soon to become known as the "water ski capital of the world."

With the development of a variety of water skis and water shows, individual swimmers and water skiers began to gain recognition. As with other sports, enthusiasts formed an organization to oversee competitions, and in 1939, its infant year, the American Water Ski Association sponsored the first National Water Ski Championships in Long Island, New York; 10 years later, France hosted a world championship.

Willa Worthington McGuire Cook (active 1940s and 1950s), a winner in the 1946 and 1947 national championships, had been discovered and encouraged by Don Ibsen to enter competitions. She represented the United States in world water skiing championships, bringing home trophies in 1949, 1950, 1953, and 1955. Worthington joined the Cypress Gardens show in 1948 and served as its star attraction for a decade.

The 1948 Olympic Games, held in London, proved to be a time for the United States to revel in the glory of its swimmers and divers who brought home eight gold medals, five silver, and one bronze as seen in Table 94. Before winning Olympic medals, several of these athletes—Wally Ris (1924–1989), Bruce Harlan (1926–1959), Bill Smith (b. 1924), Robert Cowell (1924–1960), and Alan Ford (1923–2008)—served in the U.S. Navy. Wally Ris, along with Adolph Kiefer (1908–2008), a 1936 gold medal recipient for the backstroke, worked as swimming instructors for the navy. Ann Curtis (b. 1926) took home two gold medals. In 1944, she became the first woman and first swimmer to receive the James E. Sullivan Memorial Award given annually to the most outstanding amateur athlete.

World War II affected life in the United States in a number of ways. For swimmers, one of the first signs of war came with the shortage of swim caps. Made of latex, they had long been an important part of any swimming outfit for women. The permanent wave hairstyle had been popular for many years, and it took time and money to obtain one. Thus women swimmers wanted something to protect their hair while swimming, but industry needed the rubber used in the manufacture of latex for war materials, and so bathing caps became scarce. During the postwar years, latex caps returned, frequently decorated with colorful plastic petals or leaves in an effort to make them prettier than a simple, head-fitting accessory.

Swimsuits for women evolved from 1920s athletic tank suits to 1930s bathing suits, often with small overskirts to hide the thighs, to 1940s figure-hugging numbers that could be one or two pieces. At this time, corset manufactures contributed a stretch tummy control panel to hold in the stomach and inserted bra cups to give bust support, thereby making a perfect outfit for pinup girls whose pictures could be found in army barracks, inside helmets, even on airplanes and bombs. In 1946, a daring two-piece bathing suit called a bikini, which left little to the imagination, made its debut in the Paris salon of French **fashion** designer Louis Reard (1897–1984). It would be many years, however, before this article of clothing would appear at American swimming

TABLE 94.  1948 Olympic Games: U.S. Swimming and Diving Winners

| Event | Male Athlete | Medal | Female Athlete | Medal |
|---|---|---|---|---|
| 100-Meter Back Stroke | Allan Stack | Gold | | |
| | Robert "Bob" Cowell | Silver | | |
| 100-Meter Freestyle | Walter "Wally" Ris | Event | | |
| | Alan Ford | | | |
| 400-Meter Freestyle | William "Bill" Smith | Gold | Ann Curtis | Gold |
| | James "Jimmy" McLane | Silver | | |
| 1,500-Meter Freestyle | James McLane | Gold | | |
| 200-Meter Breast Stroke | Joe Verdeur | Gold | | |
| | Keith Carter | Silver | | |
| | Robert "Bob" Sohl | Bronze | | |
| 4-×-100 Freestyle | | | Marie Corridon | Gold |
| | | | Thelma Kalama | |
| | | | Brenda Helser | |
| | | | Ann Curtis | |
| 4-×-200 Relay Team | Walter Ris, James McLane | Gold | | |
| | Wallace "Wally" Wolf, William Smith | | | |
| 10-Meter Platform Diving | Sammy Lee (first Asian American to win an Olympic Gold) | Gold | | |
| | Bruce Harlan | Silver | | |
| Springboard Diving | Bruce Harlan | Gold | | |

pools and beaches. Illustrator Pete Hawley (1916–1975) nonetheless employed provocative imagery for advertising Jantzen swimwear during the 1940s and 1950s.

In the 1940s, it became fashionable for men to wear bathing suits consisting of form-fitting briefs, but some men felt these were too revealing and continued to wear traditional boxer-style trunks. In either case, a separate top for men had by then become obsolete.

Adolph Kiefer, a champion swimmer and the owner of a swimming goods business called Adolph Kiefer & Associates, introduced the first nylon suit in 1948. Kiefer, well-known for his many international race victories, understood the advantages to be offered by this lightweight alternative to cotton and wool suits. Kiefers, as they were called, easily became the swimsuits of choice at the 1952 Olympics in Helsinki, Finland.

Swimming has wide appeal for both men and women of all ages and has been a human activity since prehistoric times. It costs little, so long as one resides near water. Swimming for fun can lead to improved physical fitness, a trimmer figure, and the opportunity to socialize with others. Competitive swimming as a sport dates back to the early 1800s in Europe. It demands disciplined training and can be in the form of distance, speed, or synchronized events. Water skiing grew up with the 20th century and, like swimming, can be done for fun or competitively. It, however, uses more equipment, including skis and a boat.

*See also:* Fads; Illustrators; Leisure and Recreation; Race Relations and Stereotyping

**Selected Reading**

Dulles, Foster Rhea. *A History of Recreation: America Learns to Play.* Englewood Cliffs, NJ: Prentice Hall, 1965.

Grimsley, Will, ed. *A Century of Sports by the Associated Press Sports Staff.* New York: Associated Press, 1971.

Wiltse, Jeff. *Contested Waters: A Social History of Swimming Pools in America.* Chapel Hill: University of North Carolina Press, 2007.

# SWING

A form of listening and **dance** music that captivated audiences in the 1930s, swing moved into the 1940s like a steamroller, seemingly unstoppable in its popularity. Yet, by 1945 and the end of World War II, other musical formats had begun to displace swing, and when the decade closed, it seemed an antique, a leftover from another time.

The style called swing had its beginnings with **jazz** and many of the popular dances from the Roaring Twenties. Musicians and bandleaders like Louis Armstrong (1901–1971), Cab Calloway (1907–1994), **Duke Ellington** (1899–1974), Fletcher Henderson (1897–1952), Earl Hines (1903–1983), Jimmie Lunceford (1902–1947), Bennie Moten (1894–1935), and Fats Waller (1904–1943), among many others, served as progenitors and pioneers in the movement, playing arrangements that featured a propulsive, toe-tapping energy that attracted listeners. These artists came from the black jazz tradition, but a handful of white bands, such as those led by Larry Clinton (1909–1985), Glen Gray (1900–1963), Ben Pollack (1903–1971), and Paul Whiteman (1890–1967), also proved receptive to the infectious rhythm in this as-then unnamed music. By the mid-1930s, with "swing" firmly ensconced as its proper title, all other forms and styles of American popular music had to take a back seat to the growing popularity of this new musical phenomenon.

Black musicians in the main nurtured swing, but white bandleaders came to dominate it. By the late 1930s, orchestras led by the Dorsey brothers (Tommy, 1905–1956, and Jimmy, 1904–1957), Benny Goodman (1909–1986), Glenn Miller (1904–1944), Artie Shaw (1910–2004), and many others had assimilated swing into their repertoires and achieved a level of commercial success never realized by any of the black aggregations that had done so much in bringing it to maturity.

The big bands that characterized swing to most audiences as a rule consisted of 12 or more instrumentalists (usually a minimum of four reeds, four brass, and four rhythm), playing carefully written arrangements that blended jazz and popular music in a way that attracted both dance and listening audiences. With the onset of the 1940s, the large aggregations fronted by Charlie Barnet (1913–1991), **Count Basie** (1904–1984), the Dorsey brothers, Ellington, Goodman, Miller, and Shaw led the way into the new decade. But close behind came innumerable others, with leaders like Benny Carter (1907–2003), Jan Garber (1894–1977), Shep Fields (1910–1981), Harry James (1916–1983), Sammy Kaye (1910–1987), Kay Kyser (1905–1985), Russ Morgan (1904–1969), and Charlie Spivak (1905–1982) keeping dancers and record buyers of all stripes happy.

*During the heyday of swing, roughly the late 1930s and early 1940s, when a band played an up-tempo number, couples took to the floor and danced the jitterbug, an outgrowth of a number of styles that had gained popularity in previous years. In this photograph, presumably taken at a USO (United Service Organizations) function or military base, a serviceman and his partner demonstrate to onlookers the necessary loose-limbered steps. (Photofest)*

Although swing remained king in the early 1940s, the entry of the United States into World War II created unexpected problems for the music industry. By 1942, the demands of the military draft (also called selective service and conscription) resulted in more and more men entering the armed forces. Almost overnight, once-large orchestras shrank appreciably in size. Small groups—sextets, quintets, quartets, and trios—played an increasingly important role in music. From an artistic standpoint, these changes led to the dominance of such groups in evolving areas of modern jazz, encouraging the exploration of new musical formats, and they occurred at the expense of traditional big band swing. The shortage of qualified male musicians led, during the war years, to the creation of "**all-girl orchestras**," a phenomenon that virtually disappeared with the end of the draft and the return of men from the various service branches.

Perhaps the strongest evidence of changing times for swing bands involved the role of vocalists—the "boy singers" and "canaries" as many called them—that began to accompany every group, large and small. Traditionally, band singers tended to stand off at the edges of the stage and only came into the spotlight when the leader called for one of their numbers. In addition, they often earned less than the musicians, since most bands usually played a number of instrumental numbers during a set. Many people, especially the leaders themselves, saw the singers as part-timers and deserving of a lower paycheck. With the war, however, the status of vocalists changed. With manpower shortages reducing the size of many orchestras, the soothing sounds of a crooner often held greater appeal for war-weary audiences than did a large, wailing sax section. Record sales and bandstand requests reinforced the growing popularity of the singers, and this perception also held true for small vocal groups. Although not immediately apparent, public taste underwent a significant shift during the early 1940s.

The war also caused the traditional mainstays for booking the many swing orchestras, such as clubs, dance halls, and **restaurants,** to cut back on their hours of operation. Lighting restrictions such as **blackouts, brownouts, and dim-outs** imposed after sunset—the most popular time for operating these venues—forced many to close early. A later nationwide midnight-to-dawn curfew effectively shut down most urban areas at night.

The **rationing** of various **food** products made serving dinners a challenge because menus could not provide many scarce items, often the very favorites of patrons. Lack of personnel, from chefs to wait staff, created additional difficulties. Getting to and from a club or restaurant also presented problems: gasoline rationing severely limited personal **travel,** and public **transportation** had been sharply reduced, to the point that many places went to weekend hours only, and a number simply shut their doors "for the duration," a phrase commonly used from 1941 until 1945. As a final blow, the federal government in 1944 decreed a 20 percent amusement tax to raise much-needed war revenue, making a visit to a nightclub too expensive for many.

If all the foregoing were not enough, two non-war-related events also contributed to the woes of the big bands. First, a simmering feud between the American Society of Composers, Authors, and Producers (ASCAP) and Broadcast Music Incorporated (BMI) caused a boycott that resulted in the protracted absence of ASCAP-related recordings over the airwaves during much of 1941. The second event occurred in late 1942, when the AFM (American Federation of Musicians), under the leadership of its president, James C. Petrillo (1892–1984), decreed that no union musicians could participate in commercial recording sessions, although this restriction did not include vocalists. Not until late 1944 did the ban come to an end, a curious chapter in American music history and one that worked to the detriment of active bands and musicians.

With its exceptions for vocalists, the AFM strictures on recordings heightened public awareness of singers and groups. The overriding cause for the erosion of the swing's dominance, however, came about because of changing tastes. Swing had run its course as America's favorite music. New approaches and new artists attracted audiences always looking for anything novel or fresh. Too many bands constantly repeated their old hits, relying on the tried and true instead of innovation, and in time this easygoing spirit no longer attracted the multitudes it had during the music's heyday. What had been new and exciting in the 1930s and early 1940s now sounded old-fashioned to a new generation of musicians and listeners.

Despite the growing signs of economic and personnel problems, several new swing bands nevertheless jumped into the already-crowded field. For example, in 1938, Les

Brown (1912–2001) introduced his new aggregation, the Band of Renown. Although it boasted no unique sound or style, the orchestra landed several long hotel and club engagements, which gave the musicians some economic stability, and Brown gained a recording contract with RCA Victor's Bluebird label, a major accomplishment. In 1940, a young singer named Doris Day (b. 1924; nee Mary Anne von Kappelhoff) briefly joined the group. She soon left but returned in 1943, a move that signaled an important change in the orchestra's image. In late 1944, Day and Brown recorded "Sentimental Journey." An immediate hit, it stayed on the charts throughout early 1945, peaking that spring. "Sentimental Journey" ultimately emerged as the No. 2 song for the year and ensured the continuing popularity of the Les Brown band at least for a while. For her part, Doris Day moved on to a solo career that culminated with remarkable success in both **movies** and recordings.

After serving an apprenticeship during the 1930s as a pianist, composer, and arranger for a number of big bands, Claude Thornhill (1909–1965) in 1940 likewise started his own orchestra. Following a rocky beginning, he found his own style that combined rich, sonorous dynamics with unusual instrumentation, including tubas, French horns, and several clarinets. With its tonal delicacy, his 1941 composition "Snowfall" captures the band's unique sound well and achieved considerable commercial success. Just as he was getting established, Thornhill chose to enter the navy, an enlistment that included playing piano with Artie Shaw's service band as well as fronting a group of his own. Fortunately, a handful of recordings he had previously made kept him in the public eye, so Thornhill soon resumed his commercial duties upon his 1945 discharge and return to civilian life. He organized a new band and hired the immensely talented Gil Evans (1912–1988) as his chief arranger. In no time, the Thornhill/Evans sound found a host of listeners, and the two musicians went on to become significant voices in the creation of new directions in modern American music—neither swing in the traditional sense nor jazz as it evolved in the 1940s.

With varying degrees of success, several other new bands attempted to buck the trends of the early 1940s. Most turned out to be short-lived, but they nonetheless produced, during their varying tenures, interesting variations on the ongoing swing motifs then passing from public favor. For example, Hal McIntyre (1914–1959) led a group that played much in the style of Glenn Miller, an approach that initially assured some club and dance hall dates.

On another plane altogether, Raymond Scott (1908–1994) led a quintet—called a "quintette" and in reality a sextet—in the late 1930s and then a big band during the 1940s. During his work with a small group, Scott proved himself a real innovator, creating such popular novelties as "The Toy Trumpet," "Twilight in Turkey" (both 1937), and "In an Eighteenth-Century Drawing Room" and "Huckleberry Duck" (both 1939). Remarkably complex in their composition and execution, these tunes and several others made their way to the soundtracks of Warner Bros.' **cartoons,** the medium in which most people gained exposure to his wacky music. The group broke up in 1939, and Scott switched to a big band, did arranging, and worked in **radio** during the 1940s. But for two years, he pioneered in the creation of offbeat novelty music that had strong jazz and swing overtones. For many, however, he will be best remembered as the man who fronted the orchestra on *Your Hit Parade* on both radio and **television** from 1949 until the show went off the air in 1957.

Another problem, related to conscription and the attrition of personnel occurring in many aggregations, pertained to the bandleaders themselves. Some received their draft notices from the government, and others felt the need to enlist. Either way, a number of the most prominent leaders soon wore uniforms instead of tuxedoes. In 1942, at the height of his popularity in the states and too old for the draft, Glenn Miller enlisted and donned an Army Air Corps uniform bearing the rank of captain. He had tried to join the navy, but officials would not allow it because of his age, 38 in 1942. But the army yielded, thus giving birth to one of the first big-name service ensembles, a huge organization consisting of a 42-piece marching unit, a jazz combo, string accompaniment, and most famously, his 19-piece Army Air Force dance orchestra. Even after Miller's untimely death in December 1944, the various groups carried on under the leadership of sideman Ray McKinley (1910–1995) until the army finally disbanded them with the return of peace in 1945.

But Glenn Miller represented only one of many bandleaders who fronted service orchestras. Miller's vocalist and saxophonist from his civilian aggregation, Tex Beneke (1914–2000), led a navy band in landlocked Oklahoma. After his discharge, and with the consent of the Miller estate, he took over the leadership of the old Glenn Miller orchestra, allowing the popular band to carry on. Conducting a navy band, for whatever reasons, seemed a magnet for a number of swing-oriented leaders. Artie Shaw also formed a unit, as did sax player Sam Donahue (1918–1974) and pianist Eddie Duchin (1909–1951), while Bob Crosby (1913–1993) wielded a baton for the Marine Corps. Trumpeter Clyde McCoy (1903–1990) enlisted in the navy's Special Services division, and many members of his band likewise joined at the same time. On the army side of things, Major Tiny Bradshaw (1905–1958) led a large dance orchestra that played for the troops overseas, and "Waltz King" Wayne King (1901–1985), a bit long in the tooth for active duty, served at a post in Chicago with a number of fine musicians in his group.

When these and other bandleaders and musicians received their discharges in 1945 and 1946, they returned to a changed musical picture. Many once-prominent swing bands were no more, others faced discouraging economic realities, and new musical styles vied for attention. During 1946, a crucial year, the accumulating problems of the war years such as declining public interest, the rise of vocalists, and new trends in music came to a head: in short order, Les Brown, the Dorseys, Benny Goodman, and Harry James broke up their bands. An era had come to a close, and those still hanging on faced an uncertain future.

*See also:* Andrews Sisters, The; *ASCAP vs. BMI* Radio Boycott and the AFM Recording Ban; Bebop (Bop); Boogie-Woogie; Cole, Nat King; Broadway Shows (Musicals); Jukeboxes; Musicals (Film); Race Relations and Stereotyping; Radio Programming: Music and Variety Shows; Rhythm 'n' Blues; Sinatra, Frank; Songwriters and Lyricists

## Selected Reading

*An Anthology of Big Band Swing, 1930–1955.* 2 CDs. Decca GRD 2–629. Compiled 1993.

McClellan, Lawrence, Jr. *The Later Swing Era, 1942 to 1955.* Westport, CT: Greenwood Press, 2004.

Walker, Leo. *The Wonderful Era of the Great Dance Bands.* Berkeley, CA: Howell-North Books, 1964.

Yanow, Scott. *Swing: Great Musicians, Influential Groups.* San Francisco: Miller Freeman, 2000.

# T

## TECHNOLOGY

In wartime, technology—the practical application of science and the creation of tools and techniques to accomplish tasks—usually makes significant advances. The pressures of war and the need to solve problems as quickly as possible bring together the best minds and available resources. The 1940s turned out to be such a period.

An era of unparalleled technological developments in many fields, some of them good, some not, the decade witnessed a continual struggle between the rational and the intuitive. World War II brought about a vastly increased level of government spending on technological research and development. No defense-related projects were too big or too small, from the Manhattan Project and the creation of the **atomic bomb** to improving the cut and fit of military uniforms. Because of the momentum for newer and better brought about by the conflict, the postwar years demonstrated little slowdown, but peace transferred that energy to a vast array of consumer products. The lists below (one alphabetical, the other chronological) mention some of the more prominent or newsworthy technological inventions and improvements that occurred during this time.

**An Alphabetical Listing of Selected Technological Achievements of the 1940s**

*Aerosol spray cans.* Although a prototype had been designed in 1927, nothing came of it. In 1941, engineers Lyle David Goodloe and William N. Sullivan (both active in the 1940s) developed the first practical aerosol can. They used chlorofluorocarbons (CFCs) as their propellants. Because of environmental concerns, CFCs were later banned and other gases substituted. Robert H. Abplanalp (1922–2003) devised an efficient nozzle, the crimp-on valve, in 1949. That same year, Edward H. Seymour (active 1940s), marketed the first commercial spray paint, available in aluminum only.

*Aqualung.* Engineer Emile Gagnan (1900–1979), working with French diver Jacques-Yves Cousteau (1910–1997), in 1943 developed a means of breathing while underwater; it came to be called an aqualung. When adopted by the navy, the device received the acronym "scuba," for self-contained underwater breathing apparatus.

*Atomic bomb.* A fearsome weapon, the most destructive of World War II, came about because of a massive effort, involving thousands of scientists and technicians, to produce a nuclear device before the Axis powers could do so. This military-civilian collaborative effort came to be called the Manhattan Project. In mid-July 1945, the team successfully exploded the first atomic bomb in a test conducted in the deserts of New Mexico. Shortly thereafter, U.S. bombers dropped two atomic bombs; one, on August 6, 1945, on the Japanese city of Hiroshima, and the other, on August 9, 1945, on Nagasaki. A few days later, on August 15, 1945, Japan sued for peace and the war came to an end.

*Automated streetlights.* In 1949, the city of New Milford, Connecticut, successfully demonstrated streetlights that would turn on automatically at dusk and turn off at dawn. Using photoelectric cells, the lights responded to changes in light. Other cities would soon adopt this new, efficient lighting system.

*Automatic washer.* In 1947, merchandiser Sears, Roebuck introduced a Kenmore (the company brand name) top-loading washing machine. Its popularity, despite its hefty price tag of $239.95 (slightly over $2,300 in 2008 dollars), would render obsolete traditional manual washing machines. Other manufacturers, aware of the Kenmore's immediate success, soon offered similar models.

*Ballpoint pen.* Hungarian Laszlo Biro (1899–1995) in 1938 patented an early example of the modern ballpoint pen, a writing instrument he had invented some years earlier. Six years later, after fleeing Europe because of World War II, Biro took out a new patent and began manufacturing his creation. By the end of the 1940s, the pen had demonstrated its usefulness, and a French firm, the Société Bic, bought Biro's patents and commenced mass producing the cheap and popular Bic pen.

*Chain reaction.* The first self-sustaining nuclear chain reaction—the process that occurs when a neutron strikes a nucleus with resultant fission, or the release of atomic energy—occurred in 1942. As part of the ongoing Manhattan Project, Italian-born physicist Enrico Fermi (1901–1954) and his colleagues initiated a controlled chain reaction beneath the playing fields at the University of Chicago, an important step in the development of the atomic bomb.

*Color television.* CBS (Columbia Broadcasting System) Laboratories, under the direction of Peter Goldmark (1906–1977), demonstrated a workable color **television** system in 1940. World War II interfered with its introduction, and not until 1950 did CBS begin broadcasting with Goldmark's invention. Because it proved incompatible with already-existing black-and-white receivers, the Federal Communications Commission (FCC) blocked its use, favoring instead a competing system developed by rival RCA (Radio Corporation of America) and made available in 1953. Even the RCA system required the purchase of a TV set able to reproduce colors; older black-and-white receivers could carry the picture but without the colors.

*Computer—digital.* During the period 1943–1944, British technicians constructed the first digital (binary) computer, the Colossus Mark I. Limited to military uses, it

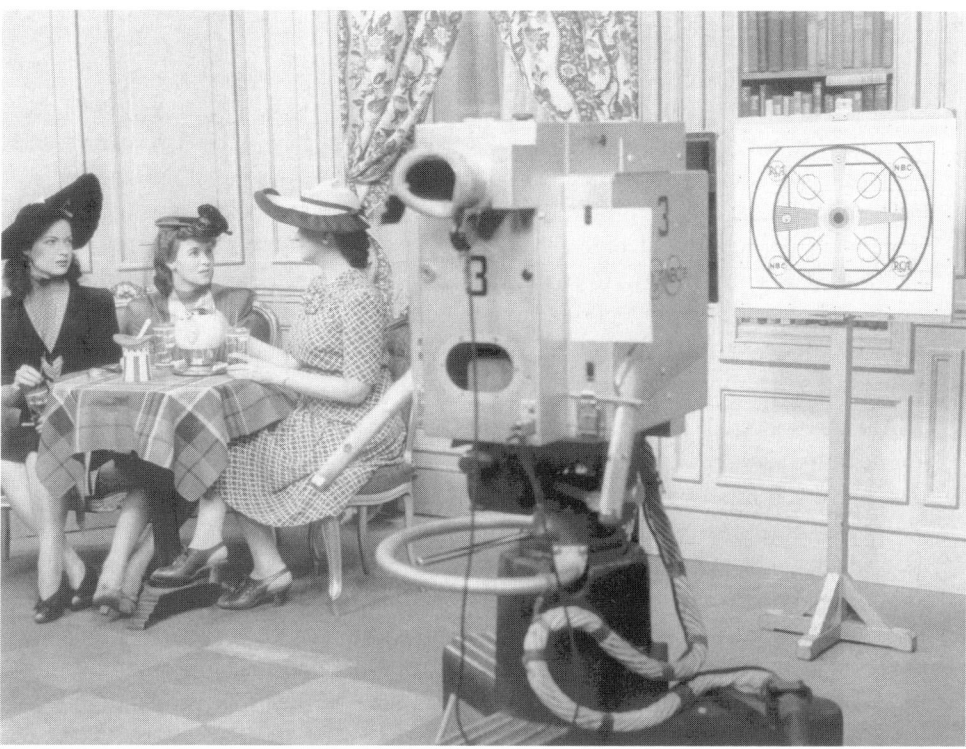

*In the early days of commercial television, the necessary equipment tended to be bulky and difficult to move. This photo shows a typical camera setup in a studio. Technicians called the image on the adjoining screen a test pattern; it allowed viewers to adjust their sets for the best picture. (Photofest)*

deciphered German codes produced by their Enigma machines; this top-secret ability hastened the end of World War II in Europe. Unfortunately, the zeal for secrecy also delayed other computer developments, because the British shared little information until years after the war.

*Cortisone.* Researchers Edward C. Kendall (1886–1972) and Phillip S. Hench (1896–1965) in 1941 identified cortisone, a steroid hormone that had previously been known as "substance X" or "compound E." They obtained it from the adrenal glands of oxen and found it useful in treating arthritis. Chemist Percy L. Julian (1899–1975) in 1948 synthesized cortisone, making possible its manufacture, thereby reducing its cost and greatly widening its availability.

*Cybernetics.* The term goes back to ancient Greece, suggesting control, such as that exerted by a steersman or governor. In the 1940s, it gained popularity because of mathematician Norbert Weiner (1894–1964) and a pioneering 1948 book he wrote that bore that title. Weiner used cybernetics to describe how any change in an environment causes other changes within that system. He expanded his ideas to mechanical and electrical applications that tend to replicate human control functions and made understandable some of the early concepts that would define how computers work.

*DDT.* The initials used to identify a chemical pesticide, dichlorodiphenyltrichloroethane, which became widely known during the 1940s. First formulated in 1894, its use as a pest control remained undiscovered until 1939. World War II witnessed military and civilian officials using the chemical freely to control mosquitoes, lice, and other disease-carrying pests. With the end of hostilities, DDT became the pesticide of choice among farmers and cooperating governments, and vast amounts of the chemical were indiscriminately sprayed on agricultural sites as well as on any areas where insects might breed. Not until much later—the late 1950s and early 1960s—did scientists begin to realize the environmental risks associated with its use. Finally banned completely in the United States in 1972, DDT continues to be employed in a handful of countries, albeit more sparingly than before, especially in those places that experience a high incidence of malaria.

*DNA.* Deoxyribonucleic acid, a long molecule that resembles a twisted ladder (or a double helix, as it came to be called), received these more easily remembered initials in 1944. It functions to encode the genetic information of all living organisms, except for some viruses that utilize ribonucleic acid, or RNA. Scientists refer to discrete segments of DNA as genes; longer structures of genes become chromosomes. Although laboratory experiments revealed the existence of DNA in 1869, science could not firmly establish its role in the transmission of genetic instructions until 1943, when researchers verified its existence and its importance. Further investigations followed this breakthrough, culminating in the double-helix model of the molecule, formulated in 1953 by molecular biologists Francis Crick (1916–2004) and James D. Watson (b. 1928), with the assistance of Rosalind Franklin (1920–1958).

*ENIAC Computer.* Scientists John W. Mauchly (1907–1980) and J. Presper Eckert Jr. (1919–1995) created a new step in computer design with their electronic numerical integrator analyzer and calculator, or ENIAC machine. It became operational in 1946. Commissioned by the U.S. military, the ENIAC weighed 30 tons, occupied more space than the average room, generated great heat, and consumed enormous amounts of electricity. Over 17,000 vacuum tubes powered its calculations; transistors (see below) had not yet been invented. Mauchly and Eckert followed the ENIAC with the considerably faster and more powerful UNIVAC (universal automatic computer) in 1951.

*Fender solid-body electric guitar.* In 1944, **radio** repairman Leo Fender (1909–1991) began experimenting with electric solid-body guitars; two years later, he formed the Fender Electric Instrument Manufacturing Company. His first model, created in 1946 and marketed in 1948, bore the name *Broadcaster.* It amplified the guitar's sound electrically, not acoustically, and did not create feedback from the player's body; its success introduced a new era in popular music, especially in **rhythm 'n' blues** and rock 'n' roll. Because of legal problems with the name, the company rechristened the guitar as the *Telecaster* in 1951.

*Fluoridation of public drinking water.* Grand Rapids, Michigan, holds the distinction of being the first U.S. community to add fluoride to its public water supply, doing so as a test city in 1945. Following considerable research, scientists determined that minute quantities of fluoride added to water would significantly reduce the likelihood of tooth decay. Despite some opposition that attempted to link fluoridation to sinister Communist plots during the **Cold War,** the United States Public Health Service had by 1951 endorsed fluoridation, and many more towns and cities adopted the practice. In addition, major toothpaste manufacturers began adding fluoride to their products. Since then, dramatic reductions in cavities among the general population have been attributed to fluoride.

*45-rpm records.* In 1949, RCA Victor introduced a new concept in phonograph recordings: the 7-inch 45-rpm disk. The company released records in this format in a futile attempt to compete with Columbia Record's 33 1/3-rpm long-playing disks [see below], which had become available to consumers in 1948. The "singles" (one two-sided disk, with a single song on each side) market had long been dominated by 10-inch 78-rpm records, but the latter possessed several disadvantages: they tended to be highly breakable, their large playing surface scratched easily, they wore out quickly with repeated playing, and they were bulky. RCA's innovative disks, pressed in durable vinyl, seldom broke, had a higher resistance to scratching, and, being smaller and lighter, could easily be transported from place to place. They also boasted a distinguishing feature—a large center hole designed for record players equipped with special spindles manufactured by RCA. It did not take competitors long to get around that disadvantage; they either manufactured spindles of their own or sold plastic "spiders," small, flexible inserts that reduced the oversized hole to conventional size and made it possible to play one of the disks on an ordinary record player, provided it offered the 45-rpm speed.

For a brief period in the early 1950s, RCA and several other labels also tried marketing 45 EPs—the EP standing for extended play. A typical EP would contain two songs per side and sometimes came packaged as albums, with two or three such disks by the same artist, the 45-rpm version of a 33 1/3-rpm disk. EPs did not capture the public's imagination, did poorly in record shops, and have largely disappeared. Within a few years, however, the 45 single had rendered the once-mighty 78-rpm record obsolete, with the last ones being pressed around 1960. Nevertheless, for virtually all albums, consumers overwhelmingly turned to the long-playing disk, and RCA had to begin issuing its own 33 1/3 recordings in 1950 to remain competitive.

*Frisbees.* The name given plastic disks, which, when tossed correctly, will spin and cover considerable distances in the air. They reputedly received their unusual name from the Frisbie Baking Company of Bridgeport, Connecticut. Young customers would occasionally keep the aluminum pie plates from the bakery, sailing them in the air for fun. Walter Morrison (b. 1920), a California resident, in 1948 refined the pie plate concept into the plastic disk so familiar today. He peddled his creation at county fairs, calling it, among other things, a "Flyin' Saucer." Wham-O, Inc., a California toy manufacturer, in 1955 bought out Morrison and attempted to market his disk as a "Pluto Platter." Tradition won the day, however, and in 1959 Wham-O trademarked the word "Frisbee."

*Frozen TV dinners.* C. A. Swanson & Sons, a Nebraska-based **food** processor, lays claim to the invention of the so-called TV dinner, saying that it introduced the product in 1953. But others preceded Swanson in the development of precooked, frozen meals. In 1944, Maxson Food Systems introduced Sky Plates for navy fliers that consisted of full, packaged dinners. They expanded into Strato Plates the following year, featuring similar frozen meals marketed to commercial airline passengers and crew members. Served on plastic plates, the food had been reheated on board the aircraft. Frozen Dinners, Inc., in 1949 sold prepackaged foodstuffs in bars and taverns in the Pittsburgh area. The company became Quaker States Foods in 1952, wholesaling frozen dinners to supermarkets throughout the East. To give Swanson its due, the company tied in the idea of eating meals while watching television and also coined the term "TV dinner."

*Hot rods.* During the late 1930s and early 1940s, a number of young men took delight in souping up old cars, altering them for speed and fast acceleration. The majority of these automotive tinkerers were based on the West Coast, but a few could be found scattered in other parts of the country. They nicknamed their vehicles **hot rods**—hot obviously for speed, but rod has never been a synonym for an automobile, so its etymology remains vague. The term "hot rod" nevertheless began appearing in the early 1940s and received dictionary recognition as a legitimate addition to American popular speech in 1945. Since those early beginnings, the hobby has become well established.

*Jeep.* In 1941, the U.S. Army announced that it wanted a sturdy, general-purpose four-by-four utility vehicle. Bantam Motors, a small Pennsylvania-based company, already had on the boards a conveyance it called the Bantam Reconnaissance Car, but the firm possessed limited production capacity. Willys-Overland Motors, Inc., a similar operation, in the meantime developed a stronger, longer-lasting engine, and the army awarded contracts to Willys and to Ford, the latter because of its large assembly lines and ability to turn out vehicles in huge quantities. From this emerged the ubiquitous Jeep, probably the best-known form of military transport in World War II. By the end of 1945, over 650,000 Jeeps had been manufactured.

The source of the name Jeep has been open to conjecture for many years. "General-purpose," or G-P, has been suggested, but the immensely popular *Popeye* (or *Thimble Theatre*) comic strip, written and drawn by Elzie C. Segar (1894–1938), contained a character called Eugene the Jeep. This cartoon figure, introduced in 1936, could do almost anything, a trait often attributed to the motorized creation the army adopted. Whatever its true roots, the name Jeep has survived into the present.

*Jet-propelled aircraft flight (U.S.).* Credit for the first flight by an aircraft propelled by a jet engine rightfully belongs to Germany. In August 1939, an experimental Heinkel HE 178 successfully flew under turbojet power. The Germans also manufactured the first operational jet, the Messerschmidt ME 262, which joined the *Luftwaffe* in 1944. Close behind came the Royal Air Force Gloster E.28/39, which flew in tests in May 1941; this aircraft would evolve into the operational Gloster Meteor in the summer of 1944.

The honor of being the first U.S. jet aircraft to fly goes to the Bell XP-59-A Airacomet; it had its maiden flight at the beginning of October 1942. Bell built a total of 66 Airacomets, but none saw combat; they instead trained pilots for flying jet aircraft. Lockheed Aircraft's P-80 Shooting Star replaced the Bell P-59s in 1945, too close to the end of World War II for combat operations.

*Microwave oven.* Percy L. Spencer (1894–1970), a Raytheon Company engineer, accidentally discovered the technology behind the microwave oven found in most contemporary kitchens. Spencer had been working with magnetrons, tubes that utilize electrical and magnetic currents to create energy in the form of microwaves. Such tubes had been created in the 1920s but, lacking any seemingly practical use, lay idle for over a decade. During World War II, Raytheon had done considerable experimental work with radar devices, including the use of magnetrons, and Spencer, when approaching one such tube in 1946, found that a candy bar in his pocket melted. Further investigation showed that microwaves could be used as a source of tightly controlled energy that would cook but without a buildup of heat.

Shortly after that discovery, Raytheon commenced work on creating a workable microwave oven that could be marketed commercially. Called Radaranges, they became commercially available in 1947; huge, expensive, heavy ovens, the company sold them to **restaurants** and institutions. Not until the early 1950s did the company market cheaper, smaller microwave ovens for home use.

*Mobile telephone.* In the days prior to World War II, scientists worked to establish a mobile system of radios and telephones for communication purposes. Led by AT&T (American Telephone and Telegraph) and its subsidiary Bell Labs, wireless radios sometimes had telephone capabilities and bore the designation radio-telephones. The government placed most civilian efforts of this nature on hold during the war years, but the military worked intensively to perfect walkie-talkies, mobile radios that soldiers could carry into battle and still have the ability to communicate with others. In 1946, with preprinted circuit boards available for civilian use, much smaller radio-telephones became a reality.

That same year, Bell Labs initiated commercial radio-telephone service, and the Federal Communications Commission (FCC) specified channels for such transmissions. A receiver could thereby pick up a signal on one channel (frequency) and transmit it to another. Antennas, strategically placed on tall buildings and poles, provided maximum efficiency. For longer distances, a signal might go to a nearby antenna and then be transferred to another closer to the designated recipient. By 1948, this service had begun to enjoy widespread use.

*Penicillin.* An early "miracle drug," British biologist Alexander Fleming (1881–1955) discovered penicillin in 1928. Quite by chance, he found that mold had formed in one of his Petri dishes, effectively killing the sample it held. This discovery led to an antibiotic that he chose to call penicillin, but it elicited little enthusiasm in the medical community, since sulfonamides (commonly known as sulfa drugs) had been introduced in the 1930s as antibacterial agents. Fleming continued to test penicillin, and with the onset of World War II, it finally gained attention. Foreseeing high numbers of wounds, both the British and U.S. governments underwrote continued experimentation and stockpiling of the drug. Because of its potency in treating various physical injuries, Fleming secured the assistance of scientists Howard W. Florey (1898–1968) and Ernst B. Chain (1906–1979) to devise ways of mass producing penicillin. By the time of **D-Day** in 1944, sufficient supplies of the antibiotic existed to treat the many wounded at the Normandy landings. Although civilians had begun to hear about penicillin, its use continued to be primarily military until the end of 1945, when it became available for widespread public use. Because of their work, Fleming, Florey, and Chain shared in the Nobel Prize for Medicine in 1945.

*Polaroid camera.* Edwin Land (1909–1991), a self-taught inventor, in the early 1930s created photographic filters and film that effectively polarized light (polarizing sunglasses eliminate glare on a bright day). In 1937, he and a number of investors formed the Polaroid Corporation; during World War II, the company developed several related products for defense work. In the postwar era, Land achieved his greatest fame and success with the 1947 Polaroid Land camera, a unique camera capable of taking pictures and then developing them in about a minute, an approach labeled "one-step **photography.**" Polaroid cameras sold well from the day of their introduction, and Land continued to refine and improve his instant cameras for the next several decades.

*Radar.* An acronym coined in 1942 by the U.S. Navy that stands for radio detection and ranging, radar has a long history. Early devices that utilized many of the principles of modern radar underwent testing in the 1900s to 1930s, and some historians argue that the development of the scientific theories behind radar date back to the 19th century. By the mid-1930s, scientists had developed devices capable of sending out radio waves that would detect obstacles (airplanes, ships, icebergs, coastlines, etc.) in their path and allow operators to know their approximate location.

In a farsighted move, the British constructed a series of large antennas across the southern approaches to England; when World War II broke out in the autumn of 1939, operators were able to detect the approach of German planes from the European mainland. In a battle of technologies, the British worked continuously to improve their detection capabilities, while the Germans worked to perfect equipment that could in turn detect the presence of enemy radar. Both sides also worked feverishly to improve systems capable of jamming the other's radar. The Allies soon had radar units small enough to be put in aircraft, allowing them to hunt and locate other planes both at night and in foul weather. These improvements even applied to the oceans; radar equipment that could detect a submarine periscope became part of the Allied arsenal.

The end of World War II and the ensuing Cold War did nothing to slow down the development of ever-more sophisticated radar systems. Both the United States and the Soviet Union ringed themselves with early-warning arrays of radar in order to know of any attempted sneak attacks. Postwar commercial **aviation** and maritime commerce also made extensive use of the technology. On a more popular level, the so-called radar gun came along in 1954. A device to measure the speeds of vehicles, police departments and highway patrols quickly adopted it to catch traffic violators. That led in 1965 to a bustling business in radar detectors, or "fuzzbusters," for drivers wishing to avoid speeding tickets. Since then, a series of improvements, both in police radar units and civilian detectors, has been ongoing.

*Refrigerator-freezer combination.* The appliance division of the General Electric Company (GE) introduced a new concept in refrigeration when, in 1947, it showed a two-door model that separated the freezer portion from the conventional refrigerator. The upper third of the unit held a freezer accessed by its own exterior door. The lower two-thirds housed a conventional refrigerator, also with a separate door. The upper freezer compartment, much larger than the traditional small box usually built into the refrigerator, allowed for the storage of considerably more frozen items, a reflection of the growing popularity of **frozen foods** then occurring. This innovation also led to fierce competition among appliance makers as they tried to improve on GE's model.

*Rubber—synthetic.* In the early days of World War II, Japanese forces had overrun most of the rubber plantations in Southeast Asia, the primary source of this strategic material for U.S. industry. In light of the worsening Asian situation, the government had begun stockpiling rubber in 1940 and had more than a year's worth set aside when the war broke out at the end of 1941. Strict civilian **rationing** of rubber products went into effect in early 1942, and **posters** and **scrap drives** implored citizens to turn in extra tires, boots, or anything else made of rubber for recycling to fill defense needs.

In the meantime, an intensive search had begun in 1940 to find a synthetic form of natural rubber that could be made in the United States. A partnership of the government, commercial rubber companies, the oil industry (petroleum by-products would be key ingredients), chemical firms, and academic research centers undertook this challenge. Efforts to synthesize rubber have a long history, dating back to the 19th century, and, although some substitutes had been found, they did not equal natural rubber. This previous research, however, did lay the groundwork for a quality synthetic, which made the war-generated quest somewhat easier.

Thanks to the cooperation of all involved parties, plus the leadership of top executives with varied areas of expertise, the daunting task proved successful in a remarkably short time; in the spring of 1942, the first bales of synthetic government rubber-styrene (GR-S)) were produced. By the end of the year, over 2,000 tons of GR-S had been manufactured, a figure that soared upward each year for the remainder of the war.

*Silly Putty.* Not all technological innovation necessarily leads to scientific or cultural advancement. In 1943, General Electric Company engineer James Wright (active 1940s) had been assigned to work on finding substitutes for natural rubber. Because the Japanese had captured most of the rubber plantations in Southeast Asia, severe shortages in U.S. rubber supplies resulted.

Wright tried combining a number of ingredients but failed to create anything that might be useful in making tires, boots, insulators, or other products requiring rubber. He did, however, concoct a gooey substance that would bounce, stretch, and resist high temperatures. Neither he nor his colleagues could find much use for it other than amusing themselves by bouncing it in the laboratory.

In 1949, Wright's gooey discovery made it into a small toy catalog at the insistence of Peter Hodgson (1912–1976), an **advertising** consultant who bought the production rights and the existing supply held by General Electric. After a year or so in the catalog, "bouncing putty" was dropped, and Hodgson took his savings and decided to market it himself. He called it Silly Putty, and placed one-ounce globs of it in red plastic eggs. After a slow start, Hodgson's product, "the real solid liquid," took off, and with effective advertising in key television time slots, it became an enduring favorite.

*Simulcasting.* The late 1940s witnessed the decline of traditional radio programming but also saw the rise of commercial television. Once-favorite radio shows were canceled or went to new TV lives on the small home screen. Occasionally, however, a popular radio show stayed on the air, went to TV also, and then technicians broadcast it over both media. This practice received the name of simulcasting, a blending of words "simultaneous" and "broadcasting." In the late 1940s, before television stations had large staffs of announcers, **baseball** games would sometimes be broadcast on radio, and a television hook-up would show the game with the radio play-by-play providing the sound. *You Bet Your Life,* a popular quiz show hosted by comedian Groucho Marx (1890–1977), ran on radio from 1947 to 1956. It also played on television from 1950 to 1961. When the show made the transition to TV, engineers simulcast the audio portion for radio. Also, in the early days of postwar **FM radio,** some AM stations would simulcast their programming over an FM affiliate in order to save the costs of running two separate stations.

*Slinky.* Richard James (1914–1974), a naval engineer, discovered the toy potential in certain types of industrial torsion springs in 1943 when he accidentally knocked over one on which he was working and watched it fall, flip, bounce over obstacles, and end upright. The reactions of neighborhood children convinced him he was on to something that might sell.

Working closely with his wife Betty (1918–2008), who came up with the name, saying that "slinky" described the motions of the spring, the couple launched their product at a Gimbel's Philadelphia department store during the 1945 Christmas season. The toy promptly sold out, and they had to manufacture more. Over time, hundreds of millions of Slinkies have since been purchased, and it continues to be one of the most successful toys of all time.

*Snorkel.* This term comes from German naval submarine jargon used during the war years; it refers to a breathing tube, or air intake, that a diesel-powered sub could extend just above the water's surface when at periscope depth to bring in fresh air. To some, this tube resembled a nose or snout, a *schnorchel.* Allied sailors Anglicized it to *snorkel* toward the end of the decade but still limited its use to submarines. In 1953, a rubber tube through which swimmers could breathe while floating face down in the water or **swimming** just below the surface became popular at beaches, and it inherited *snorkel* as its name. A verb, *to snorkel,* also entered water enthusiasts' speech, meaning to go swimming face down in the water while using this breathing apparatus.

*Sonar.* An acronym, meaning sound navigation ranging, that gained a measure of public recognition in 1946. A naval term used mainly with submarines, sonar devices allow submarines "to see" while underwater. Simply put, a sonar operator sends out pulsing sounds beneath the water's surface. When these sounds strike an object, the operator can record the echo of that meeting and thus learn the object's bearings. Although the principles behind sonar had been understood for many years, research and development of improved systems moved slowly and amid top secrecy before and during World War II. A favorite scene in submarine **movies** of the day involves a sonar operator sending out pings (sound) and awaiting the echoes. Silent and tense, both the observers on screen and the theater audience await the information sonar will provide. Is the enemy close at hand or some distance away? Since the end of the war, advances have been made, with small, sophisticated sonar devices being made commercially available to fishermen, divers, and boaters, while defense-based applications have also advanced.

*Sound barrier broken.* The speed of sound exists as a variable number, dependent on temperature, altitude, and several other factors, but it approximates 760 miles per hour (mph) at sea level. On October 14, 1947, while piloting a Bell X-1 in level flight, U.S. Air Force Captain Charles "Chuck" Yeager (b. 1923) broke the so-called sound barrier by attaining a speed of 807.2 mph. Many scientists had long understood the physics of exceeding the speed of sound, and such speeds had been attained previous to Yeager's flight; aircraft in dives (sometimes unplanned), and some top-secret experimental flights, often using rocket engines, had undoubtedly broken the mythic barrier, but lack of reliable speed measurements and secrecy kept these exploits out of record books.

The term "barrier" had arisen because of fears about turbulence (buffeting of the aircraft as it nears, and then exceeds, the speed of sound). In addition, the so-called sonic boom posed problems for those on the ground. As an aircraft exceeds 760 mph, the air around it compresses, unable to expand, with a resultant shock wave made audible as a thunderous boom to all on the ground. The success of Yeager's flight showed that the sound barrier could be broken, and with proper **design** and engineering, aircraft could be manufactured that could safely fly at supersonic speeds.

*Streptomycin.* An antibiotic drug discovered in 1943 that became useful in the treatment of tuberculosis (TB). After extensive testing, the Food and Drug Administration allowed its medical use in 1947. Administered via injections, streptomycin proved effective against bacteria that had previously displayed resistance to other treatments. Its success, when accompanied by other antituberculosis drugs, allowed the once-dreaded disease to be treated on an outpatient basis and brought about the closing of TB sanitariums.

*Suntan lotions, Coppertone.* In the 1940s, a good, visible tan, the darker the better, represented robust **health.** The notion of staying out of the sun because of its long-term injurious effects remained for future generations to discover. In light of the positive attitudes tanning elicited, Miami-based pharmacist Benjamin Green (active 1940s) in 1944 introduced a lotion designed to enhance (i.e., darken) one's tan. He called his product Coppertone, and he placed the image of an Indian chief on the label with the slogan, "Don't Be a Paleface."

Not until 1953 did Green's company create the iconic Coppertone Girl for its advertising. In **magazines** and on billboards, Coppertone presented the picture of a little girl at a beach with a frisky black cocker spaniel tugging at her bathing suit bottoms. The dog has succeeded in exposing a bit of her white, untanned buttocks, and the slogan, "Don't be a paleface!" runs across the lower part of the ad. Over time, that humorous image has become famous, and Coppertone has reaped countless benefits from it.

In addition, Green reputedly concocted a primitive sunscreen lotion around this time. U.S. troops stationed in the South Pacific suffered from excessive exposure to the tropical sun, and welcomed Red Vet Pet (for Red Veterinary Petroleum), a red, greasy salve that probably blocked some rays if applied heavily enough. But the day for true sunscreens still lay in the years ahead.

*Teflon.* Roy J. Plunkett (1910–1994), a chemist with a small firm called Kinetic Chemicals, quite by accident discovered in 1938 that a compound, polytetrafluoroethylene (PTFE) possessed an unusual characteristic. It appeared to disperse both water and oil. His company patented it in 1941 and gave it a trademarked name, Teflon, in 1945.

The huge DuPont chemical conglomerate acquired an interest in Kinetic during this time. DuPont, however, wanted to utilize PTFE for industrial and scientific purposes because it reduces friction, resists corrosion, and can be employed as an electrical insulator. A French firm created the first cooking utensil, an aluminum frying pan clad with PTFE, which it marketed as Tefal (or T-Fal in North America) in 1954. This signaled the beginning of consumer applications of PTFE. Since then, Teflon has become a popular coating and lubricant, utilized in a variety of products.

*33 1/3-rpm long-playing records.* In the summer of 1948, Peter Goldmark (1906–1977) of Columbia Records unveiled the company's long-playing record, or LP, as many called it. Pressed on durable vinyl, this new product provided about 20–25 minutes of music per side on a 12-inch disk and about 12–15 minutes on a 10-inch variety. Either way, an LP offered far more than the 3 or 4 minutes available on a traditional 10-inch, 78-rpm single. The LP played at 33 1/3 rpm and boasted microgroove technology—a much narrower groove than anything then on the market. Because LPs played more slowly, they reduced surface noise—the annoying hisses, pops, and clicks associated with 78-rpm records—but consumers had to still treat them with care to avoid scratches. In addition, the slower rotation allowed the phonograph's tone arm to be lighter in weight and the needle (stylus) could track with less pressure. Both LPs and styli therefore did not wear out as quickly. Excessive heat or improper storage could, however, warp them.

Columbia's long-playing recordings helped usher in the high-fidelity era, a time when electronics manufacturers rushed to produce improved amplifiers and speakers to accompany the new turntables needed to play such recordings. The introduction of the LP also brought about the so-called battle of the speeds, when archrival RCA Victor brought out its competing 45-rpm vinyl singles [see above]. In a tacit admission of defeat, RCA began releasing long-playing disks on its own label in 1950, but its 45s would nevertheless end up becoming the standard for singles.

*Tide detergent.* Until the 1930s, traditional laundry soaps handled almost all washday chores, often in the form of soap flakes for sudsy water. But soaps could not always clean greasy laundry or embedded dirt until Procter & Gamble, a leading U.S. manufacturer of household products, introduced Dreft, the first synthetic detergent.

Dreft used a chemical formulation that involved synthetic surfactants (a word combining "surface active agents"). Essentially two-part molecules, one portion pulled grease and dirt from laundry, and the other suspended them so that they could be rinsed away. But Dreft did an inferior job on tough cleaning, so Procter & Gamble chemists came up with Tide detergent in 1943. It, too, utilized surfactants (also called "syndets," for synthetic detergents) but added what the company called "builders" that improved the cleaning action.

After considerable testing, coupled with wartime restrictions, Tide appeared on store shelves in 1946. A runaway success, it achieved full national distribution by 1949 and has remained a top seller in the highly competitive detergent field ever since.

*Transistors.* The American Telephone and Telegraph Company, better-known as AT&T, controlled the lucrative long-distance telephone business throughout the 1940s. Because it had to employ vacuum tubes to amplify its signals, the company wanted a product more reliable and cheaper than tubes. That decision led AT&T, through its subsidiary Bell Laboratories, to explore semiconductors, a class of solid-state materials that fall somewhere between an insulator and a traditional conductor (thus its literal name, a "half conductor"). A team of physicists, consisting of William B. Shockley (1910–1989), John Bardeen (1908–1991), and Walter H. Brattain (1902–1987), with Shockley designated as the leader, in 1945 tackled the task of creating a practical semiconductor that could replace vacuum tubes.

After two years of experiments, the team found that small cylinders coated with silicon showed some promise. When, in late 1947, Bardeen and Brattain added gold and germanium (a chemical element that can function as a semiconductor) crystals to their efforts, they realized they had invented what came to be called a point-contact transistor. It could amplify electrical signals and also switch on and off, blocking the signal when necessary. Shockley joined in with the concept of a junction transistor, a device that layered, or sandwiched, two different kinds of semiconductors for better amplification capabilities. After much work, scientists announced the creation of a practical junction transistor in 1950.

Bell Labs, however, did not wait for everything to work flawlessly. At the end of June 1948, they announced the arrival of a new product, the transistor. Few knew what the word meant, let alone the potential of this new addition to modern science. For the United States, researchers mainly studied possible applications for military use. Texas Instruments, a U.S. electronics firm, marketed the first transistorized radio, the Regency TR1, in 1954 but stopped selling them after a brief time on the market in order to concentrate on other products. Because of advertising and public interest, the word "transistor" nonetheless entered everyday speech and suggested greater things to come.

Half a world away, a small Japanese manufacturer of tape recorders, Tokyo Tsushin Kogyo, also took notice. When Texas Instruments withdrew from the transistorized radio market in 1955, this company jumped in, releasing its TR-55. Realizing the difficulties that would arise with its Japanese name in the United States, the firm changed it to the now-familiar Sony. Since then, consumer-oriented transistorized products have been dominated by Asian-based companies.

*Tupperware.* Polyethylene, a versatile plastic developed in 1933, comes in two forms, high-density and low-density. Both have become familiar to consumers, with the high-density variant (called HDPE) used in making containers, piping, and automotive parts, and the low-density version (LDPE) in sheeting and packaging, especially the ubiquitous plastic shopping bag.

The virtues of both include flexibility, durability, and a resistance to other chemicals. Earl Tupper (1907–1983), an entrepreneur and inventor, recognized the potential in HDPE. He had worked briefly for DuPont during the late 1930s and knew something about plastics. He formed his own company, Tupper Plastics, in 1938 and managed to obtain some lucrative government contracts during World War II for defense-related products. He introduced a line of flexible HDPE kitchen storage containers for consumers in 1946, patenting his ideas in 1947. He called his product Tupperware.

Possibly the most original thing about Tupperware involved its air- and watertight seal. Basing his design on the covers used with paint cans, Tupper devised a locking lid, easy to close and easy to open, but one that kept items fresh and moisture-free. He also made Tupperware available in several translucent pastel colors that were fashionable at the time, such as yellow, green, orange, and pink (or, as Tupper marketed them, lemon, lime, orange, and raspberry).

Department stores, however, seemed reluctant to take on his invention, and those that did found the containers did not sell particularly well. As a result, Tupper hired Bonnie Wise (1913–1992), a marketing expert, for assistance in promoting his containers. She came up with the clever Tupperware Home Party, gatherings where Tupperware products would be sold directly to individuals. Wise capitalized on the concept of women working and socializing simultaneously. Not an entirely new idea, Hostess Plans had evolved in the 1930s with several home products firms, and Wise simply adapted it to Tupperware. She used churches, clubs, and sororities, as well as friends and neighbors, to sell to one another. Tupperware Parties became an overnight success in the early 1950s, and soon the versatile plastic could only be obtained this way—the pastel bowls with the tight lids had been withdrawn from stores.

*Zamboni.* A resident of Southern California, Frank J. Zamboni (1901–1988) displayed a knack for tinkering with machinery. His family operated an ice wholesale business in the 1930s, but as refrigeration technology improved, demand for their product declined. With their knowledge of ice, the family in 1940 opened a large skating rink in Paramount, California, which they named Iceland.

At that time, in order to keep the ice smooth and in good condition for skaters, a rink would every so often have to be temporarily closed, a situation no one liked. A tractor rolled out onto the ice, dragging a heavy scraper that would shave the surface, and workers would follow, sweeping up the shavings, hosing down the ice, and then, with squeegees, smoothing it. It all took time and involved considerable labor. As the owner of a rink, Frank Zamboni knew how tedious this kind of maintenance could be, and he resolved to improve the process.

Still using a tractor and a scraper, Zamboni devised a conveyor that picked up the shavings and any debris and brushed, wetted, and smoothed the ice all in one operation. This prototype appeared in 1947. By 1949, he had eliminated the tractor. Instead, he utilized a Jeep (see above) chassis and built a surrounding unit that contained the scraper, conveyor, brushes, and water. The resultant boxy, almost military-looking contrivance he named after himself: a Zamboni.

Since then, the Zamboni company has built hundreds of machines for **hockey** teams, ice shows, the Olympics, and, of course, countless rinks. The same firm also created, during the 1960s, Grasshoppers, mechanisms that will vacuum up the standing water on artificial grasses, such as Astroturf.

*See also:* Automobiles and the American Automotive Industry; Cartoons (Film); Civil Defense; Classical Music; Comic Strips; Crosley Automobiles; Fads; Lawns, Lawnmowers, and Fertilizers; Newspapers; Skating (Figure); Sinatra, Frank; Toys

A Chronological Listing of Selected Technological Achievements from the 1940s

| | |
|---|---|
| **1940** | Color Television |
| | Radar |
| **1941** | Aerosol Spray Cans |
| | Cortisone |
| | Jeep |
| **1942** | Chain Reaction |
| | Jet-Propelled Aircraft Flight (U.S.) |
| | Rubber—Synthetic |
| **1943** | Aqualung |
| | DDT |
| | DNA |
| | Silly Putty |
| | Slinky |
| | Streptomycin |
| **1944** | Ballpoint Pen |
| | Computer—Digital |
| | Fender Solid-Body Electric Guitar |
| | Frozen TV Dinners |
| | Snorkel |
| | Suntan Lotions, Coppertone |
| **1945** | Atomic Bomb |
| | Fluoridation of Public Drinking Water |
| | Hot Rod |
| | Penicillin |
| | Teflon |
| **1946** | ENIAC Computer |
| | Mobile Telephone |
| | Sonar |
| | Tide Detergent |
| | Tupperware |
| **1947** | Automatic Washer |
| | Microwave Oven |
| | Polaroid Camera |
| | Refrigerator-Freezer Combination |
| | Sound Barrier Broken |
| **1948** | Cybernetics |
| | Frisbees |
| | 33-1/3-rpm Long-Playing Records |
| | Transistors |
| **1949** | Automated Streetlights |
| | 45-rpm Records |
| | Simulcasting |
| | Zamboni |

**Selected Reading**
Because of the breadth of this chapter, no specific works are recommended; instead, the reader is directed to the bibliography at the end of this encyclopedia.

# TELEVISION

Following the end of World War II in 1945, a shift occurred in American broadcasting. **Radio** networks and stations, for many years the primary force in electronic communication, saw their influence gradually wane as television, once a technological curiosity, began its inexorable climb to dominance. The Big Three networks—**ABC (American Broadcasting Company),** CBS (Columbia Broadcasting System), and NBC (National Broadcasting Company)—allocated more and more of their resources to the development of television programming, all at the expense of their radio schedules. Ironically, the profits accrued from commercial radio made possible the development of commercial television. Although radio also expanded in the immediate postwar era, particularly in the number of small, independent stations, long-running network shows got canceled, and long-time stars moved to the new medium. By the early 1950s, however, and despite a lengthy holding action throughout the 1940s, American radio increasingly became a purveyor of music, news, and little else.

As early as 1938, a few television receivers, mainly those manufactured by **DuMont,** became available to the American public in limited markets. Often featuring miniscule round screens as small as three inches in diameter and priced from $125 to $600 (approximately $1,900 to $9,100 in 2008 dollars), they aroused considerable curiosity but few sales. Despite the lack of buyers, the following year saw many more manufacturers—Crosley, General Electric, Muntz, Philco, RCA, Zenith, and others—offer receivers. Appliance stores and similar outlets purchased most of these early sets as demonstration models; few individuals wanted to take a chance on such new **technology,** plus virtually no broadcasting took place outside New York City and Schenectady, New York, along with limited facilities in Chicago, Los Angeles, and Philadelphia, the sites for most experimental telecasting.

At the 1939–1940 New York World's Fair, aptly called "The World of Tomorrow," the Hall of Television stood out among the many buildings and exhibits, although Crosley, General Electric, and Westinghouse also had displays of television components elsewhere. The hall, sponsored by the RCA (Radio Corporation of America), an early leader in the development of commercial television, featured the new RCA TRK-12 model within its modernistic walls. Additionally, RCA had strategically placed TV receivers around the vast fairgrounds, broadcasting live scenes of events then occurring at the exposition. Viewers watched those exterior images, however, on DuMont receivers, not RCA models. Since DuMont had gotten the jump on its competitors by offering sets in 1938, it could supply enough receivers for the fair. RCA, of course, would eventually catch up and then far surpass DuMont and most other companies in the mass production of television components, but not in 1939. One of the most popular attractions at the fair, the Hall of Television reflected growing public curiosity about the new electronic marvel; for many visitors, it provided their first glimpse of televised images.

Despite this display of confidence about television's future, confusion marked the opening of the new decade, because broadcasters, manufacturers, and the Federal Communications Commission (FCC) wrangled over standards for transmitting and receiving television signals. In a compromise that pleased no one, the FCC in 1940 allowed a patchwork of rules to remain in place, citing the need to allow research to continue rather than freezing it at an arbitrary point.

Finally, in May 1941, with the various parties in essential agreement, the FCC approved a set of basic technical standards for commercial television. In essence, this agreement okayed 18 channels, delayed discussions about the possibilities for color television (at that time, all broadcasters provided only a black-and-white signal), and made FM (frequency modulation) the carrier for sound instead of AM (amplitude modulation). The way had been cleared for commercial television on a broad scale, and NBC's WNBT and CBS's WCBW, both located in New York City, went on the air commercially, broadcasting for about 15 hours per week. Schenectady, Chicago, and Los Angeles followed suit in late 1941. The initial programming consisted of shows that could be produced and televised within the stations' studios. To attract sponsors, an hour of prime time television in 1941 could be purchased for $120 (approximately $1,750 in 2008 dollars); a comparable hour on radio would cost 10 times as much.

Given the high cost of receivers, limited production, and the availability of programming in only a few metropolitan areas, television as a mass medium grew very slowly. Estimates place the number of sets in use in 1941 at around 10,000 to 20,000, with most of them in New York City. The outbreak of World War II in December 1941 changed everything; by May 1942, the War Production Board had banned any expansion of existing television facilities and had placed a freeze on the manufacture of new sets, explaining that those resources had to be directed to the war effort. Those already on the air had to drastically cut back operations for the duration of the conflict, effectively bringing the development of American television to a standstill. Engineers and technicians kept things running, however, and a number of advances in equipment and planning still took place.

At the same time, license applications for new television stations piled up in FCC offices, and officials knew that, with the return of peace, pressure would be on to grant allocations for broadcasters. Both television and radio transmit their signals on prearranged bandwidths, a system measured in megahertz. The narrow range previously assigned **FM radio** would be insufficient to accommodate any growing roster of stations and would require increased bandwidth. Following much spirited discussion as manufacturers and broadcasters, particularly NBC and CBS, vied for advantageous positions in any agency rulings, the FCC in 1945 gave television broadcasters 13 VHF (very high frequency) channels and changed and expanded the FM spectrum. The agreements pleased no one completely but brought enough order that it allowed for the postwar advance of commercial television. Stations then in operation had to change frequencies in order to comply and stay on the air, making 500,000 older FM radios obsolete overnight.

The FCC identified 140 metropolitan areas and allotted them a minimum of one television channel; since it had 400 licenses to distribute, a number of metropolitan areas received more than one channel. The agency also explicitly restricted channel 1 on the television spectrum to low-wattage community broadcasting. Manufacturers followed the FCC's lead and had sold at least 175,000 new black-and-white receivers by the beginning of 1948. These postwar models usually boasted a 10-inch screen and sold for an average of $375 (approximately $3,600 in 2008 dollars), making them a costly investment for most families. People with access to television signals nonetheless lined up at appliance and department stores to purchase the latest models.

Other services, particularly mobile communications, such as police and fire calls, also used the broadcast band, and their proximity to one another sometimes caused interference problems. The FCC in 1948 decreed that the bandwidth space formerly occupied by channel 1 would be turned over to mobile and other special services. In return, channels 2 through 13 would become clear-channel operations, free of electronic interference. Since that time, all VHF television encompasses channels 2 through 13, and channel 1 has disappeared.

Additional problems emerged as more television stations came on the air. Stations located in cities close together often encountered interference from one another (e.g., New York City and Philadelphia, Cleveland and Detroit), and the many pending license applications would only exacerbate the situation. Again in 1948, the FCC instituted a freeze on any new stations going on the air until all the technical problems had been ironed out. It would last until 1952, giving ABC, CBS, NBC, and others four years to work on such topics as standards for color television, eliminating electronic interference, fair and impartial allocations for new licenses, and implementing educational (noncommercial) television. The edict did not include those stations already on the air or under active construction, allowing them to continue their activities.

At the onset of the 1948 FCC freeze, only about 10 percent of the population had actually seen a television broadcast. Across the country, 34 licensed TV stations were on the air, with another 75 authorized. Out of that 109, only a few large cities had two channels, but that gave the illusion of greater availability. Many sizable communities—Austin, Denver, Little Rock, Portland (Maine and Oregon), among a number of others—had no stations whatsoever. American television therefore had to wait until the early 1950s to evolve into a true mass medium.

For consumers, the purchase of a television set in the late 1940s not only involved a significant outlay of money but also demanded time and involvement with the receiver on the part of buyers. Each time they turned on the receiver and often when they changed channels as well they had to contend with five or six knobs—horizontal, vertical, brightness, tint, channel selector, plus a volume control and an on-off switch—on the face of the cabinet. They all required attention, and too much of an adjustment with one might distort another. Stations, when they first came on the air each broadcasting day, provided a test pattern on the screen before they commenced their regular schedule. This image, consisting of static designs that included horizontal, vertical, and diagonal lines, along with shades of gray, allowed individuals to twiddle the knobs and adjust the picture until they achieved a satisfactory image, but it took practice and patience.

In addition to tuning the set, consumers also had to buy either an indoor or outdoor (sometimes both) antenna in order to pick up a station's signal. The higher an antenna reached into the air, the better the reception, so rooftops around the country soon sprouted ungainly assemblies of rigid, shaped wire attached to a pole. Inside, "rabbit ears," as some called them, two adjustable spokes or circles (the ears) on a stand, could be manipulated for a better picture. People usually placed them on tabletops, window sills, or the TV cabinet. So, before anyone could relax and enjoy a show, these television rituals had to be performed. The heavy early models also took up large amounts of space in homes; the truly portable TV still lay in the future.

In the years immediately following the war, most television stations broadcast only during the late afternoon and evening hours. Virtually all programming came into homes live—it emanated from local studio facilities as it happened, and little could be filmed or otherwise saved for later broadcast. No good way existed to preserve early television shows. Networks and stations used kinescope recording, a method utilizing a filmed image taken from a special, synchronized TV picture tube, but the results lacked definition and tended to be grainy, and the development of videotape did not occur until the early 1950s. Since not all presentations had kinescope recordings made of them, many early entertainment shows, sporting events, and news broadcasts have been lost forever; those fortunate enough to be preserved in the kinescope format tend to be less than satisfactory.

Not until 1949 did coaxial cable link the East Coast with the Midwest; true national broadcasting—Atlantic to Pacific—did not occur until 1951, and that link omitted most areas of the Rocky Mountain states. As network affiliates became connected, however, the situation changed. The three major networks dominated the prime-time evening hours (traditionally 8:00 p.m. to 11:00 p.m. EST, weeknights), causing affiliate stations to increase their on-air time. Local programming expanded, mainly in the late morning and on into the afternoon and early evening hours, and it usually consisted of cheap, easily produced and telecast material, often called filler shows. Because most broadcasters had prior experience with radio programming, they often borrowed formats that had previously been successful, such as cooking demonstrations, children's entertainment, musical interludes, and interview and talk programs. But with time to fill, they also experimented with various formats to see what worked best in the new medium.

In order to attract larger audiences, network television executives early on looked to the **movies** for a treasure trove of material. Hollywood, on the other hand, showed little inclination to supply this new rival with motion pictures. The difference between film projection at 24 frames per second (fps) and television images at 30 fps presented technicians the problem of learning how to synchronize the two. Once it had been resolved, most of the movies first shown on TV sets consisted of shorts, **cartoons,** and the like. The major studios would not release any post-1948 features to television, so stations had to make do with older, less desirable footage in the public domain, including some in the form of silent films. Not until the 1950s would the studios begin to relent and allow more recent features to be shown.

With the lack of popular films, television producers turned to vaudeville and radio for inspiration, and thus created the TV variety show. Led by the ***Texaco Star Theater*** (NBC, 1948–1953), with comedian Milton Berle (1908–2002); the long-lived ***Toast of the Town*** (CBS, 1948–1971), with host Ed Sullivan (1901–1974); and *Cavalcade of Stars* (DuMont Network, 1949–1952), a series that introduced Jackie Gleason (1916–1987), the variety show established itself as a staple of the new medium. Dave Garroway (1913–1982), an easygoing radio reporter and disc jockey from Chicago, in 1949 began *Garroway at Large,* an informal talk show that ran until 1951 and led to his tenure as host of NBC's pioneering *Today* in 1952. Garroway's relaxed format paved the way for the many talk shows that would become regular features of television programming in the years to come.

Again borrowing from radio, talent shows, such as the *Original Amateur Hour* (DuMont, others, 1948–1958), with host Ted Mack (1904–1976), and *Talent Scouts* (CBS, 1948–1958), with **Arthur Godfrey** (1903–1983), proved popular, as did countless game and quiz shows. Most of them employed simple sets—a desk, possibly some chairs or a podium, and little else. The meager prizes consisted of small amounts of cash or a modest check; not until the 1950s would the elaborate sets and large prizes in the thousands, or tens of thousands, of dollars come along, until a series of scandals, beginning in the mid-1950s, sullied the genre and caused its virtual disappearance from network programming.

A high point of these early days of television involved anthology drama series. These shows, such as *The Ford Television Theater* (CBS, others, 1948–1957), **Kraft Television Theater** (NBC, 1947–1958), *Philco Playhouse* (NBC, 1948–1955), and *Studio One* (CBS, 1948–1958), presented both adapted and original dramatic productions, usually an hour in length. They utilized the talents of the best writers and playwrights of the day and starred top performers. Because the production of virtually all network shows originated in studios located in New York City—the headquarters of ABC, CBS, and NBC—the people involved usually came from radio and Broadway, not Hollywood. Given the limitations of television at the time, dramatic shows tended to be intimate, dialog-based productions instead of action stories or anything dependent on outdoor scenes or elaborate sets. But, as the parenthesized dates above suggest, for a brief period from the late 1940s until the mid-1950s, these programs demonstrated the dramatic potential of the new medium.

Children could enjoy the late-afternoon antics on **Howdy Doody**, which debuted in 1947 on NBC and ran until 1960, one of the most popular youngsters' shows of all time. They could also watch the puppets on *Kukla, Fran and Ollie* (NBC, others, 1948–1957) or sample the variety of *Small Fry Club* (DuMont, 1947–1951). One of the first attempts to bring the classroom into the home occurred when *Ding Dong School* went on the air in 1952. Miss Frances (Frances Horwich, 1907–2001, a real-life **education** professor) presided over her charges on this NBC program that ran until 1956. *Mr. I. Magination* (CBS, 1949–1952) likewise brought a touch of fantasy to children, as did the interplanetary adventures of *Captain Video* (DuMont, 1949–1955), a series that introduced science fiction into homes. **William Boyd**'s (1895–1972) popular *Hopalong Cassidy* premiered in 1949 and ran for two years on NBC, at which time it went into syndication. One of the first Westerns presented on the small screen, Boyd had wisely

TABLE 95. Representative Television Game and Quiz Shows of the Late 1940s

| Game or Quiz Show | Network | Years |
| --- | --- | --- |
| *Ben Grauer's Americana Quiz* | NBC | 1947–1949 |
| *Break the Bank* | NBC | 1948–1956 |
| *Kay Kyser's Kollege of Musical Knowledge* | NBC | 1949–1950 |
| *Pantomime Quiz* | CBS, others | 1949–1959 |
| *Quiz Kids* | NBC, others | 1949–1953 |
| *Stop the Music* | ABC | 1949–1952 |
| *Winner Take All* | CBS | 1948–1952 |

bought the rights to his many old Cassidy movies and had no hesitation about showing them on television.

The areas of news and sports got off to a somewhat slow start. Regular network news shows commenced in 1948, when CBS tapped journalist Douglas Edwards (1917–1990) to be the anchor for *Douglas Edwards with the News,* a 15-minute summary that stations carried weekday evenings. Rival NBC followed suit in 1949 with John Cameron Swayze (1906–1995) and the *Camel News Caravan,* also a 15-minute production. The shows relied on filmed newsreel clips, but both Edwards and Swayze frequently had to read headlines directly from scripts without benefit of any pictures, either still or moving. *Meet the Press,* the longest-running show in the history of American television, preceded both Douglas and Swayze, making its debut in 1947. Created for radio by Martha Rountree (1911–1999), one of the few women prominent in early broadcasting, it easily made the transition to TV. Rountree served as the first moderator of *Meet the Press* until 1953. Its format of intensively interviewing a prominent guest has since been widely emulated. During the 1949–1950 season, CBS ran *Capitol Cloak Room,* another interview show that featured members of Congress.

Sports presented technical problems for the new medium. The bulky cameras of that era could not be easily maneuvered, so directors had to locate choice positions to cover a contest. The size of the playing fields required for **baseball** and **football** presented difficulties in giving viewers a sense of events. A baseball diamond forced cameras to be some distance from players, so what people saw on their screens tended to be tiny figures chasing a fly ball or equally tiny runners rounding the bases. Nevertheless, yearly television coverage of the World Series commenced in 1947 with NBC. The up-and-down field movement of football presented similar problems, and often viewers had no idea of who carried a ball until after a tackle or touchdown. No one even dreamed of instant replays in those early days. Not until the development of smaller, more portable cameras in the 1950s, along with better lenses and microphones, did the two sports begin to receive the coverage contemporary audiences expect.

Because they are limited to small, controlled areas, **boxing,** wrestling, and Roller Derbies enjoyed considerably more television coverage than they receive in more recent times. **Bowling** likewise could be found in some areas. A boxing ring or its wrestling equivalent needs only one or two cameras to cover virtually all the action up close. *Cavalcade of Sports* in 1946 began regular local broadcasts of Monday- and Friday-night boxing events from New York City. In 1948, the Gillette Safety Razor Company took it over, renaming it the *Gillette Cavalcade of Sports,* and broadcast the bouts over the NBC network. A popular show, it remained on the air until 1960, when questions about gambling and criminal influences in boxing forced NBC to drop it. The sponsor's tagline, "Look Sharp, Be Sharp" became one of the most familiar advertising themes of the time.

Serious professional wrestling, long a sport but never one followed by mass audiences, changed in the late 1940s. Thanks to the antics of George Wagner (1915–1963) and television, wrestling came into American homes because of the ease of capturing it for broadcasting. Wagner, a good but not outstanding wrestler, in the mid-1940s grew his hair long, dyed it blonde, and dubbed himself Gorgeous George. He would enter the ring, accompanied by valets who would spray perfume and disinfectant in order to "purify" the ring. He then proceeded to be an outrageous villain during the match, applying illegal holds, defying the referee, and deliberately playing to the crowd. He infuriated fans, caused small riots, and generally put professional wrestling on the entertainment (not sports) map. His notoriety convinced Hollywood to cast him in *Alias the Champ* (1949), one of the few wrestling movies ever made. More legitimate wrestlers, such as Lou Thesz (1916–2002), who held a variety of championships, became the "good guys," but they never generated the enthusiasm that Gorgeous George could whip up simply by climbing into the ring.

A **Roller Derby** likewise took place in a confined space, and, although watching skaters go around and around the track may sound boring, the pushing and shoving, jamming, tumbles, and pile-ups provided plenty of excitement, not unlike watching stock car racing today. A contact sport that traces it lineage back to the 1920s, Roller Derby started out as an endurance sport. Roller skaters tried to outlast the competition on a banked oval track. This arrangement carried over to early television, often with all-women teams competing. Spectacle, just as in professional wrestling, soon took over, and the more outrageous the collisions, the better fans liked it. As increasingly conventional viewing fare filled television schedules in the 1950s, both wrestling and Roller Derbies declined in viewership, although wrestling would stage a remarkable comeback some years later.

What some foresaw but many did not, television in its formative years resembled a sleeping giant that would soon awaken. As engineers worked on the technical challenges, creative people experimented with new formats designed for a small, black-and-white screen. Failures outnumbered successes, but the televised offerings grew, and in a short time it had eclipsed radio, until then the most successful purveyor of mass entertainment. In early 1949, fewer than 7 percent of American families owned a television receiver. Before the decade ended, however, TV sets could be found in about 10 percent of residences, while movie attendance and the hours spent listening to radio dropped sharply. The electronic giant, coming out of its slumber, would awaken fully soon thereafter, and the 1950s marked a time of unparalleled growth. For much of the rest of the 20th century, television showed few signs of slowing down.

*See also:* Advertising; Broadway Shows (Comedy and Drama); Broadway Shows (Musicals); Comedies (Film), Costume and Spectacle Films; Crosley Automobiles; Radio Programming: Drama and Anthology Shows; Radio Programming: Educational Shows; Radio Programming: News, Sports, Public Affairs, and Talk; Radio Programming: Quiz Shows; Skating (Roller); Westerns (Films)

**Selected Reading**
Barnouw, Erik. *Tube of Plenty: The Evolution of American Television.* New York: Oxford University Press, 1982.
Greenfield, Jeff. *Television: The First Fifty Years.* New York: Harry N. Abrams, 1977.
Reiser, J. W. "Whatever Happened to Channel 1?" www.tech-notes.tv/ [go to "History and Trivia" at the site to find this article]
Sterling, Christopher H., and John M. Kitross. *Stay Tuned: A Concise History of American Broadcasting.* Belmont, CA: Wadsworth, 1990.

# TENNIS

During the 1940s, the sports sections of **newspapers** regularly carried stories about amateur tennis championship titles won by players such as Pauline Betz (b. 1919),

Don Budge (1915–2000), Jack Kramer (1921-2009), and Bobby Riggs (1918–1995). Some of the more successful amateurs turned professional and, in attempts to promote the game, gain spectators, and advance their careers, made exhibition tours across the country. Despite these activities, many Americans adhered to a perception of tennis as a game for the wealthy played on country club or private courts, not something to pay money to see or take up as a sport.

Some aspects of life in the United States, however, gradually increased the availability of the game and expanded interest. Thanks to building programs initiated by the New Deal, the number of tennis courts provided to the public at municipal and county parks grew from just under 8,400 in 1930 to 12,075 in 1940. World War II slowed construction, and 10 years later they had only grown to a little over 13,000 courts.

Shortly after the country entered the conflict in 1941, government officials became concerned about the large number of recruits who failed the physical fitness entry requirements. **President Franklin Delano Roosevelt** (1882–1945) directed the Federal Security Agency (FSA), which included the Board of Social Security, Public Health Service, Food and Drug Administration, Office of Education, and a number of other bureaus, to initiate a campaign to correct the situation. The plan called for better nutrition for all Americans and asked schools and community centers to strengthen their physical **education** programs and engage more **youth** and adults in individual and team sports. Despite these efforts, for tennis, it would not be until the arrival of televised matches in the 1950s that the game began to attracted significant numbers of players from various economic backgrounds.

Those individuals wanting to play and dedicate considerable time pursuing tennis fell into two groups, amateurs and professionals, with each having an organization governing its activities. The United States Lawn Tennis Association (founded in 1881 and later renamed the United States Tennis Association, or USTA) represents amateur players. The Professional Lawn Tennis Association (founded in 1927 and now known as the Professional Tennis Association) serves a membership of professional tennis coaches and players.

Over the years, a recurring discussion between the two groups centered on the question of whether to continue to preserve the system that prevented amateurs and professionals from playing in the same tournaments. Jack Kramer, an active promoter of professional tennis, advocated open tennis, which would remove the restrictions. The regulation, however, held throughout the 1940s; not until 1968 did an open U.S. system come into existence, thereby giving tennis greater visibility and increased acceptance by the public.

A handful of U.S. players, both professional and amateur, still managed to became celebrities. For example, amateur Bill Tilden (1893–1953) achieved fame when he dominated the game in the 1920s, winning the men's singles title for six consecutive years, 1922 to 1927. He turned professional in 1931. Likewise, a woman, Alice Marble (1913–1990), received publicity because she ranked in the world's top 10 for four straight years, 1936 to 1939. She became a professional player in 1940.

The biggest news about tennis players occurred in 1938, when Don Budge, an amateur, made history as the first man to capture all four major tournaments considered the Grand Slam of tennis: the Australian Open, the French Open, Wimbledon, and the United States National Championships (today known as the U.S. Open). Budge joined the professional ranks in 1939 and toured the United States in 1941 with Bill Tilden. Their matches drew decent crowds and the much younger Budge easily won almost all of their 58 events.

As happened with many sporting activities, the armed forces took male players away from the game to fight in the war, thus limiting most amateur playing and completely suspending professional matches. Officials canceled the Australian and French Opens and Wimbledon. The United States, however, continued to hold both the men's and women's national amateur championship matches at Forest Hills, New York, with only U.S. individuals participating. Even with the return of players from other countries after the conflict, Americans took the U.S. title every year.

Among the most famous players of the time, Kramer joined the Coast Guard and Budge entered the Army Air Force. Once in the service, an athletic injury greatly interfered with Budge's playing but did not stop him from participating in exhibition matches that brought the game to many soldiers for the first time, and possibly served as an inspiration for some to learn the game.

Three men—Frank Parker, Jack Kramer, and Pancho Gonzales—not only won the U.S. National title, but each did so for two years in a row. All three continued to accumulate other victories in the succeeding years. Parker captured the French championships in 1948 and 1949. Gonzales turned professional in 1950 and reigned as the world's No. 1 player for eight consecutive years in the late 1950s and early 1960s.

Kramer had been on the winning U.S. National Doubles team in 1940, 1941, and 1943. At Wimbledon, he walked away with the men's doubles trophy in 1946 and 1947 and won the singles championship in 1947. He declared himself a pro in 1948 and embarked with Bobby Riggs (1918–1995) upon a national tour, which started in New York at Madison Square Garden. Despite a severe snowstorm, the match drew a large crowd. Riggs, a tennis star in his own right and a pro since 1942, had held U.S. amateur titles and a win at Wimbledon. Kramer easily beat Riggs on the tour, winning 69 out of 89 matches. All told, they grossed a healthy $383,000 (almost $3.5 million in 2008 dollars).

Whatever the American public might have felt about the appropriateness of women playing competitively, 1887 saw the first United States Women's National Singles

TABLE 96. United States Men's and Women's National Singles Champions, 1940–1949

| Year | Men's Winners | Women's Winners |
| --- | --- | --- |
| 1940 | Donald McNeill (1918–1996) | Alice Marble |
| 1941 | Bobby Riggs | Sarah Palfrey Cooke (1912–1996) |
| 1942 | Ted Schroeder (1921–2006) | Pauline Betz |
| 1943 | Joseph Hunt (1919–1945) | Pauline Betz |
| 1944 | Frank Parker (1916–1997) | Pauline Betz |
| 1945 | Frank Parker | Sarah Palfrey Cooke |
| 1946 | Jack Kramer | Pauline Betz |
| 1947 | Jack Kramer | Louise Brough Clapp (b. 1923) |
| 1948 | Pancho Gonzales (1928–1995) | Margaret Osborne duPont (b. 1918) |
| 1949 | Pancho Gonzales | Margaret Osborne duPont |

Championship matches, just six years after the inauguration of the title for men. Women's play continued uninterrupted, and, in the 1940s, the winners, as did their male counterparts, enjoyed headlines in the newspapers. USLTA ranked Pauline Betz in the world's top 10 women players for 1939 through 1946 and she topped the list from 1942 to 1944 and again in 1946. She won Wimbledon the only time she entered, in 1946, without losing a set. Betz appeared on the cover of *Time* magazine, along with a lengthy article on September 2, 1946, just days before she won her fourth U.S. title at Forest Hills. She became the only tennis player of either gender so honored during the 1940s by the magazine. In 1947, Betz turned pro; she and Sarah Palfrey Cooke toured the United States playing matches but earning far less than their male counterparts. For their efforts, they took home approximately $10,000 each (about $96,500 in 2008 dollars).

Also earning a reputation in the field of tennis, Cooke became the second mother to be a U.S. singles winner. She also appeared on a top-level men's championship list in 1945. Because the war caused a shortage of male players, officials allowed her to team with her husband, Elwood Cooke (1913–2004), a successful tennis player during the 1930s and 1940s, to play in a men's doubles tournament. They came in second.

Margaret Osborne DuPont ranked in the world's top 10 women players for 1946 through 1950 (rankings were not issued for 1940–1945). In addition to her U.S. women's singles victories in the 1940s, she won again in 1950. She also came in first at the French Open in 1946 and 1949 and at Wimbledon in 1947, giving her a total of six Grand Slam singles championships.

In addition to the skillful play of its champions, U.S. tennis offered some moments of sensationalism. One player, Gertrude Moran (b. 1923), better known as Gorgeous Gussie, became the fourth-ranked player in the world in 1949. At the time, she also shocked the tennis establishment and world by showing up at Wimbledon to play at center court in a short tennis dress that revealed ruffled lace panties along with a sweater that flattered her feminine physique. Moran may have lost the match, but she attracted attention and turned pro in 1950.

Hollywood acknowledged tennis only slightly. No feature-length **movies** of the 1940s dealt with the game per se, but four documentaries did focus on top-ranking players, and one offered lessons in the game. Warner Bros. Pictures highlighted Bill Tilden's career in a 1941 short titled *Big Bill Tilden*. Columbia Pictures countered in 1942 in its Columbia World of Sports with *Tennis Rhythm with Bobby Riggs,* a review of his career during his prime. The studio also produced a sports reel titled *Tennis Wizards* in 1947 that features Bobby Riggs and Don Budge talking about and demonstrating how to play the game. Paramount offered *Queens of the Court* (1946) in a *Grantland Rice Spotlight* with top players such as Pauline Betz, Sarah Palfrey Cooke, Margaret Osborne duPont, and others.

**Cartoons** deemed tennis worthy of being the brunt of some humor. *Tennis Racquet* (1949) has two Goofys playing a match amid much confusion. In *Tennis Chumps* (1949), Tom and Jerry take up the sport, and Tom's game suffers serious trouble in light of his opponent's (another cat) skills. Jerry the mouse, who has been carrying Tom's equipment, which includes a killer ball, saves the match for him.

Movie stars also got in the act, with *Life* magazine periodically running pictures of those who played. The January 1, 1940, issue shows Ava Gardner (1922–1990) leaping over the net, and Claudette Colbert (1903–1996) appears in the January 1, 1945, copy, smiling as she holds her tennis racket, ready for a match.

Tennis gained some popularity as a spectator sport following World War II. Recreational play gradually increased, but a significant change in the number of public courts did not occur until 1965, when the count reached almost 20,000. Country clubs continued as popular places for playing. For ambitious amateurs and professionals, the 1954 establishment of the International Tennis Hall of Fame in Newport, Rhode Island, offered an opportunity for official recognition of the best players.

*See also:* Fashion; Food; Leisure and Recreation; Magazines; Race Relations and Stereotyping; Television

**Selected Reading**
Baker, William J. *Sports in the Western World.* Totowa, NJ: Rowman and Littlefield, 1982.
Grimsley, Will. *Tennis: Its History, People, and Events.* Englewood Cliffs, NJ: Prentice Hall, 1971.

# *TERRY AND THE PIRATES* (MILTON CANIFF)

The name given a popular comic strip of the 1930s and 1940s, it broke new ground in the areas of content and drawing. Cartoonist Milton Caniff (1907–1988) created *Terry* in 1934. Prior to that, he drew a fantasy series called *Dickie Dare,* stories about a boy who dreams of adventures with heroes from the past. Caniff eventually dropped the dream sequences in favor of having Dickie accompany "Dynamite Dan" Flynn, an adult soldier of fortune, for more realistic escapades.

The 1930s marked the heyday of action-adventure **comic strips,** with popular titles like *Dick Tracy, Jungle Jim, Red Barry, Scorchy Smith,* and many others adorning the funny pages of U.S. **newspapers.** But *Dickie Dare,* awkward in its drawing and pedestrian in its plotting, enjoyed at best modest success. Caniff's luck changed in 1934, when Captain Joseph Medill Patterson (1879–1946) asked him to create a new strip set in the exotic Far East. A legend in comics circles for his unerring eye in discovering new talents, Patterson headed the Chicago Tribune–New York News Syndicate and strove to hire the best cartoonists for its staff.

When approached by Patterson, Caniff decided to set the stories in China and came up with a youthful hero he named Tommy Tucker and a companion called Pat Ryan, a "two-fisted adventurer." Patterson rejected the childlike name Tommy Tucker and suggested Terry Lee in its place. Always looking for a gimmick, Patterson proposed that the pair become involved with Asian pirates, thus the title, *Terry and the Pirates.* Together with an array of villains, usually bandits, evil warlords, or rogue military units instead of actual pirates, George Webster "Connie" Confucius plays a stereotyped Chinese who dresses oddly, speaks in strange aphorisms, and butchers the English language. Connie serves as a sidekick of Terry and Pat, but more for comic relief than for advancing any plots. For the period, however, such demeaning characterizations of racial minorities, especially Asians, appeared in many comic strips. The old image of the "Yellow Peril" had not died out, especially as war with Japan loomed, and variants abounded, from Charlie Chan to Fu Manchu.

At first, the new strip closely resembled *Dickie Dare,* but it quickly took on its own personality. By the end of the decade, Terry has grown into a young man capable of independent action. And Pat Ryan, who stood in for and resembled Dan Flynn, plays less of a role while Terry's importance increases. As the series matured, so did Caniff's drawing style. From simple line drawings, he mastered brushing in large areas of black ink that gave his work a distinctive chiaroscuro effect. This use of shadow, reminiscent of cinematic techniques, added atmosphere, especially suspense, for heightened story lines. His characters also evolved from simple cartoons to realistic figures, especially glamorous women, which soon became a specialty of his. Within a short time, *Terry* began to separate itself visually from most other action-adventure series of the era.

The popularity and circulation of *Terry and the Pirates* grew throughout the decade, and the stories take on strong topical overtones in the late 1930s. Japan launched a full-scale invasion of China in 1937, a prelude to World War II. The United States professed neutrality toward the worsening Asian problem, a situation that forced **movies, radio** shows, and other popular media outlets to more or less follow suit. In *Terry*'s case, this meant calling the Japanese the "invaders," but no doubt exists in regard to their true identity.

As the 1940s opened, war raged in Europe, and the far eastern locale that Captain Patterson had presciently suggested gained increasing attention. The "pirates" of the title disappear, and *Terry and the Pirates* moves resolutely toward war. When the United State finally has to enter the conflict in December 1941, Terry Lee—suddenly more mature than before—stands poised to fight not "invaders" but the Axis powers, especially Japan. In October 1942, he enlists in the Army Air Force, and *Terry and the Pirates* becomes one of the most earnest and patriotic of all strips. One year later, Terry has his wings, and his commanding officer, Colonel Flip Corkin, gives him an eloquent talk on duty, responsibilities, and teamwork. This memorable Sunday panel touched so many readers that it has been widely reprinted and entered in full in *The Congressional Record,* the only instance of a comic strip being so honored.

During the war years, the adventures lose some of their exotic, picaresque (a favorite term of Caniff's) qualities, becoming more military in their themes. Since Terry has become a pilot, many of the stories involve airplanes, aerial combat, and life in the Air Force. The freckle-faced Hotshot Charlie, or Chazz, another pilot, becomes an important character but at the expense of some of the more romantic and mysterious figures from the 1930s. *Terry* remained one of the best strips of the 1940s, but it mellowed, as had the cast, and it lacked some of the zest that had characterized its earlier days.

Caniff also found he had a flair for drawing beautiful, sensuous women, and never more so than in his seductive Dragon Lady. This enigmatic character reappears throughout the strip's run, usually as a femme fatale, and she plays the role to the hilt. Readers might never be really sure whose side this temptress represents, but they know she will lead most of the men she encounters to no good. Even innocent Terry occasionally falls into her clutches, although she usually takes sympathy on him. With her presence, sex entered the usually sexless comics.

Along that line, in 1943 Caniff began drawing a special weekly series for distribution only to the armed forces. Called *Male Call,* it consisted mainly of pinups of attractive women, although its lead character, aptly called Miss Lace because of her usual attire, gave the cartoons a form of continuity. Immensely popular, *Male Call* ran until 1946, and its cheesecake endeared Caniff with a generation of servicemen from all military branches.

When the war ended, and with *Terry* boasting strong circulation among subscribing newspapers, Caniff announced he was dropping the strip and moving to a competing syndicate. Contrary to common belief, cartoonists as a rule do not own their creations; they work as employees of a syndicate, which normally owns the copyrights to any strips it carries. By leaving the Tribune-News group at the end of 1946, Caniff knowingly surrendered *Terry and the Pirates*. He moved to Chicago's Field Enterprises and, at the beginning of 1947, introduced *Steve Canyon,* a new series featuring an Air Force veteran in his apparent thirties, an urbane, grown-up version of Terry Lee with a roguish wink in his eye. It would run until 1988 and enjoyed considerable popularity during most of that interval.

Despite an artist's departure or death, successful comic strips seldom disappear; the original syndicate brings in a successor and the series goes on. In the case of *Terry and the Pirates,* George Wunder (1912–1987), a former sports cartoonist and a veteran of World War II, took over the drawing and writing of the comic strip. Never Caniff's equal in either artwork or storytelling, Wunder nevertheless did a workmanlike job with *Terry,* moving from imitation to eventually giving it a new and distinctive look. He would spend more years with the series than Caniff and kept it running until 1973. During much of his tenure, he has Terry and his friends battling Communists, a reflection of the **Cold War** in the aftermath of World War II. Most followers of *Terry and the Pirates,* however, have always thought of the strip as Caniff's alone, and they tend to look on Wunder as a kind of apprentice hired to fill in for the master.

The strip's exotic Far East locale and muted references to ongoing events matched up well with the radio serials of the day. *Terry and the Pirates* received a late afternoon slot—the preferred time for most adventure serials on radio—with NBC (National Broadcasting Company) in 1937. It premiered on the air in November and continued until 1948; despite a crowded field, it brought a dash of realism to serial programming. But the adult dialogue and situations of the newspaper comic strip never transferred with complete success to radio, and Terry Lee seemed more an imitation of such juvenile favorites as Jack Armstrong.

In 1940, Columbia Pictures produced a 15-part movie serial that shared little more than its title with the comic strip. William Tracy (1917–1967) plays Terry, and Jeff York (1912–1995) takes the role of Pat Ryan. But cheap production values and little attempt to build characterizations mire the effort in mediocrity. Twelve years later, *Terry and the Pirates* reappeared on **television** in a syndicated series that lasted about a dozen episodes. John Baer (1923–2006) took Terry's part, and William Tracy, too old now to play the young hero, reappeared as Hotshot Charlie, Terry's buddy.

Milton Caniff served as a significant innovator for newspaper comics in a variety of ways. He discovered he had a gift for rapid-fire, snappy dialogue, something that allowed him to place wisecracks and one-liners throughout the speech balloons. No matter how desperate the situation, someone will utter a flippant remark at the height of the tension. *Terry* never ceases being an action strip, but one with a humorous edge. Unique for its time, the strip touches on current events of the era. Caniff's cinematic eye advanced comic art, and his drawing skills, especially with the use of large areas of black, changed the appearance of American comic strips.

*See also:* Aviation; Race Relations and Stereotyping; Radio Programming: Children's Shows, Serials, and Adventure Series; Serial Films; Youth

**Selected Reading**
Goulart, Ron. *The Adventurous Decade: Comic Strips in the Thirties.* New Rochelle, NY: Arlington House, 1975.
Marschall, Richard. *America's Great Comic-Strip Artists.* New York: Stewart, Tabori & Chang, 1997.
Walker, Brian. *The Comics before 1945.* New York: Harry N. Abrams, 2004.
———. *The Comics since 1945.* New York: Harry N. Abrams, 2002.

## *TEXACO STAR THEATER* (MILTON BERLE)

On September 21, 1948, still the early days of American **television** broadcasting, NBC (National Broadcasting Company) unveiled a new variety show for which it held high hopes. Texaco (The Texas Company), a large oil firm whose gasoline bears the corporate name, sponsored NBC's offering. The producers chose an energetic **radio** comedian named Milton Berle (1908–2002) to headline and host the proceedings.

As was the custom then, sponsors did not merely place spot advertisements along with commercials from others during the running of a show, they often wielded a heavy hand in the planning, content, casting—even the time slot when it aired—of a production. They owned the entire show, all 15, 30, or 60 minutes of it, and their name in the title often took precedence over anything else, even the stars. Thus, the *Camel Caravan,* the *Chesterfield Supper Club,* the *Colgate Comedy Hour,* the *Ford Theater,* the *Kraft Music Hall,* the *Voice of Firestone,* and many other TV shows bore a corporate or product name, and the sponsor enjoyed top billing. A carryover from radio (e.g., *The Chase and Sanborn Hour, The Jell-O Program, The Maxwell House Show Boat, The Royal Gelatin Hour*), this practice would gradually end during the 1950s. Sponsors instead bought time on a network and seldom exerted the level of control seen in the 1940s.

Raised in New York City, Berle (ne Berlinger) made his professional debut in 1914 as a child actor in silent films. Urged on by his mother, he appeared on stage in a traveling show when just 12 years of age. Berle soon thereafter began to perform as a comedian in vaudeville. By the early 1930s, with vaudeville on the wane, he moved to nightclubs and radio and found himself in demand as a guest comic on various variety shows. Quick-witted and possessed of a vast mental storehouse of jokes and one-liners at his command, he worked steadily in the medium and eventually got a radio show of his own in 1947. Philip Morris cigarettes underwrote *The Milton Berle Show* on NBC from 1947 to 1948. Although it failed to ignite strong audience interest, his radio show would serve as a stepping-stone to the *Texaco Star Theater.*

Beginning in the late 1930s and continuing until the end of the 1940s, variations on the *Texaco Star Theater* played on network radio. In 1938, the first *Texaco Star Theater* made its debut on CBS (Columbia Broadcasting System); it then went through a series of changes in hosts, formats, and networks until March 1948, when **ABC (American Broadcasting Company)** acquired the property. At first, no one person dominated, and a rotating schedule of singers, dancers, and comics appeared. This version of the show remained on radio until the summer of 1949—less than a year—but it launched Berle's career, not as a radio celebrity but as a television star. For a brief period of time, September 1948 to June 1949, Berle actually held down two jobs, and both with the *Texaco Star Theater*. Because television was still in its infancy, he hedged his bets by remaining with the ABC radio broadcasts, while polishing his TV image on the new NBC show. He need not have worried; Milton Berle, overnight, became the hottest star on television.

Radio exists as an aural medium, and no matter how physically animated a performer may be or how clownish his or her costume, the audience cannot see any of that. Sound effects may give a hint of on-stage antics but little more. Television, on the other hand, provides the images to accompany the sound. And Berle's comedic gift shone in slapstick, something he had mastered in his vaudeville experiences. Many radio stars found it difficult to make the transition to TV; they were used to talking into a microphone and doing little else, invisible to their listeners. Before the unblinking eye of a television camera, they often appeared awkward and wooden. Not so Berle.

Radio had confined the comedian, making him reliant on his wealth of jokes and little else. The camera, however, freed him. As he approached his stride on the *Texaco Star Theater*, Berle clearly considered no costume too outlandish, no stunt too foolish. The jokes and one-liners continued also, but his routines relied on their visual aspects; his gags became sight gags, a return to the vaudeville humor of years earlier. A kid with a new toy, Berle explored the possibilities of television comedy with glee.

In no time at all, the *Texaco Star Theater* dominated the ratings for Tuesday nights. The show aired at 8:00 p.m., EST, and Berle owned the hour. He called himself Uncle Milty, but fans dubbed him Mr. Television, the first superstar of the young medium. Texaco continued to sponsor the show, delighted that it continued as the No. 1 viewing attraction. The ratings wavered slightly in the fall of 1951, and Berle cut down slightly on his hectic schedule. In 1953, Texaco dropped Berle, but Buick

*During the 1940s, comedian Milton Berle struggled to establish his career on radio, but the advent of commercial television changed his fortunes. He became one of the first major stars on the new medium, and the* Texaco Star Theater, *a comedy-variety show, provided him a vehicle to fame. He wears one of his trademark zany costumes in this 1948 picture. (NBC/Photofest)*

Motors quickly picked up his contract, calling the production *The Buick-Berle Show*. It lasted two years, and then he had his own *Milton Berle Show* beginning in 1955. More changes followed, but Mr. Television remained a strong presence on American TV for the next several decades. He also appeared on Broadway and resumed acting in a number of **movies.**

*See also:* Advertising; Broadway Shows (Comedy and Drama); Broadway Shows: Musicals: Comedies (Film); Radio Programming: Music and Variety Shows; *Toast of the Town* (Ed Sullivan)

**Selected Reading**
Berle, Milton, with Haskell Frankel. *Milton Berle: An Autobiography.* New York: Delacorte Press, 1974.
Dunning, John. *On the Air: The Encyclopedia of Old-Time Radio.* New York: Oxford University Press, 1998.

## *TOAST OF THE TOWN* (ED SULLIVAN)

In June 1948, CBS (Columbia Broadcasting System) **television** welcomed a new variety show to its Sunday evening lineup, calling its offering *Toast of the Town*. It would soon become a television staple, running until June 1971. During its remarkable 23-year tenure, New York *Daily News* columnist Ed Sullivan (1901–1974) served as its one and only host. In its first year, the show appeared on home screens from 9:00 p.m. to 10:00 p.m. EST, but then shifted to its more familiar 8:00 p.m. to 9:00 p.m. slot in 1949, a position it retained until its 1971 cancellation. For most of that time, the Lincoln-Mercury division of the Ford Motor Company sponsored *Toast of the Town*.

Sullivan had begun his professional career as a newspaper reporter, first as a sports writer at several small dailies. He moved to the New York *Evening Graphic* in 1927 and eventually replaced Walter Winchell (1897–1972) as the paper's gossip columnist. During the 1930s, he moved to the New York *Daily News*, where he wrote a Broadway theater column. This position gave him considerable renown in New York's entertainment circles, and he gained experience as a **radio** emcee at various

Long-time newspaper columnist Ed Sullivan served as host of Toast of the Town *from 1948 to 1971, an unusually long run for a television show of any kind. Stiff and seemingly awkward while on camera, Sullivan showcased an endless variety of entertainers, from old vaudeville acts to the latest teen sensations. This picture captures Sullivan in a characteristic pose. (CBS/Photofest)*

events and even hosted several short-lived shows of his own. Hardly a household name outside the city, he moved into the relatively new world of television in 1948, when CBS tapped him to host its planned revue for prime time broadcasting.

Seemingly wooden in the glare of the TV cameras, shoulders back, arms stiff at his sides or tightly crossed, and with a curious, hesitant manner of speaking, Sullivan quickly became the butt of countless impressionists, and it all served to endear him to a growing public. With his wide range of acquaintances in show business, Sullivan and his staff knew how to make contact with celebrities. But he also had an eye for unknown performers, and so *Toast of the Town* gained a reputation for offering a true mix of troupers. He might schedule a concert pianist, followed by a trained dog act; from there a popular vocal group, possibly some jugglers, and maybe a ballerina would take the stage. The show perhaps could wind it down with slapstick comedians and the resident June Taylor Dancers. In the early years (1940s to 1950s), the producers featured 6 or 7 acts; later (1960s onward), the number grew to 11 or 12; either way, the show seldom suffered a dull moment.

In many respects, *Toast of the Town* resembled nothing so much as an old-time vaudeville revue. One unrelated act followed another, with everything occurring at a rapid pace, so if one performance did not appeal, perhaps the next one would. Sullivan stressed diversity at all times, and no particular theme or idea linked the entertainers on stage. The host himself, a man of few words, would briefly, often awkwardly, introduce each successive act—"right here, on our stage"—with no patter, no insider jokes, and then step away. But the audiences—both those at CBS's TV Studio 50, a venerable theater in Manhattan and the show's home for its entire run, and those at home—came to expect and enjoy this format. Although the glory days of *Toast of the Town* lay in the decades following the 1940s, Sullivan had become such an integral part of the production that the network renamed it *The Ed Sullivan Show* in the fall of 1955.

As television in its formative years strove to find the best ways to attract audiences, variety shows proliferated. That format had been successful on radio—*The Rudy Vallee Show,* which ran from 1929 to 1939, serves as a good example—and much early television owes a debt to the medium. But although many variety shows came along in the late 1940s and early 1950s, none could ever replicate the formula that Ed Sullivan and his staff created with *Toast of the Town* in 1948.

*See also:* Advertising; Automobiles and the American Automotive Industry; Broadway Shows (Comedy and Drama); Broadway Shows (Musicals); Newspapers; *Texaco Star Theater* (Milton Berle)

**Selected Reading**
Bowles, Jerry. *A Thousand Sundays: The Story of the Ed Sullivan Show.* New York: Putnam, 1980.
Harris, Michael David. *Always on Sundays: Ed Sullivan, An Inside View.* New York: Meredith, 1980.
Maguire, James. *Impresario: The Life and Times of Ed Sullivan.* New York: Billboard Books, 2006.

# TOYS

Children living during World War II might not have comprehended all of the ramifications of the United States' involvement in the conflict, but they certainly knew that something had happened with many of their favorite toys. Some could no longer be found in department stores, while others continued to be plentiful but greatly changed in materials and appearance.

Prior to 1940, cast-iron toys ranked as favorites, and the Hubley Manufacturing Company prided itself as the world's largest manufacturer of them. The firm supplied children with a wide variety of trains, fire and circus wagons, trucks, cars, motorcycles, cap pistols, and dollhouse kitchen appliances. In mid-1942, however, after a half-year of U.S. participation in the war, production of all toys utilizing metal and rubber in their manufacture ceased, an event that created a time of no more new cast-iron items, such as tin windups, tricycles, steel wagons and trucks, metal cap pistols, ice skates, roller skates, sleds with metal runners, even balloons and rubber squeak toys.

These wartime restrictions, along with a scarcity of workers, meant hard times for most toy manufacturers. Some closed their plants, while others such as Hubley, Lionel Trains, Auburn Rubber Company, Grey Iron, Fisher-Price, Manoil, and Marx retrofitted to make a wide range of war-related products including gaskets, torpedo and bomb racks, fuses for explosives, ship fenders, first-aid kits, cots, bomb crates, shell casings, pistol grips, gun plugs, and parts for hand grenades.

Adults nevertheless believed that, no matter how dire the conditions, kids needed playthings, and several toy manufacturers quickly retooled to try to make exciting toys out of wood, plastic, cardboard, and papier mâché. The wooden ones could be described as crude and lacking in detail, cardboard and papier mâché as always fragile, and plastic as brittle. But, whenever these kinds of toys appeared on store shelves, they quickly sold despite their drawbacks.

The Moline Pressed Steel Company, with its Buddy "L" line, had led the industry in pressed-steel toys; with the restrictions, it offered pine station wagons, taxicabs, Greyhound buses, and Coca-Cola trucks. After the war, the company returned to its pressed-steel toys, but ultimately cheaper plastic ones surpassed both wood and steel in demand.

Built-Rite Toys turned out cardboard items that tended to be more attractive than wooden toys. Airports, railroad stations, and forts just the right size for the five-and-dime tin soldiers bought before the war, as well as cardboard dollhouses and furniture, proved popular. Complete army fighting units, also made of cardboard, became available in 1942. Once cut out and assembled, children could use the soldiers, officers, various vehicles, weapons, bombs, and flags, all in camouflage, to replicate battles being reported on the news.

But World War II did not mean difficulties for all toy companies, as exemplified by the 1941 founding of Molded Products. The father-son team of Leslie S. Steinau and Leslie S. Steinau Jr. (both active 1940s), working in **advertising,** correctly anticipated that the war would create a shortage in consumer goods with a corresponding lack of advertising. Mindful of needing to be employed, they turned to toy making; by 1942, their Molded Products worked at full capacity manufacturing soldiers out of wood flour, starch, whiting, and water. Despite crude designs that lacked detail and a tendency to dissolve in water, the scale matched that of the prewar tin soldiers, making them a desirable purchase. One year later, another company, Transogram, also offered similar soldiers but made from wood flour, 20 Mule Team Borax, water, and unbleached white flour. Both types sold well.

*Home run king Babe Ruth dons a Santa suit in 1940 and gives out toys to good little girls and boys. Sports and entertainment celebrities frequently participated in various promotions built around the Christmas holidays (Photofest)*

In the late 1930s and early 1940s, several firms offered simple lead casting kits. The owner could melt lead bars, often in a small electric furnace that the manufacturer provided, pour the liquid lead into heated molds, and, when cool, three-dimensional lead soldiers or small artillery pieces resulted. Because of shortages, the government banned the commercial sale of lead in 1942. The kits made a comeback in the postwar years, but growing concerns about safety and the toxicity of lead sharply dampened sales.

With the exception of lead items, children, especially boys, enjoyed a tremendous selection of military-oriented toys in addition to as many miniature soldiers as they could afford. Tanks, armored cars, howitzers, destroyers, battleships, and submarines dotted merchants' shelves. And for a staged battle in an empty lot, full-size imitation pistols and rifles of all types were readily available, ranging from cheap replicas of side arms to detailed machine guns with ratchet mechanisms to suggest the rat-a-tat-tat of the real thing. Despite all the shortages of materials, manufacturers somehow found what they needed for the toy arsenal, plus everyone thought it patriotic that boys could play soldier and annihilate the country's enemies in the space of an afternoon.

After 1945 and the return of peace, the toy military hardware did not entirely disappear. The most famous battles of the recent war—Normandy, Iwo Jima, Salerno, Okinawa—could always be fought once more while still fresh in people's memories;

plus the old standbys, cowboys and Indians, found a new generation of cowpokes toting shiny plastic six-shooters, flimsy bows and arrows, and costumes complete with boots, chaps, holsters, and a small Stetson hat or a feathered headdress. These getups attracted hordes of youngsters and proved enduring favorites in the postwar era.

Three toy companies—the Holgate Toy Company, dating back to 1789; the Playskool Manufacturing Company, established in 1928; and Fisher-Price, incorporated in 1930—had led in research and development of wooden educational toys throughout the 1930s. Many of their toys sold in the early 1940s, such as Holgate's Bingo Bed and Playskool's wooden mailbox, which had been designed to develop eye-hand coordination or to teach about certain areas of employment. In 1941, even before the United States entered the conflict, Holgate sold toy army vehicles, but the company discontinued them after 1945. Playskool bought the J. L. Wright Company in 1943 and thereby added Lincoln Logs to its inventory. Fisher-Price decided to manufacture war-related items but, during the first half of the decade, also turned out a limited number of wooden toys, such as Granny Doodle and Doctor Doodle ducks.

Model kits fulfilled many of the goals of educational play and had become a significant endeavor by 1940. Although model making dates back to antiquity, it boomed in the 1930s. The Strombeck-Becker Company (founded in 1911) in 1934 introduced the novel idea of assembling and painting your own toy using kits for trains seen at the recent Century of Progress Exposition held in Chicago. They expanded to airplane kits with the China Clipper in 1936. To stimulate interest in model building, the company organized a club and awarded young builders with badges denoting skill levels based on the number of kits completed. A huge success, 1940 catalogs from StromBecker Toys offered precut wooden model kits for airplanes, navy warships, artillery, and trains.

The company drastically cut back on production of its kits during the war in order to provide wooden items for the government. Strombecker, along with two other model airplane companies, Comet and Megow, created simple kits to aid in the training of recognition of different planes and ships by those serving in military units. At the conclusion of the war, StromBecker embarked on a business plan for a full line of new and updated assembly kits, especially those that replicated the many military airplanes flown in World War II. Initially, however, the firm also continued to offer several of its prewar kits while gearing up for new lines.

Future architects, engineers, and scientists could while away long afternoons designing and building all manner of structures and devices with products made available by several long-established manufacturers. On a basic level, Tinkertoys, introduced in 1913, but popular ever since, remained available throughout World War II, since wood constituted all of the components. Similarly, Lincoln Logs, which had made their initial appearance in 1916, utilized wood for their traditional round, notched logs and allowed young builders to construct cabins, forts, farm houses, and the like. A direct competitor, Roy Toys' Log Building Sets, which debuted in the mid-1930s, boasted square-cut logs and claimed greater stability than their round counterparts. American Bricks, wooden bricks that could be arranged and stacked to form buildings, provided another construction favorite. Originally marketed by Halsam Products Company of Chicago in the 1930s, the red-stained brick continued to be turned out throughout the war years and had great popularity. In the late 1940s, Halsam turned to plastic for its bricks.

But the biggest building and construction sellers of them all were the Erector Sets manufactured by the A. C. Gilbert Company. Based on the actual building methods employed in modern skyscrapers, Erector Sets gave their owners hundreds of metal pieces that looked like the girders found on any large construction site. Tiny nuts and bolts joined these pieces in endless patterns, limited only by one's imagination. Because they employed steel and aluminum almost exclusively, virtually unavailable during the war, Erector Set sales surged in the postwar era. Gilbert, a primary source for technologically and scientifically oriented toy kits, also sold simple microscopes, along with chemistry, physics, and electricity sets. The company also carried the highly realistic American Flyer train sets.

The toy market did not ignore girls, despite its intense focus on military items. Fortunately, the war did not interrupt the production of paper dolls, although they came to consumers made from inferior stock. This popular toy has been around as long as there has been paper and artists to apply images to it. Starting in the early 1900s, women's and children's **magazines** made paper dolls readily available to a large number of children in the United States by including cut-out paper dolls on their pages. In the 1940s, such dolls continued to appear in **newspapers** and magazines, especially the popular children's periodical *Jack and Jill*. **Comic books** moved beyond the subjects of adventure and heroes to appeal to a growing girls' market by including paper doll pages.

Walt Disney characters and historical and folk figures frequently served as models for paper dolls. In 1941, Blondie, from the comic strip of the same name, joined other comic strip characters like Dick Tracy, Daisy Mae, and Li'l Abner in this medium. Many Hollywood movie stars and other celebrities also appeared, and children's publishing companies such as Whitman and Merrill issued paper doll books.

Traditional dolls and stuffed animals stand out as classic toys that have crossed all generations; because they utilized nonstrategic materials, the war affected them less than it did some other toys. The demands of the draft, however, created sudden shortages of workers that caused production difficulties. Companies such as Ideal Toy Company and Dream World nevertheless continued to manufacture dolls based on famous Hollywood stars such as Shirley Temple (b. 1928), Judy Garland (1922–1969), **Carmen Miranda** (1909–1955), and Rita Hayworth (1918–1987). Molly'es International Doll Company, famous for its Raggedy Ann and Raggedy Andy cloth dolls, presented dolls in 1940 based on characters found in the popular United Artists movie, *The Thief of Bagdad*.

Vogue Dolls, Inc., founded in 1922, issued two composition dolls from 1942 to 1944 dressed in military uniforms; one wore the brown outfits of the WACs (Women's Army Corps), and the other appeared in blue to represent the WAVES (Women Accepted for Volunteer Employment Emergency Service) in the women's branch of the navy. During the war years, the Freundlich Novelty Company also offered uniformed dolls of both servicemen and -women and in 1942 created a doll version of one of the popular World War II heroes, **General Douglas MacArthur** (1880–1964).

After 1945, doll design returned to prewar favorites, including toddler dolls that resembled young children. Jiminy Cricket, Pinocchio, and Superman, from the comics and **movies** inspired composition and wood character dolls. In 1949, Ideal introduced the Toni doll, an advertising doll for the popular Toni Home Permanent.

Ongoing **radio** shows served as another source of toys. Premiums like decoder rings, badges, toy space guns, and assorted trinkets came either in a sponsor's box of cereal or in the mail upon receipt of proofs of purchase. Easily shown off before school or during recess or lunch, these toys were treasured by many youngsters both during and after the war.

Despite the challenges of manufacturing restrictions, a few new toys emerged during the war years. Richard (1914–1974) and Betty James (1918–2008) defied the struggles experienced by many in the industry with their 1943 introduction of the Slinky, a springy wire that walks down either an inclined plane or stairs. Engineer Richard James, while working on an antivibration device for ships' instruments, accidentally knocked off the shelf a spring he had made and observed it "walking" down to the floor. He told his wife about the possibility of this device becoming an interesting toy. She agreed and suggested the name Slinky. The couple produced 400 Slinkies and convinced Gimbel's Department Store in Philadelphia to sell their creation just before Christmas 1945—a true success story, because their total supply sold out in 90 minutes. For a brief time in the late 1940s, Slinkies could be purchased in red, blue, or green. This clever plaything has continued to fascinate and delight children and adults into the present, so much so that both the Discovery and History **television** channels selected Slinky as one of the top 10 toys of the 20th century.

A wartime experiment provided another fascinating new toy, Silly Putty. Early in the war, Japan invaded rubber-producing countries in Southeast Asia to cut off supplies to the United States. To help overcome the lack of this important product, U.S. citizens donated to the government any rubber they had such as spare tires and boots. Their donations proved insufficient for military needs, and so the federal government ordered industries to find a compound that could be transformed into synthetic rubber. In an attempt to find such a product, James Wright (active 1940s), an engineer with the General Electric Company (GE) developed a substance in 1943 that could be manufactured cheaply, would bounce and stretch, and did not collect mold. It failed to replace rubber but did serve as a good caulking material.

When the war ended, Peter Hodgson (1912–1976), a marketing consultant familiar with the putty, recognized a unique potential with Wright's compound to entertain. Hodgson bought production rights and the supply held by GE and, with Easter approaching, decided to capitalize on the event. He put small amounts of the putty in plastic eggs, and sold it under the name Silly Putty. Because of the flexibility of this product and its ability to assume various wacky shapes, both adults and kids loved it. It could be used to create any number of objects, animals, or insects such as spiders and snakes, and it made effective Halloween masks when applied to the face; it could even lift comic strip images off the pages of the Sunday funnies. Silly Putty also served practical uses by picking up dirt, lint, and pet hair. It eventually evolved into a bestselling novelty of many colors and continues to fascinate all ages.

At the end of the war, the cessation of **rationing** restrictions stimulated a return to normal industrial production, and older toy manufacturers resumed their usual output of Erector Sets, American Flyer trains, science experiment kits, and whimsical and brightly colored windups. Executives from many toy firms, along with marketing and advertising professionals, anticipated the now-historic **baby boom** and realized that a new and larger customer base for toys would develop as returning servicemen married and started families.

Marketing analyses of both current and potential consumers soon revealed a desire for toys that conveyed realism. Kids and adults had seen newsreels, photographs, and Hollywood movies showing real life, people hurt, soldiers fighting in mud, and camouflaged vehicles. Accuracy and detail in toys grew in importance. Cognizant of the demand for realism, C. W. Doepke Manufacturing Company, an old industrial toolmaker, introduced a side business of heavy construction equipment toys in 1946. Under the banner of Doepke's Model Toys and copied from blueprints of real trucks and bulldozers, the miniaturized Barber-Greene high-capacity bucket loader, the Adams diesel road grader, and the Heiliner earth scraper operated just like real pieces of equipment and sold as authorized replicas. The actual brand names also appeared on these reproductions. More collector's items than toys, they found a market interested in extreme realism. Similarly, the Ertl Company specialized in farm toys and contracted with manufacturers such as John Deere and International Harvester to issue toy replicas at the same time they unveiled the latest models to farmers.

New to the business of toys, the Mound Metalcraft Company, located in a small schoolhouse basement in Mound, Minnesota, originally specialized in garden tools, a good spring/summer product. The owners, while searching for a fall/winter item to balance their enterprise, in early 1947 bought the dies and tools of Streeter Industries, which included a toy steam shovel with a wooden cab and steel base, boom, and bucket. With this die, Mound Metalcraft created a second toy, a crane, and by the end of the year had produced 37,000 units of their two products.

They named their toys Tonka, after Minnesota's Lake Minnetonka and the Sioux word *tonka,* which means great. The firm advertised realism and cultivated the idea of boys sharing the world of work with men. Tonka trucks, with their ability to withstand the toughest play, won immediate acceptance in postwar America and demand far outpaced production, making these vehicles in miniature very successful. Mound Metalcraft quickly dropped its line of garden tools, changed the company name to Tonka, and by 1949 carried 13 different vehicles and even expanded its line to include a doll hospital bed with mattress. Today, the Tonka brand has grown into a line of trucks and vehicles that have kept abreast with developments in the construction and **transportation** industries, as well as dolls and other toys aimed at girls.

The postwar years posed the problem of families reconnecting—husbands and wives, fathers and children—and toy companies were quick to advertise along these lines. Lionel Trains, because of large war-connected government contracts and restrictions on the use of metal parts, had stopped making toy trains in 1942 but resumed its prewar production in 1945. Throughout the late 1940s, Lionel met both the realism demand and parent-child bonding challenge.

Correctly scaled and detailed trains had appeared before World War II with model railroaders. In the postwar era, Lionel added an array of accessories such as coal cars, log carriers, ice containers, barrel loaders and unloaders, spotlight and beacon towers, crossing gates and signals, switchmen, brakemen, streetlights, and water towers, just to mention a few. Most Lionel Train ads, and some of those from other toy companies, appeared in adult-oriented magazines such as, *Life,* the *Saturday Evening Post,* and *Parents' Magazine.* Advertising for Lionel Trains, as well as their chief competitor, A. C. Gilbert's American Flyer series, illustrate the trend of linking toys with parents and their children, frequently picturing a father and son accompanied by a script that suggested Lionel Trains and accessories could strengthen emotional ties with fathers and sons.

Manufacturers introduced other interesting new toys during the second half of the decade. One, the Magic 8-Ball debuted in 1950 as a variation on a pocket-size fortune-telling tube named the Syco-Slate, which in turn had started out in a larger size called the Syco-Seer. The Seer, initially invented in 1946 by either or both Abe Bookman or Al Carter (both active during the 1940s), of the Alabe Toy Company, progressed through several improvements and name changes to the Magic 8-Ball status. The device's popularity and success rested on its supposed ability to help advice-seekers find answers to questions about their future. This 20-sided die offers 20 possible replies—10 positive, 5 ambiguous, and 5 negative—ranging from "all signs point to yes" to "ask again later" to "don't count on it." Since the emergence of the first Magic 8-Ball, numerous variations of the concept have appeared and gained popularity.

Japan, the wartime enemy of the United States, both before and after the conflict played a major role in the selling of toys in North America. Japan had led the world in the production of celluloid since the 1920s. A cheap commodity, the Japanese exported to customers everywhere inexpensive items such as teething rings, baby rattles, ping-pong balls, bathtub toys, dolls, farm equipment, circus figures, trains, planes, boats, and cars, along with reproductions of American comic strip characters, sports heroes, and movie stars. With the outbreak of World War II, both the production and distribution of such items to the United States stopped.

Immediately after Japan's surrender, a highly favorable exchange rate made it profitable for Japanese manufacturers to resume production immediately and once again export celluloid products all over the world. The items remained somewhat the same as before the war—figurines representing various aspects of a child's life, including ice cream wagons and vendors, dolls of all descriptions, various vehicles, skiers, animals, and clowns—but they now bore the words "Made in Occupied Japan," a requirement made by the U.S. forces occupying the country. This designation would not be dropped until 1952 and the return of an independent Japanese government. In the meantime, resourceful Japanese entrepreneurs created special mechanisms that, combined with celluloid, allowed for the production of new items such as dancing and crawling dolls, merry-go-rounds, and other toys with special functions. Even robots became available, although they were not plentiful and varied until the 1950s. But celluloid's one defect, high inflammability, raised concerns in the mid-1950s, a problem solved by the development and growing use of fire-resistant plastics.

On the home front, Ruth (1916–2002) and Elliot Handler (b. 1918), along with Harold Matson (active 1940s) in 1945 launched Mattel (a play from their names, Matt-el) out of a garage workshop to make picture frames and dollhouse furniture. Harold Matson soon sold out to the Handlers, who turned all of their attention to toys. In 1947, the Uke-A-Doodle became the first of a line of Mattel musical toys. Creation of the Barbie doll in 1959 by Ruth Handler moved the company forward and over the course of its history it expanded its many different lines of playthings. With mergers and acquisitions, Mattel entered the 21st century as America's largest toy manufacturer based on revenues.

In 1948, another West Coast garage venture carried out by two students at the University of Southern California, Arthur Melin (1924–2002) and Richard Kerr (1926–2008), resulted in the founding of Wham-O to market by mail slingshots and other projectile-firing goods. In 1955, the company acquired rights to the Frisbee, the flying disk that surged in popularity during that decade. Toy manufacturer Mattel bought out Wham-O in 1994, but the Frisbee maker became independent again in 1997 and has continued in that capacity into the present.

As the country approached the 1950s, changes continued to occur in toy manufacturing. Cast iron had become obsolete for toys, and plastic had emerged as the favored material. Tried and true science fiction toys such as Flash Gordon and Buck Rogers had fallen in popularity. The postwar phenomenon of television and the first airing of a children's program called ***The Howdy Doody Show*** on December 27, 1947, meant the arrival of more and more television-inspired toys. *Captain Video* debuted on June 27, 1949, and, in the tradition of radio, offered premiums as a way to obtain new toys—flying saucer rings, Rite-O-Lite flashlights, rocket launchers and rocket ships, secret seal rings, space fleet ray guns, and rocket balloons.

During the first half of the decade, the work of some former toy companies as military suppliers eclipsed their reputations as toy manufacturers; some never returned to toys, and others closed their doors forever with the return to peace. Most toys marketed during World War II, usually inferior to prewar ones, nonetheless continued to capture the hearts of children. The postwar era immediately gave way to a level of realism, variety, and abundance seldom seen before.

*See also:* Architecture; Cartoons (Film); Children's Films; Comic Strips; Education; Hobbies; Scrap Drives; *Superman;* Technology

**Selected Reading**
Cross, Gary. *Kid's Stuff: Toys and the Changing World of American Childhood.* Cambridge, MA: Harvard University Press, 1997.
O'Brien, Richard. *The Story of American Toys, from the Puritans to the Present.* New York: Abbeville Press, 1990.
Walsh, Tim. *Timeless Toys, Classic Toys and the Playmakers Who Created Them.* Kansas City: Andrews McMeel, 2005.

# TRAINS

England gave birth to the railroad industry in 1797 with the invention of the steam locomotive. Thirty years later, the United States saw its first train when Baltimore merchants chartered the Baltimore and Ohio Railroad. Throughout New England and in other parts of the United States, tracks spread rapidly and made the Civil War (1861–1865) the first major U.S. conflict in which railroads played a significant role, because both sides used trains to move troops and supplies. By May 1869, at Promontory Point in the Utah Territory, a golden spike joined the Union Pacific and Central Pacific railroads, marking the completion of the first transcontinental line. The industry experienced steady growth and passenger usage throughout the 19th and early 20th centuries, reaching a peak in 1920, with no other mode of **transportation** challenging its position as the primary means of **travel.**

This monopoly, however, could not last forever. Two factors caused a drop in railroad passenger travel: first, **automobiles** steadily served as a major competitor with an almost threefold increase in registrations from 1920 to 1930, growing from a little over 8 million registrants, or 7.5 percent of the population, to 23 million or 18.5 percent of the population. Second, during the Great Depression, the use of trains dropped, forcing several lines into bankruptcy. The industry managed to regain some ground with the 1934 debut of diesel-powered locomotives, which offered greater efficiency and economy, plus the introduction of streamlined locomotives and air-conditioned passenger cars with recessed fluorescent lighting. Over the next five years and the opening of the 1939–1940 New York World's Fair, passenger rail travel increased 38 percent, and trains held a major spot in the fair's Transportation Zone. But this gain proved illusory;

*Train travel grew in popularity during World War II. With peace, railroad industry administrators attempted to prevent a postwar decline by investing millions of dollars in new diesel engines, freight equipment, and passenger trains. The New York Central Railroad spent some of these dollars on a new Pullman-Standard dining car shown in this 1948 photograph. (Bettmann/CORBIS)*

fewer riders took trains with greater frequency; over the long term, the automobile rose as the transportation star, and this vehicle of choice for most people offered a serious challenge for the railroad industry.

Railroad executives, anticipating U.S. involvement in World War II, in 1939 organized to argue with the federal government against a repeat of the World War I nationalization of railroads. At that time, the government guaranteed each railroad company a net operating income with any amount above accruing to federal authorities, a situation that ultimately sent a large portion of the industry's profits to Washington. The railroad officials successfully prevented any renewal of government control, a victory that laid the groundwork for a new life for railroads.

With the attack on Pearl Harbor on December 7, 1941, and the continuing escalation of the war in Europe, the United States became engaged in a two-front conflict, which required huge shipments of military personnel and equipment to both the Atlantic and Pacific coasts. Trains could easily meet this need, and the years 1942 to 1945 saw record-setting figures for both passengers and freight volume. Efficiency also increased because runs, going and coming, contained full or nearly full cars. Profitability for the railroad industry similarly grew; in addition to the military use of trains, civilians, with

TABLE 97. Selected Train Usage Statistics, 1920–1950

| Year | Number of Operating Railroads | Number of Passengers Carried | Passenger Revenue (rounded) | Average Number Passengers per Train | Freight Revenue (rounded) | Number of Automobile Registrations (rounded) |
|---|---|---|---|---|---|---|
| 1920 | 1,085 | n.d. | $1 billion (average for 1916–1920) | n.d. | $3.5 billion (average for 1916–1920) | 8.1 million |
| 1940 | 573 | 471,000 (annual average for 1936–1940) | $420 million (average for 1936–1940) | 57 (average for 1936–1940) | 3.3 billion (average for 1936–1940) | 27 million |
| 1941 | n.d. | n.d. | n.d. | n.d. | n.d. | 30 million |
| 1942 | n.d. | n.d. | n.d. | n.d. | n.d. | 28 million |
| 1943 | 534 | n.d. | $1.7 billion | n.d. | $7 billion | 36 million |
| 1944 | 524 | n.d. | $1.8 billion | n.d. | $7.1 billion | 26 million |
| 1945 | 517 | 772,000 (annual for average 1941–1945) | $1.7 billion | 158 (average for 1941–1945) | $6.6 billion | 26 million |
| 1946 | 513 | n.d. | $1.3 billion | | $5.9 billion | 28 million |
| 1947 | 502 | 706,000 | $955 million | 110 | $7.1 billion | 31 million |
| 1948 | 485 | n.d. | $956 million | 101 | $8 billion | 33 million |
| 1949 | 481 | n.d. | $862 million | 92 | $7.1 billion | 36 million |
| 1950 | 471 | 488,000 | $815 million | 89 | $7.9 billion | 40 million |

*Note:* n.d. = no data available.
*Source: Historical Statistics of the United States, Colonial Times to 1970.* Washington, DC: Census Bureau, U.S. Department of Commerce, 1975.

**Table 98.** Total Railroad Track Mileage in the United States, 1910–1950

| Year | Miles |
|---|---|
| 1910 | 240,430 |
| 1916 | 254,037 |
| 1920 | 252,845 |
| 1925 | 249,398 |
| 1930 | 249,052 |
| 1935 | 241,822 |
| 1940 | 233,670 |
| 1945 | 226,696 |
| 1950 | 223,779 |

*Source:* John Stover, *The Life and Decline of the American Railroad.* New York: Oxford University Press, 1970.

their automobiles parked at home because of gas **rationing,** likewise turned to trains for transportation.

A booming business can have its problems, even the railroad industry. Normal operating procedures included the annual discarding of some tracks and the building of new ones. Soon after its 1920 peak, railroads experienced a steady decline in the number of miles of railroad track, creating a curtailment of service in some areas because the tracks given up exceeded any new construction. With the Great Depression, rail abandonment hastened—a condition that continued throughout the 1940s and into the present.

The demand for military rail services during World War II initially served as a boon for the industry, but it also created overcrowded trains, schedule delays, and long waits for the general public at some stations. The trains carrying troops would stop along the way at stations with **USO (United Service Organizations) canteens,** providing a good break for the soldiers but sometimes presenting frustration for other passengers. **Advertising** by the railroad companies addressed civilian usage but at the same time displayed images of fighting men headed to war and asked civilians to consider limiting their travel to absolutely necessary trips. In an attempt to help the American public understand the importance of the military use of the railroads, Columbia Pictures Corporation and the U.S. Office of War Information produced *Troop Train* in 1943, a 10-minute documentary explaining the need and difficulties of transporting military vehicles, heavy armaments, and soldiers on trains.

The heavy military train traffic experienced during the war briefly became greater once peace had been achieved; soldiers in large groups returned to the United States and used trains to get home. The greatest troop movement of the entire war occurred on August 3 and 4, 1945, when more than 20,000 solders packed into 31 trains and departed from Camp Kilmer, New Jersey, to various destinations around the country; everywhere, families excitedly greeted their loved ones home.

Railroad administrators, expecting a slight postwar decline in demand but still optimistic about future growth, immediately invested billions of dollars in new diesel engines, freight equipment, and passenger trains. To their dismay, impediments occurred. Production delays postponed delivery of a large number of new coaches, causing some lines to have to continue to use worn and unsatisfactory cars that had been in service for some time. In addition to the equipment problems, civilian passenger numbers dropped at a much greater rate than predicted. Gas rationing had ended, and the motor vehicle industry began to advertise heavily as customers lined up at dealerships. As soon as new automobiles became available, factory sales skyrocketed, and, by the end of the decade, the number of cars on the road had almost doubled since 1940, from 3.7 million to 6.6 million. Automobiles and buses made significant inroads in urban travel and, at the same time, joined airplanes for intercity travel.

For many decades, trains dominated transportation in the United States. In the 1920s and 1930s, railroad travel began to experience a decline in popularity against a growing motor vehicle industry. World War II provided a much-needed burst of energy, but the movement of 43 million military personnel in 114,000 special troop trains, while simultaneously meeting unprecedented civilian travel needs, exhausted the railroad industry. After the war ended, both passenger and freight traffic declined steadily. In 1948, as a part of his presidential campaign, **Harry S. Truman** (1884–1972) gave the industry high visibility as he traveled across the country in a famous whistle-stop campaign, addressing crowds from the rear platforms of trains. But even this could not lure passengers back onto trains because the prewar competitors—automobiles, buses, trucks, and airplanes—had gained too much in popularity and usage.

*See also:* Aviation; Leisure and Recreation

**Selected Reading**

Barger, Harold. *The Transportation Industries, 1889–1946: A Study of Output, Employment, and Productivity.* New York: National Bureau of Economic Research, 1951.

Stover, John F. *The Life and Decline of the American Railroad.* New York: Oxford University Press, 1970.

# TRANSPORTATION

During the 1900s, technological discoveries brought major changes to the lives of Americans, including the transport of people and goods over increased distance in shorter periods of time and with a greater degree of comfort. Significant transportation advancements began with the successful completion of a transcontinental rail system in 1869. Established railroad lines and new ones expanded quickly to serve industries and cities, and, by the 1920s, **trains** ranked as the nation's preferred means of travel.

By the 1930s, however, the development and mass production of **automobiles** created a popular alternative. Cars by the hundreds rolled off assembly lines in 1903. That same year, an adventurous pair, Horatio Nelson Jackson (1872–1955) and his chauffeur, bicycle racer Sewall K. Crocker (ca. 1881–1913), drove from the West Coast to the East Coast in a Cleveland-made Winton, and this publicity for auto **travel** proved invaluable. As the number of cars increased, prices tumbled. By the 1920s, thanks to competition between Henry Ford's (1863–1947) Model T at $300 and his 1927 Model A at $385 (roughly $3,690 and $4,760, respectively, in 2008 dollars) along with General Motor's annual model changes for all its cars, automobiles had made significant gains in replacing trains as the predominant means of getting around, especially in cities.

But another mode of transportation made its debut in 1903. Brothers Orville and Wilbur Wright (1871–1948; 1867–1912) successfully flew a powered aircraft at Kitty Hawk, North Carolina, and by 1914 the first commercial flights had been established. The United States Post Office in 1918 provided airmail delivery between New York and Washington, DC; two years later, the government extended the service to California. In 1923, two lieutenants with the Army Air Service completed a nonstop transcontinental flight, opening up another way for faster travel over great distances.

Still more improvements in all modes of transportation occurred throughout the 1930s, making the exhibits at the New York World's Fair Transportation Zone a major component of the 1939–1940 event. Even with war enveloping Europe and the inevitable involvement of the United States, exhibitors used the fair's theme of "Building the World of Tomorrow" to project an optimistic and comfortable future for Americans. Staying true to the message, the Transportation Zone underscored modernization and prosperity with its celebration of cars, trains, and airplanes, housing them in spectacular buildings containing breathtaking displays.

For the fair as a whole, crowd favorites included the exhibitions by the Big Three U.S. automobile manufacturers—Chrysler Motor Company, General Motors Company, and Ford Motor Company. The Chrysler exhibit, located at the forefront of the Transportation Zone, used moving pictures projected upon a map of the world to chronicle the story of transportation from the time of using one's feet to the arrival of trains, cars, and airplanes.

Audiences at General Motor's *Futurama* exhibit, created by designer Norman Bel Geddes (1893–1958), reclined in moving chairs that took them over a 36,000-square-foot scale model of a futuristic city that showed them the highway world of 1960: seven-lane roads with bridges and inviting landscapes connecting homes, farms, and industrial plants to the urban complex. The Ford Motor Company likewise envisioned a modernistic highway, the product of a collaboration between architect Albert Kahn (1869–1942) and designer Walter Dorwin Teague (1883–1960). Visitors rode sample cars over an elevated, winding half-mile "Road of Tomorrow." In addition to these shows, all three automobile companies provided convenient displays of their newest cars.

Trains also held a prominent spot in the fair, with 27 Eastern railroad lines participating. The Railroads Building, the largest at the exposition, contained various train models and dioramas. Historic locomotives, as well as new ones, such as the Pennsylvania Railroad's streamlined Model S1, designed by Raymond Loewy (1893–1986) and the largest locomotive ever built by the Altoona, Pennsylvania, railroad shops, were housed outdoors. *Railroads at Work*, a 40-minute show with 500 pieces of equipment, demonstrated every facet of railroading.

The **aviation** industry, not to be outdone, boasted a building that consisted of a long hanger section and a half-dome, which housed three Army Air Corps fighters and three navy aircraft. Scale models showed the latest technical developments, and displays highlighted the comfort and safety of flying.

In addition to the transportation exhibits, fairgoers could use a variety of ways to move themselves from one zone to another. The Long Island Railroad brought visitors to the fair and deposited them at an ultramodern terminal. Sixty-five miles of paved streets and footpaths into the fairgrounds could then be used for walking or riding one of Greyhound's sleek 160-passenger buses designed by Loewy.

The New York World's Fair closed in the fall of 1940, and a little over a year later the United States plunged into World War II, causing many of the transportation dreams shown at the fair to be put on hold and passenger usage to change rapidly. Just days after the December 7, 1941, attack on Pearl Harbor, **President Franklin Delano Roosevelt** (1882–1945) signed Executive Order 8989, which created the Office of Defense Transportation (ODT) under the leadership of Joseph B. Eastman (1882–1944). The agency had the responsibility for coordinating all domestic transportation and it acted immediately.

In succession, between January and May 1942, government regulations placed limits on purchasing tires, converted automobile production lines to military vehicle and tank production, and instituted a gas **rationing** system for all drivers. **Posters, radio** programs, newspaper articles, and advertisements emphasized the importance of all Americans accepting these sacrifices as a part of their patriotic duty and support of winning World War II. Citizens on the home front responded and drastically reduced personal travel, drove their cars less, used bus and rail transport at levels never before or since equaled, and car pooled (a term coined in 1942), walked, and bicycled more. When bicycle tires wore out and could not be replaced, this option decreased in usage.

Taxi companies, once a popular means of getting around in large cities, had struggled to stay solvent during the 1930s because of a number of issues—primarily regulations, low rates, and a questionable public image. By the end of the decade, most taxicabs were owned and operated by local entrepreneurs with only local restrictions, if any, to follow. Effective September 1, 1942, significant changes occurred for the taxicab industry when the ODT gained authority to control the operating characteristics of the country's taxi fleets. Their regulations prohibited the production of new taxicabs and stopped employment of taxis for recreational trips and deliveries. Travel in a cab within a city could not exceed 35 miles, and excursions outside city limits could not go beyond 10 miles. Throughout the war, the supply of taxis dwindled, while ridership increased. For example, in 1942, the industry, with a loss of 4.5 percent of its vehicles, experienced a 12 percent increase in passengers served. By the end of 1943, 45 cities had implemented shared riding, an efficient way to serve more people in fewer vehicles without increasing the miles traveled or gas consumed.

The two-way radio, a wartime instrument, came into common taxi use after the war, and the industry, despite being hampered by old, worn-out cars, reported a gradual increase in usage until 1949. That year, the industry experienced an 11 percent decline, a trend that continued into the 1950s as more and more people resumed driving their own cars. Even with this drop in business, the cessation of shared taxi riding plus the increased length of average trips caused by families moving to the suburbs and still using taxis, allowed the industry to maintain an acceptable level of business after 1949.

When the war ended in 1945, Americans unleashed pent-up consumer demand by purchasing new cars. Late that year, Detroit produced 75,000 automobiles, enough for two cars for each of the some 33,000 dealers across the country. In 1950, the United States Census Bureau reported a 44 percent increase in sales for new cars as compared to 1940 and a 32 percent increase in automobile registrations. So many cars on the highways required improvements in existing roads, as well as the building of new ones. The Federal-Aid Highway Act of 1944 called for 41,000 miles of interstate highways, but lack of funding delayed significant construction until the passage of another Federal-Aid Highway Act in 1956, which included the necessary money.

Other motorized vehicles—namely buses and trucks—had likewise played an important role in the development of U.S. transportation systems. By the mid-1920s, over 6,500 companies provided bus service, most of them small operations with as few as one vehicle and limited routes. Nevertheless, buses, along with greatly increased numbers of cars, pushed streetcars and trolleys off city streets. In 1927, Greyhound Bus Company, a large firm dating back to 1914, sent a vehicle from its fleet across the country, showing the feasibility and comfort of this kind of traveling. Trailways, Greyhound's only national competitor, consisted of an association of many small motor coach companies working together to enable passengers to transfer easily when traveling from one company's territory to another. During World War II, buses therefore served as an alternative for many whose cars remained parked in their driveways or garages.

In 1948, building on its publicity and success at the New York World's Fair and free of wartime restrictions, Greyhound announced a new air-conditioned luxury bus with seats for 50 passengers, each equipped with a reading lamp and radio, and large windows for good viewing of the passing scene. Other features included a lounge that would accommodate 12 riders at a time, a refrigerated cabinet, drinking fountain, and wash room and toilet. One year later, Greyhound introduced a 43-passenger Scenicruiser designed by Raymond Loewy. Borrowing an idea from the railroad industry, this two-story bus featured a glass-covered observation deck that provided an unobstructed view of the road ahead and offered an expanded baggage compartment and a public-address system for announcements and musical programs. After a series of test runs, the 40-foot-bus went into production.

Before 1900, trains carried most of the freight transported over land—a system with limitations, because they primarily could deliver only to centralized urban centers. As the decade advanced, the appearance of several innovations, such as the gasoline-powered internal combustion engine, improvements in automotive **technology,** and the development of the 18-wheel tractor-trailer, along with the building of a system of roads, gave rise to the modern trucking industry. Shortages of steel, rubber, and gasoline during World War II hampered the motor freight business, but after the war trucking companies large and small experienced steady and rapid growth.

Railroads witnessed declines in passenger travel during the 1920s and 1930s but then enjoyed a sharp increase during World War II. Restrictions on buying tires, gas rationing, and a ban on pleasure driving greatly reduced competition from cars, buses, trucks, or planes and sent civilians to trains for both business and vacation travel. At the peak of the war, more than 74 percent of city travelers rode a train. The biggest gain in railroad traffic, however, came from the military, because the railroad industry over the course of the war transported some 43 million armed forces personnel, or an average of 1 million a month. Freight trains carried more than 90 percent of all military and defense freight as well as a large amount of civilian goods.

The end of World War II brought a gradual lifting of road travel restrictions and also produced heavy traffic for the railroads, as millions of soldiers, sailors, and aviators worked their way through process centers and back home, nearly all traveling by train. While the railroads continued to handle wartime business after the war, other modes of transportation responded to peacetime civilian demand. Soon a large number of consumers returned to automobiles because of convenience and the sense of freedom they provided. They also booked flights on airplanes for their speed and efficiency for traveling great distances. Both railroad passenger and freight traffic thus declined steadily through the remaining years of the decade as well as throughout the 1950s. No matter how hard the railroads tried to lure passengers back onto trains, Americans preferred to take to the road or the skies.

In 1941, prior to the nation joining the Allied forces in the war in Europe, the airline industry had carried 3.4 million passengers, primarily business travelers, throughout the United States and across the Atlantic Ocean. World War II caught the military ill-prepared in terms of equipment and personnel for aerial combat. The major commercial airlines, American, Eastern, United, Trans World Airlines (TWA), and Pan American Airways (Pan Am), canceled many of their civilian flights and turned over some 200 of their 360 airplanes to the military. Many of their pilots became flying instructors for the armed forces.

By the spring of 1942, most aircraft factories ran 24 hours a day, six to seven days a week, to manufacture the badly needed planes. They also attempted to improve on their basic aircraft construction and military features. Countless women joined the defense workforce, bringing the labor pool to a high of 2.1 million employees. By the end of 1943, aircraft plants had turned out more than 300,000 military planes for the armed forces and the Allies. This nonstop work schedule did two things: (1) it spurred technological discoveries and improvements with airplanes ahead of what would have been accomplished in a standard work week, and (2) it contributed to challenging demands being made on the transportation industry for around-the-clock service.

After the war, airplane travel grabbed Americans' attention as never before, and commercial aviation grew rapidly. In December 1945, American and Pan Am initiated schedules to England, with the intention to expand to Amsterdam, Stockholm, and Berlin as soon as possible. TWA opened a flight from New York to Paris in February 1946. International flying benefited enormously from wartime construction of airfields at locations around the world that had been converted to civilian passenger use.

When the war ended, government travel dropped drastically, providing more seats on commercial aircraft for the average traveler. At first, airlines cut the cost of their tickets to be slightly below that of first-class and lower-berth tickets on trains. For example, in 1945, an airline ticket from New York to Chicago could be purchased for $32.85 (approximately $390 in 2008 dollars) compared to the rail ticket of $36.88 (approximately $440 in 2008 dollars). Also, at the conclusion of the war, the army turned over many of its transport airplanes to the airline companies. United acquired Douglas DC-4s, and TWA utilized the sleek four-engine Lockheed C-69, better known as the Constellation.

Throughout World War II, jet engines underwent testing and revision in laboratories. Germany started production of the Messerschmitt Me 262 in 1944, the world's first jet-powered fighter aircraft. The United States soon followed suit with the Lockheed P-80 Shooting Star in 1944, although it did not become operational until 1945, too late for combat in World War II. Development of practical commercial jet engines consumed a number of years but, once perfected, served as a big boon to the airline industry. On May 2, 1952, British Overseas Airways Corporation sent the first commercial jet flight from London to Johannesburg, giving birth to modern commercial aviation.

While the sky filled with planes, ocean liners regained use of the seas. Both prior to World War II and afterward, ocean liners served as important means of transportation for European emigration to the United States and Canada, as well as U.S. travelers who could afford a sojourn in Europe or along the Mediterranean. But during the war, civilian ocean travel ceased. The United States' vulnerability on the West Coast became apparent with the successful assault on Pearl Harbor. In early 1942, the same became true for the East Coast, when German U-boat attacks disrupted Atlantic shipping. That threat caused all transatlantic pleasure travel to cease, and authorities quickly converted cruise ships into troop carriers. After bringing soldiers back home in 1945, the ocean liner companies again refitted their vessels for cruise service and prospered. With travel restrictions to Europe lifted, eager vacationers lined up to book an ocean voyage, many having to wait a year or two for available space. Interest in air travel also grew but slowly, and it did not initially serve as an immediate competitor to ocean travel.

During World War II, the development of transportation systems in the United States for civilian use came to a standstill. Any advances that occurred stemmed from the country's focus on strengthening its military tactics and winning the war. With victory, demand for all those things not available during the war ushered in a period of rapid technological progress. The resulting prosperity created a modern transportation system that offered unequalled convenience and flexibility to its users.

*See also:* Advertising; Leisure and Recreation; Levittown and Suburbanization; Newspapers; Technology

**Selected Reading**
Bilstein, Roger E. *Flight in America: From the Wrights to the Astronauts.* Baltimore: Johns Hopkins University Press, 1984.
Gilbert, Gorman, and Robert E. Samuels. *The Taxicab: An Urban Transportation Survivor.* Chapel Hill: University of North Carolina Press, 1982.
Weiner, Edward. *Urban Transportation Planning in the United States: An Historical Overview.* Westport, CT: Praeger Publishers, 1999.
Wurts, Richard. *The New York World's Fair, 1939/1940.* New York: Dover, 1977.

# TRAVEL

By the late 1930s, many Americans owned **automobiles** and regularly took to the road—to get to their jobs, go shopping, enjoy a Sunday afternoon drive, or embark upon an extended trip for the family vacation. The nation's active entry into World War II on December 7, 1941, changed those driving behaviors and pleasant pastimes. The postwar years, however, saw a return to normalcy for a large number of citizens; they once more could travel and viewed both leisure and business excursions as part of the American way of life.

Wartime **rationing** of consumer items diverted raw materials and necessary products for the war effort and, at the same time, created shortages for civilians, forcing many to spend their vacation on their front porches. The first controls on goods for sale, issued in January 1942, included tires, an essential item for operating a car. The following month, the government called for the conversion of automobile assembly lines to the production of military vehicles and by May had placed restrictions on purchasing gasoline.

Travel for fun ceased abruptly, and, as seen in Table 99, motor vehicle sales and distances covered plummeted until late 1945 and a return to peace. New cars purchased during the war years would have been manufactured prior to February 7, 1942, the date the government ordered an end to all nonmilitary automobile production. The steady increase in automotive sales for the last half of the decade resulted in a significant jump of 44 percent, from prewar figures of over 4 million vehicles sold in 1940, to around 8 million in 1950. During this same period, the distances traveled went from a low of roughly 249 million miles in 1946 to more than 458 million in 1950, a 45.5 percent climb.

By 1940, the American Automobile Association (AAA), promoter of travel and safety since 1902, found itself riding the wave of expanded travel and growth of the tourism industry. With over 1 million members, it reigned as the largest leisure travel agency in the United States and offered many services, including customized routing maps, evaluation reports on lodgings and **restaurants,** emergency road service, and two publications: *Digest of Motor Vehicle Laws* and *Motoring in the United States.* Throughout the war years, the AAA continued to serve its members while also supporting the war effort. It made its mapping facilities available to the army, conducted

TABLE 99. Motor Vehicle Sales and Motor Vehicle Travel

| Year | **Factory Sales** (in millions of dollars) | **Vehicle Miles** (in millions) |
|---|---|---|
| 1940 | 4.5 | 302.1 |
| 1941 | 4.8 | n.d. |
| 1942 | 1.0 | n.d. |
| 1943 | 0.7 | n.d. |
| 1944 | 0.7 | n.d. |
| 1945 | 0.7 | 249.6 |
| 1946 | 3.0 | 340.7 |
| 1947 | 4.8 | 370.6 |
| 1948 | 5.3 | 397.6 |
| 1949 | 6.3 | 424.0 |
| 1950 | 8.0 | 458.4 |

*Note:* n.d. = no data available.
*Source: Historical Statistics of the United States, Colonial Times to 1970.* Washington, DC: Census Bureau, U.S. Department of Commerce, 1975.

motor-pool driver **education** classes, and monitored tire and gas rationing. After the war, the organization broadened a driver training program originally created in 1942 for veterans with artificial limbs to include all wounded veterans. In 1946, anticipating a huge postwar increase in traffic, it released *Traffic Jam Ahead,* a film that presented ways to maintain road safety.

Duncan Hines (1880–1959), a traveling salesman for a printing firm, in 1936 turned a hobby of sharing his evaluations of eating establishments with friends into a thriving business with the publication of a guidebook titled *Adventures in Good Eating.* He followed this highly successful venture with another guide, *Lodging for a Night,* in 1938, and a cookbook, *Adventures in Good Cooking,* in 1939. A second edition of *Adventures in Good Eating* became available in 1942 and sold well, primarily to families that traveled extensively to take jobs in defense plants.

The National Park Service (NPS), created in 1916 and operated by the federal government under the U.S. Department of the Interior, also encouraged travel, particularly to national parks, monuments, historical and military sites, and parkways. As occurred with motor vehicle sales and vehicle miles shown in the preceding table, visits to these areas plunged during the war years, only to rebound strongly after the end of the conflict.

In 1941, NPS facilities attracted a high of 20.4 million visits. The figures dropped to 6.6 million visits at the height of World War II. Two factors—large numbers of citizens fighting in the war and civilians not taking vacations—greatly influenced the drastic decrease in the number of traveling Americans. The Park Service surpassed 1941's record count in 1946; by 1950, it had established new highs with 30.7 million visits to NPS sites.

TABLE 100. Visits to National Parks, Monuments, and Historical and Military Sites

| Year | Number of Visitors to National Parks (in millions) | Number of Visitors to National Monuments (in millions) | Number of Visitors to Historical and Military Sites (in millions) | Number of Visitors to National Parkways (in millions) | Total Number of Visitors to National Park Service Sites (in millions) |
|---|---|---|---|---|---|
| 1940 | 7.4 | 2.8 | 5.9 | n.d. | 16.1 |
| 1941 | 8.5 | 3.7 | 7.3 | 0.9 | 20.4 |
| 1942 | 3.8 | 1.8 | 3.1 | 0.3 | 9.0 |
| 1943 | 2.0 | 1.6 | 2.9 | 0.1 | 6.6 |
| 1944 | 2.6 | 1.9 | 3.3 | 0.3 | 8.1 |
| 1945 | 4.5 | 2.5 | 3.7 | 0.4 | 11.1 |
| 1946 | 9.0 | 3.6 | 6.7 | 1.3 | 20.6 |
| 1947 | 10.7 | 4.0 | 7.6 | 1.2 | 23.5 |
| 1948 | 11.3 | 4.4 | 7.8 | 1.5 | 25.0 |
| 1949 | 13.0 | 4.9 | 8.8 | 1.4 | 28.1 |
| 1950 | 13.9 | 5.3 | 9.5 | 2.0 | 30.7 |

*Note:* n.d. = no data available.
Source: *Historical Statistics of the United States, Colonial Times to 1970.* Washington, DC: Census Bureau, U.S. Department of Commerce, 1975.

Newspaper travel coverage reflected the decline in Americans engaged in that pursuit. For example, *New York Times* reporter Diana Rice (active 1930s to 1950s) took over a biweekly column "Random Notes for Travelers" in June 1936 and, over the course of a year, featured cruises and tours to just about all parts of the world. By 1941, however, the column appeared erratically, with only 11 for the year. Topics tended to be confined to travel opportunities to Canada, Mexico, the Caribbean, South America, or within the United States. One column even focused on holding family reunions at military camps so that those in the service would not miss out on those important gatherings. No travel columns appeared in the *New York Times* for the years 1943 to 1946. They resumed in July 1947 under a new name—"News and Notes from the Field of Travel"—but still under Rice's byline.

Good roads enhance an interest in traveling by car or bus, and as a modern highway system began to develop in the United States in the 1920s, long-distance road trips became more common and required stops at places to stay. At the time, hotels tended to be located in the center of cities near railroad stations, not along the roads connecting urban areas. Out on the highway, auto camps, which initially ranged from tents on platforms to sparsely furnished rooms, provided the first lodging for travelers. In time, some of these facilities improved to offer individual cabins with more furnishings and increased privacy. Motels (a combination of the words "motor" and "hotel") soon followed; usually one long building with adjoining rooms, they offered exterior doors along the front, which allowed for easy parking and entrance to a room.

Most early motels consisted of one business under a single owner. But a few enterprising individuals built a number of lodgings within a geographic area and formed a chain under their management. Others increased their earnings by selling franchises to buyers who operated the motels under one name and shared in the profits. For example, Scott King (active 1930s to 1940s) followed the 1935 construction of his modernistic King's Auto Court in San Diego, California, with 24 more in Southern California over the next five years. In 1940, he established a co-ownership method of operating these facilities with managers under the collective name TraveLodge and set the stage for franchise growth and success that has continued into the present.

The tourist industry, as did most other businesses, struggled with a variety of challenges during World War II. Countless small motels and hotels along the highway, because of their dependence upon a virtually nonexistent automobile trade, went out of business. Hotels located near train stations, on the other hand, experienced a revival thanks to an increase in the number of rail passengers. Motels and hotels near defense plants and military camps also thrived because they provided much-needed housing to the millions who had relocated to work in the war effort or be near family members in the service.

After the conflict, many returning veterans, looking for employment and sensing a good opportunity, decided to go into the motel business. With an end to gas rationing, demand for clean, inexpensive lodging soared. These entrepreneurs opened small mom-and-pop motels, many following the guidance offered in a 1947 Veterans Administration manual, *Occupational Outlook Series,* which highlighted both the benefits and difficulties of running small tourist businesses. Others also seized upon these opportunities. California hotelier M. K. Guertin (active 1940s to 1950s) of Long

Beach, built his first Best Western in 1946, a venture that became a franchised chain and today remains known worldwide. By 1948, the country boasted 26,000 motels, twice the number available in 1939, and another 15,000 joined the ranks between 1949 and 1952, giving the country many more motels than hotels for the first time.

With peace restored, Americans eagerly returned to traveling, and in 1946 the publishing and tourist industries responded. Advertisements for the perfect vacation spot, tours, and means of travel increased in **newspapers** and **magazines.** New and updated travel guidebooks included all three of Duncan Hines's publications, with 900,000 copies sold almost immediately, and G. P. Putnam's Sons *Your Mexican Holiday,* Harcourt Brace's *The Story of Bermuda,* and Sheridan House's *The Romantic West Indies* also did well. Reinhold Publishing, anticipating that many travelers would be businesspeople, offered *Going Abroad for Business.* Curtis Publishing, located in Philadelphia, in 1946 issued a new magazine named *Holiday* and sent writer and humorist S. J. Perelman (1904–1979) and artist Al Hirschfield (1903–2003) around the world to send back witty and informative illustrated copy about their adventures.

Travel to Europe for pleasure had been restricted in 1939. German submarines patrolling the Atlantic Ocean, sometimes close to America's shores, prohibited any ocean travel east. Besides, most ocean liners and commercial airplanes had been commandeered for military transportation needs. Soon after the end of World War II, American Airlines and Pan American World Airways (commonly known as Pan Am) scheduled a limited number of flights to England, as did Transcontinental & Western Air (T&WA; in 1946 the company changed its name to the more familiar Trans World Airlines, or TWA) to Paris. Douglas Aircraft Company sold its first postwar passenger plane, a DC-6, to United Airlines with many more to follow, and Lockheed followed suit with its popular Constellation being first acquired by TWA.

At this time, most transatlantic passengers consisted of government officials and business travelers, but as the airlines acquired more planes and as governments relaxed wartime travel restrictions to Europe, many adventurous civilians crossed the Atlantic by air and ocean liner, not only to London and Paris but to Amsterdam, Stockholm, and Berlin. The American Express Company had shepherded U.S. citizens in and out of cities and museums in Europe for over 30 years; by 1947 it had reopened many of its European offices to address any concerns about expenses or to locate adequate accommodations and the other necessities for a comfortable trip. By 1949, almost 1 million people (less than 100,000 short of 1938, the last normal travel year) made their way to European and Mediterranean tourist spots. Ocean liners accounted for the major share of this trade because commercial airlines, although offering some flights, struggled with reaching agreements about assignments of air routes and setting fares.

Americans' thoughts about travel also turned to touring at home. In 1946, AAA, concerned about the **transportation** needs of the country, launched a national campaign encouraging the construction of a 40,000 mile interstate highway system that had been defined in the Federal-Aid Highway Act of 1944. The bill, however, had not authorized the necessary funds and construction had been slow. The Federal-Aid Highway Act of 1956, signed by President **Dwight David Eisenhower** (1890–1969), increased the proposal to 41,000 miles and contained sufficient dollars to commence construction, making this the largest public works project in U.S. history at that time. By the early 21st century, the Interstate Highway System totaled at 47,742 miles.

Many travelers, whatever their destination, considered cameras necessary equipment for recording scenes and adventures. The Eastman Kodak Company, founded in 1870, had introduced its Kodak Ektra Camera in 1941. It boasted a fast shutter speed that made it an advanced instrument at the time and, as with their other products, proved to be user friendly. The following year, the firm introduced Kodacolor film for prints.

The Bell and Howell Company, incorporated in 1907, quickly moved from a business of repairing movie equipment to manufacturing film projectors. By the 1920s, Bell and Howell also sold cameras and camera accessories. They produced *Action Autographs* (1949), a series of 15-minute films that highlighted unique vacation spots as well as displayed unusual or entertaining events with the intention of showing that travel experiences can be enjoyed through film.

The Allied victory and the return to peace made the postwar years a time to travel and relax, celebrate, and have new experiences. The tourist industry attempted to adjust to both situations by meeting wartime challenges and, after the conflict, capitalizing on the growing interest in travel. Bus lines built luxury coaches and airlines offered passenger services and ticket prices competitive with **trains.** Tour packages with an all-inclusive price tag could be purchased for air tours to Mexico; bus journeys to the Southwest, the Pacific Coast, or the Rockies; and train trips to national parks. By 1949, ocean liners were booked to capacity, AAA offered its first escorted tour, and Diana Rice of the *New York Times* once again wrote regularly about travel to various parts of the world.

*See also:* Aviation; Fast Food; Leisure and Recreation; Photography

**Selected Reading**

Belasco, Warren James. *Americans on the Road: From Autocamp to Motel, 1910–1945*. Cambridge, MA: MIT Press, 1979.

Rice, Diana. "Random Notes for Travelers" and "News and Notes from the Field of Travel." *New York Times,* February 4, 1940, through December 25, 1949. www.proquest.com

Rose, Mark H. *Interstate: Express Highway Politics, 1941–1956*. Lawrence: Regents Press of Kansas, 1979.

# TRUMAN, PRESIDENT HARRY S.

At the 1944 Democratic national convention, the party nominated **Franklin Delano Roosevelt** (1882–1945) for an unprecedented fourth term as president of the United States. World War II still raged, although things were going better for the Allies by then, and Roosevelt promised a continuation of his strong leadership as commander-in-chief. The public knew that Roosevelt suffered a variety of ills, including the crippling effects of polio from his younger years, but few realized the gravity of the situation. Party leaders, despite the president's diminished health, nevertheless urged him to drop then–Vice President Henry A. Wallace (1888–1965), seeing him as too liberal for the good of the ticket. Roosevelt went along with the politicians and reluctantly chose as his running mate a little-known senator from Missouri, Harry S. Truman (1884–1972; the middle initial S in his name does not stand for anything, and disagreements persist about whether to include a period following it. Truman himself sometimes omitted it, and other times used it).

In the November 1944 election, Roosevelt and Truman won, defeating Republicans Thomas E. Dewey (1902–1971) and John W. Bricker (1893–1986), and the nation looked forward to another four years with Roosevelt at the helm. But his physical liabilities overtook him and he died on April 12, 1945, having served just a few months of his new term. He had been president for over 12 years, and his death thrust Vice President Truman into office as a relatively unknown quantity. From the time he assumed the presidency, Truman faced momentous decisions, and many wondered if he would be up to the enormous job that awaited him.

*In this 1945 photograph, Harry Truman was still serving as vice president. He became the nation's 33rd president in April of that year upon the death of Franklin D. Roosevelt. (Bettmann/CORBIS)*

Born in rural Missouri, Truman had served in World War I in France, returned to Missouri and married Bess Wallace (1885–1982), and went into the men's clothing business in Kansas City. The recession of 1921 ended that venture, but with political patronage he became a judge in the Missouri court system. In 1934, with Democratic Party backing, he won election to the U.S. Senate. As a first-term senator, Truman gained little acclaim, but he campaigned tirelessly in 1940 and emerged victorious in a try for a second congressional term. He chaired several committees and began to be noticed; thus, with strong backing from several important Democrats, Truman emerged as Roosevelt's running mate in the 1944 presidential contest.

Less than a month following Roosevelt's death, Germany, on May 7, 1945, accepted the surrender terms offered by the Allies, and the war in Europe came to a close, but the fighting dragged on in the Pacific Theater. Prior to becoming vice president, Truman knew little more than other senators about specific plans for defeating the Japanese. During his first months in office, the conflict barely let up; the ferocious battle of Iwo Jima finally concluded in March 1945, but fighting on Okinawa, which had commenced in late March, would not end until June. Although virtually everyone realized victory would eventually be achieved, few knew any details relevant to the development of the **atomic bomb,** a top-secret project that had been withheld from most members of Congress. Only in the rushed days after his nomination and subsequent election did Truman become aware of the immensity of the project and how close it was to completion.

Once Okinawa fell in June, the obvious next military step involved a land invasion of the Japanese home islands. Truman and his advisors knew that such action would in time overcome the tenacious enemy defenders, but at the cost of countless American lives. On July 16, 1945, just a month after the Okinawa campaign, scientists successfully detonated a nuclear device in the desert near Alamogordo, New Mexico. With this test, Truman had to make a fateful decision: to go ahead with the invasion or to employ a nuclear weapon in an attempt to secure peace with the Japanese.

Always a decisive man, Truman opted for the latter course of action. On August 6, 1945, less than a month following the New Mexico tests, a single atomic bomb virtually wiped out the Japanese city of Hiroshima. When the Japanese government did not respond, three days later a second bomb destroyed Nagasaki. Faced with the total destruction of their country, Japanese leaders surrendered unconditionally on August 15, an event that brought World War II to a close. Truman's decision to drop the bombs has been debated ever since, and neither position, pro or con, enjoys a clear preponderance of supporters.

The end of the war, however, did not grant Truman a respite from major decisions. The **United Nations,** in the discussion and planning stages for many years, officially came into being in October, and Truman gave the fledgling organization his strong backing. An internationalist in many ways, he also supported the 1947 creation of the states of Israel and Pakistan and the 1949 formation of the North Atlantic Treaty Organization (more commonly known as NATO). Perhaps his crowning achievement involved his successful negotiations with a recalcitrant Republican Congress in the summer of 1947 to fund the Marshall Plan, a massive aid program designed to assist in the rebuilding of war-torn Europe.

Domestically, Truman characterized his policies as a "Fair Deal," borrowing on Roosevelt's New Deal. He wanted to end unfair employment practices, raise the minimum wage, and grant higher unemployment compensation. But 1946 also saw the off-year congressional elections, and Republicans and disgruntled Democrats attacked the Truman agenda, with the result that his party lost control of Congress. The president thereafter faced fierce political opposition to many of his plans.

The return to peacetime also opened up a host of other problems. U.S. labor organizations, restive under wartime restrictions against strikes and pay raises, seized the opportunity in the immediate postwar years to assert themselves. Steel plants, automotive manufacturers, shipping companies, railroads, electrical suppliers, telephone companies, oil firms, and coal producers all felt the sting of strikes, some brief and some prolonged. This wave of **labor unrest** finally caused Congress to pass the Taft-Hartley Act in June 1947. It prohibited most strikes without prior mediation, curtailed union powers, allowed right-to-work laws, and limited the practice of closed shops. Truman saw the popular bill as antilabor and vetoed it, but a conservative Congress, including many Democrats, overrode his veto. Despite his distaste for the Taft-Hartley Act, Truman would invoke its powers 12 times between its passage and 1952 in attempts to resolve continuing labor-management problems.

Truman also had to face the growing threat of Soviet expansionism during his tenure as president. In the period 1946–1947, Greece and Turkey, considered strategically important to U.S. security, were threatened by civil wars fomented by Communist-supported forces using the guise of "popular uprisings." To prevent any takeovers, he supplied the beleaguered Greek and Turkish governments with massive foreign aid, much of it military, and talked of the Truman Doctrine, a policy of containment backed by U.S. might. These actions reflected his awareness of the so-called Iron Curtain, an impenetrable military and ideological barrier then closing down on much of Eastern Europe. The Truman Doctrine attempted to block any further encroachments toward the more democratic West, and he willingly provided aid to pro-West governments needing bolstering.

When 1948 and a new presidential election rolled around, Truman found himself in difficult political territory. His general popularity appeared low, the Soviet Union cast hungry eyes on much of Europe, and his Fair Deal had realized none of its broad objectives. The Republicans nominated Thomas E. Dewey, a strong campaigner, as their party candidate for the presidency, just as in 1944. But Truman, a feisty opponent in his own right, fooled the experts by mounting a remarkable whistle stop campaign, speaking from the rear platforms of **trains** as he crisscrossed the country. When the ballots were counted, he had squeaked out an upset victory and won a second term. People liked his mannerisms and his plainspoken approach to complex problems.

The election also returned Congress to the Democratic column in both chambers. Part of Truman's campaign strategy included railing against a "do nothing" Congress, and the tactic paid off handsomely. Buoyed by his victory, an energized Truman returned to office ready to implements his plans. But new and continuing international problems held his attention, the most serious of which involved the revelation that the Soviet Union had detonated its own atomic bomb in late August 1949. Captured wartime German scientists and their Soviet counterparts, along with considerable espionage involving U.S. nuclear secrets, enabled the Communist nation to complete the research and production of a working atomic weapon well ahead of most predictions. U.S. hegemony in the nuclear arena came to an end, and Truman and his advisors had to rethink defense strategies and the relative balance of power between the two countries.

That same year, in another upset, the Western-leaning Nationalist Chinese lost their long civil war with the Communist People's Republic of China. Chang Kai-shek (1887–1975), the Nationalists' longtime leader, and his followers fled to the island of Formosa (now called Taiwan) off the mainland China coast. Invoking the Truman Doctrine, the president vowed to defend the Nationalists and sent the navy's Seventh Fleet to defend the island. Taiwan has remained a problem for United States diplomacy ever since.

As the **Cold War** heated up in the late 1940s, anti-Communist feelings rose sharply within the United States. Many conservative factions accused Truman of being "soft on Communism" (a popular phrase of the day) and responsible for placing the nation at risk against its Soviet adversary. Heated congressional investigations suggested extensive infiltration by Soviet spies in many levels of the government and the military, and several outspoken members of Congress urged loyalty oaths, immediate arrests and trials for any suspected spies, and virtual witch hunts to uncover subversion. This postwar "Red Scare" gained in intensity as international tensions rose, a wave of popular feeling that isolated Truman and his administration.

It culminated in June 1950, when North Korea, a Communist state, attacked independent South Korea. With little hesitation, Truman committed U.S. troops and planes to a United Nations effort to stop the aggression. It would prove a costly, divisive war (or "peace action"; diplomats refrained from using the word "war"), and Truman bore considerable criticism for his handling of it as commander-in-chief. There were even calls for his impeachment when, in 1951, he fired **General Douglas MacArthur** (1880–1964), the popular commander of the UN forces, for publicly disagreeing with him over military policies.

With the Korean conflict and the MacArthur incident, Truman's poll ratings tumbled. As the sitting vice president, he had taken office with the death of Roosevelt. Truman therefore remained eligible for a second full term with the upcoming 1952 election, but he decided not to run again and instead retire to private life. The Truman era drew to a close amid charge and countercharge. He would live for another 20 years and see his reputation restored. By early years of the 21st century, Harry S. Truman has steadily risen as an effective president in the eyes of most political analysts and historians. His stubborn devotion to his principles marks him as more of a statesman than his detractors would admit at the time, and many estimates now place him in the top tier of America's presidential leaders.

On a more personal level, Truman delighted the press and many citizens. He enjoyed taking brisk walks on Pennsylvania and Constitution Avenues, often unescorted, much to the chagrin of his Secret Service guards. When on vacation or playing an occasional game of golf, he favored bright Hawaiian sport shirts, topped off with a casual hat or cap. Bess, his devoted wife, stayed dutifully in the background and granted only one press conference in all her years as first lady. She answered most of the reporters' queries with a terse "no comment."

The Trumans had a daughter, Margaret (1924–2008), who had dreams of a career as a professional singer. During the mid-1940s, she began appearing in public recitals and concerts, as well as performing on **radio** and **television**. At one such event in 1950, a music critic reviewed her concert in less-than-flattering terms; outraged, her father responded in a widely publicized letter that he would break the writer's nose and do other bodily damage should he ever encounter him, and opinion sided with the president. But plain speaking characterized the 33rd president; his motto, displayed on a desk in the Oval Office, famously read "the Buck Stops Here."

*See also:* Berlin Airlift, The; General George Catlett Marshall

**Selected Reading**
McCullough, David. *Truman.* New York: Simon & Schuster, 1992.
Patterson, James T. *Grand Expectations: The United States, 1945–1974.* New York: Oxford University Press, 1996.

# U

## UFOS (UNIDENTIFIED FLYING OBJECTS)

Since time immemorial, people have seen objects in the skies they could not identify. Often others—especially those who had not witnessed the same phenomena—thought such individuals must be seeing things. Too much to drink, hallucinations, religious frenzies, sickness, and endless other explanations were put forth to explain these mysterious sightings. The advent of air **travel** in the early 20th century hardly put an end to such reports; if anything, it increased them. During World War II, pilots and crews occasionally spotted strange lights and swiftly moving shapes and dubbed them "foo fighters."

The word "foo," a nonsense term, gained popularity from the comic strip *Smokey Stover,* a widely read humor series created by cartoonist Bill Holman (1903–1987) that ran from 1935 to 1973. From its inception, *Smokey Stover* enjoyed a diverse readership, mainly for its sheer wackiness and playful use of language. "Foo" made frequent appearances in the strip and had no real significance. Service personnel began using it to designate, among several meanings, a thing or event that cannot be rationally explained. Thus, a foo fighter might be an imaginary aircraft that crews thought they saw.

The various Allied air forces duly made note of such sightings and assumed the enemy possessed secret weapons that could fly at amazing speeds and demonstrate great maneuverability. In time, however, military intelligence found that German and Japanese pilots submitted similar reports, further complicating the issue. In most cases, the objects tended to be spherical or disk-shaped, brightly lit or glowing (some even appeared to burn), and seemed to have a form of intelligence controlling them. Documents—some only declassified in recent years—accumulated, but no concrete findings emerged.

Toward the end of the war in 1945, the news media reported on the sightings of unidentified objects, particularly foo fighters, a term certain to entertain readers. Despite the publicity, little came of the articles, and the subject elicited minimal interest from the public at large. The reports continued, however, and in late June 1947, a private pilot named Kenneth Arnold (1915–1984), flying over the western part of the state of Washington, reported observing nine strange saucer-shaped objects, from his small airplane. He further said that they flew in formation at an extremely high speed and did not threaten him.

The press gave the story wide circulation, and hundreds of similar reports came in from locations not just in the Seattle region but from around the world that corroborated his descriptions. Arnold's mention of the mysterious disks as saucer-shaped soon gave rise to the popular expression "flying saucers," a term that has remained in use since then. In addition, by the late 1940s, the formal description "unidentified flying object" was simplified to UFO. It, too, has become a part of everyday language when discussing such events.

Air Force intelligence officers dismissed Arnold's experience and those of others, suggesting illusions caused by the sun, clouds, mirages, errant weather balloons, and numerous other possibilities. But the reports kept coming in. One of the most famous, recorded in July 1947, claimed that a saucerlike object crashed in the area of Roswell, New Mexico. Again, the military denied the incident but nonetheless launched an investigation. Those inquiries eventually culminated in Project Blue Book, a lengthy examination of these and related events that ran from 1947 until 1967. Although shrouded in secrecy, occasional details leaked out, and people continued to report sightings of UFOs, so that many individuals became convinced that a complex government conspiracy had come into being to discredit any dissenting testimony.

By the end of the decade, a hard core of believers in UFOs had evolved. Hollywood, in the meantime, sensing an opportunity, was gearing up to release science fiction **movies** about flying saucers and extraterrestrial visitors to Earth. The 1950s would see movies like *The Day the Earth Stood Still* (1951), *The Thing* (1951), *Invaders from Mars* (1953), *It Came from Outer Space* (1953), *War of the Worlds* (1953), *Earth Versus the Flying Saucers* (1956), and many others. For those who believed, these films, fictional as they may be, reinforced the idea of UFOs. Nonbelievers, on the other hand, could be entertained by the screenwriters' creativity.

The Air Force may have attempted to squelch any public interest in unidentified flying objects, but with few plausible explanations, they only succeeded in further firing the imaginations of many. By the end of the 1940s, UFOs, real or unreal, were firmly fixed in American popular culture.

*See also:* Aviation; Comic Strips; Newspapers

**Selected Reading**
Clark, Jerome. *The UFO Encyclopedia: The Phenomenon from the Beginning.* 2 vols. Detroit, MI: Omnigraphics, 1998.
Keyhoe, Donald E. *Flying Saucers from Outer Space.* New York: Henry Holt, 1953.
Ruppelt, Edward J. *The Report on Unidentified Flying Objects.* New York: Doubleday, 1956.

# UNITED NATIONS, THE

The name United Nations (often abbreviated as UN), suggested by **President Franklin Delano Roosevelt** (1882–1945), first appeared in a document titled "Declaration by United Nations," that China, the United Kingdom, the Union of Soviet Socialist Republics (USSR), and the United States signed on January 1, 1942, at a conference in Washington, DC. Eventually 22 other nations added their signatures as endorsements of standing together as "united nations" in fighting the Axis powers—Germany, Italy, and Japan.

Three years later, 282 official delegates from 50 countries met in April in San Francisco to establish a global organization with the aim of promoting peace, security, cooperation, and the self-determination of nations. This meeting had been preceded by extensive work and discussions at several conferences of the Allies, including the foreign ministers of Great Britain, the USSR, and the United States (secretary of state) in Moscow in 1943, and a Tehran meeting later that same year attended by President Roosevelt, British Prime Minister Winston Churchill (1874–1965), and Soviet Premier Joseph Stalin (1878–1953).

Ironically, an international group with similar goals had formed after World War I (1914–1918), a conflict that left the world devastated by an unprecedented loss of life among both soldiers and civilians along with extensive destruction throughout Europe. Calling itself the League of Nations, this body operated from 1920 to 1946, with the intention of ensuring security for its member countries and promoting peace among them, although it attained few of its objectives. The U.S. president, Woodrow Wilson (1856–1924), credited as the father of the League, received the Nobel Peace Prize for his efforts in realizing this dream. The United States Congress, however, despite the dedication of the president to this new organization, twice voted against membership and thereby destroyed any chances that the League of Nations would succeed.

*Wilson,* a 1944 American feature movie, stars Alexander Knox (1907–1995), in a role for which he received an Academy Award nomination as best actor. He plays a beleaguered president trying to establish the League of Nations against a recalcitrant Senate led by Henry Cabot Lodge (1850–1924), portrayed by Cedric Hardwicke (1893–1964). A message movie, it created obvious parallels between Wilson and Roosevelt, just as the later president also strove to get Congress's approval for his efforts. In this case, however, Roosevelt prevailed.

The work at the historic United Nations gathering in San Francisco proceeded amid heavy publicity; countless concerned private citizens followed the event thanks to the 2,600 print and **radio** reporters present that kept the world informed. The attending countries included France, which had been occupied by Germany through most of the war, but nevertheless managed to sign the charter on June 26, 1945, just one month after the end of hostilities in Europe. Poland did not have representation at the conference; it signed later and brought the original members to 51. In 2009, the number stood at 192 member states.

Certain organizational aspects of the League of Nations can be found in the later plan of the United Nations. Both identified a basic structure of a general assembly, a secretariat, a security council, and a world court. The UN system initially added two more divisions, an economic and social council and a trusteeship council. The last named, before suspending operations in 1994, supervised the administration and eventual independence of territories that had been under the mandate of the League of Nations or were colonies of nations defeated in World War II.

The primary responsibilities of the other divisions at the time of the formation of the UN also continue as follows:

*United Nations General Assembly:* Composed of representatives from all United Nations members, the assembly meets in regular session annually under a president elected from among the member states.

*United Nations Security Council:* Charged with maintaining peace and security among all members, the Security Council consists of 5 permanent representatives with veto powers from China (today known as the People's Republic of China), the USSR (today known as the Russian Federation), the United States, France, and the United Kingdom, along with 10 members serving limited terms. It is the only group in the UN that has the power to make binding decisions that member governments have agreed to carry out.

*Economic and Social Council:* Promotes international economic and social cooperation and development under the direction of a membership of 54 countries elected by the General Assembly.

*Secretariat:* Provides information and facilities needed by UN bodies for their meetings and is headed by a secretary-general.

*International Court of Justice:* Fifteen judges from around the world hear cases relating to atrocities and injustices such as war crimes, illegal state interference, and genocide. The justices meet at The Hague in the Netherlands.

On January 11, 1946, the delegates to the UN met for the first time in London while looking for a site in New York City to construct a permanent building. Philanthropist John D. Rockefeller Jr. (1874–1960) donated six blocks he owned on Manhattan along the East River between Forty-Second and Forty-Eighth Streets; the United States declared this property an international territory.

The United Nations Board of Design, an international team of 11 individuals that included such notable architects as Oscar Niemeyer (b. 1907), Le Corbusier (1887–1965; b. Charles Edouard Jeanneret-Gris), and Wallace K. Harrison (1895–1981). They reviewed the plans submitted for the building that would house the organization. Despite heated debate among the members of the board, the group finally approved four structures to be built in the International Style and to serve as a symbol of a new beginning after World War II. Work started with the largest, the Secretariat building, with occupancy occurring in 1951. The Conference building followed in February 1952 and the General Assembly building in October of that year. The Dag Hammarskjold (1905–1961) Library, named for the organization's second secretary-general, reached completion in 1961, the year Hammarskjold died in a plane crash.

With construction underway, the delegates to the United Nations worked on matters that related to the reasons for its existence. For example, the General Assembly in 1946 established the United Nations International Children's Emergency Fund (UNICEF). In 1948, the Security Council dealt with a dispute between India and the new nation of Pakistan and, in another matter, ordered a cease-fire in Palestine, along with approval of the creation of UN Relief for Palestine refugees. Problems such as these continue to plague the United Nations.

In June 1950, North Korea invaded its southern neighbor, the Republic of Korea. The Security Council called upon UN members to resist aggression by taking police action to provide South Korea with military assistance. During the summer, the U.S. Congress voted to vigorously support the United Nations' effort to halt this breach of peace. **President Harry S. Truman** (1884–1972) deployed troops to South Korea and, with UN approval, appointed **General Douglas McArthur** (1880–1964) as supreme commander of United Nations forces in Korea, thus closing out the first five turbulent years of the new organization.

The United Nations, an idea conceived with the League of Nations following World War I, had its birth during the difficult years of World War II. It officially came into existence on October 24, 1946, when the charter had been ratified by China, France, the USSR, the United Kingdom, the United States, and a majority of the other participating countries. In 1950, with the completion of one of four buildings at its headquarters in New York, the United Nations took its first major police action; others would come in the following years.

*See also:* Architecture; Cold War, The; Design; Radio Programming: News, Sports, Public Affairs, and Talk; Selective Training and Service Act of 1940 (Selective Service, or Draft)

**Selected Reading**
Bookmiller, Kirsten Nakjavani. *The United Nations.* New York: Chelsea House, 2008.
Gorman, Robert F. *Great Debates at the United Nations: An Encyclopedia of Fifty Key Issues, 1945–2000.* Westport, CT: Greenwood, 2001.
United Nations. *Charter of the United Nations.* New York: United Nations, 2004. www.un.org/en/documents/charter/

## USO (UNITED SERVICE ORGANIZATIONS)

More than a year before the December 1941 attack by Japan on Pearl Harbor, the U.S. government acknowledged the growing unrest in the world and began to prepare for the possibility of involvement in a major conflict. Shortly thereafter, Congress passed the **Selective Training and Service Act of 1940,** a law requiring all men aged 21 to 30 to register with their local draft boards. **President Franklin Delano Roosevelt** (1882–1945) promptly signed the bill and the country's first peacetime draft system came into being.

Five months later, on February 4, 1941, the USO (United Service Organizations) took form, a response to an urgent request from the president. Concerned about providing recreation and boosting morale for the rapidly growing armed forces, Roosevelt had determined that private, not government, agencies could best address the matter. Six civilian organizations—the Salvation Army, the Young Men's Christian Association, the Young Women's Christian Association, the National Catholic Community Services, the National Travelers Aid Association, and the National Jewish Welfare Board—agreed with the president and established a separate umbrella group to coordinate their efforts and resources.

*The usually sultry Marlene Dietrich in a promotional photograph for the USO; she wears an army shirt and tie instead of a slinky evening gown. The actress tirelessly worked to raise funds for the USO, war bonds, the Red Cross, and other worthy causes. (Photofest)*

The new entity quickly developed a two-pronged approach for meeting its responsibilities: (1) organized entertainment and (2) designated places for soldiers to go for recreation and relaxation. As early as May 1941, seven traveling show buses had taken performers to training camps in the United States east of the Rocky Mountains. Demand for similar shows increased rapidly, and, in order to efficiently meet the requests for entertainment, the USO formed a separate corporation, the USO Camp Shows, Inc. This division became chartered on October 30, 1941, and operated in affiliation with and supported by the USO.

Eventually, four circuits comprised the USO Camp Shows with its operating structure. The Victory Circuit, established in 1941, took full-sized revues, Broadway shows, and concerts to the larger military installations. The Blue Circuit consisted of smaller touring companies performing vaudeville-type shows at smaller bases. The Hospital Circuit, introduced in 1944, enabled entertainers to visit wards and auditoriums at U.S. military hospitals and included the Sketch Artists program. This unit involved some 170 **illustrators** and painters who drew portraits of wounded servicemen. Finally, and the most dangerous, the Foxhole, or Overseas Circuit, went as close to the front lines as possible, where entertainers of all types performed for the troops.

Participants in the USO Camp Shows included both the famous and the unknown, the young and the old, with personalities from all facets of the entertainment and sports worlds. Because it is impossible to list them all, the following examples serve as a brief introduction to the many individuals who dedicated themselves to supporting the armed forces wherever they were stationed—in training camps in the United States, in hospitals, and on the battlefields in foreign lands.

**Bob Hope** (1903–2003), well-known for more than 50 years of traveling to military bases and hospitals to show his patriotism and entertain the troops, made his first overseas tour for USO Camp Shows in 1942. Vocalist Frances Langford (1913–2005), actor Tony Romano (1915–2005), and vaudeville dancer and singer Jack Pepper (1902–1979) accompanied him.

In the spring of 1943, ventriloquist Edgar Bergen (1903–1978) and his dummy Charlie McCarthy entertained in Newfoundland, while comedian Jack Benny (1894–1974) and harmonica player Larry Adler (1914–2001) traveled to the Middle East. Comedian Joe E. Lewis (1902–1971) and dancer Ray Bolger (1904–1987), who played the scarecrow in *The Wizard of Oz* (1939), covered military bases in the Pacific, as did the *Oklahoma!* company from Broadway. Playwright and director Moss Hart (1904–1961) took the production *The Man Who Came to Dinner* to the Pacific and Australia, and actress Judith Anderson (1897–1992) offered Shakespearean plays in Hawaii. In 1944, a cast for the folk opera *Porgy and Bess* gave a preview performance at Mitchell Field, Long Island, before touring in Europe for the Foxhole Circuit. For these varied performances, Camp Show units created backdrops that would fold into suitcases and built supports that dismantled easily. Frequently, they had to improvise, such as lighting a stage entirely with flashlights.

Leading singers, vocal groups, musicians, and bandleaders participating in USO Camp Shows included **The Andrews Sisters** (Patty [b. 1918], Maxene [1916–1995], and LaVerne [1911–1967]), Fred Astaire (1899–1987), **Bing Crosby** (1903–1977), **Duke Ellington** (1899–1974), Spike Jones (1911–1965) and his City Slickers, Andre Kostelanetz (1901–1980), **Glenn Miller** (1904–1944), and **Dinah Shore** (1916–1994). An operatic concert unit that included tenor Frederick Jagel (1897–1982), violinist Isaac Stern (1920–2001), soprano Polyna Stoska (active 1930s to 1940s), baritone Robert Weede (1903–1972), and pianist Alex Zakin (1903–1990) landed in amphibious military DUKWs (commonly called "ducks") to perform for 10,000 GIs in New Guinea.

Athletes also did their share of boosting the morale of service personnel. Wrestler Nick Munday (active 1940s) went to France and Belgium, as did boxers Jack Sharkey (1902–1994) and Mickey Walker (1903–1981), while world table tennis champion Ruth Aarons (1910–1980) played the game with GIs in Normandy. **Baseball** greats Frankie Frisch (1898–1973), Carl Hubbell (1903–1988), Lefty Gomez (1908–1989), and Mel Ott (1909–1958) called on troops, and Brooklyn Dodgers manager Leo Durocher (1905–1991) took 22 people, including players, managers, and umpires, to visit the various theaters of war.

The severity of the battle zone or the roughness of a spot did not stop Camp Shows, and the entertainers often faced the same dangers as the troops. In the spring of 1944, the tent cities on the British fields and beaches bordering the English Channel received entertainers, and on July 28 of that year, just 48 days after the **D-Day** invasion, plywood appeared atop a 30-ton ammunition carrier to accommodate the group that had arrived to give a show in France. By then, units had branched out to North Africa, Sicily, and Italy. Entertainers in North Africa included actors John Garfield (1913–1952), Jack Haley (1898–1979), and George Raft (1895–1980), singer Nelson Eddy (1901–1967), and violinist Jascha Heifetz (1901–1987).

From 1941 to 1947, USO Camp Shows presented 428,521 performances and hit a peak in 1945 with 700 shows a day to audiences as large as 15,000 and as small as 25 at some distant outposts. These performances, both overseas and in the United States, meant entertainment for an audience totaling at least 173 million. In all, more than 7,000 entertainers traveled overseas.

To achieve its second charge, to provide a place for service members to gather, the USO established centers in communities close to bases across the country, using whatever available vacant space that would work, such as churches, yacht clubs, old mansions, storefronts, log cabins, and barns. The first one opened its doors on November 28,

1941, in Fayetteville, North Carolina, and by 1944, more than 3,000 such clubs had become the GIs' home away from home.

Successful operation of the USO centers required the involvement of many volunteers, a role fulfilled by more than 1.5 million people by war's end. Usually residents of the communities housing a club provided this service. In 1944, the National Recreation Association published a volunteer's handbook that gave tips on social issues, such as appropriate dress and lists of favorite refreshments to prepare. The guide also offered advice on ways of making conversation and included suggestions for acceptable topics—home, **hobbies,** schools, and **movies**—as well as subjects to avoid, mainly anything touching on military matters.

Military personnel visiting special USO clubs close to Los Angeles and New York City, the Hollywood Canteen and the Stage Door Canteen in Times Square, had the opportunity to interact with a unique set of volunteers: stars from the entertainment world who performed for the soldiers, talked with them, and served refreshments or a meal. These activities became the focus of two movies, *Stage Door Canteen* (1943) and *Hollywood Canteen* (1944). Both starred an array of actors and actresses portraying themselves as they provided this important service for those in the armed forces.

Programs at the USO centers varied as much as the places that housed them. The primary focus of all the clubs dealt with providing recreational opportunities for off-duty soldiers—a place to read, **dance,** meet and talk with people, see a movie, write letters, and enjoy free coffee and doughnuts.

By December 31, 1947, all USO clubs and facilities had closed, and the organization disbanded the Camp Shows. **President Harry S. Truman** (1884–1972) even gave the USO an honorable discharge. But in 1951, the outbreak of the Korean War revived both the clubs and touring shows. USO Camp Shows, Inc., which had evolved into a separate entity, ceased operation in 1957. The USO itself assumed all responsibility for managing the entertainment needs of military personnel around the world, a practice that has continued to the present.

*See also:* Broadway Shows (Comedy and Drama); Broadway Shows (Musicals); Canteens; *Edgar Bergen/Charlie McCarthy Show, The; Jack Benny Program, The*

**Selected Reading**

USO. www.uso.org/whoweare/ourproudhistory/

USO and USO Camp Shows. *New York Times,* March 1, 1942; July 27, 1942; April 6, 1944; August 27, 1944; September 14, 1944. www.proquest.com

Young, William H., and Nancy K. Young. *Music of the World War II Era.* Westport, CT: Greenwood Press, 2008.

# V

## V-E AND V-J DAY

Anticipation about the successful end to World War II grew throughout 1944, and two terms appeared in print and were heard on **radio:** V-E Day and V-J Day. They meant "victory in Europe" and "victory over Japan," although no actual surrenders had yet taken place. Credit for the terms often goes to James F. Byrnes (1879–1972) who, as director of the United States War Mobilization Board, used them in a 1944 speech, although others perhaps employed similar phrasing before him. The more generic Victory Day or V-Day may have preceded them, especially in Europe. An accurate etymology will probably never be discovered, but V-E Day and V-J Day quietly entered everyday American language some time in 1944.

Allied commanders correctly foresaw that, by mid-1944, with the landings at Normandy and the bold tactic of island hopping in the Pacific, the conclusion of World War II loomed in the near future. But they also knew that many more bloody battles would be fought and that the Axis powers would not surrender easily. For Americans back home, however, this sense of inevitability grew as they read about victories on all fronts, and any setbacks, no matter how bloody, seemed like delaying actions by the enemy.

On April 30, 1945, Germany's Adolf Hitler (b. 1889) committed suicide. In the chaotic aftermath of his death, his generals rushed to secure a peace with advancing Allied forces. A week later, virtually all fighting came to a halt, and the various parties reached the terms for an unconditional surrender by the following day in Berlin. **President Harry S. Truman** (1884–1972) declared May 8, 1945, as the official V-E Day, and celebrations, both in the United States and elsewhere, reflected people's relief at the cessation of hostilities.

The war in the Pacific, however, would drag on for another three months. Japan stubbornly rejected any peace overtures and vowed to fight to the last defender. Finally, on August 6 and 9, U.S. bombers dropped two atomic bombs—one on the city of Hiroshima and the other on Nagasaki. Shortly thereafter, the Japanese agreed to surrender, and on August 15, 1945, the war in the Pacific ended. Officials from both sides signed the formal documents on September 2, 1945, on the deck of the U.S. battleship USS *Missouri* in Tokyo Bay. President Truman thereupon proclaimed that date as the official V-J Day. Once again, celebrations, even more joyous and riotous than those held in May, broke out across the land. World War II had finally come to a close.

*See also:* Atomic Bomb, The; D-Day; Eisenhower, General Dwight David; MacArthur, General Douglas; Radio Programming: News, Sports, Public Affairs, and Talk

**Selected Reading**
Kennedy, David M. *Freedom from Fear: The American People in Depression and War, 1929–1945.* New York: Oxford University Press, 1999.

# VICTORY GARDENS

Immediately after the December 7, 1941, Japanese attack on Pearl Harbor and the United States' official entry into World War II the following day, government leaders asked citizens at home to organize and make necessary contributions to the war effort. One suggestion involved cultivating home vegetable gardens, a successful concept first used in World War I in both England and the United States; at the time, the two nations called them war gardens. Following Armistice Day in 1918, officials had encouraged continued production, with a name change to victory gardens, but most people turned to other pursuits and it failed to have much of an impact. With a new war, however, the idea once again received a strong, positive response. Resplendent with vegetables, fruits, and herbs, home gardens quickly appeared in America's backyards, front lawns, city rooftops, and vacant lots.

The lawn at San Francisco's City Hall exemplified how many towns and cities converted public land to vegetable gardens; other municipalities boasted communal planting areas in parks, such as one located in the Boston Commons. By now called victory gardens again, plots sprang up in Chicago's Arlington Race Track and Portland, Oregon's zoo. Even factories got into the act by using farms outside cities to grow **food** for consumption in employee cafeterias. By the fall of 1943, some 40 percent of the nation's vegetables came from these efforts, easily the most popular of all the home-front war projects.

Three situations drove the necessity for gardens: shortages of materials and food for home use, decreases in the labor force, and **rationing.** Materials, such as tin cans, utilized in food processing and canning had to be redirected to the manufacture of items for the war, thus decreasing supplies of produce and canned products available for stocking grocery and supermarket shelves. Also, the government allocated over 50 percent of commercially canned food to the military. At the same time, as thousands of men joined the armed forces, a lack of labor and **transportation** hindered the harvesting and movement of fruits and vegetables to market. Finally, the federal government, in the spring of 1942, imposed rationing to regulate the amount of commodities that consumers could buy. This included canned, bottled, and frozen fruits and vegetables, plus juices.

Along with the obvious need for victory gardens, participation in the program clearly offered other benefits. Reducing food scarcities through homegrown produce meant more food on the family table as well as fuller stomachs. Those who had a victory garden reported a feeling of satisfaction because of their participation and proudly took credit for contributing to the war effort in a way that directly helped the nation's servicemen. The planting and care of the garden offered a recreational activity for the family that sometimes included friends or neighbors. Finally, what could be seen as both a work and leisure activity also doubled as exercise.

Supporting the government's request, both agricultural and wildlife services offered assistance. The U.S. Department of Agriculture issued a 20-minute film titled *Victory Garden* to encourage participation and teach people how to plant and harvest a garden. Extension agents with this department provided seed, fertilizer, and simple gardening tools. The

*While sons, husbands, brothers, and fathers picked up rifles to fight the enemy, those on the home front picked up shovels and hoes and planted victory gardens. It was estimated that by 1943, some 40 percent of the country's vegetables came from these backyard efforts. (Library of Congress)*

U.S. Fish and Wildlife Service published leaflets alerting gardeners to ways to protect their vegetables from common pests, including rabbits, moles, rats, and groundhogs. Both pamphlets and classes offered instruction in the art of successful canning. The United States Office of War Information (OWI) issued **posters** and slogans to encourage Americans to plant and harvest a victory garden: "Plant A Victory Garden—Our Food Is Fighting," "Grow It Yourself," "Your Victory Garden Counts More Than Ever," and "War Gardens For Victory—Grow Vitamins At Your Kitchen Door," to name a few.

In addition to government agencies, various organizations contributed to the victory garden endeavor. The nonprofit Ad Council, created in 1941, encouraged the building of victory gardens and assisted with publicity efforts. **Magazines** such as the *Saturday Evening Post* and *Life* ran stories about the program and published plans for successful gardens. Photographs in the May 3, 1943, issue of *Life* show a flower garden at a townhouse complex in Los Angeles that had been converted to a vegetable plot, prisoners in Chicago working on a victory garden in their walled-in jail yard, nuns growing vegetables for the residents at a home for the aged, and a lush garden situated in a vacant lot in downtown New Orleans only one block from busy Canal Street. Even a portion of the manicured grounds of the White House were tilled. Newspaper ads suggested gardening supplies and promoted presentations on how to garden and put up canned goods.

Public service booklets published by *Good Housekeeping* magazine, International Harvester, Beech-Nut Packing Company, *House & Garden* magazine, and seed companies and nurseries taught the basics of gardening and suggested vegetables to plant. Depending on the climate and time of the year, most amateur gardeners planted squash, beans, cabbage, peppers, eggplant, peas, lettuce, kale, cucumbers, and tomatoes, although many attempted other items whenever they could.

Shortly after the 1942 announcement of the program, Grosset and Dunlap published *Food Gardens for Defense,* by M. G. (Maurice Grenville) Kains (1868–1946). Comedian Jack Benny (1894–1974), by way of his **radio** program, let it be known that he had a victory garden and perhaps convinced many to join him.

Hollywood promoted the concept through cartoons. In December 1942, MGM released *Barney Bear's Victory Garden.* The next year saw more activity. Paramount's Popeye had one in *Ration Fer the Duration,* and Warner Bros. Pictures issued three films with victory garden references. Bugs Bunny cracks garden jokes in *Jack Wabbit and the Beanstalk* and steals all the carrots from a plot in a small San Fernando Valley town in *Buckaroo Bugs.* Babbit, a take-off on comedian Bud Abbott (1895–1974) of Abbott and [Lou] Costello (1906–1959), waters his plot in *A Tale of Two Kitties,* and in a Private Snafu short, *The Home Front;* this last film shows a victory garden fertilized with horse manure.

From 1942 through 1945, the OWI collaborated with Hollywood production companies on 47 documentaries, each addressing an issue related to the war effort. One, released by Warner Bros. Pictures in 1943 and titled *Food and Magic,* stars actors Faye Emerson (1917–1983), Fred Kelsey (1884–1961), Bill Kennedy (1908–1997), and Mark Stevens (1916–1994). In this short, a carnival magician teaches his audience how to aid the war effort by producing and conserving food.

Everyone got the message. Neighbors in communities across the country gathered on weekend mornings to build and maintain individual and communal garden sites. The Girl Scouts learned how to grow seedlings and transplant them to their family's plot, and groups of schoolchildren shared the responsibilities of a garden, frequently on school grounds. Billboard advertisements for products such as Dr. Pepper and Budweiser carried gardening themes, and department stores ran films and created displays on canning. Botanical societies offered classes on a variety of topics, ranging from appropriate fruits for home gardens to both storing and canning methods.

Women enrolled in classes on the topic, and programs for women's clubs, church groups, and garden clubs frequently focused on raising and preserving food. The lawns gracing wealthy homes, such as the Charles M. Schwab estate in New York City, provided space for demonstration gardens. The FSA (Farm Security Administration) and the OWI photographed and publicized a plethora of examples of the movement: Vice President Henry Wallace (1888–1965) working in his victory garden; an empty corner in Forest Hills, New York, converted to a garden; families caring for gardens in Washington, DC, New England, the South, and the Midwest, to name but a few.

In order to maintain a high level of interest, state war councils sponsored harvest fairs where anyone could exhibit his or her best produce, and towns and cities, small and large, participated. In 1943, such an event, called Harvest Show, occupied the lobbies of RKO theaters throughout the five New York City boroughs and moved to the Pershing Square Center for the 1944 and 1945 events. Chicago gardeners showed off their successes at Soldier's Field in a festival sponsored by the *Chicago Sun* newspaper. Catherine Benso (active 1940s), a resident of Norway, Michigan, in 1944 won that year's garden record book contest and received a $1,000 savings bond from the National Victory Garden Institute for her outstanding home garden of prize tomatoes, onions, and 35 other kinds of vegetables.

In short, it became stylish to garden. Estimates indicate that Americans planted more than 15 million victory gardens in 1942 and more than 20 million in 1943. By the end of the conflict, the Department of Agriculture calculated that the program had achieved a total home-front production of over 1 million tons of fruits and vegetables worth roughly $85 million, or valued at about 4 cents a pound (approximately $1 billion and 47 cents, respectively, in 2008 money).

The businesses needed to support this effort flourished. Seed companies experienced significant success. In 1943, American families bought 315,000 pressure cookers for canning vegetables and fruits, up from 66,000 in 1942, but the supplies were limited. Some home canners utilized community canning centers that had been established for the sharing of such equipment. In March 1944, the War Production Board allowed the release of 500,000 enamel pressure cookers for home use, thus alleviating the shortage.

At the end of the war, however, with an expectation of greater produce availability and the anticipated convenience of supermarket shopping, many of the wartime gardeners put away their pressure cookers and hung up their shovels and hoes. With the postwar economic boom, if Americans did anything with the grounds surrounding their homes, they tended to concentrate on exceptional lawns, shrubs, and flower beds, not on vegetable gardens.

When the United States entered World War II, it had asked its citizens to help out in a number of ways. One of those, victory gardens, although not a new idea, had appeared across the nation during World War I and again as a Great Depression relief project. With the onset of the Second World War, victory gardens, along with the purchase of **war bonds,** conservation of raw materials, and **scrap drives,** provided those on the home front ways to support the national war effort. Millions stepped up to the challenge. Only two public examples of the successful victory garden endeavor remain active today—the Fenway Victory Gardens in the Back Bay area of Boston, which now feature mainly flowers, and the Dowling Community Garden in Minneapolis, which retains a focus on vegetables.

*See also:* Advertising; Grocery Stores and Supermarkets; Frozen Food; Hobbies; Lawns, Lawnmowers, and Fertilizers; Leisure and Recreation; Newspapers; Photography

**Selected Reading**
Lingeman, Richard. *Don't You Know There's a War On? The American Home Front, 1941–1945.* New York: Thunder's Mouth Press, 1970.

McCutcheon, Marc. *The Writer's Guide to Everyday Life from Prohibition through World War II.* Cincinnati: Writer's Digest Books, 1995.

Miller, Char. "In the Sweat of Our Brow: Citizenship in American Domestic Practice during WWII—Victory Gardens." *Journal of American Culture* 26 (September 2003): 395–409.

Victory Gardens. *New York Times,* April 12, 1942; August 30, 1942; March 13, 1943; January 12, 1945. www.proquest.com

# VOICE OF AMERICA

Officials gave this name to the external broadcasting arm of the federal government of the United States. Created in 1942 and run by the Office of War Information (OWI), the Voice of America (VOA) carried informational **radio** programming to other countries—especially Germany, Italy, and Japan, as well as those nations occupied by Axis forces. At first limited to radio signals transmitting news, it has long since grown to offer a varied menu, such as music and special interest programming. In more recent times, the organization expanded to include **television** and Internet content. When World War II ended in 1945, the government cut VOA programming sharply, and the State Department took over its operation. This arrangement lasted until 1953, when the service became part of the newly formed United States Information Agency (USIA). In both cases, the Voice of America existed as an extension of ongoing foreign policy.

Unlike private AM and FM stations in the United States, federal law, exercised through the Federal Communications Commission (FCC), exempts the Voice of America from many FCC regulations, including customary call letters or call signs. The service carries programming in numerous languages to make it accessible to nations everywhere, and bears the responsibility of presenting the culture of the United States in a positive light and promoting international goodwill. During the war years, the VOA worked strenuously to counter anti-American propaganda emanating from the Axis powers; in the postwar period, Communist propaganda became its target.

With the rise of the **Cold War** in 1946 and after, the Voice of America soon became a tool in the struggle between East and West. Officials felt the organization could be an asset in advancing American values. In 1947, VOA commenced Russian-language broadcasts aimed at the Soviet Union. In a continuing, rancorous dispute between the two countries, the Soviets attempted to jam incoming signals by blocking them with electronic interference, and American engineers worked to devise ways of countering those efforts. This radio confrontation provided reams of propaganda for both sides. The practice of jamming continued in most Soviet-controlled countries well into the 1950s and beyond.

The height of the Cold War also saw the emergence of Radio Free Europe (RFE) and Radio Liberty (RL), two broadcasting services that complemented the anti-Communist tone of VOA transmissions. RFE, founded in 1949, received most of its monies from the United States Congress. Radio Liberty came along two years later. Both emerged at a critical time in international relations and focused their attention on the Soviet Union and its Eastern European satellites. Stridently anti-Communist in the late 1940s and throughout the 1950s, the two organizations merged in 1976, citing changes in world affairs and a duplication of effort. In more recent years, the RFE/RL budget has been slashed, and most congressional funding has gone to the Voice of America.

Ever since the launching of the Voice of America, FCC rules have prevented it from broadcasting within the United States, although listeners with shortwave equipment (which most radios lack) could pick up its signals with relative ease. The FCC has stated that broadcasting VOA programming within the United States does not meet its requirements for content, although critics have charged that the commission, by forbidding VOA broadcasts within the United States, imposes it own form of censorship.

*See also:* Axis Sally and Tokyo Rose; FM Radio; Political and Propaganda Films; Radio Programming: News, Sports, Public Affairs, and Talk

**Selected Reading**

Heil, Alan L., Jr. *Voice of America: A History.* New York: Columbia University Press, 2003.

Hixon, Walter L. *Parting the Curtain: Propaganda, Culture, and the Cold War.* New York: St. Martin's Press, 1998.

Puddington, Arch. *Broadcasting Freedom: The Cold War Triumph of Radio Free Europe and Radio Liberty.* Lexington: University Press of Kentucky, 2003.

# W

## WAR BONDS

To raise funds, governments and public companies can issue bonds that promise to repay the buyer, over a certain period of time, the face amount plus a stated rate of interest. Historically, governments have helped to pay for wars through the issuance of bonds, and World War II has become a classic illustration of the effectiveness of bond drives as a means of securing money. At no other time in U.S. history—the Revolution, the Civil War, World War I—did bonds play such an important role. For example, the sale and purchase of the much-touted Liberty Bonds during World War I were so dismally low that the government ceased issuing them with the 1918 Armistice.

In 1934, **President Franklin Delano Roosevelt** (1882–1945) appointed Henry Morgenthau Jr. (1891–1967) as secretary of the United States Treasury. With the country in the midst of the Great Depression, Morgenthau turned out to be an imaginative secretary, overseeing numerous programs that helped alleviate the hardships, including the reinstatement of bonds. Congress accepted Morgenthau's opinion that they could be a secure savings instrument for all investors, including those of modest means, as well as a guaranteed source of funds for the Treasury. The sale of Series A bonds (and later series B, C, and D) commenced on February 4, 1935. Easily purchased, with a 10-year maturity, they soon gained the popular name of "baby bonds." Supported by a mail campaign, they sold steadily, primarily to wealthy individuals, banks, and corporations, not ordinary citizens as had been hoped.

Thanks in part to Morgenthau's measures, the nation by 1940 had experienced some relief from its economic problems, but the government acknowledged the reality of an impending war and the need to make preparations. Morgenthau and his advisors anticipated two economic conditions that would emerge with the advent of war: (1) inflation and (2) huge financial burdens.

*The fifth of eight war bond drives ran from June 12, 1944, to July 8, 1944, and raised $20.6 billion (approximately $252 billion in 2008 dollars). This picture shows a giant cash register erected in New York City's Times Square to tally the results, part of an estimated $42.7 million worth of donated advertising (approximately $522 million in 2008 dollars). (Bettmann/CORBIS)*

In an attempt to prevent wartime inflation brought on by rising costs, growing employment, and competition for fewer goods caused by scarcity and **rationing,** Roosevelt issued an executive order on April 11, 1941, that established the Office of Price Administration (OPA), an agency that would operate within the Office for Emergency Management. Charged with attempting to avert inflation, the OPA decided to concentrate on encouraging the American public to invest in bonds. The War Finance Committee, a group under the direction of the United States Treasury, also addressed the sale of bonds; before the war's end, it had overseen eight bond drives as well as thousands of special events that sold bonds.

It was decided that a new bond, the Series E savings bond, would be one means of defraying some of the costs associated with another war. They went on sale in the spring of 1941, along with new Series F and G offerings, designed more for institutional and commercial investors instead of the average citizen of limited means. Treasury officials called all three categories defense bonds, a name that promptly changed to war bonds after Pearl Harbor and the nation's active entry into World War II.

The Series E offering, the bond of choice for most people, initially came in five denominations, $25, $50, $100, $500, and $1,000; they could be purchased for 75 percent of face value. Thus, a $25 bond could be bought for $18.75, a $50 bond for $37.50, and so on. In addition, the Treasury Department created a special $10 bond for active members of the armed forces. Regardless of denomination, the E Bonds paid 2.9 percent interest, with a 10-year maturity.

To encourage as much citizen participation as possible, the government made the E series available to individuals only. At first, bonds could be bought at post offices and banks or at specified campaigns and special events, but officials soon broadened those restrictions to include department stores and other commercial establishments. Anyone regularly employed could also purchase them directly through payroll deductions. By 1945, the peak year, enrollment in various payroll savings plans exceeded 25 million workers.

Bond programs encouraged schoolchildren to participate by issuing Defense Savings Stamps (which superseded earlier Postal Savings Stamps). They came in 10-cent, 25-cent, 50-cent, one-dollar, and five-dollar denominations. The figure of the Minute Man, the famous statue by sculptor Daniel Chester French (1850–1931) that stands in Concord, Massachusetts, in honor of the American Revolution, became the symbol of the program, and the Defense Stamps display the iconic citizen-soldier, rifle at the ready. Boys and girls—along with many adults—traded their dimes, quarters, and other change for these stamps, pasting them in albums provided by post offices and schools. When an album reached the desired amount—usually $18.75 for children (roughly $274.50 in 2008 dollars)—it could be turned in for a bond. The weekly addition of a stamp or two became a ritual for people around the country.

On April 30, 1941, President Roosevelt went on network **radio** and urged citizens to invest in the new bonds; the following day, in a much-publicized ceremony, he purchased the first Series E bond from Secretary Mongenthau. The wartime campaign lasted until January 3, 1946, although the Series E bonds would remain available until 1980, When the proceeds from the last drive had been deposited, the government's all-out effort to sell bonds of all kinds reached nearly $186 billion (approximately $2 trillion in 2008 dollars) in funds for the war. Of that total, the Series E bonds accounted for a remarkable $33.7 billion (approximately $388 billion in 2008 dollars).

From past bond-selling experiences, the Treasury Department recognized a need to educate the American public about the safety of this way of investing in one's country. The department understood that achieving a high level of sales would require unique and extensive **advertising,** a move that could incur expenses that reduced overall yields. When estimates on the costs of advertising reached $4 million (approximately $51 million in 2008 dollars), the War Finance Committee determined that assistance from the private sector would be needed.

A speech by James Webb Young (1886–1973) in November 1941 provided a solution. Young, an advertising executive with the J. Walter Thompson agency and a lecturer at the University of Chicago's School of Business, spoke on the topic of "What Action Can Be Taken?" at the first joint meeting of the Association of National Advertisers and the American Association of Advertising Agencies. In this speech, Young emphasized that advertising's survival depended on the strength of businesses but that advertising had a responsibility to use its potential power to influence social change.

The private sector received Young's speech with a strong, positive response, which led to the immediate formation of the Advertising Council, informally known as the Ad Council. Charged with distributing public service announcements for charitable, commercial, and government organizations the council first accepted a request from Morgenthau for it to play a key role in the Series E savings bond campaign. Under the leadership of advertising executive and scholar Walter Weir (1909–1996), the agency became known as the War Advertising Council, with headquarters in both Washington, DC, and New York City, It launched a campaign to sell the public on the merits of the new Series E war bonds and by 1945 had secured in excess of $300 million (approximately $3.5 billion in 2008 dollars) in advertising time and space from media outlets.

By capitalizing on a strong sense of patriotism and encouraging an attitude of partnership with the government, the council stressed that buying bonds assured everyone a personal role in the war effort and fostered the idea of influencing others to do likewise. Constant and effective advertising of all kinds brought together untold numbers of Americans from all walks of life in a common pursuit. By purchasing war bonds, citizens saw themselves serving their country and hastening the end of the conflict.

The increased availability of money from good-paying defense jobs and a reduction in the availability of consumer products, along with rationing, gave people the wherewithal to obtain bonds—a combination that assured the success of the plan. Purchasing bonds during specific campaigns also was unusually effective. Table 101 offers basic statistics for eight such events conducted between November 30, 1942, and December 8, 1945—one in 1942, two in 1943, three in 1944, and two in 1945. The eighth and final campaign, which commenced in October 1945 and did not end until December of that year, actually occurred after the May surrender of Germany and Japan's September capitulation. Despite the formal end of the war, expenses continued long afterward, making every dollar raised important.

Each campaign had unprecedented support in donated money and advertising, exceeding stated goals so that the Treasury Department from these efforts alone collected over $156 billion (almost $1.5 trillion in 2008 dollars). Combined with the payroll savings plan, over 85 million Americans individually bought close to 800 million war bonds and raised the most money ever to help finance a war.

TABLE 101. United States Department of the Treasury War Bond Campaigns, 1942–1945

| Dates | Campaign | Goal | Total Collected Through The War Effort | Donations for Advertising the Campaign |
|---|---|---|---|---|
| November 30–December 23, 1942 | First War Loan | $9 billion | Almost $13 billion | n.d. |
| April 12–May 1, 1943 | Second War Loan | $13 billion | Over $18.5 billion | Over $4.5 million worth space from **newspapers** and $170,000 from **magazines** |
| September 8–October 2, 1943 | Third War Loan | $15 billion | Almost $19 billion | Estimated $23.4 million worth of ads |
| January 18–February 15, 1944 | Fourth War Loan | $14 billion | $16.7 billion | Almost $25 million worth of donated ads and 6 million volunteers |
| June 12–July 8, 1944 | Fifth War Loan | $16 billion | $20.6 billion | Estimated $42.7 million worth of ads |
| November 20–December 16, 1944 | Sixth War Loan | Not known | $21.6 billion | Over $11 million worth of ads |
| May 14–June 25, 1945 | Seventh War Loan | $7 billion | Over $26 billion | Over $42 million worth of ads |
| October 29–December 8, 1945 | Eighth War Loan | $11 billion | Over $21 billion | n.d. |

*Note:* n.d. = no data available.
*Source:* "Brief History of World War Two Advertising Campaigns War Loans and Bonds," Duke University Libraries. www.library.duke.edu/digitalcollections/adaccess/warbonds.html

The First War Loan Drive, conducted in November and December 1942, although financially successful, did not attract as many buyers as anticipated. Only $1.6 billion of the almost $13 billion (approximately $20 billion and $165 billion, respectively, in 2008 dollars) came from individuals, with the remainder contributed by corporations and commercial banks. The level of individual buying doubled, however, with the Second War Loan Drive. The third and fourth campaigns, likewise, attracted increased numbers of individual buyers. Some of the drives targeted specific war costs: for example, the second, which carried the name "Outfit the Outfit," focused on raising funds needed to feed, dress, and equip a soldier; the fourth emphasized the purchase of hospital equipment.

Promotional materials encouraged various demographic groups to buy bonds. The fourth campaign targeted farmers with pamphlet titles of "Our Good Earth...Keep It Ours" and "The Minute Man Was A Farmer Too." All of the drives reminded Americans that purchasing bonds ranked high on the list of what needed to be done to win World War II quickly. Judging from the results of the bond program, Americans agreed.

Although advertising and media businesses played a major role in all war bond promotions, a large number and variety of other businesses, industries, organizations, and individuals also gave impressive support in both money and time. Groups as diverse as the Daughters of the American Revolution and B'nai B'rith provided the Treasury Department with member addresses for direct mail campaigns. War bond committees, established in communities across the country and made up of volunteers, spurred on their friends and neighbors to participate and staffed booths selling bonds at theaters, public gatherings, and stores. Cashiers urged their patrons to take their change in savings stamps, and organizers often figured the price of admission to various functions in the ubiquitous stamps.

The major radio networks regularly devoted entire broadcasting days to "Radio Bond Days." During these periods, every scheduled show tied itself to buying bonds in one way or another, and announcers urged listeners to make telephone pledges for still more bonds. The Treasury Department also ran daily ads that promoted war bonds on stations across the land.

Retailers ranging from mom-and-pop operations to large companies allowed for a variety of bond-selling promotions. In addition to establishing booths at their businesses, some offered free products or services with the purchase of a bond at their store, and many devoted window display space to advertising war bonds. In fact, the Treasury Department organized advertising contests in connection with the Fifth and Sixth War Loan Drives. The War Finance Committee, which oversaw all sales, designated July 1942 as Retailers for Victory Month and asked all merchants to set aside a 15-minute period on July 1 to sell only war bonds. For the Seventh War Loan Drive, the Treasury introduced the Third Army Plan, a promotion that awarded small badges to retail employees, ranking them from private to general depending on their bond sales record.

Teachers, administrators, and students came under the Treasury's "Schools at War" program, which held bond and stamp drives. Materials provided by the government contained stories, plays, songs, and recitations that linked the buying of savings bonds and stamps to the value of democracy, citizenship, and patriotism. Some drives encouraged children to purchase stamps in order to raise enough funds for specific purposes, such as buying Jeeps or other designated pieces of military equipment.

Trade unions, although initially opposed to the foreign policy positions of the Roosevelt administration, changed their opinion and supported the federal government as the country's possible involvement in European matters accelerated in 1940. With the launching of the savings bond program, labor leaders assisted with the distribution of government pamphlets, such as *Defense Bonds for American Workers,* to a total of 15 million members of the unions.

Much of the copy generated for these campaigns showed considerable originality. Materials addressed to women became commonplace. A pamphlet titled *Mrs. Brown Goes to War,* paid for by grocery chains such as A&P, Safeway, Kroger, and Piggly Wiggly, appeared on store shelves along with canned corn and peas. In addition to in-store endorsements, **grocery stores and supermarkets,** like many businesses, promoted sales in their radio and newspaper ads.

All the major **magazines** available in the country—some 500 different titles—collaborated in July 1942 by featuring similar covers, both on newsstands and for subscribers. The covers depict a U.S. flag and the words "United We Stand," the name given this unique campaign unify the country for the struggle ahead. *Ladies' Home Journal* partnered with the Treasury Department in the publication of *Home Front Journal,* a newsletter for women serving on bond promotion committees. War stamp bouquets, made of war stamps instead of flowers, became a new table decoration or party favor and served as a way to bring the campaign directly into homes. The year 1943 saw a Bonds for Babies promotion, and a similar Bonds for Brides campaign followed with the launching of the Grandmothers' War Bond League in 1944.

Even the incarcerated became supporters of the campaigns. In 1942, prisoners at the Ohio State Penitentiary spent $6,325 (approximately $80,500 in 2008 dollars) on bonds and $1,333.75 (approximately $17,000 in 2008 dollars) on savings stamps. That same year, a defendant convicted of arson in Massachusetts received as punishment instruction to purchase $5 (approximately $64 in 2008 dollars) worth of defense stamps each week for the duration of the war. If he failed to comply, he would receive two years' imprisonment.

In addition to these innovative approaches, the Treasury also employed some classic sales techniques, such as linking the purchase of a bond to specific holidays. For Christmas 1942, a special envelope designed to hold a war bond became available as a holiday present, and the Treasury, in 1944, offered a V-Mail certificate to friends and relatives of service personnel, redeemable as a war bond.

Celebrities of all kinds turned out in record numbers in a variety of ways to support the buying of war bonds as well as assist with all eight war loan drives. For example, more than three dozen entertainment stars organized into seven groups and visited 353 cities and small towns in September 1942 with an extravaganza called "Stars Over America."

Actress Carole Lombard (1908–1942), before the first official campaign began in November 1942, appeared in January in Indianapolis, a city very near the country's population center at that time, and in one day sold $2.5 million (approximately $32 million in 2008 dollars) worth of war bonds. Her successful technique? She would only give an autograph to those who made a purchase. As a tragic consequence of her efforts, the plane carrying her back to California crashed and burned near Las Vegas, making her one of Hollywood's first wartime fatalities. Dorothy Lamour (1914–1996) followed Lombard as an early volunteer and easily brought in $30 million (approximately $382 million in 2008 dollars) during the first four days of an effort in New York City and throughout New England.

In 1943, the Hollywood Cavalcade, which crisscrossed the country to develop awareness of bond sales, showcased stars such as Lucille Ball (1911–1989), James Cagney (1899–1986), Fred Astaire (1899–1987), Dick Powell (1904–1963), and Kay Kyser (1905–1985). They paraded through dozens of towns and cities seated in army jeeps that bore their names. Singer Kate Smith (1907–1986), in a separate marathon effort, sold $39 million (approximately $485 million in 2008 dollars) worth of bonds in a 18-hour, nonstop radio session on September 21, 1943.

The motion picture industry exerted intense efforts to support the bond drives, producing **movies,** shorts, and trailers to show in theaters, schools, war plants, and other places where people gathered. In 1942, Warner Bros. Pictures distributed *Any Bonds Today?* a three-minute cartoon featuring Bugs Bunny and friends singing and dancing to promote the sale of bonds. It boasts an original 1941 number by composer Irving Berlin (1888–1989) called "Any Bonds Today?" Berlin generously donated his considerable share in royalties to the U.S. Treasury.

*Hollywood Victory Caravan,* a 20-minute short produced in the fall of 1945 for that year's Eighth Victory Loan Drive, interviews various stars on the sets of whatever film they were currently involved in. Participants include Humphrey Bogart (1899–1957), Bing Crosby (1903–1977), Bob Hope (1903–2003), Betty Hutton (1921–2007), to name but a few, along with Oregon theater executive Theodore R. Gamble (active 1940s), who served as the national war finance director.

Athletes, sports figures and teams, boxers, sporting contests, even greyhound racing events assisted the Treasury Department in promoting and selling bonds. Professional **baseball** players supported a number of activities, such as Baseball Defense Bond Day held in 1941 and an exhibition game in 1943 between the Washington Senators and Navy All-Stars. That same year, a baseball autographed by President Roosevelt and British Prime Minister Winston Churchill (1874–1965) sold for $10,000 (approximately $120,000 in 2008 dollars) in bond sales. Sportscaster Red Barber (1908–1992) raised $100,000 (approximately $1.2 million in 2008 dollars) during the broadcast of a game between the Dodgers and Giants. The 1944 **football** game between West Point and the Naval Academy, a traditional rivalry, included a war bond pitch, and proceeds from the 1943–1944 season of the Bowlers' Victory Legion were dedicated to bond purchases. Heavyweight champion **Joe Louis** (1914–1981) invested all his prize money from a 1941 match with Billy Conn (1917–1993) in war bonds; Louis also appeared on a 1942 government poster, one of just a handful that featured a black celebrity.

Musicians and writers also played important roles. From a Treasury Department request to **songwriters and lyricists** for help, several tunes with a war bond theme emerged, and sheet music of songs about war bonds became popular at schools and community club meetings. The Treasury's Writers' War Board, with the popular mystery writer Rex Stout (1886–1975) as its president, oversaw the creation of campaign slogans, **posters,** and other promotion materials and engaged the help of many authors. Novelist Pearl S. Buck (1892–1973) headed an effort called Books and Authors Rallies, events where professional writers assisted with selling bonds and sometimes auctioned off an autographed copy of one of their works. Some wrote short essays about the benefits of investing in bonds, and many allowed their book jackets to contain war bond messages.

Artists and commercial **illustrators** likewise made significant contributions, especially in the development of posters. Midway in the war, Norman Rockwell (1894–1978) joined with others to help boost sales. Rockwell allowed the original oils of his *The Four Freedoms* (freedom of speech, freedom of religion, freedom from want, and freedom from fear), a quartet of famous paintings that he had created for *Saturday Evening Post* covers, to tour the country in 1943 for a special Four Freedoms War Bond Show. These paintings, which themselves had been inspired by an often-quoted "Four Freedoms" speech given by President Roosevelt before Congress in 1941, eventually drew in over 1 million viewers on this tour. They also purchased some $133 million in war bonds (approximately $1.6 billion in 2008 dollars). During this drive, the *Saturday Evening Post,* with which Rockwell had close connections because of these and many other covers, commissioned composer Robert Russell Bennett (1894–1981) to write *The Four Freedoms,* a symphony. Notable orchestras performed it throughout the war.

Each war loan drive experienced phenomenal success and jointly obtained a level of selling to help finance the war that has never been matched, before or since. The buying of bonds helped stave off major inflation, provided a safe investment for income earned during the wartime boom, and assisted in keeping home-front morale at a high level. Finally, the program achieved overwhelming popularity across all segments of American life; it offered a way for all citizens to express patriotic attitudes and gave them a personal stake in the war.

In the immediate postwar years, a euphoric time for many, government and business leaders agreed that a savings bond program should continue. They considered the sense of thrift developed by many citizens in order to purchase savings stamps or bonds a civic virtue that needed encouragement. Less philosophical, but more practical, the argument that the purchase of government securities took cash out of circulation and thus lessened the pressures of inflation also received support. When rationing and shortages ended and more consumer goods came onto the marketplace, the urge to buy could drive up prices and create inflationary pressures, a real threat to the postwar economy.

Thus, at the beginning of 1946, with the Eighth War Loan Drive still fresh in everyone's memory, the Treasury Department created the Savings Bond Division. Its goal was to continue the already successful operations instituted during the war. The Ad Council remained, payroll savings and over-the-counter sales would carry on, as well as the savings stamp programs in the schools. The popular bond drives with parades and celebrities, however, came to a halt, and the promotion of savings bonds became more subdued. On certain anniversaries, such as **D-Day** (June 6), the Fourth of July, Pearl Harbor Day (December 7), and a few others, promotional activities increased amid a flurry of advertising, and sales picked up noticeably. But the sense of emergency had passed and the public no longer rallied to the extent it had during the 1941–1945 period.

The Department of the Treasury feared a rash of redemptions following the war, but it did not come about. People held on to their bonds, viewing them as a form of financial insurance, and many continued to buy more. A few other gimmicks received trials in the late 1940s, but most bond-selling operations continued with a business-as-usual approach while Americans slowly caught their breath after the long and painful conflict. Significant changes in bonds and their promotion would occur in the ensuing years, but the decade of the 1940s witnessed an unparalleled willingness by U.S. citizens to participate voluntarily in the purchase of bonds for the greater good of the country.

*See also:* Best Sellers (Books); Classical Music; Hobbies; Radio Programming: News, Sports, Public Affairs, and Talk; Technology

**Selected Reading**
Ad Council. www.adcouncil.org
Hoopes, Roy. *When the Stars Went to War: Hollywood and World War II.* New York: Random House, 1994.
Samuel, Lawrence R. *Pledging Allegiance: American Identity and the Bond Drives of World War II.* Washington, DC: Smithsonian Institution Press, 1997.
U.S. Department of the Treasury, U.S. Savings Bond Division. *A History of the United States Savings Bonds Program.* Washington, DC: U.S. Department of the Treasury, 1991. www.treasurydirect.gov/indiv/research/history/history_sb.pdf
War Bond Drives and Advertising. www.library.duke.edu/digitalcollections/adaccess/warbonds.html

# WAR FILMS

For much of the Western world, World War II broke out in earnest in September 1939 when Germans troops invaded Poland. In far-off Asia, the conflict had been simmering since the early 1930s; Japanese forces marched in Manchuria, began a systematic conquest of China, and defied Western requests to recognize treaties and borders. For the United States, however, seemingly protected by two oceans, a mood of isolationism prevailed in many quarters, and much of the nation turned away from foreign affairs and potential involvement.

This course of events left the American entertainment industry—especially Hollywood—in something of a quandary. Although most citizens appeared opposed to the nation's participation in what critics called "foreign wars," neither did they feel much sympathy toward the Axis powers (Germany, Japan, and Italy). The **Selective Training and Service Act of 1940,** better known simply as the draft, weighed on the minds of many young men. Entering the military meant interrupting schooling or a job, and the gloomy course of international events had young and old worrying about the prospect of a war. The motion pictures that issued from Hollywood during this period gave viewers mixed messages: most ignored current realities altogether and doled out escapist fare; a handful depicted the looming threats a bit more accurately and stressed preparedness.

Only a few studios, however, produced **movies** with an anti-Axis tone. Most others assumed a stance of studied neutrality in order not to offend anyone or keep patrons away from the all-important box office. In 1939, Warner Bros. offered *Confessions of a Nazi Spy* and *Espionage Agent*, while Producers Releasing Corporation (PRC), a small, independent studio, released *Hitler—Beast of Berlin*. In 1940, the number of such pictures increased, and more studios participated, with titles like *Foreign Correspondent* and *The Great Dictator* (both United Artists) and *The Mortal Storm* and *Escape* (both MGM). Twentieth Century-Fox produced *Four Sons* and *The Man I Married* (also known as *I Married a Nazi*).

By 1941, popular opinion had clearly turned sharply against the tyranny of the Axis powers, and the movie industry felt emboldened to shed its own lingering impartiality; it slowly moved toward the idea of U.S. involvement in a new war. Two releases that illustrate this shift are *The Fighting 69th* (1940) and *Sergeant York* (1941), both action-packed pictures about World War I; seemingly historical, they also advance the idea of Americans fighting abroad, and their enemies just happen to be German soldiers.

Other productions eschewed politics and instead glorified duty in one of the branches of the military, making service look adventurous, exciting, and even fun. Films like *A Yank in the R.A.F., International Squadron* (both 1941) and *Captains of the Clouds* and

*Following the attack on Pearl Harbor, the Hollywood studios poured a large portion of their considerable resources into patriotic war films. In the dark days of 1942, Paramount Pictures released* Wake Island. *In this studio still (from the left) a determined Albert Dekker, Brian Donlevy, Walter Abel, MacDonald Carey, and Robert Preston stand atop the sandbags, ready to take on any enemies. (Paramount Pictures/Photofest)*

*Flying Tigers* (both 1942) give audiences stories about American volunteers, young men who eagerly sign up for action with the air forces of Great Britain, Canada, and China. *I Wanted Wings* and *Dive Bomber* (both 1941) create glowing portraits of the training raw recruits receive upon joining the U.S. Army or Navy and certainly must have served as strong enlistment tools.

Some movies even put the draft and service in general in humorous terms. For example, Abbott and Costello (Bud Abbott, 1895–1974; Lou Costello, 1906–1959), a hugely popular comedy team of the 1940s, reflected this heightened awareness of all things military in a trio of 1941 slapstick films: *Buck Privates, In the Navy,* and *Keep 'em Flying*. They carried on in 1947 with *Buck Privates Come Home,* humorously showing how the draftees—now veterans—return to their civilian lives. Veteran comedians Laurel and Hardy (Stan Laurel, 1890–1965; Oliver Hardy, 1892–1957) also employed contemporary events for a pair of war enlistment movies: *Great Guns* (1941) and *Air Raid Wardens* (1943). Similarly, former vaudevillians Jimmy Durante (1893–1980) and Phil Silvers (1911–1985) went for laughs in *You're in the Army Now* (1941). **Bob Hope** (1903–2003), no stranger to topical humor, shows up as a hapless draftee in *Caught in the Draft* (1941).

Later in the conflict, with millions of Americans serving their country, Columbia Pictures released *Mr. Winkle Goes to War* (1944). It stars Edward G. Robinson (1893–1973), an actor better known for his roles as hard-bitten gangsters and law enforcement officers—as an example, he portray a determined Secret Service agent in the aforementioned *Confessions of a Nazi Spy*. In *Mr. Winkle Goes to War,* however, he appears as a mild-mannered banker unexpectedly thrust into the army. To the amazement of his friends, he returns a hero. The film suggests, both comically and realistically, how the draft became a great equalizer, making even the most unlikely candidates into soldiers.

*Mr. Lucky* (1943), another picture that deals with the draft, serves as a vehicle for the popular Cary Grant (1904–1986). In this case, however, instead of going into the army, Grant, playing against type as an amoral gambler, chooses draft dodging, a serious topic for the times. But the actor carries it off with his usual aplomb and, of course, by the ending finds redemption for his misdeeds.

Characters from the newspaper **comic strips** also got into the spirit of the early 1940s. *Private Snuffy Smith* and *Hillbilly Blitzkrieg* (both 1942), based on individuals found in *Barney Google & Snuffy Smith* by cartoonist Billy De Beck (1890–1942), brought a rural flavor to both the comic pages and theater screens in their hillbilly depictions of military life. Comedies about the war—particularly those that featured soldiers, sailors, and pilots—nonetheless remained a distinct minority, especially when the country finally plunged into the war as a combatant. In short order, U.S. troops found themselves fighting in far-flung campaigns, and, as casualties mounted, World War II and the draft quickly ceased being a source for film comedy other than in occasional flashes of humor.

In 1942 and 1943, the darkest years of the conflict, motion picture messages and images were deemed important at the highest levels of government, but initially no real plan existed for coordinating ways of dealing with the influential film industry. A mixed group of federal agencies that often competed with one another had sprung up in the period 1940 through 1941, and several felt the government should monitor the content of commercial films. To many observers, their attitudes smacked of censorship, although few of these agencies shared matching points of view about what constituted proper content in a time of war.

**President Franklin Delano Roosevelt** (1882–1945) recognized the need for a coherent voice, and he wanted a liaison between Hollywood and official Washington. Out of the squabbling came the Office of War Information (OWI) in June 1942, with journalist Elmer Davis (1890–1958) at its helm. Davis had the able assistance of Lowell Mellett (1884–1960), the former coordinator of government films and head of the Office of Government Reports, and newspaper publisher Nelson Poynter (1903–1978). Together the two men managed the Bureau of Motion Pictures (BMP) in Hollywood, a federal agency that functioned as a part of the larger OWI. With the support of Davis, they urged the film industry to produce war-related pictures that carried consistent, up-beat, pro-American content at all times for both domestic and foreign distribution. They maintained that such movies reinforced the country's image and boosted morale. The BMP asked to review scripts prior to production, and the studios complied, although they did not always accept the advice the agency offered.

While Mellett, Poynter, and the BMP were making their suggestions regarding content, the powerful War Department (superseded by the Department of Defense in 1947), a cabinet-level branch of the federal government, had earlier established its own Bureau of Public Relations in Hollywood. This group represented the interests of the various armed services and had enjoyed a long and harmonious relationship with the industry. When filmmakers needed military equipment or the expertise of service personnel, the War Department usually obliged. Movie credits often acknowledged this support—"Thanks to [the United States Army, Navy, etc.] without whose assistance this picture would not have been possible," or words to that effect—because they suggested that the action on screen presented accurate images and details about the U.S. military.

During the remainder of the war, both the OWI and the War Department proffered advice to studios, usually after reviewing scripts. Hollywood accepted this mild form of censorship, couched as "recommendations," with everyone involved denying any attempts at editing or suppressing material. Both agencies maintained that wartime movies should be "educational, inspirational, and recreational," but they disagreed on how best to achieve such goals, and a rivalry developed over authority. The OWI, more civilian and politically oriented than the War Department, argued that crime, poverty, **labor unrest,** and the like should be downplayed in order to paint an optimistic picture of life in the United States. The War Department, on the other hand, maintained that the various services knew best how to present themselves on film and that clearly stating the military objectives of the country in the conduct of the war should have priority. The department also felt it should not be subordinate to a civilian authority. Roosevelt asked that they resolve their differences behind closed doors but did not explicitly order one agency to defer to the other.

The discussions continued, with each side outwardly agreeing to work harmoniously, but still arguing the merits of their respective positions. In the end, the studios politely listened and then pretty much went ahead with their own plans, despite the well-meaning (and sometimes myopic) remarks from government agencies. To no one's surprise, no dire consequences ensued, and an increasingly conservative Congress looked askance at any governmental oversight in regard to motion pictures. In 1943, legislators slashed the OWI budget for 1944, effectively limiting its operations. The Motion Picture Bureau was shut down, and the once-powerful Office of War Information ceased functioning in 1945.

While all this infighting ensued, the War Department in early 1942 commissioned director Frank Capra (1897–1991) as a major in the U.S. Army and placed him in the Morale Branch of the Special Services Division. Essentially a public relations position, the army allowed Capra to develop a series of films designed to explain the nation's participation in the war. The department gave him free rein to employ archival and recent materials in the project, and from this work came seven remarkable documentaries bearing the collective heading W*hy We Fight.* The series commenced production in 1942 and reached its conclusion in 1945. Individually, they bore the following titles: *Prelude to War, The Nazis Strike, Divide and Conquer, The Battle of Britain, The Battle of Russia, The Battle of China,* and *War Comes to America.* Designed both for service personnel and civilians, they detailed the complexity of fighting a world war from the perspective of U.S. military forces.

Servicemen had the privilege of viewing the first film, *Prelude to War,* which finished production in October 1942, at the end of that month. In April 1943, the War Department allowed it to be shown in defense plants, and the general civilian population first saw it the next month. The others followed similar schedules and received favorable audience reactions but little commercial success. Billed as "The Greatest Gangster Picture Ever Made," *Prelude to War* did not do well at the civilian box office. People saw its topic as dated; by mid-1943, they knew the origins of World War II and wanted more immediate news. Despite their lack of public appeal, these documentaries can be seen as splendid examples of cinematic history and **art.** They also stand as blatant propaganda—not an unreasonable outcome, since the U.S. government underwrote them—one of the few examples of an official presence in the normally freewheeling realm of popular culture.

A number of other documentaries, also overseen by leading Hollywood directors and supported by various official agencies, deserve mention: *The Battle of Midway* (1942), directed by John Ford (1894–1973); *Report from the Aleutians* (1943) and *The Battle of San Pietro* (1944), both directed by John Huston (1906–1987); *Memphis Belle* (1944), directed by William Wyler (1902–1981); and *Fighting Lady* (1944), produced by Louis De Rochemont (1899–1978). Hardly in the tradition of commercial filmmaking, these hard-hitting chronicles stand, for their time, as unique records of the struggles faced by U.S. forces in all theaters of the war.

Also worthy of note, *The March of Time,* a combination of **radio** news and film newsreel, also informed the American people about the war. Underwritten by *Time* magazine, the radio version premiered in 1928 and could be heard on network stations until 1945; its movie counterpart first appeared in 1934 and continued in theaters until 1951. Over the years, they set new standards for broadcast journalism, presenting hundreds of vignettes about the news of the day, going beyond the headlines to present insightful interpretations of events.

The cinematic *March of Time* helped give birth to the contemporary docudrama, the blending of the factual documentary with dramatic additions. The shows frequently combined newsreel footage with dramatized segments, smoothly mixing truth with fiction based on fact. The approach enlivened events, creating a kind of heightened reality, but at the expense of total, unbiased accuracy.

Unlike the weekly 10-minute theatrical newsreels that chronicled recent happenings and spiced up their content with ephemera like beauty contests, sports, and the latest gadgets, *The March of Time* documentaries ran monthly for approximately 20 minutes. The producers tackled just a few important news stories during that brief time, usually handling difficult or complex events that involved politics, economics, or military subjects. Usually, one piece in particular dominated each issue of the show, receiving up to 15 minutes of discussion and dramatization. Consigned to the middle of a theater's double bill with other short subjects, *The March of Time* competed with previews and **cartoons,** so it did not always receive the attention it deserved. It nonetheless provided audiences a level of visual reporting about the war seldom achieved in conventional newsreels.

Documentaries, however, occupy a small niche in any chronicle of moviemaking during World War II. Far too many war-oriented commercial films came out between 1942 and 1945 to create any comprehensive listing; it has been estimated that, of the 1,700 or so feature movies released during those years, fully a third of them—over 500—fit the category of war films. Table 102 charts Hollywood's war films and mentions primarily those pictures produced by the major studios that focused their storylines on action and the depiction of combat. Musicals, comedies, domestic dramas, wartime romances, and many other noncombat tales have been omitted for the sake of both brevity and cohesion.

The content of the table also makes it obvious that, with the return of peace in the fall of 1945, the film industry lost no time in distancing itself from the conflict. Production of war-related films plummeted, and only in the last two years of the decade did studios once more commence creating full-fledged war pictures. With the onset of the 1950s and an ongoing war in Korea, Hollywood resumed releasing numbers of such movies, some dealing with the **Cold War,** others looking back at actions that occurred during World War II. Military combat had again become a marketable film commodity, but it had taken about five years to reach that point.

Many of the titles also suggest, such as *Stand By for Action* (1942), *Action in the North Atlantic* (1943), *Aerial Gunner* (1943), *Bombardier* (1943), *Wing and a Prayer* (1944), *God Is My Co-Pilot* (1945), and so on, that a majority of the pictures emphasize the techniques of modern warfare and the simultaneous need for a spiritual foundation in the face of formidable odds. The many stars—mostly men; this category of film offered few roles for women—can suffer mightily, as in *Bataan* (1943), *Guadalcanal Diary* (1943), *The Purple Heart* (1944), *They Were Expendable* (1945), and others, but because of the rightness of their cause they will prevail. The pictures often show setbacks on the road to victory such as *Wake Island* (1942), *Corregidor* (1943), *The Fighting Sullivans* (1944), and others, but more importantly they portray the indomitability of the American will. *The Beginning or the End* (1947), about the development of the **atomic bomb** and the emerging nuclear capabilities in warfare, contains no combat footage at all but is harrowing in its implications about mass destruction, one of the few commercial motion pictures to address this topic.

TABLE 102.   Representative War-Oriented Movies, 1940–1949

| Year | Movie Titles | Stars |
|---|---|---|
| 1940 | *The Fighting 69th* | James Cagney, Pat O'Brien |
| | *Flight Command* | Robert Taylor, Walter Pidgeon |
| | *Murder in the Air* | Ronald Reagan, John Litel |
| 1941 | *Dive Bomber* | Errol Flynn, Fred MacMurray |
| | *I Wanted Wings* | Ray Milland, William Holden |
| | *Man Hunt* | Walter Pidgeon, Joan Bennett |
| | *Sergeant York* | Gary Cooper, Walter Brennan |
| | *A Yank in the R.A.F.* | Tyrone Power, Betty Grable |
| 1942 | *Across the Pacific* | Humphrey Bogart, Mary Astor |
| | *Berlin Correspondent* | Dana Andrews, Virginia Gilmore |
| | *Danger in the Pacific* | Don Terry, Leo Carrillo |
| | *Desperate Journey* | Errol Flynn, Ronald Reagan |
| | *Eagle Squadron* | Robert Stack, Eddie Albert |
| | *Flying Tigers* | John Wayne, Paul Kelly |
| | *Half Way to Shanghai* | Kent Taylor, Irene Hervey |
| | *Invisible Agent* | Jon Hall, Peter Lorre |
| | *Joan of Paris* | Paul Henreid, Michele Morgan |
| | *Little Tokyo, U.S.A.* | Preston Foster, Brenda Joyce |
| | *Nightmare* | Diana Barrymore, Brian Donlevy |
| | *Remember Pearl Harbor* | Don "Red" Barry, Alan Curtis |
| | *Reunion in France* | Joan Crawford, John Wayne |
| | *Stand By for Action* | Robert Taylor, Brian Donlevy |
| | *Submarine Raider* | Larry Parks, Forrest Tucker |
| | *Thunder Birds* | Preston Foster, Gene Tierney |
| | *To the Shores of Tripoli* | Randolph Scott, John Payne |
| | *Wake Island* | Brian Donlevy, William Bendix |
| | *A Yank on the Burma Road* | Barry Nelson, Laraine Day |
| 1943 | *Action in the North Atlantic* | Humphrey Bogart, Raymond Massey |
| | *Aerial Gunner* | Chester Morris, Richard Arlen |
| | *Air Force* | John Garfield, Gig Young |
| | *Bataan* | Robert Taylor, George Murphy |
| | *Bombardier* | Randolph Scott, Pat O'Brien |
| | *China* | Loretta Young, Alan Ladd |
| | *Corregidor* | Otto Kruger, Elissa Landi |
| | *Corvette K-225* | Randolph Scott, Barry Fitzgerald |
| | *Crash Dive* | Tyrone Power, Anne Baxter |
| | *Cry "Havoc"* | Margaret Sullavan, Ann Sothern |
| | *Destination Tokyo* | Cary Grant, John Garfield |
| | *Edge of Darkness* | Errol Flynn, Walter Huston |
| | *Five Graves to Cairo* | Franchot Tone, Erich von Stroheim |
| | *Guadalcanal Diary* | Preston Foster, William Bendix |
| | *Gung Ho! The Story of Carlson's Makin Island Raiders* | Randolph Scott, Robert Mitchum |
| | *A Guy Named Joe* | Spencer Tracy, Van Johnson |
| | *Hangmen Also Die* | Brian Donlevy, Walter Brennan |
| | *Immortal Sergeant* | Henry Fonda, Thomas Mitchell |
| | *The Moon Is Down* | Henry Travers, Lee J. Cobb |

*(continued)*

TABLE 102. *(continued)*

| Year | Movie Titles | Stars |
|---|---|---|
| 1943 | The North Star | Dana Andrews, Anne Baxter |
| | Pilot #5 | Gene Kelly, Van Johnson |
| | Sahara | Humphrey Bogart, Bruce Bennett |
| | So Proudly We Hail! | Claudette Colbert, Paulette Goddard, Veronica Lake |
| | Submarine Alert | Richard Arlen, Wendy Barrie |
| | Wings Over the Pacific | Edward Norris, Montagu Love |
| 1944 | Days of Glory | Gregory Peck, Alan Reed |
| | The Fighting Seabees | John Wayne, Dennis O'Keefe |
| | The Fighting Sullivans | Anne Baxter, Thomas Mitchell |
| | Marine Raiders | Pat O'Brien, Robert Ryan |
| | The Purple Heart | Dana Andrews, Richard Conte |
| | Song of Russia | Robert Taylor, John Hodiak |
| | Thirty Seconds Over Tokyo | Spencer Tracy, Van Johnson |
| | To Have and Have Not | Humphrey Bogart, Lauren Bacall |
| | Wing and a Prayer | Don Ameche, Dana Andrews |
| | Winged Victory | Lon McCallister, Edmund O'Brien |
| 1945 | A Bell for Adano | Gene Tierney, John Hodiak |
| | Back to Bataan | John Wayne, Anthony Quinn |
| | Betrayal from the East | Lee Tracy, Nancy Kelly |
| | Counter-Attack | Paul Muni, Larry Parks |
| | God Is My Co-Pilot | Dennis Morgan, Dane Clark |
| | Objective, Burma! | Errol Flynn, Henry Hull |
| | Pride of the Marines | John Garfield, Eleanor Parker |
| | The Story of G.I. Joe | Burgess Meredith, Robert Mitchum |
| | They Were Expendable | Robert Montgomery, John Wayne |
| | A Walk in the Sun | Dana Andrews, Richard Conte |
| 1946 | The Best Years of Our Lives | Frederic March, Dana Andrews |
| | O.S.S. | Alan Ladd, Geraldine Fitzgerald |
| | 13 Rue Madeleine | James Cagney, Richard Conte |
| | Till the End of Time | Robert Mitchum, Guy Madison |
| 1947 | The Beginning or the End | Brian Donlevy, Robert Walker |
| 1948 | Beyond Glory | Alan Ladd, Donna Reed |
| | Command Decision | Clark Gable, Walter Pidgeon |
| | Fighter Squadron | Edmund O'Brien, Robert Stack |
| | Homecoming | Clark Gable, Lana Turner |
| | Jungle Patrol | Kristine Miller, Arthur Franz |
| | Saigon | Alan Ladd, Veronica Lake |
| 1949 | Battleground | Van Johnson, John Hodiak |
| | Malaya | Spencer Tracy, James Stewart |
| | The Red Danube | Walter Pidgeon, Ethel Barrymore |
| | Sands of Iwo Jima | John Wayne, Forrest Tucker |
| | Twelve O'Clock High | Gregory Peck, Dean Jagger |

To make the war more understandable, the studios often employed stereotyping. For the Axis nations, the images of cruel Gestapo agents clad in long, black leather coats, contemptuous of everyone around them, or of snarling Japanese soldiers, peering through round spectacles, ready to rape and pillage, may seem hopelessly dated to contemporary audiences. But at the time they constituted the *enemy*—the threat to the United States—and anything that could differentiate us from them could be, and was, employed in all branches of popular culture. Similarly, noble Britons, as in *Mrs. Miniver* (1942), and valiant Russians and Chinese in *North Star* (1943) and *Dragon Seed* (1944) fight tyranny and show themselves to be, in their two-dimensional portrayals, the proper types to have as allies.

Closer to home, the studios shifted their emphases from the rugged American individualism so celebrated in the past to the need for group cooperation. In picture after picture, smoothly functioning military units rise to any challenge. Although heroes abound, they do not seek glory for themselves but allow the group, the team, to be victorious in its mission. This approach reinforced positive attitudes about U.S. fighting forces, the idea of democracy in action.

These ideas carried over into movies about civilian life. **Rosie the Riveter,** the name of both a 1944 comedy and an iconic figure in **advertising** and public service announcements, symbolized the teamwork concept in the nation's industrial efforts at this time. Rosie epitomizes the tens of thousands of women who worked in defense plants, stepping into traditional realms of men's labor while the men go off to fight. The film industry presented this kind of imagery repeatedly in commercial motion pictures dealing with both military and civilian life and created a collective body of work that reassured a troubled nation. With teamwork, with the subordination of self for the greater national good and everyone doing his or her part, the country would prevail.

During the course of World War II, Hollywood succeeded in building a vast production machine capable of portraying virtually any aspect of the conflict. The industry strove to lift morale for millions of viewers on the home front by mixing entertainment with propaganda in hundreds of pictures. Not only did the countless war-oriented movies lift the spirits of those at home, some went to considerable lengths to explain some of the complexities surrounding the events shown on theater screens. It would be impossible to know, with any quantitative accuracy, exactly how much American motion pictures contributed to winning the war, but for the millions of people who weekly went to the movies, Hollywood's latest offerings usually diverted them from the grim headlines and news reports of the day, and in that way positively contributed to the overall war effort.

*See also:* Comedies (Film); Drama (Film); Musicals (Film); Newspapers; Radio Programming: Drama and Anthology Shows; Serial Films

**Selected Reading**
Doherty, Thomas. *Projections of War: Hollywood, American Culture, and World War II.* New York: Columbia University Press, 1993.
Koppes, Clayton R., and Gregory D. Black. *Hollywood Goes to War: How Politics, Profits, and Propaganda Shaped World War II Movies.* New York: Free Press, 1987.
Manvell, Roger. *Films and the Second World War.* New York: Dell, 1974.
McLaughlin, Robert L., and Sally E. Parry. *We'll Always Have the Movies: American Cinema During World War II.* Lexington: University Press of Kentucky, 2006.

# WESTERNS (FILM)

In the early years of the 20th century and the birth of the American film industry, one of the very first offerings bore the title *The Great Train Robbery* (1903). Directed by Edwin S. Porter (1870–1941) and released by the Edison Manufacturing Company, this pioneering effort established many of the conventions of the movie Western. Crude by modern standards, it nonetheless inspired countless directors, actors, and studios—an influence that has carried on into the present. Porter created a series of expectations in the audience, including thrilling gunfights and fisticuffs, galloping horses and breathless chases, and even the stylized outfits that countless Westerns ever since have attempted to honor and satisfy.

By the 1940s, the conventions had long been in place; audiences knew what to expect, liked what they saw, and made the Western one of the most durable and consistently profitable genres of filmmaking. The pressures of World War II may have brought about shortages in materials, restrictions on travel, and a depleted pool of male actors, but it affected the production of Westerns only in passing. They continued to roll out of the Hollywood studios, a staple of double features and Saturday matinees, and adults and children gladly paid admission to see the latest exploits of their cowboy heroes.

The larger, more prosperous studios, usually called the majors or Big Five (MGM, Paramount, RKO, Twentieth Century-Fox, and Warner Bros.), attempted to produce quality Westerns that employed their leading contract players. MGM in 1940 put Gary Cooper (1901–1961) and an all-star supporting cast in *The Westerner,* a big-budget tale about range wars, and followed it that same year with *Northwest Passage,* featuring the popular Spencer Tracy (1900–1967) and Robert Young (1907–1998). Not to be outdone, rival Twentieth Century-Fox countered with *The Return of Frank James* (1940) with Henry Fonda (1905–1982) and *Western Union* (1941) starring Randolph Scott (1898–1987), an actor destined to make some 18 Westerns in the 1940s alone, including a number for RKO. Warner Bros., usually associated with **musicals** and gritty urban crime pictures, utilized the star power of swashbuckler Errol Flynn (1909–1959) in a series of action-filled **movies:** *Dodge City* (1939), *Virginia City* (1940), *Santa Fe Trail* 1940), *They Died with Their Boots On* (1941)*,* and *San Antonio* (1945). Another competitor, Universal Studios, often consigned to the "Little Three" among studios (along with Columbia and United Artists), released a pair of 1940 Westerns with unlikely casting. *When the Daltons Rode* stars Brian Donlevy (1901–1972) and Broderick Crawford (1911–1986), whereas *Trail of the Vigilantes* features Franchot Tone (1905–1968) and Crawford again. None of these performers enjoyed particular renown in the Western genre; perhaps Universal wanted actors associated with other forms of drama to give their productions a mark of quality and thereby attract a broader audience.

Not all the production companies went in the direction of large-budget Westerns. A number of smaller, less affluent ones released countless Westerns made quickly and cheaply. Most of these studios, which fell under the name "Poverty Row," struggled for their very existence and frequently went out of business after valiant attempts to achieve financial solvency. Acquisitions and mergers muddied the details about this side of the movie business, but Mascot, Monogram, Republic Pictures, and Producers Releasing Corporation (PRC) gained the most prominence and developed the strongest distribution networks and the widest array of talents.

To meet costs, the Poverty Row studios utilized the services of relatively anonymous players and usually shot outdoor scenes on the back lots that abutted their properties. They scavenged sequences, such as pitched battles and stagecoach robberies, that had been shown in previous pictures and spliced them into new movies to save even more money. Their films, usually shorter than those released by both the Big Five and the Little Three, averaged 60 minutes instead of the customary 80- to 90-minute running time. For the most part, these productions received little publicity and tended to be shown in smaller neighborhood theaters as the bottom part of a double feature. Collectively, such movies fell into the category of what came commonly to be called B pictures, the "B" meaning they qualitatively ranked below their more expensive counterparts. For whatever reason, the term "B Western" came into widespread usage, more so than for other film genres. People rarely spoke, however, about "A Westerns" as a category when differentiating the two varieties.

Whereas the major studios could call upon recognized stars like Gary Cooper, Errol Flynn, Henry Fonda, Robert Taylor (1911–1969), and John Wayne (1907–1979), the Poverty Row organizations enjoyed no such luxury. They had their rosters of players, but few boasted any celebrity. Nevertheless, actors like Johnny Mack Brown (1904–1974), Fuzzy Knight (1901–1976), Lash La Rue (1917–1996), Ken Maynard (1895–1973), Charles Starrett (1903–1986), Bob Steele (1907–1988), Dub Taylor (1907–1994), Jimmy Wakely (1914–1982), and a host of other players found steady employment performing in endless B Westerns. Sometimes they had top billing in a film, other times they served as sidekicks, but only a handful rose to be leading men in the more expensive productions of the Big Five. For example, John Wayne paid his dues in endless minor cowboy movies during the 1930s; not until 1939 and the classic *Stagecoach* did he move from B player and begin his rise as a major star. Two other cowboy actors, **Gene Autry and Roy Rogers** (1907–1998 and 1911–1998, respectively), spent their entire careers in B Westerns but nonetheless achieved substantial fame and fortune in the later 1930s and throughout the 1940s. Similarly, **William Boyd** (1895–1972), better known to millions as Hopalong Cassidy, ran a long string of formulaic Westerns into considerable success. Such exceptions, however, do not describe the overwhelming majority of performers who got typecast as B players and dutifully labored in virtual anonymity for most of their professional lives.

Out of the hundreds of Westerns released during the 1940s, only a handful dealt with World War II; most, of course, had as their settings the 19th or early 20th centuries, and any references to a modern conflict would have been anachronistic at best. A few, however, pushed history aside and attempted to cash in on patriotic feelings. Monogram Pictures distributed a series of B Westerns featuring the Range Busters, a trio of cowboys that appeared in several dozen usually nontopical releases. But in *Texas to Bataan* (1942), they discover a Japanese spy ring, and in *Cowboy Commandos* (1943), they battle Nazi spies at a strategic mine. The scene shifts to more traditional territory in *Black Market Rustlers* (1943), where they break up a ring of racketeers trying to rustle beef to sell illegally on the **black market.** Such efforts proved the exception, and few other Westerns of any kind chose to reflect ongoing events.

The smaller studios did, however, display a fondness for series Westerns. The continuing adventures of both groups and individuals found a solid base of fans. Tim McCoy (1891–1978), Buck Jones (1891–1942), and Raymond Hatton (1887–1971) joined forces

TABLE 103. Representative Western Movies, 1940–1949

| Year | Movie Titles | Actors |
|---|---|---|
| 1940 | Arizona | Jean Arthur, William Holden |
| | Dark Command | John Wayne, Claire Trevor |
| | The Man from Tumbleweeds | Bill Elliott, Iris Meredith |
| | Prairie Schooners | Bill Elliott, Dub Taylor |
| | Rangers of Fortune | Fred MacMurray, Gilbert Roland |
| | The Return of Frank James | Henry Fonda, Gene Tierney |
| | Three Faces West | John Wayne, Charles Coburn |
| | Virginia City | Errol Flynn, Randolph Scott, Humphrey Bogart |
| | The Westerner | Gary Cooper, Walter Brennan |
| | When the Daltons Rode | Randolph Scott, Brian Donlevy |
| 1941 | Badlands of Dakota | Richard Dix, Robert Stack |
| | Belle Starr | Gene Tierney, Randolph Scott |
| | Billy the Kid | Robert Taylor, Brian Donlevy |
| | Fight Bill Fargo | Johnny Mack Brown, Fuzzy Knight |
| | Honky Tonk | Clark Gable, Lana Turner |
| | King of Dodge City | Bill Elliott, Tex Ritter |
| | North from the Lone Star | Bill Elliott, Dub Taylor |
| | Texas | Glenn Ford, William Holden |
| | They Died with Their Boots On | Errol Flynn, Olivia de Havilland |
| | Western Union | Randolph Scott, Robert Young |
| 1942 | American Empire | Richard Dix, Preston Foster |
| | Deep in the Heart of Texas | Johnny Mack Brown, Tex Ritter |
| | Down Texas Way | Buck Jones, Tim McCoy |
| | The Great Man's Lady | Barbara Stanwyck, Joel McCrea |
| | The Mysterious Rider | Buster Crabbe, Al St. John |
| | Ride 'Em, Cowboy! | Bud Abbott, Lou Costello |
| | The Spoilers | John Wayne, Randolph Scott, Marlene Dietrich |
| | Texas to Bataan | John "Dusty" King, Max Terhune |
| | Valley of the Sun | Lucille Ball, Dean Jagger |
| | Vengeance of the West | Bill Elliott, Tex Ritter |
| 1943 | Arizona Trail | Tex Ritter, Fuzzy Knight |
| | Blazing Frontier | Buster Crabbe, Al St. John |
| | Buckskin Frontier | Richard Dix, Lee J. Cobb |
| | Death Valley Manhunt | Bill Elliott, Gabby Hayes |
| | The Desperadoes | Glenn Ford, Randolph Scott |
| | In Old Oklahoma | John Wayne, Gabby Hayes |
| | A Lady Takes a Chance | Jean Arthur, John Wayne |
| | The Outlaw | Jane Russell, Jack Buetel |
| | The Ox-Bow Incident | Henry Fonda, Dana Andrews, Anthony Quinn |
| | The Texas Kid | Johnny Mack Brown, Raymond Hatton |
| 1944 | Arizona Whirlwind | Ken Maynard, Hoot Gibson |
| | Belle of the Yukon | Randolph Scott, Gypsy Rose Lee |
| | Buffalo Bill | Joel McCrea, Maureen O'Hara |
| | Fuzzy Settles Down | Buster Crabbe, Al St. John |
| | Land of the Outlaws | Johnny Mack Brown, Raymond Hatton |

| Year | Movie Titles | Actors |
|---|---|---|
| | *Nevada* | Robert Mitchum, Anne Jeffreys |
| | *Song of the Range* | Jimmy Wakely, Dennis Moore |
| | *Tall in the Saddle* | John Wayne, Gabby Hayes |
| | *Tucson Raiders* | Bill Elliott, Robert Blake |
| | *The Woman of the Town* | Claire Trevor, Albert Dekker |
| 1945 | *Along Came Jones* | Gary Cooper, Dan Duryea |
| | *Dakota* | John Wayne, Vera Ralston |
| | *Flame of the Barbary Coast* | John Wayne, Ann Dvorak |
| | *Frontier Feud* | Johnny Mack Brown, Raymond Hatton |
| | *Lone Texas Ranger* | Bill Elliott, Robert Blake |
| | *The Navajo Kid* | Bob Steele, Syd Saylor |
| | *San Antonio* | Errol Flynn, Alexis Smith |
| | *Song of Old Wyoming* | Eddie Dean, Lash La Rue |
| | *Springtime in Texas* | Jimmy Wakely, Dennis Moore |
| | *West of the Pecos* | Robert Mitchum, Barbara Hale |
| 1946 | *Abilene Town* | Randolph Scott, Ann Dvorak |
| | *Beauty and the Bandit* | Gilbert Roland, Martin Garralaga |
| | *California* | Ray Milland, Barbara Stanwyck |
| | *Canyon Passage* | Dana Andrews, Susan Hayward |
| | *Duel in the Sun* | Jennifer Jones, Gregory Peck |
| | *The Gentleman from Texas* | Johnny Mack Brown, Raymond Hatton |
| | *In Old Sacramento* | Bill Elliott, Constance Moore |
| | *My Darling Clementine* | Henry Fonda, Walter Brennan |
| | *Terror Trail* | Charles Starrett, Barbara Pepper |
| | *The Virginian* | Joel McCrea, Brian Donlevy |
| 1947 | *Angel and the Badman* | John Wayne, Gail Russell |
| | *Bandits of Dark Canyon* | Allan "Rocky" Lane, Bob Steele |
| | *Desert Fury* | Burt Lancaster, John Hodiak |
| | *The Fabulous Texan* | Bill Elliott, John Carroll |
| | *The Fighting Vigilantes* | Lash La Rue, Al St. John |
| | *Land of the Lawless* | Johnny Mack Brown, Raymond Hatton |
| | *Pursued* | Robert Mitchum, Teresa Wright |
| | *Robin Hood of Monterey* | Gilbert Roland, Chris-Pin Martin |
| | *Ramrod* | Veronica Lake, Joel McCrea |
| | *The Sea of Grass* | Spencer Tracy, Katharine Hepburn |
| 1948 | *Albuquerque* | Randolph Scott, Gabby Hayes |
| | *Blood on the Moon* | Robert Mitchum, Robert Preston |
| | *Fort Apache* | Henry Fonda, John Wayne |
| | *Four Faces West* | Joel McCrea, Charles Bickford |
| | *The Man from Colorado* | Glenn Ford, William Holden |
| | *Red River* | John Wayne, Montgomery Clift |
| | *Relentless* | Robert Young, Barton MacLane |
| | *3 Godfathers* | John Wayne, Ward Bond |
| | *Whispering Smith* | Alan Ladd, Robert Preston |
| | *Yellow Sky* | Gregory Peck, Richard Widmark |
| 1949 | *Gun Law Justice* | Jimmy Wakely, Dub Taylor |
| | *Hellfire* | Bill Elliott, Marie Windsor |

*(continued)*

TABLE 103. *(continued)*

| Year | Movie Titles | Actors |
|---|---|---|
| | *I Shot Jesse James* | Preston Foster, John Ireland |
| | *Lust for Gold* | Ida Lupino, Glenn Ford |
| | *Renegades of the Sage* | Charles Starrett, Smiley Burnette |
| | *She Wore a Yellow Ribbon* | John Wayne, Ben Johnson |
| | *Son of Billy the Kid* | Lash La Rue, Al St. John |
| | *South of St. Louis* | Joel McCrea, Alexis Smith |
| | *Stampede* | Rod Cameron, Gale Storm |
| | *Streets of Laredo* | William Holden, William Bendix |

*Note:* List does not include films by Gene Autry or Roy Rogers, which are covered elsewhere in this encyclopedia.

as The Rough Riders, undercover marshals in a series of eight Monogram pictures. The Three Mesquiteers, led by Robert Livingston (1904–1988), foiled latter-day criminals in a quasi-contemporary series that ran from 1936 until 1941. Livingston moved from the Mesquiteers to The Lone Rider series in 1942, in which he appeared in half a dozen additional features, all the while making other movies on an individual basis.

Veteran actor Duncan Renaldo (1904–1980) endeared himself to audiences by playing the roguish Cisco Kid, a character created in 1907 by the American writer O. Henry (pen name of William Sidney Porter, 1862–1910). Renaldo first portrayed him in three Monogram pictures released in 1945. At that point, former romantic film star Gilbert Roland (1905–1994) renewed his career by taking over the Cisco Kid franchise with six additional Monogram titles released between 1946 and 1947. Renaldo then reappeared as the Kid and starred in yet another five adventures produced from 1948 to 1950 by United Artists. By this time, **television** had begun searching for materials to fill air time, and Renaldo parlayed the Cisco Kid into an early TV series that ran from 1950 until 1955. The fact that two different actors portrayed the Cisco Kid at roughly the same time did not seem to faze audiences, and they willingly suspended any disbelief at the box office. In the hectic world of B Westerns, characters appeared, disappeared, reappeared, and often a number of different performers filled the roles at one time or another.

Finally, Bill Elliott (sometimes advertised as William "Wild Bill" Elliott; 1904–1965), a busy actor in Westerns, had established himself in a series of 13 feature films that ran from 1938 until 1942 in which he portrayed the legendary lawman Wild Bill Hickok. Opportunity presented itself again when he took on the role of Red Ryder in 1944. Based on a character found in a popular newspaper comic strip of the same name drawn by Fred Harman (1902–1982) and written by Stephen Slesinger (1901–1953), Elliott reprised the role in 16 features that ran until 1946. Actor Robert Blake (billed at the time as Bobby Blake; b. 1933) also appeared in this series as Little Beaver, Ryder's young Navajo sidekick, a boy who can get laughs, but also proves valuable when the need arises, which occurs frequently. Blake eventually played in more Red Ryder films than did Elliott, who bowed out of the series with *Conquest in Cheyenne* (1946); Allan "Rocky" Lane (1909–1973) came in as a replacement, and he and Blake acted in seven additional Ryder movies, concluding with *Marshall of Cripple Creek* in 1947.

Many other Western series of one kind and another played theaters around the country during the 1940s. In most of them, anything contemporary or topical proved the exception, and the vast majority of Westerns, A or B, steered clear of that kind of obvious plotting. The themes accompanying the stories could, however, be more subtle than spy rings or black marketers. In a number of pictures, such as *Western Union* (1941), *California* (1946), and *She Wore a Yellow Ribbon* (1949), the idea of westward expansion coupled with a strong sense of nationalism gave audiences reassurance about American destiny—positive, inevitable, irreversible. In a decade when the nation faced both World War II and the threats implicit in the **Cold War,** the image of the cowboy (cavalryman, Indian fighter, scout, pioneer, settler, cattle rancher, farmer) had to be comforting, even if on a subconscious level. This familiar Western mythology, repeated hundreds of times in features both good and mediocre, probably helps to account for the genre's continuing popularity.

Director John Ford (1894–1973), considered by many to be the cinematic poet of the American West, created a number of memorable Westerns that began in the late 1930s and carried through the 1940s and beyond. Quality A pictures in every respect, they reinforce the mythic story of expansion and destiny in both their stories and imagery. Often employing the glorious scenery of Utah's Monument Valley, Ford emphasized the vastness of the land, its stark beauty, and the arrival of U.S. civilization in this harsh setting. Starting with 1939's *Stagecoach* and continuing with *My Darling Clementine* (1946), *3 Godfathers* (1948), *Wagon Master* (1950), and, in particular, his epic cavalry trilogy—*Fort Apache* (1948), *She Wore a Yellow Ribbon* (1949), and *Rio Grande* (1950)—he defined the elements audiences have come to associate with motion pictures about the West.

*See also:* Comedies (Film); Comic Strips; Costume and Spectacle Films; Crime and Mystery Films; Crosby, Bing; *Howdy Doody Show, The;* Murphy, Audie; Newspapers; Radio; Radio Programming: Children's Shows, Serials, and Adventure Series; Serial Films

**Selected Reading**
Cameron, Ian, and Douglas Pye, eds. *The Book of Westerns.* New York: Continuum, 1996.
Fenin, George N., and William K. Everson. *The Western: From Silents to Cinerama.* New York: Orion Press, 1962.
Fernett, Gene. *Hollywood's Poverty Row, 1930–1950.* Satellite Beach, FL: Coral Reef Publications, 1973.
McVeigh, Stephen. *The American Western.* New York: Columbia University Press, 2007.

# "WHITE CHRISTMAS" (IRVING BERLIN)

Irving Berlin (1888–1989), one of the most successful and prolific of all 20th-century American songwriters, had a gift for touching the emotions of everyone who heard his music. The strut of "Alexander's Ragtime Band" (1911), the lilt of "Blue Skies" (1926), the nostalgia of "Easter Parade" (1933), the patriotic fervor of "God Bless America" (written in 1918 but revised and published in 1938)—the list could go on for pages, but few years between 1907 and his death in 1989 failed to produce a memorable Berlin song or two.

A favorite of both Broadway and Hollywood producers, the versatile composer usually had a show or a movie to work on during the 1930s and 1940s, arguably two of his peak decades. So it was that 1938 (or 1939; sources do not agree) saw the composer working on a number for a proposed motion picture revue that revolved around popular holidays. He called the project *Happy Holiday*. As he sketched out some lyrics for a tune about Christmas, he apparently was basking in the Arizona sun, a fact that would cause some minor changes in later versions of the song. But the project lagged, and Berlin moved on to other things, putting his notes and incomplete music aside. He had, however, a reputation for never discarding any of his compositions, knowing, as in the case of "God Bless America," that it might be used again.

A brief period passed, and in April 1941, discussions about *Happy Holiday* came back to life. By then, Berlin had roughed out a more complete score with songs for numerous major holidays, and Paramount Pictures had agreed to produce the musical. Two of the biggest names in **movies** of the era, **Bing Crosby** (1903–1977) and Fred Astaire (1899–1987), shared the lead, and Mark Sandrich (1901–1945), a man with whom Berlin had worked several times before, directed the proceedings. Playwright and novelist Elmer Rice (1892–1967) undertook the task of adapting Berlin's notes and ideas into a workable screenplay. In the midst of all this activity, the title *Happy Holiday* underwent a change and became *Holiday Inn,* an alteration that more accurately refers to the plot.

The film opened in August 1942. Given its casting, the picture enjoyed immediate box office success and would quickly become a Christmas favorite, even though it hit theaters long before the start of the holiday season. Paramount had not marketed *Holiday Inn* as a Christmas movie, because the picture recognized a number of other traditional celebrations as well. In the story, Crosby operates a small Connecticut inn that, implausibly, opens only at specific times, such as New Year's, Easter, the Fourth of July, Thanksgiving, and so on, including Christmas. Most of Berlin's music for this movie remains forgettable, such as "Abraham" for Lincoln's birthday (done in blackface, possibly the only number that dates the picture) and "I Can't Tell a Lie" for George Washington's. But "Be Careful, It's My Heart," a paean to Valentine's Day, did well for a brief time.

Had he written nothing else in his long career, Irving Berlin would, however, be remembered for another song from *Holiday Inn:* "White Christmas." Bing Crosby has the privilege of performing this number in the movie twice, but few people realize he had previously introduced it on his popular **radio** program, *The Kraft Music Hall,* a broadcast carried on Christmas Day 1941. At that time, it elicited little attention, and no transcription of that particular show has ever been discovered, so the true debut performance of "White Christmas" has been lost. Although many listeners heard Crosby on a regular basis, his rendition of the song apparently caused few ripples. In the long stretch between the December 1941 broadcast and the August 1942 release of *Holiday Inn* on film, nothing more was heard about Berlin's composition.

Everything changed when the picture began playing theaters. Paramount had expected great things with "Be Careful, It's My Heart," and the public did not disappoint the studio. It quickly climbed the charts for several weeks that summer, and the popular Tommy Dorsey (1905–1956) orchestra recorded it, with the up-and-coming crooner **Frank Sinatra** (1915–1998), who at the time sang with the band, doing the vocal honors. But after its brief moment of fame, "Be Careful, It's My Heart" entered the ranks of forgotten pretty ballads and lost its place among the hits of the day.

Not so for "White Christmas." As more and more people heard the song in the movie or over the airwaves, demand for sheet music and the phonograph record featuring the Bing Crosby rendition grew, even though the way he sings it on the Decca recording does not match exactly the version heard in the film. After the July 1942 release of the record, "White Christmas" spent 29 weeks on the 1942 hit charts and peaked in popularity and sales in late October. It even won Berlin an Academy Award for the best song in a movie.

In 1943 and 1944, his composition continued to sell at a remarkable clip. In 1945, three years following its initial release, "White Christmas" reappeared at No. 13 on the *Billboard* charts and in 1946 continued its winning ways, earning a respectable No. 20 position. Within five years, it had sold 5 million records and another 3 million copies of sheet music. After those remarkable figures, it settled into the comfortable niche of a standard, one of those widely known, often-performed songs that enjoys steady sales year in and year out. Music historians give "White Christmas" the honor of being the best-selling single recording of the 20th century, with over 100 million copies sold in the United States and abroad. This unprecedented demand caused Decca to wear out the master, and in 1947 Crosby had to return to the studio and re-record his 1942 effort, note for note, to create a fresh copy. Virtually no one could tell the difference.

The lyrics for typical 20th-century American popular songs, as constructed by Irving Berlin and most of his contemporaries, consist of a verse-chorus format. The opening verse sketches a situation or vignette, and then the chorus elaborates on the details found in that introductory section. In practice, although most songwriters provided a verse, the chorus became the portion of the song most people knew. Verses tend to be wordy and often unmelodic, whereas the chorus, with its emphasis on melody, provides familiarity. When Berlin initially wrote "White Christmas" in the late 1930s, World War II had not yet begun for the United States, and he dutifully provided a prewar verse that the subsequent chorus would expand. But by the time of *Holiday Inn*, the world situation had significantly changed.

In his original version, the speaker in the verse resides in Los Angeles amid palm trees and warmth, but he longs for an old-fashioned Christmas in New England with snow. He makes no mention of war or current events, just nostalgia for the past. But the versions heard in the film and on recording drop the verse and simply move into the wistfulness of Christmas dreams, of a Christmas that the speaker will probably not experience firsthand. With the war, and U.S. troops spread out around the globe, "White Christmas," what some have come to call a secular carol, turned out to be the perfect vehicle for summarizing these feelings. Without ever referencing the conflict in any way, it became an ideal war song, and with more and more men going overseas, families separated during the holidays, and people looking back fondly on more peaceful times, "White Christmas" in its final form turned out to be a runaway hit and an iconic musical composition from World War II.

*See also:* *ASCAP vs. BMI* Radio Boycott and the AFM Recording Ban; Broadway Shows (Musicals); Musicals (film); Smith, Kate, Songwriters and Lyricists

**Selected Reading**
Kimball, Robert, and Linda Emmet, eds. *The Complete Lyrics of Irving Berlin.* New York: Alfred A. Knopf, 2001.
Rosen, Jody. *"White Christmas": The Story of an American Song.* New York: Charles Scribner's Sons, 2002.

# WOMEN IN THE MILITARY: WACS, WASPS, WAVES, SPARS, AND OTHERS

The United States Congress approved a peacetime conscription program, or draft, called the **Selective Training and Service Act of 1940.** Induction initially applied only to men aged 21 to 30. As the likelihood of war grew, both political and military leaders recognized the need for raising the number of personnel in the nation's armed forces, and discussions included the possibility of utilizing women in the various service branches, but no actions transpired. After active hostilities broke out in December 1941, with the attack on Pearl Harbor, men from 18 to 45 greatly enlarged the size of the eligible pool of draftees, and tours of duty increased from 12 months to the duration of the war. Women, however, continued to remain exempt from conscription.

The growing pressures of World War II coupled with strained manpower resources led officials to reconsider allowing women to serve in uniform and pragmatism won out over preconceived notions. Edith Nourse Rogers (1881–1960), a member of the House of Representatives from Massachusetts, had been advocating the creation of a women's branch of the army since early 1941. After considerable debate and compromise, the Women's Army Auxiliary Corps, or WAAC, came into being in May 1942. Opposition came mainly from conservative congressmen who disliked the concept of women in the armed forces in any way, but **President Franklin Delano Roosevelt** (1882–1945) promptly signed the bill the day following its passage.

The final proposal established a corps whose duties did not involve combat. Instead, its members would take on mainly clerical and communications assignments, such as switchboard and radio operations. At no time would WAAC officers be in command of men, and pay schedules would not be commensurate with the amounts paid to men for similar work. Limitations were also placed on benefits, especially for overseas duties. Despite these inequities, Oveta Culp Hobby (1905–1995), a member of the Women's Interest Section of the War Department, assumed command of the fledgling corps with the rank of major; she would later be promoted to colonel. Although a ceiling of 25,000 recruits had initially been set, response to the new army branch proved so overwhelming that in November 1942, the secretary of war boosted it to 150,000 volunteers.

In the early days of the WAAC, when the first recruits completed basic training, they frequently received assignments to Aircraft Warning Services locations, tedious jobs requiring them to plot the positions of aircraft over or near the Eastern seaboard. Later recruits began to take over clerical and motor pool duties. The Army Air Force (AAF) eagerly accepted WAAC personnel, broadening their responsibilities to include weather forecasting, mechanical repair and upkeep, **photography** interpretation, parachute rigging, and a host of other duties; in time, the AAF used almost half of all available women. Regardless of branch, as their postings increased, these enlistees freed growing numbers of men for combat operations, thereby fulfilling the primary goal of admitting women into the military.

As was the case in every branch of the armed forces at the time, the army imposed strict racial segregation on WAAC activities and facilities. Although most of their training might be integrated, base theaters, shops, and social events remained separated. White platoons had white officers, and black units had black officers. Not until the mandated racial desegregation of the U.S. military, which did not occur until the late 1940s and early 1950s, would these practices be discontinued.

In the meantime, the army, anxious to maximize the effectiveness of the WAAC, agreed to make this women's branch a full and equal part of the service. In the summer of 1943, the Women's Auxiliary Army Corps became the Women's Army Corps and its members soon went by the familiar term "WACs." They quickly lost any stigma that the former "Auxiliary" might have carried with it. At the time of the change, those members of the WAAC were given the choice of going with the new organization or returning to civilian status. Over 75 percent chose to remain and become WACs.

The army, like any large organization performing multiple tasks, has long been divided into subgroups with varying responsibilities. For example, during the World War II years, the Army Service Forces (ASF) functioned as the supply and administrative branch that fed, clothed, housed, and equipped the millions of troops serving at any given time. The ASF made extensive use of WACs, usually without any overt prejudice toward women. From driving trucks to keeping track of soldiers in the field, WACs turned in outstanding performances, and top-ranking officers, including **General Dwight David Eisenhower** (1890–1969), praised their work. On the other hand, the Army Ground Forces (AGF), charged with providing ground units organized and trained for combat operations, turned out to be the only group reluctant to use WACs. It clung to the men-only military tradition, with the result that WACs assigned to AGF functions found themselves the victims of overly strict discipline, nonexistent promotions, and demeaning tasks not worthy of their skills or training. When the conversion from WAAC to WAC took place in 1943, over a third of those women in AGF units chose to return to civilian life, the highest percentage among all WAC groups.

With the Allied campaigns in North Africa (1942–1943), Italy (1943–1945), and Normandy (1944–1945), WACs usually came ashore only weeks after the initial landings. By the end of the war in Europe (**V-E Day,** May 8, 1945), close to 8,000 WACs held various posts in the European theater. In the sprawling Pacific, about 5,500 WACs served through **V-J Day** (September 2, 1945), primarily in New Guinea and the Philippines. Among the hardships endured by WACs, the Pacific contingent, because of poorly managed supply orders, had been issued heavy winter uniforms unsuitable for tropical climates. Many WACs in this theater suffered from skin diseases brought on by constant humidity and incorrect dress, and about 25 percent of those in island environments had to request medical transfers.

Added to health questions, a number of Pacific commanders opposed having women in the field. Headquarters thus gave them gratuitous duties instead of challenging work. In addition, many WACs found themselves confined to guarded, fenced-in compounds on off-duty hours "for their own protection." Morale, therefore, seldom stayed as high as that among WACs assigned to the European theater.

With the end of World War II, the army commenced a rapid demobilization. But roughly 10,000 WACs continued in active service, their futures in doubt. Colonel Hobby had resigned her commission in the summer of 1945, and Lieutenant Colonel Westray Battle Boyce (1926–1972) assumed command of the Women's Army Corps. She served from 1945 until 1947, whereupon Colonel Mary A. Hallaren (1907–2005) assumed the post until 1953. Although many officials favored a complete demobilization of the corps, others felt it should be retained. In June 1948, after considerable congressional deliberation, the WAC became a permanent part of the United States Army, with equal pay and benefits, and those remaining WACs were phased into the service.

The Army Air Force also utilized the skills of Women's Airforce Service Pilots (WASPs), a group of approximately 1,000 women. Hired not as military personnel but as employees with civil service status and thus ineligible for service benefits, they ferried aircraft, taught flying to AAF cadets, towed gunnery targets, and anything else that might free male pilots for combat. Jacqueline Cochran (1906–1980), a famed aviatrix who could probably fly circles around any man, was enlisted to command the WASP program as director of women pilots.

From its beginnings in 1942, the WASP program became embroiled in controversy, most of it gender-based in one way or another. Male civilian pilots felt threatened and did not want their jobs endangered by women, especially with the end of the war approaching. Many critics believed women should not fly or be in command of men, and others objected to any female presence in the armed forces whatsoever. When a 1944 proposal to militarize the WASP and grant its members full service equality, columnist Drew Pearson (1897–1969) engaged in a scurrilous campaign against the group. Although his motives remain unclear, his diatribes so inflamed both sides that a counterproposal to disband the WASP met with success. In December 1944, with the war still raging, the program came to an abrupt end, and officials declared its records as classified; they would not be made unavailable until 1979. Only in the 1980s and thereafter has an accurate history of this little-known women's unit become known.

The navy likewise created an all-women service branch popularly known as WAVES, or Women Accepted for Voluntary Emergency Service. Mildred McAfee (1900–1944; fondly known as "Captain Mac" by her associates) received a commission in the U.S. Naval Reserve as a lieutenant commander in the late summer of 1942, the first woman to hold that rank. Years earlier, in 1919, some navy nurses had carried the curious rating of yeomen (F). McAfee thus became the director of a new organization dedicated to recruiting and training women for a wide range of naval duties. The word "emergency," a political ploy to assuage some officials resistant to women in the navy, suggested that the WAVES would disband when the "emergency"—World War II—had come to an end.

As was the case with the Women's Auxiliary Army Corps, interest ran high among civilians, and within a year McAfee and her staff had 27,000 women wearing navy blue in a distinctive new uniform. In order not to repeat a mistake the WAC had made in regard to military dress, leaders of the WAVES commissioned Mainbocher, an old, established New York **fashion** house, to design the clothing the new branch would wear. Most people agreed that the World War II WAC outfits suffered from dowdiness, that they appeared too masculine to hold much feminine appeal. Mainbocher's designs blended fashion and utility and have remained little changed since the 1940s. By the war's end in 1945, almost 90,000 women served in the WAVES, second only to the Women's Army Corps.

The recruitment of WAVES to serve on shore-based naval installations thereby freed up more men for sea duties. Restrictions forbade them from serving on board any navy vessels or aircraft and they could not participate in any combat operations. In addition, the WAVES excluded all black women from enlisting until late in 1944, when a formula allowing for one black enlistee for every 36 white applicants went into effect.

Not until years later, when the desegregation of the armed forces took place, did the navy discard that artificial ratio.

At the same time as the creation of the WAVES, the Marine Corps, a distinct branch of the U.S. Navy, also received permission to form a women's contingent. Officials made no attempt to form a memorable name or acronym, and the group became the Marine Corps Women's Reserve. Like the WAVES, the distaff Marines were supposed to undertake shore-based duties to allow greater numbers of men for combat. Major (later Colonel) Ruth Cheney Streeter (1895–1990) served as their first commander and saw the group grow to over 18,000 by 1945. In 1946 and peacetime, the Marines deactivated the Women's Reserve. After 1948 and passage of the Women's Armed Services Integration Act remaining members became eligible to join the regular Marine Corps. This stipulation also held true for women in the other services as well.

The Coast Guard, recognized as an official branch of the U.S. military establishment, originally existed as an arm of the Department of the Treasury. In more recent times, it has served as a part of the Department of Homeland Security. The previously all-male service accepted women into a new unit formed in 1942, shortly after the creation of the WAVES program. Officially called the U.S. Coast Guard Women's Reserves, it operated under the command of Dorothy C. Stratton (1899–2006), a former dean at Purdue University and an officer in the WAVES. Stratton began her assignment as a lieutenant commander and soon attained the rank of captain in 1944. In order to identify women in the Coast Guard, she suggested the distinctive name of SPARS by combining the Coast Guard's motto of *Semper Paratus* and its translation, "Always Ready." She also noted that a spar, in nautical usage, consists of a supporting beam, and that her SPARS would support the Coast Guard.

The Coast Guard traditionally has fewer members than the other main services, so when the SPARS program attained a strength of over 11,000 women in 1945, it could therefore boast having the highest ratio of women enlistees and officers to men of any service branch (1 out of 16 enlisted personnel and 1 out of 12 officers). Unlike the other services, the Coast Guard was the only military branch during the war to train women officers at its own academy in New London, Connecticut. West Point and Annapolis remained men-only throughout World War II.

As with WACs, WASPs, WAVES, and Women Marines, SPARS initially served only on land in the continental United States and were barred from combat. Toward the end of World War II, SPARS also performed their duties in Alaska and Hawaii, and the range of tasks they performed expanded greatly. Demobilized after the war, like other women in the armed forces, SPARS could eventually join the regular military.

Surprisingly, American popular culture did not capitalize to any great degree on women entering the military. Perhaps a sense of patriotism in time of war or a reluctance to engage in controversy kept the subject, one seemingly ripe for exploitation or satire, muted. Cartoonist Russ Westover's (1886–1966) popular *Tillie the Toiler* comic strip had its titular heroine enlist as a WAC in 1942, one of the few comic characters to do so. Tillie accepts her new role as she would a new job, and much of the focus of the strip remains on her love life, just as it always had.

Hollywood released a short, *Women at War,* in 1943. It depicts several women, including actresses Faye Emerson (1917–1983) and Dorothy Day (1897–1975), who for various reasons enlist in the Women's Army Corps. That same year saw *So Proudly We Hail!* a story about army nurses (a group separate from the Women's Army Corps) on duty in the Philippines. It graphically depicts the grueling work and dangers they daily faced in the early days of the war from a relentless advance by Japanese forces. On the other hand, that same war plays no real part in *Here Come the Waves* (1944), a frothy musical that stars **Bing Crosby** (1903–1977) and Betty Hutton (1921–2007), the latter in a dual role. The movie simply accepts the premise that women served in the navy and focuses instead on music and fun. For most films, however, any references, visual or otherwise, to women in the military exist as background, bit parts that lend realism to a picture but add little or nothing to the plot.

The purveyors of popular music, swept up in a wave of tunes that referred to the war in many ways, did not ignore the WACs and the WAVES. A spate of songs, none destined to be hits, paid their respects to women serving in the armed forces. Such titles as "I've Got a WAAC on My Hands and a Wave in My Hair" (1942), "Wait Till the Girls Get in the Army, Boys" (1942), "In My Little G.I. Shoes" (1942), "Yankee Doodle Girl" (1943), "WAVES in Navy Blue" (1943), "The WAAC Is in Back of You" (1942), "Song of the WAC" (1944), and "One Little WAC" (1944) acknowledge the novelty of women in uniform—sometimes humorously, other times sentimentally—but collectively failed to capture the public imagination. Mediocre efforts all, they survive as footnotes to the musical history of World War II.

Children's dolls could be purchased wearing the uniforms of the various service branches, so that miniature WACs or WAVES would be dressed up reasonably authentically, but they merely reflected the wartime years when uniformed citizens—men and women—could be seen daily on city streets. Scattered newspaper and magazine advertisements also utilized WACs and WAVES to sell products, but overall, women serving in the military receive only the most perfunctory coverage in media outlets.

Conversely, despite a continuing campaign of disrespect and misunderstanding about the role of women in the armed forces, much of it fueled by a tradition-bound officer corps that felt women infringed on a previously all-male domain, U.S. military women—volunteers all—have always conducted themselves with distinction. And gradually, often grudgingly, they have won the respect of their male colleagues. Today, women serve alongside men in virtually all jobs, and few think much about it. To those pioneers from the World War II era that broke down gender barriers, the nation owes a debt of gratitude.

*See also:* Advertising; Comic Strips; Magazines; Musicals (Film); Newspapers; Race Relations and Stereotyping; Toys

**Selected Reading**
Bellafaire, Judith A. *The Women's Army Corps: A Commemoration of World War II Service.* www.history.army.mil/brochures/wac.htm
Godson, Susan H. *Serving Proudly: A History of Women in the U.S. Navy.* Annapolis, MD: Naval Institute Press, 2001.
Holm, Maj. Gen. Jeanne. *Women in the Military: An Unfinished Revolution.* Novato, CA: Presidio Press, 1992.
Morden, Bettie J. *The Women's Army Corps, 1945–1978.* Washington, DC: Center of Military History, 1992.

# Y

## YOUTH

The word "teenage," sometimes shortened to "teen" and used to denote the period of growth in persons between 13 and 19 years of age, has been in the English language since at least early in the 20th century. Advertisers and marketers initially utilized "Teenager," coined in the late 1930s, as a means of reaching adolescent girls of junior high and high school age. They soon expanded its usage to include both sexes in a developmental stage with their own patterns of behavior, values, peer interactions, and **fads,** a trend captured by *America's Youth,* a *March of Time* newsreel released in 1940.

Schools, as both a place for learning and social activities, played an important role in the formation of this identifiable age group. The proportion of 14- to 17-year-olds in high school grew from 10.6 percent of that demographic in 1900 to 51.1 percent in 1930, 71.3 percent in 1940, and approximately 85 percent in the early 1950s. This growing school population included members from various socioeconomic strata and backgrounds. Gathered together much of the year, seven hours a day, cliques formed, and the teenager's life soon revolved around peers. Instead of parents or adults, other teens served as the source for information and advice; influenced speech, clothing, entertainment, and other leisure activities; insisted on conformity; and announced approval and disapproval.

Money also served as a major impetus in the emergence of a youth culture. Parents still provided the necessities of life; some also granted a weekly allowance. This spending money, often along with pay from after-school and occasional full-time jobs, empowered teenagers to be viable consumers—a condition manufacturers, marketers, and retailers rarely ignored. Throughout the 1940s, an explosion of goods and services—**magazines,** records, clothes, dances, drinks, and **food,** to name a few—targeted this new teenage market. Promoted by various media, the purchases made by teenagers identified their lifestyle.

Like so many aspects of American culture during this time, the youth culture of the 1940s can be split into two periods: the wartime years and the postwar years. During 1940–1941, various magazines for women, such as *Ladies' Home Journal, Good Housekeeping,* and *Parents,* ran columns about, and sometimes for, teenage girls. With titles like "Trick for Teens" and "Teens of our Times," these pieces usually presented updates on dating etiquette, hints for getting along, or the latest slang.

*Life* magazine, in January 1941, included an article titled "SubDebs, They Live in A Jolly World of Gangs, **Games,** Gadding, **Movies,** Malteds & Music." Photographs show affluent teenage girls in Detroit who expect to marry well and join the ranks of high society relaxing at home wearing moccasins, drinking chocolate milkshakes at commercial establishments, and attending dances, while the text explains their special slang. Their activities of going after school to a soda fountain for a shake made and served by teenage boys who worked as soda jerks, taking in a movie, dancing a jitterbug at a high school **dance** with a well-stocked jukebox, or gathering at someone's home for a slumber party proved to be popular throughout the decade with most adolescents, not just subdebs.

In July 1941, the publishers of *Parents* began offering *Calling All Girls,* the first magazine explicitly for girls. It carried a few articles on dating, beauty, **fashion,** and manners—a clear continuation of the previous decades' emphases on an innocent, peaceful life and perceived gender-appropriate topics for girls such as behavior, appearance, and relationships. Its format resembled that found in **comic books,** a popular publishing phenomenon that attracted millions of young readers during the decade by including a number of "girl comics," an approach and feature that turned away some potential readers, mainly young women who wanted to be treated as being older than their years.

**Comic strips,** on the other hand, long a staple in U.S. **newspapers,** had early on identified teenagers as a potential audience. As far back as 1912, with Cliff Sterrett's (1883–1964) *Polly and Her Pals,* the world of adolescents became a focus. Language, fashions, and teen rituals played out frame by frame in this and other pioneering strips, such as Merrill Blosser's (1892–1983) *Freckles and His Friends* and Carl Ed's (1890–1959) *Harold Teen. Freckles* debuted in 1915; *Harold Teen* in 1919. By the 1940s, and with teenagers receiving more and more scrutiny, strips like 1941's *Teena* (by Hilda Terry, 1914–2006), 1943's *Penny* (by Harry Haenigsen, 1900–1991), 1944's *Bobby Sox* (by Marty Links, 1917–2008), and 1947's *Archie* (by Bob Montana, 1920–1975) made their appearances on the funny pages. All of the foregoing comics prospered during the 1940s and continued running well into subsequent decades. These cartoonists had opened a rich vein of humor, proved astute observers of teen virtues and foibles, and yet avoided stereotyping their characters as boorish juveniles.

At the same time the comics were going strong, a new singer on the scene, a crooner named **Frank Sinatra** (1915–1998), skyrocketed to stardom by garnering heavy media attention. His adoring and screaming female teenage fans, called bobby-soxers, stood in line for hours with their socks rolled down to ankle level and worn with loafers or two-tone saddle shoes, in hopes of getting an autograph from "Blue Eyes" before attending his show.

Concurrent with the continuous attention paid by the media to adolescents in general, as well as those wearing bobby sox or considered to be subdebs, clothing manufacturers began to increase their **advertising** directed at young women and suggested that they needed age-appropriate sizes and styles. This business-driven acknowledgement of teenagers—no longer children and not yet adults—led department stores to place clothes for girls in their own sections initially called "girls' wear" or "high school shop."

A 1944 movie, *Janie,* produced by Warner Bros. and starring Joyce Reynolds (b. 1925), Robert Hutton (1920–1994), Edward Arnold (1890–1956), and Ann Harding (1901–1981), tells a wartime story of bobby-soxers who, when not on the telephone, regularly frequent the local drugstore to buy malts and magazines and spend hours speculating about the hundreds of young GIs at a nearby army camp. Another film, RKO Radio Picture's 1947 romantic comedy titled *The Bachelor and the Bobby Soxer,* stars Gary Grant (1904–1986), Myrna Loy (1905–1993), Shirley Temple (b. 1928), and Rudy Vallee (1901–1986). It follows a teenage girl whose crush on a playboy artist creates slapstick consequences before her infatuation abates. Best-selling author Sidney Sheldon (1917–2007) won a 1947 Oscar in the category of best original screenplay for his efforts with this movie.

While bobby-soxers made headlines, stylish young men sporting zoot suits—long, fitted jackets with padded shoulders and multibutton sleeves worn with trousers with high waists and legs cut full in the thigh and pegged at the ankle—also appeared in the news. This fad originated on the West Coast with young Mexican Americans and became a short-lived teenage indulgence bordering on rebellion for boys in different parts of the country. Official production of zoot suits ceased in 1942 when, at the request of the War Production Board (WPB), clothing manufacturers reduced the amount of fabric used in men's suits. Narrower lapels and shorter jackets destroyed the zoot suit look. Even though they continued to be found on the **black market** in larger cities, the craze soon died out and never made a comeback.

Throughout the war years, an attitude of youth as a fun time prevailed for many who seemed oblivious to the conflict. They immersed themselves in the fads of the day and took advantage of increased social activities, such as extracurricular programs, sports, and dances offered by schools and community organizations. At the same time, some felt that their days of youth had been unjustly hampered by food **rationing,** little or no chewing gum, and lack of gasoline for cars for dating or for team buses going to school athletic events.

But changing conditions and uncertainties could not be completely ignored. Slogans such as "Study, Sacrifice, Save, and Serve" posted in schools underscored wartime expectations and told adolescents, especially young men, to expect an uncertain future. Students regularly participated in air raid drills as a reminder to be always alert for possible dangers. A small number, about 22 percent of those eligible, became members of the High School Victory Corps organized by the Federal Security Agency as a preinduction program for voluntary high school students. Many eagerly joined adults in raising money in war bond drives, tending **victory gardens,** and collecting for **scrap drives.**

The demands of national defense granted a new prestige to the youth of the country, especially young men. *Life* magazine, in a November 1942 issue, acknowledged the lowering of the draft age for men from 21 to 18 years with a cover story on Bob Berger, an 18-year-old undergraduate at the University of Nebraska. The cover photograph offers a typical representation of the 2.5 million newly drafted eligible adolescents—a serious youth wearing a cardigan, collared shirt and tie, carrying an armful of textbooks. Four pages of pictures reveal a pre–military service life for a young man as a mix of work and play.

With many draft-age men in service,, the government urged boys below this age group, along with girls and women, to find work in essential jobs. A number of teenagers, sensing an opportunity for freedom, service, and money, quit school and found full-time employment, while others worked part-time after school. Together, the employment figures for boys and girls 14 years or older increased from just over 1 million in 1940 to nearly 3 million by 1944, with even more taking jobs during the summer months. Educators worried about this trend, and the United States Office of Education launched a National Go-to-School Drive for the 1944–1945 academic year. Officials provided communities with a handbook on how to address the issue.

Along with growing teenage employment, fathers in military service, and mothers working, juvenile courts across the country reported increases in arrests and convictions of both boys and girls for crimes such as petty larceny, incorrigibility, and disorderly conduct. Court cases increased at such a startling pace during the war years that **President Harry S. Truman** (1884–1972), in December 1945, declared **juvenile delinquency** to be the most alarming problem in the nation since the war. A national panel consisting of representatives from groups such as Camp Fire Girls, Boys Clubs of America, Big Brother Movement, and Boy and Girl Scouts convened in 1946 to study the situation and assisted the Department of Justice in formulating plans to be distributed to social service and law enforcement agencies. Meanwhile, many localities across the country established teen centers, which offered a place for young people to gather under supervision to play ping pong, dance, and hang out. By 1947, large cities reported a noticeable drop in juvenile delinquency statistics and attributed this success to a combination of preventive measures. This trend continued through the remaining years of the decade.

In September 1944, as U.S. citizens looked forward to a return to peaceful times, a new publication for young women appeared on newsstands. Recognizing the potential of a growing teenage national market, especially girls, this periodical, titled ***Seventeen,*** focused on beauty, careers, and relationships, but also asserted that its readers were serious, intelligent, thinking young women approaching adulthood and wanting to know what was happening in the world, politically and socially. These editorial decisions proved profitable. Within six days, 400,000 copies of *Seventeen*'s premier issue had been sold, and the magazine went on to set fashion trends and answer behavior and dating questions during the postwar years. Still in publication in the 21st century, *Seventeen* achieved a circulation of 2.5 million by 1949, an audience larger than any other girl-focused publication.

At the time of the first issue of *Seventeen,* department stores strove mightily to identify and attract the teenage market. They dropped references to girls and now called their clothing sections for young women "teen-age wear" or the "teen shop." At the same time, teenagers viewed their social life as a barometer of success, and retailers stood ready to sell them the right clothes to wear; inform them on the right places to go for fun; and, with magazines such as *Seventeen,* provide them with the best advice on a wide range of topics.

Boys' fashions also moved into the limelight, and *Life,* in June 1945, ran a cover story titled "Teen-age Boys." The article leads off showing a variety of young men's outfits, from rolled jeans and white socks for school dress to a tie and oxfords for a date. It suggests that a teenage boy's day consists of a number of activities, including school, working part-time, sports, and listening to the **radio,** with the favorite being at least four hours of "goofing off," both with peers and alone. According to the magazine's story, all of this requires foods such as milkshakes, ice cream, candy, pop, sandwiches, milk, crackers, cereal, fruit, jam, butter, eggs, meat, and vegetables to be consumed at breakfast, lunch, first afternoon snack, second afternoon snack, dinner, and evening snack. This article differs in focus from a number of other publications of previous years about boys that stressed **education,** sports, work, rebellion, and outdoor adventures and also stands in sharp contrast to *Life*'s wartime coverage of draftee Bob Berger.

The radio as a popular form of mass entertainment extended to both sexes, who frequently joined their families or peers to catch a late afternoon or early evening airing of *The Lone Ranger,* ***The Edgar Bergen/Charlie McCarthy Show,*** or ***The Jack Benny Program***. Music of all kinds proved to be equally popular, and they listened to **Sinatra, Bing Crosby** and shows ranging from the **swing** bands of the early 1940s to **bebop,** country, and blues toward the end of the decade. Teenagers also regularly tuned in to *Your Hit Parade* (first aired in 1935), especially from February 1943 through December 1944, when Frank Sinatra sang on the show

In addition to listening to the radio, teenagers could be counted on to take in the latest movie, sometimes with family members, frequently with peers, or with a date—an acceptable unsupervised postwar activity. Surveys consistently reported adolescents as the most frequent and faithful customers at theaters, no matter what the movie. Wanting to exert their independence, they related to 17-year-old Willy, a young man who asks to be called William. Jackie Cooper (b. 1922) plays Willy in Paramount Picture's 1940 *Seventeen,* a film loosely based on the 1916 novel of the same name by Booth Tarkington (1869–1946).

But the subject matter hardly mattered. Young movie audiences were equally satisfied with the depictions of middle-class families as seen in Andy Hardy's family or the Henry Aldrich series; incorrigible goof-offs such as the Dead End Kids (also known as the East Side Kids or Bowery Boys); or Saturday afternoon double features of **Westerns** starring **Gene Autry** (1907–1998) **or Roy Rogers** (1911–1998).

By the early 1940s, American adolescents had emerged as an identifiable group, with the words "teenage" and "teenager" serving as acceptable descriptors. Over the course of the decade, a strong youth culture existed with its own rules for dress, language, behavior, dating, and determinations of popularity. The most admired boys had achieved the designation of star athlete, while many girls measured their standing by their degree of popularity with boys. Socioeconomic status, as in the past, continued to play a role in adolescent activities and pursuits, while fads such as wearing bobby sox or zoot suits and adoring Frank Sinatra crossed socioeconomic groups. Finally, members of the youth culture, as reported by *Life* magazine in 1950, had their idols, and those in the realm of popular culture won out. Five of the final top 12—Joe DiMaggio (1914–1999), Vera-Ellen (1921–1981), Roy Rogers (1911–1998), Doris Day (b. 1924), and Babe Ruth (1895–1948)—came from the entertainment and sports worlds.

*See also:* ASCAP vs. BMI Radio Boycott and the AFM Recording Ban; Automobiles and the American Automotive Industry; Best Sellers (Books); Beverages; Country Music; Desserts, Candy, and Ice Cream; Jukeboxes; Leisure and Recreation; Photography; War Bonds

**Selected Reading**
Considine, David M. *The Cinema of Adolescence.* Jefferson, NC: McFarland, 1985.
Palladino, Grace. *Teenagers: An American History.* New York: Basic Books, 1996.
Savage, Jon. *Teenage: The Creation of Youth Culture.* New York: Viking, 2007.
Schrum, Kelly. *Some Wore Bobby Sox: The Emergence of the Teenage Girls' Culture.* New York: Palgrave Macmillan, 2004.

# Timeline for the 1940s

Some general statistics about the decade:

U.S. population, 1940: 132 million; 1950: 149 million.

Life expectancy, 1940: 60.8 years (men), 68.2 (women); 1950: 65.6 years (men), 71.1 years (women).

1940: 75 percent of population urban or suburban, 25 percent rural; 1950: 85 percent of population urban or suburban, 15 percent rural.

Gross national product (GNP), 1940: $100 billion (roughly $1.48 trillion in 2008 dollars); 1950: $365 billion (roughly $3.14 trillion in 2008 dollars).

Federal budget, 1940: $13 billion (roughly $192 billion in 2008 dollars); 1950: $40 billion (roughly $344 billion in 2008 dollars). For comparison, the actual 2009 federal budget equaled approximately $3.1 trillion.

National debt, 1940: $43 billion (roughly $600 billion in 2008 dollars); 1950: $257 billion (roughly $2.3 trillion in 2008). For comparison,; the national debt in 2009 equaled some $12 trillion.

Some significant events occurring during the 1940s:

## 1940

The decade opens gloomily, with war already raging in Europe and Asia and the threat of direct U.S. involvement growing daily. Civilians learn new words like *blitzkrieg* (a quick, decisive attack) and *blitz* (sustained bombing of a target; literally, "lightning"). But the dark international news is tempered by good economic statistics: as the nation prepares for conflict, defense-oriented industries grow markedly and reduce any lingering unemployment left from the Great Depression; 1940 stands as a prosperous year.

In the June Republican national convention, Wendell L. Willkie, a political unknown, secures the party's nomination to run again Franklin D. Roosevelt for the presidency; although Willkie conducts a strong campaign, Roosevelt easily defeats him in November and thus gains an unprecedented third term.

CBS (Columbia Broadcasting System) successfully demonstrates a working color television setup in August. The impending war, however, prevents its wide deployment, although experimental black-and-white broadcasting continues.

The America First Committee, an isolationist group organized in an attempt to keep the country out of any European or Asian war, contests President Roosevelt's support for foreign allies and begins to attract attention and supporters.

In October, Selective Service officials draw numbers in the nation's first peacetime draft; by the end of the year, some 16 million men have been registered for possible conscription.

With the Germans and Japanese victorious in Europe and Asia, President Roosevelt throughout the year sharply increases the amount of military aid to beleaguered Britain, throwing off any pretense of neutrality. In a Fireside Chat broadcast on December 29, he coins the phrase "arsenal of democracy" to describe to listeners how U.S. industrial might will arm both the country and its allies against the Axis powers.

Despite Roosevelt's exhortations supporting hard work and unstinting sacrifice, American popular culture gives little indication of the crisis. *Gene Autry's Melody Ranch* premieres on radio, as does *Superman,* and listeners laugh at Jack Benny and thrill to *I Love a Mystery*. The movies offer a little bit of everything, from *The Grapes of Wrath* to *The Philadelphia Story,* a screwball comedy. Rodgers and Hart's *Pal Joey* opens on Broadway, Frank Sinatra croons his way to stardom, and the top recording for the year is Glenn Miller's up-tempo "In the Mood." Finally, readers buy Richard Llewellyn's gentle *How Green Was My Valley,* the No. 1 best seller for the year, a book far removed from the headlines of the day.

## 1941

In his January State of the Union address, President Roosevelt enumerates the Four Freedoms that must be defended in this time of crisis: the freedoms of speech and expression and the freedoms from want and fear. It inspires many and lives on as an American credo.

In the spring, the government establishes the Office of Price Administration to keep prices and wages in line, because record defense spending has created inflationary pressures.

Throughout the summer, as tensions rise, the United States and the Axis powers close one another's consulates, impose import and export restrictions, and freeze assets abroad. In the meantime, a series of incidents involving U.S. ships and German submarines creates a state of emergency, and the navy is given permission to attack any enemy (i.e., German or Italian) vessels operating within the nation's three-mile coastal boundaries.

Despite the growing hostilities, network radio premieres the slapstick *Red Skelton Show,* along with the situation comedy, *The Great Gildersleeve.* Moviegoers line up to see Humphrey Bogart in *The Maltese Falcon;* one of the greatest American films, Orson Welles's *Citizen Kane,* similarly debuts but not as successfully—only with time will it achieve its lasting reputation. On stage, *Watch on the Rhine,* by playwright Lillian Hellman, tackles the subject of fascism in Europe and argues against neutrality, a courageous position for the time. Jimmy Dorsey's rendition of "Amapola (Pretty Little Poppy)" holds down the No. 1 position for popular songs, and novelist A. J. Cronin's *The Keys of the Kingdom* ranks first in fiction.

In major league baseball—the teams increasingly riddled by the loss of players by the draft or through enlistment—Ted Williams bats .406 for the season and Joe DiMaggio hits safely in 56 consecutive games; fans cheer them on, and both records have never been broken.

But everything suddenly changes when, on the morning of December 7, warplanes from the Imperial Japanese Navy without warning attack Pearl Harbor, Hawaii, thereby precipitating, on the following day, a declaration of war by the United States against Japan.

Three days later, December 11, the United States also declares a state of war exists between it and Germany and Italy. On December 12, those two nations formally reciprocate against the United States. And so the year closes with World War II at last a reality, a conflict that will continue for four years.

## 1942

The year opens with the Office of Production Management, another wartime agency, ordering an outright ban on the production and sale of new cars, a ban that lasts until the end of hostilities in 1945.

In March, federal troops on the West Coast commence rounding up citizens of Japanese descent, many of whom reside in California. Although guilty of no crimes, they are placed in compounds for national security, a controversial decision. The government does not take similar measures with those of Italian or German ancestry, nor does it include those of Asian ancestry living elsewhere in the country.

After losing the Philippines to the Japanese and in retreat across the Pacific, Army Air Force pilots led by Lieutenant Colonel Jimmy Doolittle stage a morale-boosting April bombing raid on Tokyo and other key cities. It accomplishes little militarily but cheers the public and punctures the enemy's supposed invulnerability. In August, Marines storm ashore Guadalcanal, a Japanese-occupied island in the South Pacific. It signals a turn in strategy and a campaign of island hopping that will continue for the remainder of the war.

On the home front, the Office of Civilian Defense comes into being in May. Citizens from all walks of life don helmets and check their flashlights in order to serve as air raid wardens on guard against enemy planes and bombs. Blackouts, brownouts, and dim-outs become commonplace in many cities.

To avoid shortages, gasoline rationing commences in July, one of many commodities that will be strictly controlled through ration books and stamps. Children collect metals, newsprint, and kitchen grease in neighborhood scrap drives.

U.S. and British troops invade North Africa in November, the first large-scale operation against German and Italian forces. General Dwight D. Eisenhower serves as commander.

The overall picture of the war continues to look grim, and the entertainment media slowly shift gears in order to acknowledge events and create optimistic, patriotic messages designed to reassure their audiences. Radio presents *Stage Door Canteen,* a cheerful revue with celebrities entertaining the troops, while Hollywood cranks out one war-themed feature after another. Leading the list are *Casablanca* and *Mrs. Miniver,* with Humphrey Bogart outwitting the Gestapo in North Africa in the first and Greer Garson coping with any problem the war might bring in the second. Irving Berlin scores two big hits during the year: his timely musical *This Is the Army* celebrates soldiers and life in the army, and he touches everyone's sentimental side with "White Christmas," the year's top-selling record and a tune that goes on to be a recurring hit year after year. In books, escapism, more than relevance, continues to rule publishing. *The Song of Bernadette,* a religious tale about a young girl and her visions, ranks as No. 1 in fiction sales.

## 1943

To ensure maximum production, defense plants begin in February to operate on a minimum 48-hours-per-week schedule. Two months later, President Roosevelt freezes all wages and prices at their April levels in order to curb inflation and price gouging. At about the same time, the ages men can be drafted are expanded to 18 through 38; deferments will be granted only to those employed in essential wartime industries.

Throughout 1943, the traditional penny receives a zinc coating to conserve copper supplies. People nickname the altered coins "steelies."

Despite Roosevelt's objections, Congress passes the Smith-Connally Anti-Strike Act in June. This law makes union-led strikes at essential industries illegal and allows the government, if necessary, to forcibly take over a plant and operate it.

British Prime Minister Winston Churchill and President Roosevelt, having met early in the year at Casablanca, Morocco, to map strategy, convene in late November with Soviet Union Chairman Josef Stalin in Teheran, Iran, to discuss mutual cooperation. "The Big Three," as the press calls them, also discuss their ideas about the postwar era.

While world leaders meet, entertainment goes its own way. News shows abound, and listeners can learn the latest from reporters stationed in far-flung battle zones; closer to home, *The Army Hour* and *Meet Your Navy,* two musical variety presentations, keep listeners abreast of both pop music and activities within the service branches. *For Whom the Bell Tolls,* a film adaptation of Ernest Hemingway's novel about the Spanish Civil War, has a stalwart Gary Cooper battling to the end, while *Air Force* has lots of exciting shots of bomber crews in action. Similar fare can be found in movie houses throughout the year. On Broadway, one musical dominates: Rodgers and

Hammerstein's *Oklahoma!* Its unparalleled success announces the arrival of a writing team that will, in the years to come, overshadow all the competition.

In the recording field, although songwriters strive to pen patriotic war songs, they seldom find receptive audiences. So tunes like "I've Heard That Song Before" (No. 1) and "Paper Doll" (No. 2) take top honors on the music charts, much to the chagrin of government, which wants a nationally popular song about the war and even appoints a commission in an ill-fated attempt to get one. In like fashion, readers eschew books dealing with the conflict, falling back instead on old favorites. For 1943, Lloyd C. Douglas's religious epic, *The Robe,* tops the best-seller lists.

# 1944

As the year opens with the Allies increasingly taking the offensive, people realize that eventually a second front—a full-scale invasion of continental Europe—will occur, and the question becomes when. Allied troops continue their arduous march up through Italy, and virtually continuous strategic bombing of German installations throughout Europe weaken the German war machine, but much bloody fighting continues.

In the Pacific, the island-hopping tactics of General Douglas MacArthur pay off, and many formerly Japanese territories fall into U.S. hands, but at an expensive price in casualties. Formerly unknown names like Tarawa, Kwajalein, the Admiralty Islands, Bougainville, Saipan, Guam, and Leyte make newspaper headlines as marines and army troops push ever closer to mainland Japan.

On June 6, the long-awaited invasion of France begins in Normandy. The largest military operation in history, it entails hundreds of thousands of troops along with thousands of aircraft, ships, and artillery. Despite a vigorous defense by the Germans, the Allies secure a beachhead and move inland. The conflict will continue for another year, but the Normandy landings mark a partial beginning of the end for World War II. General Dwight Eisenhower commands the undertaking, which he dubs the Great Crusade.

Aware of the millions of men in uniform, Roosevelt in June signs the Servicemen's Readjustment Act, better known as the GI Bill. This legislation, containing some of the most sweeping social reforms in the nation's history, makes it possible for discharged U.S. service personnel to obtain grants for finding jobs and furthering their education. Looking to the near future and the end of the war, the government plans to cushion their transition back to civilian life. In its original form, the GI Bill will run until 1965; it contributes immeasurably to the prosperity of the postwar era and countless GIs take advantage of its generosity.

Late in June, the Republicans nominate Thomas E. Dewey, the governor of New York, as their candidate to run for president. In July, the Democrats once again place their hopes with Franklin D. Roosevelt, who will be attempting to win an unprecedented fourth term.

While the war continues its bloody course and citizens await the November election, an unexpected September hurricane strikes New England and kills over 400 people and causes untold millions in property damage.

Despite the war and the weather, November arrives and Roosevelt defeats Dewey. He has, as his running mate, Harry S. Truman, a little-known senator from Missouri.

In the Pacific, B-29 bombers pound Japan daily, launching raids from captured islands that lie ever closer to the homeland. In Europe, however, a last-ditch offensive by German troops in the days just before Christmas turns out to be one of the costliest battles of the war; called the Battle of the Bulge, it takes its toll in thousands of lives on both sides. The Allies eventually prevail and in the process destroy a significant part of German military might and will.

Spirits perceptibly rise throughout 1944, and the entertainment industry breathes a sigh of relief. Radio offers a vast menu of programming, with comedies leading the way (*The Pepsodent Show with Bob Hope, The Abbott and Costello Show*), while teary soap operas take up the afternoons (*Ma Perkins, The Romance of Helen Trent*), and kids can hear their favorite serials (*Jack Armstrong, the All-American Boy, The Lone Ranger*). Movie marquees boast an equally large selection, from the joyful music of *Meet Me in St. Louis* to the gripping submarine exploits of *Destination Tokyo*. On stage, Leonard Bernstein's *On the Town,* a musical tale about three sailors on leave in New York City, draws appreciative audiences. And once again, popular music stays with the tried and true formula of up-tempo optimism. "Swinging on a Star" tops the charts, followed closely by "Don't Fence Me In." Popularized religion momentarily takes a back seat in the world of fiction when Lillian Smith's *Strange Fruit,* a controversial, chilling story of race relations in the contemporary South, briefly rides to the top on reams of publicity. Readers will return to their more conventional choices in the upcoming years.

## 1945

February witnesses a second meeting of the Big Three—Roosevelt, Churchill, Stalin—at the Crimean resort city of Yalta. At this conference, the leaders map plans for the imminent postwar era, including the formation of the United Nations. Although outwardly cordial, tensions build and Roosevelt appears tired.

Between February and July, U.S. Marines and soldiers capture two strategic islands close to Japan, Iwo Jima and Okinawa. In Europe during this same period, U.S. troops cross the Rhine into Germany proper. But April also marks the death of Franklin D. Roosevelt, weakened by the stresses and pressures of 17 consecutive years in office. A Great Depression and a World War have simply worn him out. Harry Truman assumes the presidency that same day, April 12, and an era draws to a close.

Working desperately against time, German technicians develop the first operational wartime missile, the V-2, which replaces the primitive V-1, or "Buzz Bomb." They also produce the Messerschmitt ME-262, a true jet fighter plane. But the expertise arrives too little, too late; on May 7, 1945, Germany gives its unconditional surrender to the Allies. The victors divide the country into zones—American, British, French, and Russian—and people rejoice that Europe is once again at peace.

While the Germans try to assemble their secret devices, scientists in Tennessee and desolate New Mexico strive to perfect a fearsome new weapon. The work takes time, but on July 16 they successfully detonate an atomic bomb in the desert near Los

Alamos and it exceeds expectations. Within three weeks, on August 6, another atomic bomb, nicknamed "Little Boy," is detonated over the city of Hiroshima, Japan. Three days later, another nuclear device, "Fat Man," explodes over Nagasaki, Japan. In a subsequent series of complex negotiations defining terms that take place between August 10 and 15, the Japanese announce their intention to capitulate. The Allies accept the offer, and on September 2, 1945, Japan formally surrenders aboard the battleship *Missouri* in Tokyo harbor. The world is momentarily at peace.

As the war winds down, radio stations continue to program comedy, crime, and music for the evening hours, while the daily soap operas retain their core of dedicated listeners. In a last gasp of war films, Hollywood releases, among others, *The Story of G.I. Joe, They Were Expendable,* and *The House on 92nd Street.* For the most part, however, the studios return to musicals and nonwar dramas. *The Glass Menagerie* announces the Broadway arrival of an important new playwright in the person of Tennessee Williams.

Popular music, which has basically ignored the war, follows its familiar patterns. A novelty number, "Rum and Coca-Cola," tops the charts in a lively rendition by the Andrews Sisters, and a number of new vocalists, such as Perry Como, Doris Day, and Vaughn Monroe, signify a change in public preferences, with singers replacing the big bands. Readers choose a racy historical romance with the best-selling *Forever Amber.* The city of Boston feels otherwise, however, and bans the book, a move that only increases sales further (and the Massachusetts Supreme Court will overturn the ruling in 1947).

The demobilization of millions of U.S. service personnel begins in autumn as state, federal, and military officials attempt to address the myriad problems that will accompany this move, one that sees upward of 35,000 discharges a day. As the armed forces shrink, going from over 11 million men in 1945 to just over 1 million in 1946, the more farsighted in Washington realize that the Soviet Union, an ally in the war, is now making unreasonable demands about the occupation of Germany and casting hungry looks at the rest of Europe, especially the eastern tier of nations.

As the year ends, the Cold War, in its formative stages, begins. The term "Cold War," however, does not achieve any particular notoriety in 1945, although British author George Orwell employs the phrase in his writing. The opposite of a "hot war," the phrase remains unknown until pundit Bernard Baruch uses "Cold War" in a 1947 speech; at that time, it enters the popular vocabulary.

## 1946

Americans, inured to sacrifice during the war, delight in most consumer controls being lifted. Armed with record personal savings accumulated during the conflict, they go on a buying binge, and manufacturers rush to refit their factories to churn out automobiles, appliances, radios and television sets, the latest fashions, and any and everything else the public might desire.

For example, an RCA 10-inch black-and-white television, one of the biggest-selling models at the time, retails for about $375 (roughly $4,000 in 2008 dollars). The steep price slows sales not at all. Instant gratification of wants, after so long without, becomes the order of the day.

Organized labor, also freed from the wartime strictures imposed on it, challenges management in many industries, with thousands of walkouts and strikes during the year. One of the first major disruptions occurs in the steel industry; a January strike cripples production and results in increased wages for workers and higher prices for steel and helps trigger inflation across the board. Coal mines, automobile plants, appliance manufacturers, and railroads soon follow suit.

In a March speech given in Fulton, Missouri, Winston Churchill utters the famous words, "an iron curtain," to describe the Soviet Union's military and political seizure of much of Eastern Europe, a move that effectively seals it off from the more democratic western portion of the continent.

To make the fledgling United Nations a physical reality, philanthropist John D. Rockefeller contributes over $8 million (roughly $89 million in 2008 dollars) to the organization. The money will be used to construct a permanent headquarters in New York City along the East River.

Recognizing both the threat and promise of nuclear power, the government in August forms the Atomic Energy Commission; a civilian agency, its duties include overseeing the production and applications of nuclear components.

In another technological advance, the University of Pennsylvania in February formally unveils a computer some years in development, the ENIAC (electronic numerical integrator and computer). Crude by modern standards—it occupies an entire room and generates tremendous heat because of the thousands of vacuum tubes necessary to run it. The machine nonetheless performs complex mathematical equations in seconds and points the way to the future.

To drum up listenership, network radio begins to offer a variety of quiz shows ranging from *Winner Take All* to *Twenty Questions*. Although the prizes are pitifully small by later standards, the programming piques public interest. In contrast, a number of mature, thoughtful movies come out during the year, including *The Best Years of Our Lives* and *The Razor's Edge,* along with a sprinkling of foreign films, like *Henry V* (England) and *Shoeshine* (Italy). A rich Broadway season boasts such plays as *The Iceman Cometh, Born Yesterday,* and *Annie Get Your Gun.* Theatergoers are happy to see the Great White Way ablaze in lights once again, and the quality of the fare seems to reflect this.

The Ink Spots, a popular vocal group, have the No. 1 recording with "The Gypsy," but bebop (or simply bop), a modern, evolving form of jazz, generates considerable publicity and controversy. *The King's General,* a long, complex English romance set in the 17th century, attracts a bevy of readers, perhaps hungry for more historical fiction after the success of 1945's *Forever Amber.*

# 1947

The Voice of America, a powerful, federally funded shortwave radio network run by the State Department, begins broadcasting in Russian to counter Soviet broadcasts. Originally formed in 1942, it becomes an important propaganda tool in the Cold War.

It transmits information and entertainment to nations under Communist control and achieves considerable popularity among its foreign listeners. The Soviet Union responds in 1949 by attempting to jam (electronically block) the transmitters, but most efforts prove futile. Interestingly, the broadcasts cannot be heard within the continental United States; federal law bans them for resident citizens.

In March, President Truman articulates what has come to be called the Truman Doctrine, a foreign policy initiative that says the United States can and will provide substantial aid to non-Communist nations seeking assistance to ward off Soviet aggression. Despite heightening international tensions, Congress discontinues the peacetime draft in March but reinstates it in June 1948 amid deteriorating relations with the Communist bloc.

With minimal fanfare, President Truman in September signs the National Security Act. This important piece of legislation, along with some subsequent amendments, reorganizes the military services, changing the National Military Establishment into the Department of Defense, led by a cabinet-level secretary of defense. The United State Air Force breaks away from the army and emerges as an independent branch of the armed forces. The act also dissolves the Central Intelligence Group, formed in 1946 to replace the colorful Office of Strategic Services, the nation's World War II spy organization, and creates the Central Intelligence Agency, giving it the task of carrying out intelligence work overseas. To coordinate these changes, Congress creates the National Security Agency, a secretive council charged with overseeing all aspects of national security. In the face of a growing Russian threat, especially with evidence of Soviet espionage, few quibble about any aspects of the new law and resultant agencies.

Emboldened by the growing clamor about Communist influences in American life, the House Committee on Un-American Activities (popularly abbreviated HUAC) stages a series of investigative hearings in the fall. It charges that the entertainment industry harbors Communist supporters, especially in Hollywood. Some 300 writers, producers, and actors see their careers ruined or damaged by this investigation when the industry blacklists them and a climate of fear envelops the movie capital.

On a brighter note, the Bell XS-1, an experimental rocket-powered aircraft, successfully breaks the sound barrier in the fall, and the United States lays claim to being the first nation to do so, although several groups challenge the claim. Since the Air Force executed the XS-1 flight under strict test conditions, most aviation groups accept its validity. Within a short time, supersonic flights become almost commonplace for advanced military aircraft.

As more people purchase television receivers and the industry inexorably expands, broadcasters increase the variety of their programming, the networks sense the potential for limitless profits, and sponsors envision reaching vast audiences. The excitement gives birth to a new mass medium. Radio, the nearest competitor to television, does not accept the challenge lightly. The networks sink considerable money into new programs and schedules, and the old standbys—Bob Hope, Bing Crosby, Jack Benny, Fibber McGee and Molly—remain loyal to radio for the time being, but the novelty of the small home screen lures new video fans daily.

The movies likewise feel the pressure brought by television. Relying on superior production values and a better picture, the film industry at first tries to ignore the interloper, but as more and more families stay glued to their sets instead of going to their neighborhood theaters, movie attendance drops, and the decline does not lessen with time. Prestige films like *Gentleman's Agreement* and *Crossfire* do little to lessen the hemorrhaging of a once-reliable audience. Broadway theater, perhaps a little more removed from television than radio and the movies, offers a fine season for 1947: Tennessee Williams' *A Streetcar Named Desire* introduces Marlon Brando to the stage, and *All My Sons* gives playwright Arthur Miller his first major theatrical success.

Popular music, unaffected by the inroads television makes on other media, goes its own way. The No. 1 song for 1947 originates in Nashville, Tennessee, a town more associated with country music than big pop hits. "Near You," written and performed by bandleader Francis Craig, starts out slowly and regionally but picks up speed and finally gains national recognition in August, staying on the charts for the remainder of the year. Other artists, particularly the Andrews Sisters, cut their own versions, making "Near You" a major happening in music circles.

While people hum Craig's tune, many of them read *The Miracle of the Bells*, another in the stream of religious novels that reach best-seller status during the 1940s. Written by Russell Janney, it consists of spiritual platitudes and little else, but readers flock to it, making the book the biggest selling title of the year. An unheralded paperback mystery, *I, the Jury*, a debut novel by Mickey Spillaine, also attracts attention because of its explicit sex and violence.

## 1948

In April, the Marshall Plan, a program of generous U.S. aid to war-devastated European countries, begins to disburse funds. Originally proposed by Secretary of State George C. Marshall in 1947, the program will, by 1951, give over $13 billion (roughly $121 billion in 2008 dollars) in aid to non-Communist countries and hastens reconstruction and expands trade. In addition, the month sees most of the nations within the Western Hemisphere cooperating to form the Organization of American States. The group encourages countries to work together and resist meddling from any nonmembers.

At their June convention, Republicans nominate Thomas E. Dewey to be the party standard-bearer in the November presidential elections. The Democrats, a month later, grant Harry Truman the nomination but not without serious squabbling. A group of disaffected Southern Democrats break away from the party, call themselves the States Rights Party (or Dixiecrats), and put up South Carolina governor Strom Thurman as a third-party candidate. On the more liberal side, the Progressive Party, composed of somewhat radical Democrats and their supporters, nominate Henry Wallace. It all promises an exciting election in November.

While the political parties square off against one another, the Soviets close down land transportation into occupied Berlin in June, effectively sealing off the city. The Western Allies—England, France, and the United States—respond by instituting nonstop flights of food and other needed supplies into the beleaguered city, a response that takes on the popular name the Berlin Airlift (although officials give it the military title of Operation Vittles). Powerless, the Soviet Union finally backs down in May

1949, almost a full year later. The airlift electrifies the Free World and humiliates the Soviet Union.

Pundits' prognostications to the contrary, Truman defeats Dewey in November and the splinter parties have little effect on the election. Instead of a New Deal, his platform calls for a Fair Deal.

On radio, Ralph Edwards dispenses nostalgia, sentiment, and good feeling in *This Is Your Life,* a fall offering that lasts only until mid-1950, when it makes the transition to television, where it will remain ensconced until 1961.

In the meantime, television captures an ever-larger audience share, *The Toast of the Town,* with host Ed Sullivan, premieres in June on CBS. An instant success, this variety show will run until 1971. Three months later, NBC's *The Texaco Star Theater,* featuring comedian Milton Berle, brings more vaudeville and variety to the small screen. Newscasters like John Cameron Swayze and Douglas Edwards become celebrities in their own right and make watching the evening news part of the American TV diet. Radio, fighting a losing battle, nonetheless offers *Stop the Music,* with host Bert Parks, a quiz that challenges contestants' musical knowledge. With prizes averaging $20,000 (roughly $179,000 in 2008 dollars), it presages the huge jackpots TV will later offer.

In terms of quality, 1948 stands as a good movie year; in terms of audience, the numbers continue their decline. Despite all-star offerings like *Treasure of Sierra Madre* (Humphrey Bogart), *Red River* (John Wayne, Montgomery Clift), *Easter Parade* (Fred Astaire), and *Hamlet* (Laurence Olivier), weekly attendance falls below 75 million admissions a week—a healthy figure but considerably below the 90 million of 1945. On a more upbeat note, playwright Tennessee Williams returns to Broadway with *Summer and Smoke,* actor Henry Fonda delights in *Mr. Roberts,* and composer Cole Porter creates a memorable score for *Kiss Me, Kate.*

In music, Dinah Shore's rendition of "Buttons and Bows," taken from a Bob Hope comedy Western titled *The Paleface,* takes top honors for the year and also wins an Academy Award for best film song. More important, however, CBS, owner of Columbia Records, announces the successful development of 33-1/3 rpm long-playing vinyl records. They surpass 78-rpm disks in popularity because of their longer playing time and durability. Competing record companies, especially RCA Victor, rush to duplicate Columbia's technological feat and release long-playing records of their own.

Novelist Lloyd C. Douglas repeats with another No. 1 best seller with *The Big Fisherman,* another religious offering that purports to tell the story of Peter and his relationship with Jesus. The second-place finisher, *The Naked and the Dead,* comes from a young writer named Norman Mailer, a veteran of World War II. The plot involves the nightmarish combat on a mythic Pacific island and has become an American classic.

## 1949

Various Western European nations, along with the United States, in April establish the North Atlantic Treaty Organization, or NATO. A mutual defense pact aimed squarely at curbing Soviet aggression, real or potential, it reflects the heightened security worries facing the Free World.

Alger Hiss, an official with the State Department, goes on trial in late May for perjury regarding possible Communist connections. Although it ends in a hung jury, the proceedings mirror the mounting concern about spies and Soviet infiltration into government circles. More hearings, accusations, and ruined careers will follow as paranoia grows in some quarters about "Reds," "Commies," "Pinkos," and "fellow travelers" in public life.

People worried about Soviet military power find their fears justified in September, when President Truman announces the USSR's detonation of an atomic bomb. The unthinkable becomes real.

Labor unrest continues in several key U.S. industries, especially coal. Led by John L. Lewis, the unionized miners stage a work slowdown in December. These disputes take place in the midst of a year-long recession, a period of economic adjustment after the immediate postwar boom.

Most Americans, however, take a rosy view of things and look to a prosperous future. Congress raises the minimum wage from 40 cents to 75 cents (or from roughly $3.50 to $6.50 in 2008 dollars).

Developer William Levitt converts some former Long Island potato fields into one of the largest planned communities ever attempted in the United States. Work on Levittown had commenced in 1947 with several thousand Cape Cod–style houses for sale or for rent. By 1949, this "instant suburb" consists of thousands of homes, including larger models called ranches.

Television continues to makes gains as home entertainment. *Hopalong Cassidy,* a Western series starring William Boyd, begins a two-year run on NBC, capturing an audience of both kids and adults. *The Lone Ranger,* a comic strip character that also runs on radio, likewise debuts, becoming a fixture on ABC until 1957. CBS counters with two sentimental family shows, *Mama* and *The Goldbergs.* The first stars Peggy Wood in the title role (based on the hit 1944 play, *I Remember Mama*) and runs until 1957; the second, taken from radio's popular series that had premiered back in 1929, features Gertrude Berg recreating her original character of Molly Goldberg. *The Goldbergs* stays on CBS until 1951, then goes to NBC and later Dumont, finally ending up in syndication until 1955.

Radio continues a gradual retreat from original programming, offering instead disc jockeys and recorded music on many stations. The networks, however, still strive to come up with winning combinations, the most notable being the creation of *Dragnet,* a realistic police series with Jack Webb. It draws sizable audiences, to the point that it stays on the air until 1957, although a television version (also with the inimitable Webb) comes along in 1951, providing a choice: radio or television?

Refusing to throw in any kind of towel, the movie industry advertises something for every taste, from gritty wartime stories (*Twelve O'Clock High*) to psychological drama (*Champion*) to musicals (*On the Town*) to sophisticated comedies (*Adam's Rib*). But nothing the studios do stanches the gradual loss of audience to television. On the other hand, people line up at New York's Morosco Theatre for seats to *Death of a Salesman,* Arthur Miller's tragic portrait of Willy Loman, a defeated man. And Broadway also boasts one of the great Rodgers and Hammerstein musicals, *South Pacific,* another unqualified hit.

Although the Western-tinged "(Ghost) Riders in the Sky" dominates the music charts for 1949, and the somewhat similar "Mule Train" also makes a respectable showing, a novelty number by a real cowboy star becomes an instant classic. Gene Autry records "Rudolph, the Red-Nosed Reindeer" and establishes it as a staple for the holiday season, as enduring as any carol.

The publishing business enjoys no such luck; the No. 1 title in fiction goes to *The Egyptian,* a historical novel by Finnish writer Mika Waltari (in translation) about the age of the pharaohs. But readers do not entirely desert their more conventional preferences; *The Big Fisherman,* the leader in 1948, claims second place.

The U.S. Air Force, after a two-year investigation, denies the existence of unidentified flying objects in a lengthy report that leaves many dissatisfied with its findings.

Although the event goes relatively unnoticed, Volkswagen ships it first cars to the United States; the company sells a total of two Beetles this first year.

Finally, in Italian restaurants, bars, and kiosks across the country, a new menu offering quickly finds acceptance: pizza.

# 1950

The decade ends and a new one begins; the transition does not offer an optimistic picture of things to come. President Truman gives the go-ahead to develop a hydrogen bomb, a weapon immeasurably more powerful than the atomic bomb. In response, Soviet authorities announce that they, too, will pursue research in this direction. Plans for home bomb shelters appear in periodicals, and the government issues survival pamphlets.

In a second trial, held in January, a jury finds Alger Hiss guilty of perjury, and he receives a five-year sentence. Shortly thereafter, Wisconsin's Senator Joseph McCarthy launches a crusade to weed out Communists in government; he claims that over 200 active members of the Communist Party serve in the State Department. Although experts later debunk this particular charge, it sets off a virtual witch hunt, with McCarthy leading the attack.

Emboldened by the publicity, in March McCarthy claims, with little, if any, concrete evidence to back him, that Owen Lattimore, a ranking State Department employee, is a top Soviet agent. Lattimore chooses to contest the Wisconsin senator, and eventually a Senate committee accuses Lattimore of perjury in 1952. His career in tatters, he will continue to protest his innocence, and by 1955 all charges will subsequently be dropped, but the entire affair illustrates the poisonous atmosphere pervading Washington at that time.

If anti-Communist hearings were not enough, Tennessee Senator Estes Kefauver opens hearings on organized crime in May. They will continue on into 1951, but testimony reveals a far-flung web of gambling, prostitution, corruption, theft, and murder overseen by various organizations linked in one way or another. Cameras televise the proceedings, bringing the reality of crime into people's living rooms and making Kefauver an overnight celebrity.

On June 25, North Korean forces sweep into South Korea, the first large-scale open warfare the world has seen since World War II. The United Nations immediately responds and dispatches a multinational force led by the United States. This action results in a protracted campaign that will endure until the two sides agree on an armistice in 1953.

Because of the conflict, the country again mobilizes. Congress grants Truman power to regulate prices and wages and to impose rationing if needed. In December, just five years after the end of World War II, he declares a state of national emergency, a move that allows the country to again get on a war footing. But with anti-Communist hysteria rising, the government also squelches dissent, a menacing development for the start of a new decade that will come to be called the Age of Anxiety.

The new decade will witness the astronomical rise of television as an entertainment medium. New shows abound in 1950, such as *The Colgate Comedy Hour, Your Show of Shows, The Jack Benny Program, What's My Line?* and many others. An exodus of famous stars from radio to television exacerbates network radio's decline. NBC retaliates for the loss of Jack Benny and Edgar Bergen (along with Charlie McCarthy) by producing *The Big Show,* a celebrity-studded variety extravaganza that premieres on Sunday evenings. Hosted by Tallulah Bankhead with musical support from Meredith Willson, it costs a fortune. The network sees little return for its money and throws in the towel in 1952, the end of significant variety programming on radio.

The year also sees movie attendance drop to approximately 60 million admissions a week—still a sizable figure but down 30 million from 1945, a decline of one-third. And the losses will continue throughout the 1950s. Television simply eclipses fine motion pictures such as *All About Eve, Sunset Boulevard, Born Yesterday, The Asphalt Jungle,* and *Harvey.* The studios search for technological improvements to lure people back into theaters, but nothing outstanding appears for 1950.

Frank Loesser's *Guys and Dolls* and Irving Berlin's *Call Me Madam* brighten Broadway, as the legitimate theater follows an independent path, seemingly removed from the threat of television.

In literature, tradition continues its reign. The leading best seller, Henry Morton Robinson's *The Cardinal,* falls squarely into the religious category so favored by readers throughout the 1940s.

Patti Page warbles *The Tennessee Waltz,* the year's No. 1 tune, followed closely by the Weavers' interpretation of "Goodnight Irene." Such conservative tunes, steeped in tradition, give no hint about the momentous changes facing popular music. A noisy revolution, rhythm 'n' blues and rock 'n' roll, waits in the wings and will soon dominate.

# Selected Resources

## Bibliographical Note

As the Internet's World Wide Web (WWW) grows in thoroughness, accuracy, and ever-easier access, the number of available resource tools will continue to increase. In any work that stresses popular culture such as this encyclopedia, familiarity with invaluable sources like the Historical New York Times (www.proquest.com); the Internet Movie Database (www.imdb.com); the Internet Broadway Database (www.ibdb.com); and, for music, the bands-composers-lyricists database (www.info.net/index.html) is necessary. Access to the National Archives and the Library of Congress, two treasure troves of information on just about anything connected with the United States, can be found at www.archives.gov/ and www.loc.gov/index.html. Monetary conversions are simple, thanks to the Federal Reserve. Go to www.minneapolisfed.org/research/data/us/calc/ and the site will do the calculations. YouTube (www.youtube.com/) can unearth countless visual images. Literally hundreds of other Web sites will provide information about the 1940s, and readers are encouraged to avail themselves of these research tools.

## Audio

*American Musical Theater.* 6 LPs. Smithsonian Collection of Recordings. R 036. Compiled 1989.
*American Popular Song.* 7 LPs. Smithsonian Collection of Recordings. R 031. Compiled 1984.
*American War Songs, 1933–1947: Hitler and Hell.* CD. Trikont 0280. Compiled 1971.
*An Anthology of Big Band Swing, 1930–1955.* 2 CDs. Decca GRD 2–629. Compiled 1993.
*As Time Goes By: World War II Songs.* 3 CDs. Dynamic Entertainment DYN 3508. Compiled 2004.
*The Best Female Big Band Singers of the 40's.* CD. Chestnut CN 1007. Compiled 2005.
*Classic Songs from World War II.* 2 CDs. *Kiss the Boys Goodbye,* BMG 66702, and *Always in My Heart,* BMG 66703. Compiled 1995.

Copland, Aaron. *Copland Conducts Copland: Appalachian Spring, Rodeo, Others.* CD. CBS Records Masterworks MK 42430. 1988.
*The Country Hits of the 40s.* ASV Living Era CD AJA 5418. Compiled 2002.
*40's Hits: Country.* CD. Curb Records D2–77346. Compiled 1990.
*Forty #1 Hits of the Forties.* 2 CDs. Collector's Choice Music CCM 307. Compiled 2002.
*G.I. Favorites: The Tunes of World War II.* 2 CDs. Sounds of Yesteryear DSOY685. Compiled 2005.
*G.I. Jukebox.* CD. St. Clair Entertainment VNL14512. Compiled 2005.
*G.I. Jukebox: Songs from World War II.* CD. Hip-O HIPD-40142. Compiled 1998.
*Great Vocalists of the Big Band Era.* 6 LPs. Columbia Special Products, CBS Records. Compiled 1978.
*The Great War Songs.* 3 CDs. REDX Entertainment RXBOX31063. Compiled 2006.
*The Jazz Singers.* 5 CDs. Smithsonian Collection of Recordings. RD 113. Compiled 1998.
Jones, Spike. *(Not) Your Standard Spike Jones Collection.* 3 CDs. Collectors' Choice Music CCM-329–2. Compiled 2005.
Mercer, Johnny. *The Johnny Mercer Songbook. Vol. 1, Blues in the Night; Vol. 2, Trav'lin' Light; Vol. 3, Too Marvelous for Words.* 3CDs. Verve 314555 268–2; 314555 402–2; 314557 140–2. Compiled 1997–1998.
Popular Songs, 1946 (various artists). *Hit Parade 1946.* CD. Dynamic DYN2907. Compiled 2007.
Popular Songs, 1947 (various artists). *Hit Parade 1947.* CD. Dynamic DYN2908. Compiled 2007.
Popular Songs, 1948 (various artists). *Hit Parade 1948.* CD. Dynamic DYN2909. Compiled 2007.
Popular Songs, 1949 (various artists). *Hit Parade 1949.* CD. Dynamic DYN2910. Compiled 2007.
Popular Songs, 1950 (various artists). *Hit Parade 1950.* CD. Dynamic DYN2911. Compiled 2007.
*The Road to Nashville: A History of Country Music, 1926–1953.* 3 CDs. Sanctuary Records IGOTCD 2559. Compiled 2004.
*Rock 'n' Roll Roots: The Country Influence.* CD. Smith and Co. SCCD 1103. Compiled 2005.
*Rock 'n' Roll Roots: The R&B Influence.* CD. Smith and Co. SCCD 1105. Compiled 2005.
*Star Spangled Rhythm: Voices of Broadway and Hollywood.* 4 CDs. Smithsonian Collection of Recordings. RD 111. Compiled 1997.
*Swing Out to Victory! Songs of WWII.* 4 CDs. Intersound Records 1482. Compiled 2005.
V-Discs (various artists). *G.I. Jukebox Jive.* CD. Giant Steps GIST 002. Compiled 2003.
V-Discs (various artists). *Swinging on a V Disc.* 4 CDs. Jasmine Records JASBox 16–4. Compiled 2005.
*V-E Day: Musical Memories.* CD. ASV Living Era AJA5163. Compiled 1995.
*The Victory Collection: The Smithsonian Remembers When America Went to War.* 3 CDs. Smithsonian Collection of Recordings. RD 106–1, -2, -3. DMC3–1243. Compiled 1995.
*The War Years.* 4 CDs. Intersound CDC 1046–1049. Compiled 2003.
Wills, Bob. *Take Me Back to Tulsa: Bob Wills and His Texas Playboys.* 4 CDs. Proper Records Box 32. Compiled 2001.
*The Words and Music of World War II.* 2 CDs. Columbia/Legacy C2K 48516. Compiled 2001.

## Print and Electronic

Ad Council. www.adcouncil.org
Advertising. John W. Hartman Center for Sales, Advertising, and Marketing History. Duke University Libraries. www.library.duke.edu/digitalcollections/adaccess
Ahlstrom, Sydney E. *A Religious History of the American People.* New Haven, CT: Yale University Press, 1972.
Alinder, Mary Street. *Ansel Adams, an Autobiography.* Boston: Little, Brown, 1985.
Alinder, Mary Street, and Andrea Gray Stillman, eds. *Ansel Adams: Letters and Images, 1916–1984.* Boston: Little, Brown, 1988.
All-American Girls Professional Baseball League. Sean Lahman's Baseball Archive. www.baseball1.com/bb-data/bbd-wb1.html; www.aagpbl.org/league/history.cfm

Allen, Bob, ed. *The Blackwell Guide to Recorded Country Music.* Oxford, England: Blackwell, 1994.

Allen, Frederick. *Secret Formula: How Brilliant Marketing and Relentless Salesmanship Made Coca-Cola the Best-Known Product in the World.* New York: HarperCollins, 1994.

Allen, Frederick Lewis. *The Big Change.* New York: Bantam Books, 1952.

Alvarez, Luis. *The Power of the Zoot: Youth Culture and Resistance during World War II.* Berkeley: University of California Press, 2008.

Ammer, Christine. *Unsung: A History of Women in American Music.* Westport, CT: Greenwood Press, 1980.

Ancelet, Barry Jean, Jay D. Edwards, and Glen Pitre. *Cajun Country.* Jackson: University Press of Mississippi, 1991.

Andrews, Wayne. *Architecture, Ambition and Americans: A Social History of American Architecture.* New York: Free Press, 1964.

Anobile, Richard J., ed. *Michael Curtiz's Casablanca.* New York: Flare Books, 1974.

Antfarm [Chip Lord]. *Automerica: A Trip Down U.S. Highways from World War II to the Future.* New York: E. P. Dutton, 1976.

Armour, Richard. *Give Me Liberty.* New York: World Publishing, 1969.

Armstrong, Dan, and Dustin Black. *The Book of SPAM.* New York: Atria Books, 2007.

Armstrong, Tom, Wayne Craven, Norman Feder, Barbara Haskell, Rosalind E. Krauss, Daniel Robbins, and Marcia Tucker. *200 Years of American Sculpture.* New York: David R. Godine, 1976.

Ashe, Arthur R., Jr. *A Hard Road to Glory: A History of the African-American Athlete, 1919–1945.* 3 vols. New York: Warner Books, 1988.

Atkinson, Brooks, and Albert Hirschfeld. *The Lively Years: 1920–1973.* New York: Association Press, 1973.

Atomic Bomb. www.atomicarchive.com/historymenu.shtml

Atwan, Robert, Donald McQuade, and John L. Wright. *Edsels, Luckies, and Frigidaires: Advertising the American Way.* New York: Dell, 1979.

Austin, James C., ed. *Popular Literature in America.* Bowling Green, OH: Popular Press, 1972.

Austin, Joe, and Michael Nevin Willard, eds. *Generations of Youth: Youth Culture and History in Twentieth-Century America.* New York: New York University Press, 1998.

Awmiller, Craig. *This House on Fire: The Story of the Blues.* New York: Franklin Watts, 1996.

B Westerns. "The Old Corral." www.b-westerns.com/

Baeder, John. *Gas, Food, and Lodging.* New York: Abbeville Press, 1982.

Bailey, Robert Lee. *An Examination of Prime Time Network Television Special Programs, 1948–1966.* New York: Arno Press, 1979.

Bak, Richard. *Joe Louis: The Great Black Hope.* New York: Da Capo Press, 1998.

Baker, William J. *Sports in the Western World.* Totowa, NJ: Rowman & Littlefield, 1982.

Barbour, Alan G. *A Thousand and One Delights.* New York: Collier Books, 1971.

Barfield, Ray. *Listening to Radio, 1920–1950.* Westport, CT: Praeger, 1996.

Barger, Harold. *The Transportation Industries, 1889–1946.* New York: Arno Press, 1951.

Barnouw, Erik. *A History of Broadcasting in the United States.* Vol. 1, *A Tower in Babel.* New York: Oxford University Press, 1966.

———. *A History of Broadcasting in the United States.* Vol. 2, *The Golden Web.* New York: Oxford University Press, 1968.

———. *A History of Broadcasting in the United States.* Vol. 3, *The Image Empire.* New York: Oxford University Press, 1970.

———. *Tube of Plenty: The Evolution of American Television.* New York: Oxford University Press, 1982.

Barr, Andrew. *Drink: A Social History of America.* New York: Carroll & Graf, 1999.

Barrier, Michael. *Hollywood Cartoons: American Animation in Its Golden Age.* New York: Oxford University Press, 1999.

Barrier, Michael, and Martin Williams, eds. *A Smithsonian Book of Comic-Book Comics.* Washington, DC: Smithsonian Institution Press, 1981.

Barson, Michael, and Steven Heller. *Red Scared! The Commie Menace in Propaganda and Popular Culture.* San Francisco: Chronicle Books, 2001.

Baseball Songs. "Bibliography of Published Baseball Music and Songs in the Collections of the Music Division of the Library of Congress." Performing Arts Reading Room. www.loc.gov/rr/perform/baseballbib.html

Basie, Count. www.rutgers.edu/ijs/cb/index.html

Basinger, Jeanine. *A Woman's View: How Hollywood Spoke to Women, 1930–1960.* New York: Alfred A. Knopf, 1993.

Bastin, Bruce. *Red River Blues: The Blues Tradition in the Southeast.* Urbana: University of Illinois Press, 1986.

Batchelor, Bob, ed. *Basketball in America: From the Playgrounds to Jordan's Game and Beyond.* New York: Haworth Press, 2005.

Batterberry, Michael, and Ariane Batterberry. *Mirror Mirror: A Social History of Fashion.* New York: Holt, Rinehart and Winston, 1977.

Baxandall, Rosalyn, and Elizabeth Ewen. *Picture Windows: How the Suburbs Happened.* New York: Basic Books, 2000.

Baxter, John. *Science Fiction in the Cinema.* New York: A. S. Barnes, 1970.

Bayor, Ronald H. *Race and Ethnicity in America: A Concise History.* New York: Columbia University Press, 2003.

Becker, Stephen. *Comic Art in America.* New York: Simon & Schuster, 1959.

Belasco, Warren James. *Americans on the Road: From Autocamp to Motel, 1910–1945.* Cambridge, MA: MIT Press, 1979.

Bellafaire, Judith A. *The Women's Army Corps: A Commemoration of World War II Service.* www.history.army.mil/brochures/wac.htm

Benny, Jack, and Joan Benny. *Sunday Nights at Seven: The Jack Benny Story.* New York: Warner Books, 1990.

Benton, Mike. *The Comic Book in America: An Illustrated History.* Dallas: Taylor, 1989.

Berger, Michael L. *The Automobile in American History and Culture: A Reference Guide.* Westport, CT: Greenwood Press, 2001.

Bergreen, Lawrence. *As Thousands Cheer: The Life of Irving Berlin.* New York: Viking Penguin, 1990.

Berle, Milton, with Haskell Frankel. *Milton Berle: An Autobiography.* New York: Delacorte Press, 1974.

Bernstein, Adam. "Iva Toguri D'Aquino, 90: 'Tokyo Rose' in WWII." www.washingtonpost.com/wp-dyn/content/article/2006/09/27/ar2006092700133.html

Bernstein, Mark, and Alex Lubertuzzi. *World War II on the Air.* Naperville, IL: Sourcebooks, 2003.

Berry, I. William. *The Great North American Ski Book.* New York: Charles Scribner's Sons, 1982.

Beschloss, Michael. *The Conquerors: Roosevelt, Truman, and the Destruction of Hitler's Germany, 1941–1945.* New York: Simon & Schuster, 2002.

*Big Bands Database Plus.* www.nfo.net/index.html

Bilstein, Roger E. *Flight in America: From the Wrights to the Astronauts.* Baltimore: Johns Hopkins University Press, 1984.

Biracree, Tom. *The Country Music Almanac.* New York: Prentice Hall, 1993.

Black Gospel Music. www.arts.state.ms.us/crossroads/music/gospel/mu2_text.html

Blackbeard, Bill, and Martin Williams. *The Smithsonian Collection of Newspaper Comics.* Washington, DC: Smithsonian Institution Press, 1977.

Bliss, Edward, Jr. *In Search of Light: The Broadcasts of Edward R. Murrow, 1938–1961.* New York: Alfred A. Knopf, 1967.

Block, Geoffrey. *Enchanted Evenings: The Broadway Musical from Show Boat to Sondheim.* New York: Oxford University Press, 1997.

Bloom, John, and Michael Nevin Willard, eds. *Sports Matters: Race, Recreation, and Culture.* New York: New York University Press, 2002.

Bloom, Ken. *The American Songbook: The Singers, the Songwriters, and the Songs.* New York: Black Dog & Leventhal, 2005.

Bloom, Lynn Z. *Doctor Spock: Biography of a Conservative Radical.* Indianapolis: Bobbs-Merrill, 1972.
Blum, Daniel. *A Pictorial History of the American Theatre, 1860–1970.* New York: Crown, 1969.
Bogart, Leo. *The Age of Television.* New York: Frederick Ungar, 1956.
Bogdanov, Vladimir, Chris Woodstra, and Stephen Thomas Erlewine, eds. *All-Music Guide to Country.* San Francisco: Backbeat Books, 2003.
Bonn, Thomas L. *Under Cover: An Illustrated History of American Mass Market Paperbacks.* New York: Penguin Books, 1982.
Bookmiller, Kirsten Nakjavani. *The United Nations.* New York: Chelsea House, 2008.
Bordman, Gerald. *American Theatre: A Chronicle of Comedy and Drama, 1930–1969.* New York: Oxford University Press, 1996.
———. *Jerome Kern: His Life and Music.* New York: Oxford University Press, 1980.
Bowles, Jerry. *A Thousand Sundays: The Story of the Ed Sullivan Show.* New York: Putnam, 1980.
Bowling. www.bowl.com/recordsstats/
Boyd, Jean A. *We're the Light Crust Doughboys from Burris Mill.* Austin: University of Texas Press, 2003.
———. "Western Swing: Working-Class Southwestern Jazz of the 1930s and 1940s." In *Perspectives on American Music, 1900–1950,* ed. Michael Saffle, 193–214. New York: Garland, 2000.
Boyd, William. "Hoppy" and the Bar-20 Ranch-Hands: Unofficial Web Site of William "Hopalong Cassidy" Boyd. www.hoppyandthebar-20.50megs.com
Boyer, Paul. *By the Bomb's Early Light: American Thought and Culture at the Dawn of the Atomic Age.* New York: Pantheon Books, 1985.
Bridwell, E. Nelson, ed. *Superman: From the Thirties to the Seventies.* New York: Bonanza Books, 1971.
"Brief History of World War Two Advertising Campaigns War Loans and Bonds," Duke University Libraries. www.library.duke.edu/digitalcollections/adaccess/warbonds.html
Broekel, Ray. *The Great American Candy Bar Book.* Boston: Houghton Mifflin, 1982.
Brooks, Lou. *Skate Crazy.* Philadelphia: Running Press, 2003.
Brooks, Tim. *The Complete Directory to Prime Time TV Stars: 1946–Present.* New York: Ballantine Books, 1987.
Brooks, Tim, and Earle Marsh. *The Complete Directory to Prime Time Network TV Shows, 1946–Present.* New York: Ballantine Books, 1988.
Brown, Bob, and Eleanor Parker. *Culinary Americana: 1860–1960.* New York: Roving Eye Press, 1961.
Brown, Curtis F. *Star-Spangled Kitsch.* New York: Universe Books, 1975.
Brown, Les. *Les Brown's Encyclopedia of Television.* 2nd ed. New York: Zoetrope, 1982.
Buechner, Thomas S. *Norman Rockwell: Artist and Illustrator.* New York: Harry N. Abrams, 1970.
Buscombe, Edward, ed. *The BFI Companion to the Western.* New York: Atheneum, 1988.
Cajun Music. www.npmusic.org
Calder, Alexander. *Calder: An Autobiography with Pictures.* New York: Pantheon Books, 1966.
Cameron, Ian, and Douglas Pye, eds. *The Book of Westerns.* New York: Continuum, 1996.
Cameron, Kenneth M. *America on Film: Hollywood and American History.* New York: Continuum, 1997.
*Canteen Spirit.* PBS Home Video, 2006.
Cantor, Muriel G., and Suzanne Pingree. *The Soap Opera.* Beverly Hills, CA: Sage, 1983.
Caplow, Theodore, Louis Hicks, and Ben J. Wattenberg. *The First Measured Century: An Illustrated Guide to Trends in America, 1900–2000.* Washington, DC: AEI Press, 2001.
Capra, Frank. *The Name above the Title.* New York: Macmillan, 1971.
Carlson, Reynold E., Theodore R. Deppe, and Janet R. MacLean. *Recreation in American Life.* Belmont, CA: Wadsworth, 1963.
Carringer, Robert L. *The Making of Citizen Kane.* Berkeley: University of California Press, 1985.
Carruth, Gordon, ed. *The Encyclopedia of American Facts and Dates.* New York: Thomas Y. Crowell, 1959.
Carter, Ernestine. *The Changing World of Fashion: 1900 to the Present.* New York: G. P. Putnam's Sons, 1977.

Casdorph, Paul D. *Let the Good Times Roll: Life at Home in America During World War II.* New York: Paragon House, 1989.

Cassiday, Bruce. *Dinah! A Biography of Dinah Shore.* New York: Franklin Watts, 1979.

Castleman, Harry, and Walter J. Podrazik. *Watching TV: Four Decades of American Television.* New York: McGraw-Hill, 1982.

Chanin, Michael. *Repeated Takes: A Short History of Recording and Its Effects on Music.* New York: Verso, 1995.

Chipman, John H. *Index to Top-Hit Tunes, 1900–1950.* Boston: Bruce Humphries, 1962.

Church Attendance. *New York Times,* January 18, 1942; January 3, 1946; December 18, 1946.

Churchill, Allen. *Remember When.* New York: Golden Press, 1967.

Civil Air Patrol. www.caphistory.org/

Civitello, Linda. *Cuisine and Culture: A History of Food and People.* Hoboken, NJ: John Wiley, 2008.

Clancy, Deirdre. *Costume Since 1945: Couture, Street Style, and Anti-Fashion.* New York: Drama Publishers, 1996.

Clarens, Carlos. *An Illustrated History of the Horror Film.* New York: Capricorn Books, 1967.

———. *Crime Movies: From Griffith to the Godfather and Beyond.* New York: W. W. Norton, 1980.

Clark, Clifford Edward, Jr. *The American Home: 1800–1960.* Chapel Hill: University of North Carolina Press, 1986.

Clark, Eric. *The Want Makers: Inside the World of Advertising.* New York: Penguin Books, 1988.

Clark, Jerome. *The UFO Encyclopedia: The Phenomenon from the Beginning.* 2 vols. Detroit: Omnigraphics, 1998.

Clarke, Alison J. *Tupperware: The Promise of Plastic in 1950s America.* Washington, DC: Smithsonian Institution Press, 1999.

Clarke, Donald. *All or Nothing at All: A Life of Frank Sinatra.* www.donaldclarkemusicbox.com/

———. *The Rise and Fall of Popular Music.* New York: St. Martin's Press, 1995.

Cleary, David Powers. *Great American Brands.* New York: Fairchild, 1981.

Cline, William C. *In the Nick of Time: Motion Picture Sound Serials.* Jefferson, NC: McFarland, 1984.

Clothing Regulations and Availability: *New York Times,* January 5, 1941; April 9, 1942; October 18, 1942; August 1, 1942; February 2, 1945; November 25, 1946.

Cloud, Stanley, and Lynne Olson. *The Murrow Boys: Pioneers on the Front lines of Broadcast Journalism.* New York: Mariner Books, 1997.

Cochran, David. *America Noir: Underground Writers and Filmmakers of the Postwar Era.* Washington, DC: Smithsonian Institution Press, 2000.

Coffey, Frank, and Joseph Layden. *America on Wheels: The First 100 Years, 1896–1996.* Los Angeles: General Publishing Group, 1998.

Cogley, John. *Report on Blacklisting I: The Movies.* New York: Fund for the Republic, 1956.

———. *Report on Blacklisting II: Radio-Television.* New York: Fund for the Republic, 1956.

Cohen, Norm. *Folk Music: A Regional Exploration.* Westport, CT: Greenwood Press, 2005.

Cohen, Stan. *V for Victory: America's Home Front During World War II.* Missoula, MT: Pictorial Histories, 1991.

Coin Collecting. www.collecting-us-coins.com/pennies-cents/penny-cent.html

Collins, Max Allan. *The History of Mystery.* Portland, OR: Collectors Press, 2001.

Colman, Penny. *Rosie the Riveter: Women Working on the Home Front in World War II.* New York: Crown, 1995.

*Composers and Lyricists Database.* www.nfo.net/cal/

Considine, David M. *The Cinema of Adolescence.* Jefferson, NC: McFarland, 1985.

Cooke, Alistair. *The American Home Front: 1941–1942.* Boston: Atlantic Monthly Press, 2007.

Coontz, Stephanie. *The Way We Never Were: American Families and the Nostalgia Trap.* New York: Basic Books, 1992.

Cooper, Martin, ed. *The New Oxford History of Music: The Modern Age, 1890–1960.* New York: Oxford University Press, 1974.

Copley-Graves, Lynn. *Figure Skating History: The Evolution of Dance on Ice.* Columbus, OH: Platero Press, 1992.

Coppage, Keith. *Roller Derby to Roller Jam.* Santa Rosa, CA: Squarebooks, 1999.

Corkin, Stanley. *Cowboys as Cold Warriors: The Western and U.S. History.* Philadelphia: Temple University Press, 2004.

Corn, Joseph J., and Brian Horrigan. *Yesterday's Tomorrows: Past Visions of the American Future.* New York: Summit Books, 1984.

Costantino, Maria. *Men's Fashion in the Twentieth Century, from Frock Coats to Intelligent Fibres.* New York: Drama Publishers by Design Press, 1997.

*Country Music* Magazine Editors. *The Comprehensive Country Music Encyclopedia.* New York: Random House, 1994.

Couperie, Pierre, and Maurice C. Horn. *A History of the Comic Strip.* New York: Crown, 1968.

Cowan, Ruth Schwartz. *More Work for Mother.* New York: Basic Books, 1983.

Cox, Jim. *The Great Radio Sitcoms.* Jefferson, NC: McFarland, 2007.

———. *Music Radio: The Great Performers and Programs of the 1920s through the Early 1960s.* Jefferson, NC: McFarland, 2005.

Cox, Stephen, and John Loftin. *The Abbott and Costello Story: Sixty Years of "Who's on First?"* Nashville: Cumberland House, 1997.

Crawford, Richard. *America's Musical Life.* New York: W. W. Norton, 2001.

Cripps, Thomas. *Making Movies Black: The Hollywood Message Movie from World War II to the Civil Rights Movement.* New York: Oxford University Press, 1993.

Crosley Cars. www.crosleyautoclub.com

Cross, Gary. *Kids' Stuff: Toys and the World of American Childhood.* Cambridge, MA: Harvard University Press, 1997.

Cross, Mary, ed. *A Century of American Icons: 100 Products and Slogans from the 20th-Century Consumer Culture.* Westport, CT: Greenwood Press, 2002.

Crowther, Bruce, and Mike Pinfold. *Singing Jazz: The Singers and Their Styles.* San Francisco: Miller Freeman Books, 1997.

Crumpacker, Bunny. *The Old-Time Brand-Name Cookbook.* New York: Smithmark, 1998.

———. *The Old-Time Brand-Name Desserts.* New York: Abradale Press, 1999.

Csida, Joseph, and June Bundy Csida. *American Entertainment: A Unique History of Popular Show Business.* New York: Watson-Guptil, 1978.

Culinary Institute of America. www.ciachef.edu/admissions/about/history.asp

Cullen, Jim. *The Art of Democracy: A Concise History of Popular Culture in the United States.* New York: Monthly Review Press, 1996.

Cummings, Richard Osborn. *The American and His Food.* Chicago: University of Chicago Press, 1941.

Cusic, Don. *Discovering Country Music.* Westport, CT: Praeger, 2008.

Dahl, Linda. *Stormy Weather: The Music and Lives of a Century of Jazzwomen.* New York: Pantheon Books, 1984.

Dale, Alan. *Comedy Is a Man in Trouble: Slapstick in American Movies.* Minneapolis: University of Minnesota Press, 2000.

Dale, Rodney. *The World of Jazz.* New York: Elsevier-Dutton, 1980.

Dance, Stanley. *The World of Count Basie.* New York: Charles Scribner's Sons, 1980.

———. *The World of Duke Ellington.* New York: Charles Scribner's Sons, 1970.

Daniels, Les. *Comix: A History of Comic Books in America.* New York: Bonanza Books, 1971.

Davies, David R. *The Postwar Decline of American Newspapers, 1945–1965.* Westport, CT: Praeger, 2006.

Davis, Francis. *The History of the Blues.* New York: Hyperion, 1995.

Davis, Ronald L. *A History of Music in American Life.* Vol. 3, *The Modern Era, 1920–Present.* Malabar, FL: Robert Krieger, 1981.

Davis, Stephen. *Say Kids! What Time Is It? Notes from the Peanut Gallery.* Boston: Little, Brown, 1981.

Davis, Thomas J. *Race Relations in the United States, 1940–1960.* Westport, CT: Greenwood Press, 2008.

Dawidoff, Nicholas. *In the Country of Country: People and Places in American Music.* New York: Pantheon Books, 1997.

Dawkins, Marvin P., and Graham Charles Kinloch. *African American Golfers during the Jim Crow Era.* Westport, CT: Greenwood Publishing Group, 2000.

Delamater, Jerome. *Dance in the Hollywood Musical.* Ann Arbor, MI: UMI Research Press, 1981.

DeCillis, Tom. *Toms Zone: The* inComplete *Jukebox.* www.tomszone.com

DeLong, Thomas A. *The Mighty Music Box: The Golden Age of Musical Radio.* Los Angeles: Amber Crest Books, 1980.

———. *Radio Stars.* Jefferson, NC: McFarland, 1996.

Denisoff, R. Serge. *Great Day Coming: Folk Music and the American Left.* Baltimore: Penguin Books, 1971.

Denisoff, R. Serge, and Richard A. Peterson, eds. *The Sounds of Social Change.* New York: Rand McNally, 1972.

Denison, Edward F. *Trends in American Economic Growth, 1929–1982.* Washington, DC: Brookings Institution, 1985.

Derks, Scott, ed. *The Value of a Dollar: Prices and Incomes in the United States, 1860–1999.* Lakeville, CT: Grey House, 1999.

———. *Working Americans, 1880–1999.* Vol. 1, *The Working Class.* Lakeville, CT: Grey House, 2000.

———. *Working Americans, 1880–1999.* Vol. 2, *The Middle Class.* Lakeville, CT: Grey House, 2001.

Dettelbach, Cynthia Golumb. *In the Driver's Seat: The Automobile in American Literature and Popular Culture.* Westport, CT: Greenwood Press, 1976.

DeVeaux, Scott. *The Birth of Bebop: A Social and Musical History.* Berkeley: University of California Press, 1997.

Dick, Bernard F. *The Star-Spangled Screen: The American World War II Film.* Lexington: University Press of Kentucky, 1985.

Dickson, Paul. *The Worth Book of Softball: A Celebration of America's True National Pastime.* New York: Facts on File, 1994.

Diggins, John Patrick. *The Proud Decades: America in War and Peace, 1941–1960.* New York: W. W. Norton, 1988.

Disney Archives. www.disney.go.com/vault/archives/today.html

Dixon, Wheeler Winston, ed. *American Cinema of the 1940s: Themes and Variations.* New Brunswick, NJ: Rutgers University Press, 2006.

Dodds, John W. *Everyday Life in Twentieth Century America.* New York: G. P. Putnam's Sons, 1965.

Doherty, Thomas. *Projections of War: Hollywood, American Culture, and World War II.* New York: Columbia University Press, 1993.

Dooley, Dennis, and Gary Engle, eds. *Superman at Fifty! The Persistence of a Legend!* Cleveland: Octavia, 1987.

Dorner, Jane. *Fashion in the Forties and Fifties.* New York: Arlington House, 1975.

Doss, Erika, ed. *Looking at LIFE Magazine.* Washington, DC: Smithsonian Institution Press, 2001.

Douglas, George H. *All Aboard! The Railroad in American Life.* New York: Paragon House, 1992.

Douglas, Susan J. *Listening In: Radio and the American Imagination.* Minneapolis: University of Minnesota Press, 2004.

Drexler, Arthur, and Greta Daniel. *Introduction to Twentieth Century Design from the Collection of the Museum of Modern Art.* New York: Museum of Modern Art, 1959.

Dryer, Sherman H. *Radio in Wartime.* New York: Greenberg, 1942.

Duany, Andres, Elizabeth Plater-Zyberk, and Jeff Speck. *Suburban Nation: The Rise of Sprawl and the Decline of the American Dream.* New York: North Point Press, 2000.

Dulles, Foster Rhea. *A History of Recreation: America Learns to Play.* Englewood Cliffs, NJ: Prentice Hall, 1965.

Dunkleberger, A. C. *King of Country Music: The Life Story of Roy Acuff.* Nashville: Williams Printing, 1971.

Dunning, John. *On the Air: The Encyclopedia of Old-Time Radio.* New York: Oxford University Press, 1998.

———. *Tune in Yesterday: The Ultimate Encyclopedia of Old-Time Radio, 1925–1976.* Englewood Cliffs, NJ: Prentice Hall, 1976.

Durgnat, Raymond. *The Crazy Mirror: Hollywood Comedy and the American Image.* New York: Dell, 1969.

Duus, Masayo. *The Life of Isamu Noguchi: Journey without Borders.* Princeton, NJ: Princeton University Press, 2004.

———. *Tokyo Rose: Orphan of the Pacific.* New York: Kodansha Amer, 1979.

Eames, John Douglas. *The MGM Story: The Complete History of Fifty Roaring Years.* New York: Crown, 1975.

Eberly, Philip K. *Music in the Air: America's Changing Tastes in Popular Music, 1920–1980.* New York: Hastings House, 1982.

"Education." *New York Times,* November 5, 1940; November 9, 1941; August 23, 1942; July 18, 1943; November 5, 1943; July 30, 1944; March 20, 1950.

Edwards, Bob. *Edward R. Murrow and the Birth of Broadcast Journalism.* Hoboken, NJ: John Wiley, 2004.

Eells, George. *The Life That Late He Led: A Biography of Cole Porter.* New York: G. P. Putnam's Sons, 1967.

Eisinger, Chester E., ed. *The 1940's: Profile of a Nation in Crisis.* New York: Doubleday, 1969.

Eleanor Roosevelt Papers Project. www.gwu.edu/~erpapers/

Elliott, William Y. *Television's Impact on American Culture.* East Lansing: Michigan State University Press, 1956.

Emde, Heiner. *Conquerors of the Air: The Evolution of Aircraft, 1903–1945.* New York: Bonanza Books, 1968.

Emery, Edwin. *The Press and America: An Interpretive History of Journalism.* Englewood Cliffs, NJ: Prentice Hall, 1962.

Engelhardt, Tom. *The End of Victory Culture: Cold War America and the Disillusioning of a Generation.* New York: Basic Books, 1995.

Engen, Alan K. *For the Love of Skiing: A Visual History.* Salt Lake City: Gibbs-Smith, 1998.

Ennis, Philip H. *The Seventh Stream: The Emergence of Rocknroll in American Popular Music.* Hanover, NH: Wesleyan University Press, 1992.

Epstein, Daniel Mark. *Nat King Cole.* New York: Farrar, Straus and Giroux, 1999.

Epstein, Edward J. *News from Nowhere: Television and the News.* New York: Random House, 1973.

Erenberg, Lewis A., and Susan E. Hirsch, eds. *The War in American Culture: Society and Consciousness during World War II.* Chicago: University of Chicago Press, 1996.

Ermoyan, Arpi. *Famous American Illustrators.* New York: Society of Illustrators, 1997.

"Ernie Pyle." Indiana University School of Journalism. www.journalism.indiana.edu/resources/erniepyle/

Evangelista, Nick. "At Sword's Point: Swashbuckling in the Movies." www.classicalfencing.com/articles/swash.php

Ewen, David. *All the Years of American Popular Music: A Comprehensive History.* Englewood Cliffs, NJ: Prentice Hall, 1977.

———. *Great Men of American Popular Song.* Englewood Cliffs, NJ: Prentice Hall, 1970.

———. *A Journey to Greatness: The Life and Music of George Gershwin.* New York: Henry Holt, 1956.

———. *The Life and Death of Tin Pan Alley: The Golden Age of American Popular Music.* New York: Funk and Wagnalls, 1964.

———. *Panorama of American Popular Music.* Englewood Cliffs, NJ: Prentice Hall, 1957.

Ewen, Stuart. *Captains of Consciousness: Advertising and the Social Roots of the Consumer Culture.* New York: McGraw-Hill, 1976.

Ewen, Stuart, and Elizabeth Ewen. *Channels of Desire: Mass Images and the Shaping of American Consciousness.* New York: McGraw-Hill, 1982.
Faith, William Robert. *Bob Hope: A Life in Comedy.* New York: Da Capo Press, 2003.
Fass, Paula S. *Outside In: Minorities and the Transformation of American Education.* New York: Oxford University Press, 1989.
Feather, Leonard. *Jazz.* Los Angeles: Trend Books, 1957.
———. *The New Edition of the Encyclopedia of Jazz.* New York: Bonanza Books, 1962.
Feather, Leonard, and Ira Gitler. *The Biographical Encyclopedia of Jazz.* New York: Oxford University Press, 1999.
Fehrman, Cherie, and Kenneth Fehrman. *Postwar Interior Design: 1945–1960.* New York: Reinhold, 1987.
Felsen, Henry Gregor. *Hot Rod.* www.lib.uiowa.edu/spec-coll/MSC/ToMsC650/MsC601/felsen.html
Fenin, George N., and William K. Everson. *The Western: From Silents to Cinerama.* New York: Orion Press, 1962.
Fernett, Gene. *Hollywood's Poverty Row, 1930–1950.* Satellite Beach, FL: Coral Reef Publications, 1973.
Ferris, William, and Mary L. Hart, eds. *Folk Music and Modern Sound.* Jackson: University Press of Mississippi, 1982.
Fielding, Raymond. *The American Newsreel, 1911–1967.* Norman: University of Oklahoma Press, 1972.
Finch, Christopher. *The Art of Walt Disney: From Mickey Mouse to the Magic Kingdoms.* New York: Harry N. Abrams, 1975.
———. *Norman Rockwell's America.* New York: Harry N. Abrams, 1975.
Flexner, Stuart Berg. *Listening to America.* New York: Simon & Schuster, 1982.
Flink, James J. *The Car Culture.* Cambridge, MA: MIT Press, 1975.
Flusser, Alan. *Clothes and the Man: The Principles of Fine Men's Dress.* New York: Villard Books, 1989.
"Flying Fortress Fashions." *Life,* May 17, 1943.
Foertsch, Jacqueline. *American Culture in the 1940s.* Edinburgh, Scotland: Edinburgh University Press, 2008.
Foley, Karen Sue. *Television and the Red Menace.* New York: Praeger, 1985.
Foley, Mary Mix. *The American House.* New York: Harper & Row, 1980.
Football. *New York Times,* December 31, 1941; July 28, 1942.
Ford, James L. C. *Magazines for Millions: The Story of Specialized Publications.* Carbondale: Southern Illinois University Press, 1969.
Forte, Allen. *Listening to Classic American Popular Songs* [includes CD]. New Haven, CT: Yale University Press, 2001.
Forty, Adrian. *Objects of Desire: Design and Society since 1750.* New York: Thames & Hudson, 1986.
Fowles, Jib. *Advertising and Popular Culture.* Thousand Oaks, CA: Sage, 1996.
Fox, Stephen. *The Mirror Makers: A History of American Advertising and Its Creators.* New York: William Morrow, 1984.
Frank, Rusty E. *Tap! The Greatest Tap Dance Stars and Their Stories, 1900–1955.* New York: Da Capo Press, 1990.
Fraser, Antonia. *A History of Toys.* New York: Delacorte Press, 1966.
Fraser, James. *The American Billboard: 100 Years.* New York: Harry N. Abrams, 1991.
Fred Waring. www.libraries.psu.edu/psul/waring.html
Freedland, Michael. *All the Way: A Biography of Frank Sinatra.* New York: St. Martin's Press, 1998.
———. *Jerome Kern.* London: Robson Books, 1978.
Freeman, Larry, ed. *Yesterday's Games.* Watkins Glen, NY: Century House, 1970.
Friedwald, Will. *Jazz Singing: America's Great Voices.* New York: Da Capo Press, 1996.
———. *Stardust Melodies: A Biography of Twelve of America's Most Popular Songs.* New York: Pantheon Books, 2002.
Fuller, M. Williams. *Axis Sally.* Santa Barbara, CA: Paradise West, 2004.

Funderburg, Anne Cooper. *Chocolate, Strawberry, and Vanilla: A History of American Ice Cream.* Bowling Green, OH: Bowling Green State University Press, 1995.

Furia, Philip. *The Poets of Tin Pan Alley: A History of America's Great Lyricists.* New York: Oxford University Press, 1990.

———. *Skylark: The Life and Times of Johnny Mercer.* New York: St. Martin's Press, 2003.

Furia, Philip, and Michael Lasser. *America's Songs: The Stories behind the Songs of Broadway, Hollywood, and Tin Pan Alley.* New York: Routledge, 2006.

Fyne, Robert. *The Hollywood Propaganda of World War II.* Lanham, MD: Scarecrow Press, 1997.

Gabler, Neal. *Walt Disney: The Triumph of the American Imagination.* New York: Vintage, 2007.

Gaddis, John Lewis. *The Cold War: A New History.* New York: Penguin Press, 2005.

Galbraith, John Kenneth. *The Affluent Society.* Boston: Houghton Mifflin, 1958.

Gallo, Max. *The Poster in History.* New York: McGraw-Hill, 1972.

Gans, Herbert J. *The Levittowners: Ways of Life and Politics in a New Suburban Community.* New York: Columbia University Press, 1982.

Garraty, John A., and Mark C. Carnes, eds. *American National Biography.* 24 vols. New York: Oxford University Press, 1999.

Gehring, Wes D., ed. *Handbook of American Film Genres.* New York: Greenwood Press, 1988.

Gelber, Steven M. *Hobbies: Leisure and the Culture of Work in America.* New York: Columbia University Press, 1999.

Getz, Leonard. *From Broadway to the Bowery: A History and Filmography of the Dead End Kids, the Little Tough Guys, the East Side Kids, and the Bowery Boys Films, with Cast Biographies.* Jefferson, NC: McFarland, 2006.

Gianokos, Larry James. *Television Drama Series Programming: A Comprehensive Chronicle, 1947–1959.* Metuchen, NJ: Scarecrow Press, 1980.

Giddins, Gary. *Bing Crosby, a Pocketful of Dreams: The Early Years, 1903–1940.* Boston: Little, Brown, 2001.

———. *Visions of Jazz: The First Century.* New York: Oxford University Press, 1998.

Gies, Joseph. *Franklin D. Roosevelt: Portrait of a President.* Garden City, NY: Doubleday, 1971.

Gifford, Denis. *The Great Cartoon Stars: A Who's Who.* London: Jupiter Books, 1979.

Gilbert, Gorman, and Robert E. Samuels. *The Taxicab: An Urban Transportation Survivor.* Chapel Hill: University of North Carolina Press, 1982.

Gilbert, James. *Another Chance: Postwar America, 1945–1968.* Philadelphia: Temple University Press, 1981.

Gillett, Charlie. *The Sound of the City: The Rise of Rock and Roll.* New York: Pantheon Books, 1983.

Ginell, Cary. *The Decca Hillbilly Discography, 1927–1945.* Westport, CT: Greenwood Press, 1989.

Gioia, Ted. *The History of Jazz.* New York: Oxford University Press, 1997.

Giordano, Ralph G. *Fun and Games in Twentieth-Century America: A Historical Guide to Leisure.* Westport, CT: Greenwood Press, 2003.

Gleason, Ralph J., ed. *Jam Session: An Anthology of Jazz.* New York: G. P. Putnam's Sons, 1958.

Glickman, Lawrence B., ed. *Consumer Society in American History: A Reader.* Ithaca, NY: Cornell University Press, 1999.

Godfrey, Donald C., and Frederic A. Leigh, eds. *Historical Dictionary of American Radio.* Westport, CT: Greenwood Press, 1998.

Godson, Susan H. *Serving Proudly: A History of Women in the U.S. Navy.* Annapolis, MD: Naval Institute Press, 2001.

Golden Age Radio. *101 Old Radio Commercials.* CD. Plymouth, MN: Metacom, n.d.

Golden, Claudia. "America's Graduation from High School: The Evolution and Spread of Secondary Schooling in the Twentieth Century." *Journal of Economic History* 58 (2) (June 1998): 345–374.

Goldstein, Carolyn M. *Do It Yourself: Home Improvement in 20th Century America.* New York: Princeton Architectural Press, 1998.

Golenbock, Peter. *American Zoom: Stock Car Racing—from the Dirt Tracks to Daytona.* New York: Macmillan, 1993.

Goodman, Jack, ed. *While You Were Gone: A Report on Wartime Life in the United States.* New York: Simon & Schuster, 1946.

Goodrich, Lloyd. *Three Centuries of American Art.* New York: Frederick A. Praeger, 1966.

Goodrum, Charles, and Helen Dalrymple. *Advertising in America: The First 200 Years.* New York: Harry N. Abrams, 1990.

Goodwin, Doris Kearns. *No Ordinary Time: Franklin and Eleanor Roosevelt: The Home Front in World War II.* New York: Simon & Schuster, 1994.

Gordon, Linda, and Gary Y. Okihiro, eds. *Impounded: Dorothea Lange and the Censored Images of Japanese American Internment.* New York: W. W. Norton, 2006.

Gordon, Lois, and Alan Gordon. *American Chronicle: Six Decades in American Life, 1920–1980.* New York: Atheneum, 1987.

Gorman, Robert F. *Great Debates at the United Nations: An Encyclopedia of Fifty Key Issues, 1945–2000.* Westport, CT: Greenwood Publishers, 2001.

Gossett, Sue. *The Films and Career of Audie Murphy.* Madison, NC: Empire, 1996.

Gottesman, Ronald, ed. *Focus on Citizen Kane.* Englewood Cliffs, NJ: Prentice Hall, 1971.

Gottfried, Martin. *Broadway Musicals.* New York: Harry N. Abrams, 1979.

Gottlieb, William P. *The Golden Age of Jazz.* New York: Simon & Schuster, 1979.

Goulart, Ron. *Cheap Thrills: An Informal History of the Pulp Magazines.* New York: Arlington House, 1972.

———. *Over 50 Years of American Comic Books.* Lincolnwood, IL: Mallard Press, 1991.

Goulart, Ron, ed. *The Encyclopedia of American Comics.* New York: Facts on File, 1990.

Gourse, Leslie. *Louis' Children: American Jazz Singers.* New York: Quill, 1984.

———. *Unforgettable: The Life and Mystique of Nat King Cole.* New York: St. Martin's Press, 1991.

Gow, Gordon. *Suspense in the Cinema.* New York: A. S. Barnes, 1968.

Graebner, William S. *The Age of Doubt: American Thought and Culture in the 1940s.* Boston: Twayne, 1991.

Graham, Otis L., Jr., and Meghan Robinson Wander, eds. *Franklin D. Roosevelt: His Life and Times, an Encyclopedic View.* New York: G. K. Hall, 1985.

Grams, Martin, Jr. *The Edgar Bergen and Charlie McCarthy Show: An Episode Guide and Brief History.* www.old-time.com/otrlogs2/charlie_mg.html

Green, Benny. *Let's Face the Music: The Golden Age of Popular Song.* London: Pavilion Books, 1989.

Green, Douglas B. *Singing in the Saddle: The History of the Singing Cowboy.* Nashville: Vanderbilt University Press, 2002.

Green, Jonathan. *American Photography: A Critical History, 1945 to the Present.* New York: Harry N. Abrams, 1984.

Green, Samuel M. *American Art: A Historical Survey.* New York: Ronald Press Company, 1966.

Green, Stanley. *Broadway Musicals: Show by Show.* 4th ed. Milwaukee: Hal Leonard, 1994.

———. *Encyclopaedia of the Musical Film.* New York: Oxford University Press, 1981.

Greene, Bob. *Once Upon a Town: The Miracle of the North Platte Canteen.* New York: William Morrow, 2003.

Greenfield, Jeff. *Television: The First Fifty Years.* New York: Harry N. Abrams, 1977.

Greenfield, Thomas Allen. *Radio: A Reference Guide.* Westport, CT: Greenwood Press, 1989.

Griffith, Richard, and Arthur Mayer. *The Movies.* New York: Simon & Schuster, 1970.

Grimes, William. *Straight Up or on the Rocks: A Cultural History of American Drink.* New York: Simon & Schuster, 1993.

Grimsley, Will. *Golf: Its History, People and Events.* Englewood Cliffs, NJ: Prentice Hall, 1966.

Grossman, Gary. *Superman: From Serial to Cereal.* New York: Popular Library, 1977.

Grout, Donald Jay, and Claude V. Palisca. *A History of Western Music.* New York: W. W. Norton, 1988.

Gruber, Frank. *The Pulp Jungle.* Los Angeles: Sherbourne Press, 1967.

Grudens, Richard. *Bing Crosby: Crooner of the Century.* Stony Brook, NY: Celebrity Profiles, 2004.

———. *Chattanooga Choo Choo: The Life and Times of the World Famous Glenn Miller Orchestra.* Stony Brook, NY: Celebrity Profiles, 2004.

———. *The Spirit of Bob Hope: One Hundred Years, One Million Laughs.* Stony Brook, NY: Celebrity Profiles, 2004.

Guttman, Allen. *A Whole New Ball Game: An Interpretation of American Sports.* Chapel Hill: University of North Carolina Press, 1988.

Haas, Robert Bartlett, ed. *William Grant Still and the Fusion of Cultures in American Music.* Flagstaff, AZ: Master-Player Library, 1972.

Hackett, Alice Payne, and James Henry Burke. *80 Years of Best Sellers, 1895–1975.* New York: R. R. Bowker, 1977.

Hajduk, John C. "Tin Pan Alley on the March: Popular Music, World War II, and the Quest for a Great War Song." *Popular Music & Society* (December 2003): 497–512.

Hamm, Charles. *Yesterdays: Popular Song in America.* New York: W. W. Norton, 1979.

Handlin, David P. *American Architecture.* New York: Thames and Hudson, 1985.

Hangen, Tona J. *Redeeming the Dial: Radio, Religion, and Popular Culture in America.* Chapel Hill: University of North Carolina Press, 2002.

Harper, Dale P. "Mildred Elizabeth Sisk: American-Born Axis Sally." www.historynet.com/mildred-elizabeth-sisk-american-born-axis-sally.htm

Harris, Andrew B. *Broadway Theatre.* New York: Routledge, 1994.

Harris, Mark Jonathan, Franklin D. Mitchell, and Steven J. Schechter. *The Homefront: America during World War II.* New York: G. P. Putnam's Sons, 1984.

Harris, Michael David. *Always on Sundays: Ed Sullivan, an Inside View.* New York: Meredith, 1980.

Harris, Neil. *Cultural Excursions: Marketing Appetites and Cultural Tastes in Modern America.* Chicago: University of Chicago Press, 1990.

Harris, Rex. *Jazz.* New York: Penguin Books, 1952.

Hart, Dorothy. *Thou Swell, Thou Witty: The Life and Lyrics of Lorenz Hart.* New York: Harper & Row, 1976.

Hart, James D. *The Popular Book: A History of America's Literary Taste.* Berkeley: University of California Press, 1961.

Harvey, James. *Romantic Comedy in Hollywood.* New York: Da Capo Press, 1998.

Haskell, Barbara. *The American Century: Art and Culture, 1900–1950.* New York: W. W. Norton, 1999.

Hawes, William. *American Television Drama: The Experimental Years.* Tuscaloosa: University of Alabama Press, 1986.

Hayden, Delores. *Building Suburbia: Green Fields and Urban Growth, 1820–2000.* New York: Vintage Books, 2004.

Hayes, Joanne Lamb. *Grandma's Wartime Kitchen: World War II and the Way We Cooked.* New York: St. Martin's Press, 2000.

Hayes, Richard K. *Kate Smith: A Biography, with a Discography, Filmography, and List of Stage Appearances.* Jefferson, NC: McFarland, 1995.

Heide, Robert, and John Gilman. *Dime-Store Dream Parade: Popular Culture, 1925–1955.* New York: E. P. Dutton, 1979.

———. *Home Front America: Popular Culture of the World War II Era.* San Francisco: Chronicle Books, 1995.

Heidenry, John. *Theirs Was the Kingdom: Lila and DeWitt Wallace and the Story of the Reader's Digest.* New York: W. W. Norton, 1993.

Heil, Alan L., Jr. *Voice of America: A History.* New York: Columbia University Press, 2003.

Heisman Trophy (Football). www.heisman.com/index.php

Heller, Steven, and Louise Fili. *Cover Story: The Art of American Magazine Covers, 1900–1950.* San Francisco: Chronicle Books, 1996.

Henderson, Amy, and Dwight Blocker Bowers. *Red, Hot and Blue: A Smithsonian Salute to the American Musical.* Washington, DC: Smithsonian Institution Press, 1996.

Henderson, Mary C. *Broadway Ballyhoo.* New York: Harry N. Abrams, 1989.

Henderson, Sally, and Robert Landau. *Billboard Art.* San Francisco: Chronicle Books, 1981.

Hennessey, Maureen Hart, and Anne Knutson. *Norman Rockwell: Pictures for the American People.* New York: Harry N. Abrams, 1999.

Hentoff, Nat, and Albert McCarthy, eds. *Jazz.* New York: Grove Press, 1959.

Hentoff, Nat, and Nat Shapiro, eds. *The Jazz Makers.* New York: Grove Press, 1957.

Hess, Alan. *Ranch House.* New York: Harry N. Abrams, 2004.

Hiesinger, Kathryn. *Design since 1945.* Philadelphia: Philadelphia Museum of Art, 1983.

Higby, Mary Jane. *Tune in Tomorrow.* New York: Cowles Education, 1968.

Higgs, Robert J. *Sport: A Reference Guide.* Westport, CT: Greenwood Press, 1982.

Higham, Charles. *The Art of the American Film, 1900–1971.* Garden City, NY: Anchor Press, 1973.

Higham, Charles, and Joel Greenberg. *Hollywood in the Forties.* New York: A. S. Barnes, 1968.

Hill, Daniel Delis. *Advertising to the American Woman, 1900–1999.* Columbus: Ohio State University Press, 2002.

Hilliard, Robert L., and Michael C. Keith. *The Broadcast Century: A Biography of American Broadcasting.* Boston: Focal Press, 1992.

Hillier, Bevis. *Austerity Binge: The Decorative Arts of the Forties and Fifties.* London: Cassell & Collier Macmillan, 1975.

———. *The Style of the Century: 1900–1980.* New York: E. P. Dutton, 1983.

Hilmes, Michele. *Radio Voices: American Broadcasting, 1922–1952.* Minneapolis: University of Minnesota Press, 1997.

Hilmes, Michele, and Jason Loviglio, eds. *Radio Reader: Essays in the Cultural History of Radio.* Florence, KY: Routledge, 2002.

Hine, Thomas. *Populuxe.* New York: Alfred A. Knopf, 1986.

———. *The Rise and Fall of the American Teenager.* New York: Avon Books, 1999.

Hirshorn, Paul, and Steven Izenour. *White Towers.* Cambridge, MA: MIT Press, 1979.

"Historical and Future Population Trends." www.npg.org/popfacts.htm

*Historical Statistics of the United States, Colonial Times to 1970.* Washington, DC: Census Bureau, U.S. Department of Commerce, 1975.

Hixon, Walter L. *Parting the Curtain: Propaganda, Culture, and the Cold War.* New York: St. Martin's Press, 1998.

Hobbs, Robert Carleton, and Gail Levin. *Abstract Expressionism: The Formative Years.* New York: Whitney Museum of American Art, 1978.

Hoffmann, Frank W., and William G. Bailey. *Fashion and Merchandising Fads.* New York: Haworth Press, 1994.

———. *Sports and Recreation Fads.* New York: Haworth Press, 1991.

Holm, Maj. Gen. Jeanne. *Women in the Military: An Unfinished Revolution.* Novato, CA: Presidio Press, 1992.

Holme, Bryan. *The Art of Advertising.* London: Peerage Books, 1985.

Hooker, Richard J. *Food and Drink in America: A History.* Indianapolis: Bobbs-Merrill, 1981.

Hoopes, Roy. *Americans Remember the Home Front: An Oral Narrative.* New York: Hawthorn Books, 1977.

Hoopes, Roy. *When the Stars Went to War: Hollywood and World War II.* New York: Random House, 1994.

Hopalong Cassidy. www.hopalong.com/home.asp

Horn, Maurice. *Women in the Comics.* New York: Chelsea House, 1977.

Horn, Maurice, ed. *100 Years of American Newspaper Comics.* New York: Gramercy Books, 1996.

———. *The World Encyclopedia of Comics.* New York: Chelsea House, 1976.

Hornung, Clarence P., and Fridolf Johnson. *200 Years of American Graphic Art.* New York: George Braziller, 1976.

Horowitz, Joseph. *Classical Music in America: A History of Its Rise and Fall.* New York: W. W. Norton, 2005.

Horse Racing and World War II. *New York Times,* December 22, 1940; May, 25, 1942; January 1, 1943; December 26, 1943; August 6, 1946.

Hot Rod. www.hotrod.com/index.html

Houston, Penelope. *The Contemporary Cinema, 1945–1963.* Baltimore: Penguin Books, 1963.

Howard Johnson's. www.fundinguniverse.com/company-histories/Howard-Johnson-International-Inc-Company-History.html

"How to Use Your War Ration Book." *Genealogy Today.* U.S. Government Printing Office #16–26649–1. www.genealogytoday.com/guide/ww2/book_one_intro.html

Hughes, Robert. *American Visions: The Epic History of Art in America.* New York: Alfred A. Knopf, 1997.

Hulick, Diana Emery, and Joseph Marshall. *Photography: 1900 to the Present.* Upper Saddle River, NJ: Prentice Hall, 1998.

Hurley, Andrew. *Diners, Bowling Alleys, and Trailer Parks: Chasing the American Dream in Postwar Consumer Culture.* New York: Basic Books, 2001.

Huss, Roy, and T. J. Huss. *Focus on the Horror Film.* Englewood Cliffs, NJ: Prentice Hall, 1972.

Hyland, William G. *Richard Rodgers.* New Haven, CT: Yale University Press, 1998.

———. *The Song Is Ended: Songwriters and American Music, 1900–1950.* New York: Oxford University Press, 1995.

Inge, Thomas M., ed. *Concise Histories of American Popular Culture.* Westport, CT: Greenwood Press, 1982.

———. *Handbook of American Popular Culture.* 3 vols. Westport, CT: Greenwood Press, 1981.

Inness, Sherrie A. *Dinner Roles: American Women and Culinary Culture.* Iowa City: University of Iowa Press, 2001.

———, ed. *Delinquents and Debutantes: Twentieth-Century American Girls' Culture.* New York: New York University Press, 1998.

*Internet Movie Database.* www.imdb.com/

Jablonski, Edward. *Gershwin.* New York: Doubleday, 1987.

Jablonski, Edward, and Lawrence D. Stewart. *The Gershwin Years.* Garden City, NY: Doubleday, 1958.

Jackson, Carlton. *Hounds of the Road: A History of the Greyhound Bus Company.* Bowling Green, OH: Popular Press, 1984.

Jackson, Kathy Merlock. *Images of Children in American Film.* Metuchen, NJ: Scarecrow Press, 1986.

Jackson, Kenneth T. *Crabgrass Frontier: The Suburbanization of the United States.* New York: Oxford University Press, 1987.

Jakle, John A. *The Tourist: Travel in Twentieth-Century North America.* Lincoln: University of Nebraska Press, 1985.

Jakle, John A., and Keith A Sculle. *The Gas Station in America.* Baltimore: Johns Hopkins University Press, 1994.

———. *Fast Food: Roadside Restaurants in the Automobile Age.* Baltimore: Johns Hopkins University Press, 1999.

Jakle, John A., Keith A. Sculle, and Jefferson S. Rogers. *The Motel in America.* Baltimore: Johns Hopkins University Press, 1996.

Jandl, H. Ward. *Yesterday's Houses of Tomorrow: Innovative American Homes, 1850–1950.* Washington, DC: Preservation Press, 1991.

Janello, Amy, and Brennon Jones. *The American Magazine.* New York: Harry N. Abrams, 1991.

Jasen, David A. *Tin Pan Alley: The Composers, the Songs, the Performers and Their Times.* New York: Donald I. Fine, 1988.

Jeffries, John W. *Wartime America: The World War II Home Front.* Chicago: Ivan R. Dee, 1996.

Jenkins, Virginia Scott. *The Lawn: A History of an American Obsession.* Washington, DC: Smithsonian Institution Press, 1994.

Jennings, Jan, ed. *Roadside America: The Automobile in Design and Culture.* Ames: Iowa State University Press, 1990.

Jewell, Derek. *Duke: A Portrait of Duke Ellington.* New York: W. W. Norton, 1977.

Johnson, Judy. "History of Paper Dolls." Original Paper Doll Artists Guild. www.opdag.com/history.html

Johnson, Paul. *Modern Times: From the Twenties to the Nineties.* New York: HarperCollins, 1991.

Jonas, Susan, and Marilyn Nissenson. *Going, Going, Gone: Vanishing Americana.* San Francisco: Chronicle Books, 1994.

Jones, Gerard. *Men of Tomorrow: Geeks, Gangsters, and the Birth of the Comic Book.* New York: Basic Books, 2004.

Jones, James H. *Alfred C. Kinsey: A Public/Private Life.* New York: W. W. Norton, 1997.

Jones, John Bush. *Our Musicals, Ourselves: A Social History of the American Musical Theatre.* Waltham, MA: Brandeis University Press, 2003.

———. *The Songs that Fought the War: Popular Music and the Home Front, 1939–1945.* Waltham, MA: Brandeis University Press, 2006.

Jones, Landon V. *Great Expectations: America and the Baby Boom Generation.* New York: Coward, McCann & Geoghegan, 1980.

Jones, Max, and John Chilton. *Louis: The Louis Armstrong Story.* Boston: Little, Brown, 1971.

Jones, R. L. *Great American Stuff.* Nashville: Cumberland House, 1997.

Judd, Denis. *Posters of World War II.* New York: St. Martin's Press, 1973.

Jukebox History. www.nationaljukebox.com

Jukebox History. www.radiomuseum.org/forum/jukebox_history_of_coin-operated_phonographs.html

Jungk, Robert. *Brighter Than a Thousand Suns: A Personal History of Atomic Scientists.* Translated by James Cleugh. New York: Grove Press, 1958.

Juvenile Delinquency. *New York Times,* September 22, 1942; December 28, 1942; May 21, 1943; July 18, 1943, September 22, 1943; September 25, 1943; August 6, 1944; December 12, 1945, February 10, 1946; April 28, 1947; July 20, 1947; April 24, 1949. www.proquest.com

Kael, Pauline. *The Citizen Kane Book.* New York: Limelight Editions, 1988.

Kaledin, Eugenia. *Daily Life in the United States, 1940–1959: Shifting Worlds.* Westport, CT: Greenwood Press, 2000.

Kallir, Jane. *Grandma Moses: The Artist behind the Myth.* New York: Clarkson N. Potter, 1982.

Kammen, Michael. *American Culture, American Tastes: Social Change and the 20th Century.* New York: Alfred A. Knopf, 2000.

Kaplan, Donald, and Alan Bellink. *Classic Diners of the Northeast.* Boston: Faber & Faber, 1980.

Karolyi, Otto. *Modern American Music: From Charles Ives to the Minimalists.* Cranbury, NJ: Fairleigh Dickinson University Press, 1996.

Kashima, Tetsuden, and the United States Commission on Wartime Relocation and Internment of Civilians. *Personal Justice Denied: Report of the Commission on Wartime Relocation and Internment of Civilians.* Washington, DC: U.S. Government Printing Office, 1996.

Kaye, Marvin. *A Toy Is Born.* New York: Stein & Day, 1973.

Keats, John. *The Crack in the Picture Window.* Cambridge, MA: Riverside Press, 1956.

Keepnews, Orrin, and Bill Grauer, Jr. *A Pictorial History of Jazz.* New York: Crown, 1955.

Kennedy, David M. *Freedom from Fear: The American People in Depression and War, 1929–1945.* New York: Oxford University Press, 1999.

Kennedy, Michael. *The Concise Oxford Dictionary of Music.* New York: Oxford University Press, 1980.

Kenney, William Howland. *Recorded Music in American Life: The Phonograph and Popular Memory, 1890–1945.* New York: Oxford University Press, 1999.

Kenrick, John. *Musicals 101: The Cyber Encyclopedia of Musical Theatre, TV and Film.* www.musicals101.com/

Kern-Foxworth, Marilyn. *Aunt Jemima, Uncle Ben, and Rastus: Blacks in Advertising, Yesterday, Today, and Tomorrow.* Westport, CT: Greenwood Press, 1994.

Keyhoe, Donald E. *Flying Saucers from Outer Space.* New York: Henry Holt, 1953.

Kidwell, Brush, and Valerie Steele, eds. *Men and Women: Dressing the Part.* Washington, DC: Smithsonian Institution Press, 1989.

Kidwell, Claudia B., and Margaret C. Christman. *Suiting Everyone: The Democratization of Clothing in America.* Washington, DC: Smithsonian Institution Press, 1974.

Kimball, Robert, and Linda Emmet, eds. *The Complete Lyrics of Irving Berlin.* New York: Alfred A. Knopf, 2001.

Kingsbury, Paul, and Alan Axelrod, eds. *Country: The Music and the Musicians.* New York: Abbeville Press, 1988.

Kinkle, Roger D. *The Complete Encyclopedia of Popular Music and Jazz, 1900–1950.* 4 vols. Westport, CT: Arlington House, 1974.

Kinsey Book Reviews. *Time,* January 5, 1948; April 12, 1948; August 24, 1953. www.time.com/time/magazine/article; *New York Times,* January 4, 1948; August 30, 1953; September 24, 1953.

Kinsey Institute for Research in Sex, Gender, and Reproduction. www.kinseyinstitute.org/

Kirby, Edward M., and Jack W. Harris. *Star-Spangled Radio.* Chicago: Ziff-Davis, 1948.

Kirchner, Bill, ed. *The Oxford Companion to Jazz.* New York: Oxford University Press, 2000.

Kirkendall, Richard S. *The United States, 1929–1945: Years of Crisis and Change.* New York: McGraw-Hill, 1974.

Kitahara, Teruhisa. *Yesterday's Toys.* Vol. 1, *Celluloid Dolls, Clowns, and Animals.* San Francisco: Chronicle Books, 1989.

———. *Yesterday's Toys.* Vol. 2, *Planes, Trains, Boats, and Cars.* San Francisco: Chronicle Books, 1989.

———. *Yesterday's Toys.* Vol. 3, *Robots, Spaceships, and Monsters.* San Francisco: Chronicle Books, 1989.

Kizer, George A. "Federal Aid to Education: 1945–1963." *History of Education Quarterly* 10 (1) (Spring 1970): 84–102.

Klapp, Orrin E. *Heroes, Villains, and Fools: The Changing American Character.* Englewood Cliffs, NJ: Prentice Hall, 1961.

Kleeblatt, Norman L., ed. *Action/Abstraction: Pollock, De Kooning, and American Art, 1940–1976.* New Haven, CT: Yale University Press, 2008.

Kleinfelder, Rita Lang. *When We Were Young: A Baby-Boomer Yearbook.* New York: Prentice Hall General Reference, 1993.

Knapp, Wilfred. *A History of War and Peace: 1939–1965.* New York: Oxford University Press, 1967.

Knight, Arthur. *The Liveliest Art.* New York: New American Library, 1957.

Knight, Edgar W. *Education in the United States.* 3rd ed. Boston: Ginn, 1951.

Knott, Robert. *American Abstract Art of the 1930s and 1940s.* New York: Harry N. Abrams, 1998.

Koppes, Clayton R., and Gregory D. Black. *Hollywood Goes to War: How Politics, Profits, and Propaganda Shaped World War II Movies.* New York: Free Press, 1987.

Kostof, Spiro. *America by Design.* New York: Oxford University Press, 1987.

Kouwenhoven, John A. *The Beer Can by the Highway.* New York: Doubleday, 1961.

Kozol, Wendy. *Life's America: Family and Nation in Postwar Photojournalism.* Philadelphia: Temple University Press, 1994.

Kraus, Richard. *Leisure in a Changing America: Trends and Issues for the 21st Century.* Boston: Allyn and Bacon, 2000.

———. *Recreation and Leisure in Modern Society.* Englewood Cliffs, NJ: Prentice Hall, 1971.

Krivine, John. *Jukebox Saturday Night.* London: New English Library, 1977.

Kushner, David. *Levittown: Two Families, One Tycoon, and the Fight for Civil Rights in America's Legendary Suburb.* New York: Walker, 2009.

Lackman, Ron. *The Encyclopedia of American Radio.* New York: Checkmark Books, 2000.

Laforse, Martin W., and James A. Drake. *Popular Culture and American Life.* Chicago: Nelson-Hall, 1981.

Lahue, Kalton C. *Continued Next Week: A History of the Moving Picture Serial.* Norman: University of Oklahoma Press, 1964.

Landau, Robert, and James Phillippi. *Airstream.* Salt Lake City: Peregrine Smith Books, 1984.

Lange, Jeffrey J. *Smile When You Call Me a Hillbilly: Country Music's Struggle for Respectability, 1939–1954.* Athens: University of Georgia Press, 2004.

Lanza, Joseph. *The Cocktail: The Influence of Spirits on the American Psyche.* New York: St. Martin's Press, 1995.

Larka, Robert. *Television's Private Eye: An Examination of Twenty Years of Programming of a Particular Genre, 1949–1969.* New York: Arno Press, 1979.

Larrabee, Eric, and Rolf Meyersohn, eds. *Mass Leisure.* Glencoe, IL: Free Press, 1958.

Lash, Joseph P. *Eleanor: The Years Alone.* New York: W. W. Norton, 1972.
———. *Eleanor and Franklin.* W. W. Norton, 1971.
Lax, Roger, and Frederick Smith. *The Great Song Thesaurus,* 2nd ed. New York: Oxford University Press, 1989.
Lears, Jackson. *Fables of Abundance: A Cultural History of Advertising in America.* New York: Basic Books, 1994.
Leming, Barbara. *Orson Welles: A Biography.* New York: Viking Penguin, 1985.
Lender, Mark Edward, and James Kirby Martin. *Drinking in America: A History.* New York: Free Press, 1987.
Leonard, Neil. *Jazz and the White American: The Acceptance of a New Art Form.* Chicago: University of Chicago Press, 1962.
Leonard, Thomas C. *News for All: America's Coming-of-Age with the Press.* New York: Oxford University Press, 1995.
Lesser, Robert. *A Celebration of Comic Art and Memorabilia.* New York: Hawthorn Books, 1975.
Lesy, Michael. *Long Time Coming: A Photographic Portrait of America, 1935–1943.* New York: W. W. Norton, 2002.
Leuchtenburg, William E. *A Troubled Feast: American Society since 1945.* Boston: Little, Brown, 1979.
Levenstein, Harvey. *Paradox of Plenty: A Social History of Eating in Modern America.* New York: Oxford University Press, 1993.
Levin, Martin, ed. *Hollywood and the Great Fan Magazines.* New York: Arbor House, 1970.
Levinson, David, and Karen Christensen, eds. *Encyclopedia of World Sport.* New York: Oxford University Press, 1996.
Lewine, Harris. *Good-Bye to All That.* New York: McGraw-Hill, 1970.
Lewine, Richard, and Afred Simon. *Songs of the American Theater.* New York: Dodd, Mead, 1973.
Lewis, David L., and Laurence Goldstein, eds. *The Automobile and American Culture.* Ann Arbor: University of Michigan Press, 1983.
Lewis, Lucinda. *Roadside America: The Automobile and the American Dream.* New York: Harry N. Abrams, 2000.
Ley, Sandra. *Fashion for Everyone: The Story of Ready-to-Wear, 1870's–1970's.* New York: Charles Scribner's Sons, 1975.
Lhamon, W. T., Jr. *Deliberate Speed: The Origins of Cultural Style in the American 1950s.* Washington, DC: Smithsonian Institution Press, 1990.
Libby, Bill. *Great American Race Drivers.* New York: Cowles Book Company, 1970.
Lichty, Lawrence W., and Malachi C. Topping. *American Broadcasting: A Source Book on the History of Radio and Television.* New York: Hastings House, 1975.
Liebs, Chester H. *Main Street to Miracle Mile: American Roadside Architecture.* Baltimore: Johns Hopkins University Press, 1985.
Liesner, Thelma. *Economic Statistics, 1900–1983.* New York: Facts on File, 1985.
LIFE Editors. *"LIFE": The Second Decade, 1946–1955.* Boston: Little, Brown, 1984.
"Life Presents a Review of Fall Fashions." *Life,* May 22, 1947.
Lifshey, Earl. *The Housewares Story.* Chicago: National Housewares Manufacturers Association, 1973.
Lingeman, Richard. *Don't You Know There's a War On? The American Home Front, 1941–1945.* New York: Thunder's Mouth Press, 1970.
Lippa, Mario, and David Newton. *The World of Small Ads.* Secaucus, NJ: Chartwell Books, 1979.
Long, Robert Emmet. *Broadway, the Golden Years: Jerome Robbins and the Great Choreographer-Directors, 1940 to the Present.* New York: Continuum, 2001.
Longley, Marjorie, Louis Silverstein, and Samuel A. Tower. *America's Taste: 1851–1959.* New York: Simon & Schuster, 1960.
Louis, Joe, fights. *Joe Louis vs. Billy Conn; Ringside Remembers; Joe Louis vs. Abe Simon II; Joe Louis vs. Jersey Joe Walcott Fight 2KO (Round 11); The Negro Soldier* (1944); *Joe Louis vs. Sky High Lee.* www.youtube.com
Love, Brian. *Play the Game.* Los Angeles: Reed Books, 1978.

Lovegren, Sylvia. *Fashionable Food: Seven Decades of Food Fads.* New York: Macmillan, 1995.
Lowenthal, Leo. *Literature, Popular Culture, and Society.* Englewood Cliffs, NJ: Prentice Hall, 1961.
Lucie-Smith, Edward. *American Realism.* New York: Harry N. Abrams, 1994.
———. *Visual Arts in the Twentieth Century.* New York: Harry N. Abrams, 1996.
Luke, Tim. *American Insider's Guide to Toys and Games.* London: Octopus Publishing Group, 2002.
Lupoff, Dick, and Don Thompson, eds. *All in Color for a Dime.* New York: Arlington House, 1970.
Lupton, Ellen. *Mechanical Brides: Women and Machines from Home to Office.* Princeton, NJ: Princeton Architectural Press, 1993.
Lynch, Vincent, and Bill Henkin. *Jukebox: The Golden Age.* Berkeley, CA: Lancaster-Miller, 1981.
Lynes, Russell. *The Lively Audience: A Social History of the Visual and Performing Arts in America, 1890–1950.* New York: Harper & Row, 1985.
Macdonald, Dwight. *Against the American Grain.* New York: Vintage Books, 1965.
MacDonald, J. Fred. *Don't Touch That Dial! Radio Programming in American Life, 1920–1960.* Chicago: Nelson-Hall, 1979.
———. *Who Shot the Sheriff? The Rise and Fall of the Television Western.* New York: Praeger, 1987.
Maddocks, Melvin. *The Great Liners.* Alexandria, VA: Time-Life Books, 1978.
Magee, Jeffrey. *The Uncrowned King of Swing: Fletcher Henderson and Big Band Jazz.* New York: Oxford University Press, 2005.
Maguire, James. *Impresario: The Life and Times of Ed Sullivan.* New York: Billboard Books, 2006.
Maier, Thomas. *Dr. Spock: An American Life.* New York: Basic Books, 2003.
Malone, Bill C. *Country Music, U.S.A.* Austin: University of Texas Press, 1968.
Malone, Bill C., and Judith McCulloh, eds. *Stars of Country Music: Uncle Dave Macon to Johnny Rodriguez.* Urbana: University of Illinois Press, 1975.
Maltby, Richard. *Passing Parade: A History of Popular Culture in the Twentieth Century.* New York: Oxford University Press, 1989.
Maltin, Leonard. *The Great American Broadcast: A Celebration of Radio's Golden Age.* New York: Dutton, 1997.
———. *Of Mice and Magic: A History of American Animated Cartoons.* New York: McGraw-Hill, 1980.
Manchester, William. *American Caesar: Douglas MacArthur, 1880–1964.* Boston: Little, Brown, 1978.
———. *The Glory and the Dream: A Narrative History of America, 1932–1972.* 2 vols. Boston: Little, Brown, 1974.
Mandel, Richard D. *Sport: A Cultural History.* New York: Columbia University Press, 1984.
Mandelbaum, Howard, and Eric Myers. *Forties Screen Style: A Celebration of High Pastiche in Hollywood.* Santa Monica, CA: Hennessey + Ingalls, 1989.
Manvell, Roger. *Films and the Second World War.* New York: Dell, 1974.
*March of Time, The.* www.xroads.virginia.edu
Marcus, Stanley E. *David Smith: The Sculptor and His Work.* Ithaca, NY: Cornell University Press, 1983.
Margolies, John. *Home Away from Home: Motels in America.* Boston: Little, Brown, 1995.
———. *Pump and Circumstance: Glory Days of the Gas Station.* Boston: Little, Brown, 1993.
Margolies, John, and Emily Gwathmey. *Ticket to Paradise: American Movie Theaters and How We Had Fun.* Boston: Little, Brown, 1991.
Mariani, John. *America Eats Out.* New York: William Morrow, 1991.
Markin, Rom J. *The Supermarket: An Analysis of Growth, Development, and Change.* Pullman: Washington State University Press, 1963.
Marschall, Richard. *America's Great Comic-Strip Artists.* New York: Stewart, Tabori & Chang, 1997.
Marshall, William. *Baseball's Pivotal Era, 1945–1951.* Lexington: University Press of Kentucky, 1999.
Marter, Joan M. *Alexander Calder.* New York: Cambridge University Press, 1991.
Martin, Richard. *American Ingenuity: Sportswear, 1930s–1970s.* New York: Metropolitan Museum of Art, 1998.

Marum, Andrew, and Frank Parise. *Follies and Foibles: A View of 20th Century Fads.* New York: Facts on File, 1984.

Marx, Samuel, and Jan Clayton. *Rodgers and Hart: Bewitched, Bothered, and Bewildered.* New York: G. P. Putnam's Sons, 1976.

Marzulla, Elena, ed. *Pictorial Treasury of U.S. Stamps.* Omaha, NE: Collectors Institute, 1974.

Mathy, Francois. *American Realism: A Pictorial Survey from the Early Eighteenth Century to the 1970's.* New York: Skira, 1978.

Mattfeld, Julius. *Variety Music Cavalcade.* Englewood Cliffs, NJ: Prentice Hall, 1962.

Matthew-Walker, Robert. *Broadway to Hollywood: The Musical and the Cinema.* London: Sanctuary, 1996.

Mauldin, Bill. www.lambiek.net/artists/m/mauldin_bill.htm

———. *Up Front.* New York: Henry Holt, 1945.

May, Elaine Tyler. *Homeward Bound: American Families in the Cold War Era.* New York: Basic Books, 1988.

May, Larry, ed. *Recasting American Culture and Politics in the Age of the Cold War.* Chicago: University of Chicago Press, 1989.

Mayo, James M. *The American Grocery Store: The Business Evolution of an Architectural Space.* Westport, CT: Greenwood Press, 1993.

Mazo, Joseph H. *Prime Movers: The Makers of Modern Dance in America.* New York: William Morrow, 1977.

McAlester, Virginia, and Lee McAlester. *A Field Guide to American Houses.* New York: Alfred A. Knopf, 1984.

McArdle, Kenneth, ed. *A Cavalcade of Collier's.* New York: Barnes & Noble, 1959.

McArthur, Colin. *Underworld U.S.A.* New York: Viking Press, 1972.

McBride, Joseph. *Frank Capra: The Catastrophe of Success.* New York: Touchstone Books, 1992.

McBrien, William. *Cole Porter: A Biography.* New York: Alfred A. Knopf, 1998.

McCallum, John D. *College Basketball, USA: Since 1892.* New York: Stein & Day, 1978.

McClellan, Lawrence, Jr. *The Later Swing Era, 1942 to 1955.* Westport, CT: Greenwood Press, 2004.

McClintock, Inez, and Marshall McClintock. *Toys in America.* Washington, DC: Public Affairs Press, 1961.

McClure, Rusty, with David Stern and Michael A. Banks. *Crosley.* Cincinnati: Clerisy Press, 2008.

McCullough, David. *Truman.* New York: Simon & Schuster, 1992.

McCutcheon, Marc. *The Writer's Guide to Everyday Life from Prohibition through World War II.* Cincinnati: Writer's Digest Books, 1995.

McDermott, Catherine. *Book of 20th Century Design.* New York: Overlook Press, 1998.

McDonagh, Don. *Martha Graham: A Biography.* New York: Praeger, 1973.

McGee, Mark Thomas. *The J.D. Films: Juvenile Delinquency in the Movies.* Jefferson, NC: McFarland, 1982.

McLaughlin, Robert L., and Sally E. Perry. *We'll Always Have the Movies: American Cinema During World War II.* Lexington: University Press of Kentucky, 2006.

McNeil, Alex. *Total Television: The Comprehensive Guide to Programming from 1948 to the Present.* 4th ed. New York: Penguin Books, 1996.

McShane, Clay. *Down the Asphalt Path: The Automobile and the American City.* New York: Columbia University Press, 1994.

McVeigh, Stephen. *The American Western.* New York: Columbia University Press, 2007.

Meeker, David. *Jazz in the Movies.* New York: Da Capo Press, 1981.

Meikle, Jeffrey L. *Design in the USA.* New York: Oxford University Press, 2005.

Mergen, Bernard. *Play and Playthings: A Reference Guide.* Westport, CT: Greenwood Press, 1982.

Meyer, Susan E. *America's Great Illustrators.* New York: Galahad Books, 1978.

Meyerowitz, Joanne. *Not June Cleaver: Women and Gender in Postwar America, 1945–1960.* Philadelphia: Temple University Press, 1994.

Millard, Andre. *America on Record: A History of Recorded Sound.* New York: Cambridge University Press, 1995.

Millard, Bob. *Country Music: 70 Years of America's Favorite Music.* New York: HarperCollins, 1993.

Miller, Char. "In the Sweat of Our Brow: Citizenship in American Domestic Practice during WWII—Victory Gardens." *Journal of American Culture* 26 (September 2003): 395–409.

Miller, Chuck. "V-*Discs*." www.chuckthewriter.com/vdisc.html

Miller, William H. *The Last Atlantic Liners.* London: Conway Maritime Press, 1985.

Mintz, Steven, and Susan Kellogg. *Domestic Revolutions: A Social History of American Family Life.* New York: Free Press, 1988.

Mirtle, Jack. *Thank You, Music Lovers: A Bio-Discography of Spike Jones, 1941–1965.* Westport, CT: Greenwood Press, 1986.

Modell, John. *Into One's Own: From Youth to Adulthood in the United States, 1920–1975.* Berkeley: University of California Press, 1989.

Moline, Mary. *Norman Rockwell Encyclopedia: A Chronological Catalog of the Artist's Work, 1910–1978.* Indianapolis: Curtis, 1979.

Moon, Krystyn. "There's No Yellow in the Red, White, and Blue: The Creation of Anti-Japanese Music during World War II." *Pacific Historical Review* (August 2003): 333–352.

Morath, Max. *The NPR Curious Listener's Guide to Popular Standards.* New York: Berkley, 2002.

Mordden, Ethan. *Better Foot Forward: The History of American Musical Theatre.* New York: Grossman, 1976.

Morden, Bettie J. *The Women's Army Corps, 1945–1978.* Washington, DC: Center of Military History, 1992.

Morella, Joe, Edward Z. Epstein, and John Griggs. *The Films of World War II.* Secaucus, NJ: Citadel Press, 1973.

Morgan, Robert P. *Twentieth-Century Music: A History of Musical Styles in Modern Europe and America.* New York: W. W. Norton, 1991.

Morthland, John. *The Best of Country Music.* Garden City, NY: Doubleday, 1984.

Morton, Brian. "Swing Time for Hitler." *Nation* 277 (7) (2003): 33–38.

Motorsports. *New York Times,* January 12, 1941; August 16, 1941; December 21, 1941; May 9, 1942; July 4, 1942; August 18, 1946; June 29, 1947; June 13, 1948; October 3, 1948; January 9, 1949; September 18, 1949.

Mott, Frank Luther. *American Journalism, a History: 1690–1960.* 3rd ed. New York: Macmillan, 1962.

Mott-Smith, Geoffrey. *Guide to Popular Hobbies.* Chicago: J. G. Ferguson, 1954.

Muller, Jurgen. *Movies of the 40s.* Cologne, Germany: Taschen, 2005.

Mulvey, Kate, and Melissa Richards. *Decades of Beauty: The Changing Image of Women, 1890s–1990s.* New York: Checkmark Books, 1998.

Murphy, Audie. *To Hell and Back.* New York: Holt, Rinehart & Winston, 1949.

Murray, Albert. *Stomping the Blues.* New York: Da Capo Press, 1976.

Murray, Alice Yang. *Historical Memories of the Japanese American Internment and the Struggle for Redress.* Stanford, CA: Stanford University Press, 2008.

Mustazza, Leonard. *Frank Sinatra and Popular Culture.* Westport, CT: Greenwood Press, 1999.

———. *Ol' Blue Eyes: A Frank Sinatra Encyclopedia.* Westport, CT: Greenwood Press, 1999.

Nachman, Gerald. *Raised on Radio.* Berkeley: University of California Press, 1998.

Naremore, James. *More Than Night: Film Noir and Its Contexts.* Berkeley: University of California Press, 1998.

National College Football Champions. www.infoplease.com/ipsa/A0908943.html

National Nutrition Campaign. *New York Times,* March 24, 1941; September 4, 1941; December 8, 1941; April 5, 1942; May 25, 1942; January 11, 1943; October 3, 1943; November 19, 1943; February 5, 1944; October 6, 1944; May 13, 1945; June 1, 1947; August 20, 1947.

NFL Championship Games: A History. www.4nflpicks.com/NFL%20Championship%20Games.html

National Hot Rod Association. www.nhra.net/aboutnhr/history.html

National Museum of Roller Skating. www.rollerskatingmuseum.com

National Opinion Research Center. *The Effects of Television on College Football Attendance.* Chicago: University of Chicago Press, 1951.

National Roller Derby Hall of Fame. www.rollerderbyhalloffame.com

Needham, Richard. *Ski: Fifty Years in North America.* New York: Harry N. Abrams, 1987.

Neuberg, Victor. *The Popular Press Companion to Popular Literature.* Bowling Green, OH: Popular Press, 1983.

Neumeyer, Martin H., and Esther S. Neumeyer. *Leisure and Recreation.* New York: Ronald Press, 1958.

Nevins, Francis M. *Bar-20: The Life of Clarence E. Mulford, Creator of Hopalong Cassidy.* Jefferson, NC: McFarland, 1993.

Newhall, Beaumont. *The History of Photography from 1839 to the Present.* Boston: Little, Brown, 1982.

Newhouse, Thomas. *The Beat Generation and the Popular Novel in the United States, 1945–1970.* Jefferson, NC: McFarland, 2000.

Nobel Laureates. www.nobelprize.org/

Nourmand, Tony, and Graham Marsh, eds. *Film Posters of the 40s: The Essential Movies of the Decade.* New York: Taschen, 2005.

Nye, Russel. *The Unembarrassed Muse: The Popular Arts in America.* New York: Dial Press, 1970.

O'Brien, Ed, and Scott Savers. *Sinatra: The Man and His Music: The Recording Artistry of Francis Albert Sinatra, 1939–1992.* Austin, TX: TSD Press, 1992.

O'Brien, Kenneth Paul, and Lynn Hudson Parsons, eds. *The Home-Front War: World War II and American Society.* Westport, CT: Greenwood Press, 1995.

O'Brien, Richard. *The Story of American Toys: From the Puritans to the Present.* New York: Abbeville Press, 1990.

Oermann, Robert K. *America's Music: The Roots of Country.* Atlanta, GA: Turner, 1996.

———. *A Century of Country: An Illustrated History of Country Music.* New York: TV Books, 1999.

"Old-Time Radio Commercials: Selling Stuff during the Golden Age of Radio." www.old-time.com/commercials/

Olian, JoAnne. *Everyday Fashions of the Forties as Pictured in Sears Catalogs.* New York: Dover, 1992.

Oliphant, Dave. *The Early Swing Era: 1930 to 1941.* Westport, CT: Greenwood Press, 2002.

Oliver, Paul, ed. *The Blackwell Guide to Recorded Blues.* Cambridge, MA: Basil Blackwell, 1991.

Oliver, Valerie Burnham. *Fashion and Costume in American Popular Culture: A Reference Guide.* Westport, CT: Greenwood Press, 1996.

Olmstead, Clifton E. *History of Religion in the United States.* Englewood Cliffs, NJ: Prentice Hall, 1960.

Olney, Ross R. *Great Moment in Speed.* Englewood Cliffs, NJ: Prentice Hall, 1970.

Orbanes, Philip E. *Monopoly: The World's Most Famous Game and How It Got That Way.* New York: Da Capo Press, 2007.

Osgerby, Bill. *Playboys in Paradise: Masculinity, Youth and Leisure-Style in Modern America.* New York: Berg, 2001.

O'Sullivan, Judith. *The Great American Comic Strip: One Hundred Years of Cartoon Art.* Boston: Little, Brown, 1990.

Osur, Alan M. *Blacks in the Army Air Forces during World War II: The Problem of Race Relations.* Washington, DC: Office of Air Force History, 1977.

Oswald, Greg. *Race and Ethnic Relations in Today's America.* Burlington, VT: Ashgate, 2001.

"Our Proud History: 67 Years of the USO." www.uso.org/whoweare/ourproudhistory/

Packard, William. *Evangelism in America: From Tents to TV.* New York: Paragon House, 1988.

Palladino, Grace. *Teenagers: An American History.* New York: Basic Books, 1996.

Panati, Charles. *Extraordinary Origins of Everyday Things.* New York: Harper & Row, 1987.

———. *Panati's Parade of Fads, Follies, and Manias.* New York: HarperCollins, 1991.

Passman, Arnold. *The Deejays.* New York: Macmillan, 1971.

Patterson, James T. *Grand Expectations: The United States, 1945–1974.* New York: Oxford University Press, 1996.

Patton, Phil. *Open Road: A Celebration of the American Highway.* New York: Simon & Schuster, 1986.

Pautz, Michelle. "The Decline in Average Weekly Cinema Attendance, 1930–2000." www.org.elon.edu/IPE/Pautz2.pdf

Peacock, John. *Fashion Sourcebooks: The 1940s.* London: Thames and Hudson, 1998.

Peatman, John Gray. "Radio and Popular Music." In *Radio Research 1942–1943,* eds. Paul F. Lazarsfeld and Frank N. Stanton, 335–393. New York: Duell, Sloan and Pearce, 1944.

Persico, Joseph E. *Edward R. Murrow: An American Original.* New York: McGraw-Hill, 1988.

Pendergrast, Mark. *For God, Country, and Coca-Cola: The Unauthorized History of the Great American Soft Drink and the Company That Makes It.* New York: Charles Scribner's Sons, 1993.

———. *Uncommon Grounds: The History of Coffee and How It Transformed Our World.* New York: Basic Books, 1999.

Pepsi-Cola Canteens. *New York Times,* March 1, 1943; July 22, 1943; July 22, 1944.

Perret, Geoffrey. *Old Soldiers Never Die: The Life of Douglas MacArthur.* Holbrook, MA: Adams Media, 1996.

Peterson, Richard A. *Creating Country Music: Fabricating the Authentic.* Chicago: University of Chicago Press, 1997.

Peterson, Robert W. *Pigskin: The Early Years of Pro Football.* New York: Oxford University Press, 1997.

Peterson, Theodore. *Magazines in the Twentieth Century.* Urbana: University of Illinois Press, 1964.

Peyser, Joan. *The Memory of All That: The Life of George Gershwin.* New York: Simon & Schuster, 1993.

"Phil Spitalny's All Girl Orchestra." www.cornslaw.net/allgirlorchestra/index.html

Phillips, Ann-Victoria. *The Complete Book of Roller Skating.* New York: Workman, 1979.

Phillips, Lisa. *High Styles: Twentieth-Century American Design.* New York: Whitney Museum of American Art, 1985.

Phillips, Lisa, ed. *The American Century: Art and Culture, 1950–2000.* New York: W. W. Norton, 1999.

Photography. *New York Times,* February 22, 1942.

Pillsbury, Richard. *From Boarding House to Bistro: The American Restaurant Then and Now.* Boston: Unwin Hyman, 1990.

Pitz, Henry. *200 Years of American Illustration.* New York: Random House, 1977.

Placksin, Sally. *American Women in Jazz: 1900 to the Present.* New York: Wideview Books, 1982.

Pluto, Terry. *Tall Tales: The Glory Years of the NBA, in the Words of the Men Who Played, Coached, and Built Pro Basketball.* New York: Simon & Schuster, 1992.

Poppe, Fred C. *The 100 Greatest Corporate and Industrial Ads.* New York: Van Nostrand Reinhold, 1983.

Potter, David M. *People of Plenty: Economic Abundance and the American Character.* Chicago: University of Chicago Press, 1954.

Prendergast, Roy M. *Film Music: A Neglected Art.* New York: W. W. Norton, 1977.

Puddington, Arch. *Broadcasting Freedom: The Cold War Triumph of Radio Free Europe and Radio Liberty.* Lexington: University Press of Kentucky, 2003.

Pulos, Arthur J. *The American Design Adventure, 1940–1975.* Cambridge, MA: MIT Press, 1988.

Pyle, Ernie. *Brave Men.* New York: Henry Holt, 1944.

Quart, Leonard, and Albert Auster. *American Film and Society since 1945.* New York: Praeger, 1991.

Quinlan, Sterling. *Inside ABC: American Broadcasting Company's Rise to Power.* New York: Hastings House, 1979.

Rader, Benjamin G. *American Sports: From the Age of Folk Games to the Age of Spectators.* Englewood Cliffs, NJ: Prentice Hall, 1983.

———. *Baseball: A History of America's Game.* Urbana: University of Illinois Press, 2002.

Radway, Janice A. *A Feeling for Books: The Book-the-Month Club, Literary Taste, and Middle-Class Desire.* Chapel Hill: University of North Carolina Press, 1997.

Rae, John B. *The American Automobile: A Brief History.* Chicago: University of Chicago Press, 1965.

———. *The Road and the Car in American Life.* Cambridge, MA: MIT Press, 1971.

Raeburn, Michael, and Alan Kendall, eds. *Music in the Twentieth Century.* New York: Oxford University Press, 1989.

Ramsey, Frederic, Jr., and Charles Edward Smith, eds. *Jazzmen.* New York: Harvest Books, 1939.
Randel, William Peirce. *The Evolution of American Taste.* New York: Crown, 1978.
Rapaport, Brooke Kamin, and Kevin L. Stayton. *Vital Forms: American Art and Design in the Atomic Age, 1940–1960.* New York: Harry N. Abrams, 2001.
Rautiolla-Williams Suzanne. "The Howdy Doody Show." Museum of Broadcast Communications. www.museum.tv/archives/etv/H/htmlH/howdydoodys/howdydoodys.htm
Read, Oliver, and Walter L. Welch. *From Tin Foil to Stereo: Evolution of the Phonograph.* Indianapolis: Howard W. Sams, 1959.
Reed, Walt, and Roger Reed. *The Illustrator in America, 1880–1980.* New York: Society of Illustrators, 1984.
Reiser, J. W. "Whatever Happened to Channel 1?" www.tech-notes.tv/
Reisman, David, Reuel Denny, and Nathan Glazer. *The Lonely Crowd.* New York: Doubleday Anchor Books, 1953.
Remmers, Hermann. *The American Teenager.* Indianapolis: Bobbs-Merrill, 1957.
Reynolds, Nancy, and Malcolm McCormick. *No Fixed Points: Dance in the Twentieth Century.* New Haven, CT: Yale University Press, 2003.
Rice, Diana. "Random Notes for Travelers" and "News and Notes from the Field of Travel." *New York Times,* February 4, 1940, through December 25, 1949.
Richards, Jeffrey. *Swordsmen of the Screen.* London: Routledge & Kegan Paul, 1977.
Rideout, Walter B. *The Radical Novel in the United States: 1900–1954.* New York: Hill and Wang, 1956.
Roberts, Randy, and James Olson. *Winning Is the Only Thing: Sports in America Since 1945.* Baltimore: Johns Hopkins University Press, 1991.
Robertson, William H. P. *The History of Thoroughbred Racing in America.* Englewood Cliffs, NJ: Prentice Hall, 1964.
Robinson, Frank M., and Lawrence Davidson. *Pulp Culture: The Art of Fiction Magazines.* Portland, OR: Collectors Press, 2007.
Robinson, Jerry. *The Comics: An Illustrated History of Comic Strip Art.* New York: G. P. Putnam's Sons, 1974.
Robson, Eddie. *Film Noir.* London: Virgin Books, 2005.
Rogers, Donald I. *Since You Went Away.* New Rochelle, NY: Arlington House, 1973.
Roller Derby Events. *New York Times,* September 11, 1936; August 18, 1946; November 28, 1948.
Rollin, Lucy. *Twentieth-Century Teen Culture by the Decades: A Reference Guide.* Westport, CT: Greenwood Press, 1999.
Rome, Adam. *The Bulldozer in the Countryside: Suburban Sprawl and the Rise of American Environmentalism.* New York: Cambridge University Press, 2001.
Roosevelt, Eleanor. *The Autobiography of Eleanor Roosevelt.* New York: Harper & Brothers, 1958.
Rose, Lisle. *The Cold War Comes to Main Street.* Lawrence: University Press of Kansas, 1999.
Rose, Mark H. *Interstate: Express Highway Politics, 1941–1956.* Lawrence: Regents Press of Kansas, 1979.
Rose, Mark H., Bruce E. Seely, and Paul F. Barrett. *The Best Transportation System in the World: Railroads, Trucks, Airlines, and American Public Policy in the Twentieth Century.* Columbus: Ohio State University Press, 2006.
Rosen, Jody. *"White Christmas": The Story of an American Song.* New York: Charles Scribner's Sons, 2002.
Rosenberg, Bernard, and David Manning White, eds. *Mass Culture: The Popular Arts in America.* Glencoe, IL: Free Press, 1957.
Rosenberg, Deena. *Fascinating Rhythm: The Collaboration of George and Ira Gershwin.* New York: Penguin Books, 1991.
Rosenberg, Neil V. *Bluegrass: A History.* Urbana: University of Illinois Press, 1985.
Rosenblum, Naomi. *The Story of Women Photographers.* New York: Abbeville Press, 1994.
Rosie the Riveter (2 parts). www.youtube.com/watch?v=xo5KOCMDe68; www.youtube.com/watch?v=flWvxW4HgwQ

Ross, Alex. *The Rest Is Noise: Listening to the Twentieth Century.* New York: Farrar, Straus and Giroux, 2007.

Roth, Leland M. *A Concise History of American Architecture.* New York: Harper & Row, 1979.

Rottman, Gordon L. *Fubar: Soldier Slang of World War II.* London: Osprey, 2007.

Rowsome, Frank, Jr. *They Laughed When I Sat Down.* New York: Bonanza Books, 1959.

Ruppelt, Edward J. *The Report on Unidentified Flying Objects.* New York: Doubleday, 1956.

Sadie, Stanley, ed. *The New Grove Dictionary of Music and Musicians.* 29 vols. New York: Macmillan, 2001.

Saffle, Michael, ed. *Perspectives on American Music, 1900–1950.* New York: Garland, 2000.

Sammons, Jeffrey T. *Beyond the Ring: The Role of Boxing in American Society.* Urbana: University of Illinois Press, 1988.

Samuel, Lawrence R. *Brought to You By: Postwar Television Advertising and the American Dream.* Austin: University of Texas Press, 2001.

———. *Pledging Allegiance: American Identity and the Bond Drives of World War II.* Washington, DC: Smithsonian Institution Press, 1997.

Sanjek, Russell. *Pennies from Heaven: The American Popular Music Business in the Twentieth Century.* New York: Da Capo Press, 1996.

Sann, Paul. *Fads, Follies and Delusions of the American People.* New York: Crown, 1967.

Santelli, Robert, and Emily Davidson, eds. *Hard Travelin': The Life and Legacy of Woody Guthrie.* Hanover, NH: Wesleyan University Press, 1999.

Santelli, Robert, Holly George-Warren, and Jim Brown, eds. *American Roots Music.* New York: Harry N. Abrams, 2001.

Sarf, Wayne Michael. *God Bless You, Buffalo Bill: A Layman's Guide to History and the Western Film.* Rutherford, NJ: Fairleigh Dickinson University Press, 1983.

Savage, Jon. *Teenage: The Creation of Youth Culture.* New York: Viking Penguin, 2007.

Savage, William W., Jr. *Comic Books and America, 1945–1954.* Norman: University of Oklahoma Press, 1990.

Sayre, Nora. *Running Time: Films of the Cold War.* New York: Dial Press, 1982.

Scanlan, Tom. *The Joy of Jazz: The Swing Era, 1935–1947.* Golden, CO: Fulcrum, 1996.

Scaruffi, Piero. "A Brief History of Rhythm and Blues." www.scaruffi.com/history/rb.html

Schaub, Thomas Hill. *American Fiction in the Cold War.* Madison: University of Wisconsin Press, 1991.

Schicke, C. A. *Revolution in Sound: A Biography of the Recording Industry.* Boston: Little, Brown, 1974.

Schickel, Richard, with George Perry. *Bogie: A Celebration of the Life and Films of Humphrey Bogart.* New York: St. Martin's Press, 2006.

———. *The Disney Version: The Life, Times, Art and Commerce of Walt Disney.* New York: Avon, 1968.

Schnurnberger, Lynn. *Let There Be Clothes.* New York: Workman, 1991.

Schoenberg, Loren. *Count Basie: The Columbia Years.* Booklet accompanying *Count Basie and His Orchestra: America's #1 Band!* Columbia/Legacy C4K 87110. 4 CDs. 2003.

———. *The NPR Curious Listener's Guide to Jazz.* New York: Berkley, 2002.

Schremp, Gerry. *Kitchen Culture: Fifty Years of Food Fads.* New York: Pharos Books, 1991.

Schreuders, Piet. *Paperbacks, U.S.A.: A Graphic History, 1939–1959.* San Diego: Blue Dolphin Enterprises, 1981.

Schrum, Kelly. *Some Wore Bobby Sox: The Emergence of Teenage Girls' Culture, 1920–1945.* New York: Palgrave Macmillan, 2004.

Schudson, Michael. *Discovering the News: A Social History of American Newspapers.* New York: Basic Books, 1978.

Schuller, Gunther. *The Swing Era: The Development of Jazz, 1930–1945.* New York: Oxford University Press, 1989.

Sears, Richard S. *V-Discs: A History and a Discography.* Westport, CT: Greenwood Press, 1980.

Sears, Stephen W. *The American Heritage History of the Automobile in America.* New York: Simon & Schuster, 1977.

Segrave, Kerry. *Drive-In Theaters: A History from Their Inception.* Jefferson, NC: McFarland, 1992.

Seidman, David. *All Gone: Things That Aren't There Anymore.* Los Angeles: General Publishing Group, 1998.

Seldin, Joseph L. *The Golden Fleece: Selling the Good Life to Americans.* New York: Macmillan, 1963.

Selective Service Act of 1940. *New York Times,* June 11, 1940; September 17 through October 15, 1940; April 1, 1947. www.proquest.com

Service Flags. www.serviceflags.com/about.htm

Settel, Irving. *A Pictorial History of Radio.* New York: Grosset & Dunlap, 1967.

Settel, Irving, and William Laas. *A Pictorial History of Television.* New York: Grosset & Dunlap, 1969.

Sexton, Richard. *American Style: Classic Product Design from Airstream to Zippo.* San Francisco: Chronicle Books, 1987.

Shanken, Andrew M. *194X: Architecture, Planning, and Consumer Culture on the American Home Front.* Minneapolis: University of Minnesota Press, 2009.

Shapiro, Jerome F. *Atomic Bomb Cinema: The Apocalyptic Imagination on Film.* New York: Routledge, 2002.

Shapiro, Mitchell E. *Radio Network Prime Time Programming, 1926–1967.* Jefferson, NC: McFarland, 2002.

Shapiro, Nat. "William 'Count' Basie." In *The Jazz Makers,* eds. Nat Shapiro and Nat Hentoff, 232–242. New York: Grove Press, 1957.

Sheppard, W. Anthony. "An Exotic Enemy: Anti-Japanese Musical Propaganda in World War II Hollywood." *Journal of the American Musicological Society* 54 (2) (Summer 2001): 303–357.

Shestack, Melvin. *The Country Music Encyclopedia.* New York: Thomas Y. Crowell, 1974.

Shindler, Colin. *Hollywood Goes to War: Films and American Society, 1939–1952.* Boston: Routledge & Kegan Paul, 1979.

Sibley, Katherine A. S. *Red Spies in America: Stolen Secrets and the Dawn of the Cold War.* Lawrence: University Press of Kansas, 2004.

Sickels, Robert. *American Popular Culture through History: The 1940s.* Westport, CT: Greenwood Press, 2004.

Silver, Alain, and Elizabeth Ward. *Film Noir: An Encyclopedia of the American Style.* Woodstock, NY: Overlook Press, 1992.

Silver, Alain, and James Ursini. *The Noir Style.* Woodstock, NY: Overlook Press, 1999.

Simmon, Scott. *The Invention of the Western Film: A Cultural History of the Genre's First Half Century.* New York: Cambridge University Press, 2003.

Simon, George T. *The Big Bands.* New York: Macmillan, 1967.

———. *Glenn Miller and His Orchestra.* New York: Thomas Y. Crowell, 1974.

Simon, Mary. *Racing through the Century: The Story of Thoroughbred Racing in America.* Irvine, CA: Bowtie Press, 2002.

Singer, Arthur J. *Arthur Godfrey: The Adventures of an American Broadcaster.* Jefferson, NC: McFarland, 1999.

Sklar, Robert. *Movie-Made America: A Cultural History of American Movies.* New York: Random House, 1975.

Skolnik, Peter L. *Fads: America's Crazes, Fevers and Fantasies.* New York: Thomas Y. Crowell, 1978.

Smith, Andrew F. *Encyclopedia of Junk Food and Fast Food.* Westport, CT: Greenwood Press, 2006.

Smith, Bradley. *The USA: A History in Art.* New York: Doubleday, 1975.

Smith, C. Ray. *Interior Design in 20th-Century America: A History.* New York: Harper & Row, 1987.

Smith, Jane Webb. *Smoke Signals: Cigarettes, Advertising, and the American Way of Life.* Chapel Hill: University of North Carolina Press, 1990.

Smith, Kathleen E. R. *God Bless America: Tin Pan Alley Goes to War.* Lexington: University Press of Kentucky, 2003.

Snider, Lee. *80 Years of American Song Hits, 1892–1972.* New York: Chappell, 1973.

Smith, Leverett T., Jr. *The American Dream and the National Game.* Bowling Green, OH: Popular Press, 1975.

Smith, Robert. *Pro Football: The History of the Game and the Great Players.* New York: Doubleday, 1963.

Soares, Manuela. *The Soap Opera Book.* New York: Harmony Books, 1978.

Softball Games. *New York Times,* May 13, 1940; April 27, 1943; August 4, 1946; July 1, 1961. www.proquest.com

Solberg, Carl. *Conquest of the Skies: A History of Commercial Aviation in America.* Boston: Little, Brown, 1979.

*Solid! The Encyclopedia of Big Band, Lounge, Classic Jazz and Space-Age Sounds.* www.parabrisas.com/index.html

Solomon, Jon. *The Complete Three Stooges: The Official Filmography and Three Stooges Companion.* Glendale, CA: Comedy III Productions, 2002.

Solomon, Louis. *America Goes to Press: The Story of Newspapers from Colonial Times to the Present.* New York: Crowell-Collier Press, 1970.

Spam. *New York Times,* January 16, 1944; August 26, 1948; May 19, 1949.

Spam. *Time Magazine,* October 5, 1942; March 20, 1944; September 11, 1944; April 15, 1946; October 4, 1948; May 19, 1949.

Spigel, Lynn. *Make Room for TV: Television and the Family Ideal in Postwar America.* Chicago: University of Chicago Press, 1992.

———. *Welcome to the Dreamhouse: Popular Media and Postwar Suburbs.* Durham, NC: Duke University Press, 2001.

Spivey, Donald, ed. *Sport in America: New Historical Perspectives.* Westport, CT: Greenwood Press, 1985.

Spock, Benjamin. *The Pocket Book of Baby and Child Care.* New York: Pocket Books, 1946.

Springer, John. *All Talking! All Singing! All Dancing!* Secaucus, NJ: Citadel Press, 1966.

Stanfield, Peter. *Horse Opera: The Strange History of the Singing Cowboy.* Urbana: University of Illinois Press, 2002.

Stearns, Marshall. *The Story of Jazz.* New York: Oxford University Press, 1958.

Stearns, Marshall, and Jean Stearns. *Jazz Dance: The Story of American Vernacular Dance.* New York: Schirmer Books, 1968.

Stedman, Raymond William. *The Serials: Suspense and Drama by Installment.* Norman: University of Oklahoma Press, 1971.

"Steel Wartime Pennies." www.en.wikipedia.org/wiki/1943_steel_cent

Stehman, Dan. *Roy Harris: A Bio-Bibliography.* Westport, CT: Greenwood Press, 1991.

Sterling, Christopher H., and John M. Kitross. *Stay Tuned: A Concise History of American Broadcasting.* Belmont, CA: Wadsworth, 1990.

Stern, Robert A. M. *Pride of Place: Building the American Dream.* Boston: Houghton Mifflin, 1986.

Sterner, Alice P. *Radio, Motion Picture, and Reading Interests.* New York: Teachers College, Columbia University, 1947.

Stevenson, Isabelle, ed. *The Tony Award: A Complete Listing.* New York: Arno Press, 1975.

Stewart, Mark. *Hockey: A History of the Fastest Game on Ice.* New York: Franklin Watts, 1998.

Stilgoe, John R. *Borderland: Origins of the American Suburb, 1820–1939.* New Haven, CT: Yale University Press, 1988.

———. *Metropolitan Corridor: Railroads and the American Scene.* New Haven, CT: Yale University Press, 1983.

Stoddard, Bob. *Pepsi-Cola: 100 Years.* Los Angeles: General Publishing Group, 1997.

Stodelle, Ernestine. *Deep Song: The Dance Story of Martha Graham.* New York: Schirmer Books, 1984.

Stoltz, Donard R., and Marshall L. Stoltz. *Norman Rockwell and the Saturday Evening Post.* Vol. 2, *The Middle Years, 1928–1943.* Philadelphia: Saturday Evening Post, 1976.

———. *Norman Rockwell and the Saturday Evening Post.* Vol. 3, *The Later Years.* Philadelphia: Saturday Evening Post, 1976.

Stoltz, Donald Robert, Marshall Louis Stoltz, and William B. Earle. *The Advertising World of Norman Rockwell.* New York: Madison Square Press, 1985.

Stover, John F. *The Life and Decline of the American Railroad.* New York: Oxford University Press, 1970.

Strasser, Susan. *Never Done: A History of American Housework.* New York: Pantheon Books, 1982.

———. *Waste and Want: A Social History of Trash.* New York: Macmillan, 2000.

Strege, John. *When War Played Through: Golf during World War II.* New York: Gotham Books, 2005.

Strombecker Model Kits. www.commercemarketplace.com/home/collectair/strombecker.html

Struble, John Warthen. *The History of American Classical Music: MacDowell through Minimalism.* New York: Facts on File, 1995.

Sturcken, Frank. *Live Television: The Golden Age of 1946–1958 in New York.* Jefferson, NC: McFarland, 2001.

Sugar, Bert Randolph, and the Editors of *Ring* Magazine. *100 Years of Boxing.* New York: Galley Press, 1982.

Sudhalter, Richard M. *Stardust Melody: The Life and Music of Hoagy Carmichael.* New York: Oxford University Press, 2002.

Summers, Harrison B. *A Thirty-Year History of Programs Carried on National Radio Networks in the United States, 1926–1956.* Columbus: Ohio State University Press, 1958.

Suskin, Steven. *Show Tunes: The Songs, Shows, and Careers of Broadway's Major Composers.* 3rd ed. New York: Oxford University Press, 2000.

Swanberg, W. A. *Luce and His Empire.* New York: Charles Scribner's Sons, 1972.

Sweeney, Russell C. *Coming Next Week: A Pictorial History of Film Advertising.* New York: Castle Books, 1973.

Symons, Julian. *Bloody Murder: From the Detective Story to the Crime Novel.* New York: Penguin Books, 1972.

Tassava, Christopher J. *The American Economy during World War II.* http://eh.net/encyclopedia/article/tassava.WWII

Tawa, Nicholas E. *Serenading the Reluctant Eagle: American Musical Life, 1925–1945.* New York: Schirmer Books, 1984.

Taylor, Ella. *Prime Time Families: Television Culture in Postwar America.* Berkeley: University of California Press, 1989.

Taylor, John W. R., and Kenneth Munson. *History of Aviation.* New York: Crown, 1972.

Taylor, Joshua. *America as Art.* Washington, DC: Smithsonian Institution Press, 1976.

Tchudi, Stephen N. *Soda Poppery: The History of Soft Drinks in America.* New York: Charles Scribner's Sons, 1986.

"Teacher Shortages." *New York Times,* January 25, 1942; December 13, 1942; June 29, 1946; February 27, 1949. www.proquest.com

Tebbel, John. *The American Magazine: A Compact History.* New York: Hawthorn Books, 1969.

———. *A History of Book Publishing in the United States.* Vol. 4, *The Great Change, 1940–1989.* New York: R. R. Bowker, 1981.

Tebbel, John, and Mary Ellen Zuckerman. *The Magazine in America: 1741–1990.* New York: Oxford University Press, 1991.

"Teen-Age Boys." *Life,* June 11, 1945.

Television History. Museum of Televison. www.MZTV/mz.asp

Tennyson, Jeffrey. *Hamburger Heaven: The Illustrated History of the Hamburger.* New York: Hyperion, 1993.

Terrace, Vincent. *The Complete Encyclopedia of Television Programs, 1947–1979.* 2 vols.; 2nd ed. New York: A. S. Barnes, 1979.

Terry, Walter. *I Was There: Selected Dance Reviews and Articles, 1936–1976.* New York: Marcel Dekker, 1978.

Thomas, Bob. *Walt Disney: An American Original.* New York: Simon & Schuster, 1976.

Thomas, Ron. *They Cleared the Lane: The NBA's Black Pioneers.* Lincoln: University of Nebraska Press, 2002.

Thomas, Tony. *The Films of the Forties.* Secaucus, NJ: Citadel Press, 1975.

Thompson, Don, and Dick Lupoff, eds. *The Comic-Book Book.* New York: Arlington House, 1973.

Thompson, Neal. *Driving with the Devil: Southern Mooonshine, Detroit Wheels, and the Birth of NASCAR.* New York: Crown, 2006.

Thornburg, David A. *Galloping Bungalows: The Rise and Demise of the American House Trailer.* Hamden, CT: Archon Books, 1991.

Three Stooges, The. www.threestooges.com/

Tichi, Cecilia. *Electronic Hearth: Creating an American Television Culture.* New York: Oxford University Press, 1991.

———. *High Lonesome: The American Culture of Country Music.* Chapel Hill: University of North Carolina Press, 1994.

*Time-Life* Books. *This Fabulous Century.* Vol. 5, *1940–1950.* New York: Time-Life Books, 1969.

Toll, Robert C. *The Entertainment Machine: American Show Business in the Twentieth Century.* New York: Oxford University Press, 1982.

———. *On with the Show: The First Century of Show Business in America.* New York: Oxford University Press, 1976.

Tonka Toys. www.hasbro.com/tonka/

Trager, James. *The Food Chronology: A Food Lover's Compendium of Events and Anecdotes from Prehistory to the Present.* New York: Henry Holt, 1995.

Trahey, Jane. *Harper's Bazaar: One Hundred Years of the American Female.* New York: Random House, 1967.

Tribe, Ivan. *Country: A Regional Exploration.* Westport, CT: Greenwood Press, 2006.

"Truman." *American Experience: The Presidents.* PBS. www.pbs.org/wgbh/amex/presidents/video/truman_27_qt.html#v184

Tucker, Mark, ed. *The Duke Ellington Reader.* New York: Oxford University Press, 1993.

Tucker, Sherrie. *Swing Shift: "All-Girl" Bands of the 1940s.* Durham, NC: Duke University Press, 2000.

Tudor, Dean, and Nancy Tudor. *Grass Roots Music.* Littleton, CO: Libraries Unlimited, 1979.

Turner, Lillian. "The Singing Cowboys: Real to Reel." Points West Online. www.bbhc.org/pointswest/

Turner, Peter. *History of Photography.* New York: Exeter Books, 1987.

Turudich, Daniela. *1940s Hairstyles.* Long Beach, CA: Streamline Press, 2001.

Tyler, Don. *Hit Parade: An Encyclopedia of the Top Songs of the Jazz, Depression, Swing, and Sing Eras.* New York: William Morrow, 1985.

Ulanov, Barry. *A History of Jazz in America.* New York: Da Capo Press, 1952.

United Nations Facts. Department of Public Information. *Basic Facts about the United Nations.* New York: United Nations Publications, 2004. www.un.org/aboutun/untoday/

United Service Organizations and United Service Organizations Camp Shows. *New York Times,* March 1, 1942; July 27, 1942; April 6, 1944; August 27, 1944; September 14, 1944.

Ursini, James. *Humphrey Bogart.* Los Angeles: Taschen, 2007.

U.S. Department of the Treasury, U.S. Savings Bond Division. *A History of the United States Savings Bonds Program.* Washington, DC: U.S. Department of the Treasury, 1991. www.treasurydirect.gov/indiv/research/history/history_sb.pdf

USO. www.uso.org/whoweare/ourproudhistory/

USO and USO Camp Shows. *New York Times,* March 1, 1942; July 27, 1942; April 6, 1944; August 27, 1944; September 14, 1944.

Van Dover, J. Kenneth. *Murder in the Millions: Erle Stanley Gardner, Mickey Spillane, and Ian Fleming.* New York: Frederick Ungar, 1984.

*Variety* Books. *The Variety History of Show Business.* New York: Harry N. Abrams, 1993.

Verney, Kevern. *Black Civil Rights in America.* New York: Routledge, 2000.

Victory Gardens. *New York Times,* April 12, 1942; August 30, 1942; March 13, 1943; January 12, 1945.

Visser, Margaret. *Much Depends on Dinner.* New York: Grove Press, 1986.

*Vocalists Database.* www.nfo.net/usa/voc.html

Wachs, Martin, and Margaret Crawford, eds. *The Car and the City: The Automobile, the Built Environment, and Daily Urban Life.* Ann Arbor: University of Michigan Press, 1992.

Wainwright, Loudon. *The Great American Magazine: An Inside History of Life.* New York: Alfred A. Knopf, 1986.

Walker, Brian. *The Comics: Before 1945.* New York: Harry N. Abrams, 2004.

———. *The Comics: Since 1945.* New York: Harry N. Abrams, 2002.

Walker, Janet. *Westerns: Films through History.* New York: Routledge, 2001.

Walker, Leo. *The Big Band Almanac.* Rev. ed. New York: Da Capo Press, 1989.

———. *The Wonderful Era of the Great Dance Bands.* Berkeley, CA: Howell-North Books, 1964.

Walker, Lester. *American Shelter.* Woodstock, NY: Overlook Press, 1996.

Wallace, Aurora. *Newspapers and the Making of Modern America: A History.* Westport, CT: Greenwood Press, 2005.

Wallechinsky, David. *David Wallechinsky's Twentieth Century: History with the Boring Parts Left Out.* Boston: Little, Brown, 1995 [Previously published as *The People's Almanac Presents the Twentieth Century*].

Wallis, Allan D. *Wheel Estate: The Rise and Decline of Mobile Homes.* New York: Oxford University Press, 1991.

Walsh, Tim. *Timeless Toys: Classic Toys and the Playmakers Who Created Them.* Kansas City, MO: Andrews McMeel, 2005.

War Bond Drives and Advertising. www.library.duke.edu/digitalcollections/adaccess/warbonds.html

Ward, Geoffrey C., and Ken Burns. *Jazz: A History of America's Music.* New York: Alfred A. Knopf, 2000.

Warner, Jay. *American Singing Groups: A History from the 1940s to Today.* Milwaukee: Hal Leonard, 2006.

Watkins, Julius Lewis. *The 100 Greatest Advertisements: Who Wrote Them and What They Did.* New York: Dover, 1959.

Watters, Pat. *Coca-Cola: An Illustrated History* New York: Doubleday, 1978.

Weibel, Kathryn. *Mirror Mirror: Images of Women Reflected in Popular Culture.* Garden City, NY: Anchor Books, 1977.

Weiner, Edward. *Urban Transportation Planning in the United States: An Historical Overview.* Westport, CT: Praeger, 1999.

Weiner, Mark. "Democracy, Consumer Culture, and Political Community: The Story of Coca-Cola Advertising during World War II." *Food and Foodways* 6 (1996): 109–129.

Weinstein, David. *The Forgotten Network: DuMont and the Birth of American Television.* Philadelphia: Temple University Press, 2004.

Weiskopf, Herman. *The Perfect Game: The World of Bowling.* Englewood Cliffs, NJ: Prentice Hall, 1978.

Wertham, Frederic. *Seduction of the Innocent.* New York: Rinehart, 1954.

West, Elliott. *Growing Up in Twentieth-Century America: A History and Reference Guide.* Westport, CT: Greenwood Press, 1996.

West, James L. W., III. *American Authors and the Literary Marketplace since 1900.* Philadelphia: University of Pennsylvania Press, 1988.

Whedon, Julia. *The Fine Art of Ice Skating: An Illustrated History and Portfolio of Stars.* New York: Harry N. Abrams, 1988.

Whisnant, David E. "Forgotten Soldier Boy: War and the Politics of Country Music." Office of News and Communications, Duke University. www.dukenews.duke.edu/2003/01/country0103._print.ht

Whitburn, Joel. *A Century of Pop Music.* Menomonee Falls, WI: Record Research, 1999.

———. *Pop Memories, 1890–1954: The History of American Popular Music.* Menomonee Falls, WI: Record Research, 1986.

Whitcomb, Ian. *After the Ball: Pop Music from Rag to Rock.* Baltimore: Penguin Books, 1972.

White, David Manning, and Robert H. Abel, eds. *The Funnies: An American Idiom.* New York: Free Press, 1963.

White, G. Edward. *Creating the National Pastime: Baseball Transforms Itself, 1903–1955.* Princeton, NJ: Princeton University Press, 1996.

White, Mark. *'You Must Remember This...': Popular Songwriters 1900–1980.* New York: Charles Scribner's Sons, 1985.

White, Roger B. *Home on the Road: The Motor Home in America.* Washington, DC: Smithsonian Institution Press, 2000.

Whitfield, Stephen J. *The Culture of the Cold War.* Baltimore: Johns Hopkins University Press, 1996.

Whyte, William H., Jr. *The Organization Man.* New York: Doubleday Anchor Books, 1956.

Wicker, Tom. *Shooting Star: The Brief Arc of Joe McCarthy.* New York: Harcourt, 2006.

Wilcox, Walter W. *The Farmer in the Second World War.* Ames: Iowa State College Press, 1947.

Wilder, Alec. *American Popular Song: The Great Innovators, 1900–1950.* New York: Oxford University Press, 1972.

Williams, Anne D. *The Jigsaw Puzzle: Piecing Together a History.* New York: Berkley Publishing Group, 2004.

Williams, John R. *This Was "Your Hit Parade."* Camden, ME: Courier-Gazette, 1973.

Williams, Martin T., ed. *The Art of Jazz.* New York: Oxford University Press, 1959.

———. *The Jazz Tradition.* New York: Oxford University Press, 1983.

Willis, Barry R. *America's Music: Bluegrass.* Franktown, CO: Pine Valley Music, 1989.

Wills, Rosetta. *The King of Western Swing: Bob Wills Remembered.* New York: Watson-Guptill, 1998.

Wilson, Sloan. *The Man in the Gray Flannel Suit.* New York: Pocket Books, 1955.

Wiltse, Jeff. *Contested Waters: A Social History of Swimming Pools in America.* Chapel Hill: University of North Carolina Press, 2007.

Winer, Deborah Grace. *On the Sunny Side of the Street: The Life and Lyrics of Dorothy Fields.* New York: Schirmer Books, 1997.

Winkler, Allan M. *Home Front U.S.A.: America during World War II.* Wheeling, IL: Harlan Davidson, 1986.

———. *Life under a Cloud: American Anxiety about the Atom.* Urbana: University of Illinois Press, 1999.

Wittner, Lawrence S. *Cold War America: From Hiroshima to Watergate.* New York: Praeger, 1974.

Witzel, Michael Karl. *The American Gas Station.* New York: Barnes & Noble, 1999.

Witzel, Michael Karl, and Tim Steil. *Classic Roadside Americana.* New York: MBI, 2006.

Wojcik-Andrews, Ian. *Children's Films: History, Ideology, Pedagogy, Theory.* New York: Garland, 2000.

Wolfe, Charles K., and James E. Akenson, eds. *Country Music Goes to War.* Lexington: University Press of Kentucky, 2005.

Woll, Allen L. *The Hollywood Musical Goes to War.* Chicago: Nelson-Hall, 1983.

Wood, James Playsted. *Magazines in the United States.* New York: Ronald Press, 1956.

Woodham, Jonathan M. *Twentieth-Century Design.* New York: Oxford University Press, 1997.

Woody Guthrie. www.woodyguthrie.org/index.htm

World War II: The Home Front. www.teacheroz.com/WWIIpropaganda.htm

World War II Canteens (Ohio). Cam-Tech Publishing. www.canteenbooks.com

World War II Rationing Collection: 1942–1946. New York State Library. SC22912. www.nysl.nysed.gov/msscfa/sc22912.htm

Wright, Bradford W. *Comic Book Nation: The Transformation of Youth Culture in America.* Baltimore: Johns Hopkins University Press, 2001.

Wright, Gwendolyn. *Building the Dream: A Social History of Housing in America.* New York: Pantheon Books, 1981.

Wrynn, V. Dennis. *Coke Goes to War.* Missoula, MT: Pictorial Histories, 1996.

Wulffson, Don. *Toys: Amazing Stories behind Some Great Inventions.* New York: Henry Holt, 2000.

Wurts, Richard. *The New York World's Fair, 1939/1940.* New York: Dover, 1977.

Wyman, Carolyn. *Spam: A Biography: The Amazing True Story of America's "Miracle Meat."* Fort Washington, PA: Harvest Books, 1999.

Yanow, Scott. *Bebop.* San Francisco: Miller Freeman, 2000.

———. *Swing: Great Musicians, Influential Groups.* San Francisco: Miller Freeman, 2000.

Yaquinto, Marilyn. *Pump 'em Full of Lead: A Look at Gangsters on Film.* New York: Twayne, 1998.

Yellin, Emily. *Our Mothers' War: American Women at Home and at the Front during World War II.* New York: Free Press, 2004.

Yoggy, Gary A., ed. *Back in the Saddle: Essays on Western Film and Television Actors.* Jefferson, NC: McFarland, 1998.

Young, Jordan R. *Spike Jones Off the Record: The Man Who Murdered Music.* Albany, NY: Bearmanor Media, 2004.

Young, William H., and Nancy K. Young. *American Music through History: The World War II Era.* Westport, CT: Greenwood Publishing Group, 2005.

———. *The Great Depression in America: A Cultural Encyclopedia.* 2 vols. Westport, CT: Greenwood Publishing Group, 2007.

Zieger, Robert H. *John L. Lewis: Labor Leader.* Boston: Twayne, 1988.

Zieger, Robert H., and Gilbert J. Gall. *American Workers, American Unions.* Baltimore: Johns Hopkins University Press, 2002.

Zierold, Norman J. *The Child Stars.* New York: Coward-McCann, 1965.

Zinn, Howard. *Postwar America, 1945–1971.* Boston: South End Press, 1973.

Zinsser, William. *Easy to Remember: The Great American Songwriters and Their Songs.* Jaffrey, NH: David R. Godine, 2000.

Zuckerman, Mary Ellen. *A History of Popular Women's Magazines in the United States, 1792–1995.* Westport, CT: Greenwood Press, 1998.

# Index

AAA (American Automobile Association), 726
AAA Championship Trail Races, 485
AAFC. *See* All-American Football Conference
Aalto, Alvar, 23–24, 262
Abbott, Bud, 172, 203, 204*t*
Abbott, George, 151
Abbott, Senda Berenson, 87
ABC (American Broadcasting Company), **1–4**, 21, 183, 286, 287, 288, 459, 692
abstract expressionism, **4–8**, 7*t*–8*t*, 30
Academy of Motion Picture Arts and Sciences (AMPAS), 384
Acaro, Eddie, 391
*Action Comics*, 208, 664
Acuff, Roy, **8–10**, 9 (photo), 230
Adams, Ansel, 411, 510, 515, 516*t*
Adams, Frank David "Dooley," 392
Adams, Franklin Pierce, 568
Adrian, Gilbert, 313
*Adventures in Good Eating* (Hines, Duncan), 109–110, 588, 727
*The Adventures of Ichabod and Mr. Toad*, 276
advertising, 5, **11–15**, 37, 75, 121

automobile, 52
baseball and, 77
*Citizen Kane* and, 174
Coca-Cola, 107
design, 263
fashion and, 321
grocery stores and, 366, 367
on *The Howdy Doody Show*, 400–401
on *The Jack Benny Program*, 419
jukeboxes, 429–430
*Kraft Television Theatre* and, 438–439
lawns and, 447–448
on *The Lone Ranger*, 461
magazines and, 468
newspapers, 501
Pepsi-Cola, 107–108
radio and, 332
in *Seventeen*, 628
*Sexual Behavior in the Human Male* (Kinsey), 436
Spam, 659
stereotyping and, 538–539
war bonds, 753, 755
water skiing, 669
women's role in winning war, 336
to youth, 783

Advertising Council, 753
AEC. *See* Atomic Energy Commission
aerosol spray cans, 677
AFL. *See* American Federation of Labor
AFM. *See* American Federation of Musicians
AFR. *See* Armed Forces Radio
AGF. *See* Army Ground Forces
Airgraph, 510
Alajalov, Constantin, 405
Alison, Joan, 166
*All My Sons* (Miller, Arthur), 139 (photo)
*All the King's Men*, 278 (photo)
All-American Football Conference (AAFC), 349
All-American Girls Professional Baseball League, 78–79, 79t
Allen, Fred, 3
all-girl orchestras, **15–19**, 18t, 673
Almanac Singers, 333–334, 442–443
Almond Joy, 271
Almond ROCA Buttercrunch, 270
AMA. *See* American Medical Association
Amalgamated Clothing Workers, 47
Amateur Softball Association (ASA), 650
Ameche, Don, 482
America First Committee, 788
American Automobile Association. *See* AAA
American Bowling Congress, 128, 129
American Bricks, 711–712
American Broadcasting Company. *See* ABC
American Federation of Labor (AFL), 441, 443 (photo), 504–505
American Federation of Musicians (AFM), **40–41**, 91, 634–635, 674
American Jockey Club, 389
American Medical Association (AMA), 338
American Motorcycle Association, 488
American Newspaper Guild, 504–505

American Society of Composers, Authors, and Producers. *See* ASCAP
*The American Stud Book*, 389
American Theatre Wing, 139, 150
American Way, 392
AMI. *See* Automatic Music Instrument Company
*Amos 'n' Andy*, 550
AMPAS. *See* Academy of Motion Picture Arts and Sciences
*Anchors Aweigh*, 635
Anderson, Eddie, 418, 536
Anderson, Elmer "Elbows," 596
Anderson, Marian, 598
Anderson, Walter L., 322
Andrews, Dana, 187 (photo), 522
The Andrews Sisters, **19–21**, 19 (photo), 20t, 112, 124, 229, 249
Andriola, Alfred, 221–222
*Andy Hardy*, 172, 199t
Annenberg, Walter, 627–628
Annual Automotive Equipment Display and Hot Rod Exposition, 395
AP. *See* Associated Press
*Appalachian Spring* (Copland), 223, 616
*Apple Mary*, 216
Aquacade, 668–669
aqualung, 678
Arapaho Basin, 645
architecture, **22–28**, 263, 738
Argetsinger, Cameron, 486
Arlen, Harold, 408
Arlen, Michael, 244
Armed Forces Radio (AFR), 183, 453, 558
Armstrong, Edwin H., 330–333
Armstrong, Louis, 422, 423
Army Ground Forces (AGF), 777
Army Service Forces (ASF), 776
Arnheim, Gus, 247
Arnold, Eddy, 231
Arnold, Edward, 783
Arnold, Kenneth, 736

Arp, Jean (Hans), 262
Arriola, Gus, 214
*The Arrow*, 208
*Arsenic and Old Lace* (Kesselring), 139, 146–147
art, 4, 6, 30, 53, 404 (photo)
   *See also* abstract expressionism; design; illustrators; painting; sculpture
*Arthur Godfrey Time*, 359–360
*The Arthur Murray Party*, 288
*Artists for Victory*, 29
Artzybasheff, Boris, 405
"As Time Goes By," 168–169
ASA. *See* Amateur Softball Association
ASCAP v. BMI, **32**, **37–40**, 674
Asch, Moses, 334
ASF. *See* Army Service Forces
Assault, 391
Associated Press (AP), 505, 509
Astaire, Fred, 249, 253–254, 496, 499, 538, 774
Astor, Mary, 118 (photo)
Atherton, John C., 527
atomic bomb, 24, **42–46**, 44 (photo), 63*t*, 466, 474, 581, 678, 731–732, 744, 792–793
   Hayworth, Rita, on, 309, 453
   *New Yorker* and, 473
   newspapers and, 503–504
   Soviet Union and, 45–46, 179–180, 191, 733, 798
   technology, 191
Atomic Energy Commission (AEC), 45
Atwater, Edith, 139
Auerbach, Artie, 418
Austin, Gene, 249
automated streetlights, 678
Automatic Music Instrument Company (AMI), 427
automatic washer, 678
automobiles, 13–14, **46–53**, 48*t*, 49*t*, 74, 720–721
   postwar demand for, 723
   sales and travel, 726*t*

Autry, Gene, 25, **53–61**, 57*t*, 170, 223, 231, 547, 769
Avedon, Richard, 514–515
Avery, Milton, 5
Avery, Sewell, 189
Avery, Tex, 166
aviation, **61–70**, 63*t*–65*t*, 68*t*–69*t*, 721, 724–725
   jet, 682
   *See also* Berlin airlift
Axis Sally, **70–72**
Ayers, E. Duran, 540

B. H. Wragge Company, 321
*Babes on Broadway*, 496
baby boom, **73–76**
   education and, 75, 297
   fast food and, 323
   movies and, 491
   suburbanization and, 455
Bacall, Lauren, 120–121, 122
*The Bachelor and the Bobby-Soxer*, 306, 783
*Back at the Front*, 532
*Bad Boy*, 495
Baer, Buddy, 131, 463
Baker, George, 214
Balanchine, George, 255, 256
Ballew, Smith, 54
ballpoint pen, 678
*Bambi*, 275
Banks, Henry, 485
barbecues, 342
Barbera, Joe, 165–166
Barfield, Johnny, 124
*Barnaby* (Johnson, Crockett), 215
*Barney Google* (De Beck), 392
Barris, Harry, 247
Barrymore, Lionel, 199, 413
Baruch, Bernard, 188
baseball, **76–82**, 81*t*, 184, 345, 478, 789
   television, 697
   Triple Crown, 391
   war bonds and, 757

Basie, Count, 17, **82–85**, 82 (photo), 84*t*, 419
basketball, **85–88**, 363
Baskett, James, 520
Baskin, Burton, 325
Baskin-Robbins, 272, 325
*Batman*, 208
Battle of the Bulge, 534, 792
*Battle of Waterloo Road* (Capa), 511
Battleship, 355
*Bazooka Joe*, 310
Beard, James, 112, 342, 343
*The Beast with Five Fingers*, 386 (photo)
bebop (bop), 84, **88–92**, 194, 420, 591
Beemer, Brace, 459 (photo), 460
Begley, Ed, 242, 537
Bell, Benny, 48
Bell and Howell Company, 730
*Belle of the Yukon*, 630
Belluschi, Pietro, 23, 26
Belmont Stakes, 390
Beneke, Tex, 481, 676
Bennett, Joan, 518
Bennett, Robert Russell, 758
Benny, Jack, 196, 417–419, 550 (photo)
Benso, Catherine, 747
Benson, Sally, 271
Berg, Patty, 363
Bergen, Edgar, 291–293, 292 (photo), 552
Berger, Bob, 784
Bergman, Ingrid, 167, 167 (photo)
Berkeley, Busby, 254, 482
Berle, Milton, 2, 255, 259, 426, 644, **705–707**, 706 (photo)
Berlin, Irving, 56, 151, 156, 249, 496, 587, 619, 648, 657, **773–775**, 790
Berlin airlift, **93–95**, 190, 796–797
Bernhardt, Sarah, 525
Bernstein, Artie, 420
Bernstein, Leonard, 183, 184
Berry Brothers, 255
Bertoia, Harry, 265
Best, Willie, 384

best sellers (books), **95–97**, 98*t*–103*t*, 125, 435–437, 506, 660–661
Best Western, 729
*The Best Years of Our Lives*, **97, 104–106**, 104 (photo), 105 (photo), 176, 281, 414, 520
Betz, Pauline, 701
*The Beulah Show*, 536
beverages, 11, **106–113**, 159, 579
*Beyond Glory*, 494–495
Big Little Books, 207
*The Big Sleep*, 121
*Big Town*, 507
Bigelow, Ruth, 111
Biggers, Earl Derr, 241–242, 537
bikini, 45, 317, 670–671
*Billboard*, 591
*Billy the Kid* (Copland), 223
Birdland, 92
Birds Eye, 350
Birdseye, Clarence, 349–350
birth rates, 73–74, 74*t*
Bisquick, 268
*Black, Brown and Beige* (Ellington), 302–303
Black, Johnny S., 41
black market, **113–115**, 445, 578, 580
food, 114, 340, 341
grocery stores and, 366
blackouts/brownouts/dim-outs, **115–117**, 177, 578
Blake, Eurbie, 193
Blanc, Mel, 418, 425
Blanchard, Doc, 347
Blitzstein, Marc, 183
Block, Martin, 559 (photo)
*Blockade*, 517
*Blondie*, 172, 201–202, 201*t*, 214 (photo), 216, 218
blood transfusions, 372
*The Blue Ghost: A Photographic Log and Personal Narrative of the Aircraft Carrier U.S.S. Lexington in Combat Operation* (Steichen), 509

Blue Grass Boys, 232
blue jeans, 319
BMI v. ASCAP, **32**, **37–40**, 674
BMP. *See* Bureau of Motion Pictures
*The Bob Hope Show*, 382
bobby-soxers, 306, 320, 633–634, 782, 783
Boettiger, Anna Roosevelt, 599
Bogart, Humphrey, **117–123**, 118 (photo), 119*t*, 167, 167 (photo)
Bohannon, David Dewey, 25
BOMC. *See* Book-of-the-Month Club
Bonavita, Rosina, 606
Bonneville Salt Flats, 395, 484, 486–487
Bonney, Betty, 78
boogie-woogie, 15, 21, **123–125**, 591
book clubs, 97, **125–127**, 451
Book-of-the-Month Club (BOMC), 125
Borglum, Gutzon, 613
*Born Free and Equal* (Adams, Ansel), 411
Bosch, Carl, 448
*Boston Blackie*, 240–241, 241*t*
Boston Symphony Orchestra, 185
Boswell Sisters, 20
Boulanger, Nadia, 223
Bourke-White, Margaret, 511, 512*t*
Bow, Clara, 669
Bowery Boys, 205, 206*t*
Bowes, Edward, 288, 632
bowling, **127–129**, 449, 697
boxing, **129–134**, 462–464, 697
*The Boy with Green Hair*, 521
Boyce, Westray Battle, 777
Boyd, Edward F., 109
Boyd, William (Hopalong Cassidy), 25, 58, **134–138**, 137*t*–138*t*, 769
Boyle, Jack, 240–241
Bracken, Eddie, 196
Braddock, James J., 462
Bradley, Will, 124
Brashun, Midge "Tuffy," 595 (photo), 596
*Bread and Butter Magazine*, 577

Brecht, Bertolt, 398
Breger, Dave, 214
Brennan, Francis E. (Hank), 526
Breuer, Marcel, 24, 27
*The Brick Foxhole* (Brooks, Richard), 520
bridge, 353–354, 449
Brimsek, Frank, 380
*Bringing Up Father* (McManus), 215
Briskin, Samuel J., 414
British Open Championship, 361
Broad Hollow Steeplechase Handicap, 392
Broadcast Music Incorporated. *See* BMI
*Broadway Melody of 1940*, 496
Broadway shows
    comedy and drama, **138–145**, 141*t*–145*t*
    musicals, **148–156**, 152*t*–155*t*, 256, 798
    *See also specific shows*
Brook National Steeplechase Handicap, 392
Brooks, Richard, 520
Brown, Edward, Jr., 284
Brown, Johnny Mack, 54
Brown, Les, 78, 674–675
Brown & Haley Candy Company, 269, 270
*Brown v. Board of Education*, 541
Bruce, Nigel, 240
Brunot, James, 356, 452
bubble gum, 309–310
*Bud Abbott and Lou Costello Meet Frankenstein*, 386
Budge, Don, 699–700
Built-Rite Toys, 709
Bunshaft, Gordon, 24
Bureau of Motion Pictures (BMP), 762
Burnett, Murray, 166
Burnette, Smiley, 55
Burns, Bob "The Arkansas Traveler," 310, 311, 424
Burns, Ralph, 421–422
Bush, Vannevar, 42

Button, Richard "Dick," 639, 640
Buttram, Pat, 55–56
Butts, Alfred, 356, 452
Byrnes, James F., 743
Byron, Robert "Red," 487

C. A. Swanson and Sons, 351
CAA. *See* Civil Aeronautics Administration
*Cabin in the Sky* (Duke), 149, 304
Cadet Nurse Corps, 371
Cagney, James, 494
Calder, Alexander, 613–614
*Call Me Mister*, 156
Calloway, Cab, 306, 306 (photo), 310
Calvert, John, 244
canasta, 354
Candoli, Pete, 422
Candy Land, 356
Caniff, Milton, 222, **702–705**
canteens, 12, 21, 109, 139, **157–161**, 305
    teen, 433
Cantor, Eddie, 12, 373, 629–630
CAP. *See* Civil Air Patrol
Capa, Robert, 511, 512*t*
Capitol Records, 194
Capp, Al, 214, 218, 307
Capra, Frank, 413–415, 763
*The Captain and the Kids*, 215
*Captain Video*, 288
Carl's Jr., 322
Carney, Don, 547
Carson, Jack, 158 (photo)
Carson, Rachel, 372
Carvel Ice Cream Company, 272
*Casablanca*, 106, 120, **166–169**, 167 (photo), 176
*Casey, Crime Photographer*, 507
*The Catholic Hour*, 584
Catlett, Sid, 423
*Cavalcade of Stars*, 287–288, 287 (photo)
CBS (Columbia Broadcasting System), 1, 37, 136, 184, 286, 287, 692

CCA. *See* Comics Code Authority
CCC. *See* Civilian Conservation Corps
CDC. *See* Centers for Disease Control and Prevention
Centers for Disease Control and Prevention (CDC), 374
Central Intelligence Agency (CIA), 189, 795
Cerdan, Marcel, 131
Chain, Ernst, 371
"A Challenge to American Sportsmanship" (Roosevelt, E.), 598
*The Chamber Music Society of Lower Basin Street*, 629, 630
Chambers, Whittaker, 192
Champion, Gower, 151, 259
Champion, Marge, 259
Chandler, Raymond, 121
Chaplin, Charlie, 170, 518
Chapman, Ceil, 318
Charles, Ezzard, 132*t*, 464
*Charlie Chan*, 241–242, 242*t*, 537
Charlie McCarthy, 291–293, 292 (photo), 552
Charteris, Leslie, 243
Chase, Mary, 147
Chatterton, George Edward, 308
Cheret, Jules, 525
Chiang Kai-shek, 190–191, 733
Chicago Roller Skate Company, 642
Chicago Symphony Orchestra, 185–186
Chicago World Fair, 649
child care centers, 599
"Chiquita Banana," 344
Christian, Charlie, 420, 421
Christian, Sara, 487
Christie, Agatha, 96
"The Christmas Song," 195
Christy, June, 422
Chrysler, 46, 50*t*
Churchill, Henry, 25, 601 (photo), 603
Churchill, Winston, 187, 188, 794
Chutes and Ladders, 355
CIA. *See* Central Intelligence Agency

CIO. *See* Congress of Industrial Organizations
Cisco Kid, 772
Citation, 391
*Citizen Kane*, **173–176**, 174 (photo), 355 (photo)
Civil Aeronautics Administration (CAA), 66*t*
Civil Air Patrol (CAP), 178
civil defense, 116, **176–180**, 191
    youth and, 430–431
Civil War, 618
Civilian Conservation Corps (CCC), 447
Civilian Defense Corps, 178
Civilian Public Service (CPS), 618
Clark, Joel Bennett, 358
Clark, Tom, 433
classical music, **180–186**, 222–226, 273–274
    lacking copyright protection, 460
    radio and, 181, 185*t*, 332, 561–562
Clay, Lucius, 93, 298 (photo)
Cleveland Orchestra, 185, 186
Clifton, Nathaniel "Sweetwater," 87, 535
Clue, 357
Coachman, Alice, 535
*Coast-to-Coast on a Bus*, 546–547
Coates, Robert, 4
Coca-Cola, 11, 107–109, 299
Cochran, Jacqueline, 778
*A Code of Wartime Practices for the American Press*, 503
coin collecting, 376–377, 662–663
Cold War, 46, 69*t*, 93, 179, **187–193**, 277, 300, 397–399, 446, 474, 499, 519, 620, 733, 793
    movies and, 492–493
    newspapers and, 504
    *See also* Soviet Union
*The Cold War* (Lippmann), 188
Cole, Nat King, 52, **193–196**
Colley, Sarah Ophelia, 230–231
Collins, Ted, 646
Collyer, Bud, 476 (photo)

Columbia Broadcasting Company. *See* CBS
Columbia Records, 83, 184
*The Columbia Symphony Orchestra*, 184
comic books and strips, 25, 52, **207–213**, 210*t*–211*t*, **213–222**, 217*t*–218*t*, 219*t*, 220*t*–221*t*, 307, 460, 702
    atomic bomb in, 44, 45
    boxing, 133
    horse racing and, 392
    juvenile delinquency and, 212, 432–433
    scrap drives, 610
    serial films and, 623
    stereotyping in, 537
    youth and, 782
Comics Code Authority (CCA), 433
Comingore, Dorothy, 175, 355 (photo)
*The Common Sense Book of Baby and Child Care* (Spock), 660–661
Community Facilities Grants, 599
computers, 678–679, 680, 794
Condon, Eddie, 423
Congress of Industrial Organizations (CIO), 441, 446, 504–505
Conn, Billy, 131, 463
conscientious objectors (COs), 587, 618
Consolidated Edison Company, 443 (photo)
Constant Comment, 111
Conway, Tom, 244
Cook, Willa Worthington McGuire, 670
*Cook It Outdoors* (Beard), 342
Cooke, Sarah Palfrey, 701
Cooper, Charles "Chuck," 87, 535
Cooper, Gary, 319
Cooper, Jackie, 200
Cootie, 356
Coplan, Aaron, 181, 183, **222–226**, 224 (photo), 256, 616
Coppertone, 687
Corley, Bob, 536
Cornell, Joseph, 614–615
Correll, Charles, 536, 550

cortisone, 679
COs. *See* conscientious objectors
Costello, Lou, 172, 203, 204t
Cotton Club, 301
Council of National Defense, 36
Count Fleet, 391
country music, 8, 38, 55, **229–236**, 258
Cousy, Bob, 87
*Cover Girl*, 309
CPS. *See* Civilian Public Service
Crain, Jeanne, 521
Cranbrook Academy of Art, 262
Crawford, Broderick, 278 (photo)
Crawford, Joan, 54, 313
Crazy Horse (Chief), 613
*The Crimson Avenger*, 208
Crocker, Betty, 268, 340
Crockett, Johnson, 215
Crosby, Bing, 2, 10, 19 (photo), 21, 40, 111, 202–203, 229, **246–251**, 247 (photo), 248t, 276, 382 (photo), 383, 424, 437, 496, 538, 774
  golf and, 361 (photo), 363
  top-rated songs performed by, 250t
Crosley automobiles, **251–252**
Cross, Milton, 546–547
*Crossfire*, 281, 520
*Crusade in Europe* (Eisenhower, D.), 300
Culinary Institute of America, 590
Cummings, Robert, 408
Cunningham, Briggs, 486
Cunningham, Imogen, 515
Cureton, Thomas K., 370
Curtiz, Michael, 167
cybernetics, 679
Cypress Gardens, 669–670

Daffan, Ted, 234
Dailey, Dan, 156
Dairy Queen, 272, 324
Dale, Virginia, 538
Dameron, Tadd, 91
dance, 39, 150, **253–259**, 496
*Dance Index*, 615

DAR. *See* Daughters of the Revolution
*Dark Legend* (Wertham), 432
*A Date with Judy*, 483
Daughters of the Revolution (DAR), 598
Davidson, Jo, 613
Davies, Marion, 175
Davis, Bette, 158 (photo)
Davis, Elmer, 511, 762
Davis, Miles, 91
Davis, Sammy, Jr., 255–256
Day, Dennis, 418
Day, Doris, 19, 675
Day, Dorothy, 779–780
Day, Ned, 129
Daytona 500, 488
D-Day, **259–261**, 260 (photo), 299, 372, 480
DDT, 372, 680
de Graff, Robert, 96
de Mille, Agnes, 151, 223, 256 (photo), 256
*Dead End Kids*, 205, 206t, 432
*Death of a Salesman* (Miller, Arthur), 146
DeBeck, Billy, 392
Defense Savings Stamps, 752–753
Dell, Gabriel, 205
DeMille, Cecil B., 134, 228
Department of Defense, 189
design, 13, 23, **261–267**, 456
desserts/candy/ice cream, **267–273**
DeSylva, Buddy, 194
*Detective Comics*, 208
Dewey, Thomas E., 733
Dexter, Al, 233–234
Diamond, David, 182
*Dick Tracy*, 221–222, 246
Dies, Martin, Jr., 397
Dies Committee, 397
Dietrich, Marlene, 740 (photo)
Dietz, Howard, 156
DiMaggio, Joe, 78, 559 (photo)
"Dinah," 629
*The Dinah Shore Show*, 629, 631
Dior, Christian, 313, 317–318

Dirks, Rudolph, 165–166
Disney, Walt, 161–163, **273–277**, 274 (photo)
    *See also* Walt Disney
Dix, Dorothy, 507
Dixon, Lee, 256 (photo)
DNA, 680
Dobson, Harmon, 324
Doby, Larry, 80, 535
do-it-yourself tasks, 377–378
Dole, Charles, 644–645
Dollar Book Club, 125
dolls, 712–713
*Donald Duck*, 275, 277, 320
*The Dooleys Play Ball* (Renick), 651
Dorsey, Tommy, 124, 559 (photo), 633–634
Doubleday & Company, 125
Dowd, Elwood P., 147
*Down Argentina Way*, 481–482
Doyle, Arthur Conan, 239–240
Doyle, Geraldine Hoff, 606
draft. *See* Selective Training and Service Act of 1940
drag racing, 52, **393–397**
*Dragnet*, 546
*Dragstrip Girl*, 396
Drew, Charles, 372
Dreyfuss, Henry, 261, 262, 267
Driscoll, Bobby, 520
drive-ins, 53, **282–286**
    banks, **285–286**
    theaters, **282–285**, 283 (photo)
Duff, Howard, 544
Duke, Vernon, 149, 304
DuMont network, **286–289**
Duncan, Isadora, 257
Dunkin' Donuts, 324
DuPont, Margaret Osbourne, 701
DuPont Chemical Company, 315, 349–350
Durante, Jimmy, 635
Durham, Eddie, 17–18, 83
*Dust Bowl Ballads* (Guthrie), 333
Dykstra, Clarence, 619–620

Eames, Charles, 26, 262, 265
Eames, Ray, 26, 262, 265
Earl, Harley, 266–267
*East Side Kids*, 205, 206t
Eastman, George, 510
Eastman, Joseph B., 722
Eastman Kodak Company, 376, 510, 730
Eberle, Ray, 479
*Ebony*, 538
EC Comics, 212
Eckstine, Billy, 89, 90
*The Ed Sullivan Show*, 708
*The Eddie Cantor Show*, 630
Eddy, Nelson, 183
Ederle, Gertrude, 669
*Edgar Bergen/Charlie McCarthy Show*, **291–293**, 552
*Edible Wild Plants of Eastern North America* (Kinsey), 344
Edison, Harry, 84
Edison, Thomas, 427
education, 14, 85, **293–298**, 358
    baby boom and, 75, 297
    film as tool for, 338
    health, 336 (photo)
    Japanese American fund for, 412
    money for college, 74
    physical, 370
    radio, **555–557**, 557t
    sex behavior and, 436
Edward B. Marks Music Company, 38
Edwards, James, 522
Edwards, John Paul, 515
*Eerie*, 211–212
Eichler, Joseph, 26
Einstein, Albert, 42
Eisenhower, Dwight D., 108, 259, **298–300**, 298 (photo), 534
    fashion and, 299, 311, 313
Eisenhower, Milton S., 409–411
Eldred, William T., 644
Eldridge, Roy, 421
Ellington, Duke, 91, **300–304**, 301 (photo), 303t, 306

Elliott, Bill, 772
Ellison, James "Jimmy," 136
Elman, Dave, 375, 376
Emde, Floyd, 488
Emergency Price Control Act, 576
Emergency Rescue Committee, 597
Emerson, Faye, 779–780
Erector Sets, 712
*Escape*, 518, 555
Espionage Act, 503
*Esquire*, 308–309, 407–408, 469
*Etiquette* (Post), 506
Evans, Dale, 58, 60, 547
Evans, Redd, 606
Evans, Walker, 511, 512*t*, 514
*Everybody Comes to Rick's* (Burnett & Alison), 166
Ewell, Tom, 532
Exner, Virgil, 48, 266

Fadiman, Clifton, 568
fads, **305–312**, 320
Fair Employment Practices Committee (FEPC), 535–536, 598, 620
Fairbanks, Mabel, 638–639
Fairfax, Beatrice, 507
*The Falcon*, 244, 244*t*
Falk, Lee, 537
*Famous Funnies*, 207
*Fanfare for the Common Man* (Copland), 225
*Fantasia*, 162–163, 180, 273–274
FAP. *See* Federal Arts Project
*Faraway Hill*, 288
Farley, James A., 601
Farm Security Administration (FSA), 514
fashion, 263, **312–321**, 611
  atomic bomb and, 45
  Eisenhower, D., 299, 311, 313
  Miranda, Carmen, 482 (photo), 484
  photography, 514–515
  *Seventeen* and, 627
  youth, 319–320, 785
fast food, **321–325**, 336, 590
*The Fat Man*, 544

Fatool, Nick, 420–421
Faulkner, William, 120, 121, 521
Faye, Alice, 482, 496
FBI. *See* Federal Bureau of Investigation
FCC. *See* Federal Communications Commission
Federal Arts Project (FAP), 29, 115 (photo), 525–526
federal budget, 787
Federal Bureau of Investigation (FBI), 411
Federal Communications Commission (FCC), 1, 331, 693, 694, 748
Federal Housing Authority (FHA), 455
Federal Interagency Committee, 450
Federal Security Agency (FSA), 336–337
Federal Theatre Project (FTP), 139
Federal-Aid Highway Act, 723, 729–730
Feller, Bob, 77–78
Fellig, Arthur. *See* Weegee
Fender solid-body electric guitar, 680
FEPC. *See* Fair Employment Practices Committee
Fermi, Enrico, 43
Ferrer, Mel, 521
Field, W. C., 292
Finegan, Bill, 39
*The Fireball*, 596
First Motion Picture Unit of United States Army Air Forces, 66
*The First Nighter Program*, 553
Fischer, Leo, 649
Fisher, M. F. K., 268
Fisher-Price, 711
fishing, 449
Fitzgerald, Ella, 19
Flagg, James Montgomery, 527
Flaherty, Robert, 14
Flanders, Charles, 460
Flatt, Lester, 232
Fleer Chewing Gum Company, 309
Fleischer, Max, 163
Fleming, Alexander, 371

Flock, Truman Fontell "Fonty," 487
Florey, Howard, 371
fluoridation, 680–681
FM radio, **330–333**, 332*t*, 556, 693
FNB. *See* Food and Nutrition Board
Fogarty, Anne, 318
Foggy Mountain Boys, 232
Foley, Clyde "Red," 231
folk music, **333–335**
   labor unrest and, 442–443
Folkway Records, 334
*Follow the Band*, 606–607
*Follow the Boys*, 630
Fonda, Henry, 517
food, 93, 150, **335–345**, 361, 364–367
   black market, 114, 340, 341
   fast, **321–325**, 336, 590
   frozen, 339, **349–351**, 367, 681–682
   health and, 369
   posters, 526 (photo)
   rationing, 339–342, 579–580, 589
   *See also* beverages; desserts/candy/
     ice cream
Food and Drug Act of 1938, 371
Food and Nutrition Board (FNB), 337, 370
football, 81, **345–349**, 478, 697
   war bonds and, 757
Ford, Gerald, 72
Ford, John, 773
Ford, Ruth VanSickle, 531
Ford Corporation, 46, 47 (photo), 50*t*–51*t*, 67, 721
*Foreign Correspondent*, 518
*Fortune*, 469, 514
Foster, Dan, 489
Foster, Stephen, 39
Fouilhoux, Jacques-Andre, 261
*Four Sons*, 518
France, William "Bill," 487, 488
franchising, 323–324
Fraser, Gretchen, 645
Fraser, James Earle, 612
Frazee, Jane, 607
Frisbee, 452, 681, 716

*From Here to Eternity*, 636–637
frozen food, **349–351**, 367
   complete meal, 351, 681–682
FSA. *See* Farm Security Administration; Federal Security Agency
FTP. *See* Federal Theatre Project
*Der Fuehrer's Face*, 161–162, 275, 425
Fulbright, J. William, 297
Fulks, Joe, 87
Fuller, Charles E., 584–585
Fuller, Mary, 622
Fuller, Paul M., 428, 429
*Fun and Fancy Free*, 276
*Funnies on Parade*, 207
*Funny Pages*, 208

Gable, Clark, 318
Gaines, William M., 212
games, **353–357**, 449
*Gang Busters*, 543
*The Gang's All Here*, 482
Garbo, Greta, 313
Gardner, Ava, 309, 453
Gardner, Erle Stanley, 96
Garfield, John, 158 (photo)
Garland, Judy, 496
*Gasoline Alley* (King, Frank), 52, 214, 393
Gaynor, Charles, 156
Gebhard, Paul, 435
GED (General Equivalency Diploma), 295
Geddes, Norman Bel, 261, 262, 721
General Electric Company, 45
General Equivalency Diploma. *See* GED
General Foods Company, 349–350
General Maximum Price Regulations, 576
General Motors, 46, 51*t*, 721
*Gentleman's Agreement*, 281
*The Ghost Breakers*, 384
GI Bill (Servicemen's Readjustment Act of 1944), 25, 74, 86, 106, 284, 296, **357–359**, 791
   suburbanization and, 455

Gibson, Althea, 535
Gibson, Walter B., 476–477, 663–664
Gilbert, Peggy, 15–16
Gilbert, Ronnie, 334
Gillars, Mildred, 70–72
Gillespie, John Birks "Dizzy," 89, 89 (photo), 91, 92, 422
Girard, Alexander H., 263
Giuffre, Jimmy, 92
*The Glass Key*, 326 (photo)
*The Glass Menagerie* (Williams, Tennessee), 146
Gleason, Jackie, 259, 287–288, 287 (photo)
*Glory for Me* (Kantor), 97, 104
GNP. *See* gross national product
*Go for Broke*, 412
GOC. *See* Ground Observer Corps
"God Bless America," 587, 648
Goddard, Paulette, 254, 384
Godfrey, Arthur, **359–360**
Gold, Bill, 529
Goldberg, Rube, 270
golf, **360–364**, 362t, 364t, 452
   Crosby and, 361 (photo), 363
   Louis, Joe, and, 363
Gonzales, Pancho, 700
Goodman, Benny, 10, 16, 92, 182, 225, 419–420
Goosens, Eugene, 183
Gorcey, Leo, 205
Gordon, Dorothy, 431–432
Gordon, Ruth, 139
Gosden, Freeman, 536, 550
Gould, Chester, 221–222, 246
Gould, Morton, 181–182
Grable, Betty, 156, 309, 310, 404 (photo), 453, 482
Graham, Billy, 437, 584, 585–586
Graham, Martha, 223, 256–257, 615–616
Grahame, Kenneth, 274
*Grand Ole Opry*, 229–235
Grant, Cary, 199, 306, 507, 507 (photo), 761, 783

Graves, Jackie, 133
Gray, Harold, 214
Grayson, Carl, 425
Grayson, Kathryn, 635
Graziano, Rocky, 129, 131, 132t, 133
"The Greatest Gift" (Stern), 413
Green, Johnny, 420
Green, William, 441
*The Green Hornet*, 208, 460
Greenberg, Clement, 5, 6
Greenberg, Hank, 77–78
*Greenwich Village*, 482–483
Greyhound Bus Company, 723
Griffith, Clark, 77
Griswold, Frank, Jr., 486
grocery stores/supermarkets, 113, 338, **364–367**, 365 (photo)
Groebli, Werner, 640
Grofe, Ferde, 183
Gropius, Walter, 24
gross national product (GNP), 787
Grotell, Majlis (Maija), 266
Ground Observer Corps (GOC), 178–179
Groves, Leslie R., 42, 373
Guarnieri, Johnny, 420
Guertin, M. K., 728–729
Gustavson, Paul, 208
Guthrie, Woody, 333, 442–443

Haber, Fritz, 448
Hall, Huntz, 205
Hallaren, Mary A., 777
Halop, Billy, 205
Hammerstein, Oscar, III, 149, 151, 156, 256 (photo)
Hammett, Dashiell, 544
Hammond, John, 83, 124
Hampton, Lionel, 420
Hancock, A. G., 670
Handy, George, 422
Hanna, William "Bill," 165–166
Hansen, Howard, 182
Harding, Ann, 783
Hardy, Oliver, 205

Hargrove, Marion, 619
Harley-Davidson, 488
Harman, Fred, 537
*Harper's Bazaar*, 515
Harriman, W. Averell, 188, 644
Harris, Bill, 422
Harris, Harwell H., 26
Harris, Joel Chandler, 276
Harris, John H., 640
Harris, Roy, 181
Harrison, Wallace K., 23, 261
Hart, Lorenz, 149
Hartley, Fred, 445
Harvest Show, 747
*Harvey* (Chase), 147
Haskell, William N., 177
Haugdahl, Sig, 487
Hawkins, Coleman, 420
Hawks, Howard, 120
Hayden, Russell, 136
Hayes, Clancy, 423
Hayes, George "Gabby," 58, 136
Hayes, Helen, 139
Haymes, Dick, 19, 40, 41
Hays, Lee, 333–334, 442–443
Hayworth, Rita, 254, 309
    on atomic bomb, 309, 453
Head, Howard, 645
health, **369–374**
Hearst, William Randolph, 173–179
Heatter, Gabriel, 477
*Hedda Hopper Show*, 506
Hefti, Neal, 421–422
Heggen, Thomas, 147
Hellerman, Fred, 334
*Help Your Doctor Help You*, 369
Hemingway, Ernest, 120
Henderson, Fletcher, 420
Henie, Sonja, 638, 640, 644
*Henry Aldrich*, 199–200, 200*t*
Herlihy, Ed, 439
Herman, Woody, 92, 421–422, 423
Herman Miller Company, 264, 265
Herriman, George, 215
Herrmann, Bernard, 175–176

Hersey, John, 473
Hershey, Lewis, 620
Hershey Corporation, 269–270
*The Hidden Persuaders* (Packard), 14
*High Sierra*, 118
Hill, George Washington, 13
Hill-Burton Act of 1946, 371
Hillman, Sidney, 47
Hines, Duncan, 109–110, 588, 727
Hines, Earl, 89
Hirohito (Emperor), 48, 467
*His Girl Friday*, 507, 507 (photo)
Hiss, Alger, 192, 798
Hitchcock, Alfred, 518
Hitler, Adolph, 425, 518, 743
Ho Chi Minh, 190
hobbies, **375–379**
    Roosevelt, Franklin Delano, 601
*Hobbies*, 375
Hobby, Oveta Culp, 776
*Hobby Lobby*, 375
hockey, **379–381**, 640
Hoffman, Hans, 4
Hogan, Ben, 361, 362
Holgate Toy Company, 711
*Holiday*, 729
Holiday, Billie, 83, 423
*Holiday Inn*, 249, 496, 538, 657, 774
Holiday on Ice, 640
Hollingshead, Richard, Jr., 282–283
Hollywood Canteen, 159, 183, 742
Hollywood Cavalcade, 757
*Hollywood Hotel*, 506
Hollywood Production Code, 517
Hollywood Ten, 398–399, 398*t*, 492, 525
*Hollywood Victory Caravan*, 757
Holman, Bill, 735
*Home Country* (Pyle), 530
*Home of the Brave*, 521–522
*Home Sweet Home*, 71
Hoosier Hot Shots, 231
Hoover, Herbert, 354, 465
Hope, Bob, 196, 202, 248, 363, **381–385**, 382 (photo), 383*t*–384*t*

Hormel, George A., 658
Hormel Foods Corporation, 657–660
Horn, Ted, 486
Horne, Lena, 521
*Hors d'Oeuvres and Canapés* (Beard), 343
horse racing, **389–393**
Horwitt, Arnold B., 156
*Hot Rod*, 394 (photo)
hot rods, 52, 312, 379, **393–397**, 431, 682
Hour of Charm Orchestra, 16 (photo), 17
*House and Garden*, 448, 614
House Un-American Activities Committee (HUAC), 191–192, 277, **397–399**, 492, 504, 522, 524–525, 795
*How Green Was My Valley*, 173
*How to Cook a Wolf* (Fisher), 268
Howard, Charles S., 390
Howard Johnson's, 271, 325, 588–590
*The Howdy Doody Show*, 270, **400–401**, 401 (photo)
Howe, Louis, 601
HUAC. See House Un-American Activities Committee
Hubley Manufacturing Company, 709
Hull, Cordell, 605
Hull, Josephine, 139
Humes, Helen, 83
Hummert, Anne, 572
Hummert, Frank, 572
Humphrey, Doris, 257
Hungerford, Cyrus C., 528
hunting, 449
Hupfeld, Herman, 168–169
Hurt, Marlin, 536
Huston, John, 119, 121
Hutton, Ina Ray, 15, 16
Hutton, Marion, 479
Hutton, Robert, 783
Hyams, Marjorie, 15

*I Wanted Wings*, 315
Ibsen, Don, 669
Ice Capades, 640
Ice Follies, 640
Ickes, Harold L., 605
*Idiot's Delight*, 517
*If You Ask Me* (Roosevelt, E.), 599
"I'll Never Smile Again," 633
illiteracy, 295, 296
illustrators, **403–408**, 406$t$–407$t$, 526
  USO club, 740
  war bonds and, 758
Indian Motorcycle Company, 488
Indian Reorganization Act of 1934, 539
Indianapolis 500-Mile Race, 484, 485–486
Industrial Designers Institute, 266
*Information Please!*, 568
Ingram, Edgar W., 322
*Inner Sanctum Mysteries*, 554
In-N-Out Burger, 285, 323–324
INS (International News Service), 509
*Inside U.S.A.* (Schwartz & Dietz), 156
Institute of International Education, 297
International Confederation of Free Trade Unions, 446
*International Mobile* (Calder), 614
International News Service. See INS
International Skating Union (ISU), 638
International Sweethearts of Rhythm, 17, 18
internment camps (relocation centers), **408–413**, 410$t$, 539, 598, 604, 615, 789
*Intruder in the Dust*, 521
*The Iron Curtain*, 187 (photo), 522
Iroquois Steeplechase, 392
ISU. See International Skating Union
*It Happened in Brooklyn*, 635–636
*It's a Wonderful Life*, **413–415**
Ives, Burl, 151, 156, 334–335
Ives, Charles, 180–181

J. P. Seeburg Corporation, 428
Jack, Beau, 132$t$, 534
*The Jack Benny Program*, **417–419**, 536
Jaffe, Moe, 314
James, Henry, 633

James O. Welch Company, 271
Jameson, Betty, 363
*Janie*, 783
Jannus, Tony, 61
Japanese American Evacuation Claims Act, 412
*Japanese Relocation*, 410
jazz, 5, 39, 82, 88, 123, 193, 301, 304, **419–424**, 591
Jeep, 682
Jell-O, 200, 268–269, 419
Jenkins, David Abbott "Ab," 484
Jepson-Turner, Gladys Lyne, 639
*Jet*, 538
jigsaw puzzles, 355–356, 355 (photo), 449
jitterbug, 258, 305, 673 (photo)
job training, 74
*Joe and Asbestos* (Kling), 392, 537
John Gabel Manufacturing Company, 427
Johnson, John H., 538
Johnson, Pete, 123 (photo)
Johnson, Philip, 24, 27
Jolson, Al, 2
Jones, Bobby, 361
Jones, Isham, 421
Jones, Spike, 275, **424–426**
Jordan, Bobby, 205
Jordan, Louis, 592–593
*Joy Ride*, 396
"Juke Box Saturday Night," 428
jukeboxes, 229, **427–430**, 427 (photo), 480, 592
Jump, Larry, 645
*Jump for Joy* (Ellington), 303
Junior Mints, 271
juvenile delinquency, **430–434**, 784
   comic books and, 212, 432–433
   movies and, 432, 495

Kahn, Albert, 22–23, 261, 721
Kaiser, Edgar F., 599
Kane, Bob, 208
Kantor, MacKinlay, 97, 104

Kapp, Jack, 247
Karcher, Carl, 322
Karcher, Margaret, 322
Karloff, Boris, 243
Karns, Roscoe, 288–289
*The Katzenjammer Kids*, 215
Kayak II, 390
Kaye, Sammy, 568–569
Keefe, Mary Doyle, 607
Keeshan, Bob, 400
Kefauver, Estes, 799
Kelly, Gene, 253–254, 635, 636
Kelly, Joe, 569
Kelly, Walt, 215–216
Kennan, George F., 188, 189
Kenton, Stan, 422
Kentucky Derby, 390, 392
Kentucky Fried Chicken, 324
Kern, Jerome, 182, 381, 635
Kerry Drake, 221–222
Kesselring, Joseph, 139, 146–147
*Key Largo*, 122
Keys, Ancel Benjamin, 339
*Kid Boots*, 629
Kidd, Michael, 151
Kiefer, Adolph, 671
Kieran, John, 568
Kilroy, James J., 307
"Kilroy was here," 307–308, 308 (photo)
King, Andrea, 386 (photo)
King, Frank, 52, 214
King, Martin Luther, Jr., 541
King, Muriel, 316
King, Pee Wee, 233
King, Scott, 728
Kinsey, Alfred C., 344, **435–437**
Kinsey Institute for Research in Sex, Gender, and Reproduction, 435
Kirstein, Lincoln, 223
*Kiss Me Kate* (Porter, Cole & Abbott, George), 151
Klamfoth, Dick, 488
Klein, Evelyn Kaye, 17
Kling, Kenneth, 392, 537
Knoll, Florence Schust, 265

Knoll, Hans, 265
Knox, Alexander, 737
Knudsen, William S., 46
Koerner, Henry, 528
Kool-Aid, 111–112
Korean War, 467, 621, 734, 739, 799–800
Kostelanetz, Andre, 182–183, 184
Kracken, Jack, 462
*The Kraft Music Hall*, 248, 249, 424, 437, 774
*Kraft Television Theatre*, **437–439**
Kramer, Jack, 699, 700
*Krazy Kat* (Herriman), 215
Kroc, Ray, 323
Krupa, Gene, 421
Kubelsky, Benjamin, 417
Kubik, Gail, 183
Kyser, Kay, 568–569

La Guardia, Fiorello, 177, 216, 314
La Touche, John, 149
labor unrest, **441–446**, 504–505, 580, 732, 798
Ladd, Alan, 326 (photo), 494–495, 544
*Ladies Home Journal*, 455
Lake, Arthur, 201
Lake, Veronica, 315, 317, 326 (photo)
Lamarr, Hedy, 309, 310
LaMotta, Jake, 132*t*, 133
Lamour, Dorothy, 202, 382 (photo), 383
  war bonds and, 757
L'Amour, Louis, 135
Lampell, Millard, 333–334, 442–443
Land, Edwin, 376, 510
Landis, James M., 177
Lang, Fritz, 492
Lange, Dorothea, 411, 511, 512*t*, 514
Langley, Roger, 644
Lantz, Walter, 165
Lapidus, Morris, 263
Lapin, Aaron, 269
Lattimore, Owen, 799
Laurel, Stan, 205
Lautner, John, 263

lawns, lawnmowers, and fertilizers, **446–448**
Lawrence, Gertrude, 139
League of Nations, 737
*Leatherneck*, 396
Lee, Peggy, 19, 420
Lee, Russell, 514
leisure and recreation, 97, 348, **449–453**, 450*t*, 451*t*
Lembeck, Harvey, 532
*Lend an Ear* (Gaynor), 156
Lend-Lease Act, 575, 602–603
Lesnevich, Gus, 132*t*
*Let Us Now Praise Famous Men* (Evans, Walker), 514
Levitt, Abraham, 455–458
Levitt, Alfred, 455–456
Levitt, Helen, 511, 513*t*, 514
Levitt, William, 26, 455–458
Levittown, **453–458**, 457 (photo), 540
Levy, Julien, 614
Lewine, Richard, 156
Lewis, Fulton, Jr., 477–478
Lewis, Jerry, 205–206
Lewis, John L., 441, 444, 445, 580, 798
Leyvas, Henry, 540
Liberman, Alexander, 514
*Liberty*, 469
Liberty Films, 414
*Life*, 469, 509, 511
  rationing and, 580
*The Life and Times of the Shmoo*, 307
life expectancy, 369, 374, 787
*Life is Worth Living*, 288
*Life with Teena*, 628
*Lights Out*, 553
*Light-Up Time*, 635
*Li'l Abner* (Capp), 218, 307
Limiting Order L-85, 313, 314–315
Lincoln Logs, 711
Lionel Trains, 714–715
Lippmann, Walter, 188
Lipton Tea, 360
Liston, Melba, 15
Litchfield, Johnny, 645

Literary Guild, 125
*Little Annie Rooney*, 216
*Little Caesar*, 432
*Little Orphan Annie*, 216
"Little Steel Formula," 444
*Little Tokyo, U.S.A.*, 409
Little Tough Guys, 205, 206*t*
Livingstone, Mary, 418
Lloyd, Earl, 87, 535
Loeb, John Jacob, 606
Loewy, Raymond, 13, 48–49, 266, 721
Log Building Sets, 711
Lomax, Alan, 333
Lombard, Carole, 418
 war bonds and, 756–757
Lombardo, Carmen, 359–360
Lombardo, Guy, 489
*The Lone Ranger*, 208, **459–462**, 459 (photo), 461 (photo), 476, 537
*The Lone Wolf*, 245, 245*t*
Longden, Johnny, 391
*Look*, 455, 511
Looney Tunes, 164–165
Loring, Eugene, 223
*Lost Boundaries*, 521
*The Lost Weekend*, 282 (photo)
Louis, Joe, 129, 130–131, 130 (photo), 132*t*, **462–464**, 462 (photo), 535
 golf and, 363
 war bonds and, 757
*Louisiana Story*, 14
Lovejoy, Frank, 544
Lowther, George F., 665–666
Loy, Myrna, 105 (photo), 783
Luce, Henry, 469
Lucky Strikes, 12–13, 419, 635
Luke, Keye, 243
Lundigan, William, 521
*The Lux Radio theater*, 553
Lydon, Jimmy, 200
Lytle, Betty, 642

M. M. Cole Publishing Company, 38
MacArthur, Douglas, 298, **465–467**, 466 (photo), 467, 734, 739, 791

Macfadden, Bernarr, 469
Mack, Ted, 288
Mack, Walter S., 108
Macon, Uncle Dave, 9
MAD. *See* mutual assured destruction
"Magazine War Guide," 433
magazines, 12, 56, 96, 107, 125, 128, **468–473**, 471*t*–473*t*
 atomic bomb in, 43
 Berlin airlift in, 94
 celebrating black culture, 538
 Cold War and, 192
 gardening, 448
 lifestyle reporting, 511
 pinup girls in, 308–309
 pulp, 326, 543, 663
 skating and, 642
 Spam and, 658
 suburbanization and, 454, 455
 victory gardens and, 745
 war bonds and, 756
 youth and, 782
Magic 8-Ball, 715
Mainbocher, 314, 778
*Make Mine Manhattan* (Lewine & Horwitt), 156
*Make Mine Music*, 276
*Male Call*, 703–704
*The Maltese Falcon*, 118 (photo), 119
*The Man I Married*, 518
*The Man in the Gray Flannel Suit* (Wilson, Sloan), 319
*Mandrake the Magician* (Falk), 537
Mankiewicz, Herman J., 173
Manship, Paul, 612
Mao Zedong, 190–191
Marble, Alice, 699
March, Fredric, 104, 105 (photo), 520
*The March of Time*, 763–764
March on Washington Movement (MOWM), 535–536, 541
Marciano, Rocky, 464
margarine, 341
Marin, John, 5
Marine Corps Women's Reserve, 779

Marks, Sadye, 418
marriage, 73, 74t
Mars, Incorporated, 269–270
Marshall, George C., 108, 189, 298, 299, **474–475**
Marshall Plan, 189, 474–475, 732, 796
Martin, Clarice, 594
Martin, Clyde, 435
Martin, Dean, 205–206
Martin, Freddy, 39
Marvel Comics, 209
Marx, Groucho, 2–3, 204–205, 483, 569
Marx Brothers, 204–205
*Mary Kay and Johnny*, 288
Masters Tournament, 361
Mathews, Billy, 488
Mattel, 715–716
Mauch, Hans, 640
Mauldin, Bill, 504, **530–533**
Mauriello, Tami, 464
Maxson Food Systems, 351
May, Cliff, 26
Mays, Rex, 486
MBS. *See* Mutual
McAfee, Mildred, 778
*McCalls*, 316
McCardell, Claire, 317
McCarthy, Clem, 392
McCarthy, Joseph, 192, 225, 799
McConnell, Ed, 547
McCormack-Dick Committee, 397
McCrea, Joel, 518
McCullough, Alex, 324
McCullough, J. F., 324
McDaniel, Hattie, 536
McDonalds, 285, 322–323, 588–589
McGrane, Paul, 428
McKay, Bernie, 594
McKinley, Ray, 124, 481
McLuhan, Marshall, 14
McManus, George, 215
McNutt, Paul V., 336–337, 620
McPherson, Aimee Semple, 584
McShann, Jay, 592
Meany, George, 446

medicine, **369–374**
*Meet the Press*, 478
Mehrtens, Warren, 391
Mellett, Lowell, 762
Melodears, 16
*Melody Ranch*, 55–56, 547
*Melody Time*, 276
Menninger, Karl, 437
Menotti, Gian Carlo, 182
Mercer, Johnny, 194, 247 (photo), 408, 652 (photo)
Meredith, Burgess, 531, 614
Merman, Ethel, 148 (photo)
Merrie Melodies, 164–165
Merrill, Gretchen, 639
Metcalf, Nelson C., Jr., 12
Metro-Goldwyn-Mayer. *See* MGM
*Metronome*, 194
MGM (Metro-Goldwyn-Mayer), 165–166, 490
Mickey Mouse, 162, 212, 273, 320
microwave oven, 683
Mies van der Rohe, Ludwig, 23, 24, 26–27
Mikan, George, 87
Mike and Ike, 270
Milland, Ray, 282 (photo)
Miller, Ann, 254
Miller, Arthur, 139 (photo), 140, 146
Miller, Glenn, 12, 39, 420, 428, **479–481**, 479 (photo), 482, 559, 644, 676
Miller, J. Howard, 316–317, 528, 606
Miller, Johnny, 193
Mills Brothers, 41
Milton Bradley, 354, 355
Minton, Henry, 88
Minute Maid, 111, 350
*The Miracle of the Bells*, 636
Miranda, Carmen, **481–484**, 482 (photo), 496
*Mister Roberts* (Heggen), 147
Mitchell, Joan, 639
Mitchum, Robert, 531
Mix, Tom, 548

M&Ms, 270
mobile telephone, 683
model making, 378–379, 711
Modernaires, 479
Mohr, Gerald, 245
Molded Products, 709
Moline Pressed Steel Company, 709
Monogram Pictures, 205
Monopoly, 354, 449
Monroe, Bill, 231–232
Monroe, Rose Will, 607
Monroe Brothers, 231–232
*Montana Moon*, 54
Montgomery, Bob, 534
Montgomery, George, 631
*The Moon Is Down*, 519
Moore, Clayton, 461 (photo)
Moore, Oscar, 193
Moorehead, Agnes, 477
*The Moral Basis of Democracy* (Roosevelt, E.), 597–598
Moran, Gertrude, 701
Morgan, Henry, 2
Morgan, Julia, 175
Morgenthau, Henry, Jr., 751
Morris, Chester, 240–241
*The Mortal Storm*, 518
motels, 728
Moten, Bennie, 83
Motion Picture Alliance for the Production of American Ideals, 277
Motley, Marion, 535
*Motor Trend*, 395
motorcycle races, 488
motorsports, **484–490**
Mounds Bar, 270–271
Mount, William Sydney, 456
Mount Rushmore, 613
Mountain Dew, 112
movies, 2, 21, 57*t*, 59*t*–60*t*, 82, 84, 119*t*, 134, 137*t*–138*t*, 148, 159, 166–176, 181, 195, 202–203, 204*t*, 218, 223–224, 291–292, 299, 382–384, 383*t*–384*t*, 398, 417–418, 426, 449, 450, 461, 463–464, 477, 480–483, **490–493**, 494–495, 531–532, 630, 635–638, 636*t*, 648, 668–669
  anti-Communist, 187 (photo), 192, 399, 522
  atomic bomb, 44
  attendance, 491
  aviation, 66–67
  baby boom and, 491
  baseball, 76–77
  black market and, 114
  blacklisting and, 399, 492, 525
  boxing, 133–134
  cartoons, **161–166**, 701, 746
  children's, **169–173**, 171*t*–172*t*
  comedies, **196–206**, 197*t*–198*t*
  costume/spectacle, **226–229**, 227*t*–228*t*
  crime and mystery, 120, **236–246**, 237*t*–239*t*
  drama, **278–282**, 279*t*–281*t*
  drive-in, **282–285**, 283 (photo)
  as education tool, 338
  fashion in, 313
  film noir, 119–120, 122, 281, **325–330**, 327*t*, 328*t*–330*t*, 386–387
  football, 349
  golf, 362–363
  horror and thriller, **385–389**, 387*t*–389*t*
  horse racing, 392
  juvenile delinquency and, 432, 495
  labor unrest, 443
  monopoly, 491
  music and, 656
  musicals, **495–500**, 497*t*–499*t*
  newspapers and, 492, 501, 507
  nursing, 371
  package, 276
  pinup girl, 309
  political and propaganda, **517–525**, 523*t*–524*t*
  posters, 529
  race, 538
  racial intolerance in, 520–522
  Roller Derby, 596

Rosie the Riveter, 606–607
Selective Service and, 619, 761
serial, 172, **621–626**, 623t–624t
skating, 638–640, 641–642
skiing, 644
softball, 650
sound technology, 54, 495
stereotyping in, 537–538
swimming, 668–669
television and, 491, 695
UFO, 736
war, **759–767**, 765t–766t
war bonds and, 757
westerns, 25, 53–61, 134, 170, **767–773**, 770t–772t
youth and, 785
*See also specific movies*
MOWM. *See* March on Washington Movement
"Mr. Chad," 308
*Mr. Lucky*, 761
*Mr. Winkle Goes to War*, 761
*Mr. Wong, Detective*, 242–243
Mulford, Clarence, 134–135
Muller, Paul, 372
Mundy, Jimmy, 83
Murphy, Audie, **493–495**
Murphy, George, 156, 496
Murphy, Gerry, 596
Murphy, Turk, 423
Murray, Arthur, 258
Murray, Gerry, 595 (photo)
Murray, Kathryn, 258
Murray, Philip, 442, 446
Murrow, Edward R., 115, 562–563
Museum of Modern Art, 22
music, 258
　about conflict, 656–657
　atomic bomb and, 45
　baseball, 76
　movies and, 656
　popular, 654t–656t
　race records, 591
　radio, **558–562**
　Rosie the Riveter, 606

Selective Training and Service Act of 1940 and, 618–619
standards, 652, 656
*See also* classical music; *specific songs*
Mutual (Mutual Broadcasting System), 1, 37, 60, 85–86, 136, 348, 426, 459, **475–478**, 583, 585
mutual assured destruction (MAD), 191
"My Blue Heaven," 249
"My Day" (Roosevelt, E.), 598, 599

NAACP. *See* National Association for the Advancement of Colored People
Naismith, James, 85
NASCAR (National Association for Stock Car Auto Racing), 53, 395, 487
National Association for the Advancement of Colored People (NAACP), 372, 533–534, 620
*National Barn Dance*, 231
National Basketball Association (NBA), 86–88
National Broadcasting Company. *See* NBC
National Collegiate Athletic Association (NCAA), 85, 346
national debt, 787
National Education Association (NEA), 75
National Football League (NFL), 347, 348t, 349
National Hockey League (NHL), 380
National Hot Rod Association (NHRA), 395
National Japanese American Student Relocation Council, 411
National Labor Union, 441
National Mental Health Act, 374
National Park Service (NPS), 727
*The National Radio Pulpit*, 583–584
National Screen Service (NSS), 529
National Security Act, 189, 300, 795

National Security Agency, 795
National Security Council (NSC), 189
National Security Resources Board (NSRB), 179
National Ski Patrol, 644–645
National Speed Trials, 395
National War Labor Board (NWLB), 41, 441
*Native Land*, 443
NATO (North Atlantic Treaty Organization), 190, 300, 475, 732, 797
"Nature Boy," 195
NBA. *See* National Basketball Association
NBC (National Broadcasting Company), 1, 2, 37, 85, 286, 287, 459, 692
*The NBC Symphony Orchestra*, 184
NCAA. *See* National Collegiate Athletic Association
NEA. *See* National Education Association
*The Negro Soldier*, 463, 535
Nelson, Byron, 362, 363
Nelson, George, 264–265
Nelson, Harriet Hilliard, 3
Nelson, Ozzie, 3
Neutra, Richard, 25, 26
*New Orleans*, 423
New York Drama Critics Circle Awards, 140, 151
New York Philharmonic, 185
New York World's Fair, 23, 46, 261–262, 344, 350, 490, 510, 612, 650, 692, 721–722
*New Yorker*, 473
newspapers, 4, 56, 96, 125, 128, 179–180, 201, 213, 460, **501–508**, 506*t*, 530, 665
  Berlin airlift in, 94
  canasta and, 354
  *Citizen Kane* and, 173–174
  Cold War and, 192, 504
  comic books and, 207
  D-Day and, 261

  education and, 294
  horse racing and, 392
  movies and, 492, 501, 507
  pinup girls in, 308–309
  reporters, 507, 507 (photo)
  scrap drives, 609
  skating and, 642
  travel and, 728
NFL. *See* National Football League
NHRA. *See* National Hot Rod Association
Nicholas Brothers, 255
"Night and Day," 632
Nixon, Richard, 399, 524
Noble, Edward J., 1–2
Noble, Ray, 91, 293, 479
Noble, Sherwood, 324
Noguchi, Isamu, 263, 615–616
North Atlantic Treaty Organization. *See* NATO
North Platte Canteen, 157–158
Noskowiak, Sonya, 515
NPS. *See* National Park Service
NSC. *See* National Security Council
NSRB. *See* National Security Resources Board
NSS. *See* National Screen Service
nuclear chain reaction, 678
Nurse Training Act of 1943, 371
NWLB. *See* National War Labor Board
nylon, 315, 318, 611

O. M. Scott and Sons, 447
OCD. *See* Office of Civil Defense
ocean liners, 725
O'Day, Anita, 421, 422
O'Donnell, Cathy, 104 (photo)
ODT. *See* Office of Defense Transportation
OEM. *See* Office for Emergency Management
O'Farrell, Chico, 92
Office for Emergency Management (OEM), 29, 177
Office of Censorship, 503, 504

Office of Civil Defense (OCD), 177, 180, 609
Office of Defense Transportation (ODT), 722
Office of Health Defense and Welfare, 337
Office of Price Administration (OPA), 114, 226, 576, 752, 788
Office of Production Management (OPM), 46–47
Office of Scientific Research and Development (OSRD), 42
Office of War Information (OWI), 168, 433, 504, 511, 526, 527, 748, 762, 763
Oh Henry!, 270
O'Keeffe, Georgia, 5
*Oklahoma!* (Rodgers, R. & Hammerstein), 149, 151, 156, 256 (photo)
Oland, Warner, 241
*The Old-Fashioned Revival Hour*, 584–585
*On the Town*, 636, 792
O'Neill, Eugene, 140, 146
OPA. *See* Office of Price Administration
OPM. *See* Office of Production Management
Oppenheimer, J. Robert, 42
*The Original Amateur Hour*, 288, 632
Osborne, Mary, 15
OSRD. *See* Office of Scientific Research and Development
*Our New Music* (Copland), 225
Outdoor Advertising Association of America, 527
Owen, Maribel Vinson, 638
Owens, Jesse, 535
OWI. *See* Office of War Information

Pabst Blue Ribbon, 112
Packard, Vance, 14
Page, Walter, 83
Pagoda Chinese Restaurant, 589
Paige, Satchel, 80, 535
painting, 5, **29–32**, 30*t*, 31*t*, 32*t*–35*t*

*The Paleface*, 383–384
Pan, Hermes, 256
Pan American Coffee Bureau, 110
*Panama Hattie* (Porter, Cole), 148 (photo)
paperbacks, 96
Paramount, 490
Parker, Charlie "Bird," 89, 90 (photo), 91, 92
Parker, Frank, 700
Parker Brothers, 354, 357
Parks, Bert, 3, 569, 797
Parks, Wally, 395
Parsons, Louella, 506
*Pastor Hall*, 518
*Pat Novak, for Hire*, 544, 546
Pauley, M. J., 649
Paulsen, Carl, 527–528
Peale, Norman Vincent, 584
Peale, Ruth Stafford, 584
*Peanuts*, 175
Pearl, Minne, 230–231
Pearson, Drew, 778
Peer, Ralph, 38
Penguin Books, 96
penicillin, 371–372, 683–684
Penn, Irving, 514–515
People's Book Club, 126
*People's Song*, 334
Pep, Willie, 132*t*, 133
*Pepsi & Pete*, 107–108
Pepsi-Cola, 11, 107–109, 160
*The Pepsodent Show, Starring Bob Hope*, 381–382, 384
Perkins, Frances C., 604–605
Perry, Antoinette, 140, 151
Perry, Lincoln, 537
*Personal History* (Sheean), 518
Peter Paul Candy Manufacturing Company, 270–271
Petersen, Robert E. "Pete," 395
Petrillo, James C., 40, 674
Petty, George, 309, 407–408
*The Petty Girl*, 408
Pfeifer, Friedl, 645
PGA Championship, 361

*The Phantom* (Falk), 537
Philadelphia Orchestra, 185, 273–274
Philip Morris, 183
Phillips, Irma, 572
photography, 30, 262, 376, **509–517**, 516*t*
   in *Citizen Kane*, 175
   film noir, 122, 281, 326, 387
   staying connected through, 376
   Technicolor, 228
   travel, 730
Physical Fitness Research Laboratory, 370
Pickett, Clarence, 597
Pidgeon, Walter, 607
Pied Pipers, 633
*The Pilgrim Hour*, 585
Pillsbury, 269
*Pinky*, 521
*Pinocchio*, 162
pinup girls, 308–309, 407, 453, 703–704
Piston, Walter, 182
Pittsburgh Orchestra, 186
Pizzeria Uno, 589
Playskool Manufacturing Company, 711
Plimpton, James Leonard, 641
Plunkett, Roy J., 343
Pocket Books, 96
*Pogo* (Kelly, Walt), 215–216
Polaroid Corporation, 376, 510–511, 684
polio, 373, 601
Pollard, Red, 390
Pollock, Jackson, 6, 30
Pomeroy, Wardell, 435
Pope, Richard, Jr., 670
Pope, Richard, Sr., 669
Popeye, 214
*Popular Mechanics*, 378
*Popular Science*, 375–376, 378
population, 787
Porter, Cole, 91, 148 (photo), 151, 381, 496
Porter, Del, 425
Porter, Edward, 510
Post, Emily, 506

posters, **525–530**, 526 (photo)
   grocery stores, 367
   scrap drives, 609, 610 (photo)
   victory gardens, 745
Potsdam Proclamation, 44
Powell, Dick, 544
Powell, Eleanor, 254, 496
*Power in the Pacific: Battle Photographs of Our Navy in Action*, 509
Poynter, Nelson, 762
Pozo, Chano, 91
Prairie View Co-eds, 18
Pratt, Anthony E., 357
Preakness Stakes, 390, 392
Preminger, Otto, 492
President's Committee on Equality of Treatment and Opportunity in the Armed Forces, 540–541, 621
President's Cup, 489
Price, Vincent, 243
Prince, Wesley, 193
Professional Tennis Association, 699
Prohibition, 110, 112, 113–114
Project Blue Book, 736
Prontosil, 371
Pulitzer, Joseph, 147
Pulitzer Prizes, 147
Punsly, Bernard, 205
*Puppet Playhouse Theater*, 400
Pure Food and Drug Act, 369
Putnam, George Carson, 586
Pyle, Ernie, 504, **530–533**

race relations, **533–541**
   movies and, 520–522
radar, 684
radio, 1, 8, 12, 17, 20, 25, 37, 52, 54, 70–71, 83, 85–86, 107, 136, 148, 184, 195, 196, 224–225, 283, 291–293, 301, 341, 359–360, 375, 381–382, 417–419, 449, 480, **541–542**, 602, 629–630, 646–647, 659, 665, 692, 748–749, 798
   action, crime, police, and detective shows, **543–546**, 545*t*–546*t*
   advertising and, 332

AM, 331–332, 332t, 541, 556
children's shows, **546–549**, 548t
classical music and, 181, 185t, 332, 561–562
comedy shows, **550–552**, 551t
D-Day and, 261
drama and anthology, **552–555**, 554t
educational, **555–557**, 557t
FM, **330–333**, 332t, 556, 693
folk music and, 333
football and, 345
horse racing and, 392
husband-wife teams, 550
music and variety, **558–562**, 560t–561t
news, sports, public affairs, and talk, **562–568**, 567t
newspapers and, 501, 507
notable newscasters, 563–566
propaganda, 71
quiz shows, **568–571**, 570t
religion, 582–586, 583t
Roller Derby and, 594
schedules, 542
scrap drives, 609
serial films and, 623
serials and adventure series, **546–549**, 549t
soap operas, 216, **571–574**, 573t–574t
stereotyping, 536
technology, 331
toys from, 713
two-way, 722
war bonds and, 755
youth and, 785
Radio Berlin, 70–72
*Radio Bible Class*, 583
Radio Corporation of America (RCA), 331
Radio Free Europe (RFE), 189, 748–749
Radio Liberty (RL), 748–749
Radio Tokyo, 70–72
Raeburn, Boyd, 422
Ralston, Vera, 639
Randell, Ron, 245
Randolph, A. Phillip, 464, 535–536, 540–541
Rankin, John, 358
Rathbone, Basil, 240
Ration Board Game, 355
rationing, 11, 110, 114, 183, 214–215, 226, 271, 379, **574–581**, 575 (photo), 619
black market and, 114
butter, 268
canteens and, 159
drag racing and, 394
food, 339–342, 579–580, 589
frozen food, 350
gasoline, 29, 48, 125, 252, 484, 578–579, 722, 790
grocery stores and, 366
horse racing and, 390
*Life* and, 580
motor oils, 48
motorsports and, 484
paper, 97
removing, 341, 342, 580–581
restaurants and, 322
skating and, 642
softball and, 651
Spam and, 658
sugar, 108, 267–268, 579
swing and, 674
tires, 48, 577–578
travel and, 726
youth and, 430–431
Raymond, Alex, 214
RCA. *See* Radio Corporation of America
Reagan, Ronald, 66, 156, 399, 412, 464
Reard, Louis, 45, 317, 670–671
records, 681, 688
*Red, Hot and Blue* (Porter, Cole), 381
Red Cross clubmobiles, 110, 160
*Red Ryder* (Harman), 537, 772
Reed, Carol, 326
Reed, Donna, 413
Reeves, George, 666
refrigerator-freezer combination, 684–685

religion, **581–588**, 582*t*, 583*t*
relocation centers. *See* internment camps (relocation centers)
*The Reluctant Dragon*, 274
Renaldo, Duncan, 772
Renick, Marion, 651
Republic Pictures, 622–623
restaurants, 109, 271, **588–590**
   drive-in, **285**
   fast food, **321–325**
   rationing and, 322
Reuther, Walter, 446
Reynolds, Joyce, 783
Reynolds, Marjorie, 538
Reynolds Wrap, 342
RFE. *See* Radio Free Europe
rhythm and blues, 39, 426, **591–594**, 592*t*, 593*t*
The Rhythm Boys, 247
Riccardo, Ric, 589
Rice, Diana, 728
Richards, Johnny, 422
Richmond, Kane, 477
Rickey, Branch, 80
Rideout, Percy, 645
Riggs, Bobby, 700
Riggs, Tommy, 552
Rinker, Al, 246, 247
RL. *See* Radio Liberty
*The Road to Good Nutrition* (Roberts), 337
*Road to Singapore*, 202, 382 (photo), 383
*Road to Victory*, 509
Robbins, Irvine, 325
Robbins, Jerome, 151, 257
*Roberta* (Kern), 381
Roberts, Lydia J., 337
Robeson, Paul, 443
Robinson, Bill "Bojangles," 255
Robinson, Edward G., 122, 199, 761
Robinson, Jackie, 80, 463, 535
Robinson, Neil, 645
Robinson, Sugar Ray, 132*t*, 133, 463, 534–535
Rock, George, 426

Rockefeller, John D., Jr., 738
Rockefeller Center, 22
Rockefeller Foundation, 436
The Rockettes, 257–258
Rock-Ola Manufacturing Corporation, 428
Rockwell, Norman, 107, 317, 403–405, 528, 529, 607
   war bonds and, 404–405, 528, 758
*Rocky King, Inside Detective*, 288–289
*Rodeo* (Copland), 223, 224 (photo)
Rodgers, Jimmie, 230 (photo)
Rodgers, Richard, 149, 151, 156, 256 (photo)
Rogers, Edith Nourse, 358, 776
Rogers, Ginger, 253, 254, 499
Rogers, Roy, 25, **53–61**, 54 (photo), 59*t*–60*t*, 163, 170, 231, 547, 769
Rohde, Gilbert, 264
Roland, Gilbert, 772
*Roller Blades* (Sawyer), 642
Roller Derby, **594–596**, 595 (photo), 596, 698
Roller Skating Association, 641
Rooney, Mickey, 172, 199, 496, 596
Roosevelt, Eleanor, 269, 506, **597–600**, 597 (photo)
Roosevelt, Franklin Delano, 24, 41, 42, 46–47, 77, 86, 110, 159, 176–177, 188, 284, 313, 336, 357, 377, 409, 443–444, 466, 474, 504, 575–576, 581, **600–605**, 601 (photo), 617
   "Arsenal for Democracy" speech, 602, 788
   "Day of Infamy" speech, 603
   death of, 187, 359, 731, 792
   "Fireside Chats," 71, 602
   "Four Freedoms" speech, 404, 602, 788
   health care and, 374
   polio and, 373
   "A Prayer in Dark Times," 586–587
   race relations and, 533
Rose, Billy, 668–669
Rose, Fred, 9, 230

Rose, Mauri, 485
Rose, Wally, 423
Rose, William L., 529
Rose Bowl, 345, 347
Rosenberg, Harold, 5, 6
Rosenberg, William, 324
Rosenthal, Joe, 509–510
Rosie the Riveter, 11, 528, **605–608**, 619, 767
"Rosie the Riveter" (Rockwell), 317, 404, 607
Ross, Shirley, 382–383
Roswell, New Mexico, 736
Rountree, Martha, 478
Roventini, Johnny, 12
*Royal Gelatin Hour*, 291
RTA. *See* Russeta Timing Association
rubber, 610, 685
"Rudolph the Red-Nosed Reindeer," 56
Rudolph Wurlitzer Company, 428
Rugolo, Pete, 422
Runyon, Damon, 594–595
Rushing, Jimmy, 83
Rusk, Howard A., 436
Russell, George, 91
Russell, Harold, 104 (photo)
Russell, Jane, 309
Russell, Rosalind, 507, 507 (photo)
Russeta Timing Association (RTA), 395
Ruth, Babe, 710 (photo)
Ryder Cup Matches, 362

Saarinen, Eero, 24, 262, 265
Saarinen, Eliel, 24, 262
Saddler, Sandy, 132*t*, 133
*The Saint*, 243, 243*t*
Salk, Jonas, 373
Salvation Army, 160
Samuelson, Ralph, 669
San Francisco Ballet Company, 183
Sandburg, Carl, 224–225, 509
Sanders, Colonel, 324
Sanders, George, 243, 244
Sandrich, Mark, 774
Saroyan, Williams, 147

*Saturday Evening Post*, 403–405
Savoy Records, 91
Sawyer, Ruth, 642
Schaper, William Herbert, 356
Schauffler, Sandy, 645
Schilling, David C., 67
Schindler, Bill, 488
Schlaikjer, Jes Wilhelm, 527
Schlesinger, Leon, 164
Schlumbohm, Peter, 266
Schmeling, Max, 462, 463
Schmidt, Gottfried, 128
*Scholastic Magazine*, 609–610
Schulz, Charles, 175
Schuman, William, 182
Schwartz, Arthur, 156
Scobey, Bob, 423
Scott, Raymond, 675
Scrabble, 356, 452
scrap drives, 11, 295, **609–612**, 610 (photo), 619
  Crosby and, 249
  grocery stores and, 366
  youth and, 430–431, 609–610
Scruggs, Earl, 232
SCTA. *See* Southern California Timing Association
sculpture, **612–617**
Seabiscuit, 390
*Seduction of the Innocent* (Wertham), 432–433
*See Here, Private Hargrove* (Hargrove), 619
Seeger, Pete, 333–334, 442–443
Seiberling, Dorothy, 6
Seibert, Peter, 645
Selective Service. *See* Selective Training and Service Act of 1940
Selective Training and Service Act of 1940, 295, 336, 443–444, **617–621**, 673, 739–742, 776
  movies and, 619, 761
Seltzer, Leo, 594, 596
service flags (gold stars and blue stars), 404, **626–627**

Service Training Units (STUs), 295–296
Servicemen's Readjustment Act of 1944. *See* GI Bill
Sessions, Roger, 182
*Seventeen*, 321, **627–628**, 784–785
Sewell, Ike, 589
*Sexual Behavior in the Human Female* (Kinsey), 435–437
*Sexual Behavior in the Human Male* (Kinsey), 344, 435–436
*The Shadow*, 476–477, 543, 663–664
Shaw, Artie, 419
Shaw, Wilbur, 484, 485
Shearing, George, 92
Sheean, Vincent, 518
Sheen, Fulton J., 288, 584
*Sheena, Queen of the Jungle*, 209, 211
*Sherlock Holmes*, 239–240, 240*t*
Sherman, Harry, 134–135
Sherwood, Robert E., 104, 520
Shibley, Arkie, 52, 396
Shore, Dinah, **628–631**, 629 (photo)
Shuster, Joe, 163–164, 208, 476, 664
Siegel, Jerry, 163–164, 208, 476, 664
*Silent Spring* (Carson, Rachel), 372
Silly Putty, 685, 713
Silverheels, Jay, 461 (photo)
Simmons, Zalmon, Jr., 489
Simon, Abe, 131, 463
Simon & Schuster, 96
simulcasting, 685–686
Sinatra, Frank, 19, 40, 41, 195, 256, 306, 320, 363, **631–637**, 634*t*, 636*t*, 782
singing cowboy, 54, 60, 231, 496
Singleton, Penny, 201
Sir Barton, 390
skating
   figure, **637–641**
   roller, **641–643**
*Ski*, 644
Skidmore, Owings & Merrill. *See* SOM
skiing, **643–646**
   water, 667–672
Slack, Freddie, 124

slang, 310–312
Sleight, Rae, 157–158
Sligh, Charles R., 670
Slinky, 686, 713
Smart, J. Scott, 544
Smith, Bob, 400
Smith, David, 616
Smith, George A., 587
Smith, Kate, 344, 587, **646–649**, 647 (photo), 757
Smith, Louise, 487
Smith, W. Eugene, 511, 513*t*, 514
Smith, W. Warren, 283
Smith, Willie "the Lion," 82
*The Smithsonian Collection of Classical Country Music*, 236
*Smokey Stover* (Holman), 735
Snead, Sam, 361, 362
Snickers, 270
snorkel, 686
*Snow White and the Seven Dwarfs*, 273
*Snuffy Smith*, 392
Snyder, Esther, 323–324
Snyder, Harry, 323–324
*So Dear to My Heart*, 276
*So Proudly We Hail!*, 780
Sockman, Ralph W., 584
softball, **649–652**
Soglow, Otto, 107
SOM (Skidmore, Owings & Merrill), 24–25
*Something for the Boys*, 483
sonar, 686–687
*Song of the South*, 276, 520
*Songs by Sinatra*, 635
songwriters and lyricists, **652–657**, 757
Sons of the Pioneers, 57
sound barrier, 67, 687
"The Sources of Soviet Conduct" (Kennan), 188
"South American Way," 481
*South Pacific* (Rodgers, R. & Hammerstein), 151
Southern California Timing Association (SCTA), 393–394, 395

Southern Music Publishing Company, 38
Soviet Union, 187–193, 397–399
   atomic bomb and, 45–46, 179–180, 191, 733, 798
   *See also* Cold War
Spam, 341, **657–660**, 658
SPARs, 779
Specht, Robert, 639
speedboat racing, 488–489
Spellman, Francis Joseph Cardinal, 467, 587
Spencer, Tim, 57
Spice Islands Company, 365
Spiegelhoff, John, 488
spies, 191, 192, 398, 409
*The Spike Jones Show*, 426
Spillane, Mickey, 95 (photo)
Spitalny, Phil, 15, 16 (photo), 17
Spivak, Lawrence, 478
Spock, Benjamin, 75, **660–661**
*Spotlight Revue*, 426
*Springtime in the Rockies*, 482
Stafford, Jo, 19
Stage Door Canteen, 139, 150, 159, 742
Stalin, Joseph, 187, 188, 601 (photo), 603
stamp collecting, 376–377, 408, 601
Standard Oil Company, 14
Stanley, Frederick Arthur, 380
Stanley Cup, 380, 380t, 381
*Stars and Stripes*, 531–532
"The Star-Spangled Banner," 648
steel pennies, 611, **661–663**
Steichen, Edward, 509
Steinbeck, John, 519
Steiner, Max, 168
stereotyping, **533–541**
   in war movies, 766–767
Stern, Philip Van Doren, 413
*Steve Canyon*, 222, 704
Stevens, Clifford Brooks, 428
Stevens, George, 414
Stevenson, Adlai, 300
Stewart, Jimmy, 293, 413, 518

Stewart, Redd, 233
Stieglitz, Alfred, 515
Still, William Grant, 181, 261
Stillman, Al, 428
Stimson, Henry L., 409, 618
Stirling, Linda, 623
stock cars, 395–396, 486–487
Stockwell, Dean, 521
Stokowski, Leopold, 162, 273–274
Stone, Edward Durrell, 22
Stone, Harlan Fiske, 605
Stone, Lewis, 199
*Stop the Music*, 569, 797
Stordahl, Axel, 634
*Stormy Weather*, 306, 306 (photo)
*The Story of G.I. Joe*, 531
"Straighten Up and Fly Right," 194
Strandlund, Carl, 27–28
Stratton, Dorothy C., 779
Strayhorn, Billy, 302
*A Streetcar Named Desire* (Williams, Tennessee), 146
Streeter, Ruth Cheney, 779
streptomycin, 372, 687
*Strike Up the Band*, 496
Striker, Fran, 459, 460
Strode, Woody, 535
Stubbins, Hugh, Jr., 24
Studebaker Corporation, 48–49, 266
STUs. *See* Service Training Units
*Suburban Life*, 377–378
suburbanization, **453–458**
Suggs, Louise, 363
Sullivan, Ed, 417, **707–708**, 707 (photo), 797
Sun Valley, 643, 644
Sundblom, Haddon, 107
suntan lotions, 687
*Superman*, 163–164, 208, 476, 476 (photo), 507, **663–667**
*Suspense*, 554–555
Swift, Henry, 515
swimming, **667–672**, 668 (photo), 671t
swimsuits, 670–671
   *See also* bikini

swing, 12, 16, 19, 83, 89, 124, 182, 194, 225, 232–233, 258, 301, 419, 420, 479, 591, 633, **672–676**, 673 (photo)
Swing, Raymond Gram, 478
Szilard, Leo, 42
Szyk, Arthur, 527

Taft, Robert A., 75, 297, 445
Taft-Hartley Act, 441, 445
*Take Me Out to the Ball Game*, 636
Tanforan Assembly Center, 409 (photo)
*Tarzan*, 172
taxis, 722
Taylor, Deems, 162
Taylor, June, 259
Taylor, Robert, 518
Teagarden, Jack, 423
Teague, Walter Dorwin, 261, 262, 721
technology, 184, **677–692**
  atomic bomb, 191
  chronological listing of achievements in, 691t
  Copland and, 225
  frozen food, 351
  magazines and, 468
  motorsports, 490
  sound, 54, 495
*Teen Trouble*, 431
Teflon, 343, 688
Tehran Conference, 603, 605, 790
television, 2, 12, 16, 21, 41, 54, 85, 128, 135, 140, 166, 168, 195, 200, 228–229, 233, 285–289, 293, 375, 382, 437–439, 450, 461, 477, 581, 631, 637, 647–648, 666, **692–698**, 705–708, 798
  anthology dramas, 437–439, 696
  baseball and, 697
  bowling, 697
  boxing, 134, 697
  camera setup, 679 (photo)
  children's, 696
  color, 678, 788
  FM radio and, 331–332
  football and, 347, 697
  game/quiz shows, 696t
  Golden Age of, 439
  hockey and, 381
  horse racing and, 392
  inspired toys, 716
  movies and, 491, 695
  news, 697
  newspapers and, 501
  Roller Derby, 596, 698
  variety shows, 695–696
  wrestling, 697–698
  *See also specific programs*
Temple, Shirley, 170, 306, 783
tennis, 452, **698–702**, 700t
Terry, Paul, 165
*Terry and the Pirates*, 214, 222, **702–705**
Terrytoons, 165
*The Texaco Star Theater*, 255, 259, **705–707**, 706 (photo), 797
*Thank Your Lucky Stars*, 630
"Thanks for the Memory," 382
*That Night in Rio*, 482, 496
theaters, 449
  drive-in, **282–285**, 283 (photo)
Theatre World Award, 140, 151
*This Is the Army* (Berlin), 151, 619, 790
Thomas, George, 123
Thomas, J. Parnell, 398, 524
Thompson, J. Walter, 437
Thomson, Virgil, 181, 183
Thornhill, Claude, 675
Three Stooges, 172, 203–204
*Throttle Magazine*, 394
Tide detergent, 688
Tierney, Gene, 187 (photo)
Tilden, Bill, 699
*Till the Clouds Roll By*, 635
*Till the End of Time*, 520
*Tillie the Toiler* (Westover), 779
Tillman, Floyd, 234
*Time*, 465, 467, 469
"Time After Time," 635
*The Time of Your Life* (Saroyan), 147

timeline (1940s), 787–800
Tinkertoys, 711
Tito, Josip Broz, 189
*To Be or Not to Be*, 196, 418
*To Have and Have Not*, 120
*To Hell and Back*, 495
*Toast of the Town*, **707–708**, 707 (photo)
*The Toast of the Town*, 259, 797
Todd, John, 460
Toguri, Iva, 70–72, 70 (photo)
Tokyo Rose, **70–72**
Toland, Gregg, 173
Toler, Sidney, 241, 537
*The Tommy Riggs and Betty Lou Show*, 552
Tonka, 714
Tony Award, 140, 151
Tootsie Rolls, 270
Topps, 310
Toscanini, Arturo, 183, 184
Tough Hill, 392
toys, 53, 94, **708–716**
Trading with the Enemy Act, 503
trains, 93, 157, **716–720**, 718*t*, 719*t*, 721, 733
    decline in, 720, 723
    military service, 719, 724
    toy, 714–715
Transcontinental Roller Derby, 594
transistors, 689
transportation, 46, 61, 75, 226, 286, **720–725**
    fast food and, 321–322
    food, 340
    horse racing and, 390
    labor unrest and, 444
    restaurants and, 590
    skiing, 643–644
    suburbanization and, 455
    swing and, 674
travel, 67, 94, 282, **725–730**, 726*t*, 727*t*
Travern, B., 121
Travis, Merle, 235–236
TravLodge, 728
*The Treasure of Sierra Madre*, 121–122

Trendle, George, 459, 460
Trotter, John Scott, 424
Troup, Bobby, 52
*True Detective Mysteries*, 543
*True-Life Adventures*, 276
Truman, Harry S., 4, 6, 44, 75, 93, 128, 177, 187, 189, 300, 319, 399, 412, 433, 445, 467, 474, 600, 621, **730–734**, 731 (photo), 739, 743, 797
    on food, 342
    health care and, 374
    race relations and, 540–541
    speedboat racing and, 489
Truman Doctrine, 189, 733, 795
Tubb, Ernest, 230 (photo), 235
Tupperware, 343, 689–690
Turner, Curtis, 487
Turner, Eugene, 639
Turner, Lana, 309, 321, 453
Tuskegee Airmen, 534, 534 (photo)
Twentieth Century-Fox, 490

UAW. *See* United Automobile Workers of America
U-boats, 116
UFOs (Unidentified Flying Objects), 735–736
UMW. *See* United Mine Workers of America
Underwood, Michael, 373
Unidentified Flying Objects. *See* UFOs
United Artists, 490
United Automobile Workers of America (UAW), 443
United Mine Workers of America (UMW), 444
United Nations, 621, 732, **736–739**
    Declaration of, 603, 737
    Educational, Scientific, and Cultural Organization, 182
    Human Rights Commission, 600
    Roosevelt, Eleanor, appointed to, 600
    Secretariat, 23
United Service Organizations. *See* USO (United Service Organizations)

United States Committee for the Care of European Children, 597
United States Information Agency (USIA), 189–190, 748
United States Public Health Service, 371
Universal Pictures, 622
*Up Front* (Mauldin), 532
*Up in Arms*, 630
Upson Company, 355
*USA Today*, 505
USIA. *See* United States Information Agency
USO (United Service Organizations), 12, 18, 21, 58, 84, 126, 150, 159, 183, 230, 384, 451, 499, 529, **739–742**

VA. *See* Veterans Administration
Valentine, Helen, 627
Vallee, Rudy, 291, 306, 783
Van Dyke, William, 515
Vance, Louis Joseph, 245
Vargas, Alberto, 309, 407–408
Varipapa, Andy, 128–129
Vaughan, Sarah, 89
V-Discs, 41, 558
V-E Day, **743–744**
vending, 112–113
Verdi, Giuseppe, 183
Veterans Administration (VA), 358, 371, 728
Victory Book Rallies, 97, 126
victory gardens, 370, 379, 452, 579, **744–748**, 745 (photo)
  golf and, 362
*Victory Through Air Power*, 275
*View*, 615
Village Vanguard, 334
vitamins, 369
V-J Day, **743–744**
V-Mail, 510
*Vogue*, 316, 514–515, 614
Voice of America (VOA), 189, **748–749**, 794–795

*The Volga Boatman*, 134
*Vox Pop*, 568

WAC. *See* Women's Auxiliary Corps
Wagner, George "Gorgeous George," 697–698
*Wake Island*, 760
Walcot, Jersey Joe, 130 (photo)
*Wall Street Journal*, 505
Wallace, Coley, 464
Wallace, Henry A., 600, 730–731
Waller, Fats, 82
Waller, Fred, 669
Wallichs, Glenn, 194
Walt Disney, 161–163, 172, 180, 212, 273–277, 425, 520, 712
Walter, Rosalind, 606
Wanger, Walter, 517
War Advertising Council, 11, 13, 753
war bonds, 11, 58, 140, 150, 295, 619, **751–759**, 752 (photo)
  boxing and, 129
  campaigns, 754*t*
  Crosby and, 249
  grocery stores and, 366
  Hope and, 384
  jukeboxes and, 430
  Rockwell, Norman, and, 404–405, 528, 758
  Smith, Kate, and, 647, 757
War Powers Act, 503
War Production Board (WPB), 48, 108, 313
War Ration Program, 576, 580
War Relocation Authority (WRA), 409, 409 (photo), 539
Warm 'n Fresh Donut, 324
Warner Bros., 164, 172, 212, 277, 490
Warren, Robert Penn, 278 (photo)
Washburne, Joe "Country," 425
Washington, Kenny, 535
WASPs. *See* Women Airforce Service Pilots
*Watkins Glen Grand Prix*, 486
Watson, Lucile, 139

Watters, Lu, 423
WAVES. *See* Women Accepted for Volunteer Military Services
Wayne, David, 532
Wayne, John, 54, 319, 769
WBA. *See* World Boxing Association
"We Can Do It!" (Miller, J. Howard), 316–317, 528, 606
Weaver, Winstead "Doodles," 425
Webb, Jack, 544, 546
Weegee, 511, 513*t*, 514
*Week-End in Havana*, 482, 496
Weir, Walter, 753
Weissmuller, Johnny, 667–668, 669
Welles, Orson, 71, **173–176**, 174 (photo), 183, 355 (photo), 477
Wells, Herman B., 436
Wertham, Fredric, 432
West, Mae, 311
Westinghouse War Production Co-Ordinating Committee, 528
Weston, Edward, 510, 515, 516*t*
Westover, Russ, 779
Wham-O, 716
"What Are We Fighting For?" (Roosevelt, E.), 598
*What Happened to Mary?*, 622
Whataburger, 324
"When the Moon Comes Over the Mountain, 648
Whirlaway, 391
White, Minor, 514
White Castle, 322
"White Christmas," 56, 249, 496, 657, **773–775**, 790
Whiteman, Paul, 246, 437
*Why We Fight*, 763
WIBC. *See* Women's International Bowling Congress
Wick, Claude R., 339
Wilder, Billy, 492
William, Warren, 245
Williams, Esther, 636, 667–669
Williams, Hank, 10, 234–235
Williams, Ike, 132*t*
Williams, Mary Lou, 15
Williams, Ted, 78, 78 (photo)
Williams, Tennessee, 140, 146
Willis, Bill, 535
Wills, Bob, 232–233
Wills, Royal Barry, 26
*Wilson*, 737
Wilson, Don, 418
Wilson, Dooley, 169
Wilson, George, 396
Wilson, Sloan, 319
Wilson, Woodrow, 737
Winchell, Verne, 324
Winchell, Walter, 3–4, 72, 506
*Wings for This Man*, 66
Winter, Roland, 537
Winters, Roland, 241
Wismer, Harry, 67
*Woman's Day*, 365
Women Accepted for Volunteer Military Services (WAVES), 314, 778
Women Airforce Service Pilots (WASPs), 314, 778
*Women at War*, 779–780
women in military, 314, **776–780**
Women's Armed Services Integration Act, 779
Women's Auxiliary Corps (WAC), 314, 776–778
Women's International Bowling Congress (WIBC), 127–128
Wood, Craig, 361, 362
Wood, Garfield, 489
Wood, Morrison, 112
Woodruff, Robert W., 108
woodworking, 378
Works Projects Administration, 29, 447, 612
World Boxing Association (WBA), 130
WPB. *See* War Production Board
WRA. *See* War Relocation Authority
wrestling, 697–698
Wright, Frank Lloyd, 22, 22 (photo), 23, 24, 27, 263–264
Wright, Henry, 264

Wright, Orville, 61
Wright, Russel, 265–266
Wright, Wilbur, 61
Wrigley, Phillip K., 78
Wrigley Company, 270
Wunder, George, 704
Wurster, William W., 26
Wyler, William, 104, 414, 520
Wyman, Jane, 158 (photo)

*Yank*, 309
Yeager, Charles E. (Chuck), 67
Yeoman, Richard S., 377
*Yip Yap Yaphank* (Berlin), 151, 156, 648
York Cone Company, 270
York Peppermint Patty, 270
*You Bet Your Life*, 569
Young, Chic, 172, 201–202, 214 (photo), 216, 218
Young, James Webb, 753
Young, Lester, 83
*Your Hit Parade*, 635
*Your Share: How to Prepare Appetizing, Helpful Meals with Foods Available Today* (Crocker), 268, 340
youth, 91, 305, 430–434, **781–786**
   civil defense and, 430–431
   fashion, 319–320, 785
   oriented agencies, 452–453
   rationing and, 430–431
   scrap drives and, 430–431, 609–610
   softball and, 650
*Youth in Crisis*, 432
*Youth Runs Wild*, 432

Zaharias, Babe Didrikson, 363
Zale, Tony, 129, 131, 132*t*, 133
Zamboni, 690
Zeisel, Eva, 266
*Zero Hour*, 71–72
Ziolkowski, Korczak, 613
zoot suits, 306, 306 (photo), 320, 431, 540, 783